When Children Play

Proceedings of the International Conference
on Play and Play Environments

Joe L. Frost and
Sylvia Sunderlin, Editors

ASSOCIATION FOR CHILDHOOD EDUCATION INTERNATIONAL
11141 Georgia Avenue, Suite 200, Wheaton, MD 20902

Lucy Prete Martin, Director of Publications
Maureen D. Goldstein, Assistant Editor

Cover photographs (clockwise from upper left):
David M. Grossman, Brooklyn, NY
Joe L. Frost, Austin, TX
Nair Benedicto/Agência F4 fotografias,
Sao Paulo, Brazil
Back cover photographs:
Joe L. Frost, Austin, TX

Library of Congress Cataloging in Publication Data
Main entry under title:
When children play.
    1. Play—Congresses.   2. Playgrounds—Congresses.
I. Frost, Joe L.   II. Sunderlin, Sylvia
HQ782.W44   1985   790'.06'8   84-20477

ISBN 0-87173-107-X

CONTENTS

Part VII: Play as an Assessment Tool

PREFACE

The 47 papers in this book (with three exceptions) were presented at the International Conference on Play and Play Environments held at the University of Texas at Austin, June 29-July 2, 1983. About 120 students of play presented papers at the conference. By all accounts, this was the largest group of play scholars ever convened. Seventy-two of the papers were presented for publication. Through a "blind" review process requiring every paper to be reviewed by three colleagues holding doctoral degrees, this number was reduced to 47.

The conference, sponsored by 14 professional organizations, was attended by more than 500 participants, representing most of the United States, the Republic of China, Denmark, the Philippines, England, Greece, Canada, Korea, Mexico, Germany, Australia and Japan. A planning committee of more than forty worked for a year and a half to make the conference a success. The conference format included general session speakers, small group sessions, tours to playgrounds and a special workshop wherein 150 conference participants, directed by a group of leading playground designers, built a playground. The photograph on the cover of this book was taken at this site.

To those responsible for making the conference a whopping success this volume is respectfully dedicated.

Conference Sponsors
Pacific Cultural Foundation in Taipei, Republic of China (honorary sponsor)
American Association for Leisure and Recreation
Association for Childhood Education International
Austin and Texas Associations for the Education of Young Children
Austin Association for Childhood Education International
College of Education, The University of Texas at Austin
Family Resource Coalition
Intercultural Development Research Association
International Association for the Child's Right to Play (formerly International
    Playground Association)
National Association for Bilingual Education
Texas Association for Health, Physical Education and Recreation
Texas Department of Human Resources
Texas Elementary, Kindergarten, Nursery Educators

Planning Committee
Director: Joe L. Frost
Co-Director: Sue Wortham
Program:
Jacqueline Myers, Chairman; Larry Bruya, Marcy Guddemi, Fill Hendrix, Marian Monroe, Francine Nichols, Mercedes Perez de Colon, Pamela Lam-Yip, Judi Blalock
Media: Ron Jackson, Frances Gates Rhodes
Registration:
Marcy Guddemi, Chairman; Johanna Huggans, Patty Boyd, Marie Kodedek, Muriel Morris
Social:
Pauline Walker, Gloria Rodriguez, Co-Chairmen; Sandy Hamilton, Linda Jones, Lee Webb, Doris Wilhite, Lily Chiang, Sharon Hunsucker, Li-Peng Chen, Baoshan Lin

Transportation: Alfred James, Chairman; Steve Hoppes
Hospitality: Earline Malone, Chairman; Betty Frost, Carole Schwartz
Housing: Sandy Briley, Chairman; Suzanne Winter, Margaret Garza
Exhibits: Michael Bell, Chairman; Patty Boyd, Jim Dempsey, Steve Jensen
Special Arrangements: Linda Bell
Graphic Art: Marshal Wortham

Playground Presession
Designers/Workshop Leaders
CHRISTOPHER CLEWS, President, Learning Structures, Inc.
JIM DEMPSEY, Designs for Play
HARRIS FORUSZ, Director, Adventure Playgrounds, Inc.
JOE L. FROST, The University of Texas at Austin
HORST HENKE, Children's Playgrounds, Inc.
PAUL HOGAN, Clearing House, Inc.
ERIC STRICKLAND, University of Texas at Arlington
WILLIAM WEISZ, President, Tire Playgrounds, Inc.
MARSHAL AND SUE WORTHAM, Matrix Design

Appreciation is expressed to the City of Austin Parks and Recreation Department, the Hyde Park Neighborhood Association and St. Martin's School and Church for planning, support and provision of sites for this presession.

General Session Speakers
GRETA FEIN
Professor of Curriculum and Instruction, University of Maryland, College Park

JOE L. FROST
Professor of Curriculum and Instruction, The University of Texas at Austin

SHU-FANG LO CHIA
Professor of Child Development, Fu-Jen University, Taipei, Republic of China

GARY T. MOORE
Associate Professor of Architecture; Director, Environment-Behavior Research Institute, University of Wisconsin, Milwaukee

JENS PEDERSEN
Chairman, Planning Group for Children and Culture, Copenhagen, Denmark

BRIAN SUTTON-SMITH
Professor, Department of Education and Folklore, University of Pennsylvania in Philadelphia

INTRODUCTION

The subject matter of this book is the play of children and the environments for their play. Play is universal, knowing no national or cultural boundaries, peculiar to all ages and all races, subject to description yet defying definition; essential to the development of thought and language, yet neither; central to the transmission of culture, yet transcending culture. Indeed, if we believe Huizinga, *Homo Ludens*, man the player, is placed on the same level as *Homo Sapiens*, man the reasoner and *Homo Faber*, man the maker.

Across history and cultures, play has captured the imagination of a few scholars and drawn the scorn of most. Scientists reflect this historical disregard for play in that their intellectual concern is such that play might not exist at all and except for the writings of a few poets and philosophers, history shows little serious interest in the subject of play.

Play has been commonly viewed as wasteful and harmful, a condition undoubtedly related to man's historical disregard for childhood. As recently as the turn of this century, childhood in emerging industrialized nations was characterized by high mortality, severe punishment, hard labor and intimidating teaching, for the history of childhood is marked by centuries-long eras of infanticide, abandonment and child slavery. In the absence of historical perspective and romantic minds, play might still be regarded as frivolous and childhood as mere preparation for adulthood.

In the eighteenth century Froebel lifted play into a respectable position when he wrote, "Play is the highest expression of human development in childhood, for it alone is the free expression of what is in a child's soul."

In contrast to the romanticism of Froebel, the theories of early scholars of play—the cathartic, repetitive compulsion and surplus energy theories—are all ways of excluding children from the richer dimensions of play and thus saying that play, like childhood, is unimportant.

Portraits of the child at play represent the innate potentialities in human beings to seek and to express themselves—artistically, freely, creatively and, thus, to gain fulfillment. Play is the child's art form, the vehicle for creative expression, the primary avenue to learning and development, a source of joy and contentment.

While Plato, Aristotle, Confucius, Spencer, Schiller, Wundt, Groos, Froebel, Huizinga, Caillois and others explored the philosophical, social and cultural dimensions of play, it was left to the incomparable Piaget to focus upon its intellectual power and set the stage for 20th-century interest and inquiry.

In the past two decades, play has increasingly been recognized as the central cognitive, social and cultural activity of infancy and the pre-school years. Unfortunately, play has never received high credit among educators at the primary and elementary level. Preoccupation with sports and "basics" and misunderstanding of play have left public schools a wasteland so far as play and play environments are concerned.

The schools' disregard for play is shared by other societal groups. Families in industrialized nations allows their young to substitute television for traditional play; thus they miss play's rich, intellectual benefits, while developing anti-social tendencies and perpetuating through dramatic play the cultural mores of popular contemporary folk figures such as Bo Duke, J.R. Ewing and The Fonz. The traditional games of native children, untainted by television, are infinitely richer and more civilized.

The people of industrialized nations, preoccupied with robots and computers, substitute technology for simple tools and personal relations. The Japanese author Daisaku Ikida speaks of our overindulged children as "glass children." They have lost their toughness; so weak you expect them to break; brittle like glass; so clumsy they cannot handle scissors and knives; ready-made kits have supplanted their need for tools. But the main reason they cannot use tools is adults' fearful prohibitions.

Anuradha Vittachi writes about the substitution of machines for labor and play (*New Industrialist Magazine*). He identifies a poverty of the spirit and loneliness prevailing in the industrialized world, a deflation of the spirit, a loss of fraternity, a rupture of human relationships. One may see in accounts by writers from African, Asian and Latin American Third World countries a portrait of children at play and at work, swimming in rivers and ponds, sliding down wet hillsides, raising crops, tending animals, keeping house, playing and working in close consort with friends and family, sharing in communal fellowship and responsibility.

In contrast, children in industrialized nations are increasingly swept up by contemporary fascination with such technological devices as computers. Such interest, relevant as it is, may be misunderstood by adults. Let us not deceive ourselves that children's preoccupation with computers is motivated solely by knowledge-seeking instinct or that their keen interest is in the acquisition of subject matter. In the construction of playthings by adults for children, adult logic is typically applied to the ludic behavior of children and to the selection of their playthings. The computer is indeed a marvelous learning device, but to children it is first and foremost a plaything—learning is a bonus.

All play proceeds from, and has its existence within, a play environment designated physically or symbolically. Perhaps the ultimate representation of a play environment for children is the natural countryside, rich with sights, sounds, challenges, living things, changing features. But not all children, certainly not those in large cities and in schools, have ready access to the world of nature. Surely, this is what Sorensen had in mind when he constructed with children the first adventure playground in Emdrup, Denmark in 1943. Adults compensate—some better than others by constructing or helping children construct artificial environments. In the United States and most industrialized countries the pattern for public playgrounds was established in the early 1900's with the provision of fixed, steel single function structures installed over asphalt or concrete and designed for minimum maintenance and maximum wear. After half a century the same structures remain in place—monuments to our contempt for children's play. The heritage continues, for most contemporary playgrounds are hazardous, unchallenging, limited in function and generally unfit for the broad forms of childhood play. They are built (exclusively) from a sports-exercise mentality and generally ignore play's social, cultural, intellectual and artistic qualities.

Most play environments are constructed as though children could not think, reason, create. Only a small minority of adults seems to understand the intellectual, cultural and artistic powers of children's imaginative, dramatic or symbolic play—these playgrounds of the child's mind—and fewer still help children construct environments that promote their expression. Very few adults seem to understand that for exploiting the social, cultural, intellectual and artistic qualities of play an array of loose parts and tools is superior to an acre of fixed structures. This is not to say that fixed structures are unnecessary—certainly not the contemporary, challenging superstructures—but their functions are limited and complementary to raw flexible materials.

What then, in this paradoxical context, should our mission be? *First,* we should address the issue of distinguishing play from related variables and seeking a definition of play itself, that is, we should seek to *understand* play.

Second, we should expand the range of our research methodologies to bring new perspectives to the examination of play. Supplementing experimental approaches with observational and ethnographic methods is one promising approach.

Third, we should initiate a round of cross-cultural and cross-national studies to determine the influences of culture on play behaviors and in so doing identify more clearly the constant dimensions of play.

Fourth, we should help those concerned for children to understand that play is not the antithesis of academic endeavor, but has a central function in education as well as in learning and development. Simultaneously, we should seek further to demonstrate these connections through research.

Fifth, we need inquiry into the effects of television viewing and video games on dramatic play and their consequences for social behavior. Such inquiry will help to clarify the already established link between TV viewing and anti-social behavior and the emerging link between TV viewing and learning. We are at a beginning stage in understanding the influences of video games.

Sixth, we need to determine the effects on cultural transmission and cultural identity of the loss of folk tales, folk games and family-inspired role play.

Seventh, we should propose new directions for the design, development, and use of play environments, pledging that any similar conference conducted in the year 2000—less than seventeen years away—may see a new world of play environments for children. In no other sphere of childhood education or child development is the need more profound. Children's playgrounds are unconscionably bad.

Finally, we should transcend parochial interests and cooperate fully with organizations such as the International Playground Association and the Association for Childhood Education International to work for universal recognition of the child's right to play.

JOE L. FROST
The University of Texas at Austin

PART I: UNDERSTANDING PLAY
Introduction

The desire to understand play led scholars of the eighteenth and nineteenth centuries to develop theories of play. During the present century these early theories have been supplemented by those of contemporary scholars. Sue Wortham traces play theory development and explains how theory is tied to practice in the design and use of play equipment and playgrounds.

In the years between 1900 and 1930, outdoor play environments reflected the surplus energy, recreation, instinct and recapitulation theories. Playground design focused on recreational and organized games, with little play equipment for younger children. Since 1930, the cognitive-development and psychoanalytic theories of play as learned behavior have contributed to understanding of how children benefit from play, while the expression, arousal-seeking and competence-motivation theories attempt to explain why children are motivated to play.

Brian Sutton-Smith believes that the play theories of the past 100 years have clearly accomplished the platonic wish that the best thing play can do is imitate the more rational aspects of human behavior. He introduces a novel perspective on philosophical changes in our views of play. He proposes that there are two kinds of play, the rational and the irrational, and considers play in terms of a dimension of meaning varying between rationality at one end and irrationality at the other. Rational play is what we tend to study in the psychology of play and the playground movement. It is "idealized behavior," tending to imitate the more rational aspects of human behavior. Irrational play is more characteristic of the play research in folklore and anthropology. Sutton-Smith does not provide specific criteria for distinguishing between rational and irrational play—"games are neither inherently rational or irrational." He refers to studies of playground apparatus, sex role preferences, play and

problem-solving, etc., as "sanitized" and argues that we examine such subject matter as violent sports, libidinous foreplay and addictive gambling and that it might be more helpful for us to use descriptive records of players with each other, with games, toys and playground apparatus.

An increasing number of investigators are using observational methods in their studies of play. Joan Isenberg and Evelyn Jacob investigated, through case study methodology, how two 4-year-old girls incorporated literacy skills and knowledge of literacy artifacts into their play activities and examined the role of these activities in learning literacy. Results indicate that each girl engaged in playful literacy activities in both pretend and non-pretend contexts. When new information about literacy artifacts was presented, there was gradual incorporation of parts of that information into their play. This new information was eventually consolidated into larger units of play behavior and then repeated several times. When playing with familiar or known information, voluntary elaboration of that information was extended into new contexts. Whether or not the girls incorporated new information or elaborated on known information seemed to be related to the saliency of the information and their own current level of skill development.

In yet another observational study, Celia Genishi and John Galvan conducted a preliminary analysis of the talk of three Mexican-American preschoolers' dramatic play in which children assign the roles that they play. The aspect of talk focused on was "getting started," or how the children initiated segments of play. Analysis of transcripts from two hours of videotape showed that two general strategies were used to regulate the direction of play: "start playing" and "play by regulation." The first strategy seemed to be the more successful one. The children's social purposes and desire for controlling the kind of play to enact clearly affected the way talk was organized. Implications of these findings for the education of young children are discussed.

Since play is universally regarded as a primary vehicle or process through which learning takes place, it follows that play is also considered to be a central component of early childhood programs. Much of our understanding of play in such programs has been based on adult conceptions (theoretical and practical) of play activity. In a study by Margaret Garza, Sandy Briley and Stuart Reifel, children described their own experiences in a full-day child care program. Open-ended questions elicited the structure of daily activities from a sample of 3- to 6-year-olds. In their descriptions of play, children reaffirmed the act of play. Children as young as three have a mental picture of play as part of their daily experience in child care. Descriptions of play focused primarily either on use of materials/equipment (e.g., scooters, blocks) or on pretend play with peers, but not on both combined. The authors present a particularly intriguing discussion on the sources and meanings of children's understanding of play.

Studies of children's play are incomplete without consideration of sex role differentiation. Sex role differences in play begin during infancy and continue throughout childhood. Betty Spillers Beeson and R. Ann Williams used an observational instrument to investigate sex differences in the play activities of preschool children. As the research literature would predict, the traditionally male oriented activities (blocks, wheeled vehicles, water/sand) were sex stereotyped while the traditionally female oriented activity, art projects, was sex stereotyped. Differing from previous studies, it was observed that house play was not sex stereotyped.

Collectively these papers sample, in microcosm, the growing body of information about understanding play and represent in method and substance the expanding range of thought about this important subject.

A History of Outdoor Play 1900-1985: Theories of Play and Play Environments

SUE C. WORTHAM
Division of Education
The University of Texas at San Antonio

Play is a natural part of childhood. Children from all cultures engage in play in the process of growing and maturing into adulthood. Although children have always played outdoors, an environment designed to facilitate play in outside areas is a fairly recent phenomenon. Since the 1900's the design and purpose for playgrounds have followed theories of play, which have waxed and waned as study of child development has evolved and progressed. A brief history here of outdoor play and playgrounds is divided into two time periods: 1900 to 1930; and from 1930 to the present. Within each section, outdoor play is discussed from the perspective of the prevailing theories of play, the perception of the role of play in the child's development and characteristics of the outdoor play environment.

THEORIES OF PLAY
1900-1930

The theories of play ascribed to in the first decades of the twentieth century were first developed during the eighteenth and nineteenth centuries. From 1900 to 1930, four theories affected the perception of why and how children play: the surplus energy theory, the recreation theory, the instinct theory and the recapitulation theory.

Advocates of the *surplus energy* theory, one approach used by early theorists to explain why children need to play, maintained that when the child builds an excess of energy, active play is necessary to get rid of the surplus. Spencer, who with Schiller advanced the theory, explained that when conditions of life became easier so that an individual or animal did not need to expend all its energy in obtaining food and shelter or gaining a living, the left-over energy was used for play

(Curtis, 1916). Teachers who send restless children out for a brief recess still hold a belief that children need to release pent-up energy.

The *recreation* theory, in contrast, described as a way to recuperate from fatigue experienced from hard work, was first proposed by Guts Muths, a German teacher, to support the advocacy of physical training as a part of development. It was felt that recreative play was more beneficial than idleness when people were not at work. Play restored energy (Mitchell and Mason, 1948).

Rousseau is credited with developing the *instinct* theory, in which play is described as inherited. Beginning with and during infancy, the child engaged in behaviors and activities instinctively. Play began naturally and continued to develop as the child grew. Johnson compared instinctive play in human beings with animal development: "During this period of immaturity, the young instinctively exercise in playful ways the growing powers by the use of which their ancestors have survived in the struggle for life, as in the case of the fox or the cat" (1907, p. 5). Groos extended the instinct theory by proposing that play is a preparation for life. In *The Play of Animals* (1898) Groos held that young animals played to prepare themselves for life's activities. Gulick made the connection between the kitten playing with a string or stick and the adult cat using similar strategies as a good mouser to explain play as role preparation (1920, p. 101).

The *recapitulation* theory of play was related to the instinct theory. G. Stanley Hall, a leader of the child study movement, supported the theory, which attributed play to heredity. In play children repeated the stages in the evolution of man. As in the instinct theory, children rehearsed the activities of their

3

ancestors. Curtis supported the recapitulation theory of play as follows:

In this wild life of the savage there were certain activities which were almost universal. It was necessary to pursue and capture his game, to find it while it was hiding, to strike it down with a stick or stone or shoot it with bow and arrow. Often he had to climb trees, to vault over obstacles, or leap across brooks. At other times he himself was the hunted, and he had to flee or hide from the pursuer or to defend himself with such means as lay at hand. These were universal activities of savage man throughout the days of unrecorded history, and it is these same activities that survive in the play of the child (1916, p. 5).

The four theories in combination or as separate theories were embraced when explaining how play affected the child's development. According to writers prior to 1930, play was an important factor in growth and development of the child within the prevailing understanding of how play was beneficial.

THE ROLE OF PLAY IN THE CHILD'S DEVELOPMENT

Stages of development in play as described in the 1920's separated spontaneous play from organized games. Play was considered as instinctive, while games had to be taught to transmit the child's historical inheritance. Games were thought to have been derived from savage man.

In defining stages of play, writers did not agree on the length of interval for each period. Curtis (1916) divided development into three periods: age one through five; six to puberty; and the adolescent years beginning at about age thirteen. In contrast, Lee (1923) and Johnson (1907) described development in three-and four-year intervals.

Infants and young children were thought to engage in instinctive and imitation play. Through instinctive play the child was gaining control of the parts of the body. Fundamental physical movements were being mastered. Through imitation play, children were preparing for the adult world. Doll play and other forms of dramatic play helped the child learn adult occupations. Curtis (1916) described the young child as a little monkey that loves to run and jump and climb.

Elementary school-age children were thought to be in a period of uneven physical development. Younger elementary-age children were considered to be physically weak with a tendency to fatigue. Older elementary-age children were physically strong. Lee (1923) categorized elementary age children as in the "Big Injun" stage when games of individual competition were popular. Hunting, camping and collections were of interest to the child, with a particular interest in running games.

Teenagers were in a stage of development corresponding to tribal life. Team games were now possible, since the children were capable of organizing themselves and taking leadership roles. Sex differences in play were noted, with both boy and girl play characterized by organization of gangs or clubs, which included development of feelings of loyalty for peer groups.

CHARACTERISTICS OF OUTDOOR PLAY ENVIRONMENTS

Playground developers of the period advocated large school and public playgrounds. Plenty of space for recreational, organized games was recommended, particularly in cities where little space was available for play. School playgrounds were to serve the community, as well as the school; consequently, writers of the period advocated that the school grounds be open after school hours and during vacation with adult supervision.

Because there was much concern over the misdeeds which might occur when children, particularly teenagers, played without supervision, arrangement of the playground for organized games such as baseball, volleyball, basketball, tetherball and tennis was of primary importance. A running track and jumping pit were included for athletic competitions. Also recommended for physical development were horizontal bars for climbing and other exercises.

Of lesser importance was play equipment for younger children. The most commonly used play apparatus included the sand bin, seesaws, swings, the giant stride and slide. Swings were to be placed parallel to the fence. Girls were not to be allowed to stand up in swings because their dresses would fly up.

Slides were made of varnished wood, at first homemade, wooden structures. Other equipment was made of wood or constructed of metal pipe fittings. Under no circumstances was the apparatus to interfere with the open spaces needed for free play.

THEORIES OF PLAY
1930-1985

From 1930 to the present, newer theories have joined the classical theories in explaining children's need for play. Although contemporary theories of play have their roots in earlier periods of the history of play, they have had their most significant effect on playground development since 1950. The cognitive theory, psychoanalytic theory and play as a learned behavior all contribute to our present understanding of how children benefit from play, while the expression theory, arousal-seeking theory and competence-motivation theory attempt to explain *why* children are motivated to play.

In the *psychoanalytic* theory of play based on the psychoanalytic theory originated by Freud and redefined by Erikson, the play of children is explained as having positive and negative causes. As the child, motivated by the pleasures and rewards derived from play moves through stages of development, play has a therapeutic affect on the development of ego strength, an effect that can explain the cathartic use of play. The child uses repetitive experiences to cope with a traumatic event. By including elements of the unpleasant experience into play episodes, the child gains control of emotions involved with the event, and their impact is diminished (Ellis, 1973).

In the *cognitive* theory, Piaget described the child's play as dependent upon cognitive structures. Play is initiated by the child relative to the thinking processes available at each stage of development. As the child develops from infancy through adolescence, the child's cognitive style influences the complexity of play. Likewise, children use play as a vehicle for cognitive development. When a new behavior has been mastered or learned, the child repeats it as a playful or pleasurable experience (Ellis, 1973).

Advocates of play as a learned behavior propose that play is not explained by a theory but learned from external conditions. Play is subject to rewards and punishments. The child's subsequent play experiences are dependent upon the positive and negative reinforcers the child encounters in play activities (Sutton-Smith, 1951; Ellis, 1973).

In proposing the *expression* theory of play, Mason and Mitchell (1948) explained that man seeks to express himself and use his abilities. Play allows the individual to achieve, create and impress others to win their approval (Galgeno, 1973). This simple definition explains that individuals are motivated to play in order to express themselves in some way.

In the *arousal-seeking* theory, play activity is motivated by the need for variety or more complex interactions with the environment. The player's level of interest and play behaviors are changed to maintain the arousal (Ellis, 1973).

In *competence-motivation* theory, White (1959) determined that individuals play from a need to demonstrate their competence over the environment. In play for competence the child continues to play after variety or novelty attributed to the arousal-seeking theory has worn off, carrying on in a repetitive manner in the absence of further stimuli for arousal. Instead, the child achieves pleasure in play that results from mastery or efficiency in play behavior.

Each of these approaches to reasons for play expresses motivation from a positive orientation. The child plays to seek variety and enhanced interest in play, or the child plays to express himself or herself and impress others. The child also plays to develop competence or mastery over the environment.

THE ROLE OF PLAY IN THE CHILD'S DEVELOPMENT

Advocates of more recent theories see play as fostering well-being, creative thinking skills and cognitive development. As the child plays all facets of development are enhanced. Motor, cognitive and socio-emotional development are all increased as the child participates in play experiences. The child develops flex-

5

ibility through play. As children engage in play, arousal, desire for variety and the need for competence all come into focus. Ellis explains:

Play fosters the behavioral variability of an individual, and therefore a species, and thereby increases the probability of future adaptation to unpredictable circumstances where behavioral flexibility is an advantage (1973, p. 116).

The child develops as a result of arousal-seeking and the desire for competence. Subsequent learning combined with arousal-seeking results in an upward spiral of increasingly complex play interactions with the environment.

CHARACTERISTICS OF OUTDOOR PLAY ENVIRONMENTS

Playgrounds of the 1930's and 1940's were generally expansions of the playgrounds established in earlier decades. Team sports were still the most important kind of play with large areas of space for athletic and sports games. Outdoor fields were provided for football, basketball, volleyball, softball, tennis, shuffleboard and croquet. Stunts and free-play were also considered essential to sound growth and the development of physical skills.

Durable surfacing materials including clay, turf, sand, concrete and asphalt appeared, as well as fences around the playground. Although landscape specialists recommended trees and shrubbery, many playgrounds had none to break the flat expanse of property.

Play apparatus for younger children was still of secondary importance. A Committee on Standards in Playground Apparatus appointed by the National Recreation Association recommended a standard list of apparatus for age groups, as follows:

1. For preschool children (under 6 years): chair swings (set of 6), sandbox (in 2 sections), small slide, simple low climbing device
2. For children of elementary school age (6-12 years): swing frame 12 feet high (set of 6), slide 8 feet high (16 feet long), horizontal ladder, giant stride, balance beam, horizontal bar, seesaws, travel-

ing rings, low climbing device (Butler, 1960, p. 17)

Public park developers also suggested facilities for crafts and nature studies, as well as water play areas. Other optional facilities were tables and benches, a theater, bleachers and playhouses.

The playgrounds of the 1930's and 1940's also saw the introduction of what Lady Allen of Hurtwood labeled the "Concrete Pipe Period" (1968), when concrete pipe and concrete constructions became popular. Butler (1960) described apparatus designed by the New York Housing Authority, which included structures made of concrete blocks, cinder blocks, and airplanes and boats made of concrete.

Some playgrounds constructed were lighted for night use. Color was introduced to make play facilities more attractive.

Contemporary play environments developed since 1950 reflect in their design a more comprehensive approach to children's play needs. Although varying in nature, designs have shown attempts to provide for play experiences that reflect current understandings of the value of play. Adventure playgrounds, designer playgrounds and creative playgrounds are designed to include the child's socio-emotional, cognitive and motor development in the play opportunities provided.

The idea of adventure playgrounds originated with Sorenson, a landscape architect, who noticed children's interest in construction materials. He proposed that children should build their own playgrounds. After World War II his ideas became a reality when the Adventure Playground movement was started. Called "junk playyards" because they allowed children to use scrap materials to create their own play areas, adventure playgrounds were first established in Denmark and spread to other European countries. In England, adventure playgrounds were established on bomb sites from World War II. Over 200 such playgrounds were established throughout Britain.

Although adventure playgrounds have been less successful in the United States, designer playgrounds and creative playgrounds have made improvements over traditional playgrounds built prior to 1950. Designer playgrounds are an urban phenomenon. Designed by architects or professional playground designers, these playgrounds include various types of play experiences for community members of different ages. The overall plan is meant to be aesthetically pleasing as well. While some designer playgrounds provide highly effective play environments, others are more successful for physical design than for playability.

Popular alternatives to traditional playgrounds in the United States are creative playgrounds (Frost & Klein, 1979; Wortham & Wortham, 1983). Designed to be both functional and safe, but more aesthetically pleasing than adventure playgrounds, creative playgrounds provide for all types of desirable play activities that promote growth and development in children. A basic component in a creative playground is a multipurpose climbing structure with various entries and exits. A basic platform has ramps, ladders, slides, fireman poles, tire rafts, clatter bridges and cargo nets attached. The structure encourages socio-dramatic play and fantasy play, in addition to various types of motor activities as the child uses make-believe to change a structure into a ship, fire station or rocket. Swings and other apparatus are there to facilitate social, motor and cognitive development. Included are open areas for organized games, construction areas and opportunities for other creative activities.

Perceptions of the value of children's play have changed considerably since 1900. Outdoor play environments have evolved in response to advances in the theories of play. Although the rationale or emphasis for play has changed, there is one factor that has remained consistent: play is important for growth and learning. The outdoor playground is essential for the play experiences of both children and adults.

Bibliography

Butler, G. D. *Playgrounds: Their Administration and Operation*. New York: Ronald Press, 1960.

Curtis, H. S. *Education Through Play*. New York: Macmillan, 1916.

Ellis, J. J. *Why People Play*. Englewood Cliffs, NJ: Prentice-Hall, 1973.

Frost, J., and B. Klein. *Children's Play and Playgrounds*. Boston: Allyn & Bacon, 1979.

Galgeno, M. L. *The Historical Development of Playground and Apparatus Design from 1930 to 1973*. Unpublished master's thesis, Smith College, 1973.

Groos, K. *The Play of Animals*. New York: D. Appleton, 1898.

Gulick, L. H. *A Philosophy of Play*. New York: Association Press, 1920.

Hurtwood, L. A. *Planning for Play*. Cambridge, MA: MIT Press, 1968.

Johnson, G. E. *Education by Play and Games*. Boston: Ginn, 1907.

Lee, J. *Play in Education*. New York: Macmillan, 1923.

Mitchell, E. D., and B. S. Mason. *The Theory of Play*. New York: A. S. Barnes, 1948.

Sutton-Smith, B. "The Meeting of Maori and European Cultures and its Effects upon the Unorganized Games of Maori Children." *The Journal of the Polynesian Society* 60 (1951): 39-107.

White, R. W. "Motivation Reconsidered: The Concept of Competence." *Psychological Review* 66 (1959): 297-333.

Wortham, S., and M. Wortham. *A Place to Play: The Why and How of Building a Basic Play Structure*. Canyon Lake, TX: Matrix Design, 1983.

Play Research: State of the Art

BRIAN SUTTON-SMITH
Graduate School of Education
University of Pennsylvania, Philadelphia

In a conventional sense the state of the art in play is on a growth curve. Recently in making an analysis of articles in this area from 1880 to 1980, involving some 739 references (Sutton-Smith, 1983), I found the bias in the sources used was towards psychology and did not do justice to anthropology, sport, sociology, folklore or health. Citations ranged from a dozen or so a decade until about 1930, then jumped to about 100 in the 1950's and in the 1960's to 150, and in the 1970's to 200. From 1930 through the 1950's the literature was dominated by articles of a psychodynamic kind, such as play diagnosis, mastery of anxiety, projection, doll play, aggression in play, play therapy and the psychodynamics of those who play chess or gamble. The major names central to that movement were Alexander, Ammons, Axline, Bach, Bender, Bergler, Conn, Erikson, Frank, Freud, Isaacs, Jackson & Todd, Klein, Levy & Levin, Lowenfeld, Menninger, Moustakas, Peller, Phillips, Redl, Reider, Sullivan, Waelder and Winnicott.

There are virtually none of these psychodynamic play studies in the literature of the 1970's.

In the earlier years various correlational studies were largely concerned with the sex, age, race, language, intelligence, family, peer, and socioeconomic status—correlates of playing. Major names in the earlier years again were Ames, Buhler, Griffiths, Hurlick, Jersild, Lehmann & Witty, Markey, Marshall, Murphy, Parten, Valentine. These kinds of correlational studies have continued in considerable force through the 1970's, but the biggest growth in these last decades has been in experimental and Piagetian derived studies. The topics include in particular: exploration, arousal, curiosity, stimulus deprivation, reinforcement, problem-solving, creativity, imagination, role reversal, symbol formation and communication. Some dominant names are Bateson, Bauman, Berlyne, Brainerd, Bruner, Collard, Christie, Csikszentmihalyi, Dansky, Ellis, Fagen, Fein, Garvey, Golomb, Hutt, Johnson, Kirschen-

Table I

Number of scholarly articles or books on child play cited in Herron & Sutton-Smith (1971) and in Rubin, Fein & Vandenberg (in press) for the years from 1880 to 1980.

Category of Research	1800–1900	Decades of 1900's	1910's	1920's	1930's	1940's	1950's	1960's	1970's	Totals
Psychodynamic	—	—	—	1	28	43	69	38	5	184
Correlational	4	4	10	20	25	11	9	19	55	157
Pragmatic	4	1	7	8	23	6	17	31	23	120
Piagetian	—	—	—	—	1	1	2	14	53	71
Experimental	—	—	—	—	1	—	11	13	30	55
Anthropological-Folkloric	1	1	1	—	1	—	10	10	9	33
Animal	—	—	—	1	2	1	11	11	5	31
Social-Psychological	—	—	1	1	2	6	9	11	1	31
Theoretical	2	—	—	—	1	—	3	6	10	22
Gestalt	—	—	—	—	2	6	8	2	1	19
Historical	—	—	—	—	—	2	1	3	3	9
Communicational	—	—	—	—	—	—	2	—	5	7
TOTALS	11	6	19	31	86	76	152	158	200	739

blatt-Gimblett, Klinger, Lieberman, Matthews, McCloyd, Levy, McDowell, Nicolich, Pepler, Pulaski, Roemer, Rocissano, Ross, Rubin, Saltz, Schwartzman, Singer, Smith, Vandenberg.

In addition to this surge in articles in the 1970's, research-oriented books in play across all fields from 1970 until the present number between 20 and 30, more than the total of such books from the preceding years of the twentieth century.

RATIONAL AND IRRATIONAL PLAY

Having looked briefly at the state of play, let us turn to other considerations play researchers must take into account if we are to know what we are about. For some time the ground has been changing philosophically under our feet, and much of what we do now seems to be entirely anachronistic, of little value for the understanding of play. As a simple preliminary into a complex set of issues, let us start with the idea that there are two kinds of play: the rational and the irrational; or, rather that it is useful to consider play in terms of meaning that varies between rationality at one end and irrationality at the other.

We might consider the *major* dimension of a discussion of play as that between what is *rational and what is irrational*. Play as something rational is what we tend to study and pursue in the psychology of play and in the playground movement. Irrational play is more characteristic of the play research in folklore, and of symbolic anthropology.

A recent analysis by Mahai Spariosu (1982) of Georgia State University, Athens (Department of Comparative Literature) suggests that from Platonic thought onwards we have been dominated by a view of the world which made play, literature and aesthetics secondary to science, logic and philosophy. In this *rational* view of the universe, the best that these secondary subject matters could hope for would be imitations of the more rational order of things provided by science, logic and philosophy. The best thing that play could do would be to imitate the more rational aspects of human behavior. It can

be argued that the play theories of the past hundred years have clearly accomplished this Platonic wish. Spencer connects play with evolution; Groos makes it a kind of preparation for adult life; Freud uses it to master anxiety; Erikson sees play as a counterpart to adult planning. Piaget makes play the place to consolidate the more rational accommodative activities. Berlyne allows that in exploration and play one discovers the stimulus world; Bruner finds that problems are solved there; Lieberman finds that the playful ones are the creative ones; Singer declares that those with imagination are better than those without it; Bateson suggests that play is the original kind of metacommunication without which ordinary communication is simply impossible and the social construction of reality hardly conceivable.

From this background a skeptic might see the history of the scholarship of play in this century as a steady idealization of hitherto unacceptable subject matter. Even when moving away from academia, we find amongst the public the same idealization of play, although this time through athletics, sports, recreation and the playground movement. The steady trend of this century has been to argue that these activities, derived as they were from the social elites of the nineteenth century, would serve to socialize and integrate the poor and the immigrant into the character and mores of the politically dominant members of the society. Gary Goodman's *Choosing Sides* (1979) is a rather trenchant and probably over-simplified story of how the New England Wasps in the first decades of this century colonized the lower East Side Jews off the streets and into the new Playground Movement. According to Spariosu, however, on the edge of all this rationalization of play has hovered another major kind of play, something basically irrational. Homer, prior to Plato, contends the irrational and agonistic modes of play dominate. *The Iliad* is a war game between the gods who are both free and irrational and play with men like toys in some divine lottery. The gods themselves are like children who at one moment play with a doll and at the next dismember it to see what is inside. In Heraclitus, play as an arbitrary, sponta-

10

neous and free movement becomes a philosophical principle for the first time. This early idea of play as freedom is that it is willful and dangerous, unlike many current definitions of play as freedom, which seem to imply only its spontaneity and rationality of choice.

It is not until Nietzsche of 1844-1900 that we once again hear a full statement of the earlier Homeric view of play as a species of irrationality, perhaps not surprising with Nietzsche's generally fascistic and power-oriented philosophy. For him play is the exuberant dionysian impulse beyond good and evil that willfully engenders and destroys entire civilizations. For him the world is the play of eternal conflict. The basic kind of *being* in an entological sense is irrational play. In his work appearance, falsehood, fiction, representation, unreality and irrationality become privileged terms, supplanting such terms as essence, model, truth, reality and rationality, which have been privileged since Plato.

We are so accustomed to thinking of play as a trivial, childlike, imitative, secondary reality that it is almost impossible to grasp this view of ourselves as *played* by reality; of reality as a kind of playing. Rather, play is considered a subcategory within sensible reality. Even when, like Freud, we suggest that irrationality as "primary process" is basic, we still see it as contained by egos and superegos. Even in Freud primary process was seldom the master, but usually only the fractious servant in the house. One finds this idea that play is the basic mode of being in the more recent 20th century phenomenological literature of Heidigger and Gadamer, although in their cases this higher metaphysical status is not accompanied by the same emphasis on irrationality as with Nietzsche.

Although, like Nietzsche, they talk about play in such global terms, it is difficult for anyone trained in the natural science tradition of social science to feel much moved by their discourse. One clarity has emerged in play research of the past twenty years, which, is that it if often (though not always) possible to distinguish between exploration and play (Hutt, 1971, 1979), between play

and creative imagination (Piaget, 1951) and between play and daydreams (Singer, 1973).

INTERPRETIVE SCIENCE VIEWS OF PLAY

In moving to yet another distinction between natural social science and interpretive social science, we see natural social science as the kind in which social science models itself after the physical sciences, presupposes a determinate and determinable human reality and seeks to establish its laws by quantitative methodologies and analytic procedures.

Interpretive social science, emerging from phenomenology in this century, has had considerable impact on anthropology and sociology under such titles as ethnomethodology, ethnography and symbolic anthropology. It begins with the central notion that human sciences should focus on human meanings. A human being has to be seen as a meaning-seeking creature; it is usually only through participatory engagement with him that we can elicit his truths, seeking at the same time to understand reflexively how we are playing a role in that which we solicit.

That part of interpretive view of science seeming to have the greatest effect on play research is that developed by such leaders as Victor Turner (1974), Erving Goffman (1959, 1961) and Clifford Geertz (1973). These scholars presume to tell us about the way things mean to those whom they study, with a strong dose of Nietzsche! They assume that play forms observed are not just there in some essentialist platonic way, but are forms of action used by the participators to achieve their ends. Play is a part of the power politics of the groups in which it occurs. Play is a rhetorical not just a grammatical event (in Kenneth Burke's sense).

Victor Turner, for example, says that play forms are used by tribal members as an active technique for resolving or assuaging social conflicts when other, more direct forms, are not available. Play expresses the orectic aspect of society as compared with its normative aspect. Play forms are society's antistructure not its conventional structure. Society is divided within itself in many ways; play forms enter into the political calculus of resolution and occasionally of change. In this dialectical kind of approach, play's irrationality is seen as a fundamental part of the social constitution. To this point we are talking about play forms on an apparent and easily understood level—festivals, sports, rituals, games. But Turner gives us the more abstract, metaphysical Nietzschean kind of notion that the society as a whole is a social drama played out in this and other ways. We are approaching the notion that reality is itself a form of playing.

In Erving Goffman, small everyday situations are also interpreted through dramatistic and ludic metaphors. Members of society are constantly in rhetorical engagement for the maintenance of social equilibrium. Their plays are like those used on stage or in games. Goffman has been accused by some of a cynical manipulative view of society and by others as showing tremendous social work and mutual respect in even the most common social rituals such as walking down the street, talking over coffee and playing games. Here again, however, we have the Nietzschean view of society as a matter of the management of power, with play and games used as metaphors for illustrating that management. Whether Goffman's view is that life is a game or maybe thought about metaphorically in game terms is not quite clear. It is certainly the latter, but it may not be the former.

In Geertz, society is to be read as a text over the shoulders of the informants. Deep play (the Balinese cock fight) is just one kind of text in which members intuit the deep social divisions of their own society and learn the political lessons of leaving evil alone. The predominant metaphor here is a narrative one. Although recently, in summing up the variety of humanistic metaphors now in operation within interpretive science, Geertz (1980) has suggested that the three major varieties—life is a stage, life is a game, and life is a text—need to "get their acts together." Clearly in Geertz we are dealing with metaphors of convenience for some larger target of scientific understanding.

While play has come to the fore as an idealized subject matter within natural science, thus overcoming some portion of its prior triviality and neglect (most particular

in animal play psychology and most completely in Fagen, 1980), it has continued to be thought of largely as a rational, even if inferior, form of human socialization.

In interpretive science, conversely, play is seen as a more fundamental mode of the social structure, not simply a variation on individual behavior. Here, however, the power of play's role in the politics of society varies from the clearly metaphoric interpretive usage of Geertz, to the more ontological use of Turner. We may use our plays for insight, or we may be played by the society of which we are a part.

It is becoming a question of whose "play" is the best play with which to study play. Is the natural science position the most valid? Is the fiction that human beings behave like determinate physical matter the best assumption to make; or the fiction that they have quite different humanistic modes of their own (ludic, dramatic, text)? Whether we call science a "fiction" or paradigm or world hypothesis, our presuppositions are something to imagine before we can begin, so, not unfairly, they might be called fictions or forms of play.

NATURAL SCIENCE VIEWS OF PLAY

In returning to the natural science views of play, those we take for granted in our psychological studies of children in nursery schools, laboratories and playgrounds, we can illuminate that kind of knowledge in terms of the issues just raised.

First, despite the idealization and rationalism of the natural science grouping of approaches to play, there is nevertheless in many of them a recognition of irrational aspects as essential even if subsidiary in their theories. Thus the evolutionists who saw play as a preparation for life saw it also as a resurgence of primitive atavisms, which must be abreacted before the emergence of rationality in adolescence. Freud, of course, had his perversibility and regressions and Piaget, his distortions and concern with the preoccupation of young children with their orifices and their jealousies. Berlyne had his arousal jags, Fagen his dysfunctional play (many animals and children and adults get maimed and killed at play). Ruth Weir had her verbal nonsense, and Bateson had his paradoxes, of not meaning what you say but only the opposite of what you say, which is what you mean in any case (Sutton-Smith, 1979).

Some of the idealization and rationality of natural science play theories—Freud, Piaget (1951), Berlyne (1960), Bateson (1972)—seem to be accomplished by brushing certain play features under the carpet. Another way in which these theories have accomplished their sanitization of the phenomenon has been by studying play in high supervision situations, such as nursery schools, laboratories, clinical and supervised playgrounds. The largest sources of play studies have come from nursery schools. Quite naturally, the aim of most nursery school teachers is to rule out irrational and immature aspects of behavior; they must go to great lengths to see that what occurs is only "good" play or "clean" play. It is their duty to socialize and counter examples of irrational play. From such contexts one is sure to get a limited view of what children's play is about. In the heyday of psychoanalytic approaches in the 1930's, in dealing often with the disturbed and the deviant, analysts had an intrinsic interest in regressive and animalistic play. The works of Isaacs (1933), Lowenfeld (1935) and Winnicott (1971) are replete with irrationality. But that kind of play has not continued to be researched, dismissed perhaps as the aberrant phenomena of psychoanalysis or as the non-objective data of psychoanalysts. Not surprisingly, given the *socialization orientation* of most researchers in child psychology, most studies of preschool play have been studies of the way in which some measurement of play correlates with other measures of maturity or cognitive activity. Early childhood play literature thus pays extraordinary attention to such findings as:

1. The association between the kind of social organization of the players (solitary, parallel, associative or cooperative) and some other index of maturity (usually age, but sometimes intelligence or socioeconomic status). (It used to be the finding that more solitary players were less mature; more recent findings are that some kinds of solitary players are really quite mature.)
2. Better attached children play more maturely.
3. Children of divorced parents play less maturely.
4. Girls play with more imaginative maturity than boys.
5. The structure of toys can affect the maturity of the play.
6. Children who play together continuously with the same sex peers play more maturely.
7. Linguistic maturity and symbolic play maturity are correlated.
8. Playful children are more creative.
9. Imaginative children are less aggressive.
10. Lower class children are or are not less imaginative (a matter of dispute).
11. Children who play in their home setting play at higher levels of maturity than when playing in public settings.

One of the best commentaries on the actions of preschool play research was the study by Susanne McBride of the University of Delaware on the status of toy research amongst psychologists. In a search of the literature between 1969 and 1979 for references to the use of toys in the Journals of *Child Development, Developmental Psychology* and *Experimental Child Psychology*, she found about 30 percent of the authors of the journal articles sampled used toys in some way or other, not as objects for study, but for rewards to elicit behavior, inhibit behavior; to study mother attachment, exploration, social behavior, imitation, transgression, delay of gratification, resistance to temptation, selfishness, emotional dependence, sex role preference, object concept or response inhibition; or used in standardized procedures on infant tests. Despite copious use of toys, the cultural meaning of these objects or their function in child development and child play was simply assumed, not studied. That would seem to typify most play studies throughout this century. Part of the sanitization of play has been the result of this overwhelming unwillingness to study what play actually is (Herron & Sutton-Smith, 1971, pp. 1-3).

Study of children in playgrounds is, by and large, equally sanitized. Here the socialization of children through the provision of the proper apparatus or the proper playground context becomes the ameliorative

13

concern. We want to know how apparatus affects children's safety, their sociability or their violence (Frost & Klein, 1979). We discover, for example, that more apparatus lowers sociability and aggression, less apparatus increases sociability and aggression. Playground theorizing and research seems to be gripped into the recapitulatory notion of the human being that was so potent a force in Stanley Hall at the turn of the century. Hall's atavistic little human monkeys had a tremendous need to climb, swing, build—needs that are being catered to brilliantly in some modern playground designs. We all know that children by preference will spend very little time in most of the playgrounds that we can engineer, but that is not to say we shouldn't keep building them. They are usually better environments for play than the play areas they supplanted. Built playgrounds have street playgrounds to remind us of their limitations. There is *street play* and now, *video game arcades*, two kinds of playgrounds with play of greatly different caliber.

Children's folklore provides a great deal of at least anecdotal documentation of the nature of play during childhood. The earlier work of Peter and Iona Opie (1968), and more recently of Andrew Sluckin in his study of Oxford playgrounds, *Growing up in the Playground* (1981), my own *History of Children's Play in New Zealand*, and in the United States the accounts of Mary and Herbert Knapp (1976), Bess Jones and Bess Hawes (1972), John McDowell (1979), and others all make it clear that children's collective play is a world of power politics, incredible struggle, aggression, sexuality, parody, regression and many other non-idyllic matters. The major meaning of social play that emerges from a review of this kind of material is that it is about power and the struggle for identity within the dominance-subordination domains of one's peers. This is not the same kind of play that prevails in preschool supervised play contexts, out of which have come most definitions of play in child psychological research, such as *non-literality, flexibility, positive affect* and *intrinsic motivation* (to cite a recent example (Krasnor & Pepler, 1980).

In a context in which one is largely guarded from the worst excesses of other children, these attributes might well be useful as describing play, but in peer play none of these definitions need be of importance although they can be. In street play the extrinsic motivation to belong to the group often leads one into play one would prefer to avoid. In that play there may be unkindness, even victimization. In addition to the negative effect, behavior can sometimes be severely routinized. In such a world of peer power politics even when games are involved, it is difficult to see *non-literality* as a simple concept.

A student of mine, Linda Hughes (1983), has for four years been studying the game of Four Square as played by girls in elementary school. It is her conclusion that while the game may be a non-literal event, the gaming that goes on around the game is certainly not. These girls are playing at manners, while playing at the game; their major dimension is that of "nasty" and "nice" and they score the game by its fulfillment in this dimension rather than routinely by the action rules. Thus, if you put out a friend in a nice way, saying "Oh I'm sorry, I didn't mean to throw so hard," the friend goes out. But if the friend claims it was a nasty shot, the rest will support her in the illegitimacy of that shot. Even that statement is too simple, because your friends' support in the judgment of the shot, depends on your relationship to those friends. That is, the judgment of "nice-nasty" is dependent on the pre-existing sociometric, or the culture of peers.

In understanding a game we are involved in at least three terms—culture, gaming and games. In William Foote Whyte's *Street Corner Society* the gang's scores in bowling reproduced the linearity of the gang sociometric, a case in which there was not much "as if" at work. Most game-playing cultures are not that tightly knit; the interrelationships of culture, gaming and games can be more variable.

The "as if" definition of play is said to derive historically from the work of Schiller and Kant who see play as a mediator between reason and perception (Spariosu, 1982), but "as ifness" may also be associated

14

with romanticism and the decay of religious hegemony. In times past the sense of "otherness" was most often an attribute of the sacred. In the diminishing of that concept, this sense of "otherness" has been attributed to more naturalistic sources—sentiment, self, aesthetics and—in our day—play and even sex.

In video games, however, the Krasnor and Pepler criteria appear to serve. In this non-literal sphere, the effect is positive and exciting and one is certainly intrinsically motivated. But video games are largely solitary activities; solitary play, like nursery play, is clearly very different from that which takes place amongst neighborhood groups in the streets.

When these games became popular in 1982, many older persons declared them to be irrational forms of play leading to aggression, addiction, thence to gambling; to perceptual-motor rigidity, impulsive decision-making and a generation of passive game players. Further, this game was first perceived by many as immediately degenerative (not "as if"), rigid (not flexible), addictive (not free) and of passive (not positive) effect.

The most sanitized of all the modern research studies of play in the natural science tradition is the study of relationships between playing and problem-solving. Here is the work ethic in its finest form, based on Kohler's demonstration that even apes who play with sticks are often better at solving problems with the same sticks. The rationality of play would be well served if such a demonstration could be made within a solid evolutionary paradigm. Characteristically, children are given about ten minutes to "play with" the materials with which they will later have to solve problems; they are compared with others who haven't had that play period, but who have already been shown how to solve problems with these materials. How many of us can perform in a strange environment under the dictate to play with strange materials and strange people?

The larger question raised by this natural science tradition, however, is whether it is possible to study play with these methods. It could be that the problem is not intrinsic to natural science but to the scientists' socialization (work ethic) concerns, which overwhelm other, worthier subjects such as problem-solving, playground apparatus, preschool training programs, sex role preferences, symbolic development, creativity and reading.

The analytic, predictive mode of approach of natural science seems to indicate that what is relatively less important about play is that which is most predictable about it. It is of some management and educational value to know what to expect of the ages and sexes in terms of children's probable play activities; in this sense at least, we have profited by our natural science research tradition. But this tradition has told us little about what play *does* for the players. It might be more helpful to have further descriptive records of players and their engagement over a period of time with each other, games, toys and playground apparatus.

One of my students, Diana Kelly-Byrne (1983), has tried such a survey by playing with one child about once a month, three to five hours at a time, for a year. Her impressive discoveries about play are in the interpretive science tradition, within which one is concerned about the validity of interpretation rather than the validity of the subject matter itself. A major conclusion from her study, for example, was that her particular 7-year-old child first played with her symbolic familial concerns of mother and father powers for six months, then moved to narrating them symbolically, and finally was able to discuss them conversationally. Play was an intermediary form of idiosyncratic communication, an ancient kind of language as Bateson would have called it.

CONCLUSION

In presenting some of the larger philosophical, historical and methodological issues of importance in our current research in play, I think I have made it clear that current research agendas bring esteem to play but in a trivial and secondary fashion. The major concern is with rationality, socialization and redemption. We are unwilling to admit that violent sports, libidinous foreplay, addictive gambling, strategic war games, video games, "seven minutes in heaven," little league base-ball, Barbie doll play, playing houses, playing with toy trucks and mobiles hanging over a crib are all a part of the necessary subject matter with which we must deal if we are to deal with play. Furthermore, we must tackle the use of some or all of these phenomena as a source of metaphors for other life activities. Is it true that play and game concepts are increasingly taking the place of earlier religious and evolutionary concepts for describing human affairs and our place in the world?

If so, then games are neither inherently rational or irrational, but both. Similarly, the freedom of games can be blessed or cursed; the freedom of the dilettante or the obsessed. Again, the otherness or "as ifness" of play and games can be the fantasy of Alice in Wonderland or the demoniacal possession of professional football. The activities of the players can be a contest, a representation or a transformation. Play can be competitive or cooperative, the ultimate reality or the ultimate unreality. Whatever it is, play enters, into a dialectic with other concerns, constituting most often their antithesis within some prevailing spirit of otherness that allows us to mask our irrationality in some fashion sufficiently rational for mutual acceptance. In playing, our diverse natures are for those temporary moments thus masked and humanized in an unorthodox fashion.

Bibliography

Bateson, G. *Steps to an Ecology of Mind.* New York: Ballantine, 1972.

Berlyne, D. E. *Conflict, Arousal and Curiosity.* New York: McGraw-Hill, 1960.

Fagen, R. *Animal Play Behavior.* New York: Oxford University Press, 1980.

Frost, J. L., and B. L. Klein. *Children's Play and Playgrounds.* Boston: Allyn & Bacon, 1979.

Geertz, C. *The Interpretation of Cultures.* New York: Basic Books, 1973.

————. "Blurred Genres: The Refiguration of Social Thought." The American Scholar (Spring 1980): 165-79.

Goffman, E. *The Presentation of Self in Everyday Life.* New York: Doubleday, 1959.

————. *Encounters.* Indianapolis, IN: Bobbs-Merrill, 1961.

Goodman, G. *Choosing Sides: Playground and Street Life on the Lower East Side.* New York: Schocken, 1979.

Hans, J. S. *The Play of the World.* Amherst, MA: University of Massachusetts Press, 1981.

Herron, R. E., and B. Sutton-Smith. *Child's Play.* New York: Wiley, 1971.

Hughes, L. "Beyond the Rules of the Games: Why are Rooie Rules Nice?" In F. Manning, ed., *The World of Play.* West Point, NY: Leisure Press, 1983.

Hutt, C. "Exploration and Play in Children." In R. E. Herron and B. Sutton-Smith, eds., *Child's Play.* New York: Wiley, 1971. Pp. 231-51.

————. "Exploration and Play." In B. Sutton-Smith, ed., *Play and Learning.* New York: Gardner Press, 1979. Pp. 175-94.

Isaacs, S. *Social Development in Young Children.* New York: Harcourt Brace, 1933.

Jones, B., and B. Hawes. *Step it Down.* New York: Harper & Row, 1972.

Kelly-Byrne, D. "A Narrative of Play and Intimacy." In F. E. Manning, ed., *The World of Play.* West Point, NY: Leisure Press, 1983.

————. "The Meaning of Play's Triviality." In B. Sutton-Smith and D. Kelly-Byrne, eds., *The Masks of Play.* West Point, NY: Leisure Press, 1983.

————. "Play: The Child-Adult Connection." In B. Sutton-Smith and D. Kelly-Byrne, eds., *The Masks of Play.* West Point, NY: Leisure Press, 1983.

Knapp, M., and H. Knapp. *One Potato, Two Potato.* New York: Norton, 1976.

Krasnor, L. R., and D. J. Pepler. "The Study of Children's Play: Some Suggested Future Directions." In K. Rubin, ed., *Children's Play: New Directions for Child Development.* Vol. 9. San Francisco: Jossey-Bass, 1980. Pp. 85-96.

Lowenfeld, M. *Play in Childhood.* London: Gollancz, 1935.

McBride, S. R. "The Culture of Toy Research." In A. T. Cheska, ed., *Play as Context.* West Point, NY: Leisure Press, 1979. Pp. 210-18.

McDowell, J. *Children's Riddling.* Bloomington, IN: University of Indiana Press, 1979.

Opie, I., and P. Opie. *The Lore and Language of Schoolchildren.* New York: Oxford University Press, 1968.

Pepler, D. J., and K. Rubin. "The Play of Children: Current Theory and Research." *Contributions to Human Development* 6 (1982): 1-158.

Piaget, J. *Play, Dreams and Imitation in Childhood.* New York: Norton, 1951.

Rubin, K. "Children's Play." *New Directions for Child Development* 9 (1980): 1-98.

Rubin, K.; G. Fein and B. Vandenberg. "Children's Play." In E. M. Hetherington, ed., *The Carmichael Handbook of Child Psychology.* New York: Wiley, in press.

Sluckin, A. *Growing Up in the Playground.* London: Routledge and Kegan Paul, 1981.

Spariosu, M. "Literature and Play: History, Principles, Method." In M. Spariosu, ed., *Literature, Mimesis and Play.* Tubingen, West Germany: Gunter Narr Verlag, 1982. Pp. 13-52.

Sutton-Smith, B. "The Kissing Games of Adolescents in Ohio." *Midwestern Folklore* 9 (1959): 189-221.

————. "Play as Meta-Performance." In B. Sutton-Smith, ed., *Play and Learning.* New York: Gardner Press, 1979.

————. "One Hundred Years of Research on Play." *Newsletter of the Association for the Anthropological Study of Play* 9 (1983): 13-16.

Sutton-Smith, B., and D. Kelley-Byrne, eds., *The Masks of Play.* West Point, NY: Leisure Press, 1983.

Turner, V. *Dramas, Fields and Metaphors.* Ithaca, NY: Cornell University Press, 1974.

Winnicott, D. W. *Playing and Reality.* New York: Basic Books, 1971.

Playful Literacy Activities and Learning: Preliminary Observations

JOAN ISENBERG and EVELYN JACOB
Department of Education
George Mason University, Fairfax, Virginia

A growing body of theory and research suggests that play contributes to children's learning. Piaget (1962) discusses play as assimilation, the driving force behind learning; Vygotsky (1976) theorizes that play is foundational to later abstract thought. Other researchers (S. Miller, 1973; Sylva, Bruner and Genova, 1976) view play as a particularly productive context for learning because the dominance of means over ends results in voluntary elaboration and complication of the means. The consequences of failure are reduced, as it is voluntary and offers a temporary moratorium on frustration.

Some researchers (Calkins, 1980; Clay, 1975) have commented that children's early reading and writing efforts often resemble play. Jacob (1982b) found that many of the literacy activities of Puerto Rican kindergarten children engaged in during play at home were playful.

Little is known, however, about the characteristics of playful literacy activities or about their contribution to literacy development. Literacy, treated here as the ability to read and write, is a complex construct, involving motor and cognitive skills, knowledge of literacy artifacts and social behaviors appropriate for specific uses of literacy (Gibson and Levin, 1975; Mason, 1981; Scribner and Cole, 1981).

In view of the limited research on the role of playful literacy activities and their role in learning literacy, we conducted exploratory case studies to refine methods and answer the following questions: What are the nature and characteristics of preschool children's playful literacy activities? What functions do these activities serve in learning literacy?

METHOD

A case study research design was used to collect qualitative, naturalistic observations, an approach that allowed us systematically and inductively to identify patterns of behavior and related variables.

Two white, middle-class girls (4 years 9 months) from a preschool in Northern Virginia were selected for case studies because they were native English speakers, did not exhibit any developmental problems and were of the same age and social class.

In January, 1983, we conducted general observations at the preschool to familiarize ourselves with the school program and allow the children and project staff to become used to our presence. We also met with the children's mothers to explain their role in the study. During one week we conducted focused, non-participant observations of the children's activities at the preschool (approximately eight hours per child). Each investigator observed one child and produced observational notes and audiotape recordings of their behavior. We also photographed literacy artifacts the children made or used. (See Jacob 1982a for a detailed description of the procedures followed.) After conducting the observations we expanded our observational notes, transcribed the audiotapes and combined these data to produce narrative descriptions of each child's activities at school.

In these narrative records we identified all instances of the children's playful reading and writing activities, defining playful behavior as that which is pleasurable, has no extrinsic goals, is spontaneous and voluntary and involves some active engagement on the part of the player (Garvey, 1977). We further distinguished playful literacy activities occurring in pretend and non-pretend contexts. Pretend contexts are those in which children transform themselves or an object into another object, person, event or situation through the use of motor or verbal ac-

17

tions in a make-believe activity (Curry and Arnaud, 1974). Non-pretend contexts do not involve such transformations.

During the week of focused observations the girls' mothers recorded their daily observations of the girls' activities at home, records including descriptions of the girls' play and literacy activities. These data were transcribed, and playful literacy behaviors were identified using the procedures followed in the preschool observations.

After observations were completed, the director of the preschool, with whom the girls were familiar, met individually with each girl, talking informally with them to assess their ability to recognize the names of the children in the class and their familiarity with, and knowledge of, characteristics and uses of prescriptions. The data from these discussions were also transcribed.

RESULTS

Both the school and home environments of the children were saturated with print. In the classroom, activity areas and objects were labelled, experience charts were written and books were available in a book corner. In the homes, books, magazines and newspapers were present; moreover, each girl had her own books and magazines. Reading and writing were highly valued by both parents and staff. The school day included story time and quiet reading period. Parents frequently read to their children and supported the children's literacy efforts.

A major goal of the preschool observed was to promote learning through play. The school day included a large block of time for free play during which children chose their own activities. The housekeeping area was often arranged to stimulate pretend play on different themes for a week at a time.

Both girls engaged in playful literacy activities at home and in school. An instance of a playful literacy activity occurring in pretend play contexts at school occurred on the day the girls played veterinarians and used pretend prescriptions; Toni played for about 25 minutes and Kelly for about 65 minutes. The girls also did several playful literacy activities while pretending at home. For ex-

ample, Kelly pretended to read a menu while playing restaurant. Playful literacy activities in non-pretend contexts occurred more often and were shorter than those occurring during pretend play. Toni did three of these playful literacy activities and Kelly, six.

Pretend Play

In pretend play contexts the girls' playful literacy activities involved skills, knowledge of artifacts and social behavior associated with literacy. In this analysis we focused on their knowledge of characteristics of a particular artifact, namely medical prescriptions. During pretend play the girls gradually incorporated new information about characteristics of prescriptions into their play behavior. These new behaviors were then consolidated into larger units and repeated several times. They also voluntarily elaborated upon and extended known information or familiar skills into new contexts.

During the week of data collection one corner was arranged as an animal hospital containing stuffed animals, doctors' props (masks, caps, gloves, needles, stethoscope), x-rays and a scale.

Examples presented occurred on the third day of observation at the preschool. On the first two days the girls had played in the hospital area but had not included any literacy activities in their pretend play. On the third day at group time, the teacher explicitly introduced information about prescriptions by asking the children what a doctor does if an animal needs medicine. She explained the characteristics of prescriptions and on a small piece of paper wrote the symbol "Rx" and the name of the medicine needed. She talked about social behaviors associated with prescriptions (the doctor writes the name of the medicine and you take it to the pharmacist), and the functions of prescriptions (to get medicine for sick animals). She then showed the children a cardboard tray containing small pieces of paper and pencils, suggesting that they should write "Rx" and the medicine the animal needs on the prescription. Placing paper and pencils in the hospital area, she said the adjacent housekeeping area could be the pharmacy.

18

In non-play settings the usual cycle for using prescriptions occurs when the doctor writes a prescription and gives it to the patient who then gets it filled at a pharmacy. We used this cycle as the unit of analysis (episode) for the girls' play with prescriptions. Kelly's behavior while playing the doctor role illustrates the incorporation and consolidation of new information about prescription characteristics.

When presented with this new information, Kelly first incorporated it orally into her play, then incorporated some of it into her behavior. She incorporated "Rx" early, added writing a number later and eventually established a pattern of writing "Rx" and the number of days until the medicine would be assimilated.

From interview data it was apparent that Kelly related the prescriptions to her own experience; she said once when she was sick she had seen the symbol "Rx" on her medicine. From parent interviews and observational data we knew that Kelly could write her own name, some letters and numbers, and that she made some reversals in her writing.

After the teacher discussed prescriptions Kelly began her play in the hospital area with five other children. The teacher had introduced three characteristics of prescriptions: patient's name, the symbol "Rx," and the name of a kind of medicine. In her first episode Kelly merely labelled the artifact; in the next, she used the term "prescription" and wrote "Rx" on the blank; right after that she wrote "XR" (a reversal) on another blank. (She wrote "Rx" on the blank prescriptions in all but one of the remaining episodes in which she played the doctor role.) Kelly took the prescription to the aide, who was pretending to be the pharmacist. In talking with Kelly, the aide discussed the kind of medicine needed and introduced new information about characteristics of prescriptions. She told Kelly the number of times a day to give the medicine and wrote the number on the prescription. In later episodes Kelly orally incorporated into her play the information about type of medicine and number of times a day medicine was to be given. For example, in the next episode she said to the aide, "I

need some little pills." After playing the pharmacist role she played doctor again, writing "Rx" and a number (for number of days or number of times a day, we assume) on the prescriptions. After again playing pharmacist she returned to playing doctor, again writing "Rx" and a number on the prescriptions.

Toni's behavior while playing the doctor role illustrates the voluntary elaboration and extension of known information into new contexts. She seemed initially to incorporate the new information about the "Rx" symbol into her play, using familiar knowledge (her name) and her interest in spelling in the new context of her pretend play. From interview data it was known that Toni knew little about prescriptions, and in response to the teacher's presentation Toni said she did not know how to spell words on a prescription, but that she could write her own name on it. This seemed to be Toni's attempt to relate the characteristics of prescriptions to what she was already familiar with and interested in. Toni on her own could write her name, the letters of the alphabet, familiar names and some words. She was interested in spelling and did a lot of writing.

Toni's first three episodes were prompted by peers. In her first episode she wrote "KP TONI" on a prescription blank. (The "KP" was apparently her interpretation and reversal of Rx.) Next, she wrote "KP TO TONI," elaborating on what she previously wrote. Her next five episodes were self-initiated. First she wrote "BHHL KR," maintaining her interpretation of "Rx" reversed and adding other letters. In four subsequent events she abandoned the "Rx" equivalent and wrote letter combinations placed next to each other to resemble a word: "BTRA" in the first, "OOBR" in the second and "MWN" in the third instance.

Non-Pretend Play Contexts

During non-pretend play the girls' playful literacy activities involved familiar information and skills, which they extended into new contexts. Several examples follow.

Every morning the teacher, in taking attendance, held up each child's name card for the children to read; after they responded she then read the name aloud. Toni could recognize all but two of the children's names. She was usually the first to read a name aloud. Also she often repeated a name after the teacher had read it.

One day Toni elaborated on this pattern by replacing the initial consonant of children's names with another letter. After the teacher read "Katie," Toni said "Watie." After the teacher read the next name, "Scott," Toni said "Bott." She continued this pattern, substituting B for the initial letter in the names of six children.

Name-reading also provided a playful literacy activity for Kelly who, after attending the preschool for one month, recognized names of three classmates besides her own and when these names were held up she read them aloud spontaneously. She did not always focus attention on the name cards, often looking around the room. Sometimes she repeated the names aloud after the teacher and other children had read them.

An instance of playful literacy occurred one day with Alex's name (one of the names she could read). Noticing his name in a story written on an experience chart, Kelly walked to the chart and said "Alex" pointing to his name in the story. She repeated his name, went to where Alex was playing and again said his name to herself. Then she returned to the chart, pointed to his name at the bottom of the story and in the middle, saying playfully, "Alex, Alex, where is Alex?"

SUMMARY

Both four-year-old girls engaged in playful literacy activities in pretend and non-pretend play contexts, activities that seemed to involve two functions related to learning: the gradual incorporation of new information into the children's behavior patterns with the formation of larger units behavior and the elaboration and extension of known or familiar information to new contexts.

The girls themselves had a crucial role in determining the content and function of the activities. Their choices seemed related to the saliency of the information and their current skills. In the pretend play at school involving new information about prescriptions,

one girl, relating prescriptions to her environment, incorporated several characteristics of prescriptions into her behavior and played both doctor and pharmacist roles. The other girl, who knew little about prescriptions, chose to perform only the doctor role, focusing her activity not on characteristics of the artifact but on extending her interest in writing and spelling.

The teachers' introduction of information to the pretend play setting about prescriptions provided an important stimulus to the girls' incorporation of this information into their play, supporting the position of learning theorists (Anderson, 1982; Piaget, 1962; Simon, 1980) that learners must choose to become involved in incorporating new knowledge and skills into their own frameworks.

Exploratory studies such as ours are based on a small number of observations and raise questions rather than provide answers. Questions raised by this study include: How important are these playful literacy activities to the children's literacy development? What is the role of the specific content in these playful activities? How do family and cultural attitudes and values about specific functions of literacy influence children's incorporation of them into play? Does children's incorporation into their pretend play of information about literacy artifacts and social behaviors associated with them contribute to their literacy development? How important is the introduction of this type of information by adults?

Detailed naturalistic observations of children's playful literacy activities need to be made of more children of different ages, gender, social class and ethnicity over longer periods of time. Such information would contribute to our understanding of the role and the processes of play important to children's literacy development and provide teachers and parents with guidelines for creating environments that maximize children's development.

References

Anderson, J.R. "Acquisition of Cognitive Skill." *Psychological Review* 89 (1982):369-406.
Calkins, L. "Children Learn the Writer's Craft." *Lan*

guage Arts 57 (1980):207-13.

Clay, M. *What Did I Write?* London: Heinemann, 1975.

Curry, N., and S. Arnaud. "Cognitive Implications in Children's Spontaneous Role Play. *Theory into Practice* 13 (1974):173-77.

Gibson, E.J., and H. Levin. *The Psychology of Reading.* Cambridge, MA: MIT Press, 1975.

Jacob, E. "Puerto Rican Children's Informal Education at Home." Final report to the National Institute of Education, February, 1982a.

———. "Learning Literacy Through Play." Paper presented at the Conference on "Children's Response to a Literate Environment: Literacy Before Schooling." Victoria, British Columbia: October 1982b.

Mason, J.M. "Prereading: A Developmental Perspective." Technical Report No. 1981. Urbana, IL: University of Illinois, Center for the Study of Reading, 1981.

Miller, S. "Ends, Means and Galumphing: Some Leit-motifs of Play." *American Anthropologist* 75 (1973):87-97.

Piaget, J. *Play, Dreams and Imitation.* New York: W.W. Norton, 1962.

Scribner, S., and M. Cole. *The Psychology of Literacy.* Cambridge, MA: Harvard University Press, 1981.

Simon, H.A. "Problem Solving and Education." In D.T. Tuma and F. Reif, eds., *Problem Solving and Education: Issues in Teaching and Research.* Hillsdale, NJ: Erlbaum, 1980.

Sylva, K.; J. Bruner and P. Genova. "The Role of Play in the Problem-Solving of Children 3-5 Years Old." In J. Bruner, A. Jolly and K. Sylva, eds., *Play—Its Role in Development and Evolution.* New York: Basic Books, 1976.

Vygotsky, L.S. "Play and Its Role in the Mental Development of the Child." In J. Bruner, A. Jolly and K. Sylva, eds., *Play—Its Role in Development and Evolution.* New York: Basic Books, 1976.

Getting Started: Mexican-American Preschoolers Initiating Dramatic Play

CELIA GENISHI
Department of Curriculum and Instruction
The University of Texas at Austin

and

JOHN GALVÁN
Foreign Language Education
The University of Texas at Austin

In considering social and linguistic aspects of dramatic play, in which children assign the roles that they play, we describe and analyze the discourse of three 5-year-old Mexican-American girls in a Head Start program where both Spanish and English are spoken.

THEORETICAL PERSPECTIVE

Sutton-Smith and Heath (1981) discuss two contrasting conceptualizations or paradigms of play; the first they call the *literacy* paradigm, which is associated with psychological approaches to pretense or fantasy play. Researchers with this cognitive orientation often study the child's developing abilities to symbolize. In this sense play contributes to young children's abilities to use symbols creatively and understand printed symbols, the basis of literacy. The other paradigm is *sociolinguistic*. Both sociolinguists focusing on the social aspects of language and anthropologists study play as a kind of communication or oral performance. Some black children, for example, are socialized to use language playfully and publicly so that their talk resembles chants or the spinning of tall tales, performances learned through interaction and group participation specific to certain cultural subgroups.

The perspective of this study is based on the sociolinguistic paradigm, a conception of play as a social activity. Dramatic play is studied as talk or discourse jointly constructed by two or more children. According to Garvey (1974, 1977), social play is "a state of engagement in which the successive, nonliteral behaviors of one partner are contingent on the nonliteral behaviors of the other partner" (1974, p. 163). To engage in social play, children must possess the abilities to:

1. distinguish between reality and play
2. abstract rules for structuring play
3. cooperatively construct, or share a common image of, a theme in play.

This view of play, as cooperatively constructed, links the language of play to children's use of language in general. Cook-Gumperz (1981) proposes a general conception of children's talk compatible with Garvey's, asserting that children use talk primarily as a tool for influencing others' behavior. Spoken language is a social resource, a means of asserting one's own importance and controlling self and others. Here we investigate one way in which children can use language to control a specific kind of social interaction, by initiating segments of dramatic play. Our analysis addresses the following questions:

1. What is the content of these children's play?
2. In what ways do individual children initiate and determine the direction of dramatic play?

METHOD

The study was carried out in Brownsville, Texas, near the Mexican border, where the first author spent, first, a month locating an appropriate school or center, familiarizing herself with the staff, children and routines of the chosen day care center and specifying

23

data collection procedures, then a second month recording videotaped data.

Site

Brownsville was chosen as the ideal research site to study the play of Mexican-American children since its population of about 100,000 is largely bilingual (Spanish-English), as well as Mexican-American. Genishi set out to locate an appropriate preschool or day care center where children used Spanish and English and where dramatic play was typically scheduled. In soliciting suggestions for centers from colleagues and professionals in Brownsville, Genishi found informants tended to recommend schools and centers known to be "educational," stressing academic preparation, even at the preschool level. Emphasis on academics worked against the feature of interest for this study: opportunities to engage in dramatic play.

The County Head Start Director in Brownsville arranged for a tour with the Social Services Coordinator of the four Head Start centers in the city. Of these Genishi chose one which the Director had recommended for its cooperative staff. This center had an enrollment of 55 3- to 5-year-old children, most of whom lived in a public housing project near the center. There were three teachers, including the head teacher and three aides. The only male was the teacher of the 3-year-old group. The parents of the children in attendance met federal guidelines for low-income families eligible for Head Start. The daily schedule also conformed to Head Start regulations. Activities included: breakfast, large group work period (flannel board, etc.), music, seat work with manipulatives, lunch, nap time, snack, art, free play and outdoor activity.

Subjects

Although children were able to engage in dramatic play on some days, it was not a daily event. Genishi, therefore, decided to select a number of focal children, who engaged willingly and often in play and who were relatively talkative players, and to observe them outside the regular classroom. Although the situation was not naturalistic, the researcher was able to gather data unaf-fected by general classroom noise. Teachers suggested a list of six; five girls and one boy were chosen. Three children came from intact families, and three had mothers who were single parents. One mother was employed; one father worked in an unskilled job, whereas another was skilled; the third father was disabled.

The six were arranged in two triads, partly because of their language abilities, as conversations in both Spanish and English were desired. Group I, members of Mrs. Rios'* class, consisted of Adelita (5 yr., 5 mo. at the time of data collection), Diana (5; 4) and Mari (5; 2). All three spoke Spanish almost exclusively although they seemed to understand some English, and Adelita and Diana were just beginning to speak it. Group II, members of Mrs. DeLuna's class, were Carlota (5; 4), Evita (4; 11) and Beto (5; 5). Evita was English dominant but usually spoke to Carlota, a Spanish dominant, in Spanish. Beto was essentially monolingual in English although he understood Spanish and on occasion produced Spanish utterances for Carlota's benefit. Most of Group II's conversations, however, were in English.

Data Collection

For ease of analysis, Genishi chose triads that produced moderate amounts of talk but usually maintained one conversation or play theme at a time.

Play was videotaped in the smallest of the center classrooms with a clearly designated "housekeeping" area for dramatic play, containing child-sized furniture—kitchen cabinets, stove, dresser, mirror, dolls, a miniature shopping cart and cooking utensils. During the three weeks of videotaping the props were varied to see if the researcher could encourage particular themes.

The children had become accustomed to the researcher's presence by the time videotaping began, with the researcher giving instructions to Group I in Spanish, Group II in English. She asked them to play in the housekeeping corner and pretend that she wasn't there. This was clearly hard for them, and she was occasionally called upon to settle disputes or grant permissions. Although the

_____
*Pseudonyms are used.

24

camera and equipment were placed as far from the children as possible, they sometimes glanced at it. Play behaviors, however, generally resembled those observed in the regular classrooms.

Audiotaped recordings, producing better sound than the videotapes, were made on a recorder with a unidirectional microphone set on a window sill near the housekeeping corner. About 8 hours of play were recorded.

Data Analysis

The preliminary analysis presented here is based on talk from two-hour videotaped recordings from four taping sessions, three with Group I and one with two members of Group I and a child from their Head Start classroom. Videotapes were transcribed by the second author Galván, bilingual in English and Spanish. The transcription format included speakers, addressees, the verbatim transcript, an English translation and a description of some of the nonverbal activity. Talk was segmented according to turns, numbered on the transcript. After the transcripts were completed, Genishi viewed the tapes with the transcripts in hand to see how best to segment and analyze several kinds of discourse that could be categorized as follows:

The play-related talk was the focus of analysis, so that we next attempted to separate *negotiations*, talk about who will play what role, from *enactments*, role-played dialogue or sequences of talk in which children play or enact their roles. Enactments were initiated by means of two general contrasting *strategies*. These are "play by regulation," in which children talk about the roles they will play before enactment and "start playing," in which children skip a planning or negotiation phase and immediately begin enactment. Agreements to enact certain roles may also be nonverbal. For example, two children may sit down at a table while the third stands in the kitchen. Without verbal negotiation, the child in the kitchen may begin to play mother as the seated children play daughters. Our analysis, however, focuses on what children accomplish verbally.

Because negotiation sometimes led to enactment and sometimes not and could occur sporadically during enactment, separating negotiations from enactments was not informative. The more revealing distinction was one between *successful* and *unsuccessful*

initiating strategies. A successful strategy was defined as the first turn in at least four consecutive turns of play, involving two speakers and a single play topic or activity. The first speaker was the initiator, who wished to start a new direction or play theme. It was assumed that the fourth turn reflected cooperation or acquiescence on the part of the second speaker. An unsuccessful strategy led to fewer than four consecutive turns and, hence, lack of cooperation from the other children.

Although the categories for analysis seem adequately to describe these data, they have not been applied by other investigators. A series of reliability checks will be done in the future to test the usefulness and adequacy of the categories for these data and for the data from Group II.

RESULTS

Results are presented according to the research questions posed. The first was, what is the content of these children's play? Themes enacted were in general not surprising: playing doctor, eating in a restaurant, going grocery shopping, picking up a child from school, mopping and sweeping, feeding grandmother, mothering, going to a party, talking on the phone, eating at home, baking a cake, delivering a present, dancing and speaking English. Of these, delivering a present, dancing and speaking English occurred least often; other themes were recurrent.

The present analysis focuses on the second question, in what ways do individual children initiate and determine the direction of dramatic play? To answer this question we looked for instances when children tried to enact a role, either at the beginning of a taping session or within a session in attempts to redirect the play by reassigning roles or changing the activity (e.g., from baking a cake to getting ready for school). During the four sessions, there were 95 instances of negotiations (attempts to enact) and enactments. More than half (52) of these 95 were initiated by one child, Mari. Diana initiated 26 during the three sessions she participated in and Adelita, 15, during four sessions. Lili, a friend of Mari and Adelita but not a member of Group I, substituted for Diana one day and initiated only two enactments.

The next question posed was, how many of these initiations were successful, i.e., how many were sustained for at least four turns of speaking? Well over half (56/95) were successful. Mari again had the highest number (27), but the lowest percentage of success (52 percent). Diana was successful 61 percent (16/26) of the time and Adelita, 73 percent (11/15). Lili made two attempts at enactment, and both succeeded.

As to type of strategy for initiating enactments, neither the first, "start playing," nor the second, "play by regulation," seemed to be favored by the children. The first strategy was employed 50 times, whereas the second was used 45 times. Mari and Diana were both notably more successful when they simply started playing. Mari was successful 18 times (vs. 10 unsuccessful negotiations); Diana was successful nine times (vs. three unsuccessful negotiations). Adelita was successful six out of nine times, using the first strategy, and five out of six times, using the second.

Although few, there were enough negotiations and enactments to give a sense of individual styles of playing and, more generally, of interacting, at least within the focal triad. The following examples illustrate the contrasts between successful vs. unsuccessful negotiations and enactments, "start playing" vs. "play by regulation" strategies, and among individuals' styles of play:

Table 1
Frequency of Children's Unsuccessful and Successful Strategies for Initiating Enactments

Session	Length in Minutes	Strategy	Mari U[a]	Mari S[b]	Diana U	Diana S	Adelita U	Adelita S	Lili U	Lili S	Total
A	40	Start Playing	6	5	0	3	2	4	-	-	20
		Play by Regulation	3	2	3	1	0	0	-	-	9
B	20	Start Playing	1	6	0	6	0	0	-	-	13
		Play by Regulation	1	1	1	1	0	0	-	-	4
C	25	Start Playing	1	5	3	0	0	0	-	-	9
		Play by Regulation	5	3	3	5	0	2	-	-	18
D	35	Start Playing	2	2	c-	-	1	2	0	1	8
		Play by Regulation	6	3	-	-	1	3	0	1	14
			25	27	10	16	4	11	0	2	95
			(n=52)		(n=26)		(n=15)		(n=2)		

[a]U = Unsuccessful
[b]S = Successful
c- = Not present for this session

EXAMPLE 1: Unsuccessful strategy, "play by regulation" at the first turn, followed by unsuccessful strategy, "start playing" at the second turn:

Speaker/Addressee	Transcription and Translation	Commentary
A to M	Y yo ero la doctora. La cami . . . cómo se pone? (I'm the doctor. The shirt . . . how do you put it on?)	Attempting to figure how to put the apron on.
M to A	¿Mi hija? (Daughter?)	M "makes" A her daughter by calling her "my daughter."
A to M	¿Qué? (What?)	A seems to acquiesce, but only for this turn.
M to A	¿Me compras. . .? (Will you buy me. . . .?)	M is interrupted by D, who ends this brief interaction between M and A.

There were many examples of this type at the beginning of the first taping session. In fact, 13 minutes of interaction elapsed before a successful enactment occurred. The next example is "successful," according to our definition:

EXAMPLE 2: Successful strategy, "start playing":

Speaker/Addressee	Transcription and Translation	Commentary
D - M, A	Ding dong! Ding dong! Ding dong! Ding dong!	M and A first talk softly behind cabinet door. M moves toward kitchen area.
D-M	Yo era—tú abrías la puerta, donde estaba. Ding dong. (I was—you were opening the door, where I was.)	D moves to other side of room, away from her "door." M moves toward D.
D - M	No, ésa no es. Allá donde está el papel y ( ). Ding dong. (No, not there. Where the paper is and ( ).	D tells M to go to the door, where she has left the paper.
	Mira. Ahora venía el doctor. (Look. Now the doctor's come.) Mira (?) Ding dong! Ding dong! Ding dong!	D moves to door. M moves with paper to A, who is next to the cabinet and on a bed.
M - D	Qué— Qué quería Vd.? (What did you want?)	M is back at door with D.

27

D - M	Vd. me llamó porque—verdad que Vd. me llamó? (You called me because. Isn't it true that you called me?)	
M - D	Uh huh. Oiga. Oiga, qué es—( ) (Listen. Listen, what is—)	
D - M	Ah, que Vd. me llamó, Srta. Para que le atendiera a su hija. ¿Y dónde está? (Ah, you called me, Miss, so that I could check on your daughter. And where is she?)	
M - D	Allí está en el cuarto. (There in the room.)	Takes doll from A ("baby").
M - A	Mire. A ver, quítate—Le va a dar un beso. Es que si le da un beso, luego no va estar mala. (Look. Let's see, take off—Are you giving her a kiss. If you give her a kiss, then she won't be sick anymore.)	They walk over to A in bed.
D - M	OK, ahorita. ¡Bien mala! Sí, es. Sí es. (OK, now. Very sick! Yes, she is. Yes, she is.)	Puts stethoscope on A's chest. Says, "Very bad," gravely. Whispers to M. A whines as if uncomfortable.
M - D	Hazle mmmmmmm. (Make a noise like mmmmmmm.)	Both D and M listen through stethoscope.
D - M	No, no. Este es mío. (This is mine.)	D and M have near disagreement, probably over stethoscope.
D	¡Ya! (OK!)	D leaves, walking out her door and humming. Looks at camera and soon starts another enactment.

Example 2 is one of the most coherent interactions recorded among these three girls. The majority of exchanges though, were fluid in that roles were established but then changed within short periods, so that play themes and roles often shifted. Assignment of roles seemed tenuous; at any second they could change.

DISCUSSION

The fluidity of the children's play is not surprising; dramatic play or fantasy play is by nature fluid. Children are free to be and do what they want, so that roles and scenes of-ten shift. Once two or more children are involved, relationships among them may constrain or add to the fluidity of play. The children in Group I, particularly Mari and Diana, were in a continual conflict to see who would regulate the play. The consequences of conflict seemed to be an unsuccessful enactment, a new negotiation or interruption by a child who wanted to reassign roles or change activities, or a termination of enactment because a child refused to play an assigned role.

The general strategies the children used to negotiate roles and/or initiate enactments showed that the three focal children were able to use language to regulate and manipulate others' behavior. The more successful of the two strategies was "start playing." This was also the less subtle and less democratic strategy. Talking about who was to play or do what, "play by regulation," was proportionately less successful. Perhaps this meant that these children were already aware that action is more effective than negotiation or consulting to get what one wants. After all, action may not leave one as vulnerable to disagreement as verbal suggestions. The most coherent enactments, in fact, were those that Diana initiated by starting to play (by saying "Ding dong!" or Waitress!"), by acting as if roles were already established.

The children's own agendas and desire for controlling the direction of play clearly affected the way discourse was organized. Analysis revealed aspects of their social knowledge, some of their social agendas and general strategies for accomplishing them. A major aspect of that social knowledge was these children's conceptions of dominance in relationships. In their play mother, doctor and teacher were unsurprisingly the dominant, often coveted roles. (The available props in the housekeeping corner promoted family play, in which dominance often becomes an issue.)

The data also reflected children's abilities to structure play situations jointly according to the setting and individual actors. In addition, all three criteria that Garvey (1974) states characterize children's play—*distinction* between play and reality, *abstraction* of interactive rules embedded in play and *joint construction* of a shared image of the play episode—were present in the children's discourse. Diana and Mari (example 2) talked about the roles they played, demonstrating that they knew this was play. Further, both girls used paralinguistic cues, such as increased volume and clearer enunciation, when they played doctor or mother.

All four showed awareness of general rules of interaction. There was turn-taking; acquiescent, nonverbal behavior on the part of the "baby" (example 2) when reacting to mother and doctor; accomplishment of doctor's job when Diana diagnosed Adelita as "*bien mala*" (very sick).

Another general feature of discourse that Diana and Mari manipulated often was terms of address: *senorita, hija, mi hija* (my daughter), a term of endearment. These were socially appropriate and served to mark the roles played. A feature specific to Spanish was the use of *usted* (*Vd.* in text, *you*, formal register), as in example 2. Children at this day care center seldom used the *usted* form, so that its use to highlight the first encounter between doctor and mother was notable.

In example 2 the children jointly constructed enactments not as a venture among equals, but because Mari complied with Diana's idea of how the play should develop. Adelita was docile in the child's role and so was cooperative in enactment. This example is atypical of the data in that it is an uninterrupted enactment, but typical in its highlighting of regulation through discourse. Controlling peers' behavior and asserting one's own importance has also been shown as important to children in other recent studies (Cook-Gumperz, 1981; Genishi & Di Paolo, 1982; Schwartzman, 1978). Schwartzman, for example, found that children in the day care center she studied were much concerned with control and manipulation, and their concerns were reflected in their play. Other investigators (Corsaro, n.d.; Garvey, 1974) have presented data showing less conflict and more reciprocity. Whether or not the discourse of play highlights conflict and control, these studies and the present one demonstrate that talk is a tool for accomplishing social activities. In this study, how those activities unfold during play seems to depend on the fleeting successes of individual children's discourse strategies.

IMPLICATIONS FOR PRACTICE

The following implications might be considered:

1. These three children's play raises questions about the nature of the benefits of sociodramatic play for children. Early childhood educators often state that play is the child's way of learning because it can be a foun-

29

Table 2
Summary Across Sessions of Frequency of Children's Unsuccessful and Successful Strategies for Initiating Enactments

Strategy	Mari U[a]	Mari S[b]	Diana U	Diana S	Adelita U	Adelita S	Lili U	Lili S	Total U	Total S
Start Playing	10	18	3	9	3	6	0	1	16	34
Play by Regulation	$\frac{15}{25}$	$\frac{9}{27}$	$\frac{7}{10}$	$\frac{7}{16}$	$\frac{1}{4}$	$\frac{5}{11}$	$\frac{0}{0}$	$\frac{1}{2}$	$\frac{23}{39}$	$\frac{22}{56}$

N = 95
[a]U = Unsuccessful
[b]S = Successful

dation for creativity, flexible thinking or taking the perspective of others. Proving the existence of those benefits has been difficult. Our data indicate that much of what children accomplish in play is social—at least in the short run. Some of the advantages of play, then, lie in the play itself, in opportunities to negotiate, persuade, assert one's importance, rather than in the transfer of playlike abilities to other situations.

2. In the 1960's it was sometimes said that the play of economically poor children was less developed than that of middle-class children. Though there may be differences between the dramatic play of poor and middle-class children (Stern, 1982), our data show that the play of these three children was complex and linguistically and socially sophisticated. Like many myths about poor children, the myth about deprived forms of play is countered when one studies actual examples of their play. What may be missing in the lives of poor children is sufficient opportunity for dramatic play, rather than the abilities needed to engage in it.

3. Teachers might utilize the kinds of observations we have made when they plan their programs, including times for play. "Free play" means that children select their own activities. Teachers, however, may notice patterns of interaction in which some children verbally dominate others in a consistent way. In our data, for example, Adelita said very little while Mari and Diana said a great deal. At times teachers may want to assign children in groups to dramatic play or other language-based activities so that children like Adelita have opportunities to be the dominant or more nearly equal playmate.

References

Cook-Gumperz, J. "Persuasive Talk—The Social Organization of Children's Talk." In J. Green and C. Wallat, eds., *Ethnography and Language in Educational Settings*. Norwood, NJ: Ablex, 1981.

Corsaro, W.A. "Script Recognition, Articulation and Expansion in Children's Role Play." Manuscript, University of Indiana, n.d.

Ervin-Tripp, S. "Structures of Social Control." In L.C. Wilkinson, ed., *Communicating in the Classroom*. New York: Academic Press, 1982.

Garvey, C. *Play*. Cambridge, MA: Harvard University Press, 1977.

———."Some Properties of Social Play." *Merrill-Palmer Quarterly* 20 (1974): 163–80.

Genishi, C., and M. DiPaolo. "Learning Through Argument in a Preschool." In L.C. Wilkinson, ed., *Communicating in the Classroom*. New York: Academic Press, 1982.

Schwartzman, H.B. *Transformations: The Anthropology of Children's Play*. New York: Plenum, 1978.

Stern, V. "The Symbolic Play of Lower-class and Middle-class Children: Mixed Messages from the Literature." In L.G. Katz, ed., *Current Topics in Early Childhood Education* Vol. IV. Norwood, NJ: Ablex, 1982.

Sutton-Smith, B., and S.B. Heath. "Paradigms of Pretense." *Quarterly Newsletter of the Laboratory of Comparative Human Cognition* 3 (1981): 41-45.

Children's Views of Play

Margaret Garza, Sandy Briley and Stuart Reifel
Department of Curriculum and Instruction
The University of Texas at Austin

The degree to which children play in early childhood settings varies from program to program (Mayer, 1971), but there is nearly always some time when children are allowed to play. In some programs (e.g., Biber et al., 1971; Kamii and DeVries, 1977), where play itself is seen as a "core" educational activity, it is essential to have children "do" whatever one does when one plays, because play is seen as an important source of learning. A good deal of time, energy, planning and money go into preparing the environment and the attitudes and skills of teachers to "allow" children to play.

Because most of us educators want children to play in their educational settings, we strive to attain many resources to that purpose. Yet, our ideas of what it means to "do" play in the nursery or kindergarten are guided by our adult views of appropriate child's play; those adult views set the limits for what we "allow" children to do. That is why, in many early childhood classrooms, doll play and board games are encouraged, while rough-house play is usually not.

Thus far, most writers and researchers on play have defined certain activities *a priori* as play, then described the relationship of those activities to other behavior patterns. So far, there has been no noteworthy validation of the activity as *play* by the children who do the playing. While it is problematic to rely on verbal responses when working with young children (and impossible to gather such information during the first several years of life), we are interested in ascertaining whether children can relate aspects of their play experience, which possibly have not been considered by past researchers. There is the possibility that the phenomena we call play may or may not be play from the player's point of view. In presenting an alternative perspective on play activity that has received little attention, we propose that this per-spective merits consideration because it considers the view of the actor (i.e., the child) who is doing the playing. How can we understand children's views of their play experience? How do children in an early childhood setting describe their own play experience? The project described here was conducted to see how children describe regular experiences in child care in order to give us some insight into what children understand to be play in their early childhood program.

One approach to documenting children's experience presented by Nelson and her colleagues (Nelson, 1978; Nelson and Gruendel, 1979, 1981) relies on the idea of a cognitive script as an organizing device for daily experience, building on the idea of script used in cognitive science (Abelson, 1981; Shank and Abelson, 1977). Experiences come to be organized into structures by a person. Not only do these structures guide behavior by providing information on what is typically associated with experiences, but they also shape expectations, by virtue of the fact that structural relationships imply the presence of elements in any given experience. For example, on the second day of kindergarten children already expect a sequence of acts including "coming in," play, group meeting, class work, lunch and "going home" (Fivush, 1982). Additional acts were added to this structure by the second week of school, at which point the script for kindergarten stabilized to a large extent. This script formed the children's expectations for the school day and directed their behavior accordingly.

Two elements are characteristic of script formation: first, a statement about acts, which are memories for events as experienced. For example, a group of children questioned about lunch at school responded with statements about cleaning up for lunch, setting the table, serving food, eating food and

31

cleaning up (Nelson and Gruendel, 1981), acts comprising the event of school lunch. Earlier research has found consistent statements of acts for children as young as three (Nelson and Gruendel, 1981) who have had as little as one day's previous experience with an event (Hudson and Nelson, 1982). Children quickly come to know the "what" of what happens in an experience.

The second element of script formation is the language form used. Scripts are expressed with either "we" or "you" (in the sense of "one") combined with the timeless present tense, e.g., We go outside to play. You go to sleep at nap time. This form suggests the regular, on-going nature of the acts presented in the script. It should be possible to locate these elements in children's descriptions of their on-going play activities.

REVIEW OF LITERATURE

A sampling of the literature on classroom play experience illustrates a distinction between adults' and children's views of classroom play. Research has tended to begin either with conceptions or definitions of play or with an adult view of play as contrasted with work. These preconceptions lead to interesting findings, but they tend to ignore the possibility that adults and children might not share a common preconception about what play is. Research has leaned toward understanding behaviors we might define as play rather than the subjective understanding of play that children might have.

Earlier research has looked at the behavior of children in classroom play. For example, Shure (1963) used time-sampling to ascertain the number of appearances by children in five different free-play areas (art, book, doll, games, block) in the preschool. She found that block play and art attracted children most frequently, with boys going to the blocks more often, and girls to art. Boys tended to linger with block play for longer periods of time, as did both boys and girls looking at books. Games and dolls tended to produce play of short duration. Bott (1928) observed the frequency and duration associated with use of different types of materials. Categories for material types were empirically generated. Data revealed age-related material preferences: 4-year-olds selected "pattern toys" (beads, puzzles, peg boards) more often than younger children; younger children selected "mechanical toys" more often; "locomotor toys" (train, tricycles, doll carriage) were being used at a similar rate by both older and younger children. These studies, like most observational research on play, presume an adult definition. Children are not asked whether they are playing or what play is at school.

More recently, King (1979) looked at kindergarteners' distinctions between work and play in the classroom. After observing children in a variety of activities, King interviewed the children to determine whether they were working or playing. Children indicated that they were playing when they freely chose the activity, whereas they were working when the teacher directed them to an activity, even if that activity was a game or "fun" activity. Teachers defined many more classroom activities as play than did children. King's study takes a major step toward understanding children's views of play in schools by seeing how they define activities in which they have been observed.

In her interview study of kindergarten experience, Fivush (1982) found that a time for play was an expected part of a kindergarten script from the second day of the school year onward. Play happened before other school activities. The details of what constituted play were not explored in her study.

Fein (1983) reported findings from interviews with 5- and 6-year-olds on their distinctions between work and play. Children clearly made the distinction between the two activity types, indicating that work was an obligatory activity. In contrast, play was described mostly in terms of its functions (who decides on the activity and on the activity's goal, whether the activity is liked) or in terms of prototypical instances (types of activities).

The current study differs from the work described above, in that we attempted to have children in child care generate and describe the experiences they viewed as play. We were especially interested in describing those ongoing activities that formed children's knowledge of play experience in the program.

METHOD

Data were gathered as part of a larger study of children's experience in child care, a study investigating narrative script formation with regard to the entire day, including events such as meals, nap, story time and indoor and outdoor play activities. Fourteen children between three and six representing several ethnicities participated in the study, all non-handicapped, English-speaking children in a small (27-child), federally-funded, full-day child care program housed in the College of Education at the University of Texas at Austin. Children who spoke English as a second language were included in the study if they communicated in English in the classroom. Children were interviewed individually by the third author, the director of the center, thus familiar to all the children.

The interview began with the request, "Tell me what you do at school each day." As reported in another paper (Reifel and Garza, 1983), all the children spontaneously responded by saying they played at school and participated in other events. Most also mentioned playing outdoors at school. When the child had responded to the first request for information, specific requests were made about events, such as "Tell me more about what you play," and "Tell me what you like at school." The interview was terminated when the child had either responded to all of the predetermined, open-ended questions or had spontaneously provided information that would answer the questions. All children provided information that responded to all of the standard, open-ended directions. The interviews were tape recorded and transcribed by a graduate student who was unfamiliar with the project. Examples of responses appear as Figures 1 and 2.

The transcripts were independently inspected by the junior authors, who coded, respectively, for instances of play activities mentioned and for the language forms used

Figure 1. Responses from a girl, age 58 months.

A: I'd like you to tell me what you do at school each day.
C: Play with toys.
A: Is that all you do? No?
C: Sleep, play with all the toys, and eat.
A: Go to sleep, play with toys, and eat.
C: And sleep with the toys.
A: Still, tell me all the things you do at school.
C: Play with toys, and play with toys .... and everything.
    * * *
A: Tell me more about the things you do at school.
C: Play with stuff.
A: Play with stuff.
C: And go to the table and "write."
A: Tell me more about what you play.
C: Play with dolls. . .
A: What happens when you go outside?
C: Play.
A: Tell me . . .
C: With scooters and play houses.
A: Scooters and play houses. Tell me more.
C: And play with, play with, play with everything.

Figure 2. Responses from a boy, age 63 months.

A: Could you tell me what you do at school each day?
C: I eat lunch.
A: Is that all you do?
C: No. I eat breakfast, too.
A: Tell me all that you do at school each day.
C: I go outside each day, and I go to sleep each day.
A: Tell me about it from the beginning. What's the first thing you do when you get to school?
C: When I get to school and eat breakfast?
A: Yes.
C: And . . . I, when I get through with breakfast, we go outside. And, and I like going outside.
A: Tell me more.
C: When we come in, when we come in we do our activity; and we sing; and, and, uh, and we, uh, and we, uh, and we play with toys; and, and we clean up; and we, uh, and we, uh, cook; and, and we make stuff.
    * * *
A: What happens when you go outside?
C: We run.
A: Yes?
C: And we play with toys.

33

to describe the acts. To assess the reliability of their coding, both independently recoded four of the other's transcripts. Inter-rater reliability for coding the play acts was .79, and for the language forms was .84.

RESULTS

Across the fourteen transcripts, we found a total of 125 acts of play given by the 14 children. Twenty-six of these acts were simple statements affirming the act of play, such as "We play" or "And then I play." Among the other play acts mentioned was a wide range of responses. Only one activity (using scooters) received as many as 6 mentions, with books receiving 5 mentions, outside play 5, puzzles 4 and unspecified "toys" 4. The remaining responses ran the gamut from playing with mud to duck-duck-goose, with some mention given to dolls, trucks, blocks, friends and pretending to be girl scouts.

What was play for these children? Of the 125 acts they provided, 5.6 percent referred to pretense with materials (e.g., feeding a doll), 47.2 percent to non-pretense manipulation of materials (e.g., riding a scooter, working puzzles), 45.6 percent sociodramatic play (e.g., pretending to be girl scouts, play with friends) and 1.6 percent organized games (e.g., duck-duck-goose). These accounts of play acts appear to reflect an articulated understanding of play as either with materials or with peers, but never with both. No child described a play act as being both social and with props of any sort. Interestingly, the few instances of games with rules were reported by the oldest children, even though all children participated in such games.

Further evidence for scripts can be found in the language children used to express their knowledge of play acts. Specifically, we looked for the use of a general present tense: you and we (in the sense of "one") with present tense (e.g., You play with dolls; We play duck-duck-goose), as opposed to I with the verb in any tense (e.g., I rode on the scooter; I like puzzles).

Of the 125 acts of play given by the children, roughly half were in the general present tense and half were in present tense with a non-general pronoun (usually I, they, or no pronoun). There were few cases of the use of a tense other than the present. For many younger children (ages 3 and 4), there was a tendency to see play activities as personal, on-going activities (e.g., I play with a doll). Many older children (ages 5 and 6) appeared more likely to see play as regular activities that everyone (we, or "one") participates in (e.g., We play with toys). The limited size of the sample precluded conducting meaningful statistical tests based on age, sex or other variables.

In summary, it is apparent that children as young as three do have mental representations of play as part of their experience in child care. Play is one thing they habitually do. The language of younger children frequently reflects play as a more personal daily experience (e.g., I play with scooters), while older children see play as something everyone usually does (e.g., We play outside).

DISCUSSION

Children as young as age 3 have a mental picture of play as part of their daily experience in child care. While these data only scratch a surface of child's understanding of play, they do appear to indicate that young children have representations of their play experiences. They think of play in terms of pretense, materials, social interaction or games with rules, *not* as experience with people *and* materials. Play is clearly distinct from other functional activities in child care, such as eating and napping (Reifel and Garza, 1983).

The children's responses contrast with teachers' observations of children's play activity. Initially only the older children (4-5 year olds) used the scooters. It was not until some of the younger ones (3-4) observed the older children that they began to "use" them as motorcycles, cars and vehicles with sirens. Children would make the sounds and motions corresponding to the things they were using their scooter for, i.e., making certain hand motions and sounds to depict the specific vehicle and its actions. Outside, children used large plastic squares placed together to form a large box as a stepping apparatus to help reach a tree branch so that they could climb the tree. The inside of the box was used as a "house," often restricted to certain children during dramatic play. All the children did play with both materials and people, although they did not describe the play that way.

Teachers also noted that interactions did occur between two or more children as they pretended in the play house, using play house materials while they took pretend roles of parent and child. Much of this play was quite complex. In isolated play a child would direct all his or her attention to a doll, dressing, feeding and rocking it. A child would also cook, use the cabinets and refrigerator, set the table or sweep without interacting with anyone. The child might talk while occupied with various tasks, but the talk was not directed to another. Pretend was sometimes social and in many cases with materials.

While children did not refer to the pretend use of materials, there was much pretense with manipulatives. Blocks were used by some to house their miniature animals or make constructions on which the miniature vehicles would be used. Generally, children interacted minimally during this type of activity. Puzzles and beads were used on an individual basis, with little or no interaction with others. Unless a scheduled group time was taking place, children could go to the library area where there was usually no interaction among children as they looked at books. Sometimes they interacted with puppets, pretending to read to each other. All children participated as part of a group for songs and finger games. In sum, from the teachers' observations, children played not only as they claimed to play but also in ways that are not revealed in the scripts. Children have scriptal knowledge of some of their play activities.

While the limited sample size makes it difficult to segment this group for statistical analyses, it is still possible to notice possible developmental changes in children's descriptions of their daily play experiences. In this study, only the older children (ages 5-6) made any references to games with rules as play, despite the fact that all children played games with rules. Why are those games not remembered by younger children, and why are they remembered by older children? Is there something about the ephemeral nature of the games with rules that they played (e.g., they seldom used props) that makes the experience evanescent for younger children, or could the rules and actions of the games be at a level of complexity difficult for young children to understand? Also in this study, the younger children tended to use the first person singular "I" more often in their statements of play acts. Is this a sign of some form of egocentrism on their part, or are they simply less familiar with the use of group pronouns as they describe activities? There is a great deal yet to understand about children's development that can be explored through investigation of their views of play.

Given that these children have thoughts about their play experience, it is important to consider the source of those ideas. How do children acquire their conceptions of play? What helps children frame their understanding of experience in terms like play, work, cooperation or wasting time? How do they know that what they are doing is play? Children must constantly hear things from their parents, such as, "Run along and play" and "Are you playing in your room?" The teachers who taught the children in this study reported that they frequently described children's activities to the children as play. For example, they would say, "You like to play house" and "Are you going to play with the puzzle now?" Could this be one developmental source for a functional definition of play? Or could play also be what one does when one is not doing other things, such as working or planning? Clearly, children's understanding of play may not be as complex as that of adults', but it is possible that their understanding of play could provide insights that could help our theories become more comprehensive.

As an aside, it seems relevant to comment on the work-play distinction used in several studies (Block, 1981; Fein, 1983; King, 1979). Adults typically make a work-play distinction, as if the two were naturally occurring opposites. Children in all the cited studies did, in fact, distinguish between work and play in the classroom. One could ask, however, whether the dichotomy is one that children would make or one the researcher has made for them. Do children naturally distinguish play from work, or do they distinguish play from bedtime and play from mealtime? The evidence we have tends to suggest that children make distinctions between play and story time, between play and mealtime, and between play and nap, rather than between play and some abstract notion of work (Reifel and Garza, 1983). There is much more we need to know about children's classification categories before we can say much about the opposition of play and work in their school lives.

Where do our adult views of play come from? This question is far too complicated to address in any depth here, but we suggest that there have been theoretical and practical sources for such views. Neither source has attended adequately to one critical feature of play, that is, the child's view of what is going on. In terms of theoretical bases for play, the best current examples include the use of Piagetian theory as a basis for programmatic play (e.g., Kamii and DeVries, 1977; Honig and Lally, 1981; Hohmann et al, 1979). In these programs, play is operationalized in terms of dimensions presented in Piaget's writing, most notably, *Play, Dreams and Imitation in Childhood* (Piaget, 1962) and *The Origins of Intelligence in Children* (Piaget, 1952). Other programs have drawn on additional theoretical descriptions of play (e.g., psychoanalytic, Wernerian) as a basis for promoting play in the classroom (Biber, 1977; Franklin, 1981). The status attributed to play in theory serves as one basis for encouraging classroom play activities interpretable in terms of theory. Children are allowed to do what can be interpreted theoretically.

Practically, a tradition of appropriate play activity is passed from one generation of early childhood teachers to the next. Older teachers tell new teachers how to stimulate desirable play with sand or how to arrange materials for dramatic play. These helpful "tips" convey a sense of what is expected of children during play. In many cases, traditional information is based on good intuitions of what is good for the child. Seldom

is the information based explicitly on some theoretical description of play. Here again, children are allowed to play in ways that traditional adult experience suggests are acceptable. There is clearly nothing wrong with teachers' making decisions about play based on theory or on tradition.

By age 3, children do know that they play and that they are doing certain things (e.g., riding scooters) and not doing other things (e.g., eating lunch) when they play. How well does their view match adults' view of play? Research must be conducted to ascertain that. Until then we must be aware that if we ignore that point of view, we may be making erroneous judgments about what the behavior means to the ones producing it.

References

Abelson, R. P. "Psychological Status of the Script Concept." *American Psychologist* 36 (1981): 715-29.

Biber, B. "A Developmental-Interaction Approach: Bank Street College of Education." In M. C. Day and R. Parker, eds., *Preschool in Action*. Boston: Allyn and Bacon, 1977.

Biber, B.; E. Shapiro and D. Wickers. *Promoting Cognitive Growth*. Washington, DC: National Association for the Education of Young Children, 1971.

Block, J. "Some Neglected Parameters of the Student Role in Teaching: Play and the Work/Play Dialectic." Final Report, NIE G-80-0070, Washington, DC, 1981.

Bott, H. "Observation of Play Activities in a Nursery School." *Genetic Psychology Monographs* 4 (1928): 44-88.

Fein, G. G. "Learning Through Play." Paper read at the International Conference on Play and Play Environments, Austin, TX, July, 1983.

Fein, G. G. and K. A. Clarke-Stewart. *Day Care in Context*. New York: Wiley, 1973.

Fivush, R. "Learning About School: The Development of Kindergartener's School Scripts." Unpublished doctoral dissertation, City University of New York, 1982.

Franklin, M. B. "Perspectives on Theory: Another Look at the Developmental-Interaction Point of View." In E. K. Shapiro and E. Weber, eds., *Cognitive and Affective Growth: Developmental Interaction*. Hillsdale, NJ: Erlbaum, 1981.

Hohmann, M.; B. Banet and D. P. Weikart. *Young Children in Action*. Ypsilanti, MI: High/Scope Press, 1979.

Honig, A. S., and R. R. Lally. *Infant Caregiving*. Syracuse, NY: Syracuse University Press, 1981.

Hudson, J., and K. Nelson. "Scripts and Autobiographical Memories." Unpublished manuscript, City University of New York, 1982.

Kamii, C., and R. DeVries. "Piaget for Early Education." In M. C. Day and R. Parker, eds., *Preschool in Action*. Boston: Allyn and Bacon, 1977.

Karnes, M. B.; R. R. Zehrback and J. A. Teska. "Conceptualization of the GOAL (Game-Oriented Activities for Learning) Curriculum." In M. C. Day and R. Parker, eds., *Preschool in Action*. Boston: Allyn and Bacon, 1977.

King, N. R. "Play: The Kindergartener's Perspective." *The Elementary School Journal* 80 (1979): 81-87.

Mayer, R. S. "A Comparative Analysis of Preschool Curriculum Models." In R. H. Anderson and H. G. Shane, eds., *As the Twig Is Bent*. New York: Houghton Mifflin, 1971.

Nelson, K. "How Young Children Represent Knowledge of Their World In and Out of Language." In R. S. Siegler, ed., *Children's Thinking: What Develops?* Hillsdale, NJ: Erlbaum, 1978.

Nelson, K., and J. Gruendel. "At Morning It's Lunchtime: A Scriptal View of Children's Dialogues." *Discourse Processes* 2 (1979): 73-94.

————. "Generalized Event Representations. Basic Building Blocks of Cognitive Development." In M. E. Lamb and A. L. Brown, eds., *Advances in Developmental Psychology* Vol. 1. Hillsdale, NJ: Erlbaum, 1981.

Piaget, J. *The Origins of Intelligence in Children*. New York: International Universities Press, 1952.

————. *Play, Dreams and Imitation in Childhood*. New York: Norton, 1962.

Reifel, S., and M. Garza. "Child Care as Script: Children's Descriptions of Daily Experiences." Paper presented at the annual meeting of the American Educational Research Association, Montreal, April 1983. ERIC Document Information Service.

Shank, R. C., and R. P. Abelson. *Scripts, Plans, Goals, and Understanding*. Hillsdale, NJ: Erlbaum, 1977.

Shure, M. E. "Psychological Ecology of a Nursery School." *Child Development* 34 (1963): 979-94.

The Persistence of Sex Differences in the Play of Young Children

Betty Spillers Beeson and R. Ann Williams
Department of Elementary Education
Ball State University, Muncie, Indiana

Do sex differences in the play activities of young children persist in spite of the effort to eliminate sexist attitudes and practices?

Although the initial thrust toward eliminating sexism in our society was a concern over the limited roles and opportunities for females, the media, industry, education and government have expanded efforts toward eliminating sexist attitudes and practices for everyone.

One means of monitoring changes in our society has been through a study of children's play. A review of research (Sutton-Smith and Rosenberg, 1971) revealed that historically children's play has mirrored society's traditional attitudes toward sex roles. These traditional labelings of male and female play activities reflect the common beliefs society has held in regard to sex stereotyping. Boys are more active, noisier and messier than girls. Girls are less active, quieter and neater than boys. Boys excel in large muscle activities and girls in fine muscle activities. These are examples of how sexism tends to limit the play opportunities of children.

REVIEW OF THE LITERATURE

In the past, it was a generally accepted fact that sex role differentiation could be attributed to genetic and biological differences. Researchers continue to study and document this area, such as recent brain research indicating differences in brain functioning (Restak, 1979). Today, the importance of cultural influences on the development of sex role differentiation is also widely recognized (Birns, 1976; Samuels, 1979; Zaichkowsky et al., 1980). Sex role stereotyping found in television programs, school curricula and career opportunities is an example of often arbitrary cultural influences that shape sex roles in American society.

Sutton-Smith and Rosenberg (1971) reviewed studies of boy-girl games preferences. Through the years, boys have played games traditionally considered "masculine," and girls have played games traditionally considered "feminine." They concluded that, in the last thirty years, the differences between the sexes in game preferences have been reduced considerably.

Sex role stereotyping in play begins early and continues throughout childhood. Sex differences have been reported in the play activities of infants (Lewis, 1972), toddlers (Lowe, 1975 and Fein, 1975), preschoolers (see Table I), school age children (Lever, 1976) and preadolescents (Erikson, 1951).

There are sex differences in fantasy play (Tizard et al., 1976; Sanders and Harper, 1976). Girls enact domestic themes, while boys pretend to drive cars, trains or airplanes. In terms of sociability, girls are found to be more socially oriented in play than boys (Coates et al., 1975). Boys show a stronger preference for the same-sex playmate than do girls (Clark et al., 1969). Rubin (1977) concluded there had been little change in the play preferences of boys and girls " . . .despite the more recent emphasis on non-sexist stereotyping."

METHOD

The hypothesis tested was: there are no sex differences in the play activities of 3-, 4- and 5-year-old children.

Sample

The 50 subjects enrolled in preschool programs at a midwestern university were 25 males and 25 females ranging in age from 36 to 64 months.

39

Five play activities that previous studies had shown to be consistently male- or female-oriented were selected for this study (see Table I). Blocks, wheeled vehicles and water/sand were the male-oriented play activities; house play and art projects were the female-oriented play activities.

An observational instrument was designed by the researchers to record each subjects's daily play activities with three graduate student observers trained to use the instrument. Observations were conducted three days a week for six weeks, a total of 18 observational periods. Each observation was for a 30 minute time sample during free play.

Analysis of Data

To test the "null hypothesis" of no sex differences in the play activities, the data were analyzed using a multi-variate analysis of variance (MANOVA). This analysis revealed a significant multivariate F-ratio (Multivariate $F = 7.54$; $df = 8, 41$; $p. 0001$). The null hypothesis was rejected; there were sex differences in the play activities.

To test individual null hypothesis of no sex differences, *post hoc* comparisons of the cell means for each of the play activities were obtained by calculating univariate F-ratios. The results of the *post hoc* comparisons are given in Table II.

All three male-oriented play activities were statistically significant at the .05 level. Blocks, wheeled vehicles and water/sand were sex stereotyped with more boys than girls selecting these activities.

One of the female-oriented play activities was statistically significant at the .05 level. Art projects were sex stereotyped with more girls than boys choosing this play activity.

One of the female-oriented play activities was not statistically significant at the .05 level. House play was not stereotyped, but a play activity chosen by both boys and girls.

FINDINGS, CONCLUSIONS, IMPLICATIONS

The findings of this research differ little from those of earlier studies. The three male-ori-

Table I
Previous Studies Reporting Sex Differences In Play Activities of Young Children

Study	Sex	Findings
Rubin (1977)	Males Females	Blocks, wheeled vehicles Art activities
Tizard, Philps, & Plewis (1976)	Males Females	Tires, crates, wheeled vehicles Climbing frame
Harper & Sanders (1975)	Males Females	Sand, tractor, climbing frame Arts & crafts
Coates, Lord & Jakabovics (1975)	Males Females	Blocks Dolls, formal games
Cramer & Hogan (1975)	Males Females	Blocks, vehicles Dolls, furniture
Clark, Wyon & Richards (1969)	Males Females	Blocks, wheeled vehicles Dolls, art activities
Shure (1963)	Males Females	Blocks Doll area, art
Vance & McCall (1934)	Males Females	Blocks Housekeeping
Parten (1933)	Males Females	Blocks, trains, kiddie-kars Art activities, house play

Table II
Univariate F-Ratios for Play Activities

F-Ratios	df	MS	F	P
Blocks	1	11.21	28.29	.0001
Residual	48	.40		
Wheeled Vehicles	1	4.85	7.05	.01
Residual	48	.69		
Water/Sand	1	2.15	4.83	.05
Residual	48	.45		
House Play	1	.73	2.42	
Residual	48	.30		
Art Projects	1	1.47	5.35	.05
Residual	48	.27		

ented play activities (blocks, wheeled vehicles and water/sand) continued to be sex stereotyped. One female-oriented play activity, art projects, remained sex stereotyped. The other female-oriented play activity, house play, was not sex stereotyped, the only play activity that produced results different from those of previous studies.

This research indicates there may have been some change in the sex stereotyping of play activities of young children. If so, the change has been in only one direction. In this study, boys' play choices had expanded to include house play which had been a traditionally female-oriented play activity. The girls' play choices, however, had not expanded. If the initial thrust to eliminate sexism was a concern over the limited roles and opportunities for females, it has had little effect as reflected in this study.

It may be that the national movement towards eliminating sexism has had some impact on the sex role stereotyping of house play. The increase in working mothers resulting in fathers' helping at home and the current emphasis on the crucial role of the father in children's growth and development may also be significant.

Still another factor may be that conscientious female teachers are trying to eliminate sex stereotyping in their early childhood classrooms. Much has been written about the "lack of male-oriented play equipment and activities" in our programs.

The persistence of sex differences in the play of young children continues. Children's play activities are still restricted by sex stereotyping. Since children learn and develop through a wide variety of play activities (Lindberg 1971; Hartley, 1971; Bruner, 1975; Yawkey and Trostle, 1982), both girls and boys must be free to build with blocks, paint pictures, sculpt with water/sand, pedal wheeled vehicles and engage in house play.

References

Beeson, Betty Spillers, and R. Ann Williams. *A Study of Sex Stereotyping in Child-Selected Play Activities in Preschool Children*. ERIC, ED 186 102 (November 1979).

Birns, Beverly. "The Emergence and Socialization of Sex Differences in the Earliest Years." *Merrill-Palmer Quarterly* 22 (1976): 229-54.

Boch, R. Darrell. *Multivariate Statistical Methods in Behavioral Research*. New York: McGraw Hill, 1975.

Bruner, Jerome S. "Play Is Serious Business." *Psychology Today* 8 (1975): 80-83.

Clark, Anne H.; Sally M. Wyon and M. P. M. Richards. "Free Play in Nursery School Children." *Journal of Child Psychology and Psychiatry and Allied Disciplines* 10 (1969): 205-16.

Coates, Susan; Mae Lord and Evelyn Jakabovics. "Field Dependence-Independence, Social-Non-Social Play and Sex Differences in Preschool Children." *Perceptual and Motor Skills* 40 (1975): 195-202.

Cramer, Phebe, and Katherine A. Hogan. "Sex Differences in Verbal and Fantasy Play." *Developmental Psychology* 11 (1975): 145-54.

Erikson, E. H. "Sex Differences in the Play Configurations of Preadolescents." *American Journal of Orthopsychiatry* 21 (1951): 667-92.

Fein, Greta; David Johnson; Nancy Kosson; Linka Stork and Lisa Wasserman. "Sex Stereotypes and Preferences in the Toy Choices of 20-Month-Old Boys and

Girls." *Developmental Psychology* 11 (1975): 527-28.

Harper, Lawrence V., and Karen Sanders. "Preschool Children's Use of Space: Sex Differences in Outdoor Play." *Developmental Psychology* 11 (1975): 119.

Hartley, Ruth E. "Play, the Essential Ingredient." *Childhood Education* 48 (1971): 80-84.

Lever, Janet. "Sex Differences in the Games Children Play." *Social Problems* 23 (1976): 478-87.

Lewis, Michael. "Sex Differences in Play Behavior of the Very Young." *Journal of Health, Physical Education and Recreation* 43 (1972): 38-39.

Lindberg, Lucile. "The Function of Play in Early Childhood Education." *National Elementary Principal* 51 (1971): 68-71.

Lowe, Marianne. "Trends in the Development of Representational Play in Infants from One to Three Years." *Journal of Child Psychology and Psychiatry and Allied Disciplines* 16 (1975): 33-57.

Parten, Mildred B. "Social Play Among Preschool Children." *Journal of Abnormal and Social Psychology* 28 (1933): 136-47.

Restak, Richard M. "Viewpoint. The Other Difference Between Boys and Girls." *Young Children* 34 (1979): 11-14.

Rubin, Kenneth H. "Play Behaviors of Young Children." *Young Children* 32 (1977): 21.

Samuels, Shirley C. *Enhancing Self-Concept in Early Childhood.* New York: Human Sciences Press, 1977.

Shure, Myrna Beth. "Psychological Ecology of a Nursery School." *Child Development* 34 (1963): 979-92.

Sutton-Smith, B., and B. G. Rosenberg. "Sixty Years of Historical Change in Game Preferences of American Children." in R. E. Herron and Brian Sutton-Smith, eds., *Child's Play.* New York: Wiley, 1971.

Tizards, Barbara; Janet Philps and Ian Plewis. "Play in Preschool Centres—I. Play Measures and Their Relation to Age, Sex, and I.Q." *Journal of Child Psychology and Psychiatry and Allied Disciplines* 17 (1976): 251-64.

Vance, Thomas C., and Louise McCall. "Children's Preferences Among Play Materials as Determined by the Method of Paired Comparisons of Pictures." *Child Development* 5 (1934): 267-77.

Williams, R. Ann, and Betty Spillers Beeson. "A Follow-up Study of Sex Stereotyping in Child-Selected Play Activities of Preschool Children." ERIC, Ed 201 390 (September 1980).

Yawkey, Thomas Daniels, and Susan Louise Trostle. *Learning Is Child's Play.* Provo, UT: Brigham Young University Press, 1982.

Zaichkowsky, Leonard D.; Linda B. Zaichkowsky and Thomas J. Martinek. *Growth and Development: The Child and Physical Activity.* St. Louis: C. V. Mosby, 1982.

PART II: PLAY, LEARNING AND DEVELOPMENT
Introduction

Research indicates that children derive numerous benefits from play related to learning and development, including enhanced creativity, perspective-taking and problem-solving. Yet, after a decade of useful research, Greta Fein aptly points out, we still do not know how play works. Lack of understanding coupled with unbridled enthusiasm could lead adults to "destroy that which we are seeking to nurture" by forcing play into another adult-dominated sphere of activity.

Fein takes the reader on a tour of four surfaces that may help to understand play's contribution to children's learning: what children know about play, what developmental theorists say about play, play as framed behavior and the "innermost core" or "secondary symbolism." All these surfaces involve thinking, feeling and learning and, though not separated in real life, they are conceptually distinguished for Fein's examination.

Despite the number of experimental studies supporting the hypothesis that play fosters problem-solving, Tony Simon and Peter K. Smith raise questions about this hypothesis. Citing "weakness in design and interpretation," they review some relevant experimental work, consider methodological reservations and assess progress toward understanding the role of play in cognitive development.

The contribution of play in cognitive development frequently overshadows its role in social development. Shu-Fang Lo Chia explores play and social development in China, tracing the historical influences of play from antiquity to the present Republic of China scene. Chinese cultural influences on play are described from both family and school perspectives.

Catherine Cooper expands perspectives on social development by studying how children think about their friendships in play and academic contexts during the elementary school years. The theoretical perspective of her paper draws from work in social-cognitive development, which focuses on how children construct categories for thinking about and engaging in social behavior. Interviews were conducted with 40 middle-class elementary school-age children to examine sociometric and social-cognitive issues. Findings suggest that children's conception of a friend expands from one who possesses concrete positive qualities, to a partner in action, to an appreciation of complementarity between friends. These patterns are discussed in terms of individual differences in children's social standing in classrooms. Implications are discussed for enhancing children's relationships with peers.

Cooper's study, focusing on enhancing relationships between peers, is complemented by that of Teresita E. Aguilar, who identifies social and environmental barriers to playfulness and lists recommendations for creating a more playful atmosphere. Aguilar defines playfulness as "the perception or attitude an individual has that allows that person to behave spontaneously in an activity." She identifies several social elements as being influential according to the degree of playfulness exhibited by an individual. Social barriers are identified as social control and social approval. Environmental barriers include physical boundaries, stabilized equipment and noise factors.

The hypothesis that play is a primary medium for learning and development in young children has substantial foundations in research and theoretical literature. There are, however, many unanswered questions about the nature and extent of play's influence on cognitive and social development. Our research agenda for the remainder of the twentieth century is comprehensive and challenging.

Learning in Play: Surfaces of Thinking and Feeling

GRETA G. FEIN
Professor of Curriculum and Instruction
University of Maryland, College Park

Among the benefits which recent research indicates derive from play (Fein, 1981; Saltz & Brodie, 1982) are: *enhanced creativity* (Pepler, 1982; Dansky, 1980); *perspective-taking* (Burns & Brainard, 1979); *language* and *memory* (Saltz, Dixon & Johnson, 1977) and *problem-solving* (Cheyne, 1982). For "play activists," these results are deeply satisfying because they confirm a conviction that play is a valuable childhood experience.

But, after a decade of useful, rich research, we still do not know how play works. Still lacking is an understanding of how diverse forms of play influence these diverse functions. Suppose we encourage parents to play with their children. Suppose we train teachers to use play in the classroom. And suppose we design playgrounds, classrooms, home and programs for play. In our well-meaning adult enthusiasm to leave no corner of the child's world untouched, we may touch this world so thoroughly as to destroy that which we are seeking to nurture. We may turn play into its opposite, another adult-dominated sphere of activity.

If play contributes to children's learning, it surely does not do so directly. Because play is embedded in the child's thinking and feeling, learning in play occurs on the player's terms. The problem of play's contribution to children's learning may be looked at as a series of psychic surfaces, an outer surface within which successive interior surfaces are nestled. The outermost surface might be called "meta-ludic," what children know about play. At this, the surface of conscious awareness, what do children say about the mental and emotional aspects of play?

The *second* surface concerns what developmental theorists say about these aspects of play. We examine the distinction between play as mastery and play as assimilation (Piaget, 1952). Play as mastery is what we most often think of as play. But play as assimilation provides a perspective from which to examine how children control and contain their strange loops from manifest reality to pretend representations. Distinctions at this second surface give us entry to a third, the surface addressed in Bateson's analysis of play as framed behavior (Bateson, 1956).

At this *third* surface, we examine how children negotiate the collective symbols of make-believe, symbols that seem to touch widely shared, yet deeply personal perceptions of social life. These negotiations rest on an exquisite form of communication that directs, sustains and embellishes the collective symbolic enterprise.

Finally, at the *fourth* surface, we reach the core, the subterranean and deeply personal passageways of fear, anger, desire and hope that children often express in play. In this core, we confront what Piaget refers to as secondary symbolism and what for psychoanalytic theorists are the grand themes of emotional life (Erikson, 1977; Peller, 1954).

Although each surface involves learning, the learning is about different things, to suit different purposes.

THE MEANING OF PLAY

The continuing difficulty of play is defining it, an elusiveness that has evoked exasperation, disgust and a carefree shrug from the more courageous. There have been recent attempts to challenge the need for an operational definition with its requisite list of distinguishing features (Vandenberg, 1982) along with a proposal to use instead a definition based on prototypical instances (Matthews & Matthews, 1982).

45

Most definitional controversies have rested on adults' intuitions with little thought for the opinions of the players themselves (Fein, 1978; King, 1979). Do children use features to describe the meaning of play, or do they use prototypical instances? If the former, what features do they use and if the latter, what type of instances do they offer?

With these questions in mind, my students interviewed 28 children between the ages of 5 and 9 years. Twelve were in kindergarten or first grade, the remaining 16 in second or third grade. They came from three schools, two in blue collar, low- to middle-income communities and one in a more affluent, professional community. Altogether, 13 different classrooms were represented in the sample of children interviewed.

The children were asked to tell us what they thought play meant. To provide a contrasting category, they were also asked what work meant. Then they were asked to indicate their favorite kind of play and their favorite kind of work. Each child's responses were first coded according to whether the child gave features or instances in their definitions. If a child mentioned features, these were coded according to three main categories: (a) the locus of the decision to engage in the activity, (b) its affective aspects and (c) its goal orientation.

With respect to definitional type, 85 percent of the children used features to define work, and 86 percent used features to define play. As shown in Table 1, 54 percent used features alone to define work, whereas 50 percent used features alone to define play. Relatively few children (14 percent) used instances alone, but one-third used both features and instances in defining each realm of activity. Children apparently do not find it difficult to use features to define these activities.

Locus of decision was a feature used by children at all age levels. As shown in Table 2 children as young as 5 indicated that they were sensitive to the obligatory aspects of social situations. According to one of our kindergarteners, "Work is doing what someone tells you to do," and according to another, "Work is when you have to listen to the teacher." A third grader elaborated by saying that work is "Doing exactly what they tell you to do." By third grade, the framing of work in a system of externally imposed but internally accepted obligations, achieved a vivid economy of expression in the children's use of the verb "Do." Work is what you "Do everyday." It is "Doing something." You "Do math," "Do homework" and "Do hard work."

Deontic logic, which refers to the intuitive recognition of obligation and duty, was applied explicitly to work by even the youngest children. Although perhaps implied, this logic was not applied explicitly to play until third grade, when children first noted the voluntary aspects of play. "Play is doing anything you want to do." "Play is what no one tells you to do." In the words of one child, play is "Messing around." At an early age, work is defined by the presence of obligation. Only later is play defined by its absence. Although patient probing might have revealed similar notions in the younger children (King, 1979), it appears likely that children's conscious awareness of highly organized obligatory systems begins with school

Table 1
Number of Children Using Features and Instances to Define Work and Play

	K-1st		2nd-3rd	
	Work	Play	Work	Play
Features Alone	5	5	10	9
Instances Alone	3	3	1	1
Features and Instances	3	4	5	6
No Response	1	0	0	0
Total No. Children	12	12	16	16

Table 2
Features Used in Definitions of Work and Play
(No. of Children)

	Grade			
	K-1st (N = 12)		2nd-3rd (N = 16)	
	Work	Play	Work	Play
Locus of Decision				
Obligatory	7	0	12	0
Voluntary	0	0	0	5
Goal Orientation				
Performance Criteria	1	0	5	0
Extrinsic Reward	1	0	5	0
Achievement	1	0	6	0
Product Outcome	1	0	3	0
Affect				
Pleasure	0	6	3	13
Effort/Difficulty	3	0	2	0
Social Context				
Peers	0	2	0	3
Adults	0	0	3	0
Location				
School	0	0	2	0
Home	0	0	0	1
Outdoors	0	2	0	3

and that it is only after obligatory systems have been comprehended that the nonobligatory contrast is fully appreciated.

By third grade, children not only recognized the obligatory nature of work, but also recognized the "dos" and "don'ts" of functioning in this arena. According to these children, work is oriented towards extrinsic goals with externally provided, compelling performance criteria: finishing, paying attention, coming on time, being quiet. Work also yields external rewards: good grades and money. None of these features appeared in the children's discussions of play.

It was however, in the realm of affect that the children had the most to say about play. Fifty percent of the younger children and 75 percent of the older children said that play meant "fun." Again, there is asymmetry in their use of this feature. Although three of the younger ones said work was hard, none said that work was the *absence* of fun. By third grade, two children spontaneously noted that work was sometimes fun and sometimes not fun. In discussing their favorite work, a few older children, but none of the younger ones, acknowledged that it

was fun. Again, had the children been pressed to assess the affective characteristics of their favorite work activities, they might have acknowledged that these, too, were fun (King, 1979).

Not surprisingly, when children gave instances of work, they typically mentioned school activities. But when children gave instances of play, they mentioned objects: play is "with a ball," "with toys," "with something," or, less often, "with friends." As the term "do" characterizes work, so the term "with" characterizes play.

Although only five children gave outdoors as a feature of play, many instances of their favorite play were physical, outdoor activities—sports, bike riding, climbing, running. When persons were spontaneously mentioned, play was with peers and work was with adults. These adults were always parents, never teachers; always fathers, never mothers. But all told, work and play were presented as largely solitary endeavors; only 29 percent of the children spontaneously mentioned the companionship of others. In addition, with the exception of sports, most instances of play did not require the presence of a partner. These responses of the children appear to contradict the results of our observational research. When we observe school-age children playing in public places, they are typically in the company of peers. And yet, companionship was not viewed as a feature of play by the children interviewed.

It was both interesting and disappointing that no child identified play with intellectual satisfaction. But in this respect, work fared no better. Only three children indicated that work had anything to do with mental activity. One child said that math and science were "interesting," and another said that handwriting was "interesting." One child explained that she liked social studies because she could "find out about things."

King (1979), who asked children to classify actual school activities, reported that the children classified math games, spelling games and the like—all obligatory, teacher-controlled activities—as work, not play. In the spontaneous observations of our children learning games were mentioned by only one child, although several listed art activities as their favorite work. At times, the same activity was listed as favorite work and as favorite play. But the children were careful to stress the difference—in the words of one child, her favorite work was "making puppets" and her favorite play was "playing with puppets."

At this outer surface, it is clear that by 5 years of age children perceived work and play as relatively well-framed activities, psychologically organized around deontic issues. Academic learning was work and if other types of learning occurred in play, the children were either unaware of it or, wisely, were unwilling to share this insight with us. In this study, there is a sobering message, a paradox for those viewing play as a vehicle of learning. If adults organize play as a learning activity, no matter how pleasant and attractive in the eyes of the children, they may be converting play into work (King, 1979).

PLAY AS ASSIMILATION

Piaget's most important contribution to a theory of play is in the distinction between play as mastery and play as assimilation. In adapted thought there is an equilibrium between assimilation and accommodation; in play there is a predominance of assimilation over accommodation. Piaget cites numerous observations of his own infants to illustrate activities that begin with the infant's effort to comprehend, but continue as ". . . ludic manifestations in so far as they are carried out for mere assimilation, i.e. for the pleasure of the activity and without any effort at adaptation to achieve a definite end"(p. 92). The children we interviewed seem to fit that analysis. Piaget also talks about ludic combinations, in which the child ". . . goes from one schema to another, no longer to try them out successively but merely to master them without any effort at adaptation" (p. 93). And again, Piaget talks about activity that "is no longer an effort to learn, [but] is a happy display of known actions" (p. 93).

Recently in a study with colleagues of what happens when young children learn to use a microcomputer, we found one advantage of this situation for research is that it is highly motivating; another is that operating a computer requires the acquisition of entirely novel, easily specified, and exact schemas. Conceivably, observations of children acquiring these schemas will clarify the distinction between adaptation to achieve a definite end and the "happy display of known actions."

The study took place at the University of Maryland's Center for Young Children where June Wright and Marilyn Church are developing a preschool computer literacy curriculum, where children are as free to choose the microcomputer as block or house play. Having chosen the computer, they may do as they wish within the constraints of the program. Because the children do not have to use the computer and because, once the choice is made, they are free to explore its capabilities, this activity seems to satisfy children's criteria of play.

The curriculum begins at age 4 with two drawing programs—Scribbler and Creative Crayons—run on an Astrovision Computer. The children operate a joy stick, a knob and a few buttons. These manipulanda produce commands that separately or in sequence control the width, motion, direction, hue and intensity of a line appearing on the monitor. One command erases an image on the screen, another alters the background hue and intensity, and a combination of commands fills line drawings with color. As part of a larger study, logs were kept of each child's encounter with the computer over a period of several months. The children's verbalizations were audio-taped, and an observer kept track of what was happening on the screen (Wright & Samaras, in preparation).

These data nicely illustrate the effort as well as the pleasure of learning within a non-obligatory play context. One of the most difficult command sequences the children learned moved the cursor inside an outlined form, then filled the form with color. In one record, a child worked diligently to move her cursor inside the boundary of a small square, then gave the command to fill in the color. When the maneuver worked, she sang out: "Hey, look what I made! Look what I did! Look, look! I'm coloring the whole thing. Hey, look, I did it all myself!"

This child had achieved a goal she had set for herself, although surely the possibility was embedded in a psychologically remote, paradigmatic—and even obligatory—computer program. Another child struggled to detach a square shape from a thick line of color. Finally successful, she exclaimed: "I know I did that! Look at this! I had it switched on and off."

Mastering these commands was only the first step. Once having mastered them, the children played with the effects—changing colors and widths, backgrounds, erasing and restoring. Some engaged in self-initiated, product-oriented efforts, much in the spirit of the block work described by Seymour Papert (1981). One child, for example, built with the cursor, moving and stacking colored forms to the accompaniment of self-produced sounds of trucks, bulldozers and steam shovels. He called out in delight: "Hey, look what I made! I'm building something! You have to guess. It's a house. Look what I did!" He did not assume that the observer would know that the shapes on the screen were to be seen as a house.

The children quite often proposed symbolic representations of their computer constructions. A flash of light appearing when a color was changed became a "thunderstorm." A child making colored criss-crossing lines said, "They're sewing." When the line disappeared at the end of the screen, one child said, "It's sleeping" and when it reappeared said, "Now he woke up." Moving lines were often referred to as living things—as I, he, she, they and even it.

Discovering how to make the background black, one child said, "It's walking in the dungeon." Others referred to the effect as "night." As knowledge of how to produce the effect spread, the group played a game called "day and night." These examples show play subtly changing from play as mastery to play as assimilation. Practice of commands the children learned became embedded in their spontaneous assimilative activity.

Perhaps the most exciting moments came after the children acquired a repertoire of basic commands, when they began to create complex pretend scenarios, combining these commands in many ways. For some children, the microcomputer became a medium for the creation of animated cartoons.

One child used his mastery over the separation and movement of shapes to create adventurous, fast-paced police chase scenes.

Jon: I'm the police boy. I have policemen all the way to the top. I'm going 10 miles! Here I go! (makes the sound of screeching wheels). Here I go! Dukes of Hazard. I'm going at a fast speed. (to Bill whose shape has been following Jon's.) You're following me. Where's my line? (Bill overtakes and covers Jon's moving shape).

Bill: I gotcha!

Jon: No you don't! Hey, don't follow me! So long, Bud! (Jon pulls his shape away).

Bill: erases Jon's shape.

Jon: That makes me angry! Please don't erase me.

Another child detached a colored shape he called a car. As he moved the shape through other forms he talked to himself:

"I'm going to have to make a parking space." The parking space was an open-ended rectangle. After much maneuvering of the cursor, he slipped

49

the "car" into its "parking spot." "I got hit by a wall. Now I'm blocked in. Now I'm getting out." Suddenly, the "car" became an animal. "He's hiding. It's an animal. He's trying to get in there. I got him out."

In this monologue, the reference of "I" changes. First it is "I" the car then it is "I" who controls the animal, "him." At this point, Sam is joined by a friend.

Sam: It's a wolf.
Sue: He's speeding up the road.
Sam: And there's the stairs. Down the stairs onto the pathways, into the jail. And he stops. Down into a dark, dark room—a cave. (He darkens a part of the screen.)
Sue: I want this to be a dark, dark place. (She darkens the entire screen).
Sam: Stop! Don't darken it. (He restores a small patch of white space). Leave this space. It's a window.

In many respects, these pretend scenarios resemble those occurring in the block corner or on the playground, where there is a predominance of speech announcing tranformations, plans and ownership of objects (Goncu & Kessel, 1983).

These computer scenarios differ, however, in real time and in the sharp contrast between the child's sedentary position and the vigorous action portrayed on the screen. The scenarios also resemble the stories children sometimes tell about their drawings. The computer, however, permits a rendering of spatial motion that children of this age are ordinarily unable to achieve with graphic media. The computer drawings also permit an unusual degree of social sharing accompanied by the construction of personal and collective symbols.

Mastering the computer is dramatically different from playing with it. Mastery involves sustained attention to motor gestures and their consequences and the use of well-regulated means to attain clearly specified ends. Success brings with it an intense feeling of accomplishment and well-being. The affective state of the child during mastery is that of intense concentration. The reaction to mastery is one of explosive delight. But once a skill is mastered, a different orientation comes to dominate the activity. As Piaget astutely observed, play begins with the "happy display of known actions."

In these logs we find pretend episodes almost as intricately woven as those that appear quite regularly in sociodramatic play. At age 4 children are able to construct a system of shared meaning and then relate to one another within this constructed system.

Piaget stressed the emergence of collective symbolism, but it was Gregory Bateson who offered the idea that pretense requires a particular psychological frame, one in which the players agree that their behavior will not be taken literally. Moreover, this psychologically-framed pretend situation requires a form of communication capable of indicating to others how to interpret and respond to events occurring with the frame.

METACOMMUNICATION: THE BOUNDARIES OF SANITY

In a recent study, Holly Giffin (1983) examined the metacommunicative options available to children between the ages of 3 and 5. An important aspect of her study was its illustration of the frailty of the boundaries between reality and fantasy. The most obvious and apparent boundary is at the entrance where children say "Let's pretend," or "You be the . . ." or "Let's say this is . . . ." Giffin (1983) however, offers persuasive evidence that much of the other language occurring in play also serves metacommunicative functions. Although this language does not overtly comment on the play as playing, it nonetheless contributes to the coordination of play. Children exercise numerous metacommunicative options from within the play frame, options that seem to refer to inner layers of pretend meaning.

In Giffin's analysis these communications begin outside the frame with formal proposals ("Let's play that . . ."). Moving inwardly, there are implicit pretend proposals, prompting, storytelling, underscoring, ulterior conversation and, finally, the enactment itself. Many of these communicative options appeared in the pretend scenes our 4-year-olds created with the computer.

Enactments are constituted by the shape, placement and movement of the forms, changes in color and by events that have gone before. Ulterior conversation occurs in the comment, "You're following me." As Giffin notes, ulterior conversation is equivalent to the attempt in real life to covertly control the behavior of others: "Wouldn't you like to come to the table now?"

Underscoring and storytelling are the most frequently occurring communications in our computer episodes. Underscoring occurs when children add sound effects such as the screeching wheels of a speeding car or the motor of a working steam shovel. Storytelling, of course, provides the actual narrative of the play world. In our examples, storytelling lets us know that the moving form is a wolf, that the descending movement of the cursor means stairs and that the darkened screen is a cave and also a jail.

Prompting happens when Sue says, "I want this to be a dark, dark place" as she darkens the screen. Sam steps outside the play world entirely when he says, "That makes me angry." He steps partly in again when he says, "Please don't erase me." Although some of Giffin's metacommunicative options did not appear in these graphic pretend episodes, many did. Some options such as prompting and implicit pretend structuring seem more useful when pretend episodes involve real partners, reciprocal roles and the spaces and places of a three-dimensional, familiar object world. Giffin's analysis, however, returns us to the ultimate questions: what on earth is happening when children produce these make-believe constructions? Why do they develop special communication devices to maintain the flow of events, and why are they so prone to share these events with others?

It is helpful to remember that Bateson's interest in play stemmed from his study of madness. Because human beings so easily slip into strange loops where the nature of reality shifts ever so imperceptibly, we seem eternally confronted by the paradox of beginnings and endings. The penalty of our promethean inventiveness is the eternal search for outer realities to contain the endless recursive, self-absorbing cycles of meanings about meanings (Hofstadter, 1979). In appreciating the amazing performance revealed in young children's pretense, one comes also to appreciate the possibility that in pretense, children are marking the boundaries of sanity. These boundary-marking communicative strategies, Piaget would remind us, are not mere verbal formalisms. Rather, they must reflect fundamental structures of social knowledge. Ulterior conversation, for example, which directs action as it appears to offer options, illustrates a deontic paradox in which the individual may choose freely only from that which others have already selected for choice. In learning these boundaries, children learn the structures of psychic survival.

THE INNER CORE

Piaget's notion of play as assimilation carves a place within his general theory of adaptive thought for children's "intimate, permanent concerns, of secret and often inexpressible desires" (1962, p. 175).

But the individual may be more or less conscious of the meaning of a symbol. Every symbol may have ". . . in addition to its immediate meaning which is understood by the subject, more remote meanings, in exactly the same way that an idea, in addition to what is consciously involved in the reasoning of the moment, may contain meaning of which the subject is . . . unaware" (1962, p. 172).

At one level, then, the child who refers to a moving colored shape as a wolf going down the stairs is conscious of the immediate transformation, aware of both the immediate physical reality and its primary symbolic meaning. Sue, Sam's partner, had little difficulty grasping the transformation. Most likely, however, there are secondary meanings associated with a slinky animal imprisoned in the dark enclosure of a cave. These secondary meanings are less accessible to Sue, although the two children negotiate with respect to them. We might suspect that some secondary meanings are involved in Sam's insistence on a small window of light—a break in the pattern, much like that left by Navaho rug weavers to let the evil spirits out.

What are these unconscious affective themes that appear in the pretend games of young children? If we return to Peller's (1954) work, we are led to believe that these themes might emerge in a developmental sequence that reflects, perhaps, the child's intellectual ability to fear the disorderliness of human existence.

What might these themes be? A perusal of pretend transcripts suggests a few that appear to reflect these developmental concerns (Fein, 1983):

☐ Mastery: Mixed with the pleasure children gain from mastery are deep longings and anxieties about the consequences of incompetence. Often pretend games will be about doing things that require considerable skill (cooking, fishing or driving a speeding car) and even fantastic things that real human beings cannot accomplish.

☐ Nurturance and Attachment: In the play of 2- and 3-year-olds, a recurring theme is that of love and affection, separation and loss. Play babies go to bed reluctantly; they are left with dads and sisters while mothers do other things.

☐ Aggression: Aggressive themes become common when children reach the age of 5 years. Some of these are ritualized fantasies cast in forms borrowed from TV. Others, however, are constructed by the children themselves. The children make up bad mothers and then dispose of them. They enact tales of sibling warfare, and marital discord. Often the content is less transparent—who is this wolf that descends the stairs to a dark jail?

☐ Punishment: Aggressive themes are often accompanied by fantasies of punishment, one form of which is death. Giffin (1983) gives us an especially poignant example which occurs at the end of an episode in which the police shoot the "bad mother" whom the children had invented. The child who had orchestrated the death of the bad mother calls out: "Gramma, come save me and help me so the police don't shoot me." Gramma does not respond and so the child dies. We then hear the following lyric plea:

"And I was crying up in heaven,
And I got back alive.
Grandmother, gramma,
save me!
And I was crying."

Dylan Thomas could hardly do better.

SOME CONCLUSIONS

Although conceptually distinguishable, these four surfaces are not really separated in real life. Each surface involves some kind of thinking and feeling, some kind of learning and some kind of consolidation; some kind, but not the same kind.

Children define work according to rules for entering and rules for behaving, and only later do they apply deontic systems to the definition of play. Perhaps one must experience the involuntary aspects of social life before one is able to appreciate its voluntary aspects. Teaching children the distinction between work and play may well be a major though hidden curriculum objective during the early school years (King, 1979). The deontic framing implies situationally appropriate learning and affect: academics and achievement in school, self-initiated problem-solving and intrinsic motivation in play. There is also a message in these data for those who would design playgrounds, homes and classrooms for play, and for those who would promote the benefits of play among parents and teachers.

Children using a microcomputer illustrate a nonobligatory choice within a larger set of adult-provided options. Play as mastery involves a self-selected problem in which goals are compelling and achievable, the means constrained though well-defined and success immediately and directly discernable. Obligations, where they exist, are intrinsic rather than extrinsic (Moore & Anderson, 1969). Within this nonobligatory choice, obligations abound. Play as mastery occurs on a fine and fragile line with a self-selected, self-modulated challenge, a difficult but not impossible task. A remarkable potential of the microcomputer is that this fine line might be indefinitely adjustable.

As children gain control over the immediate stimulus environment of lines, shapes and movement, they rapidly go beyond the environment they have created. They embed a conceptually impoverished text in a rich, nonliteral context. One result, illustrated in our transcripts, is similar to a graphic display of scientific relationships. A line descending from left to right may stand for entities as diverse as diminishing math scores over successive decades or changing temperatures from summer to fall. In much the same way, the downward movement of a form may stand for these relationships or, to 4-year-olds, the display may stand for the more fanciful relationship of a "wolf going down the stairs." The deeper cognitive issue is whether the children's representational activity can be likened to the process whereby well-formed visual displays are understood as simplified models of complex reality.

Play as assimilation reminds us of how little we know when we learn something new and how long it takes for a new skill or a new idea to mellow, mature and penetrate the innermost recesses of our understanding. In our attempts to understand children's learning in play, we have dealt primarily with the short-term acquisition of arbitrary or trivial novelties. As a consequence, we lack models for understanding how new learning acquires surcharged meaning, interior connections and loose couplings with old understanding. Play in an assimilative mode draws attention to the slippage in most human thought, to the very promethean inventiveness that forges our chains as it promises liberation. It seems strange and yet fitting that Piaget, the sublime "psychologist of the real" would confront, albeit briefly, a childhood encounter with the unreal and even irrational (Sutton-Smith, 1983).

The third surface involves communicating the meaning of these representations to others and, just as important, negotiating their meanings with others. The meanings are fluid; there is ample egocentric space. And yet, the children explore and practice diverse communication techniques associated with barely perceptible shifts in individual stances toward a commmon effort.

Finally, at the fourth surface, we arrive at the boundaries between "I," "he," "she," "they" and "it." But those boundaries require a lifetime to contruct and much energy to maintain.

References

Bateson, G. "The Message 'This Is Play.' " In B. Schaffner, ed., *Group Processes: Transactions of the Second Conference.* York, PA: Josiah Macy Foundation, 1956.

Burns, S. M., and C. J. Brainerd. "Effects of Constructive and Dramatic Play on Perspective Taking in Very Young Children." *Developmental Psychology* 15 (1979): 512-21.

Cheyne, J. A. "Object Play and Problem-solving: Methodological Problems and Conceptual Promise." *Contributions to Human Development* 6 (1982): 79-96.

Erikson, E. H. *Toys and Reasons.* New York: Norton, 1977.

Fein, G. G. "Work, Leisure, and the Emperor's New Clothes." Paper presented at the conference, "The Significance of Work and Leisure in the Lives of Children and Youth." Wayne State University, October, 1979.

———. "Pretend Play: An Integrative Review." *Child Development* 52 (1981): 1095-118.

———. "The Self-building Potential of Make-believe Play: I Got a Fish, All By Myself." In T. D. Yawky and A. D. Pellegrini, eds., *Child's Play: Developmental and Applied.* Hillsdale, NJ: Erlbaum, 1983.

Giffin, H. "The Coordination of Shared Meaning in the Creation of a Shared Make-believe Reality." In I. Bretherton, ed., *Symbolic Play: The Representation of Social Understanding.* New York: Academic Press, 1983.

Goncu, A., and F. Kessel. "Are We Pretending? An Observational Study of Imaginative Play Communications." Paper presented at the American Educational Research Association Annual Meeting, Montreal, April, 1983.

Hofstadter, D. R. *Godel, Escher, Bach: An Eternal Golden Braid.* New York: Vintage Books, 1979.

King, N. "Play: The Kindergartener's Perspective." *The Elementary School Journal* 80 (1979): 81-87.

Moore, O. K., and A. R. Anderson. "Some Principles for the Design of Clarifying Education Environments." In D. A. Goslin, ed., *Handbook of Socialization Theory and Research.* Chicago: Rand-McNally, 1969.

Papert, S. *Mindstorms.* New York: Basic Books, 1981.

Pepler, D. J. "Play and Divergent Thinking." *Contributions to Human Development* 6 (1982): 64-78.

Peller, L. "Libidinal Phases, Ego Development, and Play." *Psychoanalytic Study of the Child* 9 (1954): 178-98.

Piaget, J. *Play, Dreams, and Imitation in Childhood.* New York: Norton, 1962 (originally 1945, English translation, 1951).

Saltz, E., and J. Brodie. "Pretend-play Training in Childhood: A Review and Critique." *Contributions to Human Development* 6 (1982): 97-113.

Saltz, E.; D. Dixon and J. Johnson. "Training Disadvantaged Preschoolers on Various Fantasy Activities: Effects on Cognitive Functioning and Impluse Control." *Child Development* 48 (1977): 367-80.

Sutton-Smith, B. "Play Research: The State of the Art." Paper presented at the conference "Play and Play Environments." Austin, Texas, 1983.

A Role for Play in Children's Problem-Solving: Time to Think Again

Tony Simon and Peter K. Smith
Department of Psychology
University of Sheffield, England

During the last few years there has been considerable interest in the functional importance of play for young children. Many new experimental studies apparently provide a firm basis for the hypothesis that play opportunities and play behaviors with objects do foster problem-solving skills. Although generalizations have already been made, these studies at the same time have come under closer methodological scrutiny, revealing some weakness in design and interpretation (Cheyne, 1982; Simon and Smith, 1983; Rubin, Fein and Vandenberg, 1983). In reviewing here the relevant experimental work, we will consider how strongly various methodological reservations apply, discuss whether any consensus in findings is emerging and conclude with an assessment of how much progress has been made toward an understanding of the role of play in cognitive development.

The studies under review all employed lure-retrieval problems of a convergent nature, i.e., there was only one way to solve the task. Initiated by Sylva, the paradigm follows naturally from Bruner's (1972) theoretical viewpoints while having experimental antecedents in the work of Kohler (1926), subsequently followed by Birch (1945) and Schiller (1957) on previous experience and the solving of lure-retrieval tasks in apes.

Sylva's 1974 study (see also Sylva et al., 1976 and Sylva, 1977) comprised five groups, each of which consisted of 36 children (six boys and six girls each of the ages 3, 4 and 5 years), seated at a low table to watch the experimenter tighten a "C" clamp onto the middle of a flat stick. Foll wing this, the "play" group were allowed 10 minutes of "free play" with 10 such sticks of various lengths and seven clamps. The "observe principle" group watched the experimenter connect two of the long sticks together by tightening a clamp at the overlap. The resultant long stick was a model of the one required to solve the problem; such a tool is referred to as the "solve principle." The "no treatment" control group received no further experiences before attempting to solve the problem. The "observe components" and "train components" groups either watched the experimenter make, or were trained to make, exactly the same constructions that their "yoke-mate" in the "play" group had made.

Once all children had received their pre-task experiences, they proceeded to the task session. Still seated at the table and in the presence of the same experimenter as in the pre-task session, the children were given a number of sticks and clamps. A piece of colored chalk was placed out of reach in a box with a transparent front. The child's task was to get the chalk out of the box by constructing a tool from the two longest sticks clamped together. Five hints, giving progressively more information regarding the solution, were given by the experimenter if the child a) ignored the problem for one minute, b) got up and walked about or c) repeatedly asked to leave.

Surprisingly, no solution time differences were evident among the groups, a fact in itself a curious finding since, in terms of exposure to the materials, the "play" group had five times longer than either the "training" group or the "no-treatment" controls. However, other performance differences did exist. There were significantly more spontaneous solvers (those given no hints) in the "play" and "observe principle" groups than in the control group, and the "play" children received significantly fewer hints than any other group. These varying patterns of results highlight two main problems in this paradigm: those of possible experimenter bias and the nature of the dependent variables used.

The two problems are interlinked, but let us deal first with the question of dependent variables. The main measures used in these and later studies are those of solution time, number of hints and whether or not the child was a spontaneous solver (although Sylva pays little attention to the time measure). It can be seen that all these variables are tied to the provision of hints by the experimenter. Any hints given will a) affect the hint score, b) nullify a spontaneous solution and c) less directly affect solution time, either by provision or withholding of help or in the actual time taken to give the hints. Although the procedure for hint-giving is laid down, in practice it is very difficult to carry out objectively without acting like an automaton toward the child, which she or he would find unnatural and possibly frightening. Any latitude in giving hints or responding to the child's questions could be compounded by the possibility of experimenter bias. In Sylva's and other studies there has been inadequate control for testing bias. This could occur, since the experimenter usually knew or had watched the child's pre-test condition and the child's behavior could have been influenced by expectations about that child's performance. Furthermore, without "blind scorers" some bias could also occur in the assessment stage.

The study following Sylva's was that of Smith and Dutton (1979), essentially a replication of Sylva's work with a number of details added. The materials were changed to rounded sticks and blocks to facilitate handling. After introduction to the materials, a two-minute "exploration" period was allowed for all children to become familiar with them. The subsequent "play" condition was similar, but the non-play activity was changed to a "training" procedure wherein the experimenter assisted the child in making a variety of double-stick tools, seriated them by length and then the child repeated the process unaided. When the first task was completed, a second task, innovative in relation to the training procedure, was immediately introduced. This was merely an

extension of the first, requiring the joining of three long sticks with two blocks to retrieve the prize. There were two control groups: one proceeded straight to Tasks 1 and 2 after the exploration session, while the other went straight to Task 2. Both experimental groups were equated in terms of exposure to the materials and the experimental environment, although the latter was not true of the control group.

The same experimenter was again responsible for all the sessions of this study. The childrens' performance on both tasks was assessed in terms of solution time, number of hints and spontaneous solvers. For Task 1 there were no differences in these criteria between the now evenly matched "play" and "training" groups, although both were significantly quicker and received significantly fewer hints than the control group. There were, however, no significant differences in the numbers of spontaneous solvers among the three groups.

In Task 2, however, considerable differences were apparent. The "play" group was significantly faster, received fewer hints and had more spontaneous solvers than the "training" group, which showed similar differences in relation to both control groups on all these measures, except for spontaneous solvers where no significant differences were apparent.

This, then, seemed to be the first consistent finding of the superiority of the play experience in relation to subsequent problem-solving. The same criticisms apply to this study, however, as to the Sylva study; in fact, an attempt to replicate this Task 2 result failed when adequate controls were implemented, as will be discussed later.

Vandenberg (1981), in a study, examined the effects of play and non-play experiences on the subsequent performance of 4- to 10-year-old children on two different lure problems. After a 10-minute "warm-up" period with Lego bricks, the "play" group was allowed 10 minutes to play with a number of notched sticks with holes in them and some pipe-cleaners. The "non-play" children, meanwhile, were asked questions by the experimenter about the properties of the materials. This same experimenter then took the children through the two task sessions. The first task was similar to that of Sylva, and Smith and Dutton, involving the joining of the two longest sticks to reach the lure. The second task involved the child's retrieving a piece of sponge from inside a long transparent tube by connecting several pipe cleaners to make a suitable tool. The dependent variables used were based on the hints given and the number of goal-directed actions. Vandenberg weighted the hints to account for their informational value, although a heavy weighting for the last hint may have yielded misleading results. Vandenberg found significant age effects with the older children doing better on both tasks. There was also a differential age/play effect with the 6- to 7-year olds gaining the most benefit from play. Nevertheless, the finding that the "play" group had better task scores than the "non-play" group (for the first task only) might again be due to the measure's being dependent on the hint-giving process. This could possibly have been compounded by experimenter bias because, although a "blind scorer" was used to count the hints given, the experimenter who actually gave them was aware of the children's pre-test groupings.

In trying to assess the effect of the experimenter's knowledge of the child's grouping on the experimenter's behavior and on the child's performance, Simon and Smith (1983) carried out a study that manipulated this element of the experimental procedure. The study was essentially a replication of the Smith and Dutton (1979) experiment except that two secondary experimenters brought in to test the children were unaware of the pre-test conditions of half the children that they tested, whereas they had watched the other half during their pre-test session. Manipulations of these secondary experimenters' visual and verbal contact with the child were also added in order to control for possible bias in the form of non-verbal communication.

For Task 1 the same results occurred as in the Smith and Dutton study, with a rough equality of the "play" and "training" groups. However, in Task 2 the "play" group superiority result was not replicated. Never-

theless, it was found that the "aware" and "unaware" conditions had little effect on the secondary experimenter's behavior or the child's performance. Although no direct evidence for experimenter bias was found in this study, the discrepancy in the Task 2 findings needs to be explained (especially as the Simon and Smith Task 2 result has since been replicated in another, unpublished, study (Emberton, note 1). Possible explanations are discussed in Simon and Smith (1983). The most likely explanation, in our opinion, is that in the Smith and Dutton study, a considerable number of unnecessary hints were given to the "training" children in Task 2, which actually hindered their performance. The correlation between the number of hints given and solution time is $r = 0.88$, $p < .001$. A relevant difference between the two studies may be that in Smith and Dutton (1979) the experimenter was conscious of and involved with the experimental design and hypothesis, whereas, in the Simon and Smith (1983) experiment the secondary experimenters were not involved in this way.

In an unpublished study that went some way towards removing some of the experimental problems discussed above, Darvill (note 2) carried out an extended replication of the Vandenberg study. Using the same tasks as Vandenberg, Darvill introduced an innovative version of both tasks, as had Smith and Dutton, and also manipulated the appropriateness of the pre-test materials. The main results showed no differences between the "play" and "demonstrate" groups but did show significant positive correlation between the increase in the age of the children and their success at solving the problems.

How much of a consensus of results has emerged from these studies? The most substantial finding in favor of play experiences had been that of Smith & Dutton (1979); but that now seems invalid due to nonreplication and possible experimenter bias. Discounting that, the most recurrent finding is that no differences are to be found between the experimental groups. (One could even argue from the pattern of results that any equal exposure to the materials will produce equal performance, whatever form it may take.) But we are to take this to mean that "play" and "non-play" experiences are equally potent when it comes to aiding performance on subsequent convergent lure problems? It is interesting to note that in the Smith and Dutton study, the control group that has already attempted Task 1 then solves Task 2 significantly faster ($p<.05$) than the control group attempting the problem for the first time. This is obviously relevant experience, but at the same time it is the inverse of a play experience due to the pressure of attempting to solve the problem.

Mere exposure to the materials may not be the most relevant factor. So far, all control groups have confounded exposure to the materials with exposure to the experimental environment. A study just completed by the authors, in which the control group completed the same pre-test procedure as all other children but without exposure to the experimental materials, shows the control group performing as well as all other groups on all criteria. In this study, the alternative materials control group provides (as argued by Smith and Simon, in press) a more equitable situation in all factors except experience with the relevant materials. This contrasts with studies where the control group children were presented with the problem a mere two minutes after entering the room and then performed far worse than did those in the experimental groups. This result was used to argue that there was, indeed, some real learning occurring during the "play" and "training" sessions.

But if the control children are given as much chance to settle into the environment, then our recent results suggest that this difference does not seem to occur. In these circumstances, it seems that only two minutes' exploration with the specific materials is no disadvantage. The problem is compounded by the hints procedure. This may be creating a ceiling effect which, by ensuring that almost all the children solve the problem within six to eight minutes, prevents any differences between the groups from becoming apparent. The full implications of this result are discussed in detail elsewhere (Simon and Smith, in press). It may also be that the children used in most of these studies were rather young or that this task is rather too hard for

children of this age (this is certainly suggested by the results of Vandenberg and Darvill).

It now seems plausible that results of the published lure-retrieval studies can be interpreted in a different way from a straightforward facilitator effect of play on problem-solving. Recent reviews (Simon and Smith, in press) suggest that there are serious problems in the design of this paradigm. It may be these have resulted in the lack of positive findings of a direct role for play in cognitive development. Alternatively, as the above authors also suggest, it may be that the assumptions leading to the hypothesis that play is a primary learning medium for young children are not well founded. Further naturalistic and well-controlled studies of childrens' play are needed to try to answer which of these explanations best accounts for the apparent lack of success of the lure-retrieval paradigm.

Reference Notes
Emberton, R. "Play and Problem-solving: An Investigation of the Experimentor Effects in Studies Attempting to Determine the Relationship Between the Two." Unpublished B.A. Dissertation, Sheffield University, England, 1983.
Darvill, D. "Object Play and Problem-solving in Young Children." Unpublished M.A. Dissertation, Waterloo University, Ontario, Canada, 1982.

References
Birch, H. G. "The Relation of Previous Experience to Insightful Problem-solving." *Journal of Comparative Psychology* 38 (1945): 267-83.
Bruner, J. S. "The Nature and Uses of Immaturity." *American Psychologist* 26 (1972): 687-708.
Cheyne, J. A. "Object Play and Problem-solving; Methodological Problems and Conceptual Promise." In D. J. Pepler and K. H. Rubin, eds., *The Play of Children: Current Theory and Research* Geneva: S. Karger, 1982.
Koehler, W. *The Mentality of Apes.* New York: Harcourt, 1926.
Rubin, K. H.; G. G. Fein and B. Vandenberg. "Play." In E. M. Hetherington, ed., *Carmichael's Manual of Child Psychology: Social Development.* New York: Wiley, 1983.
Schiller, P. H. "Innate Motor Action as a Basis of Learning." In P. H. Schiller, ed., *Instinctive Behaviour.* New York: International University Press, 1957.
Simon T., and P. K. Smith. "The Study of Play and Problem-solving in Preschool Children: Have Experimenter Effects Been Responsible for Previous Results?" *British Journal of Developmental Psychology* 1 (1983) 289-97.
———. *From Bananas to Marbles with Little to Show? A Play and Problem-solving Paradigm Questioned.* In press.
Smith, P. K. and S. Dutton. "Play and Training in Direct and Innovative Problem-solving." *Child Development,* 50 (1979): 830-36.

Smith, P. K. and T. Simon. "Object Play, Creativity and Problem-solving." In P. K. Smith ed., *Play in Animals and Humans*. Oxford: B. Blackwell, in press.

Sylva, K. "The Relationship Between Play and Problem-solving in Children 3-5 Years Old." Unpublished doctoral dissertation, Harvard University, 1974.

———. "Play and Learning." In B. Tizard and D. Harvey, eds., *Biology of Play*. London: Heinemann Medical Books, 1977.

Sylva K.; J. S. Bruner and P. Genova. "The Role of Play in the Problem-solving of Children 3-5 Years Old." In J. S. Bruner, A. Jolly and K. Sylva, eds., *Play: Its Role in Development and Evolution*. London: Penguin Books, 1976.

Vandenberg, B. "The Role of Play in the Development of Insightful Tool-using Strategies." *Merrill-Palmer Quarterly* 27 (1981): 97–109.

Play and Social Development in Taiwan

JEAN SHU-FANG LO CHIA
Department of Child Development
Fu-Jen University, Taipei, Republic of China

On the beautiful island of Taiwan children grow up in different environments, in cities, suburbs, towns and rural areas, in good environments and poor. In cities, whether they live in multiple dwellings, housing projects or in separate houses, they live in the usual planned areas with space for play in school playground or park. Some children are fortunate enough to live in planned areas with ample provision for recreation.

People in Taiwan realize that it is important to provide a warm, nurturing environment and to encourage children's play. Since play is one of the most important and necessary activities for children, they must have the opportunity to experience play with both familiar and unfamiliar materials in varying environments.

CHINESE PLAY AND CULTURE

Many kinds of play may be traced back to early years of the Han Dynasty (206 B.C.– 219 A.D.) such as: the Dragon dance and the Lion dance; puppet shows and shuttlecocks; jumping rope and flying kites; swinging and hopscotch; playing with bamboo and paper toys; paper cutting; chio-lian-huan (mathematical training) diagrams; playing with kaleidoscopes and bamboo instruments. Through such play activities, children can experience a wide variety of the elements of cultural and traditional play.

The Lantern Festival, which may be traced back to the early years of the Han Dynasty (206 B.C.–219 A.D.), has fostered a long tradition of fantasy in which children may delight and participate. When service to worship the North Star was held from early morning through dawn the next day, the lanterns were lit everywhere throughout the night. Another legend associates the Lantern Festival with the actual start of schools in the days of Emperor Taitsung of the Tang Dynasty (627–649 A.D.). As the Emperor was promoting an examination system for the civil service, parents often sent their children to school for a session that usually started shortly after the 15th day of the first month. On that day, every child would bring to school a delicate lantern prepared by his parents, which the teacher would light to signal a bright future.

Many lanterns for the Festival are made by elementary school children in the Republic of China for a lantern exhibition put on in a park. Children construct frames made of baked bamboo strips bent to the proper shape and covered with cellophane, oil paper or silk fabric, with a candle or small bulb for illumination. For decoration, the children paint flowers or apply colorful paper cut-outs on the outside. Lanterns are made in all shapes, colors and sizes, resembling such familiar things as lotus flowers and peonies, birds and dragons, rabbits, goldfish and even inanimate objects such as airplanes and tanks.

Nowadays, children's artistic products are less unusual because lanterns of plastic can be bought at markets or department stores.

Another favorite activity during the Lantern Festival is guessing riddles. A few days before the lantern exhibition begins, shopkeepers or community centers hand out plain unadorned lanterns with strips of paper with riddles written on them. If a riddle is guessed correctly, the strip of paper is removed and another hung in its place. Sometimes prizes of fruit, candies or stationery are offered. The Festival is not complete without fireworks to light up the sky while children parade with colorful lanterns. This joyful Lantern Festival is often regarded as a mark of the end of winter holiday, a beginning of a new semester and a return to school for children.

61

Kung Fu is an activity very popular in Taiwan as it is everywhere in the world. Children learned Kung Fu from movies and television serials but, as used popularly today, the term Kung Fu is a misnomer. In its correct and narrow use, Kung Fu means expertise in either of the two great schools of Chinese boxing: Shaolin Ch'uan (fist) or Tai Chi Ch'uan. However, it is Shaolin Ch'uan which has come to be identified with what westerners now call Kung Fu.

Some small truths may be discerned in the American Carridine Kung Fu television series. One of these is the Shaolin Temple and the frequent flashbacks to the hero's training in Kung Fu from boyhood. Shaolin Ch'uan originated at this temple in Honan province of North Central China in 519 A.D., where Master Ta Mo, a Buddhist Monk from the state of Liang, taught the temple priests the art of self defense. Out of this came the Shaolin Ch'uan school of Chinese boxing.

As the Shaolin school grew and its fame spread, strict rules were adopted and enforced to assure the practitioners that Kung Fu would not go out to misuse their strength and power. Shaolin students were chosen with care. The secrets of the masters could be shared only with those of high moral standard.

Little boys and young men of Taiwan play at Kung Fu without excessive violence, injury or damage. The spirit of Kung Fu is ancient, honorable and respected, not unnecessarily violent, and is never destructive of life. Those who have made Kung Fu otherwise are departing from both Chinese culture and history.

Play is influenced by tradition as young children imitate the play of older children, who have imitated the play of the generation of children preceding them. Thus, in every culture, one generation passes down to the next forms of play it finds most satisfactory. The influence of tradition is apparent in the seasonal patterns of children's play. Children enjoy such games as jumping rope, walking on stilts and the lion dance during Chinese New Year. With the approach of autumn, they look forward to flying kites, and, in rural districts, making windmills and sling shots.

CONTEMPORARY PRESCHOOL CHILDREN'S PLAY

Between 2 and 3 years, Chinese children tend to imagine that their toys have lifelike qualities, that they are capable of acting, talking and feeling. Toy play reaches a peak between 5 and 6 years of age. As children develop intellectually, they no longer endow inanimate objects with real-life qualities and their interest in toys declines. Another factor that contributes to a decline in toy play is that it is mainly solitary, and children want companionship.

In nursery school or kindergarten there is usually to be found a cheerful, secure environment that provides familiarity and variety, promotes good feelings and facilitates open, child-paced learning in its materials and arrangements. These environments contain toys and equipment appropriate for 3- to 6-year-old children, with certain areas reflecting a range of typical activities: for housekeeping, creative toys, arts and crafts, blocks, musical instruments, small science and reading. The typical routine includes supervised indoor and outdoor play and activities which vary among age groups.

An abundance of available playthings is designed to encourage learning at many levels of difficulty and in all areas of development, including those emphasizing physical mastery, imagination and problem-solving. Small toys and table toys, a variety of sensory and art materials and larger pieces of commercial equipment provide sensory, manipulative and peer experiences through play. With teacher guidance, they are used by young children in a way that builds intellectual, physical and social skills. Toys are an important part of the preschool child's world of daily exploration. Adults can observe toy uses to determine the child's developmental status and personal interests.

As the child grows older and more experienced, playful treatment of toys becomes more diverse and sophisticated. Both imagination and intellectual curiosity begin to contribute to play. Paper dolls are clad in colorful and detailed costumes; intricate constructions are built from modeling sets or sand. Toys are incorporated as props into dramatic play, or their treatment is governed by complex rules in games of physical or intellectual skill. All through these changes, however, toys continue to arouse curiosity and the desire to learn. They provide enjoyment in mastering their use or in understanding the properties of things, and they also continue to facilitate social contacts and assist in the expression of ideas and feelings. There are small group times during which young children can relate to others, participate with teachers and share with their peers a specific activity. Simple participatory songs and stories and finger plays help to develop social skills and allow pleasure.

Chinese preschools offer free play sessions, space and frequent opportunities for exploration, discovery and practice that enable young children to play at their pace with activities of their own choosing. There are unstructured times, open physical space and opportunities for children to express themselves, demonstrate self-reliance, try out skills and look for interesting play situations.

SCHOOL-AGE CHILDREN'S PLAY

After entering school, most children want companionship. They become interested in games, sports, hobbies and other more mature forms of play. Some are interested in reading, watching television or looking at comics. As the number of social contacts increases, the quality of school children's play becomes more social. They learn give-and-take and become interested in cooperative play activities. They have achieved acceptance in a gang and, with it, an opportunity to learn to play in a social way.

During the first three grades in school, children care little about sedentary activities until late in the day, when they are tired. Then they like to watch television or listen to stories read by the teacher. From grade four on, however, there is a gradual increase in the amount of time spent in reading, going to the movies, watching television, listening to the radio, listening to music and watching sports events.

School-age children are interested in outdoor activities, particularly as there is much emphasis on learning to play games and en-

gage in sports. Their games are structured by explicit rules that can be precisely communicated, taught and learned. Children learn to accept and adhere to a particular set of rules, because they learn that rules are the essence of games, which would not continue to exist without rigid structure.

The early school period is a desirable time to utilize the alertness and eagerness of children in the development of hobbies and interests that will serve to enrich later life. Interest in woodworking, collecting, arts and crafts and dramatics can be stimulated easily. In the years from 9 to 12, interests are strongest in group play and hobby activities. The impulse for group solidarity is strong and can be used to move a class as a group, even though individual competitiveness also characterizes this age. The wide range of group interests helps the teacher in providing a sense of solidarity, but it may also handicap school work for it encourages boisterousness. Curiosity fosters the naturally silly behavior that characterizes this age. Poking, tripping, practical jokes for boys, and incessant giggling for girls can try the teachers' or parents' patience to the breaking point.

CHILDHOOD GANGS

The childhood gang is a spontaneous local group having no imposed authorization, no socially approved aim. It is formed by children themselves, to create a society adequate to meet their needs without support from parents, teachers or youth leaders. The gang is not necessarily a product of substandard environments; it is also found in good environments. Gangs have a more definite structure than the informal groupings of younger children. Gang members are selected because they are able to do things the others enjoy doing, not because they live near each other or can do what one or two members want to do at the moment. The gang is independent of structured activities, but selects the various activities it will engage in.

The typical gang is a group made up of children with common play interests, whose primary purpose is to have a good time. From the ages of 6 or 7, boys and girls normally find increasing pleasure in being in groups of their own sex. Gang activities include group play and entertainment, making things, annoying other people, exploring and engaging in forbidden activities.

CONTRIBUTIONS OF PLAY TO CHILDREN'S SOCIAL DEVELOPMENT

By playing with other children, children learn how to establish social relationships and meet and solve the problems these relationships give rise to. Social acceptance means being chosen as a companion for an activity in a group of which one is a member. It is an index of the success with which children take their place in the social group and the extent to which other group members like to work or play with them. Certain traits are almost universal; almost all well-accepted children are friendly and cooperative, they adjust harmoniously, comply with requests, accept some denials or setbacks graciously and have good relationships with adults as well as children. They are kind, sharing, willing to take turns in any group game and show impartiality toward other members. They assume responsibilities, participate in and enjoy social activities, feel secure in their status and compare themselves favorably with their peers.

Well-accepted children are primarily group-centered rather than ego-centered. Although maintaining individuality, they conform to the broad pattern of the group, observing its rules, regulations and mores, even as they conform to the routines of the home, school or playground group. They are flexible in that they readily adapt their way of doing things to conform to social expectations. Social maturity is also shown in their social insight which enables them to size up and adjust quickly to persons in different social situations.

Before age 4, children normally want their playmates to be companions, selecting one or two from those available, preferring to play with them. At first their playmates may be of either sex, but even before they are ready to enter school, children show a preference for playmates of their own sex. They have more interests in common with children of their own sex because the playmates also will have learned, through social pressures, to play in a sex-appropriate way.

When children enter school and begin to be interested in group play, they set additional new criteria for selecting playmates. They prefer children of the same sex, size, chronological age, social maturity and interests. As they grow older, personality traits become important, especially such traits as cheerfulness, generosity, friendliness, cooperativeness, honesty, sense of humor and sportsmanship. Most children like to have playmates who are successful in games and who, as a result, have prestige in the eyes of the group, thus increasing their own prestige through association. During late childhood, boys and girls select from their playmates those who are most congenial and with whom they can communicate as well as play.

Playmates contribute to the socialization of children. From imitating their associates, children learn patterns of behavior that lead to good or poor adjustment. Children learn, for example, to be good or poor sports, cheat or play fairly, to be kind to those who are different or discriminate against them, and play the role of leader or follower successfully or unsuccessfully.

Several playmates can generally contribute more to socialization than one because each can contribute something different. One child, for example, may help companions see why they should act in a sex-appropriate way, another may demonstrate the value of being cooperative instead of aggressive, while still another may help others develop social insight and learn to be sympathetic. A single child, because of inexperience, is usually unable to do the entire socialization job successfully. By contrast, a group made up of children of different interests, abilities and backgrounds can usually do the job better.

CONTRIBUTION OF PLAY TO CHILDREN'S DEVELOPMENT OF DESIRABLE PERSONALITY TRAITS

Personality traits are a product of learning, though based on a hereditary foundation.

They are molded mainly by child training in the home and school and by imitating a person with whom the child identifies. School-age children will imitate the traits of members of the peer group, developing the characteristic methods of adjustment accepted and approved by the group.

Children soon discover that there are sex-approved and social class-approved traits. Despite these variations, children learn that certain basic traits are admired by all cultural groups. Honesty, respect for the rights of others, respect for authority and a sense of appreciation, they discover, are universally approved.

Dramatic play contributes much to children's personal and social adjustments. From practice in role-taking, children learn what the group considers appropriate for a role, whether as a pupil, a teacher or a doctor. They learn to view a situation from the frame of reference of the person impersonated, an active effort that helps develop social as well as self-insight.

From dramatic play children gain satisfaction from their own efforts instead of waiting to be amused by others. They also learn to be cooperative members of a group, playing the roles assigned by the group instead of demanding only roles of their own choosing.

Chinese children must make good personal as well as social adjustments. Because of the high social value placed on social acceptance in Chinese culture today, children are not disposed to be happy unless they are reasonably well accepted by the people who are significant in their lives. Children need guidance and help in developing patterns of adjustment and in learning how to behave in a manner that will facilitate social acceptance and affection from others.

In attaining this level of adjustment that may lead to happiness in childhood, play is the most important activity in helping children become well developed in physical, mental and social aspects. Children must have the opportunity to experience play with familiar as well as unfamiliar materials, and many play materials are not found in the home. The play group environment, therefore, is highly important in giving young children a feeling of well-being, comfort and security.

Most of the kindergarten and elementary schools in Taiwan provide good-sized, well-equipped playgrounds. We try our best to teach our children to be successful so they can function well in the society of the future that is being developed in Taiwan, Republic of China and in the rest of the free world.

Playfriends and Workfriends: Developmental Patterns in the Meaning and Function of Children's Friendships

Catherine Cooper and Deborah Edward
Department of Home Economics
The University of Texas at Austin

What makes a good playfriend? What makes a good workfriend? Our concern here is with how children think about their friendships in play and academic settings during their elementary school years, a period marked by intense preoccupation with social relationships (Hartup, 1983) and rapid growth in children's repertoire of interactional skills (Asher & Gottman, 1981; Rubin & Ross, 1982). The early elementary years are of special significance for the development of social skills, for by this time a child has mastered the basic linguistic and conversational skills of communication, including the use of referentially specific language and contingent turn-taking (Paris & Lindauer, 1982). As children enter the school they encounter a complex set of rules and expectations and opportunities for social, cognitive and emotional development. Examining how children of different ages and abilities negotiate the social and cognitive environments of the school provides an opportunity to identify basic developmental processes of social and cognitive growth and the factors that may facilitate or impede their development or expression.

Our previous work (e.g., Cooper, Ayers-Lopez, & Marquis, 1982; Cooper, Marquis, & Ayers-Lopez, 1982; Cooper, Marquis, & Edward, in press) has been designed to trace the basic processes by which children help one another in their learning. This report presents one aspect of a larger project, examining the role of children's peer relationships in learning during the elementary school years. Here we are concerned with the relations between *children's conceptions of their relations with friends* in play and work settings and their standing within the peer network, as viewed by their peers.

This work is based on themes developed by Sullivan and Piaget and integrated by Youniss (1980), which suggest that there are two key lines of interpersonal development in childhood. Interactions between children and adults give opportunities to learn the rules of social order through being tutored or guided by a mature person. In contrast, interactions and relations between children of relatively comparable power enable them to collaborate, negotiate and "co-construct" their worlds.

We begin with some key questions. First, what changes occur across the elementary school years in children's choices of friends in play and work contexts? Second, what developmental differences exist in children's conceptions of these relationships? Our expectation was that we might see an association between age and the selectivity and relational complexity of children's thinking about their friends. We were also interested in the links between age, social standing and children's conceptions of friends in play and work settings. In less adult-structured play contexts, children might have the opportunity to develop more mutually defined friendships at an earlier age.

METHOD

Subjects

As part of a larger study of children's peer learning, 40 children, ranging from 5 to 12 years, were interviewed. These children attended a Montessori elementary school that emphasized children's relationships with their peers as a key context for personal and academic development. Consequently, peer relationships were fostered by the classroom teachers, and children were encouraged and assisted in collaborative and tutoring roles. The children came from primarily Anglo, middle-class families. This study reports data from 20 children from the younger group of 5- to 9-year-olds, and 20 from the older group of 9- to 12-year-olds.

Procedures

Children were interviewed individually in a quiet room in the school to examine sociometric and social cognitive issues. Peer ratings of classmates were obtained through a "sort and explain" procedure (following Hallinan, 1981). Children were shown the names of their classmates, each written on a $3'' \times 5''$ card, and asked to sort them into piles to show which of their peers were their closest and "sometimes" workfriends and playfriends, as well as which were best as helpers in reading and math and most knowledgeable in reading and math. Following each sorting, done separately, the children were asked to explain the basis of their choices. The choices provided a map of the learning and social networks in each class, and the explanations provided insight as to developmental and competence differences in children's conceptions of relationships.

Interviews were tape recorded and transcribed. The explanations were coded using a system derived from the work of Youniss (1980) and Selman (1981). The categories distinguish children's responses on the basis of the complexity of perspective-taking, the degree to which a child shows an awareness and ability to take into account multiple points of view. In addition, action and psychologically-based explanations were distinguished at each level. The levels can be outlined as follows:

1. Focus on general attributes of person considered in isolation: "He is my friend because he is nice."
2. Focus on specific attributes: "She makes jokes."
3. Relational focus, mentioning self and other child: "She and I are table partners." "He runs faster than me."

4. Collaborative focus: "We always do spelling together." "We like each other."
5. Contingent or complementary focus: "She lets me be what I want to be." "If I don't know the answer, he will help me figure it out and not just tell me."

Our coding system was developed through scrutiny of a stratified sample of responses varying across age, class, sex and sociometric status. Coders who had not been apprised of the hypotheses of the study then categorized each statement made by each child. Reliability on each category exceeded 80 percent agreement. Following Gottman (1983), reliability checks were conducted by each coder to minimize observer drift. Disagreements were arbitrated by consensus and all protocols were reviewed by the senior researchers to ensure consistent coding.

RESULTS AND DISCUSSION

The findings can be presented in three parts: the *first* concerns the developmental and within-class differences in children's selection patterns of playfriends and workfriends. The *second* addresses the bases given by the children for their choices. The *third* involves relationships among age, sociometric standing and conceptions of relationships.

Children's answers to the questions of the form, "Who are your playfriends (or workfriends) most of the time?", ". . . some of the time?" revealed striking differences across age, as well as distinctive patterns within age group across the playfriend/workfriend categories. As indicated in Table 1, children in the older group were more selective than in the younger group in naming their peers as playfriends, workfriends, and math and reading helpers and knowers.

Of the 8 sociometric questions asked, younger children exceeded older ones in the number of children named on all (sign test $p<.004$). In addition, within age groups, children chose more of their peers as playfriends than workfriends. This may have reflected their teachers' admonitions to work in the classroom only with those who could work productively; one teacher sometimes separated children who were not able to settle into work by reassuring them that they

Table 1
Children's Choices of Workfriends, Playfriends, Math and Reading Helpers and Knowers by Age Level

Category	Number Named by Younger Children (5-9 years) N = 20			Number Named By Older Children (9-12 years) N = 20		
	Mean	S.D.	Range	Mean	S.D.	Range
Best Workfriend	4.74	4.41	1-16	3.45	1.76	1-7
"Sometimes" Workfriend	6.85	4.30	1-17	6.25	3.11	1-13
Best Playfriend	5.95	4.46	1-13	5.30	4.98	0-19
"Sometimes" Playfriend	7.00	6.57	0-26	5.65	4.10	0-13
Math Helper	9.55	6.21	1-22	3.75	3.09	0-9
Math Knower	7.25	9.43	0-40	4.35	4.56	0-17
Reading Helper	7.30	7.71	0-26	3.30	3.01	0-10
Reading Knower	5.95	8.12	0-27	3.80	4.61	0-18

might be good playfriends, but did not seem to be good workfriends that day. These findings are consistent with other studies, which document increasing selectivity in children's choices of friends across the elementary years (Hartup, in press). By examining multiple forms of friendship choices, we can trace contextual as well as developmental differences. For example, children selected more of their peers as knowers ("who knows a lot in math?") than as helpers ("who is a good helper in math?").

The second key question concerns patterns in the explanations children made for their selections of workfriends and playfriends. Table 2 shows the number of children from younger and older groups who explained their choices at each level of the relational code.

The data indicate that younger children were more likely to offer definitional or general attributes to account for their choices of workfriends ("she is my workfriend because she is old"), chi-square $(df=1) = 3.96, p<.05$, although this age difference was not seen in playfriend choices. Children in both younger and older classes more often cited qualities of their experiences or relationship with their friend ("she plays soccer with me") than only qualities of the other child. Both collaborative reasons ("we do math together") and contingent reasons ("if I make a mistake, he waits for me") were given most frequently in action contexts by both younger and older children.

Comparisons of children's conceptions of their work and play relationships indicated few differences in level of sophistication across domains, with the exception of a greater orientation toward static attributes by young children when describing their workfriends.

To explore the links between age, conceptions of friendship and sociometric standing, we focused on two children from each group as case studies. In the younger group, Sam (all names are fictitious), a 9-year-old, was chosen by few of his classmates as either a workfriend or a playfriend. He expressed only a few reasons for his choices in each area, and these were at the lower levels of relational sophistication, such as "he is my best friend," "he plays with me a lot." In contrast, Paul, an 8-year-old boy in the same group was chosen frequently by his classmates as both workfriend and playfriend. He expressed sophisticated levels of relational concepts across work and play domains. For example, in describing a workfriend, he said, "When you're behind, he'll stay and let you catch up and then start writing again." Regarding a playfriend, he said "He helps me out when I'm goalie (in soccer) and I'm not playing too well." The responses of Sam and Paul, approximately the same age, illustrate that factors other than children's ages are significant in influencing their social-cognitive level of functioning.

Among older children, two examples illustrate different qualities of high sociometric standing. Luiz, 10 years old, expressed

Table 2
Reasons Given by Children for Their Choices of Workfriends and Playfriends

Category	Workfriends		Playfriends	
	Younger	Older	Younger	Older
1. General attributes (He is nice)	10	4	7	6
2. Specific attributes				
Actions (She plays soccer)	9	9	8	9
Competence (He does it well)	1	1	2	3
3. Relational				
Attributes (She is my friend)	7	3	5	4
Actions (He draws with me)	11	10	12	8
Psychological (She likes me)	1	0	3	0
4. Collaborative				
Attributes (We are tall)	3	0	2	1
Actions (We play ball together)	4	6	4	5
Psychological (We have the same problems)	2	0	0	0
5. Contingent or Complementary				
Actions (If I mess up, he waits for me)	5	2	1	3
Psychological (She lets me be what I want to be)	0	0	1	0

reasons for his own choices at a general and definitional level. "I like him a lot, he's in my table group," he explained of his work-friend choices. "I like to work with him." His playfriends, although explained at similar levels of complexity, are expressed in more specific and differentiated terms: "I like to play cheetah with him." "He's a very good soccer player." "Me and him have this play called 'Trick News.' We act it out." It is also notable that his contexts of play were diverse. In a related study of this same group of children (Cooper, Marquis, & Edward, in press), we observed high positive correlations between children's sociometric choices and teacher ratings of those same qualities in the children. One teacher stated that she gave the highest ratings to children who helped those beyond their circle of closest friends and mid-level ratings to those who helped within their friendship groups. In Luiz's case, we may see a child whose versatility across a wide range of play contexts brings him into contact with more children, who in turn regard him as their friend.

Finally, a slightly younger but frequently chosen member of the older class, Mary, illustrates the focus on contingent and psychological qualities reported in several accounts of children's friendship development (Asher & Gottman, 1981). In describing one friend, Mary said "We're together most of the time, so we can understand each other, more than I would understand anybody else." About another friend, Mary observed, "She knows a lot of things and she's easy to work with. She won't make fun of people when they're wrong."

There are several implications in our findings. First, children's friendships can be a significant context for both social and cognitive development. No major differences in workfriend and playfriend concepts were observed, probably because of the unusual extent of peer-assisted learning that was encouraged by the teachers. In traditional schools, where peer interaction in the classroom might be considered "cheating," children could have a less differentiated understanding of their friendships with others in academic areas. A related point is that researchers and teachers will benefit from seeing children's interactions and relationships in the larger context of the classroom group, the adults' rules of classroom life and from differentiating interaction, relational and group levels of children's functioning (Hinde, 1976).

Training programs that focus on teaching low-status children behaviors displayed by peers popular with the group may be less useful than focusing on the skills of friendship (Gottman, 1983). For any given child, having a close relationship with one or two friends may have more significance than being popular with the group but very close to no one. Finally, we see in this study that a child may gain in different ways from different environments.

Acknowledgments
This work was supported by a grant to the first author from the University Research Institute of the University of Texas at Austin. We would like to express our appreciation to the teachers, children, and families of the school where the study was conducted, to Sheila McFearon and Lynn Kane for their help in coding the interviews, and to Robert G. Cooper, for his many insightful contributions to this research.

References

Asher, S. R., and J. M. Gottman, eds. *The Development of Children's Friendships*. New York: Cambridge University Press, 1981.

Cooper, C. R.; S. Ayers-Lopez, and A. Marquis. "Children's Discourse During Peer Learning in Experimental and Naturalistic Situations." *Discourse Processes* 5 (1982): 177-91.

Cooper, C. R.; A. Marquis and S. Ayers-Lopez. "Peer Learning in the Classroom: Tracing Developmental Patterns and Consequences of Children's Spontaneous Interactions." In L. C. Wilkinson, ed., *Communicating in the Classroom*. New York: Academic Press, 1982.

Cooper, C. R.; A. Marquis and D. Edward. "Four Perspectives on Peer Learning Among Elementary School Children." In E. C. Mueller and C. R. Cooper, eds., *Process and Outcome in Peer Relations*. New York: Academic Press, 1983.

Gottman, J. M. "How Children Become Friends." *Monographs of the Society for Research in Child Development* 48 (1983): No. 201.

Halinan, M. T. "Recent Advances in Sociometry." In S. R. Asher and J. M. Gottman, eds., *The Development of Children's Friendships*. New York: Cambridge University Press, 1981.

Hartup, W. "The Peer System." In P. Mussen, Gen. Ed., *Carmichael's Handbook of Child Psychology*. Vol. 3. E. M. Hetherington, ed., *Social Development*. New York: Wiley, in press.

Hinde, R. A. "On Describing Relationships." *Journal of Child Psychology and Psychiatry* 17 (1976): 1-19.

Paris, S. G., and B. K. Lindauer. "The Development of Cognitive Skills During Childhood." In B. B. Wolman, ed., *Handbook of Developmental Psychology*. Englewood Cliffs, NJ: Prentice-Hall, 1982.

Rubin, K. H., and H. S. Ross. *Peer Relationships and Social Skills in Childhood*. New York: Springer-Verlag, 1982.

Selman, R. L. "The Child as Friendship Philosopher." In S. R. Asher and J. M. Gottman, eds., *The Development of Children's Friendships*. New York: Cambridge University Press, 1981.

Smollar, J., and J. Youniss. "Social Development Through Friendship." In K. H. Rubin and H. S. Ross, *Peer Relationships and Social Skills in Childhood*. New York: Springer-Verlag, 1982.

Youniss, J. *Parents and Peers in Social Development*. Chicago: University of Chicago Press, 1980.

Social and Environmental Barriers to Playfulness

Teresita E. Aguilar
Division of Recreation and Leisure Studies
North Texas State University, Denton

Young children are naturally playful, creative, expressive and imaginative, but as time goes on, much of this spontaneity becomes suppressed by our social system. We learn that behaviors will receive support from our significant others; we also recognize that being "different" is not necessarily rewarding. Does playfulness go away permanently, or is it possible to reinstate it?

THE MEANING OF PLAYFULNESS

Playfulness can be defined as the perception or attitude that allows an individual to behave spontaneously in an activity; it is having the ability to escape, pretend, imagine and make believe whatever one chooses. The beauty of being playful is that there is little concern for rules, boundaries, expectations or the consequences of behavior.

The most important element of playfulness is the perception of freedom, *freedom from* barriers (external influences) and *freedom for* expression (internal inclinations). Although related, these two factors should be viewed separately for a better understanding of freedom.

Playfulness, like freedom, does not occur continually. To be playful, a person must possess an attitude or perception of freedom to behave at times a little differently than usual. A state of freedom, however, is not sufficient for playfulness to exist. The behaviors exhibited as a result of freedom *need* to be unexpected or unusual in order to be playful. Otherwise, behavior becomes just another non-playful act—spontaneous as it may have been.

In a sense, the concept of playfulness is narrowed to "spontaneous and unusual or unexpected behaviors that occur when a person perceives freedom from barriers and freedom to express himself/herself." If these are the most critical factors, why then is the world not full of playful people? Such conditions are not too demanding. A look at several social factors related to playfulness may help to clarify its status.

SOCIAL FACTORS RELATED TO PLAYFULNESS

We need to consider some of the social elements[1] that shape and influence our daily lives (see Figure 1). These social elements should be viewed only as potential, influential factors. Essentially, the three areas of social elements include: significant others, community institutions and organizations and inventions and creations.

Significant Others

The influence of peers, friends, family, relatives and other significant people varies among individuals. It may vary according to a person's age. For example, the immediate family is much more influential to a child than to young adults. The teenager may be more influenced by peers than by relatives or other significant people. Certain adult roles may wield significant influence over others (i.e., leaders in a recreation setting may be more influential for the adolescent than his/her teachers at school). The recreation leader is often in a better position to establish rapport with the adolescent than is the teacher because of the favorable structure within the school setting.

How does one person or group influence another's playfulness? A person in a position of authority or leadership may be seen as a desirable model. If this person is playful, he/

---

[1]The "social elements" were selected on the basis of being adjustable in a relatively short period of time. Other social elements including religion, cultural myths, beliefs systems, etc., would require a much lengthier process to change.

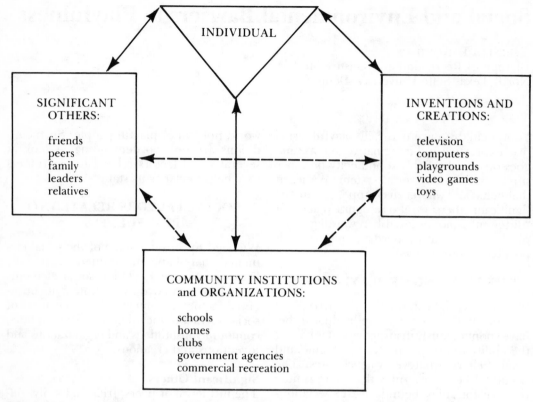

Figure 1. Basic social elements influencing an individual's potential for playfulness.

she would provide an example of playfulness for others to follow.

Significant others may also influence the idea of freedom, which is necessary for playfulness. This may happen when the classroom teacher invites students to be creative. The teacher, in this situation, is implying that the students are free to express themselves. Thus, freedom is enhanced by significant others. Community institutions and organizations also influence the playfulness of individuals.

Institutions and Organizations
The influence that institutions and organizations may have on playfulness varies according to significance to the individual. The list of institutions and organizations (see Figure 1) is a suggestion of possible structures relating to an individual's playfulness. For example, schools are community institutions with a tremendous impact on the existence of the nature of playfulness. Sometimes, in

schools when administrators and teachers must strive rigorously to maintain continuous control over the students, much of the freedom needed for the young to be playful, creative and expressive may be lost within a rigid system.

Commercial recreation establishments in a community also influence an individual's playfulness. Amusement parks are commercial markets for fun, escaping and playfulness. Although commerical, such establishments provide a safe, non-threatening environment for playfulness.

Within most sizable communities there are other institutions and organizations to provide facilities, services, programs and special events that can influence the degree of playfulness an individual may feel free to exhibit. Certainly, some communities are more supportive of playfulness than others. Certain colleges have reputations for being "party schools." Las Vegas is known as the city that never sleeps and where a wealth of "playing" is ever present. Thus, we can view the multitude of institutions and organizations in any selected community and determine to some degree whether or not playfulness is existent, supported or negated.

Inventions and Creations
Material products developed for the amusement or entertainment of society also affect the playfulness of individuals. Although computers were not developed specifically for this purpose, they are being marketed increasingly on the basis of their amusement value. Video game centers and home videos are having a phenomenal impact on both children and adults today. Toy manufacturers, aggressive marketers of myriads of playthings, have had a substantial impact on American society. Handmade, simple toys are rare. Mass-produced toys influence the degree of playfulness or imagination a child may exhibit. They are produced and marketed mostly for pleasure and entertainment.

The more successful inventions and creations in relationship to playfulness are (and will continue to be) those that allow manipulation, challenge and variety for the participant.

Another example of a creation that originated as a source of amusement and diversion was the playground. Until recently, however, most playgrounds failed to provide opportunities for manipulation and challenge for the user. Thus, these creations were not conducive to playfulness in its truest form.

EXAMPLES OF PLAYFULNESS

Mental Playfulness
Mental playfulness, often exemplified in the form of creativity, usually occurs when ideas and possibilities are being generated without the fear or inhibition of being right or wrong. Thus, freedom sets the stage. In addition, the second element of the unexpected or unusual is also a necessary condition for mental playfulness. Imagine an "idea generator" pumping around possible solutions to problems. These ideas are being tossed around like the 75 numbers in a bingo game.

No one really knows which number may come up. The number selected is unexpected even to the bingo caller, just as the ideas of the playful person are often unexpected even to that person.

Common sources of stimulation for mental playfulness are puzzles: crossword or jigsaw puzzles, riddles and other manipulative ojects. Some young persons shun such challenges, but the more playful person may dive headfirst into the challenge of solving a problem or a mystery.

Humor and Comedy
Most of us enjoy a person with a sense of humor. A playful person laughs easily and is often able to make others laugh, sometimes with the amusing facility to play with words or think of unusual ways to combine them. The essence of humor and comedy is having the freedom to do or say the unusual or unexpected.

Humorous cartoons and comic strips are examples of playfulness, where the basis of humor is often in caricature of people and absurd or exaggerated stories and situations.

BARRIERS TO PLAYFULNESS

Social Barriers
Social control is a barrier to playfulness, wherein the manner of control may be through rules, regulations, norms and expectations. We are expected to play during recess at school; we are expected to be proper at banquets. Social control is subtly exerted through advertisements by way of the media. We are subject to propaganda in education and other areas of everyday life. Both the subtle and non-subtle types serve as tools of social control. The bottom line of social control is that many behaviors and ways of thinking among the individual members of the group-at-large are regulated.

A second social barrier could be labeled social approval, an extension of social control. With social approval, individuals are seeking additional support of significant others. This becomes a barrier to playfulness when approval is sought by behaving only as expected. An example of this would be a person in a military system. The way to advance quickly is to do as expected and a little bit more. With an attitude of "I'll do anything for you," it is highly unlikely that playfulness could exist as part of that person's lifestyle. After all, it is the playful person who feels that even if he/she does something differently, life will go on.

Thus, the existence of rules, regulations and similar social constraints may be a barrier to playfulness. In addition, the intensive, exaggerated drive for social approval may be another crucial barrier.

Environmental Barriers

The environmental barriers in this study include physical and/or visible limitations as well as noise factors. The environment, *per se*, is all-inclusive with space, facilities and equipment as important components. One aspect of environmental barriers is the multitude of boundaries that exist in play situations. For example, in tennis there are lines for singles and doubles. In competitive tennis, if the ball lands anywhere outside the lines, it is called "out." The point ends there. Some players in a less competitive situation enjoy simply returning the ball in the general vicinity. Perhaps a new, more playful activity could occur on a tennis court. In fact, there is a more social version of tennis called "triples." In triples, there are three persons per team, where emphasis on competition is minimized. It seems that the inventors of triples were building on the playful possibilities.

Another environmental barrier is stabilized playground equipment which remains static and cannot be manipulated by the user. Traditional playground equipment such as slides, swings and exercise bars do little to stimulate the imagination.

A high noise level can also affect playfulness, for the atmosphere or mood of an environment can be established by the type or volume of sound.

CREATING A PLAYFUL ATMOSPHERE

If being playful means that free expression, creativity and imagination are released, then perhaps we should indeed want to provide favorable opportunities for enhanced play.

Society could benefit from the satisfying rewards of playfulness. How, then, do we go about creating a more playful atmosphere? The following list contains recommendations to consider:

○ increase the sense of freedom
○ provide an outlet for self-expression
○ encourage people to "play with" ideas rather than to "work for" solutions
○ allow for manipulation; use "people-powered" devices
○ provide risk/challenge in varying degress
○ encourage problem-solving activities
○ incorporate the arts (music, dance, drama)
○ be flexible
○ minimize or eliminate negative consequences for playful behaviors
○ allow for escapism, fantasy and imagination
○ encourage and demonstrate good humor
○ allow for experimentation/exploration

These are only a few possibilities for enhancing playfulness. An awareness of the benefits of playfulness is the initial step. It is also important to recognize the essence of playfulness, the social factors which are most influential to playfulness and the barriers which have been established by society. Finally, playfulness should be viewed as a positive characteristic or individual resource. It no longer needs to be viewed as a negative, antisocial or non-productive characteristic.

Suggested Reading

Csikszentmihalyi, Mihaly, *Beyond Boredom and Anxiety: The Experience of Play in Work and Games.* San Francisco: Jossey-Bass, 1975

Ellis, Michael J. *Why People Play.* Englewood Cliffs, NJ: Prentice-Hall, 1973.

Guilford, J.P. *Intelligence, Creativity and Their Implications.* San Diego: Knapp, 1968.

Huizinga, Johan. *Homo Ludens: A Study of the Play-Element in Culture.* London: Routledge and Kegan Paul, 1949.

Lancy, David F., and B. Allan Tindall, eds., *The Study of Play, Problems and Prospects.* West Point, NY: Leisure Press, 1977.

Levy, Joseph. *Play Behavior.* New York: Wiley, 1978.

Lieberman, J. Nina. *Playfulness: Its Relationship to Imagination and Creativity.* New York: Academic Press, 1977.

Millar, Susanna. *The Psychology of Play.* Baltimore, MD: Penguin Books, 1968.

Rubin, Kenneth H., ed. "Children's Play." *New Directions for Child Development.* San Francisco: Jossey-Bass, 1980.

Sutton-Smith, Brian, ed. *Play and Learning.* New York: Gardner Press, 1979.

Torrance, E. Paul. *Creativity.* Sioux Falls, SD: Adapt Press, 1969.

Westland, Cor, and Jane Knight. *Playing, Living, Learning: A Worldwide Perspective on Children's Opportunities To Play.* State College, PA: Venture Publishing, 1982.

PART III: HOW CHILDREN USE PLAYGROUNDS

Introduction

Before the decade of the seventies little research was conducted on how children use outdoor play environments. However, during the past ten to twelve years an ever-increasing number of investigators have directed their attention to this timely subject.

In a study by Sheila D. Campbell and Joe L. Frost, two classes of grade two children were observed for ten weeks during free play on two playgrounds, one a traditional playground with a narrow range of fixed conventional commercial equipment, the other a creative playground with an extensive variety of commercial, hand-made and movable equipment. Each child was observed for a ten-second sequence and scored on adaptations of the Piaget-Smilansky cognitive and Parten social play categories. Analysis of variance procedures carried out for each of the social and cognitive categories of play showed that *cooperative* play was the most common type of social play occupying approximately half the play time on both playgrounds, a finding consistent with play theory in respect to the age of subjects in this study. There was a significant main effect for type of playground on all other play categories. The creative playground tended to produce a wider range of play behaviors and more even scores in all categories. Significant interactions suggest the importance of sex and group as factors interacting with space and equipment.

Utilizing the same children and play environments as in the above study, Joe L. Frost and Sheila D. Campbell compared the play equipment choices of 45 second-grade children on conventional and creative playgrounds. Differences in play equipment choices are discussed. Findings indicated that children prefer action-oriented equipment over static equipment and multiple function, complex equipment over single function or limited function equipment.

In a third study conducted at the same private school, Joe L. Frost and Eric Strickland compared the play equipment choices of 138 kindergarten, first- and second-grade children in three different play environments: "unit," linked or obstacle course and creative. The creative environment attracted 63 percent of all play followed by unit environment (23 percent) and linked (13 percent). Extensive comparisons of equipment are made and implications and recommendations are drawn for equipment designers and consumers.

Contemporary play environment researchers are increasingly recommending that play environments be designed to accommodate the various play forms of children. Heather Naylor hypothesized that if such a design principle were valid, children's use of play equipment would reflect how well these items embodied such a principle. Using time sampling and tracking observations, Naylor collected data on user characteristics, play activities and equipment use at three traditional playgrounds. No clear relationship was found between amount of use and a measure of diversity of physical play. Instead, a preference order for type of physical play was established: sliding > swinging > climbing. Higher use was also associated with opportunities for social play (as well as physical) and with high novelty value. Significant differences in choice of equipment were shown by children in different age groups. Safety problems arising from children's seeking new and diverse activities were discussed.

Continuing this sequence of play equipment studies in a study by Lawrence D. Bruya, five-year-old children were assessed for the amount of time spent on and off play structures arranged in a contemporary unified or linked structure format and a traditional separated structure format. In the traditional format time spent on structures increased with age. In the contemporary format, time spent on the structures increased with age and was greater than that spent on the traditional structures. Bruya discusses findings related to peer physical contact, contact with teachers and motor patterns.

The volume of studies involving preschool and school-age children on outdoor play environments is quite large compared to a decade ago. Studies of outdoor play environments for infants, however, is only beginning to attract the attention of researchers. Connie Steele and Marjorie Nauman investigated the responses of infants under three years of age to selected outdoor equipment. Two forms of four types of equipment—sand area, slides, cubes, neutral play items—were specially designed for contrast analysis. Infants were assessed for mobility and cognitive ability for comparison purposes. No significant differences in equipment choices were noted as a function of motor ability. While playing "alone," the older group and more cognitively able children played significantly more often with the small (versus large) sandbox, the closed (versus open) cube and the horizontal (versus vertical) neutral items (cardboard logs).

In yet another study of very young children, Suzanne Winter developed an instrument for classifying toddler play, which she used in a study of outdoor play of toddlers. The results of the study indicated that the instrument provided a highly reliable method of collecting information about toddler's play. The data collected in the study revealed that the majority of the social and cognitive play behaviors of the toddlers was concentrated in the less advanced categories of the instrument. However, the toddlers were capable of some involvement in even the most complex categories. The toddlers did indicate equipment preferences associated with the gender of the child.

Michael J. Bell and Pauline Walker took the roles of participants-observers in their observational study of outdoor play interaction patterns of preschool (age 3–5) children. Their analysis of field notes and audiotape transcriptions produced a number of conclusions including: patterns and general rules were firmly entrenched in the subjects' play; developmental patterns were obvious in the formation of play groups; older children are capable of identifying the play goals of others, evaluate them with respect to personal interests and consolidate the two into a mutually satisfying play situation; the older children were able to form play groups, divided by sex; in each play group there were leaders and supporting players; there were sex differences in the group play patterns; play groups controlled an area of play space as well as play objects on the playground; control was primarily through verbal interaction and physical use of the environment; open areas were subject to territorial behavior.

Michael Henniger adds a new perspective to this section of the volume by contrasting preschool children's play behaviors in an indoor versus an outdoor environment. Twenty-eight nursery school children were each observed 20 times indoors and 20 times outdoors over a six-week period. The behaviors of the children were coded, using Smilansky's cognitive play categories and modifications of Parten's social play schemes. The data were analyzed for the total group of children, and by age and sex, to assess the differences in indoor versus outdoor play for each play category. The results indicated that the indoor environment stimulated significantly more constructive play for all groups except the girls, more dramatic play for the younger children and girls and more solitary play for the younger children. The outdoor environment encouraged more functional play for all groups and more parallel play for all groups except the older children.

For years professionals have speculated about the relative merits of free play and directed physical education activities for children. Gwen Dean investigated the differences in motor behaviors exhibited by kindergarten children on a playground during free play compared with the motor behaviors of these same children during physical education classes. She found that children engaged in significantly more "engagement" behaviors, motor behaviors and locomotor behaviors in free play. In physical education classes children engaged in more "not-engaged" behaviors, non-locomotor behaviors, manipulative behaviors and cognitive behaviors. These findings should lead to further explorations of long-held assumptions about the relative merits of free play and directed activity.

In the final selection in Part III Jacqueline Myers investigated the relationships between teacher perceptions of children's play choices and the children's perceived and actual play choices of playground equipment. The correlations between girls' and boys' perceived preferences and observed choices were evident with teachers' perceptions of children's play choices clearly related to the children's perceived choices but not to their actual, observed play choices.

Collectively, these studies provide a great deal of useful information for the design and use of children's play environments, and they raise new questions for future research.

The Effects of Playground Type on the Cognitive and Social Play Behaviors of Grade Two Children

SHEILA D. CAMPBELL
Department of Education
University of Alberta, Edmonton, Canada

and

JOE L. FROST
Department of Curriculum and Instruction
The University of Texas at Austin

Although the school playground is a largely neglected aspect of educational research, it is an aspect of the total school environment that may play a significant role in the behaviors and outcomes experienced by the child. In studies with preschool children, physical setting or the space and materials available has been found to have a significant effect on play behaviors of children both indoors and out (Clark, Wyon and Richards, 1969; Johnson, 1935; Prescott, Jones and Kritchevsky, 1972; Rubin, 1977; and Scholz and Ellis, 1975). Effects include changes in interaction levels, play complexity and child interest and involvement.

The importance of the level of interaction and complexity of play to cognitive development has been postulated by several theorists (Piaget, 1966; Sutton-Smith, 1971; Vygotsky, 1966). Several studies have demonstrated a relationship between play scores and performance on cognitive tasks. (Rubin and Maioni, 1975), skills of divergent thinking (Li, 1978; Lieberman, 1965) and associative fluency (Dansky and Silverman, 1975). These findings suggest that the relationship between the variations in physical environment and the quality of resulting play are of significant importance to educators and schools.

Other factors found to have a significant impact on play include age or stage of development, sex and group. Increasing amounts of interaction have been noted with increase in age by Iwanaga (1973), Parten (1932), Rubin (1977), and Rubin, Watson and Jambor (1978). However, Barnes (1971) reported contradictory findings that appear to be possibly related to group makeup and management. Differences across groups on play categories or similar types of behavior categories have been reported in the literature (Berk, 1973; Reichenberg-Hackett, 1962). Much of the difference appears to be an outcome of teacher management practices.

Differences in the play of boys and girls have been noted in several studies, although the findings are confusing and sometimes contradictory. Higher levels of social play in preschool girls than same-age boys were reported by Iwanaga (1973) and Smilansky (1968). Seagoe (1970; 1971a; 1971b) in studies of older children (5–11 years) reported the opposite, but noted culture and schooling effects. Other studies have found interactions between sex and other factors such as location outdoors or indoors (Harper and Sanders, 1975) and type of play materials (Busse, Ree and Gutride, 1970). Preschool girls have been reported to exhibit more play at higher cognitive levels than male peers (Moore, Evertson and Brophy, 1974; Rubin, Maioni and Hornung, 1976; Smilansky, 1968).

The study reported here was conducted to examine the effect of two contrasting playgrounds on the play behaviors of grade

81

two children controlling for factors of stage, sex and group.

METHOD

The two playgrounds used in the study were on opposite sides of a private elementary school. The traditional playground provided conventional commercial playground equipment: seesaws, a merry-go-round, swings, a slide and trapeze bars set in a row parallel to the school building with seesaws and bars at various levels at a distance on another side of a vast grass and dirt playground area, which included a backstop for baseball. The creative playground was a smaller but still extensive square area enclosed by a wire fence. The terrain was flat, mostly grassed, with a riding path, sand below the climbing structures and large shade trees along one side. There were three types of commercial climbers, a slide with a large enclosed platform, two separate tire swings on swivels, a movable seesaw, a boat, a platform structure with high sides and windows, and a quantity of large planks, crates and reels for constructing. A variety of riding, dramatic play and game equipment was stored in a corner shack to which children had access during play.

The subjects included all the children in the two grade two classes of the school. Group (class) 2A had 21 children (9m, 12f) with a mean age of 86.75 months (S.D. 4.09; range 80–95 months), and a Group (class) 2B had 24 children (14m, 10f) with a mean age of 86.72 months (S.D. 3.99; range 81–94 months). Overall there were 23 males (51 percent) and 22 females (49 percent) with a mean age of 7 years, 3 months. Both classes were taught by certified teachers, of similar age, using self-contained classrooms. Almost all the children in the school were of urban, middle-class, white background and were in their second year at the school.

The children were all tested shortly after the beginning of school in early September using tests for conservation of substance (Piaget, 1964) and number (Piaget, 1966). There were 8 male and 12 female preconservers (44 percent) and 15 male and 10 female conservers (56 percent).

Data Collection and Analysis

The coding form used for data collection was developed by the authors utilizing the Parten (1932) social categories and the Smilansky (1968) adaptation of Piaget's (1962) cognitive categories. Each child was observed twice during a free play period one day per week on each playground for a total of ten weeks. Children's names were arranged in random order, and observers began with a different child each time. Each observer was equipped with a portable tape recorder and an ear plug that emitted a beep every ten seconds. The observer located the child, watched for ten seconds and then scored for both a social and a cognitive category of play and play equipment used. The latter information is not reported here. Where more than one category of play occurred simultaneously, e.g., functional and dramatic, the theoretically higher order was coded. Coders were trained before data collection to an agreement level of 76 percent for the social categories and 94 percent for the cognitive categories. Agreement was checked by simultaneous coding on six occasions during the data collection. The percentage of agreement based on 517 codings was 74 percent for social and 88.2 percent for cognitive categories. Because no systematic trends occurred due to weather or time, these variables were not included in the analysis.

The percentage of occurrence of each social and cognitive play category was calculated from the frequency data for each child to compensate for absences during observation periods. Because there were too few occurrences in individual categories of nonplay, these were collapsed to form a single category, *not play*. Approximately 2 percent of the data was obtained for each child on each playground. (Range 1.6 percent to 2.3 percent; only 2 children less than 1.9 percent.) Using the percentage scores, a series of 4 way ANOVA's [playground (2) × sex (2) × stage (2) × group (2)] with one factor (playground) repeated was carried out for each of the social and cognitive categories of play and the non-play category. To avoid the inconvenience of unequal cell size, a set of scores was randomly selected to equal the smallest cell blocked on the factors sex, cognitive stage and group. The means for the percentage of occurrence of cognitive play categories are presented in Table 1 and for social play categories in Table 2. A summary of the significant effects for the ANOVAs is presented in Table 3, which also shows the grand means for the ANOVA subjects and the total sample.

RESULTS

Cognitive Categories

There were highly significant differences in the frequency of cognitive categories scored on the two playgrounds. Scores for the cognitive categories are presented in Table 1. Functional play was the most common type on both playgrounds but it was significantly higher (p < .001) on the traditional playground, amounting to over three-fourths (77.9 percent) of the play versus less than half (43.7 percent) for the creative playground. The differences in dramatic play were even more pronounced. There was significantly more (p < .001) dramatic play observed on the creative (37 percent) than on the traditional (2 percent) playground. There was a significant difference between playgrounds (p < .005) for constructive play which occurred infrequently on either playground, 3.9 percent on the creative and 0.2 percent on the traditional. Games-with-rules play was also low-scoring, but occurred significantly more often (p < .005) on the tra-

ditional (6.9 percent) than the creative (2 percent).

The only significant effect for constructive play was the main effect (p < .005) for playground. There was a significant (p < .05) main effect for group in the functional play category where group 2A exhibited higher scores on both playgrounds.

There was a significant two-way interaction (p < .05) for playground by sex for functional play. Boys (74.7 percent) and girls (81.1 percent) showed about the same amount of functional play on the traditional playground but boys (34.1 percent) decreased more than girls (53.4 percent) on the creative playground. There were no other interactions in this category. For dramatic play there was a significant interaction affect (p < .01) for playground × sex. Both boys (1.7 percent) and girls (2.2 percent) scored about the same low levels of dramatic play on the traditional playground. Girls increased to about half (28.9 percent) the level of boys (45.2 percent) for dramatic play on the creative playground. There were no other interactions in this category.

There was a significant (p < .001) three-way interaction effect for playground × sex × group for games-with-rules play, but scores in this category were very low. Girls and boys in both Groups 2A and 2B showed similar low games-with-rules play on the creative playground (range = 1.0 to 2.7 percent). Girls of both groups scored slightly higher with scores of 4.2 percent for each group on

Table 1
Cognitive Categories of Play
Means for Percentage of Occurrence

Variable	Sex				Stage				Group				Overall Average	
Playground	Traditional		Creative		Traditional		Creative		Traditional		Creative		Traditional	Creative
					Precon-server	Con-server	Precon-server	Con-server						
Play Category	Female	Male	Female	Male					2A	2B	2A	2B		
Functional	81.1	74.7	53.4	34.1	78.6	77.4	45.9	43.8	84.9	71.0	47.2	40.4	77.9	43.7
Constructive	0.0	0.5	3.4	4.4	0.0	0.5	2.6	3.9	0.0	0.5	3.4	4.4	0.2	3.9
Dramatic	2.2	1.7	28.9	45.2	2.6	1.3	39.1	37.1	1.2	2.7	31.5	42.6	2.0	37.0
Games With Rules	4.2	9.7	1.8	2.2	5.8	8.0	1.3	2.0	2.1	11.8	2.7	1.3	6.9	2.0
Not Play	12.5	13.4	12.5	14.1	13.0	12.9	11.1	13.3	11.8	14.1	15.4	11.3	13.0	13.3
TOTAL	100.0	100.0	100.0	100.0	100.0	100.1*	100.0	100.1*	100.0	100.1*	100.2*	100.0	100.0	99.9*

*Rounding Error

the traditional playground, but the large increase shown (Table 1) for Group 2B and for boys on the traditional playground is due almost entirely to the score of 19.4 percent for games-with-rules play for Group 2B boys.

There were no main or interaction effects for cognitive stage, and scores for these categories were very close. There were no four-way interaction effects.

Social Categories

Cooperative play was the most frequently occurring category of social play on both playgrounds, 45.6 percent on the traditional and 50.2 percent on the creative. Scores for the social categories are presented in Table 2.

Significantly more ($p < .001$) solitary play occurred on the creative playground (11 percent) than on the traditional playground (3.4 percent) and significantly more ($p < .05$) associative play on the creative playground (12.8 percent) than on the traditional (8.5 percent). There was significantly more ($p < .001$) parallel play on the traditional playground (29.5 percent) than on the creative (12.6 percent).

The only significant effect for solitary play was the main effect for playground ($p < .001$). All other categories of social play exhibited interaction effects. A significant ($p < .05$) two-way interaction occurred for playground × group for associative play. The two groups had almost the same amount of associative play (8.8 percent and 8.1 percent)

on the traditional playground. Group 2A remained the same (8.8 percent) on the creative playground, whereas Group 2B doubled (16.8 percent) the associative play.

There was a significant two-way effect ($p < .05$) for sex by stage in associative play, although there were no main effects for either sex or stage. Boy preconservers scored higher (12.4 percent) than boy conservers (10.0 percent) on associative play, but the change was in the opposite direction for girls where preconservers were lower (6.9 percent) than conservers (13.3 percent). There were no other interaction effects for associative play.

There was a significant ($p < .005$) three-way playground × stage × group interaction for parallel and cooperative play. Both conservers and preconservers in Group 2B and the conservers in Group 2A showed a decrease in the amount of parallel play from the traditional to the creative playground, whereas Group 2A preconservers showed a slight increase. All four groups had scores within a range of 8.7 percent to 14.5 percent on the creative playground, but scores on the traditional ranged from 3.1 percent for 2A preconservers to 45.1 percent for conservers in group 2B. Added to this was a significant ($p < .05$) interaction effect for sex × group. Girls in Group 2B exhibited a higher incidence (30.3 percent) of parallel play than all the other groups (2B boys—18.6 percent, 2A boys—18.1 percent, 2A girls—18 percent) across both playgrounds.

For cooperative play, 2A preconservers (46.7 percent to 62.9 percent) and 2B con-

Table 2
Social Categories of Play
Means for Percentage of Occurrence

Variable	Sex				Stage				Group				Overall Average	
Playground	Traditional		Creative		Traditional		Creative		Traditional		Creative		Traditional	Creative
					Precon-server	Con-server	Precon-server	Con-server						
Play Category	Female	Male	Female	Male					2A	2B	2A	2B		
Solitary	2.6	4.2	8.3	13.8	4.3	2.6	11.2	10.9	4.2	2.6	12.8	9.2	3.4	11.0
Parallel	33.5	25.6	14.9	10.4	27.4	31.8	11.3	14.0	24.6	34.5	11.1	14.2	29.5	12.6
Associative	6.8	10.2	13.4	12.2	7.7	9.2	11.5	14.1	8.8	8.1	8.8	16.8	8.5	12.8
Cooperative	44.7	46.6	50.8	49.6	47.6	43.7	54.9	45.5	50.6	40.7	51.9	48.5	45.6	50.2
Not Play	12.5	13.4	12.5	14.1	13.0	12.9	11.1	15.6	11.8	14.1	15.4	11.3	13.0	13.3
TOTAL	100.1*	100.0	99.9*	100.1*	99.9*	100.2*	100.0	100.1*	100.0	100.0	100.0	100.0	100.0	99.9*

*Rounding Error

84

servers (32.8 percent to 50.1 percent) both increased the level of cooperative play on the creative playground. The preconservers in 2B remained about the same (48.6 percent and 47.0 percent) but the 2A conservers decreased from 54.5 percent for cooperative play on the traditional to 40.9 percent on the creative. In addition there was a significant two-way interaction effect (p < .005) for sex × stage, the result of a difference in the direction of change for boys and girls between preconservers and conservers. Girl preconservers (55.6 percent) scored higher than girl conservers (39.9 percent), whereas boy preconservers (47.0 percent) scored slightly lower than boy conservers (49.2 percent).

There were no other interaction effects for the social play categories. A summary of the significant effects for the ANOVA is presented in Table 3.

There was no significant difference in the non-play category which occurred about the same (13.3 percent, 13 percent) on both playgrounds.

DISCUSSION

Despite some variations due to other factors, the results of this study support the contention by ecological psychologists that environment has a significant effect on behavior (Gump, 1975). The presence of different equipment and materials on the creative playground had a marked effect across all play categories. Constructive and solitary play appear to be most affected by type of playground alone and less subject to the effect of other factors such as group and sex. Although constructive play occurred infrequently, it appeared to the coders that this was one category where boys and girls interacted cooperatively in common activity. Otherwise boys tended to play with boys and girls with girls.

Solitary play increased markedly on the creative playground. This is attributed to the wider range of equipment permitting children to play apart from others on or with separate pieces of equipment. Though solitary, the children exhibited a range of cognitive activity, similar to the findings of Moore, Evertson and Brophy (1974), who take issue with the categorization of this play as lower in a hierarchical order.

Functional play predominated in the cognitive categories, a finding which might be expected for playground activity; however, the presence of construction and dramatic play materials clearly stimulated the occurrence of these types of play on the creative playground, whereas the absence of these materials on the traditional playground resulted in more functional and parallel play, where children played side by side on pieces

Table 3
Summary of Significant Effects for ANOVA
Category of Play

	Solitary	Parallel	Associative	Cooperative	Not Play	Functional	Constructive	Dramatic	Games-with-rules
Grand Mean (ANOVA)	7.2	21.1	10.6	47.9	13.1	60.8	2.1	19.5	4.4
Mean (All Subjects)	(7.4)	(21.5)	(10.4)	(49.3)	(11.4)	(60.1)	(2.5)	(21.3)	(4.6)
Playground	[1]F=21.81****	F=35.83****	F=5.38*			F=45.44****	F=14.57***	F=150.06****	F=13.93***
Sex		F=6.60*				F=12.11**		F=5.51*	
Cognitive Stage				F=8.97**					
Group		F=7.11*	F=3.51[2]	F=8.67**		F=7.79*		F=3.51[2]	F=6.11*
Playg × Sex						F=5.18*			F=3.67[2]
Playg × Stage									
Playg × Group			F=5.55**						F=17.32****
Sex × Stage			F=5.26*		F=15.48***				
Sex × Group		F=5.65*			F=4.37[2]				F=8.81**
Stage × Group		F=9.38**							
Playg × Sex × Stage									
Playg × Sex × Group									F=12.47****
Playg × Stage × Group		F=11.14***			F=11.45***				
Sex × Stage × Group								F=3.06[2]	
Playg × Sex × Stage × Group									

[1]df in all cases = 1,16 [2]p < .10 *p < .05 **p < .01 ***p < .005 ****p < .001

of equipment and in more games-with-rules play.

Recent theory suggests that cultural and schooling influences create differences in the behavior of boys and girls (Lee and Voivodas, 1977). These appear to have been operating here to create sex differences in play, which interacted in turn with playground variation and group differences. Boys tended to monopolize the boat and play house climbing structure on the creative playground for their imaginative activities, which involved a good deal of highly active, rough and tumble activity that seemed to intimidate the girls. At any rate, the latter tended to retreat to the climbing structures where they engaged in appropriate climbing activities, which would be coded functional play. Unfortunately, some play was inappropriately coded when occasionally a girl was involved in dramatic activity with the boys but was using the climbers as a place of safety from capture. The coder would be unaware or uncertain of this. This undoubtedly led to the sex difference for functional play on the creative playground.

Although the two types of playgrounds exhibit similar effects on both groups for most categories, there are two significant playground × group interactions that appear to relate to differences in teacher management activities. In the functional category, the difference was the result of higher levels of imaginative activity accompanying active play on either playground by both boys and girls in group 2B. This difference appeared to be attributable in part to variations among the teachers in encouragement, participation in and acceptance of this play type as well as to the presence of one boy in Group 2B, whose play was almost totally imaginative and who provided leadership and stimulation to others.

The significant three-way interaction for games-with-rules play occurred mainly because of differences in teacher behavior. It appeared that teachers deliberately stimulated this type of play on the traditional playground by providing games equipment in order to relieve pressure on the limited equipment and provide something for children to do. Seagoe (1971a) has suggested

that there is school/teacher influence on co-operative-competitive play occurrence. Teachers did not attempt to stimulate this type of play on the creative playground, possibly because they felt there were sufficient other opportunities. One teacher was more active in stimulating this type of play than the other which, coupled with the almost exclusive participation in this type of play by boys, led to the interaction effect for playground × sex × group.

Although games-with-rules play scores are low, it is worth noting that the dearth of this type of play did not result in a lack of cooperative experiences. Associative and cooperative play increased on the creative playground despite a decrease in games-with-rules. It appeared that these children utilized any type of material or equipment as a basis for cooperative activity. Much of the functional play was of a cooperative nature, swinging torsos simultaneously to move a tire swing or merry-go-round, or one child pushing another on a swing. The reduction in the amount of games-with-rules play, where there are other opportunities and less support for games by teachers, may reflect the possibility that children of this age prefer cooperative, non-competitive activities. This study discounts the frequent tendency to assume games-with-rules play is important in fostering cooperative behavior. Games-with-rules foster cooperation in the sense of agreement to conform; other types of activities are equally successful in creating cooperative behavior and appear to be more appealing to children. Follow-up studies of this implication are important to our understanding of child development and program planning.

The predominance of cooperative play despite the variation in playground is an important finding of this study. Cooperative play represented approximately half the play on both playgrounds, a finding that lends support to play theory, which predicts an increase with age for this higher level of interaction. The levels of cooperative play found here for 7-year-olds are substantially higher than those reported for 5-year-olds by other researchers (Barnes, 1971; Parten, 1932; Rubin, Maioni and Hornung, 1976; Rubin,

Watson and Jambor, 1978). Furthermore, the coders sometimes found it difficult to distinguish between associative and cooperative play, a difficulty reported also by Rubin (1977), who proposed combining these two categories to form a single category of Group play, a procedure that would yield a score of almost two-thirds (63 percent) for interactive social activity. It appears that children of this age prefer to interact cooperatively without regard to playground characteristics. Cooperative interaction also occurred without regard to cognitive play type. Children cooperated in making a swing spin for functional play, in using the construction materials to build, in dramatic activities and games-with-rules. This nesting of cognitive and social categories has been discussed by Rubin (1977a) and appears to be an important consideration in carrying out play research.

No explanation can be offered for the stage effects noted that produce inconsistent effects interacting with playground, group and sex. The failure of this study to obtain significant and consistent effects for cognitive stage may have resulted from several factors: the narrow chronological age span (fifteen months) of the subjects; a faulty assumption that the narrow range of tests accurately measured conservation level; an incorrect assumption that there is a relationship between conservation, as measured by tests, and play behaviors; or the existence of complex, not understood, relationships between stage behaviors and sex or activity.

Not play also remained constant across playgrounds at approximately 13 percent suggesting that, given the choice, children of this age tend to engage in play activity unaffected by environmental characteristics. The not play scores were mainly a result of teachers' using enforced passivity and isolation at the side of the playground as a disciplinary measure for classroom misdemeanors. Failing to anticipate this possibility, we had asked teachers to carry on as usual. Otherwise, children were allowed a free choice of activities, and there was an extremely low incidence of non-participatory behavior.

Overall, the findings of this study suggest

the need for thoughtful design and the introduction of a variety of equipment, materials and space to create playground environments providing balanced opportunities for play as the creative playground was able to do. Play theory suggests that some types of play behaviors are more desirable than others for their contribution to socialization and cognitive development. If this premise is accepted, then the creative playground scoring higher for associative, cooperative, constructive and dramatic play would appear to provide more opportunity for development. The apparent interrelationships among factors of sex, the constitution of the group and teacher effect suggest an additional need for awareness and consideration of these factors in playground supervision and management.

Finally, the effects of playground, sex and group found in this study suggest that some of the differences within and between studies reported by other researchers (Barnes, 1971; Rubin, Maioni and Hornung, 1976) may have been due to differences in the physical and social characteristics of the environments. Researchers need to provide complete descriptions of these characteristics to enable meaningful comparisons between studies.

References

Almy, M.; with E. Chittenden and P. Miller. *Young Children's Thinking*. New York: Teachers College Press, 1966.
Barnes, K. E. "Preschool Play Norms: A Replication." *Developmental Psychology* 5 (1971): 99–103.
Berk, L. E. *An Analysis of Activities in Preschool Settings* (Final report). Washington, DC: National Center for Educational Research and Development, November 1973. (ERIC Document Reproduction Service No. ED 099 131)
Busse, T. V.; M. Ree and M. Gutride. "Environmentally Enriched Classrooms and the Play Behavior of Negro Preschool Children." *Urban Education* 5 (1970): 128–40.
Clark, A. H.; S. M. Wyon and M. P. Richards."Free Play in Nursery School Children." *Journal of Child Psychology and Psychiatry* 10 (1969): 205–16.
Dansky, J. L., and I. W. Silverman. "Effects of Play on Associative Fluency in Preschool-aged Children." *Developmental Psychology* 9, 1 (1973): 38–43.
Goldschmid, M. L., and P.M. Bentler. *Concept Assessment Kit Conservation Manual*. San Diego, CA: Educational and Industrial Testing Service, 1968.
Gump, P. V. "Ecological Psychology and Children." In E. M. Hetherington, ed., *Review of Child Development Research* vol. 5. Chicago: University of Chicago Press, 1975.

Harper, L. V., and K. M. Sanders. "Preschool Children's Use of Space: Sex Differences in Outdoor Play." In R. C. Smart and M. S. Smart, eds., *Readings in Child Development and Relationships*. New York: Macmillan, 1977.

Iwanaga, M. "Development of Interpersonal Play Structures in Three-, Four- and Five-year-old Children." *Journal of Research and Development in Education* 6 (1973): 71–82.

Johnson, M. W. "The Effect on Behavior of Variation in the Amount of Play Equipment." *Child Development* 6 (1935): 56–58.

Lee, P. C., and G. K. Voivodas. "Sex Role and Pupil Role in Early Childhood Education." In L. G. Katz, ed., *Current Topics in Early Childhood Education*. Norwood, NJ: Ablex, 1977.

Li, A.K.F. "Effects of Play on Novel Responses in Children." *Alberta Journal of Educational Research* 24 (1978): 31–36.

Lieberman, J. N. "Playfulness and Divergent Thinking: An Investigation of Their Relationship at the Kindergarten Level." *Journal of Genetic Psychology* 107 (1965): 219–24.

Moore, N. V.; C. M. Evertson and J. E. Brophy. "Solitary Play: Some Functional Considerations." *Developmental Psychology* 10 (1974): 830–34.

Parten, M. B. "Social Participation Among Preschool Children." *Journal of Abnormal and Social Psychology* 27 (1932): 242–69.

Piaget, J. *Play, Dreams and Imitation in Childhood*. (C. Gattegno and F. M. Hodgson, trans.) New York: W. W. Norton, 1962. (Originally published, 1951.)

———. "Development and Learning." In R. E. Ripple and V. N. Rockcastle, eds., *Piaget Rediscovered: A Report of the Conference on Cognitive Studies and Curriculum Development*. Ithaca, NY: Cornell University, 1964.

———. *The Psychology of Intelligence*. (M. Piercy and D. E. Berlyne, trans.) Totowa, NJ: Littlefield, Adams, 1966. (Originally published, 1947.)

Prescott, E.; E. Jones and S. Kritchevsky. *Day Care as a Child-rearing Environment*. Washington, DC: National Association for the Education of Young Children, 1972.

Reichenberg-Hackett, W. "Practices, Attitudes, and Values in Nursery Group Education." *Psychological Reports* 10 (1962): 151–72.

Rubin, K. H. "Play Behaviors in Young Children." *Young Children* 32 (1977): 16–24.

Rubin, K. H., and T. L. Maioni. "Play Preference and Its Relationship to Egocentrism, Popularity, and Classification Skills in Preschoolers." *Merrill-Palmer Quarterly* 21 (1975): 171–79.

Rubin, K. H.; T. L. Maioni and M. Hornung. "Free Play Behaviors in Middle- and Lower-class Preschoolers: Parten and Piaget Revisited." *Child Development* 47 (1976):414–19.

Rubin, K. H.; K. S. Watson and T. W. Jambor. "Free Play Behaviors in Preschool and Kindergarten Children." *Child Development* 49 (1978): 534–36.

Scholtz, G. J., and M. J. Ellis. "Repeated Exposure to Objects and Peers in a Play Setting." *Journal of Experimental Child Psychology* 19 (1975): 448–55.

Seagoe, M. V. "An Instrument for the Analysis of Children's Play as an Index of Socialization." *Journal of School Psychology* 8 (1970): 139–44.

———. "A Comparison of Children's Play in Six Modern Cultures." *Journal of School Psychology* 9 [1971(a)]: 61–72.

———. "Children's Play in Three American Subcultures." *Journal of School Psychology* 9, 2 [1971(b)]:167–72.

Smilansky, S. *The Effect of Sociodramatic Play on Disadvantaged Preschool Children*. New York: Wiley, 1968.

Sutton-Smith, B. "The Playful Modes of Knowing." In *Play: The Child Strives Toward Self-realization*. Washington, DC: National Association for the Education of Young Children, 1971.

Vygotsky, L. S. "Play and Its Role in the Mental Development of the Child. *Soviet Psychology* 12 (1966): 62–76.

Equipment Choices of Primary-Age Children on Conventional and Creative Playgrounds

Joe L. Frost
Department of Curriculum and Instruction
The University of Texas at Austin

and

Sheila D. Campbell
Department of Education
University of Alberta, Edmonton, Canada

The present study is one of a series conducted at a private school where four different types of play environments were constructed for research purposes. The study reported here utilized two of the play environments, a "conventional" playground and a "creative" playground. The major purpose was to determine the differences in equipment choices of children on the two types of play environments.

Despite a growing concern for the quality of experience that children obtain from the environments in which they function, the majority of outdoor playground environments continues to be hazardous, unintegrated and inappropriate for facilitating the various types of play engaged in by young children (U.S. Consumer Product Safety Commission, 1975; Vernon, 1976). Isolated examples of a different kind of playground do exist in Texas and a few other states, but there has been little attempt to examine the nature of experience they provide.

The importance of type of equipment and its arrangement has been of concern for some time to playground designers in such countries as England, Sweden, Denmark and other European countries (Bengtsson, 1972; Cooper, 1970; Frost, 1978; Utzinger, 1974). In Canada the Children's Environments Division of the Central Mortgage and Housing Corporation is devoted to ensuring quality

environments for children, especially in playground areas in housing developments. Discussions at the United Nations "Habitat" Conference in Vancouver, Canada, were related to the provision of outdoor environments designed to meet children's developmental play needs.

Since the early studies of Johnson (1935), there have been sporadic and some recent signs of interest in the impact of playground space and equipment on the behavior and experiences of children. Johnson found that undesirable behavior decreased with the addition of a substantial quantity of equipment to two playgrounds and increased on a third playground where equipment was removed. In addition, with less equipment, she noted less bodily exercise, more play with sand and dirt and more organized games being played.

Comprehensive studies on the arrangement and use of space in respect to young children have been carried out by researchers at Pacific Oaks College (Prescott et al., 1972). In studying child-rearing environments, they began with the basic premise that "... settings in which events and behavior occur possess inherent regulatory features. . ." (p. 38). They identified a number of criteria that affected the quality of space, including degree of organization, complexity and variety of equipment and the ratio of play opportunities to the number of children. They reported a significant relationship between the quality of space and the behaviors observed in children: high

Reprinted with permission from *Lutheran Education* (September/October 1978).

quality space was associated with interested and involved behavior by young children. Prescott *et al.* also found that free choice and free play periods stimulated more responses than did structured/supervised play on the exceptionally interested and involved portion of a rating scale.

In the present study, the equipment choices exhibited on two playgrounds were examined, one traditional and lacking the features identified as high quality in the Pacific Oaks studies; the other incorporating a careful organization of space, varied and complex equipment and a wider range of play opportunities for the child.

METHOD

The subjects for the study were 45 children in two second-grade classes at a private school. The children attending this school are almost exclusively white, from middle- to upper-middle socioeconomic status.

Beginning early in the school year and continuing until ten weeks of two-day observations were complete, trained observers recorded data on children engaged in free play on one day each week on the conventional playground and one day on the creative playground. They used a Playground Behaviors Checklist developed by the investigators that allowed categorization of equipment choices. An equal number of observations were recorded for each child during the first, middle and last third of the play period (Goodenough, 1928; Helmstader, 1970).

Before the actual study the observers engaged in a pilot project to develop skill in using the checklist and to establish inter-coder agreement. The levels reached were 75.5 percent for the social categories, 93.5 percent for the cognitive categories and 92 percent for the equipment categories. Agreement levels were checked (and sustained) an additional six times during the progress of the study.

The conventional playground is 15 years old and consists of a merry-go-round, seesaws, swings, slide, trapeze bars and an area for organized games. The creative playground was constructed from a variety of

commercial and hand-made equipment and an array of loose parts. It was designed to accommodate the cognitive and social types of play coded in this study. A list of all equipment is provided in the following section.

RESULTS

Because of the differences in range and type of equipment on the two playgrounds, no direct comparison was possible. Equipment choices are summarized in Table 1.

There were marked differences in popularity of equipment between the two play environments (Table 2). On the conventional playground the swings were the most popular, followed in order by merry-go-round, seesaw, games equipment, climbing apparatus, slide and tactile materials and miscellaneous materials. No equipment (19.6 percent) included about a 50/50 split between "not play" and games such as "chase."

There was a more balanced usage of equipment on the creative playground. The most used equipment (play house) accounted for 13 percent of the observations while the least used (slide) accounted for 3.1 percent. The equipment more likely to be used for dramatic play predominated, with the play house, movable materials, boat, riding equipment and tactile materials accounting for 50.2 percent of the observations. The equipment designed primarily for functional play (climbing apparatus, swing, seesaw, slide) accounted for only 22.9 percent of the observations.

Use of games equipment on the creative playground totaled 4.1 percent versus 11 percent on the conventional playground. "No equipment" usage was about the same for both playgrounds.

CONCLUSIONS AND IMPLICATIONS

The dominant choices of children on both playgrounds were for movable equipment or features. Children preferred action-oriented over static equipment. On the conventional playground children selected action-oriented swings, merry-go-round and seesaw over fixed climbing apparatus and slide. On the creative playground the play house (supplied with movable props for dramatic

Table 1
Equipment Choices on Conventional and Creative Playgrounds

Equipment	Conventional %	Equipment	Creative %
Climbing Apparatus	7.7	Climbing Apparatus	10.4
Chinning bars	.0	Jungle gym	3.8
Horizontal ladder	1.3	Teepee climber	5.5
Trapeze	6.4	Tire climber	1.0
		Tree	.1
Games Equipment	11.0	Games Equipment	4.1
Baseball	.0	Baseball	.0
Basketball	.8	Basketball	.4
Football	6.5	Football	.5
Rubber ball	2.8	Rubber ball	3.2
Other	.9	Other	.0
Seesaw	11.0	Seesaw (movable)	3.7
Slide	5.1	Slide	3.1
Swings	23.7	Swing (tire)	5.7
Merry-go-round	19.9		
Tactile Materials	1.6	Tactile Materials	6.5
Dirt/mud	1.2	Dirt/mud	.0
Sand pit	.4	Sand box	6.3
Other	.0	Other	.2
		Play house	13.0
		Movable Materials (spools, crates, planks)	12.1
		Boat	10.9
Miscellaneous	.2	Miscellaneous	4.4
		Dressup clothes	.2
		Spring horse	.5
		Table	1.4
		Tools	.0
		Wheelbarrow	.4
		Wagon	.0
		Other	1.9
		Riding Equipment	7.7
		Big wheel	5.0
		Pedal car	1.3
		Tricycle	1.2
		Two-wheeler	.2
No equipment	19.6	No equipment	18.3
Total	99.8		99.9

Table 2
Popularity Rankings of Equipment:
Conventional Versus Creative Environments

Conventional		Creative	
Equipment	Per cent	Equipment	Per cent
Swings	23.7	Play house	13.0
Merry-go-round	19.9	Movable materials	12.1
Seesaw	11.0	Boat	10.9
Games & equipment	11.0	Climbing apparatus	10.4
Climbing apparatus	7.7	Riding equipment	7.7
Slide	5.1	Tactile materials	6.5
Tactile materials	1.6	Swing	5.7
Miscellaneous	.2	Miscellaneous	4.4
No equipment	19.6	Games equipment	4.1
		Seesaw	3.7
		Slide	3.1
		No equipment	18.3

play) was the most popular equipment followed by movable materials and the boat (rocked by the children to stimulate sea travel).

On the creative environment, no single piece of equipment received over 13 percent of the play and the pattern of use across equipment declined in small increments to 3.1 percent for the slide. The percentage of play was balanced across a wider range of equipment than was the case for the conventional playground. Equipment designed primarily for functional play (creative playground) received less than one-fourth of the observations and equipment designed primarily for dramatic play received over half of the observations.

In sum, the children's play revealed preferences for action-oriented equipment, or materials and equipment that supported complex dramatic play, over single function equipment. The preference for dramatic play props by 7- to 8-year-olds is inconsistent with Piaget's conclusion that dramatic play reaches its zenith somewhere between ages 3 and 6 and gradually disappears at about age 7 in favor of games with rules. The explanation for this apparent inconsistency may be that traditional playgrounds are poorly equipped to accommodate mixed forms of play and teachers and other adults push children, subtly and prematurely, into games with rules. On conventional playgrounds and in structured "physical education" periods, dramatic play may be bypassed in favor of sports-oriented games with rules and directed perceptual-motor activities. We have observed that the intensity and duration of motor activity during certain forms of dramatic play often exceed that provided by directed play classes.

References

Bengtsson, A. *Adventure Playgrounds.* London, England: C. Lockwood, 1972.

Cooper, Clare. *The Adventure Playground: Creative Play in an Urban Setting.* Berkeley, CA: Center for Planning and Developmental Research, 1970.

Frost, Joe L. "The American Playground Movement." *Childhood Education* 54 (1978): 176–82.

Frost, Joe L., and Eric Strickland. "Equipment Choices of Young Children During Free Play." *Lutheran Education* 1014 (1978): 34–46.

Goodenough, Florence L. "Measuring Behavior Traits by Means of Repeated Short Samples." *Journal of Juvenile Research* (Juvenile Deliquency) 12 (1928): 230–35.

Helmstadter, G. C. *Research Concepts in Human Behavior.* New York: Appleton-Century-Crofts, 1970.

Henniger, Michael L. *Free Play Behaviors of Nursery School Children in an Indoor and Outdoor Environment.* Unpublished doctoral dissertation, The University of Texas at Austin, 1977.

Johnson, M. W. "The Effect on Behavior of Variation in the Amount of Play Equipment." *Child Development* 6 (1935): 56–68.

Prescott, Elizabeth; Elizabeth Jones and Sybil Kritchevsky. *Day Care as a Child-Rearing Environment.* Washington, DC: National Association for the Education of Young Children, 1972.

U.S. Consumer Product Safety Commission. *Hazard Analysis: Playground Equipment,* 1975.

Utzinger, R. C. *Some European Nursery Schools and Playgrounds.* Ann Arbor, MI: Architectural Research Laboratory, University of Michigan, 1970.

Vernon, Elizabeth A. *A Survey of Pre-Primary and Primary Outdoor Learning Centers in Texas Public Schools.* Austin, TX: Unpublished doctoral dissertation, University of Texas at Austin, 1976.

Equipment Choices of Young Children During Free Play

Joe L. Frost
Department of Curriculum and Instruction
The University of Texas at Austin

and

Eric Strickland
Center for Professional Teacher Education
The University of Texas at Arlington

Presently, many claims and assumptions are being made regarding the appropriateness of various types of playground equipment. Manufacturers offer dozens of types, and for each type there are many variations. Within communities, neighborhoods and schools, individuals and organizations are with increasing frequency designing and building their own play environments, using raw materials, manufactured equipment or combinations of these.

In the main, play equipment is selected by custom. With few exceptions, school playgrounds offer the typical jungle gym, merry-go-round, see-saw, slide and swings, installed over concrete, asphalt or hard-packed earth (Vernon, 1976). They are hazardous (Consumer Product Safety Commission, 1975) and provide primarily for one form of play—exercise or gross-motor (Frost and Campbell, 1977).

Research comparing types of play environments and equipment therein is limited, but the conclusions thus far favor adventure/creative playgrounds over other types. For example, Haywood, Rothenberg and Beasley (1974) compared the play activities taking place on three types of playgrounds; traditional, contemporary and adventure. The more varied adventure playground elicited a broader language focus, a wider range of play activities and more extensive use by children. Vance (1977) reporting on data from 14 agencies in five states with adventure playgrounds found that the adventure playgrounds outdrew conventional playgrounds; they were maintained less expensively; there was greater community participation; and the number of injuries was about the same as, or fewer than, on conventional playgrounds.

Frost and Campbell (1977) found that children alternating play sessions between a traditional and a creative playground engaged in exercise or gross motor play over 77 percent of the time and in dramatic play less than three percent on the traditional playground. On the creative playground (play house, wheel vehicle area, sand and water areas, storage and loose parts, and a variety of play structures) dramatic play occupied 40 percent and exercise play 43 percent of the time. The conclusion of Frost and Campbell that type of equipment in a play environment significantly influences the type of play engaged in by children is supported by Henniger's (1977) study.

Although the evidence supporting a need for modification of play environments is accumulating, the investigators found no studies of children's play choices on contrasting types of environments. The major purpose of this study was to compare children's equipment choices on three outdoor environments during free play.

METHOD

Subjects
The subjects for this study were 138 children enrolled in two kindergarten, two first- and two second-grade classes at Redeemer Lu-

theran School in Austin, Texas. With two exceptions (one Mexican American and one black), the children were of Anglo-Saxon origin and all were middle- to upper middle-class. Approximately 97 were children of Redeemer Church members; the remainder were children of non-member parents.

The Play Environments

The three play environments were designated: play environment A, play environment B, and play environment C (Figure 1).

Play environment A consisted of a complex unit structure built from Western red cedar by Educational Systems, Inc. and donated for research purposes. This structure contains interior and exterior space for climbing and dramatic play, two horizontal tire swings, a slide, fireman's pole and ladder. It was installed in a sand area for safety and complementary sand-equipment activities. The retail cost of this structure was about $5000 at the time of installation (1977). According to the manufacturer,

This massive piece of equipment will accommodate up to fifty students, while being compact enough to allow a single instructor control of an entire class in an educational learning environment.

Play environment B included 16 different pressure-treated pine structures including balance beams, chinning bars, obstacle climbers, suspension bridge, slide, jungle gym and related equipment. The equipment was installed by the manufacturer (Creative Playgrounds Corporation) in an integrated or linked "play 'n learn" pattern or obstacle course designed to "aid in the development of a wide range of perceptual-motor skills necessary for cognitive development." Sand areas were constructed as safety fall zones in critical areas. The retail cost of this equipment was about $5000 at the time of installation (1977).

Play environment C was constructed by parents, children and teachers of Redeemer School according to designs furnished by the researchers. A mix of relatively inexpensive commercial equipment and raw building materials was used. The cost breakdown was approximately as follows:

commercial slide	$500.00	(donated)
fort	125.00	(built)
boat and car	—	(donated)
sand	50.00	
storage shed	100.00	
table (picnic type w/ benches)	100.00	
climbers (3 types)	—	(built)
wheel vehicles	200.00	
wheel vehicle track (old conveyor belt)	—	(donated)
old tires, spools, barrels, etc.	$100.00	(donated)
railroad ties and utility poles	150.00	
hardware for building	100.00	
TOTAL	$1,425.00	

The figure of $1,425 is approximately equal to that cost which would be incurred without donations. In other words, any group could likely reproduce play environment C at this cost, assuming no charge for labor. An illustrated booklet describing how the total play environment was developed is available.[1]

Data Collection

The data were collected by teachers of the subjects following a training and trial session. During one 30-minute free play session a week for six weeks, the observers observed and coded the equipment being used by each child. The equipment choice of each subject was coded three times during each play period: once after the children were settled into their play, once at the mid-point of the period and once just before leaving the playground.

Observations were written directly on a scale map showing outlines of each play structure (Figure 1). Each child's initials were written directly on the map according to his actual play location. Any choices not included on the map were written at the bottom. All children present were coded three times for each play session. Absences from school were ignored in collection and treatment of data.

During all play sessions the teachers allowed the children to make their own equip-

[1] Frost, Joe L., and Libby Vernon. *Development of a Play Environment*. Austin, TX: Texas Education Agency, 1978.

94

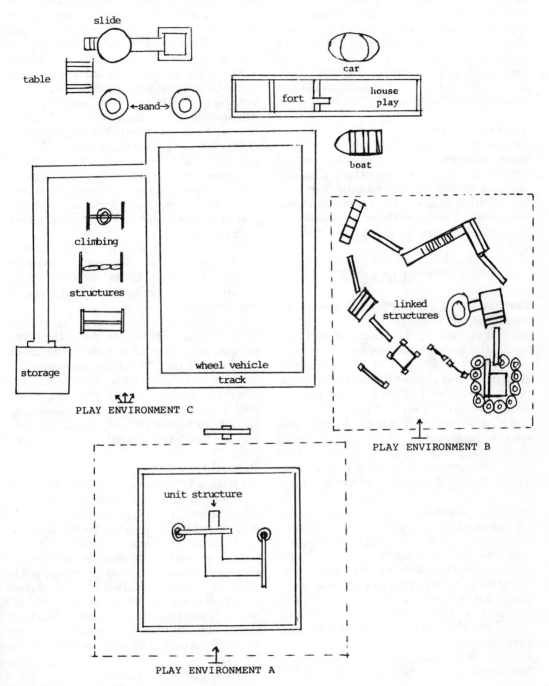

Figure 1. Layout of Play Environments.

ment choices, intervening only to prevent hazardous activity, assist with conflicts or engage in normal conversation. Teachers neither encouraged nor directed children to choose any particular type of equipment or form of play. They moved randomly about the playground to avoid attracting children to any particular area.

Treatment of Data

The data were initially analyzed for frequencies and percentages, then coded on IBM cards for computer analysis of individual play patterns, sex differences and for determining significance levels of equipment choice differences. The more elaborate analyses are reported in a separate publication.

RESULTS

Comparison of Three Play Environments Including All Subjects

As seen in Table I, play environment C was by far the most popular of the three environments with 63 percent of the observations (equipment choices). Play environment A was second with 23 percent and Play environment B third with 13 percent.

An examination of the results for these environments one at a time in greater detail shows that Environment C elicited a wider range and greater balance of choices than Environments A and B. Choices included, in decreasing order, wheel vehicles (9.93 percent of all observations, even though second-grade children were not allowed to use them), games with rules (9.63 percent), fort and housekeeping equipment (8.20 percent), play without equipment (6.65 percent), the complex slide (5.72 percent), loose parts (5.61 percent), old car and boat (4.56 percent), sand areas (4.37 percent), climbing structures (3.67 percent) and seesaw (2.44 percent).[2]

The most popular area in Environment A was the swing area, which accounted for 11.29

percent of all observations. The top of the platform accounted for 4.72 percent and the inside of the structure 2.59 percent. The sand pit surrounding the structure including play with loose parts accounted for 3.83 percent.

Environment B was broken down into six areas for coding subjects' choices: climbing structures A, B, C, D, E, suspension bridge, horizontal ladder, chinning bar and balance beams. In this environment the most-used equipment was climbing structure A (3.52 percent of all observations), which included a wooden ladder, chain ladder, platform and fireman's pole, all surrounded by a sand area bordered by tires. All other structures each accounted for two percent or fewer observations.

In terms of actual observations (times a child was coded as using equipment) playground C attracted 1641 children; playground A, 600 children and playground B, 345 children.

The subjects were playing on or with equipment in over 90 percent of the observations. In only 1.12 percent of all observations were they "watching, unoccupied or being punished." Playing chase or unidentified movement (running/walking) occupied 6.65 percent of all observations and special attractions (pile of leaves, tree, etc.) occupied 1.55 percent.

Related Data

To reduce fall hazards sand areas were constructed around most climbing structures. These areas were frequently used for sand play in addition to areas specifically constructed for such play. Including the surrounding sand area, play environment A elicited 23.20 percent of all observations. The sand area alone accounted for 3.83 percent of all observations. No sand play was observed around play environment B. Sand play on the original play environment accounted for 4.37 percent of all observations (see Table II).

When play environment A is viewed as a single play structure it compares much more favorably. Through selection of functionally equivalent structures from play environment C, a meaningful comparison can be made (Table III). The percentage of all ob-

---

[2]One additional type of equipment was removed from the play environment as a result of previous studies. The spring mounted animal seat was, among all equipment examined, the least popular and perhaps the least functional for kindergarten and primary children.

Table I
Playground and Equipment Choices—
All Grade Levels, All Equipment

	Kindergarten (n = 34)		First Grade (n = 48)		Second Grade (n = 56)		Totals Reported		
	#obs	% obs	# obs	% obs	# obs	% obs	# obs	% obs	
	767	100	927	100	892	100	2586	100	
PLAY ENVIRONMENT A	145	18.90	245	26.43	210	23.54	600	23.20	23.20
Swing	51	6.65	118	12.73	123	13.79	292	11.29	
Platform	2	.26	66	7.12	54	6.05	122	4.72	
Inside	54	7.04	11	1.19	2	.22	67	2.59	
Slide	6	.78	3	.32	11	1.23	20	.77	
Sand area—loose parts	20	2.61	6	.64	11	1.23	37	1.43	
Sand only	12	1.56	41	4.42	9	1.01	62	2.40	
PLAY ENVIRONMENT B	52	6.78	134	14.46	159	17.83	345	13.34	13.34
Climbing Structure A	13	1.69	28	3.02	50	5.61	91	3.52	
Structure B	20	2.61	22	2.37	10	1.12	52	2.01	
Structure C	2	.26	7	.76	5	.56	14	.54	
Structure D			9	.97	1	.11	10	.39	
Structure E	3	.39	9	.97	9	1.01	21	.81	
Bridge	7	.91	15	1.62	15	1.68	37	1.43	
Balance Beams			24	2.59	28	3.14	52	2.01	
Horizontal Ladder	6	.78	9	.97	4	.45	19	.73	
Chinning Bar	1	.13	11	1.19	37	4.15	49	1.89	
PLAY ENVIRONMENT C	570	74.32	548	59.12	532	59.64	1641	63.46	63.46
Boat	23	3.00	8	.86	11	1.23	42	1.62	
Car	24	3.13	27	2.91	25	2.80	76	2.94	
RR Tie Sand area	12	1.56	15	1.62	21	2.35	48	1.86	
Tire Sand area	9	1.17	32	3.45	24	2.69	65	2.51	
Slide	69	9.00	33	3.56	46	5.16	148	5.72	
Platform	22	2.87	15	1.62	15	1.68	52	2.01	
Swing	4	.52	7	.76	2	.22	13	.50	
Slide	43	5.61	11	1.19	29	3.25	83	3.21	
Big Wheel	169	22.03	68	7.34	not allowed to use		237	9.16	
Other Wheeled Veh.	19	2.48	1	.11	n.a. to use		20	.77	
Seesaw	16	2.09	34	3.67	13	1.46	63	2.44	
Fort (inside)	57	7.43	41	4.42	25	2.80	212	8.20	
Housekeeping	43	5.61	44	4.75	2	.22			
Climbing Structures	46	6.00	20	2.16	29	3.25	95	3.67	
Structure A	15	1.96	9	.97	19	2.13	43	1.66	

Table I (continued)
Table I (continued)
Playground and Equipment Choices—
All Grade Levels, All Equipment

	Kindergarten (n = 34)		First Grade (n = 48)		Second Grade (n = 56)		Totals Reported	
Structure B	4	.53	7	.76	3	.34	14	.54
Tire Swing	27	3.52	4	.43	7	.78	38	1.47
Loose Parts	35	4.56	65	7.01	45	5.04	145	5.61
Spools	12	1.56	19	2.05	27	3.03	58	2.24
Barrels	20	2.61	41	4.42	7	.78	68	2.63
Tires	1	.13	1	.11			2	.08
Other	2	.26	4	.43	11	1.23	17	.66
Games with Rules	8	1.04	84	9.06	157	17.60	249	9.63
Football	6	.78	70	7.55	101	11.32	177	6.84
Other ball	2	.26	14	1.51	56	6.28	72	2.79
Sitting/Standing	7	.91	11	1.19	11	1.23	29	1.12
Watching/ unoccupied	5	.65	7	.76	11	1.23	23	.89
Being punished			4	.43			4	.15
Watching cat	2	.26					2	.08
Running/Walking	21	2.74	49	5.29	102	11.43	172	6.65
No Props (chase, Monster, Big Foot, Gorilla)	21	2.74	49	5.29	102	11.43	172	6.65
Other	12	1.56	16	1.73	12	1.35	40	1.55
Volleyball	2	.26					2	.08
Pile of Leaves	8	1.04					8	.31
Trees			1	.11			1	.04
Storage Shed			1	.11			1	.04
Table	2	.26	14	1.51	12	1.35	28	1.08

Table II
Play Environment Choices and Sand Play

	# obs.	% obs.	Structure(s) (no sand play)	%	Sand Play	%
Unit Structure	600	23.20	501	19.37	99	3.83
Linked Structure	345	13.34	345	13.34	0	—
Original Playground	1641	63.46	1528	59.09	113	4.37
Totals	2586	100	2374	91.80	212	8.20

Table III
Play Environment A Vs. Functionally Equivalent Structures from Original Playground

Equipment	# obs.	% obs.	Total %	Total #
Play Environment A (minus sand area)	501	19.37	19.37	501
Play Environment C Slide (including tire swing)	148	5.72	17.59	455
Fort	212	8.20		
Climbing Structures	95	3.67		

servations was 19.37 (501 observations) for the unit structure and 17.59 (455 observations) for equivalent structures from play environment C.

Play Environment Choices and Grade Level

The examination of data by grade levels (Table I) allows a comparison for each play environment and for each item of play equipment.

The kindergarten children chose play environment C in 74.32 percent of the observations; play environment A in 18.90 percent and play environment C in 6.78 percent (Table IV).

The first grade and second grade children were almost equal in their choice of play environments: play environment A in 26.43 and 23.54 percent of observations respectively; 14.46 percent and 17.83 percent for play environment B; 59.12 percent and 59.64 percent for play environment C.

Play environment C with its wider array of features was much more popular with kindergarten children (74.32 percent) than it was with first-grade children (59.12 percent) and second-grade children (59.64 percent).

Play Environment A: The outstanding differences noted across grade levels on play environment A were as follows: the first- and second-grade children played on the swings about twice as frequently as did the kindergarten children. They also played on the outside of the structure much more frequently than did the kindergarten children. Play inside the structure decreased dramatically with increased grade level or age. A similar pattern was found for play with loose parts in the sand area (see Table I).

Play Environment B: Although there were exceptions for some equipment, the general pattern of play on environment B was increasing use with increasing grade level. Total use by second graders was about four times that by kindergarten children (see Table I).

Play Environment C: The play patterns observed on play environment C across grade levels were as follows: The boat and car were about twice as popular with kindergarten children as with first and second graders. Sand play was somewhat more popular with first and second graders. The slide was more popular with kindergarteners.

Table IV
Play Environment Choices by Grade Level

	Kindergarten		First Grade		Second Grade	
	# obs.	% obs.	# obs.	% obs.	# obs.	% obs.
Play Environment A	145	18.90	245	26.43	210	23.54
Play Environment B	52	6.78	134	14.46	159	17.83
Play Environment C	570	74.32	548	59.12	532	59.64

The kindergarten children used the wheeled vehicles about three times as frequently as the first graders. Second graders were not allowed to use these vehicles. The fort and housekeeping area underneath were very popular with kindergarten children (7.43 percent and 5.61 percent respectively) but decreased rapidly in popularity with increase in grade level. There was little difference between grade levels in use of climbing structures A and B and the adjacent tire swing.

Loose parts were popular with each grade level (4.56, 7.01, and 5.04 percent). The greatest variation found in the study was the dramatic increase in games with rules from level to level (kindergarten, 1.04 percent; first grade, 9.06 percent; second grade, 17.60 percent). There was very little unoccupied behavior at any grade level. Playing without props (equipment or materials) increased with grade level (2.74, 5.29, 11.43 percent). There was little difference between grade levels on "other" equipment.

CONCLUSIONS AND IMPLICATIONS

The reader should bear in mind that the context of this research was free play. The conclusions might differ substantially under conditions of directed play such as those frequently found in physical education classes. The subjects were allowed to make their own choices without direction or coercion by adults. We believe that certain types of adult intervention are important in children's play, but adult intervention was not a variable in the present study.

Three Play Environments, All Subjects
When play environments A, B and C are viewed as three separate play environments and free play is the nature of the activity, environment C is the children's choice by a substantial margin. This appears to have resulted from: (1) the existence of a wider range of equipment; (2) the opportunity to express self in a wider variety of play forms (cognitive and social); and (3) the availability of action-oriented equipment (e.g., wheel vehicles and loose parts) that could be used alone or in combination with other equipment.

The results of this study suggest that it is faulty logic to assume that a single structure (play environment A) or combination of structures (play environment B) designed primarily for one form of play (gross-motor or exercise) is sufficiently varied to accommodate the free play choices or developmental play needs of young children. It also appears that the linking structures to facilitate continuity of action sequences may be less important in attracting children to play than type of equipment provided.

On play environment C the play activity was quite diverse with several types of equipment making substantial contributions to the total observations. Even though many types of equipment were used, the wheel vehicles were clearly the most popular equipment (though not used by second graders). On play environment A, the one *movable* feature, the swings, accounted for about half of the play, while on play environment B the most *complex* climbing structure accounted for over one-fourth of the play. Collectively, these results indicate that children prefer equipment that does something (is movable) and/or that is complex (offers several play options). Further, it appears that children prefer play equipment that can be adapted to their play schemes (movable and complex equipment) rather than stationary play structures which require children to adapt themselves to the limitations of the equipment.

These conclusions might appear to be at odds with research on toys. The results generally show that simple, raw toy materials are most popular and stimulate greater interest in play. Two factors seem to explain this apparent conflict: (1) In the present research loose parts were not available in great variety or quantity and tools for building were not available; consequently, the effects of their existence could not be adequately tested. (2) The major structures in the present study were of a fixed or permanent variety. It appears that in order to attract children structures must be complex if they are not modifiable or movable.

Permanent structures are more popular in the context of sand and/or loose parts. On play environment A the sand area, provided for protection in falls, accounted for about one-fifth of the play in that environment. The absence of sand play in environment B may have been due to the relatively small sand areas and their relative inaccessibility.

The results suggest that, on the one hand, play environments A and B should not be considered "complete" play environments, since they do not foster a wide range of play behaviors. On the other hand, environment C was designed to accommodate exercise play, construction play, dramatic play, games with rules and to stimulate social interaction. An earlier study (Frost and Campbell) revealed the type of play most frequently engaged in on various types of equipment. This evidence, coupled with informal observations during the present study, suggests that exercise or gross-motor play is the most frequent form occurring on environments A and B. In environment C there appears to have been a reasonable balance between exercise, dramatic play and games with rules. Equipment for construction play was not available in any of the three environments in sufficient quantities to attract much activity. In sum, the play environment that is designed to foster one particular type of play does so, but children prefer broader options. This seems consistent with the nature of children's play development. If adults want for children dramatic or gross-motor or whatever form of play, they need merely to provide appropriate props.

Play Choices and Grade Level

The results across grade levels were that the younger children (kindergarten) chose environment C much more frequently (74 percent) than they chose other environments. Equipment (e.g., boat, car, wheel vehicles, housekeeping) designed or selected for dramatic play was more popular with the younger children. This was expected since dramatic play is a dominant type for 5-year-olds. But games with rules jumped from one percent of all observations for kindergarten children to 18 percent for second graders. Games with rules are typically very popular with 7- to 8-year-olds. Again, the most popular playground for children is the one with equipment and space that accommodate various forms of play.

As grade level increased, competitive activity and exercise activity increased. The play structures in environments A and B appear to be scaled for 3- to 6-year-olds. However, their popularity increased with grade level. Two conclusions seem warranted: (1) Fixed structures that primarily accommodate exercise play are less popular with younger children (4–6) than with older children. (2) The structures might be redesigned to present greater challenge for older children (6–9).

Collectively, the three environments attracted the children to play in one form or another. Unlike the patterns frequently observed in conventional playgrounds, there was little unoccupied activity. Children were active in well over 90 percent of the observations. There were few behavior problems, and no injuries more serious than simple scrapes and bruises were reported.

References

Consumer Product Safety Commission. *Hazard Analysis—Playground Equipment.* Washington, DC, 1975.
Frost, J. L., and S. Campbell. "Play and Equipment Choices of 2nd Grade Children on Two Types of Playgrounds." Unpublished research report. Austin: The University of Texas, 1977.
Hayward, D.; M. Rothenberg and R. Beasley. "Children's Play and Urban Playground Environments: A Comparison of Traditional, Contemporary and Adventure Playground Types." *Environment and Behavior* 6, 2 (1974): 131–68.
Henniger, M. L. "Free Play Behaviors of Nursery School Children in an Indoor and Outdoor Environment." Unpublished doctoral dissertation. Austin, TX: The University of Texas, 1977.
Vance, B. "The President's Message." *American Adventure Play Association News* 1, 4 (Fall 1977): 1.
Vernon, E. A. "A Survey of Preprimary and Primary Outdoor Learning Centers/Playgrounds in Texas Public Schools." Unpublished doctoral dissertation. Austin, TX: The University of Texas, 1976.

Design for Outdoor Play: An Observational Study

HEATHER NAYLOR
Department of Psychology
University of Surrey, Guildford, England

The literature on children's playgrounds suggests that traditional, fixed equipment playgrounds are poor places for children to play. Hole (1966) and Holme and Massie (1970) show the failure of traditional playgrounds in terms of low attendance rates by children compared to alternative outdoor play places such as roads and pavements. Hayward *et al.* (1974) show that children's traditional playgrounds not only have low attendance rates when compared to either contemporary or adventure playgrounds, but are also the settings for only a limited number of play forms. Wolff (1975) showed that a group of visually handicapped children playing in a fixed playground exhibited less socially cooperative play than when playing in an adventure playground.

The emphasis of the two previous studies has been to demonstrate the poor quality of play environments found at traditional playgrounds and to show the improved quality found in adventure play settings. Although the aim of such studies often appears to be to persuade those providing playgrounds to adopt these new types, in England at least designers still seem to base their designs on the choice of items from manufacturer's catalogs. As this is the almost universal state of affairs in England at the moment, the emphasis of this study is upon the *improvement* of fixed playgrounds and their equipment as places for play. While it is acknowledged that the ideal playground might have relatively little fixed equipment, this study specifically examines fixed items.

No designed item can be improved without some guiding principles to aid thinking. Otherwise, the problem-solving process is undirected and can only proceed by trial and error. Some understanding is necessary of what constitutes the end point of the design (in this case the occurrence of play) and of how the design achieves this end point.

In searching theoretical literature on play for some guiding principles for playground design thinking, one theory of play examined carefully was that of Bruner (1972), which stresses the adaptive value to individuals of playing. A general strategy of "playing" that has short-term costs will in the long term benefit the individual who adopts such a strategy over one who does not, achieving this through increasing an individual's knowledge and skills before these become critical for survival.

Using this as a theoretical framework, it can be proposed that the best environment for play will be one in which the child gains most knowledge and greatest skill competence. In more detail, it will be an environment that offers opportunities to gain these things in a rich variety of modes e.g. physically, socially and cognitively. This means offering the facilities for a wide range of play types. It will also be an environment offering the greatest range of possibilities for skill and knowledge acquisition within these modes.

Two design principles can now be outlined: 1) that successful play equipment design would provide for a variety of play modes; 2) that successful play equipment design would provide for a range of opportunities within each play mode, where successful is defined in terms of amount of use.

HYPOTHESES

The first problem addressed by this study is: can design principles needed to help solve the problem of poor playground design be extracted from theoretical work on play? Second, are these principles the right ones to lead to good playground design?

The latter point can be made into testable hypotheses. The extent to which existing equipment items embody these design principles can be compared with their popularity, reasoning that if these principles work in producing good play environments, then the extent of their embodiment in existing designs should be reflected in the amount of use these items receive.

Hypothesis 1 The *range of play activities within one play mode* will be positively related to the amount of *use* observed on an item.

Hypothesis 2 The *number of play modes* observed on an item will be positively related to the amount of *use* on an item.

The nearer a piece of equipment comes to "perfection" as defined by the two principles, the larger the expected amounts of play on it.

METHODS

Subjects

Subjects were any persons entering a playground during the observation periods. Each subject was assigned to one of four age categories: (a) 0–5 years, (b) 5–11 years, (c) 11–18 years, (d) 18+ years. These ages correspond to school leaving/joining ages which helped in the allocation of subjects to the different categories. Subjects were also designated either male (M) or female (F). Characteristics of observed subjects in time-samples at each of the three playgrounds is shown in Table 1.

Subjects for tracking observations were taken one at a time, from the first person to enter the playground after the researcher, to the next person to enter after that subject had left. Characteristics of these subjects are shown in Table 2.

Playgrounds

The three local fixed playgrounds chosen had sufficient number and variety of items to allow comparisons. Their high attendance figures also allowed internal comparisons. Equipment at each playground is presented in Table 3.

Procedures

Observations were carried out on fine days in the school summer holidays for maximization of numbers. The two methods used were:

Time sampling

At each site observations were made every 15 minutes for one day between 10 am and 5:30 pm, approximately. Each observation noted the number of subjects on each piece of equipment, their characteristics and play activities. In this case "on" means either in physical contact with the equipment, or about to be. Any social interaction and the participants was also noted (peers or parents). Records of users numbered 345, 706 and 475 at Broadwater Park, Stoke Park and Lion Green respectively.

Tracking

All users were monitored during their time on the playground. Items visited, time spent and play activities were all recorded. The 70 children from the three sites were observed for a total length of time of 20 hours and 12 minutes.

RESULTS

The separate results from the two methodologies are discussed first before evaluation of the hypotheses which use combined data from the two sources.

Table 1
Sex/Age Characteristics of Subjects Observed in Time-Samples

| | SEX | | AGE | | | | |
	Male	Female	0–5	5–11	11–18	18+	Total
Broadwater Park	202	143	107	212	19	9	345
Stoke Park	399	307	253	430	23	0	706
Lion Green	211	264	124	301	48	2	475
	812	714	484	943	90	11	1526

Table 2
Sex/Age Characteristics of Subjects Tracked in Playgrounds

| | SEX | | AGE | | | | |
	Male	Female	0–5	5–11	11–18	18+	Total
Broadwater Park	11	11	5	15	2	—	22
Stoke Park	13	6	6	12	1	—	19
Lion Green	15	13	9	15	4	—	28
	39	30	20	42	7	—	69

Time-sampling Data

The total number of observations of users of equipment is shown in Figure 1 (p. 106). The most popular pieces of equipment were as shown in Table 5 (p. 107). The average number of users per time-sample were:

Broadwater Park	Stoke Park	Lion Green
10.8	23.6	16.4

Most users were in the 5–11 (b) age group, 61.8 percent, with 31.7 percent below 5 years old. Only a few teenagers were observed on equipment (5.9 percent). The differential use of equipment between age groups was tested using X^2 and found to be significant at each playground.

The differential use of equipment by the sexes was also tested using X^2 but was not found to be significant. However, there were differences at the playgrounds in overall at-tendance figures, with 53.2 percent of observations referring to males and only 46.8 percent to females.

The total numbers of observations of users interacting with their peers termed "talk-ing," as this was the most common form of interaction, are shown in Figure 2 and Table 7 (pp. 108 and 107, respectively).

Those users interacting with their parents were mostly in the under-5 age group (79 percent = (a), 21 percent = (b). Most inter-action occurred while the child was using the cradle swings (38 percent), with lesser amounts associated with large swings (20 percent), slides (18 percent) and other items.

Tracking Data

A large number and variety of different ac-tivities were recorded for each piece of

Table 3
Equipment List for Each Playground

Broadwater Park	Stoke Park	Lion Green
Cradle Swings	Swings	'Jungle Gym'
'Jungle Gym'	'Moonprobe' : Space module frame	Seesaw
Contour slide	'Deltaglide' : rocket frame and slide	Slide
Pipes : concrete, hollow	'Joywheel' : roundabout	Swings
Tunnel	'Spiraglide' :helter-skelter	Cradle swings
Fort : wooden with gallery.	Cradle swings	Wendy House : wooden, with slide
Swings	Pipes : concrete, hollow.	Bars : wooden, with ladder and rope
Mound	Log pyramid	Tire swing : cable glide with tire seat.
Logs : old tree trunks.	Train: concrete model	Spring animal : rocking figure
	Cylinders: solid concrete	
	Frame: old swing frame	

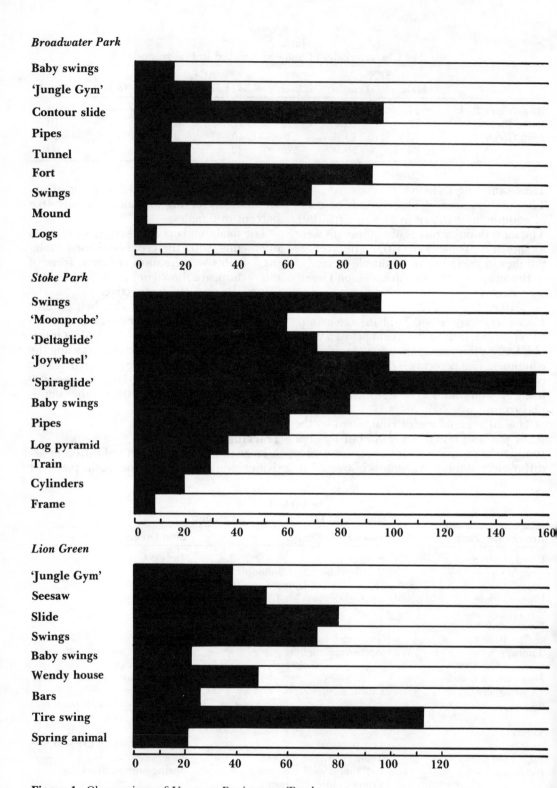

Figure 1. Observations of Users on Equipment: Totals.

Table 4
Total Observations of Subjects on Equipment for Each Playground

Broadwater Park	No.	Stoke Park	No.	Lion Green	No.
Cradle swings	15	Swings	95	'Jungle Gym'	39
'Jungle Gym'	29	'Moonprobe'	58	Seesaw	52
Contour slide	95	'Deltaglide'	70	Slide	80
Pipes	14	'Joywheel'	98	Swings	72
Tunnel	21	'Spiraglide'	155	Cradle swings	23
Fort	91	Cradle swings	83	Wendy House	49
Swings	68	Pipes	59	Bars	26
Mound	4	Log pyramid	35	Tire-swing	113
Logs	8	Train	28	Spring animal	21
	345	Cylinders	18		475
		Frame	7		
			706		

Table 5
Most Popular Items

Broadwater Park, Godalming	contour slide	fort	large swings
Stoke Park, Guildford	helter-skelter (spiraglide)	roundabout (joywheel)	large swings
Lion Green, Haslemere	tire-slider	slide	large swings

Table 6
X^2 Values for Age × Equipment Use

Broadwater Park	$X^2 = 57.326$	d.f. = 8 significant at 0.005
Stoke Park	$X^2 = 64.248$	d.f. = 10 significant at 0.005
Lion Green	$X^2 = 58.248$	d.f. = 8 significant at 0.005

Table 7
Observations of Subjects "Talking" on Equipment

Broadwater Park	No.	Stoke Park	No.	Lion Green	No.
Cradle swings	0	Swings	21	'Jungle Gym'	0
'Jungle Gym'	4	'Moonprobe'	7	Seesaw	23
Contour slide	17	'Deltaglide'	12	Slide	16
Pipes	4	'Joywheel'	22	Swings	23
Tunnel	2	'Spiraglide'	15	Cradle swings	2
Fort	40	Cradle swings	3	Wendy House	20
Swings	29	Pipes	21	Bars	0
Mound	1	Log pyramid	14	Tire-swing	51
Logs	7	Train	7	Spring Animal	2
	104	Cylinders	13		137
		Frame	6		
			141		

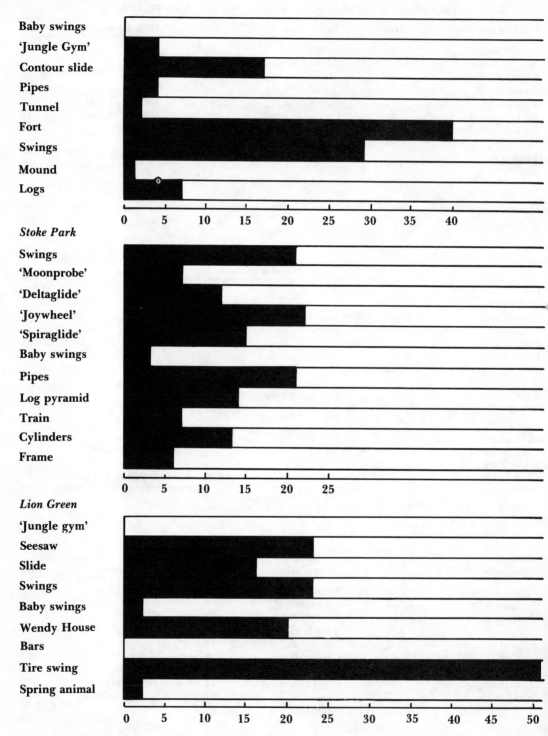

Figure 2. Users "Talking" on Equipment: Total Observations.

equipment. Due to the limitations of an observational methodology, social and cognitive play activities could not be assessed reliably and so are not reported here. Analyses are thus confined to detailed physical activities. Simplified data on social play are available within the time-sampling work.

Lists were drawn up of all observed physical activities. The continuous flow of physical movement was divided up at points where it appeared that the child changed some distinguishing feature of its motion, e.g., direction, speed, part of body used. Thus on a slide, sliding down head first was counted as different from feet first, which was different again from climbing the ladder to the slide. Frequencies of each of these actions were calculated; the modal physical actions for each item are shown in Table 8.

In many cases the modal action is the one referred to in the name of the item, e.g. swinging on a swing, sliding on a slide. The number of types of action to account for 50 percent of all action observed on equipment ranged between 1 and 5, with a mode of 1. This shows that the bulk of equipment studied is used in only very limited ways by the majority of children.

Table 8
Modal Physical Action for Each Piece of Equipment

	Modal Activity	% in Mode
Broadwater Park		
Cradle swings	Swinging pushed by parent	71.4
'Jungle Gym'	Climbing vertically up	48.6
Contour slide	Sliding down feet first	61.8
Pipes	Walking through	66.7
Tunnel	Walking through	50.0
Fort	Going up ladder	36.0
Swings	Swinging self sitting	53.4
Mound	Climbing around	22.2
Logs	Standing on	50.0
Stoke Park		
Swings	Sitting on swing, swinging self	27.8
'Moonprobe'	Climbing up ladder	28.8
'Deltaglide'	Sliding down wing, feet first	35.7
'Joywheel'	Sitting on, spinning	46.5
'Spiraglide'	Sliding down slide feet first	36.1
Cradle swings	Swinging pushed by parent	24.1
Pipes	Crawling through	50.0
Log	Climbing vertically	75.0
Train	Climbing in/on trucks	33.3
Cylinders	Standing on top	46.2
Frame	Climbing up end	50.0
Lion Green		
'Jungle Gym'	Climbing vertically up	38.7
Seesaw	Seesawing	44.8
Slide	Sliding down slide feet first	44.4
Swings	Sitting on swing, swinging self	57.4
Cradle swings	Sitting in being pushed	40.0
Wendy House	Climbing up roof laddering	30.5
Bars	Climbing up bars	29.0
Tire-slide	Taking tire to platform	28.5
Spring animals	Rocking	56.8

Combination of Data Sources and Evaluation of Principles

The hypotheses can be examined by combining use data from time-sampling observations (the larger data base) with tracking data on the range of activities. Using actual data to assess the range of activities on equipment is superior and more realistic in estimating this range.

Hypothesis 1

To test whether the range of play activities within one play mode (here physical play) is positively related to amount of use of an item, use figures from time-sampling data are combined with range of activity figures from tracking data. At each playground items are grouped together according to their scores on an index of activity flexibility. This index is the number of observed activities needed to describe at least 50 percent of all observed activities on an item. These figures compared with those for use are shown in Table 9.

There is no clear relationship between the index of flexibility and use. Also, the number of actions forming the index is invariably low, ranging from 1 to 5.

If the same analysis is redone but the equipment is regrouped according to the *type* of physical actions normally observed, a pattern emerges. This concerns three activities seen at all three sites. There is a constant preference order as evidenced by use, for sliding, then swinging and then climbing, as shown in Table 10.

Hypothesis 2

To test whether the number of play modes observed on an item is positively related to the amount of use in that item, overall use figures from time-samples can be combined with data also from time-samples on the number of play modes shown. As this was an observational study only, physical and to a limited extent social play modes were assessed. This means that a rigorous testing of this hypothesis is not possible.

Instead it is possible to compare items which have the same range and type of physical play actions but support different levels of social play. These comparisons must neces-

Table 9
Number of Activity Types
Accounting for 50% Activity vs. Mean Use Score

Equipment in Group	No. of activity types	Mean use score
Broadwater Park		
Cradle swings, 'Jungle Gym,' Contour slide, Pipes, Tunnel, Swings, Logs	1	35.7
Fort, Mound	3	47.5
Stoke Park		
Pipes, Logs, Frame	1	33.7
Swings, 'Moonprobe,' 'Deltaglide,' 'Joywheel,' 'Spiraglide,' Cylinders	2	82.5
Cradle swings, Train	3	55.5
Lion Green		
Swings, Spring animals	1	46.5
'Jungle Gym,' Seesaw, Slide, Cradle swings, Wendy house, Tire-slide	2	59.3
Bars	5	26.0

Table 10
% Use Score vs. Equipment Grouped by Modal Physical Activity

Type of Activity	Equipment in Group	% Use Score	Rank
Broadwater Park			
Climbing	Fort, 'Jungle Gym,' Logs, Mound	38.3	1
Sliding	Contour slide	27.5	2
Swinging	Swings, Cradle swings	24.0	3
Walking through	Pipes, Tunnel	10.2	4
Stoke Park			
Sliding	'Spiraglide,' 'Deltaglide'	31.9	1
Swinging	Swings, Cradle swings	25.2	2
Climbing	'Moonprobe,' Train, Logs, Frame	18.1	3
Spinning	'Joywheel'	13.9	4
Walking through	Pipes	8.4	5
Standing on	Cylinders	2.6	6
Lion Green			
Sliding	Slide, Wendy house	27.2	1
Pulling tire	Tire-slide	23.8	2
Swinging	Swings, Cradle swings	20.0	3
Rocking	Seesaw, Spring animals	15.4	4
Climbing	'Jungle Gym,' Bars	13.7	5

sarily be between items at the same site. Table 11 shows the comparison of two climbing items at Broadwater Park and two sliding items at Lion Green.

This table illustrates that items with two predominant play modes, i.e., physical and social play, support more play than similar items with only one play mode. (The pairs of items are comparable in terms of size, number of persons who could use them and accessibility.) The Fort is sufficiently popular to overtake "swinging" items, which would normally precede it in popularity terms.

DISCUSSION

In looking at the physical play on equipment, we find that of 29 items studied here 14 had just one activity that characterized what was going on there for at least half the observed time. In other words, children seemed to be constrained in what they were able to do. Referring to the earlier discussion suggesting that a range of play opportunities be provided, it is apparent that many play designs are inadequate in this respect. Despite their limitations however, some of these

Table 11
Comparison of Same Site, Same Action Items
Supporting Different Levels of Social Play

	Climbing Items (Broadwater Park)	Amount of Use	Sliding Items (Lion Green)	Amount of Use
High level of Social Play	Fort	91/345	Tire-slide	113/475
Low level of Social Play	'Jungle Gym'	29/345	Slide	80/475

one-use items are more popular than other multi-use items suggesting that the first principle (that items with greater diversity of physical play should be more popular than those with less) is incorrect or at least inaccurate. Instead, the determining factor here appears to be the opportunity for movement. This is often fast, not controlled by the child (rather by gravity or centrifugal forces) and requires a minimum of effort on the part of the child for considerable effect.

While children are learning less about their own capabilities than they might on other equipment, they are learning how external factors work on their bodies, how to stop or land effectively and how to cope with the adrenalin from the thrill of the experience. The opportunities for advancement may be greater than first realized. It may simply be that the adrenalin "rush" associated with the movement is short-circuiting an arousal mechanism that prompts play.

Not only does the factor of movement cloud the evaluation of the first principle, but also the very small range of physical actions found for items may have been insufficient to show a relationship, should one exist. Further work comparing items with a larger variation in number of actions would shed light on this.

Although the majority of equipment only promotes physical play, a resulting rise in use occurs if social play is also encouraged, e.g., the Fort which is used both as a gathering/lookout point and for climbing, and the Tire-slide which is used for sliding but is also the setting for considerable social interaction and co-operation. These two results do suggest that equipment combining two or more play modes would be more successful than equipment with only one mode (the second principle).

The interaction between the first and second principles and the movement factor needs further investigation. For example, is equipment with a large variety of physical play possibilities more popular than one with opportunities for a variety of play modes but with only a limited range of activities in each?

How does the movement factor interact with the different play modes?

As for physical play and age, the playgrounds seemed underequipped for younger children. There was less equipment that they could comfortably and safely use. Older children used more or less everything. For both age groups there was little or no provision for socializing. While parents were often provided with places to sit and talk, there were no comparable facilities for children.

Although no sex differences were observed for equipment use, it was noticeable that there were more boys attending the sites, an imbalance that raises questions. Are there fewer girls because the playground is less suited to their play demands than to those of boys? Or is the reduced number of girls a result of parental policy and discouragement? These questions await further investigation.

Some interesting points on safety have arisen from the study. One is that some children do find a variety of ways in which to use equipment, which could increase the probability of an accident. The tendency of children to progress from asking, "What can it do?" to "What can I do with it?", called specific and diversive exploration by Hutt (1970), is well known. These exploratory testings by children should be brought to mind when making design decisions. Some of these new non-standard actions will be harmless, while others may endanger both the actor and others, circumstances that would give rise to immediate increased costs from playing.

CONCLUSION

The most popular pieces of equipment are those that either combine a number of higher order play types or offer the opportunity for no-effort movement. This in part vindicates the principle of diversity of opportunity, but the preference for movement not initially postulated needs further theoretical understanding.

References

Bruner, J. S. "Nature and Uses of Immaturity." In J. S. Bruner, A. Jolly and K. Sylva, eds., *Play—Its Role in Development and Evolution*. New York: Penguin Books, 1976.

Ellis, M. J. *Why People Play*. Englewoods Cliffs, NJ: Prentice-Hall, 1973.

Hayward, D. G.; M. Rothenburg and R. R. Beasley. "Children's Play and Urban Playground Environments." *Environment and Behaviour* 6, 2 (1974): 131–68.

Hole, V. *Children's Play on Housing Estates*. London: HMSO, 1966.

Holme, A., and D. Massie. *Children's Play: A Study of Needs and Opportunities*. London: Michael Joseph, 1971.

Hutt, C. "Specific and Diversive Exploration." *Advances in Child Development and Behaviour* 5 (1970): 119–80.

Wolff, P. M. *Exploring the Influence of the Play Environment on the Social Behaviour of Visually Handicapped Children*. Unpublished master's thesis, University of Surrey, Guildford, 1975.

The Effect of Play Structure Format Differences on the Play Behavior of Preschool Children*

LAWRENCE D. BRUYA
Division of Physical Education
North Texas State University, Denton

The variety of structures available for use on playgrounds has provided us with a broad spectrum of options. Traditional structures, usually constructed of metal and cemented securely beneath the surface, are quite different from some contemporary structures. Frequently, contemporary play equipment is constructed primarily of wood but in combination with selected metal fixtures, sometimes securely held in the ground by cement but frequently, partly or entirely, freestanding (Bruya & Buchanan, 1977a; Bruya & Buchanan, 1978; Bruya, 1979a; Shaw, 1976).

Traditional structures differ from freestanding and modular contemporary structures in other ways as well. Traditional metal and contemporary wooden structures are usually placed differently in relationship to other playground equipment. In other words, the relationship between structures, or the format of the playground, differs.

Traditional separated structure formats distribute single-use play events (Beckwith, 1979) in far corners of the playground. Contemporary unified or linked structure formats differ from a separated, more even spacing of plan events on the traditional format playgrounds by incorporating a visually stimulating and complex environment usually in a central area. Such arrangement implies that structures designed for children's use should provide multiple choices through a combination of events in an arousal-raising and complex environment (Bowers, 1979).

Because of the distinct differences in design for traditional and contemporary playgrounds, many educators, park boards and parents are now addressing the problem of selecting an appropriate design format for structures distributed on the playground. As a result, the problem often considered by decision-makers is, "which design format best provides for the developmental needs of our children?" More specifically, the problem of how each of these formats affects the play behavior of children appears to be central to the issue (Beckwith, 1979).

In an attempt to provide some insight into the effect of traditional *vs* contemporary formats on selected play behaviors of children, contemporary and mostly wooden structures were selected for use in the study, primarily because of their free-standing characteristics, thus allowing changes in playground format. Essentially these structures were placed in two configurations reflecting first, the traditional, separated or non-linked format, then the contemporary unified or linked format. During both treatments, a surface of 8 to 10 inches of river-washed pea gravel was maintained under the structures and held in place by a containment wall to provide for the children's safety should falls occur (Besson, 1979).

On and off the structure two behaviors were selected for study, based on pilot studies and observation suggesting that children used differently formated structures in different ways. Motor patterns chosen for use by children during play on differently formated structures were selected for data collection based on an earlier study by Bowers (1975). Teacher contact and contact with peers were also selected for data collection, since pilot studies suggested that contact with teachers and supervisors seemed to increase when equipment was traditionally formated.

METHOD

Subjects

Three age groups were selected for study, a mixed ethnic group of 18 3-year-old, 25 4-

*This study was funded partly through the Research Office at North Texas State University (NTSU's #35718, 35579, 35540).

115

year-old and 15 5-year-old children, randomly selected. These children were from lower middle-income brackets and were members of a day care center and of a preschool matched for similarities in program. All subjects in each age group participated in both treatments with group size differences due to absenteeism from the care facility. Informed consent was obtained from all subjects.

During treatment the regular teachers in attendance were provided a shaded sitting area and asked to encourage the children to re-enter the perimeter of the playground (the ground cover containment barrier) if they happened to wander over for teacher attention. The only time the teachers were asked to interact with the children was when an accident occurred or if fighting and/or crying behavior persisted. It should be noted, however, that due to the age of the subjects and teacher behaviors this interaction was not controlled as closely as the experimenter would have liked.[1]

Apparatus

The structures utilized for this study were especially designed by Simpson of Play Plan Inc. through a round table discussion involving N. Simpson, L. Bruya and H. E. Buchanan. This discussion was necessary at the onset of product development to insure that all structures developed would be compatible with research design. These same structure ideas were later reproduced by Timberform Playground Equipment Company and marketed under the trade name Timbercraft.

The traditional separated structure format included contemporary, independent, free-standing structures placed in a separated or traditional format (see Figure 1). Use of this structure required the child to mount one structure, dismount, traverse the

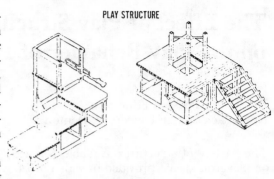

PLAY STRUCTURE

Figure 1. Traditional separated structure format with contemporary wooden structures of the type used in the study.

ground cover surface, remount the next structure, etc.

The contemporary unified or linked structure format included independent freestanding structures placed in a combined or contemporary format. Use of this structure required the child to mount the structure at any one of several entrances, move to another structure without dismounting, etc. (see Figure 2). The complexity of the playground was greater on the contemporary unified or linked structure format than on the traditional separated structure format due to the

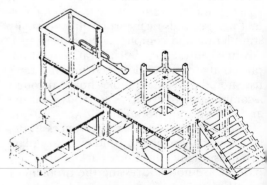

PLAY STRUCTURE

Figure 2. Contemporary unified linked structure format with contemporary wooden structures of the type used in the study.

---

[1]It became evident at the onset of the study that clinging behaviors heretofore had been allowed. This necessitated discussions with the teacher prior to data collection to insure that these children returned immediately to the play area during the treatment session. On two occasions, the experimenter found it necessary to reinitiate the discussion with the teacher during treatment.

unified or linked nature of the contemporary structures.

Procedure

Four play periods (4 periods before data collection on each of the formats and for each of the age groups) were conducted in an attempt to normalize play patterns on the structure, thus decreasing the effect of novelty in the environment. Following this series of non-data collection play periods in which the novelty associated with the equipment was thought to decrease, data collection began in each of the 30-minute play sessions. Four play sessions were conducted for each of the treatments. A total of 240 minutes of play behavior for each age group were observed for the combined traditional and contemporary format structures or 120 minutes each. The order of the presentation was assigned using a table of random numbers with the traditional format applied first.

Four observers were trained prior to data collection using a data collection form designed especially for the study. Reliability between observers was established at the .92 level using the percent agreement method recommended by Langendorfer (1983).

Upon arrival at the playground the subjects were randomly organized in a line to enter the wooden fenced-in playground. Each child was then randomly placed along the containment perimeter at designated intervals, and the same instructions were used for each session.

Instructions: "Today we have one half hour to play on the playground. Who remembers the rules for the playground?
1. Don't throw sand.
2. Don't throw gravel.
3. Don't push.
Is everyone ready? Off you go."

Subjects were assigned a number corresponding to the designated interval along the containment barrier and selected for observation, using a table of random numbers.

To compare the two arrangements of equipment, traditional format *vs* contemporary format, a simple, time-spent-on and time-spent-off the play structure was computed using a 15-second time sampling technique. "On" was defined as "the play structure supported the weight of the child," while "off" was defined as "the force absorption surface under and surrounding the structure(s) supported the weight of the child."

Motor patterns selected for use by children during play were also recorded. Physical contacts between children as well as physical contacts with the adult supervisor were also scored.

RESULTS

Based upon 120 minutes of play on the traditional format and on the contemporary format for each age group, percentage of time spent on and off the structure was computed. On the traditional format structure 3-year-olds spent 48 percent of their time on and 52 percent of their time off. Four-year-olds spent 53 percent on and 47 percent off. The 5-year-old group spent 57 on and 42 percent off. In other words, the time spent on the structure when in a traditional separated structure format increased with age (see Figure 3) and the time spent off the structure decreased with age.

On the contemporary format structure the 3-year-olds spent 54 on and 46 percent off.

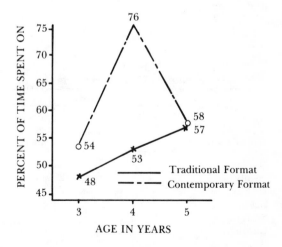

Figure 3. Percent of time spent on the traditional and contemporary format play structures for 3-, 4-, and 5-year-old children.

117

The 4-year-olds spent 76 on and 24 percent off, while the 5-year-olds spent 58 on and 42 percent off. As Figure 3 shows, the time spent on the linked structure did not fit a linear function for the contemporary format structure as it apparently did for the traditional format structure.

Motor patterns selected for use by the child during play on the traditional and/or contemporary format were similar for all age groups. For the traditional format the three patterns selected for use most often by all groups were standing 34 percent, sitting 22 percent, and holding on 22 percent. For all groups the contemporary format produced the same top three patterns selected for use: standing 32 percent, sitting 28 percent, holding on 22 percent. Other less often selected patterns produced similar results (see Table 1).

Physical contact with peers and adult supervisors and teachers was also of interest. Originally physical contact was defined as any intentional touching behavior, which included hand-holding, arms around shoulders and could even have included touching involved in fighting behavior, such as a slug or hit. For the duration of this study, however, no fighting behavior occurred during data collection. Thus, any reported touches were the kind recorded during play or during conversation.

For the traditional format, 3-year-olds were actually in contact with peers 8 percent of the time. For the contemporary format this time increased to 20 percent. Four-year-olds spent 11 percent of their time on the traditional format structure in physical contact with their peers while 5-year-olds spent 16 percent. On the contemporary format structure, 4-year-olds spent 10 percent of their time in contact with peers while 5-year-olds increased drastically to 30 percent (see Table 2). For the group as a whole, across ages— peer physical contact occurred 11 percent of the time for the traditional format and 18 percent of the time for the contemporary format.

When physical contact with the teacher or adult supervisor was considered, the traditional format and the contemporary format accounted for different percentages of time spent touching. Touches with the teacher occurred 2 percent of the time on the traditional structure while occurring .9 percent of the time on the linked structure.

DISCUSSION

For all three age groups (3-4-5 years) an increase in time spent on the structure can be expected to occur when using a contemporary format as compared to a traditional format. Choices and options made available during play through use of the unified or linked format, and repeating and crossing routes of movement on the structure, apparently assisted in the continuance of play behavior on the structure. Probably, a greater time spent off the traditional format structure was due to the fact that more "off" time was required to traverse from one separated structure to the next.

Table 1
Motor Patterns Used During Play

| Motor Pattern[a] | Group | |
	Traditional Format N = 58	Contemporary Format N = 58
Standing	34%	32%
Sitting	22%	28%
Holding on	22%	22%
Leaning	14%	14%
Swinging	12%	14%
Climbing	6%	5%
Running	8%	4%

[a]Only motor patterns used by the children more than 4% of the time are reported here.
Note: Percentages equal more than 100% because two or more patterns sometimes occurred simultaneously.

Table 2
Percent of Time Observed in Intentional Physical Contact with Peers

| Age | Format | |
	Traditional	Contemporary
3 years	$\overline{X} = 8\%$	$\overline{X} = 20\%$
4 years	$\overline{X} = 11\%$	$\overline{X} = 10\%$
5 years	$\overline{X} = 16\%$	$\overline{X} = 30\%$

One indication in the literature (Burke, 1977; Bowers, 1976; Bruya, 1979b) implies that complexity may account for differences in behavior. As greater numbers of play events are combined, the complexity of the structures is said to increase (Bruya & Buchanan, 1977b). This is related to the idea that increases in complexity will increase arousal. Arousal-seeking is said to be a major reason for children's play behavior (Ellis, 1973; Levy, 1978). In other words, as complexity is increased so too is the arousal level or the desire to play. Thus, the fact that play events in combination will increase time spent participating indicates that in the eyes of preschool players, the whole may be greater than the sum of each of the singular events, a supposition that this implies an interactive nature of play events in combination, which in turn increases play behavior in children.

The data depicted in Figure 3, which would imply that contemporary structure use probably peaks out in preschool, implies that a contemporary format is most arousing and increases the time spent on a structure at age four, indicative of a true trend or an artifact of the cross-sectional study. The group of 4-year-olds selected appeared to be particularly rambunctious, a finding which, if characteristic of only this group rather than the general population as a whole, may have skewed results. Robertson, Williams and Langendorfer (1980) might suggest that a true longitudinal study be instigated to determine whether the subject population used for this study or the structure format caused this curvilinear function.

It should also be noted that much of the "off" behavior consisted of chasing-running with frequent but momentary standing when it appeared as if the runner might be trying to locate the "it." Reviewing Figure 3 and the results of motor pattern use records recorded in Table 1 should make it possible to understand this explanation since relatively large percentages of running and standing were recorded.

Generally, there was a lack of differences between the two formats concerning the selection of motor patterns for use during play, a lack that might be attributed to a fairly constant pool of motor patterns from which a child could choose. It is possible that these same children would use approximately the same patterns no matter what the configuration of the equipment. This is supported across populations by Bowers (1975) and seems to be constant across structures in this study.

Results of the physical contact portion of the study would seem to indicate that this variable deserves further consideration. Apparently the contemporary format increases peer contacts while decreasing contact with the adult supervisors. If this finding is supported in future studies, important implications for social behavior may be drawn for the differences between traditional and contemporary formats.

References

Beckwith, J. *Accident Management on Elementary School Playgrounds*. Unpublished manuscript, 1979.
Besson, E. H. "Briefing Memorandum: Public Playground Equipment." In the *U.S. Consumer Product Safety Commission Report*. Washington, DC: Consumer Product Safety Commission, 1979.
Bowers, L. (Project Director). *Play Learning Centers for Pre-school Handicapped Children: Research and Demonstration Project Report*. Tampa, FL: College of Education Professional Physical Education Program, University of South Florida, 1976.
———. *Principles of Design for Playgrounds*. Tampa, FL: University of South Florida, Film-Library-Rental Services, 1979. (Film)
Bruya, L. D. "The Play Environment as an Effector of Mobility and Communication in Deaf-blind Children." In D. M. Compton, M. G. Burrows and P. A. Witt, eds., *Facilitating Play, Recreation, and Leisure Opportunities for Deaf-Blind Children and Youth*. Denton, TX: North Texas State University Press, 1979(a).
———. *Play Environments for the Deaf-Blind Child: Considerations for Mobility and Communication*. Dallas, TX, 1979(b). Fourth in a series of Curriculum Development Programs for Deaf-Blind Children and Youth, South Central Regional Center, 2930 Turtle Creek Plaza, Suite 207, Dallas, TX 75219.
Bruya, L. D., and H. E. Buchanan. *Play or Replay: A Choice for the Future*. Paper presented at the meeting of the Texas Association for Health, Physical Education and Recreation, Dallas, TX, Nov. 1977(a).
———. *An Evaluation of a Play Environment and the Effect*

of *Changing Structural Complexity on the Observed Motor Behavior of Preschool-age Children* (NTSU 35718). Denton, TX: North Texas State University Research Grant, 1977(b).

———. "The Effect of Changing Structural Complexity on the Observed Motor Behavior of Preschool-age Children." In C. B. Corbin, ed., *Symposium Paper: Teaching Behavior and Sport History* (Vol. 1). Washington, DC: American Alliance for Health, Physical Education and Recreation Publications, 1978.

Burke, D. *Behavior-Environment Interactions: A Field Study.* Paper presented at the meeting of the Society for Research and Child Development Biannual Meeting, New Orleans 1977.

Ellis, M. J. *Why People Play.* Englewood Cliffs, NJ: Prentice-Hall, 1973.

Langendorfer, S. Personal communication, 1983.

Levy, J. *Play Behavior.* New York: Wiley, 1979.

Roberton, M. A.; K. Williams and S. Langendorfer. "Prelongitudinal Screening of Motor Development Sequences." *Research Quarterly for Exercise and Sport* 51 (1980): 724–31.

Shaw, L. G. *The Playground: The Child's Creative Learning Space* (HM20743-04A1). Gainesville, FL: The Bureau of Research, College of Architecture, University of Florida, 1976.

Infants' Play on Outdoor Play Equipment

CONNIE STEELE
Department of Home and Family Life
Texas Tech University, Lubbock

and

MARJORIE NAUMAN
Department of Child and Family
Stephen F. Austin University
Nacogdoches, Texas

Infants from four months to 3 years of age practice gross motor skills many hours daily— rolling over, reaching, pulling up, crawling, walking, climbing, jumping, running and kicking, but outdoor play facilities seldom include equipment constructed for use by children under 3 years to exercise gross motor activities (Frost & Klein, 1979). So far, no empirical study has been located that demonstrates responses of infants to specific pieces of outdoor play equipment. Yet infants and toddlers need opportunities to exercise their bodies and explore varied environments, and logically it is the out-of-doors that could expand opportunities for the infant's motoric and cognitive learnings. Lack of research to determine how the children use the equipment (Thompson, 1976) may be directly related to provision of adequate playgrounds. Before provision of infant/toddler playgrounds, then, research should be undertaken to determine what kind of outdoor play equipment could most appropriately be provided for children from 1 to 3 years of age.

The purpose of this exploratory study was to describe the extent to which infants under 3 years of age responded to equipment developmentally designed for children ages 1 to 3 years for their out-of-doors play.

INFANTS' DEVELOPMENTAL NEEDS

It seems reasonable to use infants' emerging motor and cognitive abilities as the basis for appropriately designed equipment for outdoor play. According to Bayley (1969), a child's motor abilities influence interactions with the environment. These motor abilities progress from rolling over at 4 months to "ascending stairs without resorting to all fours" at 2 years (Sinclair, 1973). Piaget and Inhelder (1967) suggested that the child develops concepts about space in a certain sequence beginning with proximity, separation, the relation of spatial succession, enclosure and continuity—in that order (Thompson, 1976). Furthermore, a child's perceptions and cognitions during the sensorimotor period initiate qualitatively different responses to various environments (Piaget, 1954). Qualitative differences in cognition during the first three years of life can be taken into consideration in the design of outdoor environments. Developmental cognitions can be observed in the child's responses regarding: (1) visual pursuit and realization of the permanence of objects; (2) the means for obtaining desired environmental events; (3) vocal and gestural imitations; (4) beginning recognitions of causality; (5) the construction of object relations in space, and (6) development of schemes for relating to objects (Uzgiris & Hunt, 1975).

Body proportions of infants and their size differentiations are crucial factors in encouraging their utilization of any piece of equipment (Montessori, 1912/1964). Detailed charts of body measurements do not include specifications for children under 3

121

years of age—except averages for heights, weights and head circumference (U.S. Department of Health, Education, and Welfare, 1977). Additional measurements of the infants' leg length, arm length, stepping height, and comfortable "crawl-over" height are needed in order to design pieces of playground equipment that will encourage the child's play thereon.

SELECTION OF PLAYGROUND EQUIPMENT FOR INFANTS' PLAY

Since few playgrounds have been described in the literature constructed with the child under 3 years of age as the intended participant, selection of playground equipment specifically designated for infants is not commonly practiced.

To determine what equipment was most frequently used currently by children under 6 years of age, Nauman (Reference Note) combed the literature describing playgrounds for young children (Evans & Saia, 1972; Huntington, 1972; Henniger & Frost, 1976; Hogan, 1974; and Staniford, 1979). She found that some form of sand was most commonly listed as part of the playgrounds described. Slides, as fixtures were the second most frequently mentioned. Other pieces of outdoor play equipment included wooden boxes, climbing structures, water, wheeled vehicles, tunnels, rocking boats and/or horses and walking boards. One source—Evans & Saia, 1972—pertained to *Day Care for Infants* and prescribed sand, water, dirt, building materials, climbing structures, wheeled vehicles, as equipment; and utilizing indoor activities such as art, woodworking, creative movement, dancing, singing and reading in the outdoor playgrounds.

Another factor in selection of designs for infants' play in the out-of-doors is the level of complexity/flexibility of a piece of equipment (Prescot, 1972). Gramza, Corusk, and Ellis (1972) in a study with 3- and 4-year-olds found that all children in the study enjoyed the more complex piece of equipment. The preferred piece for the older children was that which essentially could be used for more than a single function. It was not known if the same concepts of complexity/flexibility should be adapted to the design of outside play equipment for children less than 3 years of age.

Subjects.
Infants and toddlers between the ages of 10 and 35 months who were walking at the time of the first observation participated in the present study. The children were enrolled in a university child development center, where all children were Caucasian from middle- to upper-middle-class families, 13 infants and toddlers in all (7 males; 6 females). Subjects were divided into two age groupings for comparisons of activity; the younger group (mean age = 13.6 months; range from 10 to 20 months) was comprised of six infants (3 males; 3 females); the older group (mean age = 26.5 months; range from 21 to 35 months) included seven infants (4 males; 3 females).

Subjects' Motor Skills.
Since it was assumed that the child's ability to move from one place or piece of equipment or from one person to another would influence the frequencies of involvement with the play equipment, only children who were walking were included in the study. Also, a child's ability to jump forward as differentiated from walking was predicted as influencing the outcomes of the data. Subjects were labelled as belonging to one of two mobility groups: walking but not jumping, and jumping forward with two feet together. Easily observed when compared to a "running" behavior, "jumping forward" is a task accomplished between 20 and 30 months of age (Bayley, 1969). Each child was asked to jump over a line taped to the floor as demonstrated to the child. Hesitant children were encouraged to jump by being commanded, "Jump with me." Each child was given three trials and classified as "jumping forward" if jumping occurred on one of the trials. Eight children were categorized as "walking but not jumping," and five as "jumping with two feet together."

Subjects' Cognitive Abilities.

It was posited that a child's level of cognitive processes would influence his/her preference for specific pieces of equipment as well as the child's level of involvement with selected play items. Prior to the present study, Nauman (Reference Note) tested the administration of the six subscales of the Uzgiris and Hunt scale with three infants—11, 19, and 27 months of age. As Zachry (1978) had also found, three of the subscales resulted in same placement of the infants—i.e., as when all six subscales were used, in either (a) sensorimotor Stage 5 or below, or (b) sensorimotor Stage 6 and above. Therefore, these three subscales were administered to the 13 infants in the present study to determine each child's stage of cognitive development, as it was assumed that the child's concepts about the permanence of objects, causality and space would predict the child's utilization of the selected pieces of outdoor play equipment: Scale I—Visual Pursuit and the Permanence of Objects; Scale II—Development of Means for Obtaining Desired Environmental Events; and Scale V—Construction of Object Relations in Space. The results showed six children below Stage 6 but having attained Stage 4, and seven children at or above Stage 6 on the three scales.

PROCEDURES TO DEVELOP OUTDOOR PLAY EQUIPMENT FOR INFANTS

Infants' Measurements

As the basis for the design of outdoor play equipment proportional to the sizes and bodies of infants and toddlers, measurements of height, head circumference, leg length, arm length, stepping height, and height for crawling-over were taken from 15 infants, ranging from two and one half years to 35 months of age (Nauman, Reference note).

Selected Designs

To design outdoor play equipment that would elicit optimal responses from children aged 10 to 35 months, attention was focused on sensorial, kinesthetic and spatial understandings. Sandboxes were considered appropriate for sensorial development. Slides afforded the potential for learning about gravity and kinesthetic involvement. Cubes were predicted as providing learning about enclosure in space. To consider the variable concerning simple *vs* complex design that Gramza et al. (1972) and Prescot (1972) had questioned regarding playground equipment, two forms of each type of equipment were introduced to the infants in the present study. To control for color, all equipment pieces were painted green.

Sand

Sources suggested use of sand in large areas (O'Brien, 1979; Evans & Saia, 1972) or in small areas (Honig & Lally, 1977; Hogan, 1974), but no research supported either form as more appropriate than the other for a child this age. Therefore, two forms of sand were used: 50 square feet of sand surface in a 6' × 8' sandbox, and 2 square feet of sand surface contained in a tire.

Slides

Two forms of slides to elicit kinesthetic and spatial development were designed, one constructed with steps to the slide, a railing on a platform and the slide. The other provided a more complex unit for play, as it included a tunnel, steps and the slide.

Cubes

Gramza (1970) in his study of children's play in enterable cubes, found that children showed considerable interest in encapsulation as they explored varied spatial relationships. Therefore, two types of cubes were constructed; one cube was open, having only two solid, vertical sides with no overhead topside; the other cube form provided almost total encapsulation, having three solid sides, the fourth side with a round, child-sized opening, and the topside with a round, child-sized opening.

Neutral logs

To determine if infants and toddlers need specially designed pieces of equipment or if they would simply use anything placed on the playground, two cardboard boxes (10"

123

$\times$ 12" $\times$ 18") painted green and taped shut were also provided for outdoor play.

MEASUREMENT OF INFANTS' PLAY ON SELECTED PIECES OF OUTDOOR EQUIPMENT

The following levels of responses to the selected pieces of outdoor play equipment were theorized as possible by infants from 10 to 35 months of age:

(a) No attention to equipment —i.e., no physical contact with or attention to the piece of equipment

(b) Inactive play —i.e., contact with the piece but no attention—e.g., sitting on or in the piece of equipment

(c) Showing attention to equipment —i.e., attention to but no physical contact with piece; watching others on piece; moving toward piece, eyes focused on it

(d) Active play —i.e., attention to and physical contact with piece or a portion of any piece of equipment.

During a pilot study four observers, not aware of the purpose of the study, were trained to 100 percent agreement in observing responses of seven children (aged 8 and a half to 28 months of age) to the four selected pieces of equipment.

The four trained observers completed two sets of observations of each of the 13 children. Since a child this age may be drawn to or repelled from toys because of the presence of other children (Mueller & Rich, 1976), conditions were observed when the child was alone with the equipment and when the child was with three other children. For each observation, university students not involved in the study selected pieces so that one of the two forms of each type of equipment appeared in every playground. Since each sandbox was stationary within a separate 15' $\times$ 20' plot, the students chose one of the sand arrangements for each observation and then randomly placed the other four pieces— one of the slides, one of the cubes, and both of the logs (one in a horizontal position, the other vertical) in any configuration around or adjacent to the sandbox. Selection oc-

curred so that each piece of equipment appeared three times across the "alone" and "group" observations for each child. For each of the observations, a child's behaviors were noted on score sheets for six 5-minute time periods. Each 5-minute period contained 10 time samples; each child was observed for 3 seconds alternating with 12 seconds for recording the child's behaviors—noting the piece or pieces of equipment used and the level of response by the child observed. Frequencies of all categories of play and instances of active play with the pieces of equipment were summed across the three observations for "alone" play for each child as well as across the three observations for "group" play for each child. Means for the younger/older children mobility groupings and cognitively grouped children are listed in Tables A and B.

RESULTS

To test for differences in frequency of infants' play with outdoor equipment as a function of the independent variables of motor ability, age or cognitive level, the dependent variable—scores of the frequency of play with each piece of outdoor playground equipment—was analyzed by use of the Mann-Whitney U statistic. No significant difference was noted as a function of motor ability. Members of the groups of children dichotomized by age and cognitive ability were the same children; therefore, results considering the independent variables of age and cognitive level are the same.

While in the "alone" condition, the older group and more cognitively able children played significantly more often with the small sandbox ($U = 62.5$; $p < .01$), with the closed cube ($U = 58.0$; $p < .05$), and with the neutral horizontal log ($U = 59.0$; $p < .05$) than did the younger children. In the group situations, there were no differences in play frequencies between the groups with any of the forms of play equipment—except that older, Stage 6 or above cognitive ability children, utilized the slide with tunnel significantly more often ($U = 57.5$; $p < .05$) than did the less cognitively able, younger children.

To determine whether or not children's

Table A
Differences in Play According to Infants' Age and Cognitive Level

	ALONE PLAY			GROUP PLAY		
	10 to 20 months	21 to 35 months	Mann Whitney "U"	10 to 20 months	21 to 35 months	Mann Whitney "U"
	Mean	Mean		Mean	Mean	
Large sandbox	.379	.371	50.5	.245	.346	52
Small sandbox	.184	.492	62.5***	.079	.210	56
Closed cube	.058	.157	58*	.066	.078	55.5
Open cube	.362	.07	38.5	.262	.092	38
Simple slide	.175	.257	49.5	.225	.3	52
Slide w/tunnel	.416	.225	41.5	.108	.264	57.5*
Horizontal log	.014	.115	59.0*	0	0	---
Vertical log	0	.003	.06	0	0	---

*$p < .01$
***$p < .05$

Table B
Differences in Play According to Infants' Mobility Level

	ALONE PLAY			GROUP PLAY		
	10 to 20 months	21 to 35 months	Mann Whitney "U"	10 to 20 months	21 to 35 months	Mann Whitney "U"
	Mean	Mean		Mean	Mean	
Large sandbox	.337	.435	38	.409	.56	40
Small sandbox	.246	.25	46.5	.284	.165	31
Closed cube	.068	.18	44	.08	.105	41
Open cube	.303	.05	23	.262	.19	34
Simple slide	.209	.235	33	.39	.275	30
Slide w/tunnel	.383	.13	25.5	.362	.235	32.5
Horizontal log	.028	.06	41	0	0	---
Vertical log	0	.003	1.4	0	0	---

play responses to one piece of equipment were related to another, Pearson product-moment correlations were calculated. No significant correlations were found between any of the play equipment pieces—even those considered to be a pair of forms for the same type of play equipment.

DISCUSSION

The present study was an attempt to describe the extent to which infants under three years responded actively to pieces of equipment designed specifically for their outdoor play. Since the data revealed no differences in children's frequency of play with the equipment dependent on motor abilities, the study appears to demonstrate that once children acquire the skill of walking, they become involved with the pieces of equipment at the same activity level as older, more motor-capable infants and toddlers. Admittedly, the scoring of the study did not assess levels of competence with each piece of equipment but only activity level. However, since both physical ability groups of children used the pieces frequently, it is evident that by constructing the equipment based on physical measurements of body and size for the age range observed, the pieces were appropriate for evoking responses from both motor-ability groups.

Cognitive ability and age appear to make a difference, as frequency of use by the older children of the small sandbox, the closed cube and the neutral horizontal log is significantly greater. The fact that both younger and older children played frequently with the larger sandbox in both the "alone" and the "group" situations would encourage persons providing infant playgrounds to construct the larger sandbox for children from 10 to 35 months. The "tire" sandbox becomes an interesting place for play when the child approaches 2 years.

The closed cube providing encapsulation was a feature more often attracting the older and more cognitively advanced subjects, a similar conclusion to that reached by Gramza (1970) in his study of 4-year-olds. The younger, less cognitively advanced children when playing alone almost universally avoided the closed cube in favor of play with other types of equipment. Their response may have been due to the fact that it was rather dark inside the cube and, once inside, there was only one opening from which the smaller children could look out, since they were not tall enough to look out the ceiling opening. It appears from the results that the older, Stage 6 and above, children may have been drawn to this piece because of these same challenging qualities. Therefore, it is recommended that some form of encapsulation be provided for older, Stage 6 and above cognitive ability children but such equipment should be avoided on playgrounds for below Stage 6 infants.

Children of the older age and higher cognitive ability level seemed to be attracted to play with the neutral horizontal log. Frequency counts of the raw data showed that the significantly greater use of the neutral horizontal log by the older children was indicated principally by inactive play—not by active play—resulting in no significant difference between younger and older children when differences in active play were analyzed. (See Tables A & B.) Of particular note is the fact that neither younger nor older, neither walking nor jumping, nor more cognitively able children used the neutral vertical log. Such an item is not an attractive object for a child this age.

The slide with the tunnel was used more frequently by Stage 6 and above children than by younger children. As shown by Gramza, Corusk and Ellis (1972), the complexity of this piece may have attracted the older, Stage 6 and above, children when other children were present. The fact that this piece of equipment could accommodate several children doing different activities at the same time may have contributed to its greater frequency of use in group situations by the older children.

While younger, less cognitively advanced children did not show significantly more use of any of the pieces of equipment than the older, Stage 6 and above children, the younger group utilized all the pieces of play equipment, although the closed cube was minimally used especially when the children were "alone" on the playground. Equipment most used by the younger children in the "alone" condition in order of preference were: the slide with the tunnel, the large sandbox, the open cube, the small sandbox, simple slide and, occasionally, the closed cube. The younger children in the "group" condition used all pieces of equipment in descending frequencies as follows: open cube, large sandbox, simple slide, slide with tunnel and, minimally, small sandbox and closed cube.

For both "alone" and "group" conditions, the younger child was most attracted to the large sandbox and the open cube. The slide with tunnel may have been especially attractive to the very young child when older children were not around and the item could be freely explored. Additional research is needed to clarify this preference.

Differences in frequencies of active play due to age may have been affected by children's past experiences (or lack of experience) with slides, steps, cubes, tunnels and tires used in designing the pieces of equipment. While younger children did not play with the pieces as much as the older ones, they did attend to them and thus became familiar with elements they may not have encountered previously.

Future designs for infant/toddler playgrounds should consider such findings as:

a) Infants from 10 to 20 months more frequently engage in active play in outdoor playgrounds with a large sandbox, an open cube without cover and a simple slide than with restricted play sites such as a "tire" sandbox, enclosed cubes or space in a tunnel.

b) Small sand areas elicit a high degree of active play by older toddlers—especially when alone in the play area—no matter what other types of equipment are available.

c) Encapsulation is a quality of play equipment that attracts toddler play when children are alone. Care should be taken in designing any enterable space for infants as it appears to be something that the very young tend to avoid.

d) Complexity and flexibility should be considered in designing playground equipment for toddlers, as evidenced by their frequent use of the slide with tunnel that allowed several children to use it simultaneously and permitted its use in a variety of ways.

Reference Note

Nauman, M. M. "Exploratory Study of Infant/Toddler Involvement with Selected Outdoor Equipment." Unpublished thesis, Texas Tech University, Lubbock, Texas, 1981.

References

Bayley, N. *Bayley Scales of Infant Development*. New York: The Psychological Corporation, 1969.

Evans, B., and G. Saia. *Day Care for Infants*. Boston: Beacon Press, 1972.

Frost, J. L., and B. L. Klein. *Children's Play and Playgrounds*. Boston: Allyn and Bacon, 1979.

Gramza, A. F. "Preferences of Preschool Children for Enterable Play Boxes." *Perceptual and Motor Skills* 31 (1970): 177–78.

Gramza, A. F.; J. Corusk and M. J. Ellis. "Children's Play on Trestles Differing in Complexity: A Study of Play Equipment Design." *Journal of Leisure Research* 4 (1972): 303–11.

Henniger, M. L., and J. Frost. "An Infant Group." In M. D. Cohen, ed., *Selecting Educational Equipment and Materials for School and Home*. Wheaton, MD: Association for Childhood Education International, 1976.

Hogan, P. *Playgrounds for Free*. Cambridge, MA: MIT Press, 1974.

Honig, A., and R. Lally. *Infant Caregiving: A Design for Training*. New York: Open Family Press, 1972.

Huntington, D. "Play of Young Children." *Young Children* 21 (1972): 33–36.

Montessori, M. *The Montessori Method*. (A. E. George, trans.) New York: Schocken, 1964. (Originally published, 1912.)

Mueller, E., and A. Rich. "Clustering and Socially-directed Behaviors in a Playgroup of One-year-old Boys." *Journal of Child Psychology and Psychiatry* 17 (1976): 315–22.

Piaget, J. *The Construction of Reality in the Child*. New York: Basic Books, 1954.

Piaget, J., and B. Inhelder. *The Child's Conception of Space*. New York: Norton, 1967.

Prescot, E. *Day Care as a Child Rearing Environment*. Washington, DC: National Association for the Education of Young Childen, 1972.

Sinclair, C. B. *Movement of the Young Child*. Columbus, OH: Merrill, 1973.

Staniford, D. J. "Natural Movement for Children." *Leisure Today* (October 1979): 14–17.

Thompson, D. "Space Utilization: Criteria for the Selecton of Playground Equipment for Children." *Research Quarterly* 47, 3 (1976): 472–83.

U.S. Department of Health, Education, and Welfare. National Health Survey. *NCHS Growth Curves for Children: Birth-18 years, United States*. Hyattsville, MD: National Center for Health Statistics, November 1977, r.

Uzgiris, I. C., and J. M. Hunt. *Assessment in Infancy: Ordinal Scales of Psychological Development*. Urbana, IL: University of Illinois Press, 1975.

Zachry, W. "Ordinality and Interdependence of Representational and Language Development in Infancy." *Child Development* 49 (1978): 681–87.

Toddler Play Behaviors and Equipment Choices in an Outdoor Playground

SUZANNE M. WINTER
Division of Education
The University of Texas at San Antonio

With mothers of young children joining the labor forces in rapidly escalating numbers (American Families and Living Arrangements, 1980), this country is experiencing an increase in the enrollment of young children in child care centers. To equip these centers with rich play environments, equipment preferences and play behaviors of young children need to be determined. Although progress has been made toward this goal, previous studies have tended to focus upon the play of children in two age spans: infancy and the preschool years. Comparatively little data have been collected that would contribute to a better understanding of the play of toddlers. The few studies including toddler subjects have used indoor settings for examination of toddler play behaviors.

The purpose of this investigation was to develop and use a comprehensive instrument for recording the social and cognitive play behaviors and the equipment choices of toddlers in an outdoor playground environment. The following questions initiated and guided the study:

1. What types of social and cognitive play behaviors are exhibited by toddlers in an outdoor playground environment? Are the play behaviors of toddlers influenced by their gender?

2. When a selection of stationary equipment and loose parts have been provided, which items will be chosen most frequently by toddlers? Are these equipment choices related to gender?

3. What percentage of the social and cognitive play behaviors sampled are associated with each item of play equipment used by the toddlers?

REVIEW OF THE LITERATURE

Parten (1932) and a number of subsequent studies found evidence that involvement in higher levels of social play increases with the age of the child (Iwanaga, 1973; Sponseller and Lowry, 1974; Bronson, 1975; Rubin, Watson and Jambor, 1978; Sponseller and Jaworski, 1979). Other studies have prompted the question of whether age actually does play a role in the social play behaviors exhibited by children (Mueller and Lucas, 1975; Smith, 1978; Bakeman and Brownlee, 1980). A study by Howes (1980) suggests another variable to be considered as a possible influence upon the social play forms manifested by toddlers: toddlers who had more experience with their peers were able to attain higher levels of social play than their less experienced counterparts.

Research of the cognitive play of children has generally supported Piaget's (1962) theory that the cognitive complexity of children's play is age related. Piaget theorized that "practice" play, which involves repetitive motor actions and the simple manipulation of objects precedes the more complex "symbolic" games. Subsequent studies of cognitive play have agreed that this pattern is evident in the play of young children (McCall, 1974; Fenson, Kagann, Kearsley and Zelazo, 1976; Largo and Howard, 1979; Shimada, Sano and Peng, 1979; Ungerer, Zelazo, Kearsley and Kurowski, 1979). Controversy has surrounded the category Piaget (1962) called "games with rules," which he considered to be the most complex cognitive play form in which children's games were governed by established rules. Contrary to Piaget's sequence of play development, researchers have reported that game-type interactions occur during the play of infants

Figure 1. Map of Playground.

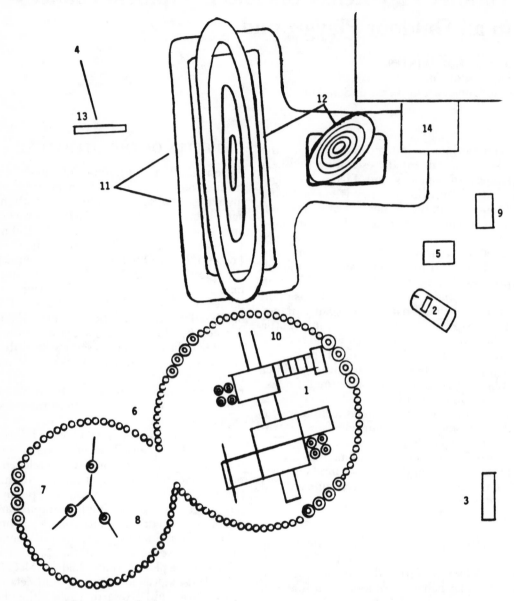

Numbers correspond to those used in Figure 2.

and toddler peers (Vincze, 1971; Sponseller and Lowry, 1974; Eckerman and Whatley, 1977; Goldman and Ross, 1978; Bronson, 1981; Mueller and Brenner, 1977). In contrast to Piaget's category definition, the rules for the infant and toddler games were ob-

served to arise spontaneously. Furthermore, these rules were found to be implicitly understood by the toddlers and only temporary in nature, findings that suggest Piaget's sequence of cognitive play development may be incomplete. The research seems to indicate a need for a category to capture the rule-governed games of infants and toddlers, which are less complex than those of older children.

The choices of play materials made by young children have been the focus of some research studies. Children as young as 9½ months have been found to indicate preferences for certain play items over others (Kearsley and Zelazo, 1979). Several studies have suggested that associations may exist between the equipment choices and the gender of the child (Benjamin, 1932; Fein, Johnson, Kosson, Stork and Wasserman, 1975; Kearsley and Zelazo, 1979). Furthermore, studies by DeStefano (1976) and Eckerman and Whatley (1977) have indicated that certain play materials seem to elicit more social interaction among infants and toddlers.

Amount of equipment available may also have an effect upon the social play of toddlers. There is evidence that children engage in more social interactions (Ramey, Finkelstein and O'Brien, 1976), which are sustained for longer periods when no play materials have been provided (Vandell, Wilson and Buchanan, 1980). In contrast, other studies have reported that the presence of play objects facilitates social interactions among infants and toddlers (Mueller and Lucas, 1975; Eckerman, Whatley and Kutz, 1975; Mueller and Brenner, 1977).

The nature of the social and cognitive play of toddlers and the effects of the equipment provided in their play environments are still obscure.

METHOD

Setting

The playground of the Hyde Park Baptist School in Austin, Texas, was chosen as the site for the study. The focal point of this creative playground was a superstructure incorporating a variety of climbing and sliding equipment. Figure 1 shows a diagram of the playground environment. Figures 2 and 3 provide a listing of the stationary equipment and loose parts to support the playground activities.

Procedures

This research study was undertaken in 5 phases:

Phase I—Collection of Anecdotal Data. Eleven male and 9 female subjects aged 24 to 34 months (mean = 30 months) were systematically observed by the investigator over a 3-month period. The investigator manually recorded an anecdotal description of the social and cognitive play behaviors and the

Figure 2. Stationary Equipment List.

1. Superstructure
   a. Barrel
   b. Bars, assorted
   c. Bars, horizontal
   d. Bars, parallel
   e. Clatter bridge
   f. Climber, 4-tire
   g. Climber, 5-tire
   h. Pole, vertical
   i. Slide, wide
   j. Slide, barrel
   k. Steering wheel

2. Automobile

3. Bench
4. Climber, V-shaped
5. Playhouse
6. Post enclosure
7. Swing, sling
8. Swing, tire
9. Table, picnic

Other Playground features:
10. Sand pit
11. Wheeled vehicle track
12. Grassy mounds
13. Grassy area, flat
14. Storage and bathroom facility

Definition:

Stationary Equipment—This term refers to play apparatus that is in a fixed position on the playground. However, moveable parts may be attached to the stationary apparatus as in the case of a swing assembly. This term may also refer to play apparatus which is too heavy to be transported about the playground by toddlers (e.g., picnic table, V-shaped climber).

131

Figure 3. Loose Parts List.

1 Balance Beam, portable	1 Hoppity Horse
2 Balls, 6″ & 9″ diameters	1 Ladle
1 Barrel, tire	4 Muffin Tins
1 Bathtub, infant	1 Potato masher
1 Broom	3 Pots, cooking
4 Cable spools, 33″ diameter	Sand
4 Cable spools, 30″ diameter	3 Scoops
4 Collanders	2 Sifters
12 Containers:	1 Spoon, large
3 half gallon	1 Tea Set
3 margarine dishes	1 Telephone, wooden
3 drinking cups	1 Tire, automobile
1 square cup	10 Tricycles
2 aluminum cups	2 Trucks:
6 Crates, plastic	1 wooden
1 Doll	1 metal
3 Funnels	1 Wagon

Definition:

Loose Parts—This term refers to any portable toy or apparatus which has been placed on the playground for use in supporting the play activities of children. These pieces of equipment are not affixed to the playground. Therefore, they are able to be transported freely by individual children or groups of children.

equipment choices of each child during a 60-second interval. Ten observations were recorded for each child.

Phase II—Designing the Instrument. The investigator located and examined the existing cognitive and social play scales. During analysis of these instruments, the researcher categorized the anecdotal descriptions of play behaviors collected in Phase I, an analysis revealing that some cognitive categories described play forms too advanced for use in analyzing the play of toddlers. For example, the toddlers in this study did not engage in Piaget's (1962) category, "games with rules" inherited from previous generations, but did engage in game-type interactions in which mutually understood rules arose spontaneously and were temporary in nature. In addition, the investigator found that play involving vestibular stimulation (e.g., swinging, sliding) was not captured by existing cognitive categories.

Following an examination of existing social play instruments, the investigator determined that the following variable should be addressed in the instrument for this study:

1) the type of communication among children, 2) the distance of the subject from other children and 3) the direction of a child in relation to others.

The investigator's aim was to devise social and cognitive play categories more specifically defined than existing systems. The intent was to provide a vehicle by which one might obtain a more accurate description of the play of toddlers than previous scales have afforded. The completed instrument is shown in Figure 4. Figure 5 represents an abbreviated version of the categories that were developed.

Phase III—Pilot Study. To evaluate the effectiveness of the instrument, a 3-day pilot study was conducted in which the investigator observed 9 male and 11 female subjects from 25 to 35 months (mean = 27 months). Each subject was observed during a 30-second interval until a total of 90 seconds of play per child was recorded. As a result of the pilot study, the time-sampling interval was judged to be adequate for data collection.

Phase IV—Final Study. Attempts were made

Figure 4. Inventory of Toddler Play and Play Equipment.

Child: _____   Date: _____   Coder: _____

SOCIAL	EQUIPMENT	LOOSE PARTS	
__ Independent	__ Automobile	__ Balance Beam	__ Spoon, large
__ Proximal	__ Barrel, superstr.	__ Ball	__ Tea Set
__ Relational	__ Bars, assorted	__ Barrell, 3-tire	__ Telephone
__ Interactive	__ Bars, horizontal	__ Bathtub, infant	__ Tire
	__ Bars, parallel	__ Broom	__ Tricycle
COGNITIVE	__ Bench	__ Cable Spool, large	__ Truck
__ Repetition	__ Clatter Bridge	__ Cable Spool, small	__ Wagon
__ Combination	__ Climber, 4-tire	__ Collander	__ Other (specify)
__ Constructive	__ Climber, 5-tire	__ Containers, assorted	
__ Conversion	__ Climber, V-shaper	__ Crates, plastic	
__ Animation	__ Playhouse	__ Doll	COMMENTS:
__ Role-play	__ Pole, vertical	__ Funnel	
__ Spontaneous Games	__ Post enclosure	__ Hoppity Horse	
	__ Slide	__ Ladle	
__ NONPLAY	__ Slide, barrel	__ Muffin Tin	
	__ Steering Wheel	__ Potato Masher	
	__ Swing, sling	__ Pots, cooking	
	__ Swing, tire	__ Sand	
	__ Table, picnic	__ Scoop	
	__ Other (specify)	__ Sifter	

Figure 5. Inventory of Toddler Play and Play Equipment (abbreviated category definitions).

SOCIAL PLAY

Independent—The child plays alone at a distance from others or facing away from others.

Proximal—The child chooses to play near others although he continues to play in his own way. The child does not communicate with other children.

Relational—The child plays as he sees fit without involving others. However, he does communicate with other children using verbal or nonverbal modes of communication.

Interactive—A child plays with one or more peers in a common activity. Conversation is relevant to the activity.

COGNITIVE PLAY

Repetition—The child performs motor actions at least twice in succession. The child's repetitive actions may be an effort to sustain an activity which provides vestibular stimulation.

Combination—The child performs two or more motor movements in an identifiable pattern. This category also refers to vestibular stimulation activities in which the child is actively engaged (e.g., pumping legs to swing). The child may also place two or more objects into spatial relationships. The child may choose to place himself into a spatial relationship with other objects.

Constructive—This form represents goal-oriented play in which the child tests hypotheses or creates end products.

Conversion—The child uses a concrete object to symbolize another absent object. The child may use gestures to indicate that an object is being symbolized rather than a concrete object.

Animation—The child pretends that an inanimate object is alive (e.g., a child growls for a toy lion) or operational (e.g., a child moves a toy truck).

Role-play—The child portrays the role of a real or imaginary character.

Spontaneous Games—The child engages in playful interactions with another peer. These interactions are governed by mutually understood rules which arise spontaneously and are temporary in nature. The children alternate turns in performing actions and may reverse roles during the game.

133

to exert some control over the loose parts available for play and over the behaviors of the teachers. Two coders, unfamiliar with the research of children's play, observed the play of 7 male and 5 female subjects, ranging in age from 25 to 34 months (mean = 29 months). Thirty-five children not involved in the study were present on the play environment along with the 12 subjects. At the beginning and end of the study, the coders established 80 percent agreement in their choices of social and cognitive play categories for two sets of 10 observations each. Data collection for the final study involved each coder's working independently using an alphabetized list of the subjects. Each coder began with a different name to avoid simultaneous observations of a child. A prerecorded audiotape was used to insure the uniformity of the 30-second intervals of the time-sampling sequence. Each subject was observed 40 times for a total of 20 minutes of play time recorded for each child over a 13-day period.

Phase V—Analysis of Data. An analysis of the data was performed using the Statistical Analysis System (SAS) statistical computer package. Frequency counts for each form of play and the various pieces of equipment

were calculated. Cross-tabulations were computed for: 1) the association of the child's gender with each form of play, 2) the association of the child's gender with particular pieces of equipment and play materials, and 3) the association of forms of play with particular pieces of equipment.

RESULTS

The most frequently occurring form of social play was found to be the proximal type at 60.9 percent. The relational and independent categories followed at 18.9 and 17.2 percent respectively. The interactive form accounted for the smallest portion of the play of the subjects at 3.0 percent. Table 1 summarizes the frequencies and percentages of social play forms associated with gender.

The most common form of cognitive play was the combination category, accounting for more than half of all the cognitive play behaviors sampled (53.2 percent). The repetition category ranked second in prevalence at 36.3 percent. The remaining categories showed considerably lower percentages: constructive (3.5 percent), spontaneous games (3.0 percent), conversion (2.2 percent), animation (1.5 percent), and role-play (.3 percent).

Table 1
Social Play Associated with Gender

Category	Male	Female	Row Total
Independent	45	24	
	65.2%	34.8%	69
	19.7%	13.9%	100%
Proximal	138	107	
	56.3%	43.7%	245
	60.3%	61.8%	100%
Relational	43	33	
	56.6%	43.4%	76
	18.8%	19.1%	100%
Interactive	3	9	
	25.0%	75.0%	12
	1.3%	5.2%	100%
COLUMN TOTAL	229	173	402
	57.0%	43.0%	100%

N = 402 play behaviors coded
For each cell: frequency = number of play behaviors coded
        row % = percentage of the total number of play behaviors coded within the category which could be attributed to each gender
        column % = percentage of the total play behaviors which were coded in each play category by gender

An examination of the cognitive play of each gender revealed that the most prevalent form for both boys and girls was combination with the repetition form ranking second. Table 2 summarizes the frequencies and percentages of cognitive play categories associated with gender.

An analysis of the association of the social and cognitive play categories with the pieces of equipment revealed a predictable relationship. The most prevalent forms, proximal and combination, were also most frequently associated with the items of equipment chosen by the toddlers.

Equipment choices recorded for the toddlers indicated that the loose parts were preferred over the stationary equipment. Sand was the most popular play material as indicated by its use in 22.0 percent of the observations involving a play item. The tricycle and the assorted containers followed at 7.9 and 7.7 percent respectively.

The highest frequency for stationary equipment was for the category termed "other" at 4.4 percent. This finding can largely be explained by the fact that the platforms of the superstructure connecting the various pieces of equipment were not listed as separate items on the instrument. The post enclosure and the swing assembly were used by the toddlers in 3.5 percent of the observations. The wide slide followed in popularity at 3.0 percent usage. Table 3 represents the preferences of toddlers by gender and as a group for items used 10 times or more.

DISCUSSION

The social play findings of this study agree with those of Parten (1932). Each social play

Table 2
Cognitive Play Associated with Gender

Category	Male	Female	Row Total
Repetition	90	56	146
	61.6%	38.4%	100%
	39.3%	32.4%	
Combination	120	94	214
	56.1%	43.9%	100%
	52.4%	54.3%	
Constructive	7	7	14
	50.0%	50.0%	100%
	3.1%	4.1%	
Conversion	1	8	9
	11.1%	88.9%	100%
	.4%	4.6%	
Animation	5	1	6
	83.3%	16.7%	100%
	2.2%	.6%	
Role Play	1	0	1
	100.0%	0.0%	100%
	.4%	0.0%	
Spontaneous Games	5	7	12
	41.7%	58.3%	100%
	2.1%	4.0%	
COLUMN TOTAL	229	173	402
	57.0%	43.0%	100%

N = 402 play behaviors coded
For each cell: frequency = number of play behaviors coded
              row % = percentage of the total number of play behaviors coded within the category which could be attributed to each gender
              column % = percentage of the total play behaviors for each gender which were coded in each play category

135

Table 3
Usage of Preferred Equipment by Gender

Equipment	Male		Female		Both	
	N	%	N	%	N	%
Stationary						
Automobile	10	41.7	14	58.3	24	3.6
Posts	10	43.5	13	56.5	23	3.5
Slide, wide	16	80.0	4	20.0	20	3.0
Playhouse	8	61.5	5	38.5	13	2.0
Swing, sling	4	40.0	6	60.0	10	1.5
Loose Parts						
Sand	65	44.8	80	55.2	145	22.0
Tricycle	41	78.8	11	21.2	52	7.9
Containers	12	23.5	39	76.5	51	7.7
Tea Set	12	30.0	28	70.0	40	6.1
Scoop	13	47.4	15	52.6	28	4.2
Funnel	7	33.3	14	66.7	21	3.2
Cooking pots	8	40.0	12	60.0	20	3.0
Wagon	12	92.3	1	7.7	13	1.9
Crates	7	53.8	6	46.2	13	2.0
Muffin Tin	4	33.3	8	66.7	12	1.8
Broom	9	90.0	1	10.0	10	1.5

preferred equipment = items used 10 or more times

male/female

$$\% = \frac{\text{N for male or female}}{\text{N for both}}$$

Both

$$\% = \frac{\text{N for both}}{\text{Total N}}$$

Total N = number of times that any piece of equipment was used during play (660)

category captured a portion of the play behaviors engaged in by the toddlers, but the majority of those play behaviors were concentrated at the low end of the scale. More than half of the social play was categorized in the proximal category alone. Furthermore, the lowest percentage of the play behaviors was categorized in the interactive category representing the most complex form. The findings of this study do offer evidence that at age 2 years, children are more actively involved in the less complex forms of social play.

In addition to age, other variables may have influenced the social play outcomes of this study, such as the fact that 35 other children rather unfamiliar to the 12 subjects were also playing on the playground during the data collection period. The Bronson (1975) study suggested that unfamiliarity of children may have an inhibiting effect upon their social interactions, a factor that may account for the low incidence of interactive play recorded for the toddlers.

Another influence that may have affected toddlers' social play behaviors was the large number of small toys accessible to them. In a similar situation, DeStefano (1976) found that social interactions among children were discouraged.

The cognitive play findings of this study lend some support to Piaget's theories concerning this type of play. The two lowest categories, combination and repetition, accounted for a clear majority of all the cognitive play engaged in by the toddlers (89.5 percent). A low incidence of the symbolic play forms is also consistent with Piaget (1962) but the low incidence of the symbolic play categories may have been related to the small number of pretend play props available to the children. A number of studies have suggested that the presence of toys closely resembling real objects is very important in fostering symbolic play in young children (Piaget, 1962; Fein, 1975; Fein, 1979; Golomb, 1979; Jackowitz and Watson, 1980).

An interesting finding was that the toddler's play was almost as likely to be a spontaneous game (3.0 percent) as a symbolic form when the conversion, animation and role-play categories were collapsed (3.9 percent total). Perhaps the game play of toddlers requires a level of cognition similar to the level needed for pretend play participation.

An examination of the cognitive play of the toddlers by gender revealed more similarities than differences. The few differences discovered occurred in the less frequently performed symbolic play categories. Similarly, few differences were found in the social play of male and female toddlers. However, there was some evidence suggesting that the females may be slightly more social in their play when compared to the males.

Analysis of the data on equipment choices revealed that the toddlers preferred the loose parts over the stationary equipment. The abundance and the accessibility of the loose parts may partly account for their frequent use. The versatility of these items may also have contributed to their popularity, a reasonable explanation if one considers the virtually infinite number of possible ways to play with sand, the most popular play material.

Gender may be another factor that influenced equipment choices. In this study, males and females were found to differ in their preferences for both stationary and loose items. A clear pattern was evident in the choice of loose parts. Boys were found to prefer items involving active gross motor participation (e.g., tricycle, wagon, balance beam). In contrast, items most popular with the girls were those requiring fine motor manipulation and more sedentary activity (e.g., sand, tea set, cooking pots).

This study found that the toddlers engaged the majority of the time, in the less complex play forms but occasions were recorded in which they engaged in more advanced play. Furthermore, the data indicated that the toddlers did have equipment preferences influenced by gender.

IMPLICATIONS

The results of this study indicate that the Inventory of Toddler Play and Play Equipment, which proved to be a highly reliable method of collecting data, would be a feasible instrument to be used by practitioners in the field of child care. The instrument was used successfully by paraprofessionals following only a brief training period.

The fact that the categories of the instrument are more specifically defined than those of previous systems leads us to yet another conclusion, that this inventory would enable researchers to scrutinize the play of toddlers even more thoroughly than existing instruments have allowed.

This study also has implications for the design of playground environments for toddlers. Results suggest that the equipment in toddler playgrounds should provide opportunities for a child to engage in a full range of play behaviors from the simplest to the most complex forms. Gender differences found in equipment choices indicate that the preferences of both male and female toddlers should be considered in planning outdoor play environments. Therefore, a balance should be achieved between the play equipment involving gross motor action and items requiring fine motor manipulation.

Many questions concerning the play of toddlers remain unanswered. Do all groups of toddlers engage in the same types of play behavior? What kinds of play behaviors do toddlers exhibit in other play settings? How is the play of toddlers affected when the type and amount of equipment is varied? The instrument developed for this study could prove to be a useful tool in the search for answers to these questions.

References

American Families and Living Arrangements. Current Population Reports, Series 23, no. 104, Bureau of the Census. Washington, DC: U.S. Government Printing Office, May 1980.

Bakeman, Roger, and John R. Brownlee. "The Strategic Use of Parallel Play: A Sequential Analysis." *Child Development* 51, 3 (1980): 873–78.

Benjamin, H. "Age and Sex Differences in Toy Preferences in Young Children." *Journal of Genetic Psychology* 41 (1932): 417–29.

Bronson, Wanda C. "Developments in Behavior with Agemates During the Second Year of Life." In Michael Lewis and Leonard A. Rosenblum, eds., *Friendship and Peer Relations.* New York: Wiley, 1975.

———. *Toddler's Behaviors with Agemates: Issues of Interaction, Cognition and Affect.* Norwood, NJ: Ablex, 1981.

DeStefano, C. T. "Environmental Determinants of Peer Social Behavior and Interaction in a Toddler Playgroup." *Dissertation Abstracts International* 36 (1976): 5861B–62B. (University Microfilms No. 76-11, 147.)

Eckerman, Carol O.; Judith L. Whatley and Stuart L. Kutz. "Growth of Social Play with Peers During the Second Year of Life." *Developmental Psychology* 11, 1 (1975): 42–49.

Eckerman, Carol O., and Judith L. Whatley. "Toys and Social Interaction Between Infant Peers." *Child Development* 48 (1977): 1645–56.

Fein, Greta G. "A Tranformational Analysis of Pretending." *Developmental Psychology* 11, 3 (1975): 291–96.

———. "Pretend Play: New Perspectives." *Young Children* 34, 5 (1979): 61–66.

Fein, G.; D. Johnson; N. Kosson; L. Stork and L. Wasserman. "Sex Stereotypes and Preferences in the Toy Choices of 20-month-old Boys and Girls." *Developmental Psychology* 11, 4 (1975): 527–28.

Fenson, Larry; Jerome Kagan; Richard B. Kearsley and Philip R. Zelazo. "The Developmental Progression of Manipulative Play in the First Two Years." *Child Development* 47 (1976): 232–36.

Goldman, Barbara D., and Hildy S. Ross. "Social Skills in Action: An Analysis of Early Peer Games." In Joseph Glick and K. Alison Clarke-Stewart, eds., *The Development of Social Understanding* Vol. I. New York: Gardner Press, 1978.

Golomb, Claire. "Pretense Play: A Cognitive Perspective." In Nancy R. Smith and Margery B. Franklin, eds., *Symbolic Functioning in Childhood.* Hillsdale, NJ: Erlbaum, 1979.

Howes, Carolee. "Peer Play Scale as an Index of Complexity of Peer Interaction." *Developmental Psychology* 16, 4 (1980): 371–72.

Iwanaga, Margaret. "Development of Interpersonal Play Structure in Three-, Four-, and Five-Year-Old Children." *Journal of Research and Development in Education* 6, 3 (1973): 71–82.

Jackowitz, Elaine R., and Malcolm W. Watson. "Development of Object Transformations in Early Pretend Play." *Developmental Psychology* 16, 6 (1980): 543–49.

Kearsley, Richard B., and Philip R. Zelazo. *Sex Typed Differences in the Spontaneous Play Behavior in Infants 9½ to 15½ Months of Age.* ERIC Document Reproduction Service, 1979. (ED 168-699).

Largo, Remo H., and Judy A. Howard. "Developmental Progression in Play Behavior of Children Between Nine and Thirty Months. II: Spontaneous Play and Language Development." *Developmental Medicine and Child Neurology* 21, 4 (1979): 492–503.

McCall, Robert B. "Exploratory Play and Manipulation in the Human Infant." *Monographs of the Society for Research in Child Development* 39, 2, Serial No. 155 (1974).

Mueller, Edward, and Jeffrey Brenner. "The Origins of Social Skills and Interaction Among Playgroup Toddlers." *Child Development* 48 (1977): 854–61.

Mueller, Edward, and Thomas Lucas. "A Developmental Analysis of Peer Interaction Among Toddlers." In Michael Lewis and Leonard A. Rosenblum, eds., *Friendship and Peer Relations.* New York: Wiley, 1975.

Parten, Mildred B. "Social Participation Among Preschool Children." *Journal of Abnormal and Social Psychology* 27 (1932): 243–69.

Piaget, Jean. *Play, Dreams and Imitation in Childhood.* New York: Norton, 1962.

Ramey, C.; N. W. Finkelstein and C. O'Brien. "Toys and Infant Behavior in the First Year of Life." *Journal of Genetic Psychology* 129 (1976): 341–42.

Rubin, Kenneth H.; Kathryn S. Watson and Thomas W. Jambor. "Free-play Behaviors in Preschool and Kindergarten Children." *Child Development* 49, 2 (1978): 534–36.

Shimada, Shoko; Rygoro Sano and Fred Peng. *A Longitudinal Study of Symbolic Play in the Second Year of Life.* ERIC Document Reproduction Service, 1979 (ED 197-814).

Smith, Peter K. "A Longitudinal Study of Social Participation in Preschool Children: Solitary and Parallel Play Reexamined." *Developmental Psychology* 14 (1978): 517–23.

Sponseller, Doris B., and Anne P. Jaworski. *Social and Cognitive Complexity in Young Children's Play: A Longitudinal Analysis.* ERIC Document Reproduction Service, 1979 (ED 171-416).

Sponseller, Doris B., and Matthew Lowry. "Designing a Play Environment for Toddlers." In Doris Sponseller, ed., *Play as a Learning Medium.* Washington, DC: National Association for the Education of Young Children, 1974.

Ungerer, Judy A.; Philip R. Zelazo; Richard B. Kearsley and Katherine Kurowski. *Play as a Cognitive Assessment Tool.* ERIC Document Reproduction Service, 1979 (ED 176-858).

Vandell, Deborah Lowe; Kathy S. Wilson and Nola R. Buchanan. "Peer Interaction in the First Year of Life: An Examination of Its Structure, Content, and Sensitivity to Toys." *Child Development* 51 (1980): 481–88.

Vincze, M. "The Social Contacts of Infants and Young Children Reared Together." *Early Child Development and Care* 1 (1971): 99–109.

Interactive Patterns in Children's Play Groups

Michael J. Bell
Department of Curriculum and Instruction
The University of Texas at Austin

and

Pauline Walker
Department of Curriculum and Instruction
The University of Texas at Austin

Within the first few months of life (Collard, 1972; Bower, 1977) children's play can be observed in many and varied settings. The complex set of play behaviors come in many forms (Garvey, 1977). Of the wide array of play situations that can occur with a group of young children, this study addresses social play as it occurs within a play group and the interaction between children from the perspective of the participant observer.

Beginning with the pioneering work of Parten (1932), the free play behaviors of young children have been carefully studied. Parten's social play research, along with the more recent work of Barnes (1971), and Rubin, Maioni and Hornung (1976) centered around the indoor play choices of young children. Piaget (1962) gave greater insight into the play of young children with his discussion of cognitive play and its developmental nature. Play behaviors have been identified as a distinctive instrument of cognitive development (Flavell, 1977). Rubin and Maioni (1975) used Piaget's cognitive play categories to code the classroom play behaviors of preschool children, supporting Piaget's hypothesis that cognitive play is developmental. Parten's findings and Piaget's assertions concerning the cognitive play categories were used to assess indoor play behaviors of young children. A review of current literature makes it clear that outdoor play behaviors have been overlooked.

This research addresses the questions: 1) What manner of social play can occur within a play group made up of young children? 2) What behaviors do young children exhibit in regard to their play group's play space and the objects found in their play space?

METHOD

Subjects and Setting

The subjects for this study were twenty-three, 3-, 4- and 5-year-old children from two classrooms at a Central Texas day care center located in a middle-class neighborhood and affiliated with a local church. It consisted of three classrooms in a building on the north side of the play area. The two groups shared a wide range of experiences during the school week—meals, field trips, special activities, swimming lessons and free play time.

The play area, a skewed rectangular shape, approximately 60′ × 100′, was considered to be adequate in quality and complexity based upon a rating scale developed by Frost and Klein (1979). There were two "house structures," one made of logs to resemble an open-air fort, the other constructed to resemble a house. The area contained a sandbox (12′ × 12′), a stationary play car, a large stationary boat and six swings adjacent to the open-air fort. A large climbing structure surrounds the trunk of a tree in the southeast corner of the play area, slide, ladder and tire climber attached to the platform, which stands four feet above ground level. Three climbing apparatuses were in the center of the play area: a wooden triangular climber, a metal chain climber and an upright truck tire. The ground cover on this play area was sub-standard, three-fourths of it hard-packed dirt and sand. An informal survey of the parents revealed a high frequency of injury among the children.

Procedures and Limitations
The researchers collected field notes during the observation period, recorded notes in outline form during free play time. Immediately following daily observations, a researcher wrote notes on each area of the outline, a method developed from a trial-and error-process as suggested by Bogdan and Biklen (1982). It was found to be difficult to write elaborate notes in the field, nor could the researchers depend on the total recall of an hour-long observation period. A micro-cassette recorder was used to record children's language during their interactions with peers, teachers and the researchers. Initially, the children were curious as to the reason for carrying a tape recorder around the play area, but their interest waned with repeated use during daily observations.

During the ten-week observation period, the senior author found it necessary to share ideas and comments with others in the area of early childhood education. Most reactions to the findings were simply to substantiate ideas and trends, as described by Mehan (1979). Based upon these positive interactions, another researcher brought to the site to familiarize herself with the participants and the setting, recorded field notes during her observations. Her schedule of observation was not concurrent with that of the primary researcher. Therefore, the pattern of one or two researchers on site varied.

The analysis of the field notes and transcriptions of the audio tapes was a process of identifying characteristics and trends, a process allowing the researchers to recognize characteristics of play group behaviors and behaviors concerning children's play space at this site.

RESULTS

It can be inferred from the field notes and transcriptions of audio tapes that patterns and general rules were firmly entrenched in the outdoor play behavior of the subjects.

The children from the younger classroom did not form play groups during the observation period, played with each other only infrequently, these interactions lasting for no more than 15 minutes. Interactions consisted of onlooker and parallel forms of social play. For example, a girl three years, five months of age ran about the playground with arms extended, yelling "Superman!" or "Supergirl!" depending on the cue from her teacher. A boy from her class, age 3 years, 11 months, would imitate her posture and follow her path around the playground. On two occasions during the observation this pattern became a game of chase. In all other examples observed this game ended abruptly when the girl stopped running. The other child stopped at the same time or ran to the swings, while maintaining the "Superman posture" and lay across the swing on his stomach. On one occasion the researcher asked the boy about this activity:

OB: What are you doing, Superboy?
  D: Flying!
OB: Can Supergirl fly?
  D: Yes. . . (pause). . . not really.
OB: Can you really fly?
  D: (Pause). . . Watch, I can go high.
OB: Great, you can really fly!

It was evident that this boy had elaborated on the Superman theme by flying on the swing. The younger children frequently "picked up" play themes from their peers. Rarely were the extensions of play themes shared between peers or among play groups made up of younger children (age range: 2.5–4.0 years).

These observed behaviors are consistent with Parten's social play categories and developmental trends that she identified throughout her research, but Parten failed to provide an explanation as to why this developmental trend occurs in play group behavior. What are older children capable of that allows them to form and sustain social interactions during free play? From the observations made during this study and the related literature on social development (Green, 1933a & 1933b; Rubin, 1975; Russell, 1956), it could be assumed that older children are capable of identifying the free

140

play goals of others, evaluate these goals with respect for their interests at the moment and consolidate the two into a mutually satisfying play situation. To illustrate this aspect of social play, this interaction was taken from a transcription of audio tape:

C: How are we going to catch them?
Z: I don't . . . I'm going to put you in jail! (under platform)
C: Let's get 'm . . . (girls)
Z: I want to be the police.
C: I know . . . . we'll be the police and put them (pointing at the girls) in jail!
Z: Yeah, let's get the robbers!

It is evident that the two goals were initially in conflict, which was solved by Chris, who accommodated his friend's wishes and satisfied his own desire to chase the girls. One could judge this to be a remarkable cognitive feat for a 5-year old child.

Younger children, ages 2.5–4.0, did not at any time exhibit skills in goal identification during the observation period. For example, two girls from the younger classroom pushed, shoved, hit and bit each other over which child was to "drive" the play car. This conflict went on for a period of five minutes, until the classroom teacher sent both crying children to "time out." These conflicts were rare; usually one child would relent to the other child's wishes. This example is consistent with the thinking of most cognitive theorists and could be an explanation as to why developmental trends are observable in the social play of young children.

There were two distinct play groups formed prior to the observation period. A play group was determined to be two or more children sharing a peer relationship and devoting most of their free play time engaged in any form of social play with other members of the play group. The two play groups were made up of children from the older preschool classroom. The older boys, Chris, Zach, Wesley and Mark were the members of the male play group. Their ages ranged from 4 years, 6 months to 5 years, ten months. The median age for the male play group was 5 years, 1 month. Ano, Stacey, Laura and Aurora were the members of the female play group, with age range from 4 years, 5 months to 5

years, 4 months. Median age for the female play group was 5 years, 1 month.

Chris, described by his teacher and peers as being "bright" and "smart," was found by the researchers to be open to interactions with adults. In a previous example, it is clear that Chris was able to manipulate peers and ideas concerning play schemes. It was common to hear him suggest "setting a trap," "hide" or chase another child to the members of his play group. He was adept in various social skills such as, negotiations, story telling and peer relations. Chris was very expressive when giving orders or making suggestions to his play group. His use of voice, facial expressions and physical movements suggested enthusiasm and confidence in the value of his play ideas. On a number of occasions, when a member of his play group passively resisted a play scheme by not participating in the activity, Chris would modify his suggestion, implore, coax or lie to encourage the child's participation. It appeared to the researchers that Chris devoted as much time to leadership and procedural activities as he did to carrying out the group play schemes.

Ano, the leader of the female play group, had the same characteristics as Chris, but her play group rarely dissented or decided not to participate in a suggested play scheme. The female play group stayed together more consistently during play and procedural activities than the male group. The researchers could not determine the reason for this difference. When the children were asked why their groups always stayed together, they replied, "We're friends!" Perhaps the bonds of friendship in the female group were stronger than in the male play group. The researchers observed less competitiveness and aggressiveness in the female play group, but more verbal confrontations.

Zach complemented the male play group well, with his unique personality and group role. He was clearly not the leader, but his influence on the daily play schemes was clear. Zach did not exhibit the exuberant leadership behaviors displayed by Chris. He seemed to lack the observable aggressiveness and dominant behavior that was a part of Chris' leadership behavior. One could raise questions as to Zach's feeling about his secondary role in the play group. He was talented in various social skills and had the ability to elaborate on play schemes and consolidate ideas of others into play schemes, but he was not the leader. Possibly all of his play goals were not being met, which could have raised his level of frustration in play situations. He remained an active member of the group and appeared to enjoy the various procedural activities and play schemes. The degree to which Zach was frustrated within the play group may be a question of little value, but, his leadership skills were evident to both researchers. Questions will remain concerning his role within the group and his relationship to his friends.

In each play group two children fulfilled the supporting roles. The researchers referred to these children as "followers." In the male play group, Mark and Wesley demonstrated a variety of behaviors that supported the leadership behaviors of Chris and Zach. Mark was a quiet follower, rarely suggesting play schemes or making suggestions about procedural activities. Wesley freely suggested play schemes and expressed ardent opinions concerning playground rules, rituals and procedures. He was keenly aware of the teacher-imposed rules and would not hesitate to remind his peers of these rules at appropriate moments. He never "told" on one of his friends when they were in violation of the playground rules, but he did use this behavior against any children during verbal confrontations.

The qualities of active participation and cooperation were observable in the followers in each play group. For example, their consistent enthusiasm for suggested play schemes facilitated procedural activities and aided the group play activities. Whether these qualities were imposed on the followers through a process of social learning or through their need to assume a position of responsibility within the play group, regardless of their subordinate position, is a question requiring further investigation.

Aurora and Laura were identified as the "followers" in the female play group. The distinctive feature of their behavior was their ability to construct sociodramatic play situations and elaborate on roles assigned to them by the play group leader, Ano. On one occasion Laura grew from a crying infant to a teenager, then to a lady driving a sports car, simply to change location from the play house to the open area and incorporate a "Big Wheel" into her individual play schemes. The followers in the male play group rarely elaborated on a sociodramatic play theme or moved from one play role to another to meet their needs. One cannot be certain if it was the boys' immature cognitive abilities and lack of social experience that limited the ability to create and elaborate sociodramatic play themes. Rubin, Maioni and Hornung (1976) suggest that the frequency of pretend play in preschool children is low when compared to other forms of play behaviors and gradually increases in kindergarten age children. An explanation for the behaviors observed in this case is that the female play group could have had more experience in various forms of social play, since there was little difference in age between the two play groups.

These two groups controlled a large area of playground play space. The male play group dominated play on the superstructure and adjacent boat and the nearby play house, an area surrounding the superstructure and loose tires usually scattered there. The female play group controlled the open-air log cabin in the northwest portion of the playground and adjacent swing sets through verbal interaction with children outside their play group and the physical use of the environment. The researchers observed few instances of actual confrontation between a member or members of a play group and other children concerning play space or a play object. One could infer that this was due to the researchers' entry into the environment after the midpoint of the school year. It was evident that the majority of the children had found areas within the boundaries of the playground where they could play as they chose. Despite these limitations, researchers observed instances of possessive behavior toward objects and a degree of territoriality, a behavior related to possessions and objects that occurred when children from outside the play group entered the house, climbed into the boat or onto the superstructure or crawled under the superstructure while the male play group was present. Generally one member of the group would say, "Get outta here!" "We're playing in here" or simply push or chase the interloper out of the area. Rarely did the pushing or chasing appear to be a game, but some could consider this a form of play. It appeared to be an aggressive response to another child's action. Wesley often asked for the teacher's help in such cases, probably due to his concept of authority and his teacher's role in maintaining order. He was generally unsuccessful in that he would get a lecture on sharing with others, but he persisted in seeking a teacher's help in confrontations.

A trend associated with sociodramatic play did appear during the observation period, when objects that fulfilled roles other than their primary functions during pretend play were considered possessions by the play groups and other children. On several occasions members of a play group explained the nature of their play scheme and the role of disputed objects. Children from outside the play group would listen to the group's "story" and give up their attempt to gain possession of an object. In some cases children returned objects to the play group's area. For example, this situation occurred between Zach and Sophie, a girl from Zach's class who was not a member of any play group:

The male play group had built a castle out of the loose tires near their play house. Sophie climbed up the side away from the boys and put her arm in the top tire, as if to pull herself up or take the tire down. Zach pulled up the other side of the castle and put his arm in the tire in a similar manner.

Zach: No, Sophie!
(Sophie and Zach tugged at the tire in opposite directions)
Sophie: But I want it for over there! (pointing)
Zach: We're using it for a castle and Wesley gets inside of there.
Sophie: (laughing) Could I get in there?
Zach: No, we're using it. (He tugs at the tire again)
Sophie removed her arm, stood erect on the stack of tires, then backed down to the ground and ran off to get a tricycle.

The children did not appear to be concerned with open areas, but focused their attention and possessive behaviors towards structures and objects in a given area. Possessive behavior, therefore, could be misinterpreted to be a form of territorial behavior. The researchers never observed an instance when a member of a play group asked or forced another child out of an open area. Play group members' possessive behavior was directed only toward objects and structures in the group's play area.

SUMMARY

Frequent and diverse social interactions took place in the context of the play group. The recordings and observations of these social interactions provided insight into the large quantity of social knowledge exchanged between children when they are at play. During this investigation, the researchers identified patterns and rules governing dramatic play, roles that children assume within the context of the play group and the degree of control groups have over the play setting. The play groups in this study were well established and organized. Each child understood his or her role as a member of a play group and supported the roles assumed by other children. The leadership role within a play group required an understanding of each child's social knowledge and ability to incorporate this knowledge into play schemes.

The children rarely expressed their intention to exclude other children from joining their play group or entering into their play space. Children who were not members of a play group were excluded from joining a group due to their lack of knowledge of particular play schemes and the roles of the group members in various schemes. These children lacked group social experiences and the exchange of social knowledge as it occurs in the play group context. In many cases, children's efforts to gain access to play groups was deterred by misunderstanding the play scheme or the intentions of the play group.

Play group members directed possessive behaviors toward objects and structures in their immediate play area and toward objects incorporated into dramatic play schemes.

Frequently, confrontations occurred over objects, which required children to exchange social knowledge concerning play schemes and intentions. Confrontations concerning play space never occurred, and play group members rarely directed possessive behavior toward open play areas.

References

Barnes, K. "Preschool Play Norms: A Replication. *Developmental Psychology* 5 (1971): 99–103.

Bogdan, R., and S. Biklen. *Qualitative Research for Education: An Introduction to Theory and Methods.* Boston: Allyn and Bacon, 1982.

Bower, T.G.R. *The Perceptual World of the Child.* Cambridge, MA: Harvard University Press, 1977.

Collard, R. "Exploration and Play in Human Infants." *Journal of Health, Physical Education, and Recreation* 43, 6 (1972): 35–38.

Corsaro, W. A. "Entering the Child's World: Research Strategies for Field Entry and Data Collection in a Preschool Setting." In J. Green and C. Wallet, eds., *Ethnography and Language in Education Settings.* Norwood, NJ: Ablex, 1981.

Flavell, J. H. *The Developmental Psychology of Jean Piaget.* Princeton, NJ: Van Nostrand, 1977.

Frost, J. L., and B. L. Klein. *Children's Play and Playgrounds.* Boston: Allyn and Bacon, 1979.

Garvey, C. *Play.* Cambridge, MA: Harvard University Press, 1977.

Green, E. H. "Friendship and Quarrels Among Preschool Children." *Child Development* 4 (1933): 237–52 (a).

———. "Group Play and Quarrelling Among Preschool Children." *Child Development* 4 (1933): 302–07 (b).

Greer, B. "First Days in the Field." In P. Hammond, ed., *Sociologists at Work.* New York: Doubleday, 1967.

Harper, L. V., and K. M. Sanders. "Preschool Children's Use of Space: Sex Differences in Outdoor Play." *Developmental Psychology* 11 (1975): 119.

Headley, N. E. *Education in the Kindergarten.* New York: American Book, 1966.

Heath, S. B. "Ethnography in Education." In P. Gilmore and A. Glatthorn, eds., *Children In and Out of School.* Washington, DC: Center for Applied Linguistics, 1982.

Isaacs, S. *The Nursery School.* London: Routledge and Kegan Paul, 1932.

Johnson, M. V. "The Effect on Behavior of Variation in the Amount of Play Equipment." *Child Development* 6 (1935): 56–58.

Lindfors, J. W. *Children's Language and Learning.* Englewood Cliffs, NJ: Prentice-Hall, 1980.

Parten, M. B. "Social Participation Among Preschool Children. *Journal of Abnormal and Social Psychology* 27 (1932): 243–69.

Piaget, J. *Comments on Vygotsky's Critical Remarks Concerning the Language and Thought of the Child, and Judgement and Reasoning in the Child.* Cambridge, MA: M.I.T. Press, 1962.

Rubin, K., and T. Maioni. "Play Preference and Its Relationship to Egocentrism, Popularity and Classification Skills in Preschoolers." *Merrill-Palmer Quarterly* 21, 3 (1975): 171–79.

Rubin, K.; T. Maioni and M. Hornung. "Free-Play Behaviors in Middle- and Lower-class Preschoolers: Parten and Piaget Revisited." *Child Development* 47 (1976): 414–19.

Rudolph, M., and D. H. Cohen. *Kindergarten: A Year of Learning.* New York: Appleton-Century-Crofts, 1964.

Russell, D. H. *Children's Thinking.* New York: Ginn, 1956.

Sanders, K. M., and L. V. Harper. "Free-Play Fantasy Behavior in Preschool Children: Relations Among Gender, Age, Season, and Location." *Child Development* 47 (1976): 1182–85.

Slobin, D. *Psycholinguistics.* Glenview, IL: Scott, Foresman, 1979.

Strauss, A. *Psychiatric Idealogies and Institutions.* New York: Free Press, 1964.

Tizard, B.; J. Philps and I. Plewis. "Play in Preschool Centers: Play Measures and Their Relation to Age, Sex, and I.Q." *Journal of Child Psychology and Psychiatry* 17 (1976): 251–64 (a).

———. "Play in Preschool Centers: Effects on Play of the Child's Social Class and of the Educational Orientation of the Center." *Journal of Child Psychology and Psychiatry* 17 (1976): 265–74 (b).

Underwood, B. "Some Relationships Between Concept Learning and Verbal Learning." In H. J. Klausmeier and C. W. Harris, eds., *Analysis of Concept Learning.* New York: Academic Press, 1966.

Vygotsky, L. S. *Thought and Language.* Cambridge, MA: M.I.T. Press, 1962.

Preschool Children's Play Behaviors in an Indoor and Outdoor Environment

MICHAEL L. HENNIGER
Division of Early Childhood Education
Central Washington State College, Ellensburg

Observational investigations of children's free play behaviors have frequently focused on either the social or the cognitive aspects of their play. Those studies concentrating on the social dimensions of play generally used categories developed by Parten (1932). With occasional modifications, the work of Shure (1963), Barnes (1971) and Tizard, Philps and Plewis (1976a, b) all used Parten's social play categories to describe the interactive aspects of the free play of nursery school children.

Studies describing the cognitive aspects of children's play often used categories developed by Piaget (1951) and elaborated upon by Smilansky (1968). Both Eiferman (1971) and Rubin and Maioni (1975) used these cognitive play categories in their observations of the play of children. A study by Rubin, Maioni and Hornung (1976) used both the cognitive play categories as defined by Smilansky (1968) and Parten's (1932) social play categories in observations of children's free play behaviors.

Very little is known about the cognitive and social play behaviors of children in outdoor environments, and still less has been done to compare children's play indoors and outdoors. Sanders and Harper (1976) compared the imaginative play of preschool children in both environments and found boys and older children performed more make-believe play outdoors than girls and younger children. Tizard *et al.* (1976b) found social class differences in indoor and outdoor play, with working-class children selecting outdoor play significantly more often than middle-class children and engaging in higher levels of play in that environment.

To investigate further the relationships between children's indoor and outdoor play, the present study was undertaken, with di- rect observations of preschool-age children made both indoors and outdoors using Smilansky's (1968) cognitive play categories and modifications of Parten's (1932) social play categories. Indoor *vs* outdoor comparisons were made for each of the play categories.

METHOD

Setting

Children. A total of 28 nursery school children from the two morning groups in the University of Texas (Austin) Child Development Laboratory were observed for the study. Seven boys and six girls from the older group (mean age 5.0 years) and eight boys and seven girls from the younger group (mean age 4.0 years) made up the sample. The children were predominantly Caucasian and from middle-class families.

Environment. The indoor environment in the nursery school consisted of eight centers with different materials placed each week, including a dramatic play area, a manipulative toy corner, a house-keeping center, a music area, a science table, a block area and a quiet/puzzle area.

The outdoor environment contained a variety of fixed and movable equipment. Stationary equipment included a treehouse platform with slide and steps, a jungle gym, a sandbox, a concrete bike path, a water play area and a swing set. Movable equipment, rearranged and/or changed each week, consisted of a boat, a steering wheel mounted in a box, metal triangular climbing structures with ladders, a tepee-type climber, large wooden crates, metal barrels and an assortment of wooden boxes and tires. Storage facilities outdoors gave children ready access to tricycles, numerous sand toys, water play

145

materials, shovels, rakes, balls, chairs, ropes, traffic signs and wagons.

Procedure

Play categories. The cognitive play categories as defined by Smilansky (1968) were used to assess children's cognitive play in the two environments. In addition, the social aspects of their play were evaluated using modifications of Parten's (1932) social play categories. Many of the ideas of Iwanaga (1973) were used to restructure these social play categories as follows:

1. *Solitary Play*—The child's play takes place without the involvement of his peers. There is an absence of attempts to make social contacts with other children. Verbalization and gestures are primarily egocentric and not directed toward others. The child shows no prolonged interest in looking at other children and may attempt to exclude these children from joining the play.

2. *Parallel Play*—Two or more children are engaged in a similar activity. There is a maintained awareness of and contact with these other children by frequently looking at, talking to and/or touching them. Maintained awareness may also be indicated by the frequent checking and showing of each other's work.

3. *Complementary Play*—The child initiates and engages in play activity where differentiated roles assigned to self and others are acted out independently as the children play together. The children involved develop and agree upon a general play plan, assign specific roles for each of the participants, then proceed to enact their specific roles with little additional concern for the play of the rest of the group.

4. *Cooperative Play*—The child initiates and engages in play activity where either differentiated or undifferentiated roles are assigned to self and others. The quality of visual, verbal and physical contacts indicates that children are aware of changes in peer behaviors. There is a greater adjusting of each child's behavior in response to the shifts and adjustments of the behavior of others. The respective roles are not carried out independently but are developed and modified in interaction with other children as they play their roles.

Observations. A prepared checklist with children's names and the social and cognitive play categories was used to observe each child during free play for a 30-second time interval. After a child had been observed and his play behaviors coded, the researcher moved to the next name on the checklist for observation. Each day the order of observation was changed. Children were observed a total of 20 times indoors and 20 times outdoors over a six-week period. A minimum of ten children had to be present before observations could be made, and no observations were made when the head teacher was absent.

The author was the sole observer during data collection. In order to check the reliability of the coded play behaviors, a second person was used at both the beginning and the end of the study to establish interrater reliabilities averaging .81 and .82 respectively.

Data analysis and results. The first task of data analysis was to tally the number of play behaviors each child exhibited for each of the play categories both indoors and outdoors. The mean number of observations for each play category was then computed for both environments with the total sample being grouped by age and sex. These indoor and outdoor means were compared for significant differences using a t-test for correlated means. Table 1 presents the indoor and outdoor means and t-tests showing significant differences for each of the play categories.

DISCUSSION

It is important to emphasize the fact that the children and settings used to compare indoor and outdoor play in this study were not typical of most nursery school programs. Both environments had a wide assortment of equipment and materials to enhance the play of young children, highly skilled teachers and a low adult-child ratio of one to five, an optimal situation for observing play. Despite the fact that this optimal setting might have limited the author's ability to generalize from

Table 1
Indoor and Outdoor Means for the Social and Cognitive Play Categories
(Including t-Tests Showing Significant Differences)*

Category	Total (n=28) In	Total (n=28) Out	Older (n=13) In	Older (n=13) Out	Younger (n=15) In	Younger (n=15) Out	Male (n=15) In	Male (n=15) Out	Female (n=13) In	Female (n=13) Out
Social										
Solitary	4.07	3.25	3.83	4.15	4.67	2.47	4.47	3.20	3.61	3.30
					(t=3.21 p<0.01)					
Parallel	8.36	10.32	8.38	9.15	8.33	11.33	8.33	9.87	8.38	10.84
	(t=−3.44 p<0.01)				(t=−4.86 p<0.001)		(t=−2.43 p<0.05)		(t=−2.45 p<0.05)	
Complementary	1.00	0.79	1.00	0.92	1.00	0.67	0.67	1.13	1.38	0.38
Co-operative	2.46	2.39	2.54	3.38	2.40	1.53	2.47	2.80	2.46	1.92
					(t=2.23 p<0.05)					
Cognitive										
Functional	0.43	6.79	0.15	5.15	0.67	8.20	0.40	6.07	0.46	7.61
	(t=−11.72 p<0.001)		(t=−7.69 p<0.001)		(t=−10.33 p<0.001)		(t=−8.64 p<0.001)		(t=−8.61 p<0.001)	
Constructive	6.86	3.18	7.30	3.62	6.47	2.80	7.47	2.33	6.15	4.15
	(t=5.42 p<0.001)		(t=2.87 p<0.05)		(t=5.56 p<0.001)		(t=6.48 p<0.001)			
Dramatic	8.29	6.36	7.38	8.00	9.07	4.93	7.73	8.13	8.92	4.30
					(t=4.57 p<0.001)				(t=5.42 p<0.001)	
Games	0.29	0.36	0.38	0.77	0.20	0	0.33	0.47	0.23	0.23

*t was not computed when both the indoor and outdoor means for a category were less than 2.

the study, important conclusions can still be made about children's play in this situation.

The most comprehensive statement to be made about play compared indoors and outdoors is that both environments are valuable in stimulating the various play types. For example, while construction play was enhanced more by the indoor environment, the outdoor environment stimulated more functional play. For other types of play, such as cooperative play, observations indicated that nearly equal amounts occurred in the two environments. Thus, one environment should not be favored over the other; the settings complemented one another by stimulating different important play types.

The more specific conclusions concerning indoor and outdoor play can be divided into two parts: those dealing with the indoor environment, and conclusions about the outdoor environment.

Indoors

Traditionally, the indoor play area has been considered the most valuable environment for the development of the child, as indicated by the amount of research generated in this environment compared to the outdoor setting. Other indications are the amount of materials present in the indoor environment and the percentage of total budget often invested there.

This study has raised serious questions about the validity of placing so much emphasis on the indoor environment. Despite the undeniable values of free play in an indoor setting, this environment is limited in its ability to stimulate certain important play types and is only equivalent to the outdoor environment in stimulating some others.

The indoor environment seemed to foster three types of desirable play behaviors. The incidence of indoor dramatic play was significantly larger for both the girls and the younger children, and since dramatic play is viewed as an important vehicle for the development of social relationships, this finding seemed important. Garvey (1977) saw dramatic play as important to the child's understanding of ". . . classes of individuals and their relationships of categories and types of goals, and of the possible actions and sequences of action that can be employed to accomplish these goals" (p. 81).

The indoor environment should be structured to stimulate this type of dramatic play for boys and older children as well as for girls and younger children. Perhaps new equipment would help both groups, particularly if teachers were to renew their efforts to encourage the boys to become involved in indoor dramatic play. Even small increases in imaginative play indoors would yield positive results.

The indoor environment had a strong effect on constructive play as well. The groups observed showed a consistent trend to engage in more constructive play indoors than outdoors. Since such play helps in the development of fine motor skills and gives children the opportunity to develop their creative skills, the indoor environment provides still another fertile situation for growth.

It should be noted that the nursery school teachers took considerable time each week in planning and changing the materials and equipment placed in the indoor and outdoor environments. This careful planning influenced the amounts of constructive play observed in each environment, but if their planning had included more woodworking or art activities outdoors, the differences observed in constructive play in the two environments might have been eliminated.

The indoor environment had a tendency to stimulate more solitary play among the nursery school children. Although significantly different from the outdoor environment only for the younger group of children, the trend was for more solitary play to occur indoors. Although a primary goal of most nursery school programs is to develop in children the skills necessary to interact with other children, it is also important for children to feel comfortable in playing alone, because every person needs a healthy balance between social time and time spent alone. A positive relationship between solitary play and high intelligence has been proposed (Strom, 1976). Further research might clarify the values of solitary play.

Outdoors

Results from the present study seem to warrant a re-evaluation of the importance of the outdoor environment in children's play. With the right equipment and careful teacher planning and encouragement, any desired play type could be stimulated in the outdoor environment, for this setting has definite advantages over the indoors for certain types of play and for certain children.

The outdoor environment, for example, stimulated nearly all the functional play observed in the nursery school setting. These repetitive muscle movements are valuable in developing motor skills and in developing feelings of success and self-worth for certain children.

The outdoor environment stimulated social play as well. Cooperative play, the highest level of social play, was observed in nearly equal amounts in both environments. The only significant difference for the groups observed was the young children's preference for cooperative play indoors. When the needs of individual children are considered, finding no significant differences in cooperative play in the two environments may be particularly important. It is possible that some children are more inhibited socially in the indoor environment. For example, limitations of space, floor covering and noise levels may prevent the occurrence of the more active play that often encourages boys to get involved in the higher levels of social play. A stimulating outdoor environment could encourage this important type of play.

The dramatic play of boys and the older children was strongly influenced by the outdoor environment, where both groups engaged in more play of this type. Considering the boys' preference for more active dramatic play roles, the outdoor environment seemed to be an important stimulus, enhanced by activity-producing materials and greater freedom found outdoors. Also, there are wider varieties of dramatic themes because equipment and materials being often less detailed give the older child an option of using simpler, less complicated materials in ways to meet imaginative needs and interests.

References

Barnes, K. "Preschool Play Norms: A Replication." *Developmental Psychology* 5 (1971): 99–103.

Garvey, Catherine. *Play*. Cambridge, MA: Harvard University Press, 1977.

Iwanaga, M. "Development of Interpersonal Play Structure in Three-, Four-, and Five-year-old Children." *Journal of Research and Development of Education* 6, 3 (1973):71–82.

Parten, M. B. "Social Participation Among Preschool Children." *Journal of Abnormal and Social Psychology* 27 (1932): 243–69.

Piaget, J. *Play, Dreams, and Imitation in Childhood*. London: Heinemann, 1951.

Rubin, K., and T. Maioni. "Play Preference and Its Relationship to Egocentrism, Popularity and Classification Skills in Preschoolers." *Merril-Palmer Quarterly* 21, 3 (1975): 171–79.

Rubin, K.; T. Maioni and M. Hornung. "Free-play Behaviors in Middle- and Lower-class Preschoolers: Parten and Piaget Revisited." *Child Development* 47 (1976): 414–19.

Sanders, K. M., and L. V. Harper. "Free-play Fantasy Behavior in Preschool Children: Relations Among Gender, Age, Season, and Location." *Child Development* 47 (1976): 1182–85.

Shure, M. "Psychological Ecology of a Nursery School." *Child Development* 34 (1963): 979–92.

Smilansky, S. *The Effects of Sociodramatic Play on Disadvantaged Preschool Children.* New York: Wiley, 1968.

Strom, R. "The Merits of Solitary Play." *Childhood Education* 52, 3 (1976): 149–52.

Tizard, B.; J. Philps and I. Plewis. "Play in Preschool Centers—II. Effects on Play of the Child's Social Class and of the Educational Orientation of the Center." *Journal of Child Psychology and Psychiatry* 17 (1976b): 265–74.

———. "Play in Preschool Centers—I. Play Measures and Their Relation to Age, Sex, and I.Q." *Journal of Child Psychology and Psychiatry* 17 (1976a): 251–64.

Motor Behavior of Kindergartners During Physical Education and Free Play

GWEN DEAN MYERS
Consultant in Early Childhood Education
Cincinnati, Ohio

There are differing opinions as to how children might best be helped to reach their genetic potential in physical development. Proponents of strenuous activity programs suggest that a structured program of vigorous physical activity be included in the school curriculum to provide stimulation of physical growth. Others maintain that the natural play instincts of children are sufficient to promote growth, that the inherent drive for physical activity in young children is evident to anyone who has observed them in unstructured play situations (Seefeldt, 1974). They suggest a well-designed school playground, one that encourages movement exploration.

Are children's natural play instincts sufficient to promote play active and vigorous enough to develop the motor strengths and skills needed in adult life? The present study addresses this question in part by describing in motoric terms what children do when they play. Comparisons are made between the motor behaviors exhibited by kindergarten children when given an opportunity to interact in two different environments, a physical education class and a playground during free play.

REVIEW OF RELEVANT RESEARCH

The contribution of play to physical development, muscle skills and coordination is apparent in children's ritualized games, such as tag or hide-and-seek and, later on, football or soccer (Arnaud, 1974). The development of physical skills is obvious in these games, but it may also occur in other activities involving covert role-enactment not evident to the observer unless the child reveals such role-enactment.

Little in the way of actual research supports the casual observation that children play actively enough to promote physical development. The literature may be limited in this area because of a preoccupation with play's contributions to the cognitive and affective development of the child. Several studies were found, however, which investigated children's motor behaviors during free play.

A study (Clark, et al., 1969) that may relate only peripherally to the present investigation, since it was concerned with free play in an indoors setting, examined the behaviors of 40 children during their free play period. The researchers found that girls spent more time in activities involving sitting at a table and fine motor manipulation while boys preferred activities that required gross motor movements.

Another study, more closely related to the present research was conducted by Dean Funk (1969) in which he attempted to answer the question, "Will a planned physical education program be more effective than a non-planned program with regard to improvement in physical performance . . .?" Data were collected from 38 trainable mentally retarded children, 20 of whom designated as the experimental group were given a 30-minute planned physical education program each day for 54 days, during which period the control group of 18 children had a free activity program. Physical fitness tests (straight arm hand, sit-ups, medicine ball throw, and standing long jump) were then administered to all the children. Funk found no significant gains on three of the four above-mentioned tests. Significance at the .05 level was reached on the sit-up tests for the experimental group.

It has been observed (Hardiman, et al., 1975) that even when a variety of equipment and materials is available, some children re-

151

frain from interacting with the equipment and thus do not develop skills. This self-restraint from engaging in physical activities may be due to lack of interest in the activities, lack of coordination and skills and/or general slowness in motor development. In studies reporting that contingent teacher attention effectively increases children's use of playground equipment, (Buell, Stoddard, Harris and Baer, 1968; Hall and Broden, 1967; Johnston, Kelley, Harris and Wolf, 1966) Hardiman, Goetz, Reuter and Le-Blanc (1975) combined the use of primes (suggestion to the child), contingent attention and training sessions to assess a child's engagement and skill in six large motor activities. The subject was a 4-year-old girl medically diagnosed as having cerebral palsy. Before the study, she had spent her outdoor playtime sitting on a low table or standing near a teacher. The six large muscle activities that the researchers trained her in were: navigating a ladder and some steps, sliding, rolling, climbing and walking a low balance board. It was found that although contingent adult attention and primes for increasing engagement in motor behavior were demonstrated to be effective, such attention was insufficient to increase motor skill. By contrast, training sessions were found to be effective for increasing motor skills. These results suggest that the universal use of primes and differential attention may not lead to gains in motor skill if a child does not have such skills.

Hovell, Bursick, Sharkey and McClure (1978), in a study closely related to the present investigation, attempted to evaluate elementary students' voluntary physical activity during recess. Three hundred students, third through sixth grade were observed for five minutes over a six-week period. Every five seconds their activity levels were rated as no activity, moderate or vigorous. The observations took place on a school playing field where the students were engaged in a 20-minute period of free-play. Results showed that the students engaged in physical activity for only about 60 percent of their recess time. The observers reported that most of the children spent much of their recess time standing in line waiting their turn to run races,

"come to bat" or kick a ball or casually moving about talking with friends. Only rarely did they report a child engaged in sustained vigorous activity. Finally, the researchers compared the students' level of activity with an adult aerobic standard, which showed that the children engaged in only about half as much activity as that performed by the adult standard. The authors concluded that elementary students obtained relatively little exercise during recess periods and that children do not voluntarily engage in sufficient aerobic activity during recesses to be likely to increase their cardio-respiratory fitness.

The above study failed to take into account the effect that the play environment might have had on the level and amount of the children's physically active play. All the children in the study had to stimulate their play was a large grassy field and some playing balls.

HYPOTHESES

The following hypotheses were tested:
1. There will be no significant differences in the frequency of observed behaviors of children on the playground as compared with observed behaviors of these same children in physical education class for each of the 43 variables on the observation form.
2. There will be no significant differences in the frequency of observed behaviors of children (when tabulated by their sex), on the playground as compared with observed behaviors (tabulated by sex), of these same children in physical education class for each of the 43 variables on the observation form.
3. There will be no significant differences in frequency of observed behaviors of children when tabulated by their skill level as ranked by the physical education teachers: on the playground as compared with observed behaviors tabulated by skill level; of these same children in physical education class for each of the 43 variables on the observation form.

SUBJECTS AND SETTING FOR THE STUDY

A kindergarten class of 16 children was selected at random. Children who received special services (i.e., motor lab rehabilitation, speech therapy and psychological counseling) were omitted from the study. Of the 12 remaining children who participated, six were females, six were males. The children were ranked according to their motor skills by their P.E. teachers.

For several reasons the Crockett Elementary School in San Marcos, Texas was selected as the setting: 1) the kindergartners spent an equal amount of time each day in physical education class and in free play on the playground; 2) the physical education teachers held B.S. degrees in Elementary Physical Education; and 3) the playground had been designed to promote children's play.

PROCEDURE

Using a prepared checklist, an observer recorded the children's motor behaviors in their 35-minute physical education class and on the playground during their 35-minute free play period. Each child was observed four times during each 35-minute period. Data were collected for a total of 26 days over a nine-week period, transferred to computer cards and subjected to analysis of variance using the *Statistical Package for the Social Sciences* subroutines chi square and Spearman correlation coefficients for rank order data.

FINDINGS

The test of Hypothesis One found correlations significant at the .05 level for particular types of behavior in free play and in P.E. Children were observed to display more engagement behaviors, motor behaviors and locomotor behaviors in free play. In P.E., children were observed to display more not-engaged behaviors, non-locomotor behaviors, manipulative and cognitive behaviors. Therefore, the null Hypothesis One was rejected.

The behaviors observed in P.E. can be explained in terms of that environment's structure. That is, more time was involved in P.E. in getting out supplies, waiting in line for a turn to run a relay race and listening to instruction than occurred in free play, simply because there were no supplies to be got out, no organized games that involved waiting for a turn to participate and no one giving instructions or lectures. Thus, more time in

free play on the playground was spent in active physical participation.

The test of Hypothesis Two found no significant differences between the sexes in relation to free play and P.E. on any of the subcategories considered. Two of the individual 43 variables were found to vary by sex by environment to a significant degree. These were waiting and pushing, with girls engaged in more waiting behaviors on both environments than boys and pushing behaviors occurring more frequently for boys in P.E., more frequently for girls in free play. However, when analyzed by category, these differences disappear so that the null Hypothesis Two cannot be rejected.

Because all children participated in all activities planned for the class period in P.E., any differences between the sexes in terms of chosen activities or amount of time spent in an activity were non-existent. In P.E., the plans were for everyone to do the same activity at the same time. The fact that girls spent more time waiting than boys in P.E. was probably due to the luck of the draw or a coincidence of sampling schedule. The same could be said for the pushing behaviors that boys exhibited in P.E. Observed pushing behaviors of girls in play can be attributed to their favorite dramatic play theme, "prisoner," which they played day after day. A girl was "captured," pushed around the playground until "jail" was reached, then shoved forcefully into a "cell" and "locked up." Boys seldom participated in this game.

The test of Hypothesis Three found no significant differences between skill level and types of behaviors displayed in P.E. In free play, however, significant differences were found at the .05 and .01 levels for skill level and types of behaviors displayed. Students ranked above average displayed less not-engaged and more engaged motor and engaged-but-not-motorically behaviors than did students ranked average or below average. Because no significant differences were found in P.E. in relation to skill level the null Hypothesis Three cannot be rejected; however, for free play the null hypothesis is rejected.

Teachers, by nature of the structure of the P.E. class, insisted that all the students engage in all activities planned for the period.

153

Thus, for the purposes of this study, in P.E. class a leveling process occurred in which distinction between individuals tended to disappear. It is interesting to note that in free play, the students judged above average in motor skills were the more physically active ones. Apparently motor skill has some relation to the amount of involvement a child seeks in free play.

The findings of this study indicated that children are more physically active in free play than they are in a physical education class and that sex is not a good predictor of how actively a child plays. Furthermore, children who are above average in motor skills play more actively than children who are average or below average in motor skills.

References

Aldis, O. *Play Fighting*. New York: Academic Press, 1975.

Anderson, H. "Domination and Integration in the Social Behavior of Young Children." *Genetic Psychology Monographs* 19 (1937): 343–408.

Arnaud, S. "Some Functions of Play in the Educative Process." *Childhood Education* 51 (1974): 72–78.

Barnes, K. "Preschool Play Norms: A Replication." *Developmental Psychology* 5 (1971): 99–103.

Bayley, N. "The Development of Motor Abilities During the First Three Years." *Society for Research In Child Development Monographs* 1 (1935): 1–26.

Bayley, N., and H. Jones. "Environmental Correlates of Mental and Motor Development: A Cumulative Study from Infancy to Six Years." *Child Development* 8 (1937).

Bengtsson, A. *Environmental Planning For Children's Play*. New York: Praeger, 1970.

Brazelton, B. "Are There Too Many Sights and Sounds in Your Baby's World?" *Redbook* 137, 5 (1971).

Breckenridge, M., and L. Vincent. *Child Development*. Philadelphia: Sanders, 1955.

Broadhead, G. "Social Class Correlates of Gross Motor Performance in Special Education." *Rehabilitation Literature* 35 (1974): 331–35.

Clark, A.; S. Wyon and M. Richards. "Free-play in Nursery School Children." *Journal of Child Psychology and Psychiatry and Allied Disciplines* 10 (1969): 205–16.

Collipp, P., ed. *Childhood Obesity*. Boston: Publishing Sciences Group, 1975.

Corbin, C. *A Textbook of Motor Development*. Dubuque, IA: Brown, 1973.

Cratty, B. *Social Dimensions of Physical Activity*. Englewood Cliffs, NJ: Prentice-Hall, 1967.

Cravioto, J. "Nutritional Deficiencies and Mental Performance in Childhood." In D. Glass, ed., *Environmental Influences*. New York: Rockefeller University Press, 1968.

Curtis, H. *Education Through Play*. New York: Macmillan, 1915.

Davis, R. "The Effect of Perceptually Oriented Physical Education on Perceptual Motor Ability and Academic Ability of Kindergarten and First Grade Children." Paper presented at the annual convention of AAHPER, Anaheim, California, April 1974.

Dennis, W. "A Description and Classification of the Responses of the Newborn Infant." *Psychological Bulletin*, 31 (1934): 9–33.

Dennis, W., ed. "Environmental Influences upon Motor Development." *Readings in Child Psychology*. Englewood Cliffs, NJ: Prentice-Hall, 1963, 83–94.

Dennis, W., and M. Dennis. "Cradles and Cradling Practices of the Pueblo Indians." *American Anthropology* 42 (1940).

Edwards, N. "The Relationship Between Physical Condition Immediately After Birth and Mental and Motor Performance at Age Four." *Genetic Psychology Monographs* 78 (1968): 257–89.

Ellis, M. *Why People Play*. Englewood Cliffs, NJ: Prentice-Hall, 1973.

Espenschade, A. "Motor Performance in Adolescence." *Society for Research in Child Development* 5 (1940).

Frankenburg, W., and J. Dodds. "The Denver Developmental Screening Test." *Journal of Pediatrics* 71 (1967).

Friedberg, P., and E. Berkeley. *Play and Interplay*. New York: Macmillan, 1970.

Frost, J., and S. Campbell. "Play and Equipment Choices of Conserving and Preconserving Children on Two Types of Playgrounds." Unpublished research report, The University of Texas at Austin, 1977.

Frost, J., and B. Klein. *Children's Play and Playgrounds*. Boston: Allyn and Bacon, 1979.

Funk, D. "The Effects of a Physical Education Program on the Educational Improvement of Trainable Mentally Retarded."

Gesell, A. *The First Five Years of Life*. New York: Harper, 1940.

Gifford, P. "The Effects of High Resistance and High Repetition Physical Activity on the Body Composition of Prepubescent Boys." *Dissertation Abstracts International*, 1974 (University Microfilms no. 74-12, 022).

Goldberg, S., and M. Lewis. "Play Behaviors in the Year-old Infant: Early Sex Differences." *Child Development* 40 (1969): 21–31.

Goodenough, F. "Measuring Behavior Traits by Means of Repeated Short Samples." *Journal of Juvenile Research* 12 (1928): 230–35.

Gulick, L. *Philosophy of Play*. New York: Scribner's, 1904.

Gutteridge, M. "A Study of Motor Achievements of Young Children." *Archives of Psychology* 34, 244 (1939).

Groos, K. *The Play of Animals*. New York: Appleton, 1898.

Halverson, L., and M. Robertson. "Motor Pattern Development in Young Children." *Research Abstracts*. Washington, DC: American Association for Health, Physical Education and Recreation, 1966.

Hardiman, S.; E. Goetz; K. Reuter and J. LeBlanc. "Primes, Contingent Attention, and Training: Effects on a Child's Motor Behavior." *Journal of Applied Behavioral Analysis* 8 (1975): 399–409.

Harrow, A. *A Taxonomy of the Psychomotor Domain*. New York: Longman, 1978.

Herkowitz, J. "Sex-role Expectations and Motor Behaviors of the Young Child." In M. Ridenour, ed. *Motor Development: Issues and Applications*. Princeton, NJ: Princeton Book, 1978.

Hetherington, C. "Fundamental Education." *American Physical Education Review* 15 (1910): 629–35.

Hovell, M.; J. Bursick; R. Sharkey and J. McClure. "An Evaluation of Elementary Students' Voluntary Physical Activity During Recess." *Research Quarterly* 49 (1978): 460–74.

Howes, C., and J. Rubenstein. *Peer Play and the Effect of the Inanimate Environment*. Washington, DC: Eastern Psychological Association, 1978. (ERIC Document Reproduction Service, ED 163 323.)

Huizinga, J. *Homo-Ludens—A Study of The Play Element In Culture*. Boston: Beacon Press, 1950.

Humphrey, J. *Child Development Through Physical Education*. Springfield, IL: Charles C. Thomas, 1980.

Johnson, M. "The Effect of Variation in the Amount of Play Equipment." *Child Development* 6 (1935): 56–68.

Keller, R. "A Comparison of Two Methods of Teaching Physical Education to Secondary School Boys." Unpublished doctoral dissertation, The University of Illinois at Urbana, 1963.

Kepler, H. *The Child and His Play*. New York: Funk and Wagnalls, 1952.

Knoblock, H. *et al.* "The Relationship of Race and Socioeconomic Status to the Development of Motor Behavior Patterns in Infancy." *Psychiatric Research Reports* 10 (1958).

Parten, M. "Social Participation Among Preschool Children." *Journal of Abnormal and Social Psychology* 27 (1932): 243–69.

Piaget, J. *Play, Dreams, and Imitation in Childhood*. New York: Norton, 1962.

Pratt, R. "The Concept of Play in American Physical Education." Doctoral dissertation, Ohio State University, 1973 (University Microfiche no. 1688).

Rarick, L. "Exercise and Growth." In Paterson and Hallberg, eds. *Background Readings for Physical Education*. New York: Holt, 1966.

Rarick, L.; J. Widdop and G. Broadhead. "The Physical Fitness and Motor Performance of Educable Mentally Retarded Children." *Exceptional Children* 36 (1970): 509–19.

Roberton, M. "Stages in Motor Development." In M. Ridenour, ed., *Motor Development: Issues and Applications*. Princeton, NJ: Princeton Book, 1978.

Rubin, K.; T. Maioni, and M. Hornung. "Free-play Behaviors in Middle- and Lower-class Preschoolers: Parten and Piaget Revisited." *Child Development* 47 (1976): 414–19.

Samuels, H. "The Effect of an Older Sibling on Infant Locomotor Exploration of a New Environment." *Child Development* 51 (1980): 607–09.

Scholtz, G., and M. Ellis. "Repeated Exposure to Objects and Peers in a Play Setting." *Journal of Experimental Child Psychology* 19 (1975): 448–55.

Seefeldt, V.; J. Haubenstricker and S. Reuschlein. "Why Physical Education in the Elementary School Curriculum?" Unpublished manuscript, Michigan State University, Lansing, 1974.

Shirley, M. "The Motor Sequence." In W. Dennis, ed., *Readings in Child Psychology*. Englewood Cliffs, NJ: Prentice-Hall, 1963.

Siedentop, D. *Physical Education: Introductory Analysis*. Dubuque, IA: Brown, 1972.

Siedentop, D.; D. Birdwell and M. Metzler. "A Process Approach to Measuring Teaching Effectiveness in Physical Education." Paper presented at the AAHPER Research Symposium in New Orleans, 1979.

Significance of The Young Child's Motor Development. Proceedings of a conference sponsored by The American Association for Health, Physical Education and Recreation and The National Association for the Education of Young Children. Washington, DC, 1971.

Singer, B. "Stability and Change in Motor Behavior." In L. Rarick, ed., *Human Growth and Development*. New York: Academic Press, 1973.

Smilansky, S. *The Effects of Sociodramatic Play on Disadvantaged Preschool Children*. New York: Wiley, 1968.

Spencer, H. *Principles of Psychology*. New York: Appleton, 1896.

Strickland, E. "Free Play Behaviors and Equipment Choices of Third Grade Children in Contrasting Play Environments." Unpublished doctoral dissertation, The University of Texas at Austin, 1979.

Sutton-Smith, B. "The Playful Modes of Knowing." In Curry and Arnaud, eds., *Play: The Child Strives Toward Self-Realization*. Washington, DC: National Association for the Education of Young Children, 1971.

Tanner, J. *Education and Physical Growth*. London, University of London Press, 1961.

Tauber, M. "Girls' Physically Active Play and Parental Behavior." Paper presented at the biennial meeting of the Society for Research in Child Development, San Francisco, 1979. (ERIC Document Reproduction Service, ED 172-912.)

Teeple, J. "Physical Growth and Maturation." In M. Ridenour, ed., *Motor Development: Issues and Applications*. Princeton, NJ: Princeton Book, 1978.

Ulrich, C. *The Social Matrix of Physical Education*. Englewood Cliffs, NJ: Prentice-Hall, 1968.

Wade, C. "Effects of Teacher Training on Teachers and Children in Playground Settings." Unpublished doctoral dissertation, The University of Texas at Austin, 1980.

Wellman, B. "Motor Achievements of Preschool Children." *Childhood Education* 13 (1937): 311.

Wickstrom, R. *Fundamental Motor Patterns*. Philadelphia: Lea and Febiger, 1977.

Widdop, J. "The Motor Performance of Educable Mentally Retarded Children with Particular Reference to the Identification of Factors Associated with Individual Differences in Performance." Unpublished doctoral dissertation, University of Wisconsin, 1967.

Perceived and Actual Playground Equipment Choices of Children

JACQUELINE MYERS
Consultant
Austin, Texas

Children's play choices are influenced both by the playground equipment available to them and the design of the playground itself (Holme & Massie, 1970; Johnson, 1935; Scholtz & Ellis, 1975). In a study of two contrasting neighborhoods in England, Holme & Massie (1970) found significant differences in children's play choices. Children living in a newly developed housing area with many paths and little motor traffic spent more time in passive home-oriented activities, such as sitting about and reading. Children living in a centuries-old residential neighborhood with busy streets and trash-filled vacant lots engaged in more active, away-from-home and traditional group games, such as throwing a ball against a wall and football. Mothers in both areas wanted better play facilities for their children, with the mothers from the older area also wanting more play space. Children's play there occurred mostly on sidewalks, stairwells and in busy streets. Large neighborhood playgrounds in both areas attracted children, with team ballgame areas holding children's interest and keeping them in attendance longer than other areas of the playground.

The equipment, or lack of it, provided in play environments affects the quality of play. Johnson (1935) compared the activities of preschool children on the same playground before and after changes in the amount of equipment available. Behavior was variously identified as bodily exercise, play with materials, undesirable behavior, games and contact with teachers. After a reduction in play equipment, children played more with sand and dirt, engaged in more games, received less bodily exercise but had more social contact. With an increase in equipment, children showed a decrease in bodily exercise, had more play with materials and less undesirable behavior. The children appeared to be resourceful with or without equipment and played with what was available.

More complex play environments containing a variety of equipment will hold children's interest for a longer period of time than less complex play environments. Scholtz & Ellis (1975) found that preschool children tended to interact more with materials than with peers in a high complexity indoor environment. After the novelty wore off in a low complexity environment, these children preferred to play with their peers.

Large outdoor play structures accommodating several children at a time afford opportunities for more complex play. Research using Piaget's cognitive categories of play combined with Parten's social play categories has found that children will have more social contacts and engage in richer dramatic play when large platform structures and items such as stripped-down cars and boats are provided (Frost & Campbell, 1977; Frost & Strickland, 1978). These items appear to attract more children for longer periods of time.

Since adults are the decision-makers when planning and purchasing play equipment, their perceptions of children's play choices are important. The extent to which adult's perceptions of children's play choices coincide with those of the children need to be ascertained. Since children are the ones who will be using the equipment, their ideas ought to be solicited by the adults and included in the planning. When planning for outdoor play environments, equipment should be selected that will provide a variety of play opportunities for many children.

157

Children can select their favorite equipment from pictures. Bishop, Peterson & Michaels (1972) found that 8- and 9-year-olds were able to select their favorite playground equipment using photographs as stimulus materials, picking out their favorite equipment from as many as 15 photographs of their playground. One month earlier, photos of the children playing on the same equipment had been taken. A positive correlation was found between the children's choices of pictures of playground equipment and their interactions with the equipment during play (Peterson, Bishop, Michaels & Rath, 1973).

In her studies of children's play in several cultures, Seagoe (1970, 1971) interviewed children about their favorite play activities and found that children around the age of seven were able to write out their answers to questions on paper, while younger children responded well to questions asked by an adult. Her questions centered on what the children liked to play best at home, school and in other places.

Much of the research on children's play has focused on indoor settings (Parten, 1933; Piaget, 1962; Rubin, Maioni & Hornung, 1976; Smilansky, 1968). Outdoor play environments do not have the physical limits that indoor environments have, making data more difficult to collect. Systems for studying play indoors and outdoors have been developed (Parten, 1932; Piaget, 1962; Seagoe, 1970) with each system indicating play behaviors that can be identified, described and classified into categories. Although none of these play category systems includes play equipment as a contributing factor, studies of children's play equipment choices have been conducted using play category systems (Frost & Campbell, 1977; Frost & Strickland, 1978; Myers, 1981).

This study examined the relationships between teachers' perceptions of children's play choices in an outdoor play environment and the children's perceived and actual play choices in that environment. How playground equipment was utilized by children was also investigated, including the number of children using each item of equipment and the number of times children were actually observed using each item of equipment.

METHOD

Subjects were 56 second-grade pupils, 25 girls and 31 boys and their teachers in a school with two different styles of playgrounds for use during free play periods. The traditional playground had standard playground equipment found on playgrounds throughout the United States: metal swings, slides and jungle gyms. The creative playground contained wooden platform structures, tire swings and loose parts for the children to use in building their own play environment. Both playgrounds had large grassy areas and sand pits.

Data for the study were gathered by observations of the children during free play periods and through individual interviews with the subjects using an instrument based on the Play Report developed by Seagoe (1970). Photographs of the playground equipment were used as stimulus materials to aid the children in indicating their preferred choices of playground equipment. A tape recorder was used to gather observational data during the outdoor play periods. As each piece of equipment was observed in rotating order, the names of the children playing on it were listed, along with a short description of the activity. Observational data, gathered during two 3-week periods, one in the fall and one in the spring, were transcribed verbatim and tabulated onto coding sheets. Equipment items were ranked by frequency of choice, with the favorite item being chosen the most number of times.

Limitations of the study include: 1) a small sample predominantly from a white, middle-class background; 2) play choices limited to the equipment provided on the playgrounds; 3) the 4-month time lapse between the two observation periods. Weather is a definite factor in conducting outdoor studies, as cold or wet weather is not suitable for observing children in outdoor play. It was assumed that the data base collected in the fall might not be as reliable as that collected in the spring. It was also assumed that the teachers would have minimal influences on the children's play choices and that the children were equally familiar with all the available equipment.

RESULTS

The correlation coefficients for children's perceived and observed preferences of playground equipment and their comparisons with teacher's perceived preferences are summarized in Table 1. A position correlation between the children's perceived and observed preferences was found, which is supported by the findings of Peterson, Bishop, Michaels and Rath (1973).

Children's perceived preferences of playground equipment were positively correlated with the teachers' perceived preferences of play equipment for their students ($p \leq .01$). The girls' perceived preferences and the teachers' preferences had the highest correlation ($p \leq .001$) in the study. The fact that both teachers were female may have been an influence on this finding. A non-significant positive correlation was found between the teachers' perceived preferences and the

children's observed choices of playground equipment ($p \leq .29$). The correlation between the teachers' perceptions and the boys' observed choices of playground equipment was lower ($p \leq .12$) than the teachers' perceptions and the girls' observed choices ($p \leq .07$). Neither correlation was significant.

The teachers did not make a wide range of choices of playground equipment for their students, selecting a total of nine items out of more than 30 choices available on both playgrounds. All the teachers' choices were on the creative playground. The children were observed to play on all but three items available. One teacher indicated many of her children would play ball games and chase, a form of tag, while the other teacher indicated more equipment use by her students.

During the interview, the children selected 19 favorite items of equipment, 11 on the creative playground, and eight on the traditional playground. Children were observed spending most of their time on 12 items, seven on the creative playground and five on the traditional playground.

Table 1
Correlation Coefficients for Children's Perceived and Observed Preferences as Compared with Teachers' Perceived Preferences

	Total Group (N = 56)		Boys (N = 31)		Girls (N = 25)	
	r	p	r	p	r	p
Child Perceived Preference vs Child Observed Preference of Play Equipment[a]	.35	.06	.48	.007	.48	.007
Teacher Perceived Preference vs Child Perceived Preference of Play Equipment[b]	.53	.002	.39	.025	.63	.001
Teacher Perceived Preference vs Child Observed Preference of Play Equipment[b]	.19	.29	.28	.12	.32	.07

[a]N = 30
[b]N = 33

159

A chi square analysis between playgrounds indicated that a significantly greater number of children preferred the creative playground rather than the traditional playground ($X^2 = 5.16$, $p \leq .05$, df 1). This is supported by Strickland (1979) who observed these same children actually choosing to play on the creative playground when they had a free choice between the two. When the data from the two classrooms in this study were analyzed separately, marked differences were found. In one classroom a significant number of children preferred the creative playground ($X^2 = 4.32$, $p \leq .05$, df 1) while the children's preferences in the second classroom did not approach significance ($X^2 = .89$, $p \leq .35$, df 1). Both teachers expected their students to prefer the creative playground.

The frequency of choice or number of times a child was observed on an item of equipment was tested with chi square analysis for both fall and spring observations on each playground. Differences were expected in the amount of use each item of equipment received, with more complex equipment having more play options expected to attract more children for longer periods of time. Significant differences were found. Results are in Table 2. Ball games occupied a large part of the boys' time all year. A small group of boys in one classroom played either football, kickball or basketball almost exclusively throughout the study. There were other boys who did not touch a ball. Much of the boys' time during ball play was spent in discussion and argument about rules and their application. Boys also spent much time in the fall on the dirt mound playing "King of the Mountain," and in the spring playing in the loose parts area.

Girls preferred the swings on both playgrounds. They also spent time talking in small groups and playing chase, in which they chased boys around the playground, neither of these activities involving the active use of playground equipment. Although chase was not indicated as a favorite pastime, more than two-thirds of the children played it sometime during the study, with more girls than boys involved.

Some equipment attracted greater numbers of children than others. The length of time the equipment was in use was not considered, but the percentage of children using each item of equipment was determined with the V-Stat Library Distat Program. On the traditional playground, the dirt mound in the fall and the metal climbers in the spring were used by more than 70 percent of the children. Eighty-seven percent of the boys played "King of the Mountain" on the dirt mound, running around and rolling down the slope in their struggles to occupy the top. The play theme used by more than 75 percent of the boys on the metal climbers was outer space, based on the *Star Wars* movies. Countdowns of "5-4-3-2-1-blastoff!" were heard when the children climbed up and jumped off at "Blastoff!" Determining who were the captains and officers of the spaceships occupied considerable time. The loose parts areas on the creative playground attracted 80 percent of the children. The large linked structure containing bars, slides, balance beams, platforms and other items, attracted 84 percent of the girls on the creative playground. They spent their time sitting, talking, or doing tricks on the bars and beams. Ballgames of all types were played by most of the boys, with only one girl playing ball. More girls than boys played on the swings.

Low-interest items during the playground observations were the horizontal ladders and

Table 2
Frequency with Which Children Used Playground Equipment
on the Creative and Traditional Playgrounds

Playground	Fall		Spring		df
	Expected	Chi Square	Expected	Chi Square	
Traditional	53.31	626.11	114.23	654.00	12
Creative	83.80	963.55	73.15	1316.82	19

chinning bars on the traditional playground, which were located along the fence near a busy street. The horizontal ladder and chinning bars on the creative playground were part of a large integrated wooden structure and received more use. In their study of how the placement of equipment affects play, Witt & Gramza (1969) found that children preferred to play on equipment located toward the center of the playspace and tended to ignore equipment placed along the edge of the play area.

CONCLUSIONS

The children in this study did tend actually to play on the equipment they said they preferred, as indicated by the significant correlations reported between the children's perceived and actual choices of playground equipment. A change in interests may have occurred between the time of the interview and the time of the observations, particularly between the fall observations and the spring interviews. Peer pressure also played a role; the boys reported making plans for the free outdoor play time when they first arrived at school. The role of peers in selecting play activities has not been well documented, particularly in the primary grades. Playing with friends may be more important than playing a favorite game. Also, if a favorite activity requires a group, a child cannot engage in it by himself.

The teachers' perceptions correlated more highly with the girls' perceived and observed choices than with the boys' choices. Whether this would be true for male teachers and boys is not to be conjectured, although teachers are often responsible for requesting equipment and planning activities for children. The influence of teachers on children's play choices is present, but how it operates and what forms it takes are not well known. Children's outdoor play activities have been found to be influenced by the educational orientation of the staff (Tizard, Philps & Plewis, 1976). Seagoe (1971) found that schools with structured programs tended toward more teacher-directed play and more team sports. Whether these types of influences are operating in individual classrooms, and to what degree, is open for study.

The teachers in this study did not make a wide range of choices of playground equipment. Since they limited their choices to one playground, they apparently were not aware of what children preferred to play on the other playground or why. Their ideas of where the children would choose to play were limited in scope and they indicated that all the children would use less than half of the equipment available to them. Perhaps asking the teachers for their perceptions later in the school year would have given closer correlations. While the teachers easily selected three items of equipment for some children, they found it difficult to select with other children. The teachers in the pilot study conducted the previous spring had the same difficulties. Their perceptions correlated more closely with the children's perceived choices rather than with their actual choices, a result possibly caused by the children's use of such a wide variety of equipment or by the teachers not being fully aware of the peer group structures among their pupils.

Equipment accommodating many children doing different activities appeared to be selected most frequently by the largest number of children. While the traditional swings were nearly always full, only four children could swing at one time with little interaction occurring during swinging. When resources are limited, complex equipment providing multiple activities appears to be the better choice for playgrounds than single-use equipment such as traditional swings and slides. The boys appeared to prefer equipment accommodating large, active play groups as indicated by the large groups of boys who played on the dirt mound, the metal climbers and in ballgames. The girls preferred equipment providing smaller, quieter play groups, and they did not often participate in large, boisterous group activities.

That children did play on the equipment they said they preferred, should be an indication that children should be involved in the selection of new equipment for playgrounds. Perhaps the teachers could serve as intermediaries between children and the adult planners by gathering information from the children and presenting it to the planners. How to involve children in planning for their play should be an important consideration of adult planning committees.

References

Frost, J. L., and S. Campbell. "Play and Equipment Choices of Conserving and Preconserving Children on Conventional and Creative Playgrounds." Unpublished research report, The University of Texas at Austin, 1977.

Frost, J. L., and E. Strickland. "Equipment Choices of Young Children During Free Play." *Lutheran Education*, 114 (1978): 34–46.

Holme, A., and P. Massie. *Children's Play: A Study of Needs and Opportunities*. London: Michael Joseph, 1970.

Johnson, M. W. "The Effect on Behavior of Variation in the Amount of Play Equipment." *Child Development* 6 (1935): 56–68.

Myers, J. "Children's Perceived vs. Actual Choices of Playground Equipment as Viewed by Themselves and Their Teachers." Unpublished doctoral dissertation, The University of Texas at Austin, 1981.

Parten, M. B. "Social Participation Among Preschool Children." *Journal of Abnormal and Social Psychology* 27 (1932): 243–69.

———. "Social Play Among Preschool Children." *Journal of Abnormal and Social Psychology* 28 (1933): 136–47.

Peterson, G. L.; R. L. Bishop; R. M. Michaels and G. J. Rath. "Children's Choice of Playground Equipment: Development of Methodology for Integrating User Preferences into Environmental Engineering." *Journal of Applied Psychology* 58 (1973):233–38.

Piaget, J. *Play, Dreams, and Imitation in Childhood*. (C. Gattegno & F. M. Hodgson, trans.) New York: Norton, 1962.

Rubin, K. H.; T. L. Maioni, and M. Hornung. "Free-play Behaviors in Middle- and Lower-class Preschoolers: Parten and Piaget Revisited." *Child Development* 47 (1976): 414–19.

Scholtz, G. J. L., and M. K. Ellis. "Repeated Exposure to Objects and Peers in a Play Setting." *Journal of Experimental Child Psychology* 19 (1975): 448–55.

Seagoe, M. V. "An Instrument for the Analysis of Children's Play as an Index of Degree of Socialization." *Journal of School Psychology* 8 (1970): 139–44.

———. "Children's Play in Three American Subcultures." *Journal of School Psychology* 9 (1971):167–72.

Smilansky, S. *The Effects of Sociodramatic Play on Disadvantaged Preschool Children*. New York: Wiley, 1968.

Strickland, E. V. "Free Play Behaviors and Equipment Choices of Third Grade Children in Contrasting Play Environments." Unpublished doctoral dissertation, The University of Texas at Austin, 1979.

Tizard, B.; J. Philps and I. Plewis. "Play in Pre-school Centers—II: The Effects on Play of the Child's Social Class and of the Educational Orientation of the Center." *Journal of Child Psychology & Psychiatry* 17 (1976): 265–74.

Witt, P., and A. Gramza. "Position Effects in Play Equipment Preferences of Nursery School Children." ERIC Document Reproduction Service, University of Illinois at Urbana, 1969 (ED 045 185).

PART IV: TRENDS IN DESIGNING AND DEVELOPING PLAYGROUNDS
Introduction

A playground movement is gaining force throughout the industrialized world. As more and more children reside and attend school in urban areas, the need for playgrounds increases. These are, of course, adult inspired and frequently adult designed and manufactured and may be considered "artificial" environments. But they are necessary, for the challenges of nature—the countryside, the farm, animals, crops, trees, hills, streams—cannot be readily transported into heavily populated, limited-space areas such as the school or the city neighborhood. Consequently, adults build or, preferably, assist children to build playgrounds.

Joe L. Frost describes the playground movement in the United States, emphasizing reasons for the movement, and links it to the influences of European play environments. The deficiencies of traditional or conventional playgrounds are now well documented, and steps are under way in many sections of the country to correct them. Four major types of playgrounds—traditional or conventional, designer or contemporary, adventure, creative—now exist. The future promises a new wave of interest and new perspectives on playground design and development.

In his comprehensive essay, Gary T. Moore highlights numerous new playground design perspectives. He begins with an overview of "child-environment theory" as it pertains to play, reviews much of the available research on play and play environments and compares designated and neighborhood play environments. Finally, he draws implications for a new approach to the planning and design of play environments. These include: development of environmental policy, provision for a full variety of play activities, play environments and play locations, provision for interaction between children and adults, provision for a "network" of play by linking together elements of the play environment system and provision for studying play environments.

Studying play environments has already begun. Marian L. Monroe conducted an extensive assessment of 54 Title XX day care center playgrounds in Texas. Analyses of the operational characteristics and composite playground scores found no significant relationships between the composite scores and center capacity, daily rate, age, building origin, decision-maker, director's education, trained caregiver percentage, group sizes, staff tenure, vandalism or public playground usage. Significant relationships were found between the composite scores and center auspices, composite scores and level of enrollment, composite scores and caregiver degrees and composite scores and staff training on playgrounds. The study also provides specific information for improving playground safety and for meeting children's developmental play needs.

Perhaps the most ingenious and exciting playgrounds in the world are the adventure playgrounds of Denmark. Originated as recently as 1943, these playgrounds have already influenced playground conceptions throughout most of the industrialized world. Jens Pedersen, Chairman of the Danish Planning Group on Children and Culture, takes the reader on an intriguing tour of Danish adventure playgrounds, pointing out history, political underpinnings, playground characteristics, family and community influences and staff and child responsibilities. He believes that the adventure playground itself is less important than the idea or philosophy behind them: " . . . transforming a barren, passive and observer-type existence into an active life based on self-fulfillment."

In contrast to the natural and hand-made qualities of play materials on adventure play-

163

grounds, most playgrounds are equipped with manufactured equipment. Jay Beckwith notes that new "post/deck/event" equipment is now replacing traditional swings, slides and climbers. Beckwith is the creative force behind much of the improvement in modern play equipment. He believes that good playground equipment should be complex, linked, flexible, challenging, developmentally relevant, safe and durable. The play equipment of several manufacturers is compared for type and range of play events offered and for material specifications. In addition, safety and durability are discussed.

Continuing the theme of equipment design, Lawrence D. Bruya considers the appearance of contemporary structures on many school and park playgrounds. These structures are both different in definition as well as in the design characteristics upon which they are based. In the creation of play environments for children, designers may involve three distinct decision sets: (1) Predesign Considerations—(a) human factors, (b) safety, (c) materials; (2) Design Considerations—(a) play events, (b) accessibility, (c) linking, (d) modular concept; and (3) Post Design Considerations—(a) trained play leaders.

No discussion of modern playgrounds is complete without considering safety. Michael Henniger, Eric Strickland and Joe Frost illustrate the hazardous characteristics of conventional playgrounds, present statistics on playground injuries and trace the history of yet unfilled efforts to develop national standards for manufactured play equipment.

A pioneer in the playground movement, Paul Hogan, assists communities and agencies in designing and constructing their own playgrounds. One of his unique projects, the outdoor play environment for Children's Hospital, National Medical Center, Washington, D.C., is presented here. The project featured cooperative design by nurses, doctors, physical therapists, psychiatrists, administrators, child life program staff, the donor and Hogan himself. The design included a water play system, tree house and gathering place, ramps for wheelchairs, picnic gazebo, swing and cable ride, rubber matting in fall areas. Other features are under development.

Another unique type of playground designed by Ellen Booth Church is called the music playground. Growing out of a strong belief that music and movement are essential in child development, Church's playground is a place where children can pound, tap, blow, pour, jump, roll, strum or bang with a wide variety of materials. The design is similar to that of an exercise trail with each piece of apparatus connected to the music trail. The music materials include those that can be added to an existing playground and those requiring major construction work.

Talbot, trained in architecture, sensitive to the nature and aesthetic qualities of environments, proposes that living plants be a major component of play environments. The use of plants in children's outdoor environments opens up a new yet ancient way of creating playspaces, which increases a child's learning abilities, creativity and imagination. When used judiciously, vegetation helps children develop increased spatial and sensory awareness, practical knowledge about construction, awareness of natural processes and greater sense of wonder. Specific suggestions are included on how to approach the landscaping of a playground or schoolyard; practical ideas concerning the use of trees, shrubs, vines, grass and groundcover; and tips on starting a children's garden. More than just ornamentation, plants are an essential design tool element for anyone wishing to increase the educational value of their playspaces.

The American Playground Movement

JOE L. FROST
Department of Curriculum and Instruction
The University of Texas at Austin

A playground movement is brewing throughout the United States. From a small beginning on the West Coast and in a few scattered cities during the past several years, new, exciting playscapes are now springing up in communities, large and small, across the nation. The movement is long overdue, for the traditional American playground of concrete and steel contrasts sharply with the natural, adventure playscapes of certain other countries. True to American tradition of diversity, the new playscapes have no common source of inspiration or theory and no singular style or design. They spring from the creative thought of professional architects, designers, educators and psychologists; and they frequently engage the energy of parents, teachers and children.

Although the reasons for the American playground movement are multiple and complex, four factors appear to be central: (1) backlash of the cognitive emphasis in early childhood education, (2) influence of European play environments, (3) increasing awareness of deficiencies in traditional American playgrounds and (4) accumulation of experience with new types of playgrounds. In addition, research on play is contributing to the new look.

BACKLASH

Early research in experimental programs for young children during the mid-1960s left the illusion of supremacy for cognitive-academic programs in promoting intellectual development and academic growth. This reflection was to be shattered by later analyses (Bronfenbrenner, 1974; Frost and Kis-

Reprinted from *Childhood Education* (February 1978): 176–82.

singer, 1976) which opened serious questions about the effects of narrowly conceived approaches on more dynamic, less readily measured dimensions of development, particularly social, conative and affective. In addition, the intuition and experience of many professionals led them to distrust easy solutions or packaged programs and to turn their attention back to the "whole child." Not that cognitive development was set aside for other concerns—rather cognition was viewed as an integrative element in total development. Similarly, the preoccupation with academics was gradually tempered with the understanding that fundamental processes mediate development and allow—indeed promote—cognition and later or concurrent academic growth.

Chief among these processes is *play* (Bijou, 1976; Dattner, 1969; Ellis, 1973; Feitelson and Ross, 1973; Frank, 1968; Herron and Sutton-Smith, 1971; Omwake, 1963; Piaget, 1962). Fundamental to its expression is the existence of a facilitating environment or playscape (Frost and Campbell, 1977; Gramza, 1972; Henniger, 1977; Johnson, 1935; Rubin, 1975; Seagoe, 1971; Smilansky, 1968). Currently, even in the face of the ill-conceived, undefined, unorganized "back to basics" squabble, more and more adults who work with young children are realizing this need and lending their energies to the playground movement.

EUROPEAN PLAY ENVIRONMENTS

During recent years, American educators traveling abroad have reported with increasing fervor about play environments so radical in nature as to defy precise description. Labeled "eyesores" and "junkyards" by some and enthusiastically praised by others, the

165

adventure playgrounds* of several countries, notably England, Sweden and Denmark, have one and perhaps only one factor in common—children of all ages love to play there. Beyond this common feature, the designs are as diverse as the children who make them, for many adventure playscapes are indeed child designs.

Adults play a role. They fence off a vacant lot, provide a storage house stocked with tools and haul in loads of scrap material and hire a play leader (see Lambert, 1974). Afterward, children are essentially free to build houses and climbing structures; dig in the earth; care for gardens and animals; or simply play with basic materials, sand, water and dirt.

The adventure playground was the brainchild of a Danish architect and professor, D. Th. Sørenson (Bengtsson, 1972:12). He proposed his idea in the 1930s and the practical revolution began in 1943, in Emdrup, near Copenhagen. Sørenson and the Workers' Cooperative Housing Association provided bricks, boards, posts and tools for construction for children ages four to seventeen. The children working together in mixed age groups constructed caves, buildings, chairs, tables and other functional pieces. As huts and equipment outlived their usefulness, they were demolished and rebuilt.

The adventure-playground idea has since been implemented in Great Britain, Switzerland, Denmark, Japan and to some small extent in the United States. In some European countries, the people of the neighborhoods devastated in World War II began to work with children to develop new, imaginative play environments. One common pattern in Great Britain has been the provision of a playhut, a lavatory, heating and cooling facilities with two full-time play leaders to help children plan and do the things they attempt to do. The site is fenced and covered by comprehensive insurance.

In Denmark certain areas are defined in the playground. A main building serves for the supervisor, for storing tools to be checked out, and for first aid and lavatory. The playground is divided into the following: a storage area for building materials, a cave-digging and construction area, a communal area for adults and children to meet, a pet stable, asphalt for skating and cycling, a stage for plays, a bonfire site for cooking and warming, a fixed equipment area for climbing equipment and for sand and water, a garden, and a nature area left wild.

Common needs are evident across countries: (1) assuring an adequate supply of building materials such as lumber, crates, tools and nails; (2) providing supervisors or play leaders with the skills needed to help children with their construction problems and who are warm, friendly, open and supportive (in the United States it is difficult to convince communities that children need play leaders for public play areas); (3) securing support and cooperation of adults who initially view adventure playgrounds as eyesores or junkyards and who believe that play activities breed aggression and destructiveness in children.

The adventure playground is a remarkable experiment in providing for children's imaginative play using natural and scrap materials. It stands in stark contrast to the expensive, manufactured, hazardous, exercise-oriented playground of America.

DEFICIENCIES OF TRADITIONAL AMERICAN PLAYGROUNDS

Traditionally, the American playground is an arena of concrete and steel, comprised typically of a jungle gym, merry-go-round, slide, seesaw and swings, all designed and used primarily for one form of play—exercise. Additional natural forms of play—construction and make-believe or dramatics—are generally ignored. Frequently no equipment is provided to accommodate these forms of play and no sentiment for their expression. In sum, traditional playgrounds are developmentally inappropriate for the children who use them (see Vernon, 1976). Among the most prominent sites—public schools, private schools, day care centers and community parks—public schools are in a state of greatest need. This problem is largely due to tradition in design and purpose, a

---

*The Swedes prefer the term "building playgrounds," and the Danes prefer "play environments."

166

common set of equipment geared to developing motor skills in a middle elementary age group, now complicated by ever-increasing enrollment of fives, fours and even infants in public school contexts.

Traditional American playgrounds are unduly hazardous. A report by the U.S. Consumer Product Safety Commission (1975) is only one of several now available to support this contention (see also Bureau of Product Safety, 1972; McConnell et al., 1973; National Recreation and Park Association, 1975; for Canada see Wilkinson and Lockhart, 1976.) The National Electronic Injury Surveillance System records about 800,000 injuries per year requiring emergency room or more extensive treatment. These reports are horror stories of strangulations, hangings, entrapments, fractures, hematomas, concussions and amputations. Examples:

☐ A seven-year-old girl was killed when she fell from a swing set onto concrete, fracturing her skull.
☐ A two-year-old and a four-year-old girl strangled in separate accidents when their ponchos caught on a projecting member of a slide.
☐ Eight children of varying ages were hanged by swing ropes on chains.
☐ A finger of a nine-year-old girl was amputated by an exposed moving part of a merry-go-round.

And the list goes on and on. A major cause of serious injuries and deaths is falling onto hardpacked earth, asphalt or concrete—a problem that can be remedied simply by providing 8–10 inches of sand under all climbing and moving equipment. A second contributing factor is equipment that is poorly manufactured, installed and maintained. No mandatory standards presently influence the manufacture of play equipment in America. A preliminary set *has* been developed by the National Parks and Recreation Association under contract with the National Consumer Safety Commission, and a few manufacturers have placed themselves under voluntary standards. But tens of thousands of American playgrounds remain in use with antiquated equipment installed on hard surfaces, and many manufacturers continue to make and sell equipment of slipshod design and hazardous features (e.g., exposed bolts, moving elements too close together, lack of protective railings, heavy swing seats up to thirty or forty pounds, entrapment angles, flimsy chains, weak connecting points, protruding elements, sharp and jagged points).

Finally, it should be noted that elimination of undue hazards from play is a responsibility not only of those who design, build and install equipment but of teachers and other adults who work with children. One group is primarily responsible for making play equipment safe for children, the other for making children safe for playgrounds. Insecure, poorly coordinated children are unsafe for any playground. They *learn* to be safe by having many opportunities to express themselves in a rich, varied play environment of graduated challenge; by testing themselves over and over again—motorically, cognitively and socially.

NEW TYPES OF PLAYGROUNDS

Energy to revitalize American playgrounds is coming from many people, representing a wide range of professions and interests. Among the architects are Paul Friedberg and his inner city play parks (Friedberg, 1970); Richard Dattner and his ingenious New York City creations including an "ancient play garden" outside the Egyptian Temple at the Metropolitan Museum of Art (Dattner, 1969); Naud Burnett of Dallas and Ron Hartley of Jackson, Mississippi (Joyner, 1976), and their appealing designs for city parks.

Among those involved in helping schools and communities develop their own creative or adventure playgrounds are Jay Beckwith, a San Francisco designer (Hewes and Beckwith, 1974) who had personally designed and supervised the construction of many California playgrounds. Over a period of years the staff of Pacific Oaks College (Ellison, 1974) created one of America's finest playgrounds through ingenuity and inexpensive materials. Paul Hogan, president of the Playground Clearing House in Phoenixville, Pennsylvania (Hogan, 1974), promotes the concept of building playgrounds *with* people and has done so successfully in well over 100 Pennsylvania communities. Among the professors, Herb Wong, University of California, Berkeley, develops environmental yards for children and integrates indoor/outdoor learning strategies. Jack Mahan of Palomar College (Mahan, 1976), Joe Frost of the University of Texas at Austin, and Barry Klein (Frost and Klein, 1979) of Georgia State University assist schools, parents and community groups in designing and building playgrounds using scrounged materials. Gerry Fergeson of Pacific Oaks College and Reba Southwell of the Mississippi College for Women are among the few people involved in creating infant and toddler play yards.

The creations of these people differ from site to site (no two are alike), depending upon such factors as audience, availability of materials and human resources, site, finances and community restrictions. Three fairly distinct types are most prominent: the designer's playground, the adventure playground and the creative playground. The traditional playground is described along with these for comparison purposes.

The Traditional Playground. A formal playground consisting of commercial equipment constructed from metal and fixed in concrete. Typical equipment includes jungle gym, merry-go-round, seesaw, swing and slide, all designed for gross-motor play and limited involvement. (Some manufacturers are now producing high quality wood products for integration into imaginative playscapes.)

The Designer's Playground. A formal playground created by a professional architect or designer, usually of high esthetic quality, with variable function equipment and linked play zones. The equipment is frequently a mix of expensive commerical wood sculpture, metal apparatus and an assortment of timbers (e.g., railroad ties); natural stone and concrete are used for terraces and climbing.

The Adventure Playground. A highly informal playground utilizing a fenced area, storage facility with tools, a wide range of scrap building materials and one or more play leaders. Children are free to express themselves, with assistance as needed, in a wide range of creative forms of play. Tools and building materials are frequently supplemented with opportunities for cooking, gardening and caring for animals.

The Creative Playground. A semiformal playground constructed creatively from existing commercial equipment, purchased or gift equipment and an infinite range of scrounged materials (e.g., tires, lumber, telephone poles, railroad ties, cable spools, scrap pipe). Frequently planned and constructed by parents, teachers and children utilizing the help of a playground specialist, it includes permanent equipment, sand and water, and an array of loose parts to accommodate all forms of play. Areas for special activities such as art, gardening and caring for animals are frequently included.

A few general questions help to compare the merits of different types of playgrounds:

☐ Is the equipment durable and relatively safe?
☐ Is it properly installed and maintained?
☐ Is it of appropriate size for the age group? (For an item-by-item analysis see National Recreation and Park Association 1976.)
☐ Does the playground provide for work/play activities such as art, gardening and science projects?
☐ Are a variety of loose parts available, for sand and water play, wheeled vehicle play, dramatic play, building?
☐ Is the playground designed to involve large groups of children simultaneously?
☐ Is the playground esthetically pleasing?
☐ Is it economically feasible?

Among these four types, the "traditional playground" is rated unacceptable from both developmental and safety perspectives. Many designers' playgrounds are constructed from sound esthetic and safety assumptions, but frequently have functional restrictions—due primarily to absence of movable materials such as sand and water play equipment, wheeled vehicles, tools and materials for construction, and dramatic play materials. Designers' playgrounds are located primarily in public areas such as city parks, cost $50,000 to $250,000, and are limited to fixed equipment to prevent vandalism and theft. Most do not have play leaders or special areas for gardening, animals, etc., and practically none have proper storage facilities. With remediation of such shortcomings, these play environments could be developed into outstanding play centers.

For every criterion except esthetics (in the adult sense), the adventure and creative playgrounds must be given high marks. They are inexpensive, can accommodate large numbers of children simultaneously, are relatively safe (given normal maintenance and supervision), and most important accommodate every major form of play. The "eyesore" problem of adventure playgrounds is perhaps a major reason for their limited acceptance. The creative playground is a compromise between the formal, commercial setting and the "junk" environment. But both the adventure and the creative playground can be constructed by people of all ages working together, and herein is powerful strength.

THE FUTURE

Adults are beginning to realize that children, who after all are the consumers of play equipment, can make choices when given alternatives and that they can give creditable help in designing, building and maintaining their own playgrounds. The involvement of children, parents and community groups will increase as more and more successful projects reveal the advantages in reduced vandalism, community pride and functional products. Although the improved commercial equipment will continue to be used, the problem of ever-rising prices will force many groups to "scrounge" for surplus and discarded materials and to organize themselves for work days. It is highly important that such groups secure experienced help and search the literature on playground construction, for many bad playgrounds have resulted from good intentions.

As the playground movement grows, school designers will give greater attention to the preservation of the natural landscape immediately surrounding schools as the first, essential step in creating high-quality integrated indoor-outdoor learning environments. School boards and administrators will increasingly seek funds and professional assistance in designing the total play-recreational-sports environment for all age groups. The citizens of more and more communities in the near future will realize that playgrounds are a viable alternative for TV and boredom and a *major vehicle for learning*. They will construct exciting, functional play environments and seek facilitative play leaders as they grow to understand that the cost in human effort and material resources is a wise investment in children.

References

Bengtsson, A, ed. *Adventure Playgrounds*. New York: Praeger, 1972.

Bijou, S.W. *Child Development: The Basic Stage of Early Childhood*. Englewood Cliffs, NJ: Prentice-Hall, 1976.

Bronfenbrenner, U. "Is Early Intervention Effective? A Report on Longitudinal Evaluations of Preschool Programs," Vol. 2. Washington, DC: Department of Health, Education and Welfare, 1974.

Bureau of Product Safety, *Public Playground Equipment*. Washington, DC: Food and Drug Administration, Sept. 13, 1972.

Consumer Product Safety Commission. "Hazard Analysis: Playground Equipment." Washington, DC: Bureau of Epidemology, Apr. 1975.

Dattner, R. *Design for Play*. New York: Van Nostrand Reinhold. 1969.

Ellis, M.J. *Why People Play*. Englewood Cliffs, NJ: Prentice-Hall, 1973.

Ellison, G. *Play Structures*. Pasadena, CA: Pacific Oaks College, 1974.

Feitelson, D., and G.S. Ross. "The Neglected Factor—Play." *Human Development* 16 (1973): 202–23.

Frank, L.K. *Play Is Valid*. Washington, DC: Association for Childhood Education International, 1968.

Friedberg, P.M. and E.P. Berkeley. *Play and Interplay*. New York: Macmillan, 1970.

Frost, J.L., and S. Campbell. "Play and Equipment Choices of Conserving and Preconserving Children on Two Types of Playgrounds." Unpublished research report. Austin: The University of Texas, 1977.

Frost, J.L., and J.B. Kissinger. *The Young Child and the Educative Process*. New York: Holt, 1976. Chap. 4.

Frost, J.L., and B.L. Klein. *Children's Play and Playgrounds*. Boston: Allyn & Bacon, 1979.

Gramza, A.F. "A Measured Approach to Improvement of Play Environments." *Journal of Physical and Health Education and Recreation* 43 (1972): 25–54.

Henniger, M.L. *Free Play Behaviors of Nursery School Children in an Indoor and Outdoor Environment*. Unpublished doctoral dissertation. Austin: The University of Texas, 1977.

Herron, R.E., and B. Sutton-Smith. *Child's Play*. New York: Wiley, 1971.

Hewes, J.J., and J. Beckwith. *Build Your Own Playground*. Boston: Houghton, 1974.

Hogan, P. *Playgrounds for Free*. Cambridge, MA: MIT Press, 1974.

Johnson, M.W. "The Effect of Variation in the Amount of Play Equipment," *Child Development* 6 (1935): 56–68.

Joyner, L. "The Changing Playscape." *Southern Living* 11 (1976): 51–55.

Lambert, J. *Adventure Playgrounds: A Personal Account of a Playleader's Work as Told to Jenny Pearson*. London: Cape, 1974.

Mahan, J.L. "The Palomar College Discovery Structure Learning Environment." San Marcos, CA: Unpublished paper, 1976.

McConnell, W.H.; J.T. Parks; and L.W. Knapp, Jr. *Public Playgrounds Equipment*. Iowa City: University of Iowa College of Medicine, Oct. 15, 1973.

National Recreation and Park Association. "Proposed Safety Standard for Public Playground Equipment." Arlington, VA: National Recreation and Park Association, 1976.

——. "Summary of In-depth Accident Studies Received from 1-9-74 to 6-17-75." Mimeographed paper. Arlington, VA: National Recreation and Park Association, 1975.

Omwake, E.B. "The Child's Estate." In A.J. Solnit and S.A. Provence, eds., *Modern Perspectives in Child Development*. New York: International Universities Press, 1963.

Piaget, J. *Play, Dreams and Imitation in Childhood*. New York: Norton, 1962.

Rubin, K.H., and T.L. Maioni. "Play Preference and its Relationship to Egocentricism, Popularity and Classification Skills in Preschoolers." *Merrill-Palmer Quarterly* 21 (1975): 171–79.

Seagoe, M.V. "A Comparison of Children's Play in Six Modern Cultures." *Journal of School Psychology* 9 (1971): 61–72.

Smilansky, S. *The Effects of Sociodramatic Play on Disadvantaged Preschool Children*. New York: Wiley, 1968.

Vernon, E.A. *A Survey of Preprimary and Primary Outdoor Learning Centers/Playgrounds in Texas Public Schools*. Unpublished doctoral dissertation. Austin: University of Texas, 1976.

Wilkinson, P.F., and R. Lockhart. *Safety in Children's Formal Play Environments*. Toronto: Ministry of Culture and Recreation, 1976.

Organizations

American Adventure Play Association, P.O. Box 5430, Huntington Beach, CA 92646 (Bill Vance, President)

Danish Playground Society, Virkefeltet 2,2700, Brønshøj Copenhagen, Denmark (Helga Pedersen, Director)

Handicapped Adventure Playground Association. 3, Oakley Gardens, London, SW3 5HQ, England (Mrs. D.R. Bearman, General Secretary)

International Playground Association. Treasurer: Miss M.E. Otter, 12 Cherry Tree Dr., Sheffield S11 9AE, England (American correspondent, Paul Hogan)

London Adventure Playground Association. 25 Ovington Sq., London SW3 1LQ, England.

Playground Clearing House, Inc., 26 Buckwalter Rd., Phoenixville, PA 19460 (Paul Hogan, President and American correspondent for the International Playground Association)

Swedish Council for Children's Play, Socialstyrelsen S-106 30, Stockholm, Sweden (Eva Insulander, Head of Office)

State of the Art in Play Environment

GARY T. MOORE
Environment Behavior Research Institute
School of Architecture and Urban Planning
University of Wisconsin, Milwaukee

Play as talked about in the child environment literature is both poorly defined and broadly used, tending most frequently to mean any and all spontaneous activity not adult directed but initiated by the child or children themselves. *Environment* as used here is meant as physical, both the designed and the natural environment at all scales from play structures to the entire urban fabric.

The basic questions addressed here are: What do we know from the scientific literature about the relations between the physical environment, children's play behavior and subsequent development? How do we explain the findings, and how do we use them in applications to environmental policy, planning and design? In investigating these questions, we will look at both designated playgrounds and neighborhood play spaces and make some comparisons between the two.

OVERVIEW OF CHILD-ENVIRONMENT THEORY AS IT PERTAINS TO PLAY

A child spends the most time in informal, outdoor play settings. Children are the greatest users of public outdoor space, often at a ratio of ten to one to adults' use, and spending a much greater proportion of time outdoors (Cooper-Marcus, 1974), much of it in spontaneous play in neighborhoods, around the dwelling unit and on designated playgrounds. How can we conceptualize the importance of this time for the child?

Toward an Interactional-Ecological Theory of Child-Environment Relations

It is a truism to say that unstructured and spontaneous play is an important part of development (Garvey, 1977; Piaget, 1951; Singer, 1973; Herron & Sutton-Smith, 1971).

It is through unstructured, child-initiated play that the child is often most free to explore, test and learn from feedback from the environment. This is the instrumental view or value of play.

Many theories of child development have extolled the value of the child's interaction with his or her environment (cf. Herron & Sutton-Smith, 1971). In Piaget's theory (e.g., Piaget, 1951; cf. review in Hart & Moore, 1973), there are four functional invariants or biological givens: adaptation, assimilation, accommodation and equilibration. Piaget holds that the child is consistently *adapting* to the world and thus to the physical environment in an active, not passive way. This adaptation, which also involves changing the environment, is the wellspring of development or its motivation. Development is modulated by two opposing but complementary forces—assimilation and accommodation. *Assimilation* is the changing and incorporation of information into the child's schemes— or structures—of thinking and behaving, while *accommodation* is the changing of the structures to partially conform to, or account for, the new information. Information, in its broadest meaning, comes from the environment, that is, from all that is outside the organism. Thus the child and the environment are in a delicate balance, almost a dance, with the child both altering information and experiences to fit with existing ideas (selective attention, selective hearing, selective meaning), while simultaneously altering his or her cognitive structures to conform to the information. When these reciprocal and complementary functions of assimilation and accommodation are in balance, Piaget refers to this as *equilibration*. Equilibration occurs, then, when there is a balance between schemes and information from the environment.

These periods of equilibration are the major cognitive structures so familiar in Piaget's theory. But true equilibration occurs for only short periods of time, for the driving force of adaptation will insure that the child seeks out and is confronted with new information or experiences only too ready to challenge and topple—or disequilibriate—the status of existing ideas.

While Piaget's work has been most notable for its focus on *cognitive structures* and the processes of cognitive development, we must not lose sight of *motor* and *social-emotional* development, both of which proceed in much the same manner. Piaget himself has dealt with both, showing the role of sensori-motor development and sensori-motor schemes in the foundation of cognitive development and showing some fascinating interactions between intellectual and social development in his 1942 College de France lectures (Piaget, 1963).

In the case of play and its specific role in development, pragmatists (like equipment manufacturers, most school boards and many playground designers) stress motor play and motor development, while it may seem that most theorists stress cognitive development. Recent writers have tried to give a more equal balance to all three major areas of development (Singer, 1973; Garvey, 1977; Moore, Cohen, Oertel & Van Ryzin, 1979; Rubin, 1980), and it is this holistic view we must adopt when considering research and the design of play environments.

From the above, we have seen several major propositions of the theory, including a notion central to the author's present work, namely that of the integral and reciprocal *interaction* of the child and the environment. But this theoretical notion would lead us not only to expect the child to *develop* as a function of new information (assimilation and accommodation) but also to *change* the environment, both through changing it cognitively (thinking about it differently) and changing it physically (constructing one's own play spaces). There may be a more complex feedback system operating than that proposed by Piaget, the mutual change or development of *both* the child and the environment and the interaction between changing the environment and further development.

The "environment" impinging on child development is not only physical or designed environment but also social and cultural; the child and the total socio-physical environment are united in a complex ecology. This would lead us to hypothesize that the interactions *between* social and physical environment may be more important to the child's experience and development than either taken in isolation.

RESEARCH ON PLAY AND PLAY ENVIRONMENTS

If the child develops through feedback from interactions with the environment, the character of the physical setting available for spontaneous play would be expected to affect the types and degree of interaction. What is known currently about the effects of the physical setting of play on child behavior and development?

Some research studies have reported on various aspects of child-environment relations from the geographic scale (Hart, 1977) to the child's home (Parke, 1978), but most studies do not differentiate between indoor and outdoor settings. The investigation of setting differences in play (between different buildings or between outdoor versus indoor settings) has received only scant attention (Krasnor & Pepler, 1980), with most studies focusing on the number of materials, types of toys available and social aspects of the play environment, without paying attention to possible effects of the molar physical environment, the geographic and architectural environment (e.g., see the latest "New Directions in Child Development" sourcebook—Rubin, 1980).

Studies, about equally divided between designated playgrounds and neighborhood contexts, have been conducted on children's spontaneous play as a function of the character of different types of outdoor environments, Altman & Wohlwill (1978), Baird & Lutkus (1982), and Weinstein & David (in press). Two findings replicated many times are that children are the greatest users of public outdoor space (Bjoklid-Chu, 1977;

Cooper-Marcus, 1974; R. Moore & Young, 1978), while as little as 15 percent of children's time is spent at designated playgrounds (Auslander, Juhasz & Carrusco, 1977; Cooper-Marcus, 1974; Hole, 1966).

Research on the Impacts of Designated Playgrounds on Child Development

In the past ten to 15 years there has been a renewed interest in the design of children's play environments and on the impacts of design on behavior. Two architects, Friedberg (1969, 1975); Friedberg & Berkeley (1970) & Dattner (1969), were early forerunners in the design of children's play facilities, whose designs and writings have led to important new ideas and much criticism. Friedberg argued for what he called "linked play," play among all age groups, including adults and the elderly, and argued that complexity and wide potential choice would stimulate linked play behavior. Dattner saw play as a child's way of learning and argued for increasing the number of interactive possibilities between the child and the environ ment. But neither designer made provision for their designs to be evaluated—what are now called "post-occupancy evaluations" (Moore, 1982); their processes of design were intuitive and the product assessed at best by subjective, casual observations, if at all (Derman, 1974).

Yet there is in this country a continuing plethora of traditionally-styled playgrounds comprised of play equipment selected from one or more of the available manufacturers' catalogs. These traditional playgrounds have been touched by neither designer nor scientist. Much of the current literature on children's play environments seems to be a reaction to, and negative criticism of these traditional playgrounds (e.g., Frost & Klein, 1979).

Several studies have looked at children's preferences for and uses of different manufactured play equipment. Hutinger (1955) found increases in upper body strength in third-grade children after playing on horizontal ladder play equipment. Morris (1955) found similar results with children from grades 1 to 3 on a wide variety of gymnastics-like playground equipment. Thompson (1976) found more use of horizontal bars than other types of equipment. Hayward, Rothenberg & Beasley (1974), Brower & Williamson (1974) and Brown (1980) however, found movable equipment preferred and used more than static equipment. Brown (1980) found, furthermore, that multifunctional play structures promoted more use and moderately more social, language and motor behaviors than single-use equipment. Gabbard (n.d.) has found, however, that after the second-grade year, play activity on all forms of traditional play equipment decreases at increasing rates.

In another set of studies on conceptual aspects of play environments, Callecod (1974) found that third-grade children overwhelmingly preferred and used playgrounds with high degrees of "challenge," "novelty" and "complexity," characteristics that according to Berlyne (1960) and Ellis (1973) should increase arousal and promote exploratory behavior. Similarly, Krudinier (1978) found more imaginative play in more "encapsulated" outdoor play settings. Some of the author's own work, as yet unreported, has shown that play environments high also in "loose parts" lead to more cognitive, social-cognitive and cognitive-motor play than settings lower in "loose parts."

These latter studies begin to tell us about the *quality* of the environment related to play and to development, not just what happens *vis a vis* a particular piece of equipment, but how development is related to design quality of play environments. Admittedly, the independent variables are constructs comprised of many specific variables, but rating scales were developed in all three studies to provide reliability for the environmental measurements. Further, the resulting constructs are closer to the language of design and thus can lead more readily to translation and application.

A further set of studies has looked at traditional versus designed (or, so-called but misnamed "creative") playgrounds. Ellis (1970) and Frost & Klein (1979) have provided seething critiques of traditional playgrounds relative to designed ones. Ellis (1970) stated, "Playgrounds in general are dupli-

173

cated from site to site in a monotony of stereotyped apparatus designed to catch the adult's eye," (p. 3) and that traditional playgrounds are "no more than a large combination of large playthings placed together . . . (to) provide opportunities for gross motor activity by simulating, in galvanized steel, some primitive jungle setting" (p. 137). Frost & Klein (1979) added, "Typically the American playground is a collection of single-function equipment—merry-go-round, seesaws, jungle gyms, slides, and swings—designed primarily for exercise" (p. 46).

What does the research literature say about the differences between traditional and designed play environments? While Brown (1980) noted no differences on a range of social, language and motor behaviors between more versus less contemporary designed playgrounds, Van Valkenberg (1978), Strickland (1979), Hayward et al., (1974), and Gabbor (n.d.) all found greater, longer and more varied use of contemporary designed playgrounds than traditional playgrounds. Strickland (1979) also found more complex cognitive and social play behaviors on the designed playgrounds.

Another line of research on designated playgrounds has looked at adventure playgrounds built by children themselves. In much of the literature and discussions about children's play and play settings the argument is prominent that children will engage in more developmentally supportive behaviors on adventure playgrounds (those with loose parts for the children to build their own play environment) than on traditional or even contemporary playgrounds (Cooper, 1970; Nicholson, 1971; Spencer, Tuxford & Dennis, 1964).

Though not made explicit in the literature on adventure playgrounds, the implicit theory behind them is essentially (if informally) Piagetian. It is believed by its proponents that, "Children love to interact with variables, such as materials and shapes; smells and other physical phenomena, such as electricity, magnetism, and gravity; media such as gases and fluids; sounds, music and motion; chemical interactions, cooking, and fire; and other humans and animals, plants, words, concepts, and ideas" (Nicholson, 1971, p. 30).

Sorenson, the Danish landscape architect, and his followers argued that the greater the variety of experiences available to a child in the formative years and the greater the opportunity for creative and constructive play, the more rapid the development of cognitive skills (cf. Cooper, 1970). Nicholson (1971) summed up the theoretical position: "In any environment, both the degree of inventiveness and creativity, and the possibility of discovery, are directly proportional to the number and kind of variables in it" (p. 31). He called this the "theory of loose parts." Other exponents argued that the nature of constructive activities with loose parts would also lead to more cooperative behavior among children (Allen, 1968; Benjamin, 1974; Lambert & Pearson, 1974). Only four studies look at this issue empirically and carefully, and the results are somewhat contradictory. Based on semi-structured observations, Cooper (1970) reported a greater variety of activities, ages, cross-age interaction and group sizes on London adventure playgrounds than on comparable traditional playgrounds. She also reported two community benefits: reduction in neighborhood vandalism and greater community involvement.

One of the few studies to compare traditional and alternative types of playgrounds was that of Hayward, Rothenberg, & Beasley (1974), in which they compared traditional equipment playgrounds, contemporary playgrounds and adventure playgrounds designed by architects or landscape architects. Using behavior-mapping methods, behavior setting records and interviews with a sample of children, they found that children spent more time and engaged in more cognitive play activities on adventure playgrounds than on contemporary or traditional playgrounds. While moveable equipment was greatly preferred over static equipment on the traditional playgrounds, multiple equipment was preferred over isolated items on the contemporary sites, and building and clubhouse activities were preferred at the adventure play settings. They also found more adult participation with children on adventure playgrounds. Similar findings are reported in a less rigorous study by Thompson & Rittenhouse (1974). Van Ryzin (1978) found, however, that the percentage of time spent in environmental manipulation (a measure of cognitive activity) was high (60–82 percent of the time on a sample of adventure playgrounds in London) but was independent of the number of manipulables present. Thus, while there is some evidence for increased cognitive play activities on adventure playgrounds compared to other types of designated playgrounds, reasons are not clear. Do we attribute this cognitive activity to: self-selection, significant others involved in the setting, the character of the physical setting or some combination of these factors?

Controlling somewhat for these factors through quasi-experimental research procedures and the analysis of covariance (Moore, 1983d), one of the author's as yet unreported studies, has found that the greater incidence of cognitive, cognitive-social, cognitive-motor and cooperative play activities is related to the character of the physical settings and in particular, the quantity of loose parts available.

Research on the Impacts of Neighborhood Play Settings on Child Development

Less than 15 percent of children's time outdoors is spent on designated playgrounds, and while research would suggest that more time might be spent, and with greater benefits if more appropriate play environments were provided (contemporary designed and adventure in particular), the fact remains that most children's time outdoors is spent on undesignated settings. The claim, or hypothesis, has been advanced, furthermore, that children engage in a greater range of developmentally supportive behaviors in neighborhood play settings (front yards, corner lots and back alleys) than on designated playgrounds (Clay, 1971, 1972; Wood, 1976). Many observational studies have been conducted of children's play in everyday neighborhood settings and around the child's dwelling unit.

The hypothesis that children prefer and make greater use of the everyday outdoor environment than designated playgrounds is supported by many studies. Brower (1977) found that children's play extended throughout the neighborhood, with porches, sidewalks, curb areas and stoops being the most heavily used. R. Moore (1980) found that natural areas accounted for over one-quarter of all favorite play places, while designed schoolyards and playgrounds accounted for less than 10 percent. Hart (1979) found that children preferred natural landscapes, that the spatial richness and meaning children attach to the environment was related to their access to natural areas and elements, and that children's experience and memory for places was related to their ability to modify their environment. Bishop and Foulscham (1973) found that small scale elements in the environment such as kiosks, telephone booths and vacant lots were favorite places.

In a recent review, R. Moore & Young (1978) identified 34 studies relating to neighborhood play settings. One study (R. Moore, 1978) indicated that of 72 environmental elements mentioned by children as favorite play places, only two (the child's own home and streets) were mentioned by more than 50 percent of children. A similar study by Maurer & Baxter (1972) showed that children emphasized homes, natural features and other built structures in that order as being favorite play spaces. An analysis of six residential behavior-mapping studies done in the period 1971 to 1977 (based on charts in Moore & Young, 1978) leads this author to the conclusion that, in general, children's favorite neighborhood play places are 1) paved areas (streets, sidewalks and paths), 2) front yards and porches, public open space (including woods, grassy areas and open fields) and 3) backyards, with designated playgrounds again at the bottom of the list.

It is therefore clear from these studies that children prefer and use informal neighborhood spaces as much as six to one over designated playgrounds and that they also prefer and use natural features and everyday urban features in the environment more than specially built areas.

While we can make conclusions about preferences and use from the research literature, less is known about the impacts on children's development. In one study, Hart (1977) found that children's environmental learning was related to the amount of exploration possible of the surrounding environment and of the territorial range permitted by their parents. This study, plus earlier work by Anderson & Tindall (1972), have shown that territorial range is gender-related, little girls being given much less freedom to explore their environment and thus to learn about the environment.

Comparison of Designated and Neighborhood Play Environments

In another part of a study by the author and associates, we looked at the types of developmentally-related play behaviors occurring in neighborhood settings in comparison to adventure playgrounds, with the objective of empirically comparing designated playgrounds with informal neighborhood play spaces in terms of demonstrating actual impacts on behavior, not just children's stated preferences. A quasi-experimental field study was conducted, using observational instruments (Moore, 1983 c). Subjects were randomly selected from all children using outdoor areas of an inner-city neighborhood during the summer of 1977, including those using an adventure playground in the heart of the neighborhood. The children ranged from 3 years, 6 months to 14 and were 99 percent black. Based on random space and time sampling, 391 observational cells were recorded, some involving as many as 30 children; in all, more than 6000 children observed at play. A highly structured observational instrument, a behavior map was used to record all play behaviors in which the children were engaged (26 different behaviors) and where they occurred (31 different types of settings).

What is being found is: there are significantly more cognitive play behaviors on adventure playgrounds than in neighborhood play settings (40 percent of all behaviors observed on adventure playgrounds versus only 10 percent in the neighborhood—see Table 1); furthermore, from two to as much as 10 times more fantasy, constructive and cooperative play is evident on adventure playgrounds (see Table 2).

The gender and/or age composition of groups involved in play is significantly related to five of the six categories of play studied (see Table 3, columns 2 and 3). In addition, there are significant interactions between the physical environment and both age and gender in affecting social-motor and social-cognitive play (Table 3, columns 5 through 7). While most play occurs in same-age and same-gender groups (75–84 percent), these findings indicate that mixed-age and mixed-gender groups engage in more social types of play in informal neighbor-

Table 1
Frequencies and Proportions of Types of Play Observed
(N = 814 cases) in Adventure Playground and Neighborhood Play Settings

	Adventure Playground		Neighborhood Play Settings		
	Freq	Prop	Freq	Prop	X^{2a}
Social-motor	24	.06	299	.19	14.19**
Motor	33	.08	181	.11	4.99
Cognitive-motor	6	.02	142	.09	6.49
Cognitive	161	.40	165	.10	22.50***
Social-cognitive	38	.10	143	.09	8.54
Social	138	.34	685	.42	9.65*
Totals	400		1615		

[a] All 2×5 tables; df = 4.
*p < .05
**p < .01
***p < .001

Table 2
Frequencies and Proportions of Constructive, Fantasy, and
Cooperative Play (N = 814 cases) in Adventure Playground and
Neighborhood Play Settings

	Adventure Playground		Neighborhood Play Settings		
	Freq	Prop	Freq	Prop	X^{2a}
Constructive Play	151	.21	43	.02	213.23***
Fantasy Play	31	.04	51	.02	17.18**
Cooperative Play	313	.43	585	.21	9.61*
Totals	733[b]	.68	2758[b]	.25	

[a]All df = 4.
[b]Totals include all 26 behaviors observed including 6 levels of solitary to cooperative play.

*p < .05
**p < .01
***p < .001

hood play settings than on adventure playgrounds. Thus, the picture as it has emerged to this point is that a combination of the physical environment, the social characteristics of children and the interaction between physical and social variables affects the type of play in which children engage.

We have found a type of trade-off or balance between designated adventure playgrounds and neighborhood settings (Moore, Burger & Katz, 1979). While the adventure playground seems to provide for considerably more cognitive play, and traditional playgrounds and playing fields for more

Table 3
Analyses of Variance on Six Types of Play Observed (N = 814 cases) in
Adventure Playgrounds and Neighborhood Play Settings

	Play Environment (E)	Gender (G)	Age (A)	E×G	E×A	G×A	E×G×A	Residual
Social-motor								
MS	.02	1.46	1.28	.67	1.30	.39	1.37	.35
F	.07	4.13*	3.62*	1.89	3.68*	1.10	3.87**	
Motor								
MS	.06	.93	.78	.08	.11	.07	.15	.13
F	.42	6.96***	5.86***	.62	.79	.55	1.10	
Cognitive-motor								
MS	.39	.26	.36	.00	.04	.02	.03	.12
F	3.32	2.22	3.11	.00	.31	.18	.26	
Cognitive								
MS	1.13	.61	.17	.02	.06	.02	.05	.11
F	10.56***	5.67**	1.63	.22	.54	.15	.48	
Social-cognitive								
MS	.16	.56	.11	.27	.03	.18	.17	.06
F	2.75	9.35***	1.83	4.47*	.49	2.95**	2.83*	
Social								
MS	.04	3.11	1.40	.12	.05	.08	.04	.08
F	.50	38.58***	17.33***	1.47	.65	.95	.45	
df	1	2	3	2	3	6	4	694

*p < .05
**p < .01
***p < .001

motor play, neighborhood settings are highest in social play. While cognitive play is high on adventure playgrounds (40 percent of observed behaviors being construction or fantasy behaviors), it is in the middle of the list in neighborhood settings (7–10 percent of the behaviors). Conversely, social play is high in neighborhood settings (42 percent of the time being watching, talking or walking in groups), but lower on adventure playgrounds (6–10 percent—see Table 4). Adults are more in evidence in neighborhood settings and tend to play a supervisory role, while playing a more involved or observational role on the adventure playgrounds (Table 5). What seems to be emerging is a

Table 4
Order and Mean Percentage of Occurrence of Specific Play Behaviors in Adventure Playground and Neighborhood Play Settings[a]

Adventure Playground				Neighborhood Play Settings		
	M	SD	Rank		M	SD	Rank
Construction	.83	1.16	1	Observing	.69	1.36	1
Talking	.60	1.41	2	Talking	.40	1.19	2
Fantasy	.17	1.02	3	Walking	.34	.85	3
Observing	.16	.63	4	Wheel toy play	.31	.70	4
Raucous play	.10	.52	5	Transiting	.24	.71	5
				Gross motor play	.20	.69	6
				Inf. ball games	.13	.78	7

[a]Mean number of behavioral observations during each play type was observed; 1.00 = every observational cell. Of 26 observed behaviors, all behaviors greater than or equal to 10% of the time are shown.

Source: From Moore, Burger & Katz (1979)

Table 5
Proportion of the Time that Different Types of Interactions Occur in Adventure Playground and Neighborhood Play Settings

	Adventure Playground	Neighborhood Play Settings	χ^2
Age			
Same-Age Groups	.84	.77	
Mixed-Age Groups	.16	.23	3.43
Gender			
Same-Gender Groups	.75	.75	
Mixed-Gender Groups	.25	.25	.00
Ethnicity			
Same-Ethnic Groups	1.00	.99	
Mixed-Ethnic Groups	.00	.01	.00
Person/People With			
Self Only	.66	.59	
Other Peers	.32	.00	
Teenagers	.01	.06	
Adults	.02	.35	265.82***
Role of Other Person			
Involved	.27	.15	
Supervising	.03	.45	
Surveillance	.70	.40	34.99***

***p < .001

Source: From Moore, Burger & Katz (1979)

type of complementary relationship among various settings—no one type of play setting seems to provide for all of children's play activities and developmental needs, and while one provides for one type of play, others including adventure playgrounds and neighborhood play settings provide for other types of play and development.

This interpretation is concordant with the environmentally-based theory of play suggested at the beginning, with evidence supporting four components of the theory: that there are three important components to play—cognitive, motor and social-emotional; that development through play is an interaction of the child with his or her total environment; that adults and significant others play an important role in interaction with the environment; and, therefore, that development through play is a function of the total social-physical environment. The findings support the interactional-ecological theory of child-environment relations and point out some of the linkages between the architecturally-designed environment and the social system as they independently and in concert influence development.

IMPLICATIONS FOR A NEW APPROACH TO THE PLANNING AND DESIGN OF PLAY ENVIRONMENTS

The current state of the art of the research literature leads us to some new implications for environmental policy and the planning and design of play environments. Listed here are a few implications to be summarized in a forthcoming book. For an interim report, see Cohen, Hill, Lane, McGinty & Moore, 1979.)

1) We must develop environmental policy for "play environments," not just "playgrounds" as static entities located in well-defined locations. All environmental settings are the necessary subject matter of both research and design. We must look at the total environment of play.

2) Policy makers, recreation leaders and educators should provide for the full variety of play activities, not just motor or physical play. We need to provide for cognitive, social and motor play and for their integration (Figure 1, p. 180).

3) Planners should provide all three types of designated play environments discussed in the research literature—traditional, contemporary and adventure. As different types of play have been found to occur on each and no one is sufficient for children's needs, all three types complement each other and should be provided in proximity to each other.

4) Planners and designers should provide not only for play but also for the interaction of children with older siblings, adults and significant others, providing for the total ecology of the socio-physical environment of play. This means making opportunities for adults of all ages to be involved with children, rather than segregating children's areas from adult areas (Figure 2, p. 181).

5) Planners and designers should also provide a variety of types of play environments at different, but appropriate locations, e.g., adventure play yards in housing areas, small and large parks and adjacent to youth activity centers. Contemporary play environments should be installed in shopping centers, amusement parks and dotted throughout inner-city areas. No one type of location is sufficient. (See Table 6, p. 181.)

6) We should not only provide well-known types of play environments but develop and study new notions of play environments, like the natural play environments where children can interact with nature, such as the European adventure environments and Swedish and Canadian creative play environments where children of all ages can build and develop through doing. (See Figures 3a–c, pp. 182–84.)

7) We should provide not only new and innovative types of designated play environments, but also improve the whole fabric of children's play in urban, suburban and rural environments. Special attention should be given to the

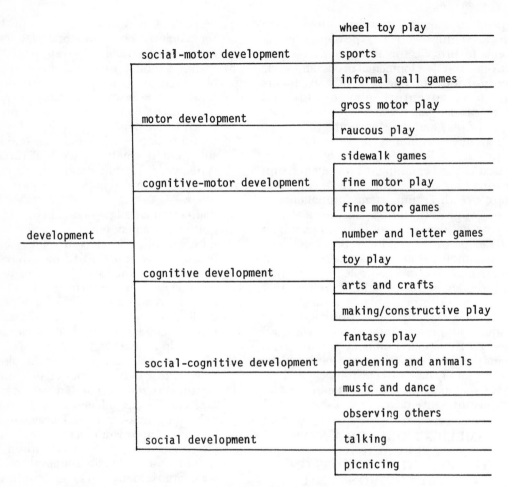

Figure 1. Relationship between 18 observable play behaviors and three major categories of play (motor, cognitive and social). (From Moore, Cohen, Oertel and Van Ryzin, 1979.)

"neighborhood of play" including developed play areas; paved play areas for ball play and informal motor play; grassy areas for formal and informal games for all ages; and a variety of play areas for different age groups—all of these within the normal fabric of the neighborhood. (See Figure 4, p. 185.)

8) Recreation and urban planners should provide a "tiered park system," that is, a planned system of district parks and play areas ranging in scale from intermediate-sized district parks through small vest-pocket parks in residential areas, to special play areas at other children's facilities like schools, youth activity centers and child care centers,

right down to neighborhood-based play areas. (See Figure 5, p. 186.)

9) We should work for "home-based play yards" by rethinking the entire design or adaptive redesign, of residential areas so that developmentally appropriate play can more readily occur close to home. (See Figures 6a & b, pp. 187 & 88.)

10) We still need special integrated play environments, called in Scandinavia "comprehensive play environments," for all ages and types of play—infants toddlers, preschoolers, school-age children, adults—and developed play areas as well as grassy areas, natural areas and hard surface areas, and including

Figure 2. Providing for the interaction of children with older children and adults.

Table 6
Recommended Appropriate Locations for Different Types of Outdoor Play Environments
Appropriate Locations

TYPES OF OUTDOOR PLAY ENVIRON-MENTS	Child Oriented Facilities			Family Housing Areas		Parks		
	Child Care Centers	Youth Activity Centers	Elem. & Jr. High Schools	Family Housing Area/each 10 to 50 units	Family Housing Area/each 50 to 100 units	Small Parks 3 to 5 acres	Large Parks 5 to 25 acres	Very Large Parks/25 to 250 acres
Home Based Play Yards				●				
Creative Play Yards	●					●	●	●
Adventure Play Yards		●				●	●	●
Natural Play Yards	●	●	●			●	●	●
Play/Learning Environments for Handicapped Children	●	●	●				●	●
Comprehensive Play Yards					●	●	●	●

Source: After Cohen, Hill, Lane, McGinty & Moore (1979)

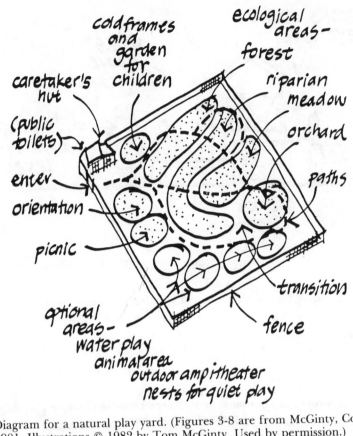

cold frames and garden for children

ecological areas—forest

caretaker's hut

riparian meadow

(public toilets)

orchard

enter

paths

orientation

picnic

transition

fence

optional areas—water play animal area outdoor amphitheater nests for quiet play

Figure 3a. Diagram for a natural play yard. (Figures 3-8 are from McGinty, Cohen & Moore, 1981. Illustrations © 1982 by Tom McGinty. Used by permission.)

adventure, creative and natural play yards. (See Figures 7a & b, pp. 189 & 90.)

11) We must repair and prepare our neighborhoods for a "network of play" by linking together all other elements of the play environment system and thus make paths to and from the child's home, other parks, schools and favorite children's places, thus making for safe play opportunities along the way. (See Figures 8a & b, pp. 191 & 92.)

Although more implications from the current research on play-environment relations could be discussed, these eleven implications show that the research is of *theoretical* interest (very important, for we need to discover and understand more about the environmental components of play) and of *practical* importance to educators, policy makers, planners and designers. The research to date suggests some very important conclusions that run counter to "standard operating procedure" all across the country; for example, the preponderance of traditional, catalog-selected playgrounds. The literature shows they support only one aspect of child development, and even that not very well after about the second or third grade. There is continued attention to designated playgrounds even to the more innovative type despite the well-replicated finding that children spend up to 85 percent of their outdoor time in other, neighborhood and home-based play settings.

Reference Note

The behavior mapping instrument used in this study, and instructions for its use, are available by writing to the Center for Architecture and Urban Planning Re-

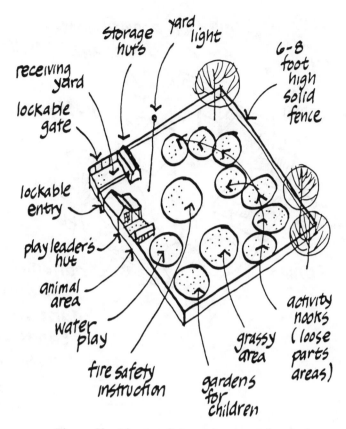

storage huts

yard light

receiving yard

6-8 foot high solid fence

lockable gate

lockable entry

play leader's hut

animal area

water play

fire safety instruction

gardens for children

grassy area

activity nooks (loose parts areas)

Figure 3b. Diagram for an adventure play yard.

search, University of Wisconsin-Milwaukee, Milwaukee, WI 53201.

References

Allen, M. *Planning for Play.* Cambridge, MA: MIT Press, 1968.

Altman, I., and J.F. Wohlwill, eds. *Children and the Environment.* New York: Plenum, 1978.

Anderson, J., and M. Tindall. "The Concept of Home Range: New Data for the Study of Territorial Behavior." In W.J. Mitchell, ed., *Environmental Design: Research and Practice.* Washington, DC: Environmental Design Research Association, 1972.

Auslander, N.; J.B. Juhasz and F.F. Carrusco. "The Outdoor Behavior of Chicano Children in Colorado." *Man-Environment Systems* 7 (1977): 214–16.

Baird, J.C., and A.D. Lutkus, eds. *Mind, Child, Architecture.* Hanover, NH: University Press of New England, 1982.

Benjamin, J. *Grounds for Play.* (An extension of *In Search of Adventure*). London: Bedford Square, 1974.

Berlyne, D.E. *Conflict, Arousal, and Curiosity.* New York: McGraw-Hill, 1960.

Bishop, J., and J. Foulsham. *Children's Images of Harwich.* Kingston Polytechnic Institute Architectural Psychology Research Unit, Environmental Education Research Report No. 3, 1973.

Bjorklik-Chu, P. "A Survey of Children's Outdoor Activities in Two Modern Housing Areas in Sweden." In B. Tizard and D. Harvey, eds., *The Biology of Play.* London: Spastics International Medical Publications, 1977.

Brower, S.N., and P. Williamson. "Outdoor Recreation as a Function of the Urban Housing Environment." *Environment and Behavior* 6 (1974): 295–345.

Brown, J.G. "Playground Design and Preschool Children's Behaviors." Paper presented at the Environmental Design Research Association meetings, College Park, MD, April 1982.

Callecod, R.L. "Play Preferences of Selected Grade-school Children on Varying Types of Playground Equipment." Unpublished master's thesis, University of Illinois, Urbana, 1974.

Clay, N. "Miniparks: Diminishing Returns." *Parks and Recreation* 6, 1 (1971): 22–26.

———. "Landscapes for Urban Play." *Architectural Forum,* 137, 7 (1972): 34–39.

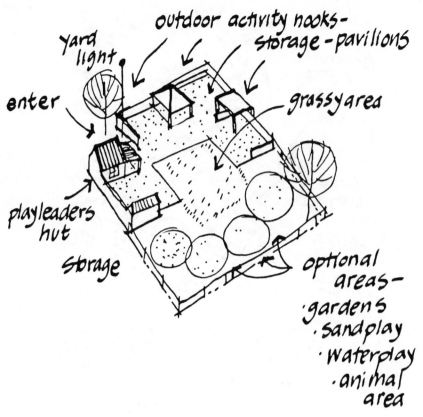

Figure 3c. Diagram for a creative play yard.

Coates, G. and E. Bussard. "Patterns of Children's Spatial Behavior in a Moderate-density Housing Development." In D.H. Carson, ed.), *Man-Environment Interactions.* Stroudsburg, PA: Dowden, Hutchinson and Ross, 1974.

Cobb, E. *The Ecology of Imagination in Childhood.* New York: Columbia University Press, 1977.

Cohen, U.; A.B. Hill; C.G. Lane; T. McGinty and G.T. Moore. *Recommendations for Child Play Areas.* Report to the U.S. Army Corps of Engineers, Center for Architecture and Urban Planning Research, University of Wisconsin-Milwaukee, 1979.

Cooper, C.C. "Adventure Playgrounds." *Landscape Architecture* 61 (October 1970): 18–29.

Cooper-Marcus, C. "Children's Play Behavior in a Low-rise Inner-city Housing Development." In D.H. Carson, ed., *Man-Environment Interactions.* Stroudsburg, PA: Dowden, Hutchinson and Ross, 1974.

Dattner, R. *Design for Play.* Cambridge, MA: MIT Press, 1969.

Derman, A. "Children's Play: Design Approaches and Theoretical Issues." *Man-Environment Systems* 4 (1974): 69–88.

Ellis, M.J. *Why People Play.* Englewood Cliffs, NJ: Prentice-Hall, 1973.

Friedberg, M.P. *Playgrounds for City Children.* Wheaton, MD: Association for Childhood Education International, 1969.

———. *Handcrafted Playgrounds: Designs You Can Build Yourself.* New York: Vintage, 1975.

Friedberg, M.P., and E.P. Berkeley. *Play and Interplay: A Manifesto for New Design in the Urban Recreational Environment.* New York: Macmillan, 1970.

Frost, J.L., and B.L. Klein. *Children's Play and Playgrounds.* Boston: Allyn and Bacon, 1979.

Gabbard, C. "Playground Apparatus Activity Among Children: Traditional Versus Contemporary Apparatus." Unpublished paper sent to the author, n.d.

Garvey, C. *Play.* Cambridge, MA: Harvard University Press, 1977.

Hart, R.A. *Children's Experience of Place.* New York: Irvington, 1977.

Hart, R.A., and G.T. Moore. "The Development of Spatial Cognition: A Review." In R.M. Downs and D. Stea, eds., *Image and Environment: Cognitive Mapping and Spatial Behavior.* Chicago: Aldine, 1973.

Hayward, D.G., M. Rothenberg and R. Beasley. "Children's Play and Urban Play Environments: A Comparison of Traditional, Contemporary, and Adventure Playground Types." *Environment and Behavior* 6 (1974): 131–68.

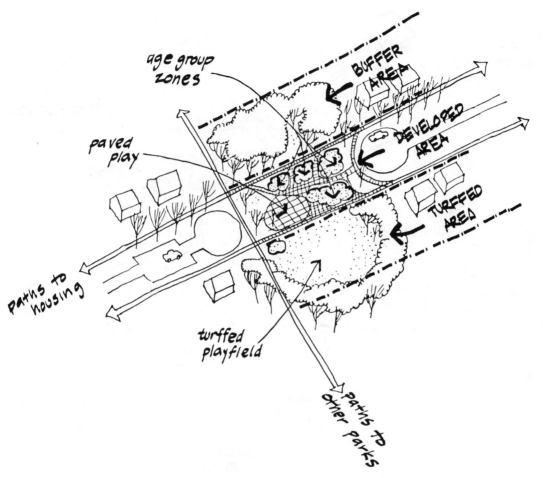

age group zones

paved play

BUFFER AREA

DEVELOPED AREA

TURFFED AREA

paths to housing

turffed playfield

paths to other parks

Figure 4. Planning for the neighborhood of play.

Henniger, M.L. "Free Play Behaviors of Nursery School Children in an Indoor and Outdoor Environment." Unpublished doctoral dissertation. The University of Texas at Austin, 1977.

Herron, R.E., and B. Sutton-Smith. *Child's Play*. New York: Wiley, 1971.

Hole, W.V. *Children's Play on Housing Estates*. London: Her Majesty's Stationery Office, Building Research Station, 1966.

Hutinger, P.W. "Effect of Systematic Horizontal Ladder Exercises upon Upper-Body Strength of Third-grade Children." *Research Quarterly* 26 (1955): 159–62.

Krasnor, L.R., and D.J. Pepler. "The Study of Children's Play: Some Suggested Future Directions." In K.H. Rubin, ed., *Children's Play*. San Francisco: Jossey-Bass, 1980.

Krudinier, W.P. "The Effects of Encapsulation on Preschool Children's Imaginative Play." Unpublished master's thesis, University of Illinois, Urbana, 1978.

Lambert, J., and J. Pearson. *Adventure Playgrounds*. Harmondsworth, England: Penguin, 1974.

Mauer, R., and J.C. Baxter. Images of Neighborhood Among Black-, Anglo-, and Mexican-American Children." *Environment and Behavior* 4 (1972): 351–88.

McGinty, T., U. Cohen and G.T. Moore. *Play Environments: Planning and Design of Children's Outdoor Play Environments*. Final report to the U.S. Department of the Army, Office of the Chief of Engineers, Washington, DC, TM 5-803-11, 1982.

Millar, S. *The Psychology of Play*. Harmondsworth, England: Penguin, 1968.

Moore, G.T. "Some Effects of the Organization of the Socio-physical Environment on Cognitive Behavior in Child Care Settings." Paper presented at the Society for Research in Child Development meetings, Detroit, April 1983(a).

———. "Effects of the Definition of Behavior Settings on Children's Behavior." Paper presented at the American Psychological Association Meetings, Anaheim, CA, August 1983(b).

———. "An Empirical Test of Design Patterns for Children's Environments." In D. Joiner, ed., *People and the Physical Environment Research*. Wellington, New Zealand: New Zealand Ministry of Works and Development, 1983(c).

———. "Teaching Design Evaluation, with Results from Case Studies of Playgrounds, Schools, and Housing for the Elderly." *Design Studies* 4 (1983): 100–14(d).

———. "The Role of the Socio-physical Environment

185

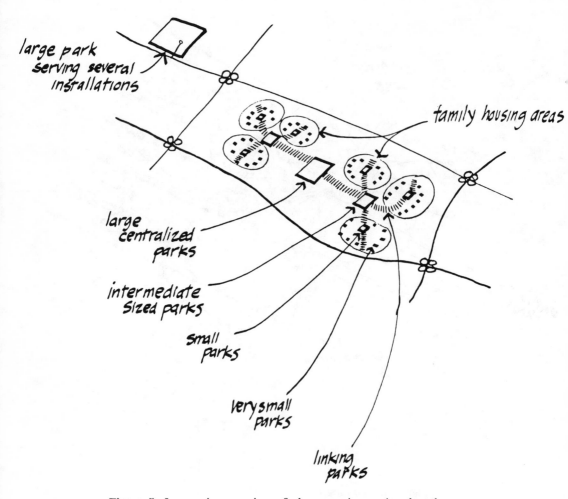

large park serving several installations

family housing areas

large centralized parks

intermediate sized parks

small parks

very small parks

linking parks

Figure 5. Integrating a variety of play areas into a tiered park system.

in Cognitive Development." In C.S. Weinstein and T. G. David, eds., *Spaces for Children: The Built Environment and Child Development.* New York: Plenum, in press.

———, ed. "Applied Architectural Research: Post-occupancy Evaluation of Buildings." Special issue of *Environment and Behavior* 14, 6 (1982).

———. "A Critique of Research in Child-Environment Relations." Paper presented at the Childhood City Workshop, Environmental Design Research Association meetings, Washington, DC, April 1981.

Moore, G.T.; U. Cohen; J. Oertel and L. Van Ryzin. *Designing Environments for Handicapped Children.* New York: Educational Facilities Laboratories, 1979.

Moore, G.T.; H. LeS. Burger and E. Katz. "Adventure Playground and Neighborhood Play Compared." In A.D. Seidel and S. Danford, eds., *Environmental Design: Research, Theory and Applications.* Washington, D.C.: Environmental Design Research Association, 1979.

Moore, R. "Collaborating with Young People to Assess their Landscape Values." *Ekistics* 281 (1980): 128–35.

Moore, R., and D. Young. "Childhood Outdoors: Toward a Social Ecology of the Landscape." In I. Altman and J.F. Wohlwill, eds., *Children and the Environment.* New York: Plenum, 1978.

Morris, M. "Measured Effects of Children in the Primary Grades from Use of Selected Playground Equipment." Unpublished doctoral dissertation, Iowa State University, 1955.

Nicholson, S. "How Not to Cheat Children: the Theory of Loose Parts." *Landscape Architecture* 62 (1971): 30–34.

Parke, R.D. "Children's Home Environments: Social and Cognitive Effects." In I. Altman and J.F. Wohlwill, eds. *Children and the Environment.* New York: Plenum, 1978.

Payne, R.J. and D.R.W. Jones. "Children's Urban Landscapes in Huntington Hills, Calgary." In P. Suedfeld and J.A. Russell, eds., *The Behavioral Basis of Design,*

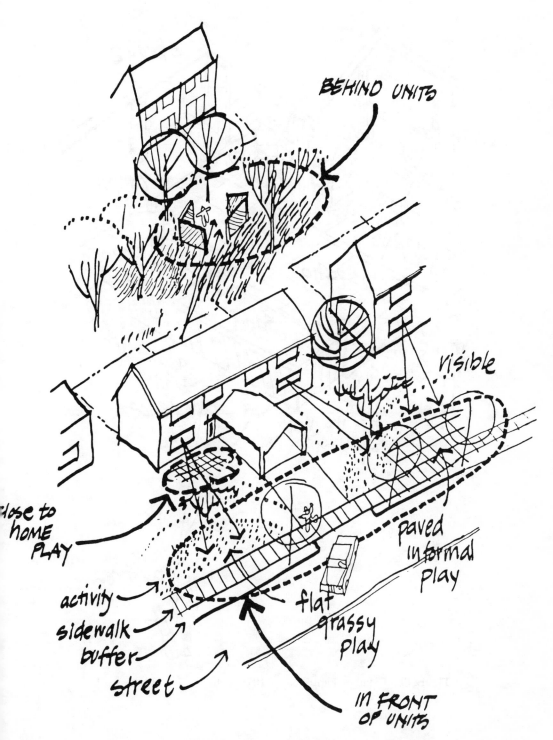

Figure 6a. Providing a range of different home-based play areas in immediate proximity to the home by redesigning everyday neighborhood spaces: overall diagram.

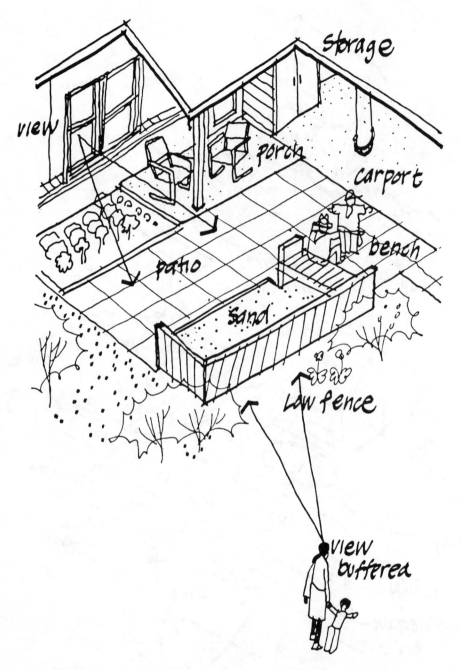

Figure 6b. Detail of Figure 6a (p. 187): a child-oriented back yard.

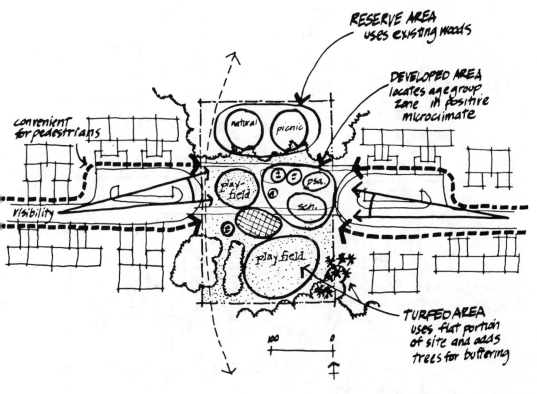

RESERVE AREA
uses existing woods

DEVELOPED AREA
locates age group
zone in positive
microclimate

convenient
for pedestrians

natural   picnic

play field

psa.

sch.

visibility

play field

TURFED AREA
uses flat portion
of site and adds
trees for buffering

100   0

Figure 7a. Comprehensive play environments for all ages: location relative to housing areas and the street pattern.

Vol. 2. Stroudsburg, PA: Dowden, Hutchinson and Ross, 1977.

Piaget, J. *Play, Dreams, and Imagination in Childhood (La Formation de Symbolole*, orig. French ed. 1946). New York: Norton, 1951.

————. *The Psychology of Intelligence.* (*La Psychologie de L'Intelligence*, orig. French ed. 1947). New York: Humanities Press, 1963.

Rubin, K.H., ed. *Children's Play.* San Francisco: Jossey-Bass, 1980.

Saegert, S., and R.A. Hart. "The Development of Environmental Competence in Girls and Boys." In M. Salter, ed., *Play: Anthropological Perspectives.* Cornwall, NY: Leisure Press, 1978.

Singer, J.L. *The Child's World of Make-Believe: Experimental Studies of Imaginative Play.* New York: Academic, 1973.

Sorenson, C. "Junk Playgrounds." *Danish Outlook* 4, 1 (1951): 311–16.

Spencer, J.; J. Tuxford and N. Dennis. *Stress and Release in an Urban Estate: Study in Action Research.* London: Tavistock, 1964.

Strickland, E. "Free Play Behaviors and Equipment Choices of Third-grade Children in Contrasting Play Environments." Unpublished doctoral dissertation, The University of Texas at Austin, 1979.

Thompson, D. "Space Utilization: Criteria for the Selection of Playground Equipment for Children." *Research Quarterly*, 47 (1976): 472–83.

Thompson, F.C., and A.M. Rittenhouse. "Measuring the Impact" (of adventure playgrounds). *Parks and Recreation* 9, 5 (1974): 24–26, 62–63.

Van Ryzin, L. "Environmental Manipulability in Children's Play Settings." In A.D.D. Siedel and S. Danford eds., *Environmental Design: Research, Theory and Applications.* Washington, DC: Environmental Design Research Association, 1979.

Van Valkenberg. "The Design Implications of Grade-School Children's Use of and Attitudes About Two Play Areas in Carle Park, Urbana, Illinois." In W.E. Rogers and W.H. Ittelson, eds., *New Directions in Environmental Design Research.* Washington, DC: Environmental Design Research Association, 1978.

Weinstein, C.S., and T.G. David, eds. *Spaces for Children: The Built Environment and Child Development.* New York: Plenum, in press.

Wood, D. "Early Building: Some Notes on Kids' Dirt Play." Paper presented at the American Association for the Advancement of Science meetings, Boston, February 1976.

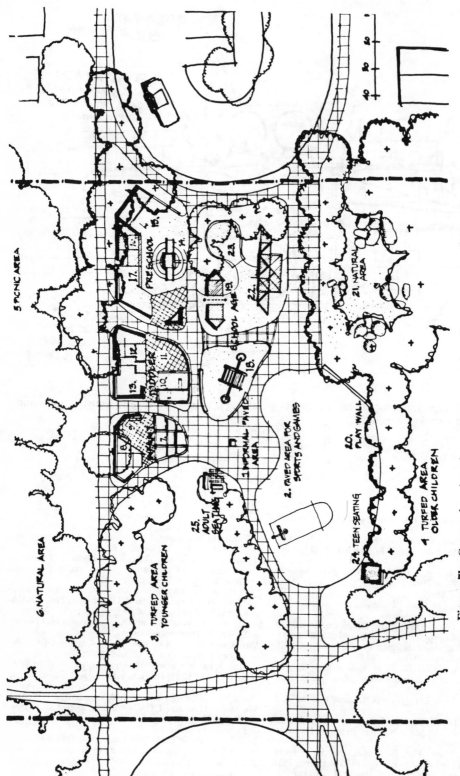

Figure 7b. Comprehensive play environments for all ages: internal organization.

1. INFORMAL PAVED AREA
2. PAVED AREA FOR SPORTS AND GAMES
3. TURFED AREA YOUNGER CHILDREN
4. TURFED AREA OLDER CHILDREN
5. PICNIC AREA
6. NATURAL AREA
7.
8.
9.
10. PLAY WALL
11.
12.
13.
14.
15.
16.
17.
18.
19.
20. PLAY WALL
21. NATURAL AREA
22.
23.
24. TEEN SEATING
25. ADULT SEATING

PRESCHOOL

SCHOOL AGE

TODDLER

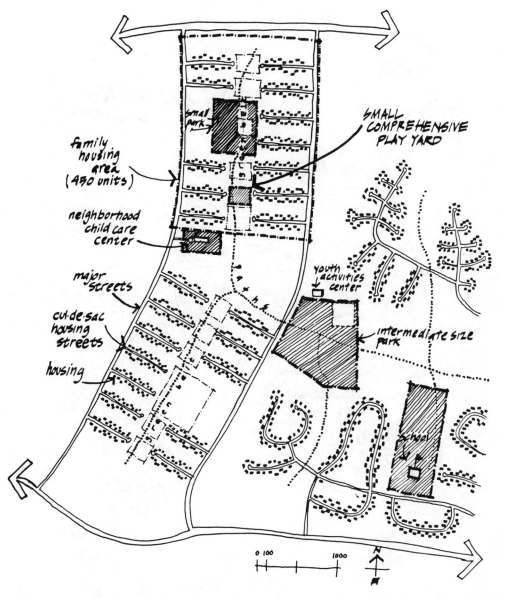

Figure 8a. Providing for the network of play by linking together all the other parts of the play environment system by a series of safe—and playful—paths. Here: overall path network.

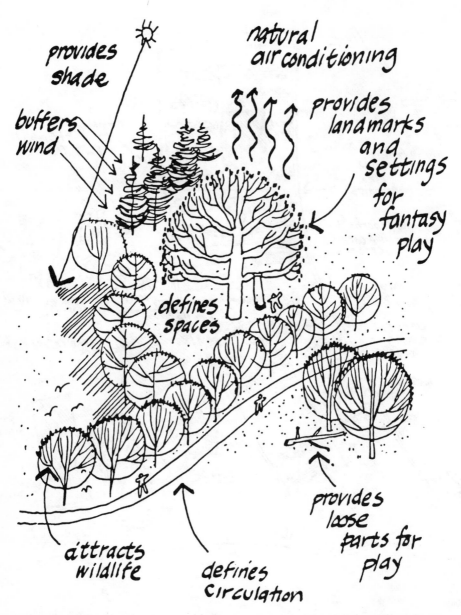

provides shade

natural air conditioning

buffers wind

provides landmarks and settings for fantasy play

defines spaces

attracts wildlife

defines circulation

provides loose parts for play

Figure 8b. Micro-climates for play along the way. (See Figure 8a, previous page.)

An Evaluation of Day Care Playgrounds in Texas

MARIAN L. MONROE
Texas Department of Human Resources, Austin

In Texas, 4,028 day care centers with the capacity to serve 293,737 children per day influence the growth and development of children (Texas Department of Human Resources, 1982). This number compares with the 227,935 preschool and kindergarten children enrolled during 1981–82 in the Texas public schools (Wilson, Note[2]). Most children spend at least one hour a day on the day care center playground. This translates into children's spending millions of hours on day care playgrounds each year. These hours should be used to meet children's developmental needs, and the playgrounds should be safe and engaging.

Playgrounds strongly influence the quality of the play experience, so important to the growth and development of children. There are, however, several questions to be asked about day care center playgrounds: What do day care center playgrounds offer? Do the playgrounds need improvement? What are the obstacles to improvement? How do we measure these?

PURPOSES OF THE STUDY

The first purpose was to determine the content, relative safety and functions (developmental provisions) of day care center playgrounds in Texas. Content included surfacing, natural characteristics, play equipment and materials, zoning, storage and other features. Relative safety pertained to the existence of safety features, appropriateness of design and level of maintenance. Development provisions related to the opportunities for children to enhance their intellectual, social and physical capabilities. The determination of these elements served as an indication of how well suited the day care playgrounds were to the needs of children.

The second was to gather demographic information regarding certain operational characteristics of the centers, center auspices, staff experience, location, capacity, enrollment, rates and playground maintenance arrangements.

The third was to examine the relationships between designated playground and operational characteristics.

REVIEW OF LITERATURE

Play influences all aspects of children's development including social, cultural, affective, cognitive, language, and physical skills and abilities (Fein and Clark-Stewart, 1973; Moore, 1974b; Butler, Gotts & Quisenberry, 1978; Frost & Klein, 1979; Pellegrini, 1979; Robins & Yahrais, 1980). Through play children discover their world, develop their senses, exercise their muscles and make social contacts. Play is the language of children and through it they express their ideas and emotions (Bettelheim, 1972).

Content of Playgrounds. The amount, variety and creativity of children's play are influenced by amount of space, equipment and materials available (Parten, 1933; Kritchevsky, Prescott & Walling, 1969; Fein & Clark-Stewart, 1973; Smith, 1974; Moore, 1974b; Garvey 1978; Frost & Klein, 1979). Some materials have greater play value than others. Play behaviors have been observed to differ on traditional and creative playgrounds (Campbell & Frost, note 1). Complex play structures are more interesting to children than simple ones (Kritchevsky et al., 1969). Smith (1974) observed more social interactions among children when the amount of equipment was decreased, but he also observed that more aggressive behaviors were included in the interactions.

A playground offering a variety of surfaces, equipment and materials should be zoned to facilitate the flow of activities, have storage and support the forms of play chil-

193

dren engage in naturally (Frost & Klein, 1979), such as:

Active play. Active play requires space and equipment for large muscle development including open space for games. Both hard and soft surfaces contribute to the variety of activities a playground can support. Smaller items are also needed for children to gain experience in manipulating activities, using repetitive motions and thereby developing coordination.

Dramatic play. The main focus is on the exercise of imaginations and the creation of roles. Common playground elements are playhouses, costumes, cans, boxes, dolls, old vehicles, toy vehicles and miscellaneous junk.

Construction play. An area with appropriate equipment and accessory materials gives children opportunities to spontaneously build and rebuild their surroundings. Items promoting this activity are moveable and junk materials, work benches, tools and building materials.

Nature and pets. The provision of living things makes it possible for children to observe and interact with natural objects such as trees, plants, animals, water and gardens. Accessories include digging tools, hoses, animal cages, magnifying glasses, seeds, bulbs and watering cans.

Creative play. An area provision frequently overlooked allows children to explore and act on materials to bring about changes. Such small protected spaces for individual and quiet activity contribute to this type of play.

Safety. In 1978, the U.S. Consumer Product Safety Commission found that there were 93,000 playground-related injuries treated in hospital emergency rooms, a number made even larger had reports of children treated in physicians' offices been included. Major factors contributing to playground safety include: sturdy equipment geared to children's needs and capabilities; appropriate spacing between items; proper surfacing underneath climbing and moving structures; designs without hazardous features; secure anchoring of stationary equipment; sufficient maintenance to keep the equipment and surfacing in good repair (Frost & Klein, 1979; Gabbard, 1981; Henninger, Strickland & Frost, 1981).

194

RESEARCH PROCEDURES

There were 443 Title XX day care centers in Texas serving children 3 years old and older. A random sample (stratified by geographic areas and purchase arrangements) containing 56 centers was selected for study. Descriptions of the playgrounds and operational characteristics were collected from the centers by 14 trained raters using two instruments, the *Modified Playground Rating System*, a modification of the *Playground Rating System* (Frost & Klein, 1979), and the *Questionnaire for Interview of Day Care Center Director*.

FINDINGS

Characteristics of Centers. Included in the study were 40 nonprofit and 14 commercial centers located in middle-class, low-income and impoverished neighborhoods. The mean age of the centers was 8.2 years; 18 sites had originated as day care centers. The capacities ranged from 20 to 357 children (median capacity of 69), and 33 centers were underenrolled. Most centers (mode) were licensed to serve children from birth through 13 years. On the average (mean), centers were open 11 hours per day and charged $4.71 to $12.20 per day.

In 11 centers the director was in charge but was not the decision-maker; in 13 others the directors' decisions were subject to approval by owners, boards, others. Among the 54 directors, only 13 directors had a master's, bachelor's or associate degree or CDA credential.

In the 54 centers there were 470 caregivers. Of the 170 with caregivers with some formal training in child development or early childhood education, only 94 had an associate degree or more. Caregivers in 41 of the centers had participated in training on play during the preceding year, including 19 instances of training on playground. The staff averaged estimated tenures of .3 to 8.5 years per center.

The size of the groups using the playgrounds ranged from 7 to 66 children with a median size of 20 children. The groups' median usage of the playgrounds was 1½ hours per day. The mean expenditure for playground improvement and maintenance was $675.00 per year, and 46 of the directors reported that some playground improvements were planned (38 within the next year). Nearly half the centers (26) had experienced vandalism during the preceding year. The occurrence of vandalism on these playgrounds ranged in frequency from once a year to every day and in severity from throwing trash on the playground to burning a storage building and contents. The majority (35) of the centers were close enough for children to walk to public playgrounds. Use of public playgrounds ranged from never to every day with a median usage of 19 days per year.

Characteristics of the playgrounds. Contents observed on the playgrounds included surfaces and natural characteristics, play equipment and zoning, storage and other characteristics. As shown on Table 1, some surfaces and natural characteristics occurred with higher frequencies than others. Grass was the most common surface (76 percent of the playgrounds), and trees were the most common natural feature (85 percent of the playgrounds). Many playgrounds contained a variety of surfaces and natural features.

All 54 playgrounds contained at least one play structure or other piece of active play equipment. Traditional equipment greatly outnumbered other items. Apparatus used for climbing and balancing (332 on 51 playgrounds) and swings (209 on 43 playgrounds) were the stationary equipment most often found. Portable equipment consisted mainly of tires, tricycles, big wheels, wagons, other wheel toys and hollow blocks. As shown in Table 2, tires (289 on 34 playgrounds) and wheel toys (383 on 43 playgrounds) were the most common types of portable equipment.

Only half the centers linked their play areas together: 57 percent used vertical treatments and 83 percent used horizontal treatments of their space; 94 percent were fenced; and 65 percent contained storage. A large portion of the playgrounds offered easy access to few, if any, of the comfort elements such as drinking water (54 percent), water for grass and play (61 percent), toilets (48 percent), wraps (44 percent) and seating (41 percent). Although 40 playgrounds had some type of transition aid, these items linking indoor and outdoor activities were limited.

Playground ratings. Twenty content, ten

Table 1
Playground Surfaces and Natural Characteristics
N = 54 Playgrounds

Characteristic Observed	Number Observed	Playground with the Characteristics		Playgrounds with 2 or more char.	Range per Playground
		Number	Percentage		
Hard surfaces	56	40	74%	14	0 to 2
Concrete	27	25	46%	2	0 to 2
Asphalt	9	9	17%	0	0 to 1
Other	12	12	22%	0	0 to 1
Network of Paths	8	8	15%	0	0 to 1
Sand area	47	33	61%	12	0 to 3
Large grassy areas	66	41	76%	17	0 to 4
Mounds	20	15	28%	1	0 to 4
Grassy incline	15	12	22%	1	0 to 4
Digging	5	5	9%	0	0 to 1
Trees	229	46	85%	4	0 to 15
Natural areas	29	20	37%	4	0 to 6
Gardens	14	14	26%	0	0 to 1
Water Supplies	NA	41	76%	15	0 to 3
Faucets	56	41	76%	11	0 to 3
Hoses/Sprinklers	43	34	63%	8	0 to 3
Fountains	10	10	19%	0	0 to 1

Table 2
Portable Equipment for Active Play
N = 54 Playgrounds

Equipment Items	Number of Items	Playgrounds with Equipment Item		Playgrounds with 2 or more Items	Range per Playground
		Number	Percentage		
Tires	289	34	63%	30	0 to 40
Tricycles					
Big Wheels	254	40	74%	39	0 to 16
Wagons/Other					
Wheel Toys	129	35	65%	25	0 to 13
Hollow Blocks	102	6	11%	6	0 to 50
Boxes	44	8	15%	7	0 to 11
Barrels	37	19	35%	10	0 to 5
Rocking Boats	30	19	35%	7	0 to 4
Saw Horses/Triangles	28	14	26%	9	0 to 4
Ropes	26	11	20%	5	0 to 12
Big Spools	23	14	26%	7	0 to 3
Boards	12	6	11%	2	0 to 4
Logs	5	3	6%	2	0 to 2
Snap Wall Sets	3	3	6%	0	0 to 1
Trampolines	2	2	4%	0	0 to 1
Pulleys	1	1	2%	0	0 to 1

safety and ten functional characteristics of the playgrounds were rated as 0 = non-existent, 1 = non-functional, 2 = poor, 3 = average, 4 = good and 5 = excellent. Content characteristics receiving highest mean scores (using these ratings) were boundaries (3.5), zoning (2.9), trees and natural areas (2.9), simple play structures (2.9) and access to comfort items (2.8). Elements receiving the lowest mean scores were provisions for pets (.2), gardens (.7), mounds (.8), dramatic play structures (1.0), super play structures (1.1), and construction play areas (1.4). Other mean scores were water (2.6), creative play (2.5), private places (2.5), grassy areas (2.5), storage (2.2), transition aids (2.1), hard surfaces (2.0) and complex structures (1.7). The mean score for the content of playgrounds was 39.9 (100 points possible).

The safety features and their mean scores were protective fences (3.8), fall zones with non-compacted materials (1.3), appropriate equipment sizes (3.4), freedom from litter and other noxious objects (3.9), nondefective moving parts (3.5), freedom from protrusions and sharp objects (3.3), safe swing sets (3.1), safety equipment such as railings

and padding (3.2), securely anchored equipment (3.3) and structurally sound equipment (3.6). The mean overall score for the ten safety features was 32.5 out of a possible 50.

The combination of surfaces, natural characteristics, equipment and materials and the manner in which these are organized determine how well a playground functions to meet children's needs. The playgrounds in the study were rated on their potential for supporting ten developmental functions as shown in Table 3. The mean score for the combination of all ten functional characteristics was 29.7 out of 50.

Scores ranging from 26.5 to 85 for the combination of contents, safety features and functions of playgrounds indicated large differences among the physical characteristics of playgrounds. The mean score for this composite of characteristics was 51 out of 100. Extrapolating from the ratings, the playgrounds in the sample could be classified as follows: Excellent—none, good—5, fair—25, poor—22 and non-functional—2. Although this indicates a fairly normal distribution for a group of scores, it also illus-

Table 3
Functions of Playgrounds
N = 54

Function	Mean Score	Median Score	Range	Number of Playgrounds Scoring 0 or 1
1. Encourages Play	3.6	4	1 to 5	1
2. Stimulates Senses	3.0	3	0 to 5	1
3. Nurtures Curiosity	2.4	3	0 to 5	11
4. Encourages Children's Interaction with Resources	2.5	3	0 to 5	9
5. Promotes Interaction Among Children	3.1	3	1 to 5	1
6. Promotes Children's Interactions with Adults	3.1	3	2 to 5	0
7. Supports Social and Physical Needs	3.0	3	1 to 5	4
8. Complements Cognitive Play	2.9	3	1 to 5	3
9. Complements Social Play	3.4	3.5	1 to 5	1
10. Promotes Social and Intellectual Development	2.7	3	0 to 5	7
Total Functions	29.7	30.0	16 to 50	—

trates that much can be done to improve all the playgrounds.

Relationships between center characteristics and playground scores. Some center characteristics may influence the playgrounds they offer. the relationship between composite playground rating scores and the operational characteristics of centers was tested using either a Spearman rho rank order correlation or median test for differences. The findings were:

1. The playground scores of non-profit centers were significantly higher (0.1 level) than those of commercial centers.

2. A weak correlation (rho = .31) was found between playground scores and the daily rates charged by the centers.

3. Centers with capacity enrollment had significantly higher playground scores (0.1 level) than under-enrolled centers.

4. A very weak correlation (rho = .14) was found between playground scores and center capacity.

5. A very weak correlation (rho = .19) was found between playground scores and age of the center.

6. The playground scores for centers that had always been used as day care centers were not significantly different from the scores for other centers.

7. The playground scores for centers in which the director made playground decisions were not significantly different from the scores for other centers.

8. The playground scores of centers in which directors had degrees in child development or early childhood education were not significantly different from the scores of other centers.

9. A very weak correlation (rho−.05) was found between the playground scores and the percentage of caregivers with training in early childhood education or child development.

10. The playground scores for centers in which at least one caregiver possessed an associate or higher degree in early childhood education or child development were significantly higher (.05 level) than the scores of other centers.

11. The playground scores of centers in which staff participated in training on play during the preceding year were not significantly different from the scores of other centers.

12. The playground scores of centers in which staff participated in training on playgrounds during the preceding year were significantly higher (0.05 level) than the scores of other centers.

13. The correlation (rho = .45) between the playground scores and the average tenure of staff in the centers was not strong enough to be considered significant.

14. The correlation (rho = .29) between the playground scores and the group sizes was not significant.

15. The playground scores of centers that had been vandalized during the preceding year were not significantly different from scores of the centers in which the playgrounds had not been vandalized (difference barely discernable).

16. A very weak correlation (rho = .11) was found between the playground scores and the frequency of public playground usage.

DISCUSSION

An analysis of the playground contents and the composite scores suggests much needed improvement. Placing resilient materials in the fall zones and removing or remodeling some traditional equipment would make many of the playgrounds safe. Meeting children's developmental needs will require more effort. Nearly 75 percent of the playgrounds need to add opportunities for children to interact with living things through gardens, natural areas, birdhouses and feeders, cages for visiting animals and support materials. Provisions for dramatic play do not exist on 50 percent of the playgrounds and could be enhanced on others. Although all centers had some characteristics that would support active play—a variety of surfaces, space for running or organized games and more diverse equipment were needed to promote the use of all motor skills.

Pervasive throughout the study of relationships was the fact that non-profit centers had significantly higher playground scores. Whatever caused this to occur could have contributed to the higher scores for centers that were enrolled to capacity, had staff who participated in training on the topic of playgrounds and had a caregiver with an associate or higher degree in child development or early childhood education. The percentage of caregivers with some formal training in child development or early childhood education (miscellaneous coursework) was fairly evenly distributed between nonprofit and commercial centers. There was no significant correlation between this characteristic and the playground scores. Most of the vandalized centers were non-profit centers, and the vandalism did not result in lower playground scores.

The relationship between higher scores and centers with caregivers having an associate or higher degree in child development or early childhood education, but not between the scores and the percentage of caregivers with miscellaneous formal training in these fields, may indicate that a controlled sequence of training makes the most difference in staff performance. Similarly, the relationship between higher playground scores and staff training on the topic of playgrounds, but not between scores and staff training on the topic of play, may indicate that transfers of knowledge are not being made from general play information to the specifics of playgrounds. The findings regarding the relationship between playground scores and the average tenure of staff should be considered as inconclusive. A moderate correlation was found, and a stronger correlation might have resulted with more sensitive data than that of an estimated average tenure.

Other factors may also have influenced the relationships. Day care rates do not always reflect the true cost of care because of donated goods and services. Quality may be influenced by the importance ascribed to playgrounds, their location and size. The talents of the personnel who plan and maintain playgrounds, including their ability to mobilize resources, must be considered.

In summary, all playgrounds in the study could be improved. Improvements are needed regarding playground content, safety and function. To improve playgrounds, day care staff need more training on the specifics of playground development and maintenance. The achievement of excellent playgrounds, however, may also depend on good center management, adequate and predictable resources, along with center staff having sufficient child development or early childhood education to value playgrounds.

References

Allen, A., and E. Neterer. "A Guide to Play Materials." In *Play: Children's Business*. Wheaton, MD: Association for Childhood Education International, 1974.

Baker, K.R. *Let's Play Outdoors*. Washington, DC: National Associaton for the Education of Young Children, 1974.

Bettelheim, B. "Play and Education." *School Review* 81 (1972): 1–13.

Butler, A.L.; E.E. Gotts and N.L. Quisenberry. *Play as Development*. Columbus, OH: Merrill, 1978.

Dickerson, M. *Developing the Outdoor Learning Center*. Little Rock, AR: Southern Association on Children Under Six, 1977.

Ellison, G. *Play Structures*. Pasadena, CA: Pacific Oaks College and Children's School, 1975.

Fein, G., and K.A. Clarke-Stewart. *Day Care in Context*. New York: Wiley, 1973.

Frost, J.L., and B.L. Klein. *Children's Play and Playgrounds*. Boston: Allyn and Bacon, 1979.

Gabbard, C. "Ideas for Improving Playgrounds." *Texas Child Care Quarterly* 5 (1981): 18–21.

Garvey, C. *Play*. Cambridge, MA: Harvard University Press, 1978.

Gillet, P. "Designing a Special Playground." *Children Today* 6 (1977): 13–17.

Hartley, R., and R.M. Goldenson. *The Complete Book of Children's Play*. New York: Crowell, 1963.

Hendrickson, J.M.; A. Tremblay; P.S. Strain and R.S. Shorey. "Relationship Between Toy and Material Use and the Occurrence of Social Interactive Behaviors by Normally Developing Preschool Children." *Psychology in the Schools*, 18 (1981): 500–04.

Henniger, M.L. "Free-play Behaviors of Nursery School Children in an Indoor and Outdoor Environment." In P.F. Wilkinson, ed., *In Celebration of Play*. New York: St. Martin's Press, 1980.

Kritchevsky, S.; E. Prescott and L. Walling. *Planning Environments for Young Children: Physical Space*. Washington, DC: National Associaton for the Education of Young Children, 1969.

Moore, R.C. "Anarchy Zone: Kid's Needs and School Yards." *School Review* 83 (1974a): 621–45.

——. "Patterns of Activities in Time and Space: The Ecology of a Neighborhood Playground." In D. Canter and T. Lee, eds., *Psychology and the Built Environment*. New York: Wiley, 1974b.

Parten, M.B. "Social Play Among Preschool Children." *Journal of Abnormal and Social Psychology* 28 (1933): 136–47.

Pellegrini, A.D. "The Relationship Between Kindergarten Play and Achievement in Prereading, Language and Writing." *Psychology in the Schools* 17 (1980): 530–35.

Robins, L.N., and H. Yahraes. "Antisocial Children as Adults." *NIMH Science Monographs: Families Today* Vol. II (Stock number 017–024–00956–3). Washington, DC: U.S. Government Printing Office, 1979.

Rouard, M., and J. Simon. *Children's Play Spaces: From Sandbox to Adventure Playground*. Woodstock, NY: The Overlook Press, 1977.

Sanoff, H., and J. Sanoff. *Learning Environments: A Developmental Approach to Shaping Activity Areas for Children*. Atlanta: Humanics, 1981.

Smith, P.K. "Aspects of the Playgroup Environment." In D. Canter and T. Lee, eds., *Psychology and the Built Environment*. New York: Wiley, 1974.

Texas Department of Human Resources. *Child Care Licensing Annual Report*. Author, 1982.

U.S. Consumer Product Safety Commission. *A Handbook for Public Playground Safety: General Guidelines for New and Existing Playgrounds* (Vol. 1). Washington, DC: U.S. Government Printing Office, 1981.

Reference Notes

1. Cambell, S.D., and J.L. Frost. "The Effects of Playground Type on the Cognition and Social Play Behaviors of Grade 2 Children." Unpublished paper, The University of Texas at Austin, 1977.
2. Wilson, B. Personal Communication from Texas Education Agency, October 29, 1982.

The Adventure Playgrounds of Denmark

JENS PEDERSEN
Chairman, The Planning Group on Children and Culture
Advisor to the Danish Minister of Culture

During the past hundred years a great deal of effort has been spent in improving the social, health and educational conditions for children in Denmark. Nowadays, our efforts are equally concentrated on giving children the possibility, on their own terms, to develop their creative talents and personalities and become familiar with those traditions, civilization and culture, which they will eventually take over. In other words, our efforts are directed toward ensuring that childhood does not merely become a "waiting room" (where they wait to become adults), but becomes a life with its own content and meaning.

WHY WE BUILD PLAYGROUNDS

Grownups need more than their houses to rest in after they've finished working. They need room for practicing sports or hobbies. In the town they need gardens and parks for mental recreation and perhaps to remind them of the countryside they never see any more.

Children also need surroundings that satisfy their needs, places where they can run about, exercise and train their muscles, develop emotionally and intellectually and find an outlet for their quite natural desire to be active. But the grownups' world is not entirely suitable for children's activities and is likely to be dangerous and full of prohibitions against children.

For more than a hundred years, ever since the changes in society created the big towns and separated the home from the place of work, we have been building playgrounds for children. It is an international phenom-

201

enon, a good phenomenon. In a playground there is enough room for the child to run about and train his or her muscles, find an outlet for energy; within certain limits there is room for imagination.

For the very young child who has just started running around by himself or herself, the playground is a rich world where challenges are to be met and courage tried out. True, there are dangers in this place, but without its being dangerous for the child in the adult sense.

But for the slightly older child, swings to swing on and see-saws to see-saw on are not enough. The young child's playground does not contain the possibility of *doing anything*; it cannot be used for anything other than what it was constructed for. The slightly older child soon exhausts the possibilities of such a playground, and it begins to be boring!

PLAY AS CULTURAL DEVELOPMENT

Among the many different definitions of culture I have met during the years I have been concerned with children and culture, the following is the most fascinating: "Culture is the answer mankind produces to the challenges it meets." This is clearly an anthropological definition, providing a good explanation of the entire history of mankind and explains equally well why man is still researching.

When applied to children's play the definition contains two concepts we ought to realize for our children: 1) We ought to take care that children in their world, in play and not from duty, are faced with challenges; 2) We must construct their physical world in such a way that they are also able to provide their own answers to these challenges.

To get the chances to discover oneself, not only as a biological being but as a cultural one and not only as an individual but also as a part of a totality bigger than oneself, is a fundamental right for every human being. Without this possibility, culture ceases to exist. For a child it is a question of discovering himself or herself by *doing* something with hands and imagination. The child has to gain experience by way of personal experiences, not by being taught by others, usually

grownups. This is the challenge and the answer for the child. But the "classical playground" does not provide much possibility for learning by experience, because it does not contain possibilities for handling basic elements like fire, water and earth or for creating something of one's own out of raw materials such as wood, stone, clay and soil. It does not offer possibilities for contact with plants and animals, not just in affectionate play but in situations demanding care and responsibility. And it does not provide many situations for building up a constructive comradeship where the desired goals are attained through cooperation and life as a whole function by virtue of mutual consideration.

The problems involved in the classical playground can also be summed up by saying that it is a *public* playground, for its very purpose is that it must be kept open and available for anyone to use, for many different purposes and for unlimited time. With such unrestricted use, a public playground has to be composed of a rigid and unalterable construction with immovable fixtures.

Children can never feel the same attachment to, or experience the same challenge in, something ready built as for something they themselves have built up through the processes of thinking, discussing, altering, then setting to work with hands and heart. For this, another type of playground is needed, a playground that children feel they themselves own because they can make something out of it, furnish and use it, see it function and grow. The type of playground best able to satisfy these important children's needs is that which has become internationally known as the Adventure Playground.

HISTORY OF THE ADVENTURE PLAYGROUND

A little more than forty years ago the first adventure playground was built in Denmark. It is characteristic that the first such playgrounds were the results of architectural considerations in designing modern urban districts and residential areas rather than the results of pedagogic deliberations as to how playgrounds should be equipped.

A pioneer within this field of town planning, the landscape architect and professor at the Danish Academy of Fine Arts, C. Th. Sørensen, was the actual originator of adventure playgrounds. As early as 1931, in his book, *Park Policy in Provincial Towns*, he presented his thesis about the importance of green open spaces in town planning. But he also advocated that recreational areas in the close vicinity of dwellings should likewise be made suitable for children and their mothers. He incorporated play areas in the green spaces and here he went further than anyone else in advocating that these playgrounds should be equipped to satisfy the fundamental needs of children: the need to do something oneself, to create something.

Thus, already two of the most important concepts concerning the adventure playground are represented: 1) It should be near the dwelling, preferably incorporated as a naturally integrated part of the residential area; 2) It should be so equipped as to appeal to children's activity and imagination, a place undergoing "eternal change" and not composed of unyielding finished constructions.

However, there is a long way between a theory and its realization. In this case about 12 years elapsed before the first adventure playground, "Emdrup," became a reality. There are, naturally, some specific reasons why our first adventure playground was built here. At that time Emdrup lay in a not very attractive corner of Copenhagen, and it was not fully developed until the 60's, so there were no complaining neighbors around. The entire residential area was developed by "socialt boligbyggeri" (The Social Building Association), a semi-public building society, which was not obliged to build according to normal profit terms.

Thus it was, that our first adventure playground also became a social and educational experiment. It was a social experiment—because from the start it was incorporated in a residential area designed for working and lower middle-class people, who seldom chose their own dwellings and were scarcely likely (if they ever did choose) to give highest priority to possibilities for their children's activity. It was an educational experiment because in this playground, in its equipment and acknowledged purpose, the results of many years' deliberation were integrated.

It was a playground where children were allowed *to build* their own houses right from the start, *to plan* the area themselves, *keep pets*. Because all these possibilities were present, although there was scarcely one ready-made thing, the children had also to learn to function in a group and as a group. By the end of the 40s, even before many more adventure playgrounds had been built in Denmark, the idea spread over the whole of Europe and also to other parts of the world. The "Lollard Adventure Playground" in London and the "Robinson Spielplatze" in Zurich are typical examples.

Today we have somewhere around 200 in Denmark. At first glance this approximate figure would seem to indicate that the idea of adventure playgrounds had become a fiasco in the very land that gave birth to the idea, especially when we consider that the number of "classical" playgrounds runs into thousands. But adventure playgrounds are not a fiasco to those children who have experienced them. They know they are a success.

A reason we do not know the exact number of adventure playgrounds, especially in the large towns, is that it has been customary to build these playgrounds on empty demolition sites. Obviously, they have been allowed to remain only until the sites come due for rebuilding. So the total number of playgrounds that have existed and still do exist since the whole idea started is considerably greater than the present statistics would show.

SOME EXAMPLES OF ADVENTURE PLAYGROUNDS

All adventure playgrounds are institutions. That is:
1) They are built in accordance with current legislation.
2) They receive public support toward running costs.
3) An adult staff is appointed to lead the playground.

4) Children have to be members in order to use the playground.
5) The number of members is limited.
6) The children have to report to the leaders on entering and leaving the playground.
7) There is a fixed set of rules (often worked out by the children and adults in fellowship) for using the playground.

Junk Playground in Emdrup. This is the original adventure playground built in 1943 and visited by people from all over the world. Its organization still shows how the original ideas were put into practice. The total area is about 6,000 square meters with room for 85 children. There are four adults on the staff. The playground comprises nearly all the elements of a combined playground, as follows: 1) area for building and gardens; 2) communal area for play and ball games; 3) office, workshops, washroom, living room; 4) conventional, classical sandbox; 5) various storerooms; 6) conventional playground with play equipment; 7) bonfire site.

This playground contains possibilities for: actual *building* (where the children are divided into small "families"); hobbies (woodwork and ceramic workshops); handling fire; conventional play and communal games. In addition, it is a year-round playground. It is traditional in character because, as in the original adventure playground, everything had to be learned from experience and for a number of years this playground had to raise the running costs by itself.

Bispevang Adventure Playground is laid out in a natural hollow surrounded on all sides by a rampart; the total area is 15,000 square meters. Two hundred and twenty-five children may be members; there are nine adults on the staff. This playground is a combined one, with a building area, *Ekkodalen*, upper part; a place for various animals, *Stalden* in the middle and an area for general play as well as conventional playground, *Andegaarden*, lower part.

Emphasis is placed on stimulating the children's social sense. The various domestic animals are shared by all the children, though a particular child may be made responsible for one animal. The houses are built by groups of up to six children. A special feature of this playground is that during the summer small groups of children may be given permission to stay overnight in their houses.

In the "Villa" there is a kindergarten class every morning for about 15 preschool children, who also take part in the daily activities (looking after the animals, cleaning up). Many of the children using this playground live in tower blocks (high-rise apartments) nearby, lacking there the possibilities for activities such as those taking place on the playground.

Tingbjerg Adventure Playground This playground, created by Jorgen Andersen, a prominent Danish social and educational leader, has a rather special function and history. The total area is 18,000 square meters. The members are 375 children and young people with 17 adults on the staff. The playground was built in 1967 in conjunction with a large residential area of 6,000 inhabitants and lies in an old marsh in northwest Copenhagen. The entire residential area and playground are closed off by a busy motorway leading to the center of Copenhagen. The residents of this new area tend to regard their town as an entity, and there are tremendous local enthusiasm and solidarity for the adventure playground, which not only houses the local youth club but also functions as a center of festivities for everyone in Tingbjerg.

With all its various functions, this playground expresses Jorgen Andersen's ideas about what a playground should be in order to belong to the whole town. Here all kinds of play are possible from the conventional to the decidedly creative. Here children become familiar with the elements—earth, fire and water—and with domestic animals. The playground is so organized as to provide challenges from the very young child to the young adult, and it can be used the year round.

One of Andersen's ideas is that children should become more involved with animals, that a child should be allowed to have an animal as a pet all through the summer and that these animals should be "proper" animals, not just pets—horses, cows, pigs and

goats. So the playground has a large enclosure for the animals to graze in and for the children to ride in or drive a horse-and-cart.

An adventure playground like "Tingbjerg" cannot be built just anywhere, least of all in urban areas already fully developed. But "Tingbjerg" is almost the perfect model of what can be done when building an entirely new town and sufficient land has been set aside for this purpose.

Nowadays "new towns" like Tingbjerg are cropping up all over especially in areas of extensive slum clearance.

SOCIAL LIFE ON THE PLAYGROUND

All the playgrounds described are institutions under the supervision of a paid adult staff on duty all during opening hours, whose most important job is to help the children with the things the children themselves want to do and make sure that the workshops, living rooms and stables are in order. Most playgrounds are open on weekdays: a few such as "Tingbjerg" are also open on Sundays. The daily routine stretches from morning to evening. It is usually the kindergarten children who come during the morning, whereas the school children and young people (if they also are members) come during the afternoon and evening.

It is characteristic in institutional playgrounds that daily life functions as an interplay between children and adults. It is fundamental that parents should feel easy about sending their children to the playground without having to be there themselves to look after them. That is why children must report their arrival and departure to the staff. The children are also duty-bound, if there are animals, to come regularly to

take their part in tending them. Therefore, membership is required to use the playground; a child may lose his or her membership by staying away. The children themselves pay a small contribution every month, which does not cover actual running costs. Though the wages of staff and rent are paid out of public money, more money has to be raised.

In many places children and their parents make great efforts to raise money, organizing collections and parties. During special weeks children take on some small paid job and give their earnings to the playground. In this way they gain some practical insight into the realities of costs and economy.

OUR ADVENTURE PLAYGROUND EXPERIENCES

The experience of adventure playgrounds in Denmark during the past half century may be summed up under: 1) Organization, 2) Adults and Children, 3) The Planning of the Playground, 4) The Adventure Playground as an Aid to Socialization.

Organization. Adventure playgrounds have to be organized, incorporated into and adapted to a system. We find it reasonable that there should be laws and regulations governing the initiatives we take on behalf of children and young people, rules to ensure that all children are offered equal conditions and chances without regard to their social status and/or their parents' incomes. This is one of the most important principles underlying the philosophy of the Welfare State.

But also important are rules that prevent anything bad, substandard or directly unsafe or dangerous used to the detriment of

205

children. Much harm is done if a playground has to give up after only a few months' use because of lack of funds or staff. It is the children who bear the brunt.

In the individual playground the concept of organization is a question in a different sense. Adventure playgrounds are not "pretty" according to ordinary adult aesthetic criteria. The children's houses are not beautiful buildings; adventure playgrounds are often known as "junk playgrounds." So we try to create local support and understanding before establishing a playground. The adults in the district concerned should be the playground's friends, not its enemies.

Acceptance. This must include an understanding on the part of grownups that it is a child's right to leave home clean and tidy in the morning and come home dirty with torn clothes in the evening. It is a pity if a child is not allowed to take active part in an adventure playground because he or she cannot avoid getting dirty in the process.

Adults and Children. Every adventure playground needs adults with broad outlook and experience. It is only in novels and films that children can manage everything and know everything if left completely to themselves. The role of the adult must be to *help*, help with all the practical things children cannot possibly know beforehand, help set things going and sort out all the unavoidable conflicts between the children. Above all, adults must help the children organize that playground. Without democracy any "adventure" rapidly ends as pure "junk."

It is important as long as we insist that the adventure playground also be an educational experiment that the children have an *influence* in the running of it. This is desirable if the playground is so organized as to consist of a democracy in which the children take over more and more of the decision-making. Our experience has shown us that "democracy" functions best in those playgrounds where it has arisen gradually in accordance with the attitudes and wishes of those children using the playground.

The Planning of the Playground. When some early adventure playgrounds were laid out and named "junk playgrounds," it was a widespread theory that they ought to consist exclusively of specific building activities—building houses, cultivating gardens, keeping animals—but the theory did not stand up. Children are also people with natural desires for variation and relaxation. The best playground is that which contains elements of both the classical and the adventure playgrounds.

Since every adventure playground is a place where many people come, it is important to make room for the various elements such as playing with earth, water and fire; activities concerned with building, gardens and animals; communal games; places for peace and quiet; but it is also important to provide for the physical separation of these different activities.

This is the reason that many playgrounds are divided into lots with different functions, thereby helping to maintain the necessary order in the playground and helping the individual child to understand that order is both necessary and pleasing. A way of attaining and maintaining order is to ensure that the number of children on a playground is in keeping with the playground's size, a good reason for introducing the concept of membership. In an area richly populated with children, regulating membership may, of course, create problems in excluding some. But knowing that overcrowded playgrounds don't work in these situations, we choose to do the best we can for some of the children instead of doing a "poor best" for all. To build as many playgrounds as there is need for is no easy solution. Money, land and political backing are needed, and there is no surplus of these commodities in the 80s.

Nor is it a matter of indifference as to where the adventure playground is sited. As in the case of the classical playground, it is important for the playground to be near the children's homes, but it must not become a campus to which children have to be transported. They should be able to run straight there from home and preferably without having to cross streets with heavy traffic.

Another important demand is that the playground be kept open the year round. Many of our original adventure playgrounds were open only during summer. That gave children too little time, not only for their activities but also to get to know each other and become comrades. To keep a playground open the year round in Denmark, however, it is necessary to have brick-built heated houses, which are expensive to build and necessarily involve political decisions. Thus, plenty of space, proximity to the dwelling-house, a well-thought-out design and building facilities are essential preconditions for building adventure playgrounds. Children come to regard them as *their playgrounds*, particularly as they are allowed to leave their own built houses standing through the winter.

This may seem obvious, but there is more to it than that. For many years it was customary for the summer season to end with the children themselves pulling down their own houses and making the playground ready for the next summer, not altogether unreasonable from an educational point of view. Summer season play strengthened the feeling of many children that no one took their endeavors seriously; they were just playing! We have discovered that no sooner did we start taking the children so seriously that we respected their efforts and let their houses remain until they themselves wished to pull them down than a number of *educational behavioral problems solved themselves*.

THE ADVENTURE PLAYGROUND AS AN AID TO SOCIALIZATION

The adventure playground is one of the means by which we can transfer the child from the role of observer to that of actor, the role where the child is allowed to so something and see the result of efforts. The adventure playground teaches the child some elementary things about the nature of culture "the answer to challenges," but it goes beyond this. The child can also meet with challenges when busy doing something on his or her own.

The adventure playground demands co-operation and fellowship. One child cannot build a house, but soon finds out the necessity of becoming a social being and forming a group that can cooperate in building. Therefore, life in the adventure playground demands the development of tolerance, of seriously showing consideration for others who will in turn show consideration for oneself. The child learns not only what helpfulness is and what it is worth but also the advantage of being able to compromise and learning that having all one's own personal demands fulfilled does not necessarily lead to happiness.

If suitably organized, the adventure playground can provide practical training in democracy, wherein the child's own influence can be brought to bear, while learning at the same time to respect decisions already approved.

And not least, in our time in which we have experienced societal and technical developments that have rendered some of the old virtues superfluous and pushed us more and more into the roles of "observers," neglecting to teach our children these virtues, it is necessary to construct playgrounds in which these traditional attitudes toward life, at one time so vital for life's very maintenance, once again become central.

Adventure playgrounds alone cannot resolve that crisis in civic discipline that is largely rooted in the fact that we have created a society in which more and more people, and especially children and young people, have become superfluous.

It may not even be necessary to build many more adventure playgrounds as long as we endeavor to keep the ideas behind them alive; that of transforming a barren, passive and observer-type existence into an active life based on self-fulfillment, while at the same time trying to create possibilities for this self-fulfillment.

Equipment Selection Criteria for Modern Playgrounds

JAY BECKWITH
Build Your Own Playgrounds, Inc.

AN EMERGING STANDARD

If you have paid attention to the recent playground equipment catalogs you will notice that most manufacturers have a "system" product consisting of posts, decks and attached playevents. Designs in this format are emerging as the new standard for playground equipment, replacing traditional swings, slides and climbers that have remained unchanged for the last half-century.

A new approach to playground design is very needed and welcomed. Playgrounds are a fitting place for creative innovation. Over the last decade we have seen such diverse products as stacks of lumber from Timberform, carnivals from GameTime and western towns from Patterson-Williams. As interesting as these products are, none of them has proven to be as successful as the straightforward Post/Deck/Event design first popularized by Landscape Structures.

While unique products will always be available, we will see continued standardization towards this format. Such a trend is both inevitable and to some extent desirable. The purpose of this article is to increase consumer awareness of the function of this new type of playground equipment and the range of features and options available.

Standardization has a number of positive aspects. Without a degree of product uniformity competitive bids would not be possible. Similarity of design leads to a body of experience on equipment function, durability and popularity. Such information in turn results in refinements which enhance the product's total performance. This process can be observed in many consumer products from computers to automobiles. Nowadays it is possible to drive any car on the market because the controls are very similar. This has increased safety and made the rental car industry possible. But such uniformity has not prevented the creation of a very wide assortment of autos.

As buyers and specifiers of playground equipment we have a great deal of power to influence the features and options which will be available in the future. It is an important responsibility to apply criteria to our purchases which will support the emergence of effective and excellent products.

In an article on playgrounds, "It's Time for Creative Play" (*Parks and Recreation*, September 1982) I pointed out the need for creative play experiences for children and the qualities a good playground should exhibit. Those attributes can be briefly summarized as:

Complex: The environment should contain as many different types of experiences as possible.

Linked: Playevents should be connected to create a natural "flow" of play activity.

Social: The total environment should foster interaction between children and playevents should be designed for group use.

Flexible: Playground flexibility can be both mechanical, i.e., equipment mounted on springs, or functional, i.e., events which can be used in many different ways.

Challenging: Creative playgrounds contain events which require motor coordination, balance ability, flexibility and strength.

Developmental: Playgrounds should offer events which will challenge a wide range of skills and ages.

Safe: Modern playgrounds must conform to the Consumer Product Safety Commission's guidelines. The safe playground not only has fewer accidents, but also encourages more inventive and creative play because the children are able to take greater risks with less fear of injury.

These six principles, when applied to playground design, produce environments in which the children play longer, show less aggressive and more cooperative behavior, have improved self-concepts, develop better language skills, and engage in more novel and physically demanding motor activity than on traditional playgrounds.

To the six principles we must add a seventh requirement: Durability. Playground equipment has to be nearly indestructible. This is imperative not only because most agencies have limited maintenance capacity, but also because equipment failure may lead to injury and all its negative consequences.

APPLYING THE STANDARDS

Currently there are several products which appear to be so similar that it is difficult to be certain that your selections are the very best possible. Thus some method by which the features and benefits of various systems can be contrasted would be useful.

Product comparisons are always of limited value because the products keep changing, the person doing the rating cannot be totally objective, and your specific application may not be fully examined. However limited, ratings do help clarify our thinking and provide a model on which we can build our own evaluations. Given that the following information will be something less than the whole story, let us examine a variety of products along the criteria we have determined as offering improved benefits. The products selected for comparison are those available nationally and manufactured by companies established more than five years. While other manufacturers may offer similar products, their long term performance is not known and their availability and support are problematical.

PLAYEVENT CHART

In our six criteria we listed complexity, challenge and development as positive qualities. A complete analysis of each product would be impossible in this short article. Instead we can only evaluate the types of playevents each

system offers with the assumption that an environment which presents many different types of play activities will tend to offer complexity and challenges appropriate to a variety of ages.

One of the surprising aspects of the chart is the number of systems which offer similar types of events. It is also interesting to note that certain systems offer so few activities. The "X" on the chart indicates that the event is common to the standard catalog designs. An "O" indicates that the event is available as a catalog option.

To satisfy the criteria of complexity and challenge for a creative play environment the system ought to have a total of fifteen or more features. Systems which scored twenty or better offer much more design flexibility and improved benefits for the children.

EVALUATING SAFETY

All of the products listed on the chart are manufactured by established and reputable companies. Most of these systems have been in production for a number of years. In general the systems are as safe as or safer than traditional equipment. One could purchase any of these products with full confidence that no extraordinary hazards would be introduced into your playground.

While these are all quality systems, there are choices you can make which will further reduce hazards. As noted earlier, the Consumer Product Safety Commission (C.P.S.C.) has identified falls as the greatest single playground hazard. There are three ways to reduce this hazard: place a fall-absorbing material under equipment, lower the height of equipment, and install safety rails which will reduce the likelihood of falls.

Selecting the best fall-absorbing material to place under your equipment is a complex problem. There is no ideal material. The Consumer Product Safety Commission has produced a booklet which provides a summary of their recommendations. Both Volumes I and II of *A Handbook for Public Playground Safety* are available from the C.P.S.C. by calling (800) 638-2772. Discussing the problems with the regional repre-

*Playevent Chart

Manufacturer/Product	To/Fro Swing	Tire Swing	Exerglide Swing	Single Slide	Wide Slide	Wave Slide	Spiral Slide	Roller Slide	Fire Pole Slide	Banister Slide	Tunnel Slide	Ladder Climber	Net Climber	Arch Climber	Log Climber	Tunnel Climber	Rope Climber	Tire Climber	Turning Bar	Chinning Bar	Parallel Bars	Horizontal Ladder	Ring Treck	Track Ride	Balance Beam	Suspension Bridge	Balance Cables	Balance Chain	Log Roller	Ramp	Crawl Tunnel	Rails at 38"	Rails Non-Climbable Panel	Steering Wheel	TOTALS
Game Time																																			
DuraScapes	X	X		X		X	X		X		O	X		X				X		X	X	X	X		X	X					O	X	X		9
Timb "R" Scapes	X	X		X			X		X		O	X		X				X		X	X	X	X		X	X					O	X	X		19
Mod "U" Logs	X					X	X		X			X	X	X				X		X	X	X	X		X	X					X	X	X		21
Landscape Structures																																			
Playstructures	X	X		X		X	X		X		X	X		X						X	X	X	X		X	X					X	X	X		22
Mexico Forge																																			
Playboosters	X	X	X	X		X	X	X	X		X	X	X	X	X				X	X	X	X	X		X	X	X	X		O	X	X	X		31
Miracle																																			
Mark IV	X	X		X	X	X	X		X		X	X	X				X		X			X			X				O			X	X		8
Natureville	X	X		X	X	X	X		X		X	X	X	X			X		X						X				O				X		15
Steelville	X			X	X	X	X		X		X	X	X	X					X			X													15
Northwest Design Products																																			
BigToys	X	X		X	X		O		X			X		X				X			X	X			X	X	X							X	11
Schoolyard BigToys	X	X		X	X		O		X			X	X	X	X			X				X			X	X	X	O			X		X	X	23
Timberform																																			
Play Towers	X			X	X	O			X			X													X	X					X	X	X		7
Play Areas				X	X	O			X			X	X	X	X				X	X	X				X			X	X						15
Play Platforms	X	X		X	X	X						X	X						X	X	X							X	X		X	X	X		11

*Data taken from 1982/83 Catalogs

211

Material Specifications

Manufacturer/ Product	Posts	Decks	Panels	Metal Finish	Post Pre- servative	Fastening Method
Game Time						
Durascapes	Aluminum	Douglas Fir	None	Powder Coated	None	Hex
Timber "R" scapes	*Pine	Pine	Pine	Galvanized	"Os- mose"	Hex
Mod "U" logs	Pine	Pine	Pine	Galvanized	"Os- mose"	Hex
Landscape Structures						
PlayStructures	Redwood	Douglas Fir	Douglas Fir & Plastic	Galvanize & Anodize	Redwood	Allen
AlumaCore	Douglas Fir Over Aluminum	Douglas Fir	Douglas Fir & Plastic	Galvanize & Anodize	Redwood	Allen
Mexico Forge						
Playboosters	Steel	Redwood	Plastic	Powder Coated	None	Torx with "Lock-Tight"
Miracle						
Mark IV	Steel	Steel	Steel	Enamel	None	Allen & Hex
Natureville	Redwood	Steel	Redwood	Galvanized	Redwood	Allen & Hex
Steelville	Steel	Steel	Steel	Powder Coated	None	Allen & Hex
Northwest Design Products						
BigToys	Pine	Pine	Plastic & Pine	Galvanized	CCA	Allen
Timberforms						
Play Areas	Douglas Fir	Douglas Fir	Douglas Fir & Plywood	Galvanized	NIE- DOX-10	Hex

*Optional Redwood

sentatives of equipment manufacturers is also an excellent procedure.

Reducing heights of equipment is more controversial. Many people feel that the higher a playevent the more children will like that activity. This assumption has not been investigated in any systematic way, and may or may not be true. The contention is that older children at least require such height if they are going to use the playground at all. It is presumed that very young children will be intimidated by such equipment and not use it. This assumption is without merit as accident statistics contain a significant number of cases in which astonishingly young children fell from equipment up to 14 feet in height. One must assume that any equipment placed in a public unsupervised playground will be used by all ages.

There are indications that a complex and challenging play environment will attract and interest children of all ages even though the height of apparatus is limited to the minimum which allows the events to function. Several manufacturers produce equipment on which the highest deck is just eight feet. There is no evidence to suggest that such playgrounds are less enjoyed by children and considerable support for the contention that they are less hazardous.

The C.P.S.C. has also made a specific recommendation about safety railings: Elevated Surfaces—It is recommended that an elevated surface located more than 30 inches above the underlying surface and intended for use as a platform, deck, walkway, landing, transitional surface, or similar walking surface have a protective barrier at least 38 inches in height. The protective barrier should completely surround the surface except for necessary entrance and exit openings. The intent of this recommendation is to prevent falls through the barriers, preclude the possibility of entrapment and discourage climbing.

There are three types of enclosure systems which meet this requirement: solid panels, wood slat panels, and pipe rails with vertical barriers. Several manufacturers have enclosures which consist of two or more horizontal rungs. These fail to meet the guideline for non-climbability. They also introduce a new hazard—children commonly sit on such rails and hook their feet into the lower rungs. One good shove and the child falls back off the structure breaking both legs in the process.

Wood slat enclosures are offered by Timb"R"scapes, Mod"U"Log, Natureville, and Landscape Structures. Solid panels are the solution on Steelville. Both Landscape Structures and Playboosters offer a solid panel with a clear bubble which allows for child supervision. A particularly elegant solution is offered by Playboosters. This rail consists of a single horizontal bar at 38 inches and two vertical bars connecting from the top rail to the Deck. This completely satisfies the C.P.S.C. guideline, offers total supervision, and is very inexpensive.

The last place for poor railing detail must go to certain Timberform designs which expose children to significant heights with no railings at all.

A final consideration is the material used for deck construction. Children not only fall from structures, they also fall against them. Striking a steel edge of deck is more damaging then impacting on a wood deck. Wooden decks have the additional benefit of improved traction when wet. Wood edge decks are available with Timb"R"scapes, Mod"U"logs, Landscape Structures, Playboosters, BigToys and Timberform products.

CONSIDERING DURABILITY

As with the issue of safety, one can generally assume that products manufactured by any of these well-established national companies will offer acceptable durability and adequate field support. There are, however, considerable differences between products that will affect their long term service.

The primary distinction between these systems is the material used for the upright support posts. Wood-based systems cannot come close to matching the long term durability of metal. Three types of wood are offered: redwood, pine and Douglas fir. Douglas fir is by far the strongest of these woods, but it also does not absorb pressure treating well. The pine woods are generally

213

treated with a copper compound which has well established preservative qualities. Timberform's NIEDOX-10 is claimed to be non-toxic, but is a relatively new compound with unknown performance characteristics. Redwood has some natural rot and insect resistance but, as with all organic materials, will vary from piece to piece.

Two systems combine the durability of metal posts with the safety advantages of wood decks, AlumaCore and Playboosters. Natureville is notable because it uses wood posts and steel decks, the exact opposite of the preferred combination. Durascapes offers a wood deck but it is edged with steel channel.

Galvanizing has been the favorite finish for steel where long term durability was desired. In the last few years a new technology has emerged called "Powder Coating." This is a polyester resin which is applied dry and baked onto the metal. This allows the introduction of color and has durability at least as good as galvanizing. There is also some evidence that this plastic coating is less conductive, making it cooler in summer and less "sticky" in winter.

Making structures vandal resistant is another step toward improving durability. In the last few years there has been a disturbing tendency to use common hex-type bolts for the construction of these systems. This means that such units can be disassembled with tools readily available. A good deterrent to such vandalism is the use of "Allen"-style fasteners. The best system is Playboosters', which uses "Torx"-type fasteners.

Timberform solves the hardware problem by covering each bolt head with a wooden cap. This is only a partial solution, however, because it prevents the periodic tightening that all wooden structures require. Wood naturally swells and shrinks as it changes in moisture content with different weather conditions. This dimensional instability causes the attachment hardware to loosen. BigToys has done an excellent job designing fittings which accommodate such expansion and contraction of wood. Most other systems require frequent retightening, especially during the first year after installation.

The use of plastic has become popular recently. These are "space age polymers" with incredible strength. Unlike brittle and combustible fiberglass these plastics are very tough and durable. While they cannot match steel components, they are more durable than wood and offer a pleasant softness and smoothness which makes the playspace more "kid-friendly." Their relative low cost means that replacement, if necessary, would be a trivial expense.

CONCLUSION

While traditional playgrounds will continue to serve the children of America for many years, they are being replaced by a new concept in playground equipment, the Creative Playground. These environments offer all the traditional play activities, but also provide greater challenge and improve interaction between children.

While there are several manufacturers of such equipment who provide high quality products, there are significant differences in the number of features offered, in safety detailing, and in durability. Using the information in this article will help the buyer or specifier select those products which will provide the most benefits and will form the basis of comparison with other products. Such informed purchases will in turn influence manufacturers to standardize the more successful components. We should expect to be able to choose among several truly excellent systems in the coming years.

Design Characteristics Used in Playgrounds for Children

LAWRENCE D. BRUYA
Division of Physical Education
North Texas State University, Denton

The "play environment" as opposed to the traditional concept of a playground is intended to increase play opportunities for children. Although work by Ellis (1973) and Levy (1978) provides some implication for the application of theory to design, the actual theory-design relationship has been defined by playground consultants across the country (Hewes, 1974; Beckwith, 1980 a&b; Dattner, 1974; Simpson, 1978; Williams, 1979a; Stueck, 1980). Their work on the creative playground concept is apparently based on an unarticulated assumption. This assumption that all uses of the environment are in keeping with the child's play has forced the provision of options, integrated and multiple play events, height reductions and a switch to wood, which many companies now use as their preferred material.

PRE-DESIGN CONSIDERATIONS

Several decisions precede the design process. Bowers (1976) describes the first consideration as the human factor, which means that an analysis of the needs of the people who will use the structure should be undertaken, with their strengths and weaknesses determined.

A procedure outlined by Williams (1979b) suggests that a designer must first consider the population of players and their motor pattern characteristics. Using a client/activity matrix that plots individual children and their probable motor use patterns and an equipment/activity matrix that lists use patterns the equipment is likely to support, a player/equipment match-up is generated, which indicates the number of players who will or will not benefit from the inclusion of certain play events. Through careful selection of play events, based on an assessment of the human factor, many persons concerned with children's play think it possible to develop a child's success-oriented view of himself.

Of course, the consideration for human factors is of no use if the structure is not also safe. The design process that primarily accounts for safety in traditional equipment (slides, monkey bars) is the railing or "primary safety system." In descriptive terms, railings act as hand holds as well as a containment barrier for elevated surfaces.

The "secondary safety system" recommended by the National Recreation and Park Association (1976) to the Consumers Panel is the ground cover system. Of the many materials tested for force absorption qualities, several were ranked either acceptable or unsatisfactory and extremely hazardous (Table 1).

One additional system for safety is best described as an "intermediate safety system" (Bruya, Sullivan & Fowler, 1979). It is made up of netting surfaces attached to a structure on an angle (45°–60°). As a passive system it slows the speed of the fall and decreases the angle before momentum is built up. The overall play structure equipped with an in-

Table 1
Rank Ordering of Force Absorption Materials

Category	Material	Depth
Satisfactory	sand (clay free)	6–8 in.
	pea gravel (river-washed)	6–8 in.
	bark chips	6–8 in.
Unsatisfactory	matting (artificial)	2 in.
	grass	any depth
	packed dirt	
	asphalt	
	concrete	

215

termediate safety system takes on a pyramid quality not unlike the safety system of adjacent platforms of which Bowers speaks (1976).

The third pre-design variable is concerned with the materials used to build the structure. Each material has advantages and disadvantages associated with it (Table 2). These materials really fit into two groups: those prepared professionally and marketed by companies and those that are not. The professionally prepared materials are more expensive but have advantages over the others in ease of construction and maintenance.

Reclaimed materials require front load, preconstruction or preparation time necessary to ready them for use. Free or reclaimed materials require: 1) heavy labor commitments but low initial cost; 2) increased time and knowledge of design to make the design fit the materials; 3) increased maintenance due to material quality. In other words, reclaimed materials may provide lower initial costs, which are sometimes later offset by increased maintenance and cost of replacement.

DESIGN CONSIDERATIONS

Jay Beckwith was the first to describe the concept of the play event and apply it to the design of play environments while establishing a ranking system for existing play events (Beckwith, 1979). Basically, a play event is that part off the structure with play value:

Table 2
Materials Frequently Used for Constructing
Play Equipment for Children

Material	Advantages	Disadvantages
Metal	indestructible low maintenance	cold to the touch unyielding to blow to falling children dangerous if welds break requires great deal of preparation to construct (welds, cuts)
Wood	warm to the touch easily shaped blends into the environment easily replaced yields somewhat to blows to falling children	slivers possible preservative infections must be tightened periodically yields to fire and carving
Fiberglass	curves and round edges yields to blows to falling children can be colorful	fatigues yields to vandalism requires a great deal to construct (forms, etc.) semi-sharp edges when it breaks
Plastic	see-through panels yields to blows curves and round edges possible	yields to vandalism construction preparation extensive price prohibitive
Reclaimed Materials	free or nearly free parent built	design must fit materials time spent in preparation of materials high maintenance can have greater potential for injuries (inferior materials) construction mistakes due to amateur labor

the slide, ladders, ropes, nets, suspension bridges and other equipment providing a reason or desire to get to a certain location on the structure to "play."

Complexity as a design variable has only recently been discussed in relationship to play structures (Burke, 1977; Bowers, 1976). Complexity is defined in two distinctly different but related concepts (Bruya & Buchanan, 1979). Complexity concept one includes accessibility and occurs when the number of entrances or exits is changed through the increased use of play events (Fowler, 1980). Concept two includes a linking (Bruya, 1979 a&b) or unified concept (Shaw, 1976). Linking as a design variable has been demonstrated to be of value in increasing the time spent playing on a structure (Bruya, 1980). Implied play routes are achieved through placement of platforms in adjoining proximity so that the child can move from one event to another without dismounting the structure. Because of the space provided by platforms and access through alternate routes to chosen events, a child may choose to defer play on any one event at the last minute and still continue to be involved.

A recent development in play structure design employs a modular concept (Shaw, 1976; Bruya & Buchanan, 1978). Usually freestanding but moveable structures allow the rearrangement of the play environment and the addition and/or elimination of play structures in an organized manner. This concept was first successfully used in 1978 in commercially-prepared play environment modules by Simpson for research purposes (Bruya & Buchanan, 1979).

The increased flexibility provided by moving these structures, and thus redesigning the play environment, appears to be this design variable's greatest strength. Rearrangement can lead the child to the selection of new combinations of play events by rerouting the play behaviors, thus providing the stage for the use of different combinations of skills and fantasies.

POST-DESIGN CONSIDERATIONS

The use of trained play leaders can greatly enhance play opportunities (Mergen, 1980;

Bruya, 1979c). If we presume that the child comes to the play setting with a pre-formulated exploratory behavior strategy (see Figure 1) and we consider that an appropriate play environment provides a supportive and at the same time arousing and complex environment with many options and choices, the use of the play leader as an intervening curriculum has validity for increasing options when all play patterns have perseverated, thus effectively eliminating further explorations. For all children, but especially for handicapped children, it is imperative that the play environment provide progressively more difficult events based on sensory strengths. Successful play is more likely to occur if the assessment of a child's needs and strengths and the selection of play events to meet these needs and strengths is accurate (described earlier in the discussion of the human factor). However, limitations do exist even in matching equipment to children. One limitation may be the perseveration of a play pattern that has proven successful. Basically, this means that a child—especially a handicapped child—will repeat successful play patterns and be unable to generate new options spontaneously.

At this juncture two possibilities exist. The first depends upon a chance play behavior such as a slip or push that redirects the child to another of the available options, effectively breaking a perseveration in play pattern. The use of the newly presented option and the resultant play behavior may be more complex, more difficult or both. At this point the child will experience either success or failure when experiencing the new event. A failure requires an intervening play leader to guide the child back to successful experiences.

If, however, a child does not elect new options, the intervening play leader is required to break the chain of perseverated play patterns. The task off the play leader is to guide the child to a new option and help plan its successful use. Through intervention, the play leader is able to guide the child to increased opportunities for success and the likelihood of perceived competency, increased ability to plan solutions to problems, increased confidence in motor ability

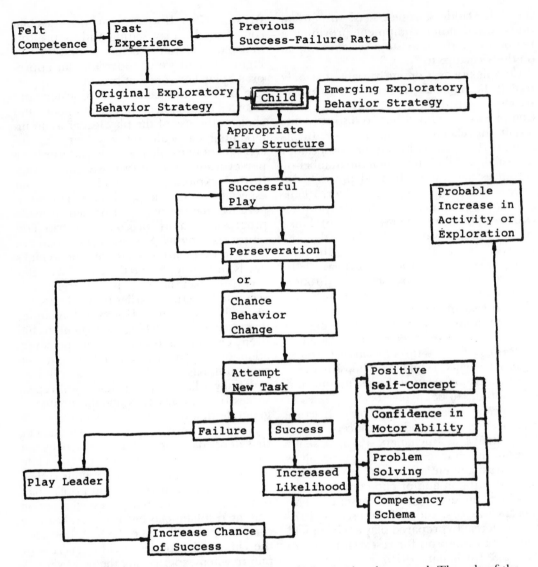

Figure 1. A model describing the child and play behavior on the playground. The role of the play leader, including use as an intervening curriculum, is shown. (From "A Model for the Play Environment Relationship to Children" by Lawrence D. Bruya and Peter K. Hixson, paper presented at The Anthropological Association for the Study of Play, 1980.)

and potentially more positive concept of self, since success is likely under the guidance of a play leader. Through this increased awareness of the ability to cope with the environment, increases in activity and exploration are possible.

A newly emerging exploratory strategy is affected as a result of this interaction with the play leader. The new behavior strategy then plays a role in future approaches to the play environment.

CONCLUSIONS

The focus of the discussion has been on the variables used to design children's play environments. Pre-variables, design variables and post-design considerations have all been

218

Table 3
Play Environment Design Variables Summary Table

Predesign Considerations	Design Variables	Post Design Considerations
• Human Factors • Safety • Materials	• Play Events— Accessibility • Linking • Modular Concept	• Play Leader

shown to play an integral part in the formation of a total environment for play (see Table 3).

Human factors, safety and material are much-needed prerequisite considerations if the environment is to work well for children. Play events, accessibility and the modular concept can be used to integrate options and choices for play within the environment. Finally, the play leader can act as a valuable support person to move children to new options for play, taking into account the need for greater and more frequent successes. Through successful interaction of all these parts it is easier to arrive at a consistent approach to the design of a play structure and the environment for children.

References

Beckwith, J. "Accident Management on Elementary School Playgrounds." Unpublished manuscript, 1979.

———. *Schoolyard Big Toys* (catalogue). Tacoma, WA: Northwest Design Products, 1980a.

———. *Make Your Backyard More Interesting than T.V.* New York: McGraw-Hill, 1980b.

Bowers, L. *Principles of Design for Playgrounds* (film). Tampa, FL: University of South Florida, Film-Library-Rental Services, 1976.

Bruya, L. D. *Play Environments for the Deaf-blind Child: Considerations for Mobility and Communication* (videotape). Dallas, TX: 1979a. Fourth in a series of Curriculum Development Programs for Deaf-blind Children and Youth, South Central Regional Center, 2930 Turtle Creek Plaza, Suite 207, Dallas, TX 75219.

———. "The Play Environment as an Effector of Mobility and Communication in Deaf-blind Children." In D. M. Compton, M. G. Burrows and P. A. Witt, eds., *Facilitating Play, Recreation and Leisure Opportunities for Deaf-blind Children and Youth.* Denton, TX: North Texas State University Press, 1979b.

———. "Factors in the Design of Play Environments." Paper presented at the meeting of the National Therapeutic Recreation Society Special Institute at the National Recreation and Park Association Convention, New Orleans, LA, October 1979c.

———. "Observed Motor Behavior on Linked and Non-linked Play Structures." Paper presented at the meeting of the Association for the Anthropological Study of Play, Ann Arbor, MI, April 1980.

Bruya, L. D., and H. E. Buchanan. "Complexity in an Outdoor Play Environment." In C. Gabbard, ed., *Texas A&M Conference on Motor Development and Movement Experiences of Children.* College Station, TX: Texas A&M Press, 1979.

Bruya, L. D., and P. A. Hixson. "Model for the Play Environment Relationship to Children." Paper presented at the meeting of the Association for the Anthropological Study of Play, Ann Arbor, MI, April 1980.

Bruya, L. D.; M. Sullivan and C. L. Fowler. "Safety on the Horizontal Ladder: An Intermediate Catch System." In C. Gabbard, ed., *Texas A&M Conference on Motor Development and Movement Experiences of Children.* College Station, TX: Texas A&M Press, 1979.

Burke, D. "Behavior-environment Interactions: A Field Study." Paper presented at the meeting of the Society for Research and Child Development Biannual Meeting, New Orleans, LA 1977.

Dattner, R. *Design for Play.* Cambridge, MA: The MIT Press, 1974.

Ellis, M. J. *Why People Play.* Englewood Cliffs, NJ: Prentice-Hall, 1973.

Fowler, C. L. "The Effects of Differing Levels of Play and Complexity on the Equipment Usage and Non-usage of Three-, Four-, and Five-year-old Children." Unpublished thesis proposal, North Texas State University, Denton, 1980.

Hewes, J. J. *Build Your Own Playground: A Sourcebook of Play Sculptures, Designs, and Concepts from the Work of Jay Beckwith.* Boston, MA: Houghton, 1974.

Levy, J. *Play Behavior.* New York: Wiley, 1978.

Mergen, B. "Playgrounds and Playground Equipment, 1885–1925: Defining Play in Urban America." In H. B. Schwartzman, ed., *Play and Culture.* West Point, NY: Leisure Press, 1980.

National Recreation and Park Association. *Proposed Safety Standards for Public Playground Equipment.* Arlington, VA: National Recreation and Park Association, 1976.

Shaw, L. G. "The Playground: The Child's Creative Learning Space" (MH20743-034A1). Gainesville, FL: The Bureau of Research, College of Architecture, University of Florida, 1976.

Simpson, N. *K-3, Timbercraft* (catalogue). Portland, OR: Columbia Cascade Timber Company, 1978.

Stueck, L. Personal communication, 1980 (Play Structures, Inc., 116 E. Rutherford, Athens, GA 30605).

Williams, R. *Exceptional Play* (catalogue). Lawrence, KS: Exceptional Play, 1979a.

Williams, R. "Considering the Options: Playgrounds for Special Populations." Paper presented at the meeting of the 57th Annual International Convention of the Council for Exceptional Children, Dallas, TX, 1979b. (Available from CEC-ERIC, 1920 Association Drive, Reston, VA 22091.)

219

X-Rated Playgrounds:
Issues and Developments

MICHAEL HENNIGER
Director, Early Childhood Education
Central Washington State College, Ellensburg

ERIC STRICKLAND
Center for Professional Teacher Education
The University of Texas at Arlington

JOE L. FROST
Department of Curriculum and Instruction
The University of Texas at Austin

The development of American playgrounds is in an infant state. Although increased emphasis on providing safe, quality play spaces for children has been evident in the American playground movement[1], most playgrounds are still hazardous and unsuited to the play needs of children. Because adults have accorded a less than honorable place for childhood play, little progress has been seen in playground development during this century. The prevailing attitude has been one of causal indifference, evidenced by the failure to develop standards for the manufacture of playground equipment, the perpetuation throughout this century of outmoded thinking about playgrounds and the tacit acceptance of crippling injuries and deaths of children on America's X-rated playgrounds.

HISTORY OF AMERICAN PLAYGROUNDS

Although the first American playground was established in Boston in 1868,[2] playgrounds did not become a part of American culture until 1886 when Froebel's sandgardens for little children were transplanted from Germany. As playgrounds grew in number and popularity, conflicts over their control and governance led to the establishment in 1906 of the Playground and Recreation Association of America (later renamed the National Recreation Association). One of the Association's first tasks was to draft an Outline for Playground Law, with the hope that this law would be adopted nationwide. The recommendations dealt with size of playgrounds, equipment, funding, time limits for use, supervision, and governing organization. Although these recommendations did not become law, their influence was widespread.

In 1928, a committee of the National Recreation Association developed a set of guidelines for selecting playground equipment. For children under six, it was felt that playgrounds should include chair swings, a sandbox, a small slide, and a low climber. For children between six and twelve the playground should provide larger swings and slides, a horizontal bar, and optional equipment such as seesaws and low climbing devices. Standards for equipment selection included the specifications that swings should be constructed of galvanized pipe with seats of hardwood. Slides should be wide enough for only one child (to facilitate taking turns) and have an eight inch platform at the top to allow the child to get settled before sliding down. Climbing structures should consist of

[1]Frost, J. L. "The American Playground Movement." *Childhood Education* 54 (1978): 176–82.

[2]Curtis, H. S. *The Play Movement and Its Significance.* Washington, DC: McGrath Publishing and National Recreation and Park Association, 1977. (Originally published 1917.)

This article is reprinted with permission from the JOURNAL of Physical Education, Recreation, and Dance, June 1982, pp. 72-77. The JOURNAL is a publication of the American Alliance for Health, Physical Education, Recreation and Dance, 1900 Association Drive, Reston, VA 22091.

various arrangements of galvanized tubing. The committee agreed that such design would ensure safety, durability, economical maintenance, simplicity of supervision, and developmental values.[3] Little could they imagine in that early period the lasting effects of these guidelines. Today, most playgrounds in America and around the world reflect this early influence—massive, single function metal equipment, rigidly fixed in place and installed over concrete, asphalt or hard-packed earth, functional from a managerial perspective but hazardous and developmentally unsound for young children.[4]

While this tradition for playground development was evolving in the United States, a radically different tradition was developing in parts of Europe. The first adventure playground, often referred to as a "building yard or junk playground," was established in 1943 in Emdrup, Denmark. Basically, the adventure playground is an enclosed area in which children use raw materials to construct and reconstruct their own play world, under the supervision of trained play leaders. These playgrounds give children opportunities to build, garden, cook over fires, care for animals, and experience the joy of creating something unique. At present, they represent a small proportion of all playgrounds in Denmark and other Scandinavian countries. Most are of the traditional variety.

Lady Allen of Hurtwood visited the Danish adventure playgrounds after World War II. Seeing in these playgrounds an appropriate vehicle for children's play, Lady Allen exported the idea to England where such playgrounds flourished.[5] In spite of the existence of the American Adventure Playground Association—formed in 1976,[6] these playgrounds still have not gained the popularity in the United States that they richly deserve.

Little change occurred with respect to American playground equipment and safety from the turn of the century to the late 1960s. Indeed, an examination of playground equipment catalogues of the 1920s and the 1960s indicates little, if any, change in the type of equipment avaliable. However, owing primarily to the rise of the adventure playgrounds in European countries,[7] the renewed emphasis on early childhood education during the 1960s,[8] and the focus on the British Infant School,[9] a small proportion of America's playgrounds began to get the attention they deserved. Along with attending increasingly to creative design, thoughtful adults were beginning to address the issue of safety on American playgrounds.

THE PROBLEMS OF SAFETY

It is reasonable to say that *no* playground is entirely free from hazards. If there were such a play space, children would probably not use it! A certain amount of risk-taking seems to be necessary for creative outdoor play. But most playgrounds today provide far too many opportunities for children to be seriously injured during the course of their play. These safety hazards are caused by inappropriate design and placement of equipment, inadequate maintenance, or improper surfacing underneath and around playground equipment. Interestingly enough, good design can *increase* play challenge while reducing injuries.

Inappropriate Design and Placement. One of the difficult situations faced by many elementary schools today is trying to meet the vastly different playground equipment needs of children in kindergarten through the sixth grade with a very limited budget. It would

[3]Butler, G. D. *Recreation Areas: Their Design and Equipment* (2nd ed.). New York: Ronald Press, 1958.

[4]Vernon, E. A. "A Survey of Preprimary and Primary Outdoor Learning Centers/Playgrounds in Texas Public Schools." Unpublished doctoral dissertation, The University of Texas at Austin, 1976.

[5]Allen, M. *Planning for Play.* Cambridge, MA: M.I.T. Press, 1974.

[6]Frost, J. L., and B. L. Klein. *Children's Play and Playgrounds.* Boston: Allyn and Bacon, 1979.

[7]Bengtsson, A. *Adventure Playgrounds.* New York: Praeger, 1972.

[8]Frost, J. L. *Early Childhood Education Rediscovered.* New York: Holt, 1968.

[9]Plowden, B., et al. *A Report of the Central Advisory Council for Education (England) Department of Education and Science* Vols. I and II. London: H. M. Stationery Office, 1976.

make sense when purchasing a slide, for example, to buy one that was shorter and of less slope for the younger children and one that was taller and more challenging for older children. Money constraints often make this difficult, with the result that only one slide is purchased and a safety hazard is built into the playground. No matter which slide is selected, safety may be compromised. Younger children on a more challenging slide often lack the motor skills necessary to safely use the equipment, while older children tend to "show off" and take unnecessary risks on developmentally inappropriate equipment.

The actual placement of playground equipment in the designated play area can also lead to potential hazards. Typically, it is desirable to cluster equipment into zones to accommodate use of soft surfaces and to stimulate action and enhance dramatic play, but equipment that is placed too close together can lead to unnecessary injuries. For example, a child who gains momentum from leaping out of a swing needs some space to regain control to avoid running or stumbling into a hazard in an adjoining play space. The opposite problem of too much space between pieces of equipment can lead to difficulty in adult supervision. For example, extensive areas frequently have corners of buildings blocking the supervisor's view of a portion of the playground. Consequently, children's play cannot be observed.

Inadequate Maintenance. The playground equipment found on most school campuses receives a great deal of use and abuse. While a single piece of equipment may be used by literally hundreds of children each week during school hours, after school usage may be even greater. And in the latter situation, there is frequently no adult supervision to prevent children from damaging the equipment. Further, most schools' custodial crews are not trained to detect playground hazards, and they are not in the habit of regularly checking playground equipment for potential hazards. The end result is that equipment designed for creative play often has sharp edges, exposed bolts, and broken pieces to cut, scrape and frustrate young children.

The overall upkeep of the play area is another problem. Because playgrounds are not closed off after school hours, children and adults alike use them in a variety of unconventional (and sometimes undesirable) ways. It is not unusual to see people walking their dogs, practicing golf, or enjoying their favorite snack food or drink on school playgrounds. If periodic inspection and cleanup of the grass and grounds are not made, the playground area becomes cluttered with litter and is a potential health hazard for young children.

Improper Surfacing. By far the greatest safety hazard found on playgrounds today is the poor surfacing materials under and around the equipment. This surfacing is responsible for most of the serious injuries that occur on American playgrounds. Analysis of public playground equipment related injuries as determined by the National Electronic Injury Survey System revealed:

Seventy-one percent (66,000 of 93,000 reported in 1977) of public playground equipment-related injuries resulted from falls. Falls to the surface accounted for 55,000 of this total ... No one general type of equipment can be identified as more hazardous than other types ... Falls to paved surfaces account for a disproportionately high number of injuries and severe injuries relative to the amount of paved surfacing in use.[10]

Many pieces of play equipment have been installed directly upon asphalt or concrete surfacing. Although this makes children, buildings, and grounds easier to keep clean, the chances of serious injury are increased dramatically. Even with normal amounts of padding installed over the asphalt or concrete, this play equipment is less safe than the same equipment installed in sand or similar loose material.

A careful analysis of playground equipment installed over dirt or grass highlights other problems associated with surfacing. Heavy usage of such equipment invariably leads to hard packed earth. Hard packed earth may not appear as dangerous as asphalt or concrete, but often leads to the same

---

[10]Rutherford, George W. Jr. "Injuries Associated with Public Playground Equipment." Washington, DC: U.S. Consumer Product Safety Commission, 1979.

223

kinds of injuries for young children.[11]

Injury Statistics. It is difficult to predict with a high degree of accuracy how many children are injured each year on playgrounds. The best estimates available to date come from the National Electronic Surveillance System[12] which indicate that in 1977 an estimated 150,773 children were injured on U.S. playgrounds with great enough severity to be treated in a hospital emergency room.

The Consumer Product Safety Commission[13] estimated that approximately 78% of all playground injuries were to children under ten years of age. The CPSC found that the types of injuries could be rank ordered as follows: lacerations, contusions/abrasions, fractures, strains/sprains, concussions, and hematomas.

Figure 1 describes the breakdown of these injuries by cause. As noted earlier, the most serious problem on playgrounds today is the surfacing found under and around play equipment. Falls to a hard packed surface account for 59% of the estimated injuries. Further elaboration of this data indicates that nearly half of the falls lead to head injuries

ranging in severity from minor scalp bruises to death.[14]

Figure 2 emphasizes the types of equipment responsible for playground injuries. Although climbers account for 42% of the total estimated injuries, it can be seen that no one type of equipment is relatively free from injuries. That is, all playground equipment contributes to the injury statistics. The National Recreation and Park Association[15] added another interesting statistic when it found that only a small percentage of reported injuries involved equipment failure or broken equipment. This is probably a reflection of the durability of most manufactured equipment.

Two other injury statistics are worthy of note. Rutherford[16] found that playground layout and equipment spacing also affect injury counts. Approximately 9% of the reported injuries could be accounted for by these factors. Finally, the hazard analysis conducted by the CPSC indicated that 36 death certificates were issued between 1973 and 1977 for playground related injuries. Although this figure is small (and incomplete), it is truly unfortunate when even one young person's life is brought to an end so needlessly.

[11]National Bureau of Standards. *Impact Attenuation Performances of Surfaces Installed Under Playground Equipment.* Washington, DC: Consumer Product Safety Commission, 1979.

[12]National Electronic Injury Surveillance System. "Hazard Identification and Analysis." *NEISS Data Highlights* 1, 5 (Nov. 1977).

[13]Consumer Product Safety Commission. Hazard Analysis–Playground Equipment, 1975.

[14]Mahajan, B., and W. Beine. *Impact Attenuation Performance of Surfaces Installed Under Playground Equipment.* Washington, DC: National Bureau of Standards, 1979.

[15]National Recreation and Park Association. Proposed safety standard for public playground equipment, 1976.

Figure 1
Estimated Injuries by Hazard Pattern*

Hazard Pattern	NEISS Estimate for 1977	Percentage
TOTAL	92,600	100%
Falls to Surface	55,000	59%
Falls—Struck Same Equipment	10,300	11%
Falls—Struck Another Piece of Equipment	700	1%
Falls—Subtotal	66,000	71%
Impact with Moving Equipment	7,100	8%
Protrusions, Sharp Edges & Points	4,500	5%
Fell Against, Onto, or Into Equipment	7,600	8%
Unknown	7,300	8%

224

Figure 2
Estimated Injuries by Type of Equipment*

	Number of Injuries	Percent of Injuries	Percent of Equipment
Swings	21,277	23%	20%
Slides	15,049	16%	12%
See-Saws	4,371	5%	6%
Climbers	38,650	42%	51%
Merry-Go-Round	7,332	8%	5%
All Other	5,881	6%	6%

*From: Rutherford, G.W. *HIA Hazard Analysis Report*, Washington, D.C.: U.S. Consumer Product Safety Commission, August 1979.

The sobering aspect of these statistics is that most of these injuries and deaths can be prevented! Thoughtful adults can eliminate most of the unnecessary hazards and provide play spaces for children that are still challenging and fun. The primary needs with respect to improving playground safety are: (1) mandatory standards for the manufacture of play equipment, and (2) education of manufacturers, designers, teachers, parents and the public-at-large about the nature of play and playground safety.

STANDARDS FOR PLAY EQUIPMENT

An effort was made by the Committee on Accident Prevention of the American Academy of Pediatrics[16] as early as 1969 to develop playground equipment design standards. The intent was to produce a set of voluntary standards for manufacturers. However, the standards were not adopted and no legislation was proposed. The effort never reached beyond the first draft and was abandoned in 1971.

In 1972 two separate actions on playground safety set in motion events aiming toward the establishment of mandatory standards for playground equipment. In the first of these actions, the United States Food and Drug Administration's (FDA) Bureau of Product Safety (BPS) issued a report, *Public Playground Equipment*[17] revealing a dismal picture of playground hazards and injuries

in the United States. At this time playground equipment ranked eighth on the Consumer Product Hazard list.

In the second of these actions, the Consumer Product Safety Commission (CPSC) supported a request of the Food and Drug Administration that the University of Iowa[18] study safety on public playground equipment. The Iowa Study collected accident/injury data from the National Safety Council, the National Electronic Injury Survey System (NEISS) and several indepth studies provided by the CPSC. The study also examined child behavior contributing to accidents, e.g., equipment misuse, and anthropometric data (ages of children and sizes of equipment). This report influenced subsequent studies on playground surfaces by the Franklin Testing Institute and anthropometric data and strength of children by researchers at the University of Michigan.

About the same time the Iowa Study was being conducted, the Playground Equipment Manufacturer's Association and the National Recreation and Park Association were developing a set of proposed equipment standards. Their resulting draft, *Proposed Technical Requirements for Heavy Duty Playground Equipment Regulations*[19] was viewed

[16]Committee on Accident Prevention of the American Academy of Pediatrics. *Proposed Voluntary Standard for Children's Home Playground Equipment*. Evanston, IL: American Academy of Pediatrics, 1969.

[17]Bureau of Project Safety. *Public Playground Equipment*. Washington, DC: Food and Drug Administration, Sept. 13, 1972.

[18]McConnell, W. H., et al. *Public Playground Equipment*. Iowa City: College of Medicine, Oct. 15, 1973.

[19]Consumer Product Safety Commission. *Proposed Technical Requirements for Heavy Duty Playground Equipment Regulations*. Washington, DC: The U.S. Consumer Product Safety Commission, Nov. 14, 1973.

as a voluntary standard. A member of the group developing these standards, Elaine Butwinick, criticized the work: "I find the standards are being drawn up by industry with only token input by other members. The Task Force has only met twice ... At the October (1973) meeting the standards were not discussed directly, and at a later industry meeting there was only one member who was not from industry present."[20]

Beginning in 1974 the standards influenced several manufacturers to state in their catalogues that they had adopted voluntary regulations, marking an important step in improving playground equipment safety. The CPSC developed a list of limitations of the voluntary standards, and activity toward mandatory standards came to a halt.

In 1974 the CPSC received two petitions from Butwinick and Sweeney[21] to initiate the development of standards for both playground equipment and playground surfaces. Butwinick's petition was later endorsed by the Americans for Democratic Action and Consumer's Union. The CPSC commissioned a Federal Register call for proposals to develop a standard. The National Recreation and Park Association, the only bidder, was granted a contract. Their committee of citizens and representatives from industry formulated a draft, *Proposed Safety Standards for Playground Equipment.*[22]

Considerable controversy resulted from this document. Industry was concerned that adoption could lead to unacceptable retooling expenses. Playground designers feared that the standards could stifle imagination and creativity. The CPSC identified problems of "inadequate technical rationale, validity, repeatability and reproductibility of

the test methods, and so forth,"[23] and authorized the National Bureau of Standards (NBS) to revise the recommended equipment standard and conduct impact tests of various playground surfaces. The NBS completed two reports in 1978[24,25], followed by another one in 1979.[11] The CPSC decided to make these reports available to the public as a handbook so that "manufacturers would be able to use the information in designing new equipment and purchasers could use the reports in selecting equipment and designing playgrounds."[23] Before publishing the reports, the CPSC decided to receive comments from interested parties on the contents of the reports and on the idea of publishing the reports as a handbook. A notice of this request was printed in the Federal Register on October 4, 1979.

A thorough analysis of the three documents revealed a great deal of useful information not yet sufficiently refined to serve as a standard *or* as a handbook. For example, the language in sections on testing methodology was too technical for most consumers; home playground equipment was excluded from the reports; no impact testing was performed on the most common playground surface, soil; and perhaps best illustrating the general state of the reports is the fact that the orientation was toward conventional, outmoded equipment. There was not a single drawing or photograph of a well-designed contemporary play structure in any one of the three documents. The illustrations represented bad design, unjustifiable expense, and excessive hazards, such as swings with heavy board and animal seats, restricted areas between moving parts, protruding elements on moving parts, excessive heights,

[20]Butwinick, E. Petition Requesting the Issuance of a Consumer Product Safety Standard for Public Playground Slides, Swinging Apparatus and Climbing Equipment. Washington, DC: U.S. Consumer Product Safety Commission, 1974.

[21]Sweeney, T. Petition to the Consumer Product Safety Commission. Cleveland Heights, OH: Coventry School PTA, May 1974.

[22]National Recreation and Park Association. Proposed Safety Standard for Public Playground Equipment. Developed for the Consumer Product Safety Commission. Arlington, VA: The Association, 1976.

[23]Consumer Product Safety Commission. "Public Playground Equipment: Request for Comment on National Bureau of Standards Reports and Possible Notification Rules Regarding Surfacing." *Federal Register* 44 (Oct. 4, 1979): 57352–55.

[24]National Bureau of Standards. *Suggested Safety Requirements and Supporting Rationale for Swing Assemblies and Straight Slides.* Washington, DC: Consumer Product Safety Commission, 1978.

[25]National Bureau of Standards. *Suggested Safety Guidelines and Supporting Rationale for Public Playground Equipment.* Washington, DC: Consumer Product Safety Commission, 1978.

narrow platforms, etc. In addition the illustrations were generally of single function equipment (narrow slides, limited access and entry, and narrow ladders), which limits child involvement and promotes stand-in-line and one-at-a-time activity.

THE PRESENT AND THE FUTURE

In April 1981, the Consumer Product Safety Commission published two volumes on public playground safety[26], resulting from the National Bureau of Standards reports and the recommendations of contracted reviewers. Volume I: *General Guidelines for New and Existing Playgrounds* was written for the general use of responsible officials and parents. It discusses playground related injuries and contains sections on planning new playgrounds and making existing playgrounds safer. Volume II: *Technical Guidelines for Equipment and Surfacing* is more technical than Volume I and is intended for use mainly by manufacturers, installers, school and park officials and others concerned with technical criteria for playground equipment.

These two volumes culminate over a half century's search for guidelines, standards and/ or laws to regulate and guide the manufacture, installation and use of playground equipment. These handbooks, if widely disseminated, could indeed have extensive positive influence in improving play equipment and playground safety. They represent a substantial amount of research and technical expertise and they bring together in concise, simple form many major essentials of play equipment and playground safety.

However, two major problems remain. First, the published handbooks contain essentially the same errors as the preliminary National Bureau of Standards Reports from which they were derived. The illustrations and explanations are of exclusively "old type" metal equipment and feature numerous hazards such as push-pull two person gliders with board seats, heavy animal type swings with "projectile-like" noses and legs, and high narrow slides with narrow platforms at the top which coincide with the guidelines developed by the National Recreation Association over a half century ago![27] Despite the rapidly growing use of modular wood equipment featuring play structures of considerable challenge, flexibility and appeal, not one illustration or example acknowledges their existence.

This critical omission means that consumers and manufacturers are not alerted to the common hazards resulting from poor design, manufacture, installation and use of such equipment. For example, many designers install upright utility poles in fall zones underneath structures, leading to serious injuries through falls onto the projecting surfaces. Further, such omission gives tacit approval for the manufacture, purchase and use of hazardous, "old fashioned" equipment and restricts the reader in learning about the benefits of newer equipment.

Second, the decision of the Consumer Product Safety Commission to publish handbooks in lieu of promoting mandatory standards for manufacturers leaves the way open for continued development and sale of equipment hazardous beyond any reasonable criteria. Although the CPSC is correct that such factors as ground surface, equipment use, supervision and maintenance are responsible for most playground injuries, certain grossly hazardous devices, heavy wood, metal and plastic swing seats, shearing devices on moving equipment, and protruding elements could be largely eliminated by a simple set of mandatory standards.

The necessary steps toward improvement of America's X-rated playgrounds include the implementation of the CPSC Guidelines, and the early revision of the Guidelines to correct errors and omissions, and the development of mandatory standards for the manufacture of play equipment. The playground movement is indeed in an infant state, but the recent efforts of professionals from many disciplines and organizations are beginning to pay dividends in improved play environments for children.

[26]Consumer Product Safety Commission. *A Handbook for Public Playground Safety. Volume I: General Guidelines for New and Existing Playgrounds*. Washington, DC: U.S. Government Printing Office, 1981.

[27]Consumer Product Safety Commission. *A Handbook for Public Playground Safety. Volume II: Technical Guidelines for Equipment and Surfacing*. Washington, DC: U.S. Government Printing Office, 1981.

A Hospital Playground

PAUL HOGAN
Playground Clearinghouse, Inc.
Phoenixville, Pennsylvania

Children's Hospital, National Medical Center, Washington, D.C. had been in its new location only a few years when it received a $60,000 donation to develop a playground, the money to be spent over a three-year period with the Hospital expected to add to the gift.

The design for a playground which the building's architect had submitted was rejected by the child-life program staff as being both overpriced and inaccessible to many of the convalescing children.

Playground Clearing House was called in the Spring of 1981 to offer a presentation and participate in a design symposium. The existing site, immediately adjoining the front entrance of the hospital consisted of a fenced-in macadam and grass area of less than one-half acre with three backless benches and a totem pole over 20 feet tall.

The basic design criteria required that the playground serve children in wheelchairs and on rolling stretchers. Some children were confined to full-sized hospital beds; others were completely ambulatory but had speech and hearing disorders, psychiatric problems, particular motor malfunctions or a combination of several handicaps.

At the design symposium attended by nurses, doctors, physical therapists, psychiatrists, administrators, child-life program staff, the donor of the gift and the author/builder, many excellent ideas and suggestions for the new playground were offered. Some had to be rejected because of potential problems of either health or safety, such as a plan submitted for a wisteria-covered arbor to provide shade for children who were sensitive to sunlight. That idea had to be discarded when it was pointed out that some of the children were allergic to bee stings and wisteria was a natural attraction for bees.

It was generally agreed that not only should convalescing children play to the maximum of their capabilities so that the play environment might provide a half-way home experience for those who were homeward bound, but should also meet the needs of those children either terminally ill or who would be severely handicapped permanently. The play facility had to be many things to many children.

Except for her keen desire that the children should have some sort of water play facility, the donor made no specific requests or restrictions. Everyone on the planning committee agreed on the importance of a water play system and the developmental challenges such play could offer. The builder was confronted with leaks, faulty drainage, problems of wheelchair accessibility, misuse and mud. It wasn't until the second year of development that both the hospital staff and the builder were satisfied with the water play system. Even now, the builder sees a need for more improvements to this very popular item.

Problems began when the initial water trays made of pressure-treated wood swelled when wet and shrank when dry. A fiberglass liner worked for a few months but eventually crumbled under intermittant pressure as its wooden support tray was dampened and dried.

The second year the builders installed in the wooden trays stainless steel inserts six inches deep and fitted with four-inch overflow pipes, which flowed into the next lower tray and finally into a ground drain directly connected with the bottom tray. For one reason or another the shiny overflow pipes kept disappearing. The bottom tray used as a wading pool was soon knocked from its place, disconnecting the drain line. This dislocation caused clogging, mud puddles and an unhealthy bog-like environment.

229

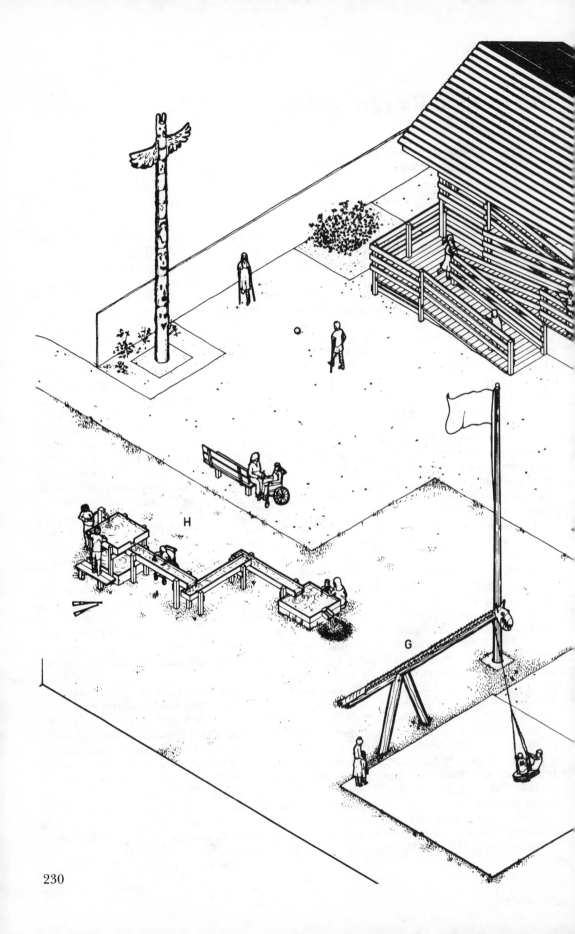

H

G

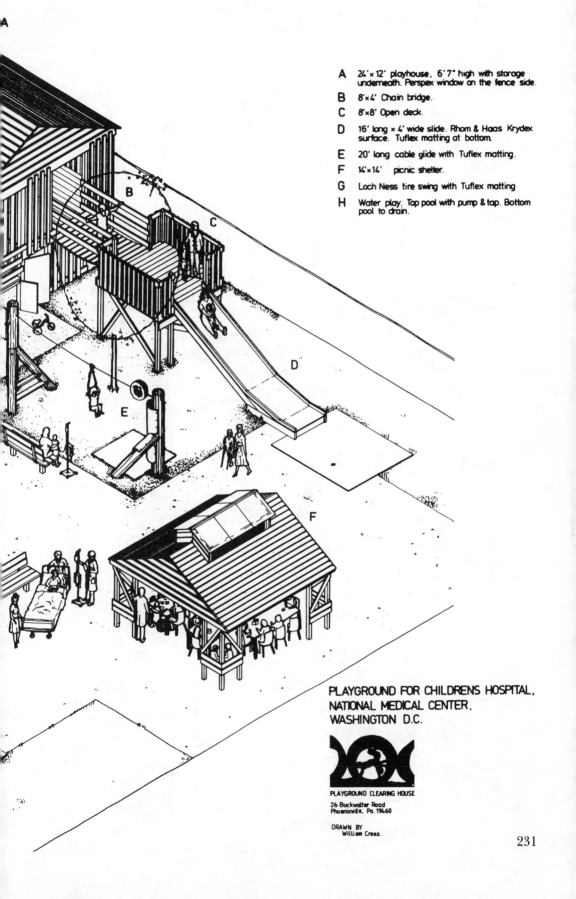

A 24' × 12' playhouse, 6' 7" high with storage underneath. Perspex window on the fence side.

B 8' × 4' Chain bridge.

C 8' × 8' Open deck.

D 16' long × 4' wide slide. Rhom & Haas Krydex surface. Tuflex matting at bottom.

E 20' long cable glide with Tuflex matting.

F 14' × 14' picnic shelter.

G Loch Ness tire swing with Tuflex matting

H Water play. Top pool with pump & tap. Bottom pool to drain.

PLAYGROUND FOR CHILDRENS HOSPITAL, NATIONAL MEDICAL CENTER, WASHINGTON D.C.

PLAYGROUND CLEARING HOUSE

26 Buckwalter Road
Phoenixville, Pa. 19460

DRAWN BY
William Crees.

231

CHAIN BRIDGE

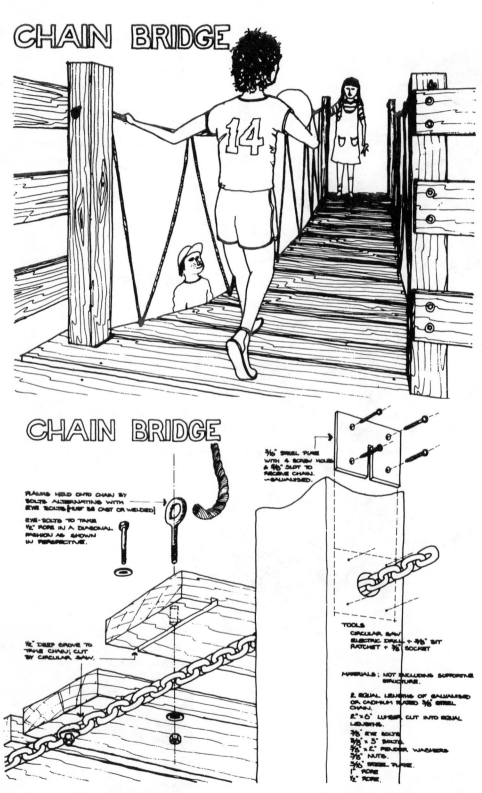

CHAIN BRIDGE

PLANKS HELD ONTO CHAIN BY BOLTS ALTERNATING WITH EYE BOLTS (MUST BE CAST OR WELDED).

EYE-BOLTS TO TAKE ½" ROPE IN A DIAGONAL FASHION AS SHOWN IN PERSPECTIVE.

3/16" STEEL PLATE WITH 4 SCREW HOLES & 3/8" SLOT TO RECEIVE CHAIN. -GALVANISED.

½" DEEP GROVE TO TAKE CHAIN; CUT BY CIRCULAR SAW.

TOOLS

CIRCULAR SAW.
ELECTRIC DRILL + 3/8" BIT
RATCHET + 5/8" SOCKET.

MATERIALS; NOT INCLUDING SUPPORTING STRUCTURE.

2 EQUAL LENGTHS OF GALVANISED OR CADMIUM PLATED 3/8" STEEL CHAIN.
2" X 6" LUMBER CUT INTO EQUAL LENGTHS.
3/8" EYE BOLTS.
3/8" X 3" BOLTS.
3/8" X 2" FENDER WASHERS.
3/8" NUTS.
3/16" STEEL PLATE.
1" ROPE.
½" ROPE.

232

The builder has since installed a wooden platform so that wheelchairs will not get stuck in the mud. Drains under the platform carry off any spilled water via a flexible drain connection tied in with the bottom tray drain. The problem of disappearing overflow pipes must still be addressed, with several alternatives yet to be tried.

THE TREE HOUSE

The focal point of the playground was an elevated structure, a tree house to serve as a gathering place. The tree house was 12 feet wide and 24 feet long so that the 12-foot lengths of lumber could be used in an efficient and modular way. The floor of the tree house was 42 inches above ground and was entered by a long ramp with two switchbacks. Originally, the ramp was about ten degrees in pitch and had just one switchback, but this steep grade proved too much for the electric wheelchairs to mount. By lengthening the slope, adding another switchback and reducing the grade, it became possible for a young quadriplegic patient to ascend the ramp using his mouth-controlled electric wheelchair.

The ramps and switchbacks had to be wide enough to accommodate rolling stretchers on which children were strapped. All life-support equipment such as intravenous feeding devices and breathing assistance machines had to be accommodated as well.

The tree-house roof was made of two-inch by six-inch pressure-treated lumber nailed in place with a half-inch gap between boards. The gap not only allowed for lumber movement (swelling and shrinking) but permitted an air flow that reduced the temperature by as much as 20 degrees on hot days. The side of the tree house facing the street had two large plexiglass windows. One of the quarter-inch thick, four-by-eight-foot units was placed high to allow ambulatory and wheelchair confined patients to see all the street activity. The other unit was placed at deck level so that small children and those who liked to crawl could also watch the passing scene.

An additional exit from the tree house led to a slightly shaky but safe suspension bridge, which was in turn connected to a six-foot square sliding board launch platform. The less handicapped children could climb on the slide for a trip back to the ground. The four-foot wide board could accommodate either several children at a time or a child with a nurse or member of the child-life staff. Made of white plastic rather than stainless steel, the slide was cool in the summer and warm to the touch in winter. Since children sometimes investigate things by licking them, plastic was substituted for the more usual materials, which could have damaged a child's tongue in cold weather.

The picnic gazebo was built to accommodate two large tables, with ends extended two feet beyond the legs so that children in wheel chairs or on gurneys could pull up close to join their friends. The picnic shelter roof followed an ancient Arabian design which included a small secondary roof/skylight ventilator. Built upon the "venturi principle" that allows for the suction of air or liquids into a larger stream of air or liquid when the larger air mass passed over the main roof of the shelter, this ventilator permitted the hot dormant air inside the gazebo to be sucked out through the natural ventilator and replaced by cooled fresh air flowing through the open sides of the structure. This rapid and natural change of air had a decided cooling effect and created a considerable reduction of temperature inside the shelter. After two years this natural air conditioning system seems to be working quite well.

ACTIVE PLAY

For active play a cantilever swing and cable ride were installed. The utility pole holding the tire swing had a carved dragon's head complete with big teeth and a red plastic tongue. The back and legs of the dragon were covered with the saw-toothed cut tread of old tires to give it a fearsome look. The rubber spinal plates were, however, soft and flexible to the touch.

The swing seat made from a commercial large auto tire was mounted in a horizontal position and suspended by three chains, so it could accommodate three children at once. Even a severely handicapped quadriplegic

233

child could be placed in the tire seat, much as one would ride an innertube in water. In such cases, a nurse or child-life staff member had to hold the life support system while someone else pushed the child in the swing,

The concrete surface under the swing area was covered with a thick soft commercial rubber matting glued to the surface with a strong outdoor epoxy adhesive.

The cable ride, sometimes called a "flying fox," was a 20-foot cable stretched between two utility poles, installed eight feet above ground level to prevent anyone's accidently running into it. One end of the cable was secured six inches higher than the other end so that a gentle slope was provided to facilitate gliding on the pulley system. As commercial pulley systems available were too

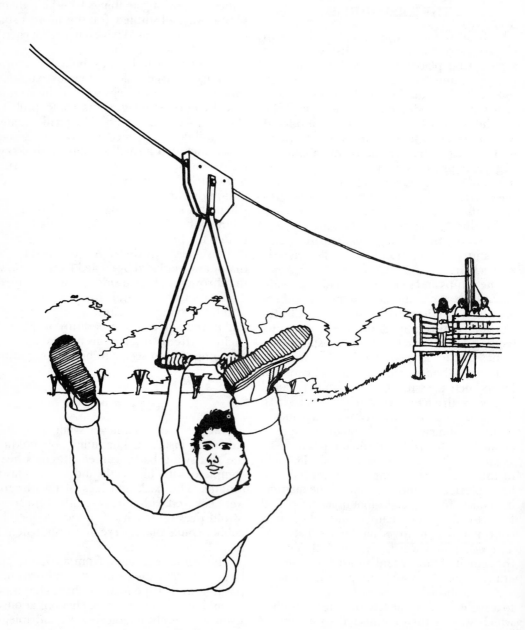

heavy and lacked bearings, the builder designed and built a system (trolley) made of aluminum with teflon bearings, which need no grease or maintenance.

Small steps were placed at the upper end of the ride and a heavy-duty rubber conveyor belt was placed under the cable. Placing the belt directly on the ground allowed the groundskeepers to mow without interference. The lower pole was encased in a soft rubber cushion in case a child could not slow down enough to dismount. A monkey ring suspended from the trolley gave children a means of grasping the handle and letting go with little trouble.

Other parts of the first-year plan included adding backs to the existing benches and creating four small wooden cars in which children could pretend to drive. These cars, designed to be stationary, were made from a single sheet of plywood and a few two-by-fours and mounted on four Volkswagen tires. The cars could bounce but not be moved. The children brought out sets of four small dollies from their play room, placed the cars on the dollies and pushed them all over the concrete surface of the play yard. They took turns as drivers and pushers with minimal supervision from adults.

SECOND-YEAR DEVELOPMENT

The plans for the second year of construction included a rubber-covered concrete half basketball court, a playhouse, a toy and tool storage house and several other items of play equipment. A vibrating balance beam attached to three half-buried tires, a set of chinning bars, a fire pole, a huge off-the-road tire also half-buried in the ground, and a cargo net for climbing were all designed, constructed and installed with the dual purpose of assisting in the development of large motor skills and promoting play.

The playhouse had two doors, one of them Dutch style. Two extra-large casement windows allowed the children to jump in and out in their play. A front deck on the playhouse simulated an old West country store porch with ramps so that children in wheelchairs could use the facility as readily as those without physical handicaps. Wear and tear on the doors and windows were severe; all the hardware had to be replaced with heavy-duty commercial hinges and catches. The tool house, like the playhouse, was eight-feet-square so that both units were not only architecturally compatible but could be moved about if future needs required such moves.

The large off-the-road tire donated by a local truck tire dealer, set on edge halfway into the ground, was used for both climbing and crawling into. It was so large that several children could fit inside the tire while others could climb on top. The inside curvature of the tire created an interesting echo of any sound. The children often experimented with this echo phenomenon, and one could hear loud screams and soft whispers emanating from the apparently abandoned tire.

The cargo net was placed so that it could also serve as a grandstand facing the basketball court. One side of the net was vertical, while the side facing the court was set at a 45-degree angle. Children who were unable to climb the vertical side were encouraged to start out on the diagonal side and thus improve their climbing skills. The frame for the net was made from six-by-six inch beams with the top beam serving as a perch for children watching basketball play.

The two-level chinning bar and climbing fire pole offered a playful way to develop upper body muscles and coordination. A climbing rope was first suggested, but potential maintenance problems and fear of over-the-fence escape by some of the children caused the substitution of a one-and-a-half inch galvanized steel pole. Thus the children could still develop their climbing skills, but the placement of the pole prevented their swinging up and over the boundary fence.

A two-inch layer of topsoil and new sod was placed where construction had torn up the ground. The subsurface was poor, consisting of rock and sand fill, and a high level of care and maintenance was required to keep the new as well as the old grass from dying.

The third-year development plan is not yet formalized. As there is little room for more equipment in the existing area, thought is being given to spending the funds on items

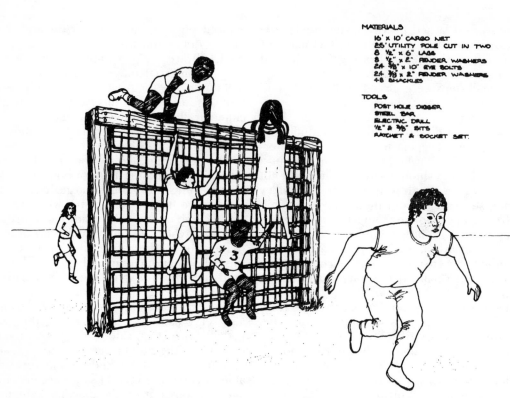

MATERIALS

16' x 10' CARGO NET
25' UTILITY POLE CUT IN TWO
8 ½" x 6" LAGS
8 ½" x 2" FENDER WASHERS
24 ⅜" x 10" EYE BOLTS
24 ⅜" x 2" FENDER WASHERS
4-8 SHACKLES

TOOLS

POST HOLE DIGGER
STEEL BAR
ELECTRIC DRILL
½" & ⅜" BITS
RATCHET & SOCKET SET.

CARGO NET

MATERIALS

A LONG LENGTH OF 3 PLY ROPE
A QUANTITY OF WOODEN OR STEEL STAKES
2 STEEL EYE THIMBLES.

TOOLS

HEAVY HAMMER OR MALLET.
NEEDLE-NOSED PLIERS OR
    MARLIN SPIKE.

APPROXIMATE FORMULA TO FIND HOW MUCH ROPE IS NEEDED:

$$\text{LENGTH OF ROPE} = \left(L' \times \left[\frac{W''}{G''}+1\right]\right) + \left(W' \times \left[\frac{L''}{G''}+1\right]\right) \text{ FEET.}$$

WHERE   L = THE LENGTH OF THE CARGO NET,
        W = " WIDTH   " " " " "
        G = THE GRID SIZE OF THE CARGO NET.

1 TYING A SIDE SPLICE KNOT....

UNRAVEL ROPE TO BE JOINED ABOUT 8"

IF USING NYLON ROPE, SEAL ENDS WITH A FLAME. IF USING HEMP ROPE DEAL WITH STRING, TWINE OR TAPE.

OBSERVE CAREFULLY HOW EACH STRAND HAS TO BE THREADED

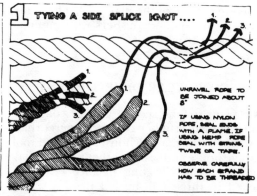

2 ... SIDE SPLICE KNOT...

... UNTWIST MAIN ROPE INSERT INDIVIDUAL STRANDS ONE AT A TIME BEGINNING WITH N° 1....

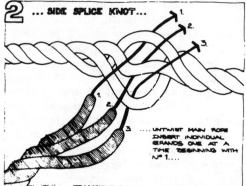

3 ... SIDE SPLICE KNOT...

... PULL UP INDIVIDUAL STRANDS UNTIL THEY ARE ALL TIGHT....

PULL TIGHT

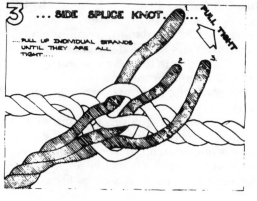

236

that will contribute to the small muscle development of the children. Outdoor musical instruments, curved radar-like dish antennas for speech therapy, speaking tubes similar to those on ships and smaller mechanical devices to promote sensory awareness and physical skills are presently being reviewed. Close cooperation with staff, donor and builder continues and a well-balanced playground is expected to be completed soon.

The Music Playground:
A Place for Creative Thinking and Play

ELLEN BOOTH CHURCH
Early Childhood Department
State University of New York, Farmingdale

Where would you go if you wanted to experience and experiment with sound, music, movement and rhythm? If you were a young child, probably to the kitchen cabinets to get out the pots and pans or perhaps the desk drawer in a classroom, or the block area, possibly even the bathroom! Unfortunately, what often happens in these experimental adventures is that the child is stopped by the parent or teacher because of making too much noise or a mess.

How would it be if there were a place where children could go to pound, tap, blow, pour, jump, roll, strum or bang with a wide variety of materials in a setting designed for just that purpose? There is such a place where divergent, creative thinking is encouraged, trial and error supported and self-expression stimulated, a place where movement and music are synonymous, a comfortable place where children can use thinking skills to process and problem-solve. This place is the Music Park Play Area that is being developed at the State University of New York (SUNY), Farmingdale.

The concept of the Music Park is simple. It is a play area consisting of newly-designed apparatus that enables children to explore their world through sound, music, movement and rhythm. These "play pieces" afford children the opportunity to experiment, hypothesize and problem-solve while using their minds and bodies. Included in the area are existing structures found in most playgrounds, which have been modified to encourage movement and music-thinking. The purpose of these designs is not just the opportunity to make a great deal of unrelated noise but to present children with open-ended opportunities actually to have an effect on the environment.

Playgrounds can be expensive undertakings. The ideas presented here are purposefully prepared with the use of scavanged materials and low-cost pieces. The Music Park is something, it is hoped, which could be easily replicated by nursery schools, child care centers and elementary schools, if not in its entirety, certainly in part. Therefore, the majority of the ideas and apparatus are simple and easy to build. Some suggestions really require only a teacher or care-giver to look at their existing play structures in new, more open-ended ways. With the addition of a few novel props, a whole new world of experience opens to the child and teacher!

MUSIC AND MOVEMENT THINKING

Why would a school want to include a music and movement component in the play area? Are music and movement so important to a child's development?

Traditionally, schools have thought of music, movement and drama, as "extras" or "frills" to the educational program. Often music is confined to a special large group once a day or maybe a few times a week, in sessions frequently structured to include some singing or perhaps a new dance to learn. Assembling children in large groups does not give them much chance for individual self-expression or even the opportunity to experiment with sound, pitch or rhythm. Since the teacher usually has a plan for the way children are to use the music or movement, there is no free time for "messing around" with instruments, sounds or movements. Of course children need to learn new songs and dances and enjoy their accomplishments, but educators need to provide time for children to use their thinking skills in a musical environment.

Two problems usually arise in an educational setting—time and space. Time is often limited for the teacher, pressed with the many activities to be crowded into a day—meeting times, art activities, snack-time. And yet most schools provide an outdoor time for children, so if the proper materials were available for children during outdoor play in the form of a music park, they could have ample time to experience this important "music play."

Space is always at a premium in the classroom. It would be ideal if all buildings had rooms equipped with a music center that provided children with a variety of materials they could experiment with to produce sounds, pitches and rhythms. Unhappily, this would be difficult in terms of space and because of the necessary noise such a center would produce. Therefore, a Music Park can provide the space and the noise buffer necessary for children to freely explore in a highly stimulating area.

When educators think of developing activities that encourage thinking skills, they include areas such as language, math, science and social studies and rarely include music and movement, which give ample opportunities for children to use and expand these skills in an exciting format. Hans Furth and Harry Wacks in their book, *Thinking Goes to School*, discuss the fact that movement and thinking are interdependent. They feel that many children do not do well in some academic tasks because they have not developed the movement-thinking necessary to complete these tanks. They speak of the thinking implied in body movement. The process questions of how, why, and when are essential in this thinking. Movement and music activities can be an excellent source of processing experiences.

For example, if you ask a child to move to some music as if he or she were a machine, that child has to think about how a machine would move, where it would go and when it would stop. Then, if you slow down the speed of the music and say the machine is breaking down, the child must process this information and solve the problem of how a machine would move as it broke down. Later, when you ask each individual machine to join another and become a two-part machine, you are motivating the children to think out the new problem of how two persons be a machine and work together. During the exercise the children are using their minds to enable them to solve problems with their bodies.

The same process holds true for music-making activities. Children can be provided with kitchen gadgets, tools, rocks and other such objects and asked to see how many different sounds they can make. In this situation they have materials to encourage them to process the many possibilities of sound in an object. The thinking can be extended further by requesting children to make similar or contrasting sounds; a wet sound or a dry sound. Extending this even further can produce an orchestra of kitchen sounds that can be put to music. It is surprising how much problem-solving can be produced by a child presented with a piece of paper and asked to make as many sounds as possible. There is no right or wrong answer to these activities. Children are presented with materials in such a manner that the process, not the product, is important.

These types of thought-provoking activities are the foundation of the Music Park concept. In essence, the playground is an open-ended creative space where children use music and movement-thinking skills, problem-solving skills and logical thinking skills in a supportive environment designed to encourage divergent thinking.

THE MUSIC PARK

The gate invites the child to touch, feel, move, make noise as he or she enters a new land. All around are things on which to walk, jump, run, climb or slide, each one producing a new sound, rhythm or melody. The walkway is specially constructed of many types of materials that make a sound as the child enters. The apparatus beckons the child to manipulate, change, think about it. There are places in which to climb and strum "strings," places to produce sound with feet, hands, the whole body. All around are thought-provoking possibilities. Here is a spot where children can use minds and bodies to process, experiment, manipulate and express, a park where children are the main activators to make it all work.

The design of the Music Park is somewhat similar to the concept of exercise trails or golf courses. Each piece of apparatus is connected by a specially-designed music trail; there is a flow or continuity from one section to another. Children are free to follow the trail or use each structure at random. The materials in the play area can be divided into two categories: those that are easily constructed or added to existing play structures commonly found in a play yard; those requiring major construction work.

APPARATUS TO ADD TO A PLAYGROUND

Music Trail. In most playgrounds pathways and trails can be added to their area—trails going from apparatus to apparatus or perhaps skirting the perimeter of the yard. A trail can be used with shoes, tricycles and what are called "fantasy feet." The path is constructed of such materials as brick, slate, wood slices, stones, cement blocks, indoor/outdoor carpeting, rubber mats, marble or granite and tile, with each material in a separate section large enough (mostly four feet by three) to allow full exploration of its individual sound character. The sections flow into one another.

Fantasy Feet. The experience of traversing the music trail can be extended by the addition of homemade "fantasy feet," which are margarine tubs (plus lids) or inverted sand pails. Each tub has a rope loop attached to two sides to form a long handle. A child places a foot on top (which is really the bottom) of the tub and holds the handle loop as he or she walks. Empty inverted sand pails make a hollow clip-clop noise. The sound varies with the part of the trail walked on. The margarine tub with lid can add another dimension to the activity, by putting an ever-changing assortment of objects inside; dry beans, for example, or pebbles, screws, nails, cut straws, bells, buttons, rice, shells, paper clips and tacks, making for a variety of sound as children walk.

Musical Fence. Most early childhood play spaces are fenced in by either chain link or wood fencing, ideal places to set up experimentation areas. Here is a giant wall providing a background for children to manipulate or produce sounds and rhythms. Scavenged materials or "glorious junk" requested from parents can be painted in non-rusting paint in bright colors and hung on the fence to invite children to touch. A few suggestions are: film cans, wooden spoons, egg beaters, pie plates, sleigh bells, coconut halves, cookie sheets, sand paper blocks, bike tires.

The Music Discovery House or Table. Essential to the Music Park is the area where children can make their own discoveries about sound, rhythm and tone, a place where a constantly changing array of materials invites exploration. Ideally, this would be a "discovery" house, perhaps a shed with a large work table with lock-up storage compartments below that would hold a changing collection of "musical goodies," at one time all kitchen gadgets, at another tools or even toy vehicles. Art materials needed to construct simple musical instruments would be available; the walls would be decorated with music-related pictures, such as rebus posters or picture charts of familiar songs so that children could add songs to their "instrumental" music.

Sand/Water Area. The simple addition of different materials in this area makes possible a music-related activity. Clear, one-inch plastic tubing is cut in diminishing lengths and sealed at the bottom. These are used by the children to fill with sand or water to produce different tones when tapped. Plastic yogurt or margarine containers and lids can become maracas when filled with sand or pebbles.

Movement Area. The movement area should be a semi-flat, either grassy or sandy area, large enough for at least six young children to move in without restraint. Adjacent is a trunk (or moveable container from indoors), filled with movement-inspiring props, such as scarves, hats, streamers, kites, beach balls, puppets, balloons. This collection would be frequently changed to add to a child's enthusiasm and excitement. A portable cassette player used occasionally will bring more music into their movement.

Wind Chime Tree. A musical area would not be complete without wind chimes dangling from a tree in the play yard or the top of a swing set. There are many excellent materials for making wind chimes: various-sized aluminum pipe, ceramic tiles, clay flower pots, nails, wooden spoons, bamboo sticks, shells and bottle caps. Children are usually eager to help and are quite capable of assisting in the making.

NEW PERMANENT STRUCTURES

The Harp Box. A four-by-eight-foot plywood structure invites children to enter and experiment. Inside, a child can be enveloped by the sounds produced by strumming the "harp strings" strung across the various geometric-cut windows. Steel string is strung from eye hook to eye hook to fill up each window opening, carefully spaced so that neither fingers nor heads can be caught in the wire. The harp can be played from inside or out.

Infants' and Toddlers' Slit Drum. The slit drum is a three-by-two foot plywood box with a number of slits in the top and sides, cut with a coping saw to allow free vibration. The slit drum will play different sounds depending on the area hit and the striking object (stick, hand or mallet). Infants and toddlers can sit on the ground around this giant version of the traditional drum box and bang to their hearts content!

Drum Box Balance Beam. Older children use a larger version of the slit drum box as a balance beam constructed of drums of various heights. Each beam has a sliding door to allow entrance inside the box, where a changing supply of materials is hung to sound as the child walks across the beam.

In a nearby container are objects for children to experiment with: bells, tambourines, wind chimes, rattles, kitchen gadgets and tools.

Steel Drum Sculpture and Net Climber. Children are fascinated by the sound of steel drums. The Music Park took this interest into consideration when developing a climbing piece consisting of a sculpture of multilevel steel drums and a cargo net climber. Here, children can make this sculpture reverberate with feet or mallets. The net is attached to a higher end of the sculpture to afford entrance to the top. Interspersed throughout the net small objects are hung to sound when the net moves.

Tire Swing. The tire swing in the Music Park is horizontally hung at the top of hanging apparatus with a large gong on either side. As a child swings back and forth the gong is rung by an attachment on the rope. Many small materials can be added and sealed into the inside section of the tire to sound as the tire moves.

Old Washboard Wall. A new sensory experience for young children as they explore the possibilities of sound, touch and sight is at the old washboard wall, which is a sheet of plywood on posts as the base for attaching five old-fashioned washboards and five wooden spoons. Children "play" the washboards with the wooden spoons attached to the wall by ample lengths of plastic rope.

SUMMARY

In a music playground the different apparatus chosen for any particular play area would reflect the age and level of the children using it. Many items in this playground are appropriate for several ages because each child brings to musical play an individual mode of thinking. An essential underlying concept of the design is that children tend to find their own levels with these pieces, turning them into objects to fit their needs or concepts at the time. The apparatus is not static, but flowing and changing with the involvement of the children. As Vernice Nye wrote in her book *Music for Young Children* (Dubuque, IA: Brown, 1979), ". . . the development of competencies in self-experience, acceptance of others, and positive and secure feelings about self result from freedom of expression, experience in music and creative movement."

Plants in Children's Outdoor Environments

TALBOT
Architect
Austin, Texas

Because plants are an integral part of our natural habitat, it would seem evident that they should be a major component in children's outdoor environments. Yet designers (like myself) and educators alike usually overlook the obvious: vegetation is perhaps the best tool we have for creating meaningful places for children. Isn't the discrepancy just too great between the wonderlands we see illustrated in children's literature and the dry, mechanical equipment we actually build for them? The loss is not merely aesthetic, but a creative and educational loss as well.

Since learning is a major outcome of child's play, good playspace design should focus on education. Below is an abbreviated list of educational objectives children's environments should fulfill, with suggestions as to how plants, whether in a children's garden or a designer's landscape, can be used to meet these objectives.[1]

EDUCATIONAL OBJECTIVES

Awareness of Three Dimensions Within the Playspace

The air space above the ground we walk on is voluminous, fluid and dense. Like fish in the ocean, we take this third dimension for granted. And yet the incredible popularity of such folk heroes as Tarzan, Spiderman, Wonder Woman and Luke Skywalker is based in part on our subliminal wish to travel easily through all three dimensions.

The upper volume of a playspace should be as accessible to children as the surface area. "Spacewalking" among branches, trunks and vines is a way youngsters can defy gravity and become aware of the layers of space that comprise the total playground. Simply placing a swingset or slide close to foliage will heighten, through visual contrast, the sensation of speed and diagonal motion through space.

A few medium-sized trees located together can hold a platform, treehouse, suspension bridge or overhead support for a swing. A stout branch or cantilevered spar can also hold a swing, climbing rope, rings or trapeze (see Figure 1). Just as swinging and sliding heighten spatial awareness, passing time in a treehouse deepens it.

I have even built platforms in a large dead cedar. I brought the tree "back to life" by planting wisteria to climb its trunk and hanging a birdfeeder in its branches. A lesser alternative is to import a dead, sound tree trunk with a few major branches to be climbed by the children.

Sharpening of All the Senses

Of course, there are no senses to which plants cannot appeal with abundance and variety, in contrast to the token sensory stimulation of the usual man-made playgrounds. An area rich with flora encourages a child's senses to develop and take in more: the visual sensuality of shifting, dappled light through foliage; the different sounds leaves make in the wind; the many tactile sensations provided by different types of bark; the scents of flowers and herbs; the colors changing with the weather.

Crape myrtle has a smooth, silvery, sinewy bark. Cottonwoods and sycamores flutter softly in the wind. Honeysuckle, gardenia and mimosa have unforgettable smells. Lamb's ear is a soft, velvety garden plant children can grow. Mulberry trees and loquats bear tasty fruit.

---

[1] Examples cited are specific to Central Texas, but are applicable to some southern and south central states. Contact horticultural professionals for suggestions specific to your area.

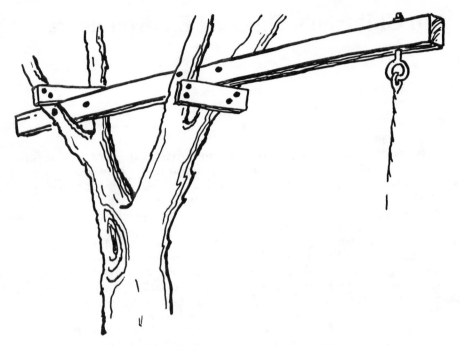

Figure 1. A man-made "branch"

Place fragrant plants upwind, at entries or along tight passageways. Hang wind-chimes or colored transparencies from branches. Use a mixture of plants that offer something special during each season, such as berries, blooms, fruit or pods. Start a small fruit orchard or make a grape arbor out of a walkway or car park. And by all means, if you're starting on a new site, keep as much of the original vegetation as you can.

Encouragement of Construction by the Children: Knowledge of Basic Tools and Concepts of Mechanical Advantage

A landscape in which plants are carefully arranged can encourage young builders; plants can offer a variety of materials with which to work. For instance, a tight grove of trees might suggest the addition of platforms, walls or a lean-to. A bamboo hedge might encourage the carving out of hideaways; and it can provide stalks for further construction. Hanging even a simple clothesline, let alone a swing or hammock, becomes an impossible task when the yard is barren.

Children gain a basic knowledge of physics as the result of such activities, a learning made easier when a heavily planted yard makes a handy setting for the practical use of the six simple machines: leaves might be hauled in a wheel-barrow (*wheel, lever*); a *pulley* could be hung from a branch; firewood could be split with a *wedge*; a *ramp* might lead to a tree platform; and a hanging basket might be held up by a *hook screw*.

Plants also expand the selection of materials useful to crafts, building and dramatic play. Besides bamboo, such "loose parts" include leaves, needles, sticks, logs, grass, flowers, gourds, natural dyes, vines, nut and seed pods.

Increased Contact with Nature: Protection from the Weather

The more plants there are in the play yard, the better the chance that it will harbor wildlife and resemble a natural setting. A variety of native plants will give children a sense of being within nature rather than just outdoors. Besides providing incentive for going outside, plants can increase the usefulness of the playspace by keeping it shady and glare-free in the summer while allowing the sun to penetrate in the winter. Deciduous foliage should be to the south of the yard and on south or west walls. Evergreen bushes can be used to block winter winds. Placement of spreading trees over high-use areas can minimize the effects of rain.

Exposure to a Context
That Changes with Time

Unlike play equipment which only deteriorates, plants change dynamically and cyclically with time. The changes in the landscape invoke greater sensitivity, increasingly complex responses and new modes of awareness in the children. This becomes especially apparent when the children have a hand in growing the plants themselves. The growth of the landscape then becomes linked with the growth of those in it.

Variation of the Playground to Allow
for Different Activities

A space can be defined by varying the heights of plants, proportion of vegetation to open space and density and location of planting. Greenery can be used to subdivide the playground with visual and acoustical barriers: (hedges, trellises, espaliers); natural ceilings (overhanging trees, arbors); light/shade patterns (denser or sparser canopies, full sun); traffic definers (hedges, trellises, raised beds, groundcover) and particular use areas (garens, climbing trees, bush shelters). Thus, settings for various play, social and educational interests can be "grown."

For example, group games can be encouraged by fewer upright plantings coupled with a grass carpet, whereas climbing can be encouraged by a few choice trees or shrubs. An outdoor classroom, swing area or performance arena might be defined by one or more tall overhanging shade trees with bushes around the edges. Hedge mazes, construction sites, private sitting places, flower beds and even science-ecology areas can be landscaped into the schoolyard or playground.

Stimulation of Imagination

Children's environments should be unconventional, landscapes of dreams and daydreams, meticulously detailed with eccentricities, hiding places, shadows, curves, offering the promise that there is always more. Build and plant together with the children. Let nature help. Man-made objects serve their purposes but they need something else which only Nature offers, filtered light, mustiness of dense foliage flowers and fruit, birds and insects. The *spirit* of a place is essential; it is the state of mind and heart the child experiences, something that is sensed. Any environment we create that doesn't take this into account will fail in the larger sense.

LANDSCAPING CHILDREN'S ENVIRONMENTS

Here are a few suggestions for designing an outdoor facility for children or adding to one already existing.

1) *Clarify your goals.* Look at how landscaping will best support your play, educational and social objectives. What ages and types of children are there? Which activities need to be segregated, which encouraged or discouraged? Is it important to consider weather modification or transition spaces between indoors and outdoors? What will it take to make your grounds comfortable, inviting and useable?

2) *Get advice from a local expert.* Contact your local green thumb—a parent, garden clubber, an interested amateur or your county extension agent.

3) *Send a questionnaire to local professionals.* Explain your intention to local nursery owners, landscapers and related professionals, asking for recommendations for trees, low and tall shrubbery, vines for both upright and overhead uses, grass and other groundcover, garden plants that children can grow themselves and any helping publications.

4) *Become familiar with native plants.* Plants that are native or have been adapted to the area, hardier and easier to maintain and connected with the locale's natural history, can often be found and transplanted for free and are ecologically honest. Become aware of poisonous plants that might inadvertently be used.

5) *Get inspiration from children's literature.* The landscapes given us by such illustrators as

Rackham, Dulac, Nielson, Froud and Disney offer wonderful alternatives to modern store-bought playscapes. Artists' versions of never-never land are as close as the library or book-shop.

6) *Consider the children.* Involve the children in all phases of the landscaping, from choosing the species to maintenance and harvest (if any). The experience will be educational in every sense of the word, the work load will be more evenly spread and the children will be less thoughtless in their treatment of the plants. Make suitable childproof barriers to protect the most vulnerable plants.

7) *Care for landscape.* Keep a strict feeding, watering and pruning schedule. Plant more than needed—the attrition rate may be as much as 50 percent. If you suspect a tree is dying, immediately plant another nearby to replace it.

8) *Select appropriate vegetation.* The basic plant types most useful in children's environments include trees, vines, shrubbery, grass and ground cover and garden plants.

Substitute species and design solutions fitting to your own eco-climate.

Trees are most important; playspaces must have trees to frame, shade and beautify. Trees give a sense of power and longevity (trees live longer than any other living thing). Just as climbing a tree augments a child's visual and spatial capabilities, planting one extends a child temporally and spiritually.

Basic tree arrangements are: *umbrella*, a single shade tree forming an outdoor room; *pair*, two trees flanking a point of passage; *avenue*, a path lined with a double row of trees whose branches form a continuous canopy overhead; *courtyard*, a space open to the sky surrounded by walls of trees; *grove*, a random cluster of trees tightly spaced to give intimacy; *orchard*, rows of fruit trees (Alexander, 1977) (see Figure 2).

These arrangements can be augmented with shade-loving understory plants for further definition, such as creating an ornamental gateway using a pair of spring-blooming trees, one or two pairs of all-bear-

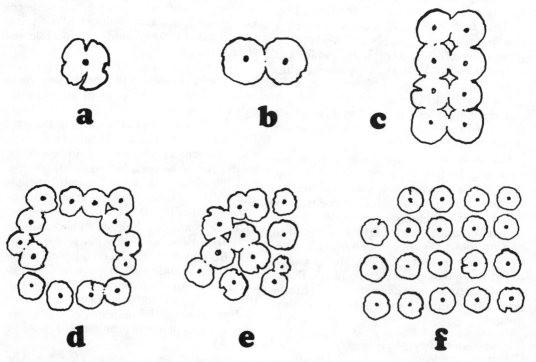

Figure 2. Basic tree arrangement (in plan): a) umbrella, b) pair, c) avenue, d) courtyard, e) grove, and f) orchard

ing bushes, all set in two matching raised beds of evergreen groundcover (see Figure 3). A courtyard could focus on a hedge maze or garden.

In general, choose rot-resistant, hard-timbered varieties such as oaks and ashes. Intermixing fast- and slow-growing trees serves both the present generation and the generations to come. When attaching something permanently to a tree, use bolts, eyebolts or heavy screws. Never ringbark a tree by wrapping it with rope. When adding structures to trees that move in the wind, allow for that motion by using sliding or hanging connec-tions to attach the main supports (see Figure 4, p. 248).

Shrubbery. Much of the quiet play of childhood takes place under bushes. Children love to carve out rooms and make dirt excavations in the shady places among the trunks. Taller shrubs can make the same basic spatial arrangements as trees, but the spaces will be smaller and more erratic. Larger bushes can even support a small treehouse.

Hedges can be made child- and animal-proof by co-planting them with inconspicuous wire fencing that disappears as the hedge matures. For added height, grow

Figure 3. An ornamental gateway

247

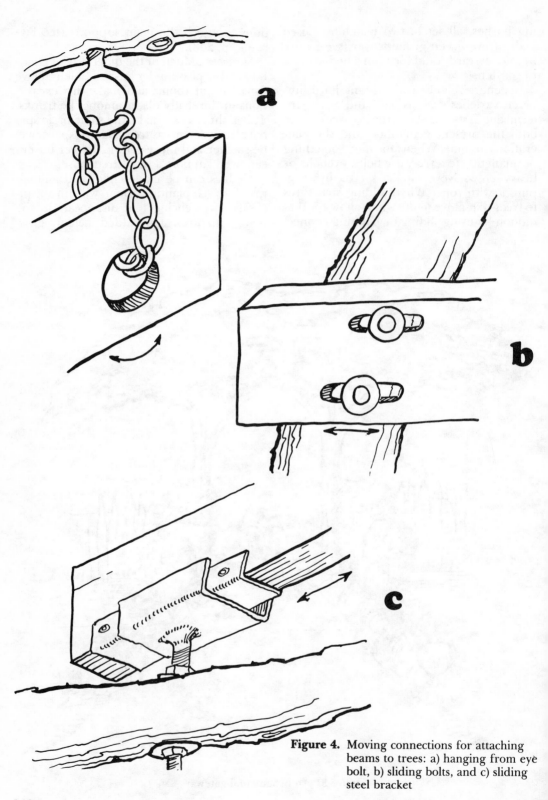

Figure 4. Moving connections for attaching beams to trees: a) hanging from eye bolt, b) sliding bolts, and c) sliding steel bracket

hedges in raised beds. Groupings of various-sized shrubs in conjunction with walls, trees and berms (narrow hedges) make good settings for hide-and-seek, chase games, sitting areas, playhouses and construction. Shrubbery is preferred by much wildlife over tree and field.

Vertical and Horizontal Vines. Buildings with roses or passion-flower softening their edges are more memorable than bare walls. Fast-growing vines help mask unsightly areas, cover fences, provide shade, cut glare and make the transition from building to grounds. Well-tended vines give a feeling of order and repose, a sense of enhanced quality of life, an aura of age and solidity; in short, the things that make a child feel at home.

Trellised porches and patios make excellent semiprotected and inviting outdoor classrooms. Walkways can be made special by using trellised overhead climbers such as grapes, clematis or Carolina jasmine for partial enclosure and shade. Widened to include a porch swing, play space, herbaceous border and an occasional focal point, the path becomes an attractive, meaningful place where a child can linger before moving on. Walkways such as these give definition, character and a feeling of shelter to the play yard (see Figure 5).

Simple, upright trellises or "green fences" can be used to define paths or form free-standing traffic barriers. In fact, trellises may be substituted in most situations calling for hedges, such as wind-breaks or mazes with the added advantages of being taller and quicker to mature. Trellises will have greater visual (and actual) solidity if thick columns are used, which might be made of from laminated lumber, concrete, logs, steel or possibly clay pipe. The basic post-beam support system should be filled in with painted wood lathe, galvanized fencing, sidewalk mesh, rebar or even cast-off bedsprings. Whatever infill is used, the vines will soon cover it.

Grass and Groundcover. Grass is alive, not a carpet. Although good for sports and unstructured play, it will not last on paths or fall zones under equipment, nor will it cushion long falls. In high-wear situations where grass is still desired, gravel, stones, pavers or "grasscrete" spaced to allow grass to grow through may be a workable compromise. Although not as soft, the creeping grasses rejuvenate better and are tougher than tussock-forming varieties. Grasses with the widest leaves and thickest stems are generally the most wear-resistant. Other groundcover to be used where traffic is low: herbs, wild-flowers, trailing shrubbery, creepers and mosses.

Making at least part of the yard a cross between the wild and the cultivated allows its natural tendencies to thrive, and it will be easier to maintain. Shorter plants tightly intermingled among larger ones keep out volunteer "weed." To make level changes, use loosely-spaced boulders or blocks where falls aren't a problem and treated lumber or tires where resilience is needed. Build retainers informally and naturalistically, filling cracks and small spaces with trailing plants or fragrant herbs. This type of gardening is not only more ecologically correct, but lends itself better to a child's flights of imagination.

Plants Children Can Grow. All children, even the handicapped, have an innate desire and capability to grow things. With a little help they can grow most fast-growing vegetables, herbs or flowers. Social skills (cooperation, sharing, respect for others, responsibility), as well as learning skills (problem-solving, intuitive reasoning, flexibility), come naturally while cultivating a garden. There is always something for everyone to do: digging, making raised beds, planting, mulching, feeding, controlling weeds and pests, composting, general tending and harvesting.

Little more is needed than a fenced enclosure in the sun, a water source and nearby storage for tools. The layout can be anything from irregular to geometric—let the children decide.

Consider spinoff activities: growing ethnic foods, keeping a personal garden journal, having a special garden song, making a sitting place, studying nutrition, adorning the garden, eating a "harvest salad," expanding into a community garden for all ages.

Play and education are tools for cultural evolution. The playground of today sets the pattern for the world of tomorrow. We who are responsible for children's environments

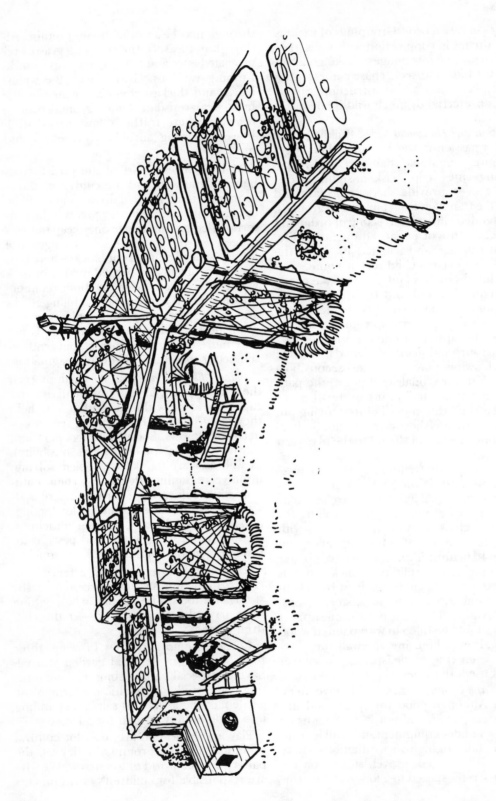

Figure 5. A trellis made with utility poles, treated lumber, used bedsprings, a second hand geodesic climber and wire

can be of great service to future generations by the seeds we plant now.

References

Alexander, Christopher, et al. *A Pattern Language*. New York: Oxford University Press, 1977.

Recommended Reading
(listed in order of usefulness)

A Pattern Language by Christopher Alexander et al. New York: Oxford University Press, 1977. Especially useful are sections 51, 57, 59, 71, 74, 104, 119–121, 160–163, 169–178, 203, 226, 238, and 241–248.

The Environment of Play by John Mason. West Point, NY: Leisure Press (P.O. Box 3, zip 10996), 1982.

Sunset Book Series by the editors of *Sunset Books* and *Sunset Magazine*. Menlo Park, CA: Lane Publishing. Particularly *How To Build Walks, Walls and Patio Floors; Garden and Patio Building Book; How To Build Fences and Gates;* and *Children's Rooms and Play Yards*.

Planning Environments for Young Children: Physical Space by S. Kritchevsky, E. Prescott and L. Walling. Washington, DC: National Association for the Education of Young Children, 1969.

Garden Art by Lorraine Marshall Burgess. New York: Walker, 1981.

The Tree House Book by David Stiles. New York: Avon Books, 1979.

The Findhorn Garden by The Findhorn Community. New York: Harper & Row, 1975.

Four Arguments for the Elimination of Television by Jerry Mander. New York: Morrow, 1978.

Planning for Play by Lady Allen of Hurtwood. London: Thames and Hudson, 1968.

PART V: INDOOR PLAY ENVIRONMENTS AND PLAY MATERIALS

Introduction

The behavior of children is affected by their physical environment and their play materials. Consequently, professionals are interested in learning about the provision of conditions and settings for optimum development.

In a study by Sheila D. Campbell and Nancy Dill, children in three rooms—two experimental, one control—of a large day care center were measured under two density conditions, regular and compacted, for use of settings, setting specific behavior, social interaction, social play and cognitive play. Following data collection, children were interviewed with the use of a scale model of the playrooms; staff were also interviewed. Quantitative measures did not support the expected effect for increased density but interview data did. Reasons for the discrepancy are discussed. Interaction effects were noted for some behaviors for factors of room (group), time of day and specific children. Implications are presented for research methodology and interpretation and day care teaching practice and standard-setting.

Sharon T. Teets provides additional insight into the influences of indoor environment on child play behavior. The purpose of her research was to determine whether improving the quality of space in preschool classrooms would facilitate desirable behaviors in the children in the classrooms. In a study conducted in three phases, 11 two-year-olds, 14 three-year-olds and 14 four-year-olds were observed in a classroom judged to be of low space quality. The quality of the space was improved, then returned to its original condition. During the second and third phases of the study, children were observed again. Behavior during each phase was coded in the following categories: child-child interaction, teacher-child contacts, use of materials in appropriate areas and level of involvement with materials.

A three-way analysis of variance (class × phase of study × behaviors) was performed for each category of behavior. During the second phase of the study when the quality of space was improved, there were more verbal interactions among children, more verbal interactions between teachers and children and more appropriate use of materials. There were more incidences of constructive play and fewer instances of non-interactive and onlooking behavior. In addition, there were fewer incidences of random behavior and deviant conduct. Changes in the physical environment of a preschool classroom appear to produce changes in the behavior of the children occupying the classroom.

For many years researchers have explored various dimensions of children's behavior through their toy play behaviors in indoor settings. Charles H. Wolfgang set out to determine whether or not preschool age children who have working mothers and who have been in day care for most of their lives differ from children of previous studies in their preference for gender-specific toys. Thirty-five preschoolers from a center committed to changes in stereotypic gender responses to toys and occupational attitude were given the Preschool Play-Materials Preference Inventory, which is a dichotomous, forced choice picture inventory. Boys preferred carpentry, number cards, color pegs, puzzles, number shapes; girls preferred toy house furniture, housekeeping corner equipment, large doll play, letter shapes, clay modeling. In categories for all subjects, the order of preference was Physical Play, Symbolic Play, Constructional Fluids, Constructional-Structured, and Letters-Numbers. Boys preferred Constructional-Structure, and

Letters-Numbers, while girls preferred significantly more Constructional-Fluids. The results were nearly identical to the findings on play preferences collected over the last 50 years.

Adults in schools are more influential in the selection and provision of play materials than are children. Virginia R. Green investigated six demographic variables of inservice preschool teachers and other preschool center personnel (244) to determine the predictive variables for the type of play materials the adult preferred. Multiple regression analysis was used with the demographic variables acting as controls for the variable of interest, personality type. A significance was established for adult education level and geographic location in preference for academic and make-believe materials. Adults who indicated a high preference for make-believe and low preference for academic materials appear also to be of the higher education level. In addition, men more often than women preferred physical-type play equipment.

Perhaps the most influential playthings on the contemporary scene are video games. In recent years, multitudes of children and youth have flocked to video-game arcades to participate in this new craze. Steven B. Silvern, Peter A. Williamson and Terry A. Countermine focus on the issue of whether playing video games is good or bad for children. Twenty-six children were paired into same sex, similar age dyads and allowed to play with toys and competitive video games on alternate days. Video tapes of the play sessions were coded to determine children's aggression toward persons and things. Post hoc comparisons showed that aggression at baseline was higher than after the competitive game. The results of this preliminary study thus indicate that participation in video games may have a cathartic effect on players.

The Impact of Changes in Spatial Density on Children's Behaviors in a Day Care Setting

SHEILA D. CAMPBELL
Early Childhood Consultant
Sherwood Park, Alberta, Canada

and

NANCY DILL
Kelsey Institute of Applied Arts and Sciences
Saskatoon, Saskatchewan, Canada

A number of research studies have demonstrated complex interactions between spatial factors and children's play behaviors. Play behaviors of preschool children are influenced by total amount of space (Doke and Risley, 1972), organization of play areas (Hoffman, 1976; Kinsman and Berk, 1979; Prescott, Jones and Kritchevsky, 1972); setting in which play occurs as well as size of setting and type of equipment (Shure, 1963) and density of the play area (Loo, 1972, 1976, 1979; McGrew, 1979; Rohe and Nuffer, 1977; Shapiro, 1975). The effect of environmental influence on preschool children has been most frequently measured by play behaviors, in particular, social play behaviors such as social interaction, antagonistic behavior and behavior appropriate to the setting. However, play behaviors in preschool children are also influenced by personal characteristics such as age (Parten, 1932; Rubin, Maioni and Hornung, 1976) and sex (Clark, Wyon and Richards, 1969; Coates, Lord and Jakabovics, 1974).

In the one environment in which children are found with increasing frequency—the group day care center—the important aspect of that environment is the density, which is defined as the amount of space available to each child. Minimum space-child ratios are specified in most day care regulations and guidelines in Canada and the United States, but these ratios vary from $1.92m^2$ (20 sq. ft.) per child to $5.70m^2$ (60 sq. ft.) per child (Canadian Council on Social Development, 1973; Center for Social Work Re-

search, 1977; Child Welfare League of America, 1972; Mathien, 1978). Despite universal support for some type of ratio, however, there is limited empirical evidence on which to base decisions about appropriate density. The project discussed here was initiated to investigate the effects of variations in spatial density on the behaviors of day care children, particularly during periods of self-selected activity, with the expectation of finding significant differences in play and other behaviors when the amount of space was reduced.

METHOD

The project was carried out over a two-year period in a large urban area in Canada where the authors were granted unhampered access to a large municipally-operated day care center with four playrooms almost identical in size, shape, amount and type of equipment and materials, organization of space, time, curriculum content and caregiver practices. One, (Room C), was used as a control room with a constant density based on average daily attendance of $4.3m^2$ (46.2 sq. ft.) per child. Two were used as experimental rooms (Room A and Room B) where the density was varied during the project. During the first two weeks and the final two weeks of data collection, the experimental rooms were in a regular, low density condition with ratios of $4.38m^2$ (47.1 sq. ft.) per child and $4.29m^2$ (46.1 sq. ft.) per child respectively (see Figure 1). For the middle three

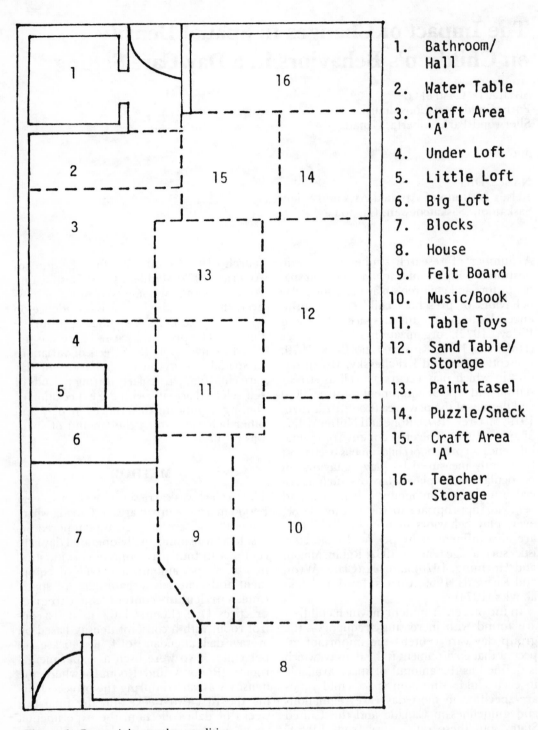

1. Bathroom/ Hall
2. Water Table
3. Craft Area 'A'
4. Under Loft
5. Little Loft
6. Big Loft
7. Blocks
8. House
9. Felt Board
10. Music/Book
11. Table Toys
12. Sand Table/ Storage
13. Paint Easel
14. Puzzle/Snack
15. Craft Area 'A'
16. Teacher Storage

Figure 1. Room A in regular condition.

weeks, the space was reduced to create a high density condition in each room of $2.7m^2$ (29.1 sq. ft.) per child (see Figure 2).

The playrooms averaged twenty registered children with an age range of 3.3 to 5.9 years and a similar range of backgrounds. Scores for children who were not present for 65 percent of the data collection were not used in the analysis, resulting in a total of 43 subjects with approximately equal numbers from each room and evenly divided for age and sex.

Data collection involved both quantitative and qualitative methods. Quantitative data included time sampling measures of setting use, setting specific behavior, social interaction and type of social and cognitive play. Qualitative measures of behavior included density preference of children and staff perceptions of density impact. Following the return of regular density, children from the experimental rooms were interviewed with the use of a specially constructed model of the room. The interview sample of 12 children included five males and five females with half the group from each age range, older and younger. Each staff member, two full-time and one part-time for each experimental room, was interviewed individually with the use of a loosely structured, open-ended format.

All data collected in the room scan and child scan were processed to provide frequency and percentage scores for the categories studied for each of the three time periods. Control room scores were used as a benchmark for determining a normal variation. Detailed information on instrumentation, methodology, data analysis and a full report of the findings including tables and graphs is available in other sources (Note 1). Findings and conclusions can only be summarized here.

FINDINGS

Setting Use
The most significant results will be discussed separately for each measure. Because of some differences in organization of space and teacher practice from room to room, comparisons of setting use were not always possible. Where comparisons were possible, scores for the use of centers were highly consistent across both experimental and control rooms regardless of density conditions of year. The slight variations in use that did occur were not greater than the variation in the control room and were often inconsistent in direction between the experimental rooms. The block center illustrates nicely the generally high consistency of overall use along with the inconsistency of sub-grouping scores from room to room and from time to time. Table 1 portrays the patterns of Block Area use for all children, males, females and older and younger groups.

Setting Specific Behavior
Setting specific behavior accounted for a minimum of 95 percent of the children's behavior when activities within each setting were observed. This finding was consistent across density conditions, across room, and across sex and age groupings.

Social Interaction
Scores for social interaction are presented in Table 2. The variations in social behavior scores in the control room were of similar, not greater, magnitude to the scores obtained in the experimental rooms. Children spent the majority of the time in small groups in all rooms regardless of sex and age. Variations for sex and age were not consistent across rooms.

Certain individual children presented a more extreme reaction to density than most other children. Table 3 gives behavior scores for Child 7 whose level of group behavior dropped sharply in the compacted density (Time 1 = 50 percent group; Time 2 = 25 percent group; Time 3 = 42 percent group) with correspondingly higher levels of solitary and parallel behavior.

Social Play Scores
The social play scores presented in Table 4 again show that variations for the experimental rooms across the three time periods did not vary more than the control room scores and that there was no consistent direction for the slight variations that did occur. However, the scores for all rooms did

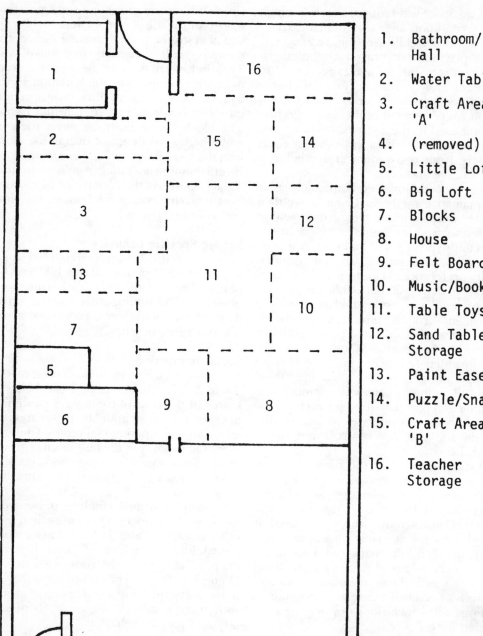

1. Bathroom/Hall
2. Water Table
3. Craft Area 'A'
4. (removed)
5. Little Loft
6. Big Loft
7. Blocks
8. House
9. Felt Board
10. Music/Book
11. Table Toys
12. Sand Table/Storage
13. Paint Easel
14. Puzzle/Snack
15. Craft Area 'B'
16. Teacher Storage

Figure 2. Room A in compacted condition.

Table 1
Mean Percentage Use of Block Area

	Male	Female	All	Older	Younger
Room C (control)					
Time 1	31.8	16.0	23.6	18.1	32.4
2	24.6	17.2	20.5	14.6	30.2
3	39.3	15.7	25.9	21.8	32.7
Mean	31.9	16.3	23.3	18.2	31.8
Room A					
Time 1	11.8	5.3	8.8	9.7	8.2
2	13.7	10.0	11.9	11.7	12.3
3	24.0	18.1	19.3	21.3	20.3
Mean	16.5	11.1	13.3	14.2	13.6
Room B					
Time 1	26.1	7.0	18.1	14.4	20.8
2	10.6	8.6	8.5	6.2	8.9
3	21.2	3.8	14.8	11.6	16.1
Mean	19.3	6.5	13.8	10.7	15.3
All Rooms	22.6	11.3	16.8	14.7	20.2

vary consistently between morning and afternoon data collection periods. The mean percentage of solitary play for all three rooms remained constant at 13.8 percent for both morning and afternoon as did non-play at 27.8 percent of the time. All rooms showed a higher level of parallel play with language in the afternoon (a.m. 19.7 percent; p.m. 23.7 percent) and a lower level of cooperative play (a.m. 26.0 percent; p.m. 18.5 per-

cent). Despite consistency of increase for all rooms, there were still overlapping scores between rooms. For example, Room B afternoon scores for cooperative play were lower for afternoon (Time 1 = 22.4 percent, Time 2 = 23.6 percent, Time 3 = 22.7 percent) than morning (Time 1 = 26.0 percent, Time 2 = 27.3 percent, Time 3 = 28.1 percent) but one was higher, and one equalled the morning scores for Room A (Time 1 =

Table 2
Mean Percentage of Social Interaction

Room	Solitary	Parallel	Group	Watching	Transition
Room C					
Time 1	10.3	12.7	68.8	2.7	2.8
2	9.5	11.6	70.9	3.3	2.5
3	9.4	6.7	75.8	3.1	2.8
Mean	9.7	10.3	71.8	3.0	2.7
Room A					
Time 1	8.7	16.7	66.5	4.3	1.2
2	7.5	20.9	64.5	3.5	1.1
3	10.4	17.1	65.3	3.7	1.2
Mean	8.9	18.2	65.4	3.8	1.2
Room B					
Time 1	12.4	12.5	66.5	4.2	2.0
2	13.5	15.0	64.3	2.7	2.4
3	15.6	8.4	68.2	1.2	3.8
Mean	13.8	12.0	66.3	2.9	2.7
All Rooms	10.8	13.5	67.8	3.2	2.2

22.7 percent, Time 2 = 21.7 percent, Time 3 = 24.1 percent), and the Room B afternoon mean score (22.9 percent) was higher than the Room A morning mean score (22.8 percent).

Cognitive Play Scores

For the cognitive play categories, variations in the scores for the experimental rooms across the three time periods were not significantly greater than variations within the control room. Where scores did show changes between compacted and regular conditions, the direction of change was not consistent across the two experimental rooms. There were no significant changes in cognitive play due to time of day, sex or age, but Room B showed 5 percent higher level of imitative/

Table 3
Mean Percentage Scores for One Child

	Solitary	Parallel	Group	Watching	Transition
Child No. 7					
Time 1	24	15	51	6	1
Time 2	45	20	25	4	4
Time 3	41	8	42	0	5
Mean Room B	13.8	12.0	66.4	3.5	2.7

Table 4
Mean Percentage Scores for Social Play and Non-Play
within each Room over Three Time Periods*

	ROOM			
	A N = 16	B N = 12	C N = 16	TOTAL N = 44
Solitary Play				
Time 1	15.3	11.2	11.7	
2	14.1	15.0	13.6	
3	15.3	15.3	12.8	
Mean	14.9	13.8	12.7	13.8
Parallel Play—				
no language				
Time 1	7.5	11.9	15.7	
2	10.9	8.4	11.4	
3	12.5	9.8	13.6	
Mean	10.3	10.0	13.6	11.3
Parallel Play—				
with language				
Time 1	22.9	23.0	21.7	
2	18.3	19.4	22.4	
3	19.5	22.8	25.6	
Mean	20.2	21.7	23.2	21.7
Coordinated Play				
Time 1	19.3	24.2	23.1	
2	19.1	25.5	23.6	
3	20.8	25.4	19.2	
Mean	19.7	25.0	22.0	22.2
Non-Play				
Time 1	30.0	26.8	26.7	
2	32.6	29.6	27.3	
3	25.3	24.9	27.4	
Mean	29.3	27.1	27.1	27.8

* Due to computer truncation of scores percentages do not total to 100.

dramatic play and a 7 percent lower level of constructive play than the other experimental room or the control room.

Child Preferences

Of the ten children interviewed, three consistently and four most frequently stated that they preferred the room in the regular larger space. All the boys, two consistently and three inconsistently, preferred the larger space. However, inconsistency in the responses of five children suggested that findings must be considered tentative. Older children were more articulate in expressing their reasons for space preference. The children who preferred the larger area gave reasons such as: lack of space in the block, house or table toy area when the space was smaller; not bumping into each other or the furniture and limitations to the kind of play possible, particularly in the block area. Children who preferred the smaller area gave reasons such as being able to sleep closer together in nap time or specific occurrences such as the use of blankets hanging from the loft area.

Staff Perceptions

Staff members were asked to comment on what they had perceived as happening during the decrease in the amount of space for the following categories: program changes, where children played in the room, the social interactions in the child group, emotional climate, staff reactions to the change and staff-child interactions. Finally, they were invited to speculate on probable changes in their teaching practice if the space reduction had been permanent. Staff in both rooms generally reported numerous changes in the behaviors of the children and themselves as a result of the reduction in space.

Staff in Room A agreed there had been a reduction in the use of the house and block centers but stated that use of the table toy and water table areas remained the same. The former change was not supported by the room scan data, the latter was. Room B staff differed among themselves about changes in use of space. Changes reported by individual staff members and not contradicted in other interviews included shorter length of stay in the house area, along with

a general difficulty in the children's becoming involved in activity in an area and leaving in frustration. Teachers reported different use of areas, e.g., use of the book/music area for group play. Another commented on the "layering" effect, noting that children were playing on and under tables and equipment. Another observed that children were moving materials from one area to another.

Teachers also reported program changes related to portions of the day other than scheduled for free playtime. They remarked that the limited space restricted offerings of dramatics and creative dance, games, larger motor and science activities. Themes were cancelled as there was no space to set out materials. They found it difficult to work with a small group of children at a time without disturbing other children. The staff spent more time in planning and in tidying.

With respect to social and emotional behaviors in the children, the staff reported that there were more interactions between the children and an increase in agonistic interactions such as disagreements and fighting. They found the children noisier, more active and less focused. Arguments created a "ripple" effect, with nearby children becoming involved in the altercation. As a result, staff intervened more frequently to prevent the disagreements from spreading. Children with prior problems, low frustration levels and social or emotional difficulties were noted to be involved in more confrontations and conflicts.

All staff preferred the regular, larger area. During compacted density, they felt the increased proximity to the children increased the demands of the children on the staff, produced a tendency to refer to staff more often and created a requirement for more staff intervention, direction and management. One member commented that the increased proximity allowed staff to be more aware of what was happening among the children, but she felt the nearness to be emotionally draining. Others reported increased tension and fatigue and less patience with the children.

If the reduction in space were to be permanent, the staff concurred they would remove some of the furniture and equipment, rotating the items in use at one time. They felt their programs would be more teacher-directed with less free play and more passive whole group activities.

In summary, the percentage scores for setting use, setting specific behavior, social interaction, social and cognitive play were remarkably consistent, and any variation across times and rooms was not consistent for density conditions. Scores across density conditions and sub-groupings for the experimental rooms generally remained within the ranges exhibited by the control room where no density changes occurred. Where the experimental rooms did have scores outside the normal range, the scores were not consistent across rooms and did not exhibit the same pattern of change.

The majority of variation in scores appeared to be explainable by room or by the interaction of changes in the organization of space and room. Scores for subgroupings of age and sex did not show significant variation during higher density.

Qualitative data obtained from interviews suggested a high level of consensus among children and staff in their preference for the larger space. Children and staff reported a definite and generally undesirable impact of the reduced space on child and staff behaviors.

CONCLUSIONS

The results from the quantitative and the qualitative data of the research project presented very different pictures about the effect of variations in spatial density on children in a day care center. The quantitative data did not provide support for a significant impact on reduced density on child behaviors. The interview data, tentatively in the case of children but strongly for the adults, indicated a significant effect for the reduction in space.

There appear to have been several reasons for the discrepancy between the quantitative and the qualitative data. First, although teacher perceptions in one room about use of centers appeared to conflict with data from the room scans, it is important to note that the room scan data represented only one

hour of a ten-hour day whereas teacher perceptions reflected the total time. Teacher comments on program changes clearly did not refer only to free play time, thereby supporting the assumption that teachers were considering the totality of the day. Although both child and staff perceptions may have been influenced by a predetermined bias on the part of the adults, their perceptions of change effects corresponded with findings of other studies where increased density resulted in higher scores for agonistic behavior and lower involvement (Phyfe-Perkins, 1980).

Teacher and child comments along with post-data collection discussion among the trained observers suggested that another explanation may have been the failure of the quantitative methodologies to measure the quality of the experience. For example, although the amount of solitary and group activity remained consistent in the limited space, the solitary activity was much less focused and the group activity was much more agonistic. Although block setting use and constructive play remained consistent despite spatial changes, there was less elaboration of play and children were more often frustrated and irritated by constraints in the compacted space. Although dramatic play continued apace in less space, the level of play organization deteriorated and the plot and action were more diffuse and wandering. Obviously, attempts to measure children's play behaviors must focus on the quality as well as the quantity of the experience.

Previous studies have reported a failure to find an impact for density or crowding, and Smith and Connolly (1976) have suggested a lower threshold effect of 15 to 25 sq. ft. per child before any effects are noted. The failure of the present study to attain density levels below $2.7m^2$ (29.1 sq. ft.) might explain the lack of effect in the quantitative data. However, it appears possible that studies that have not been able to find effects for density (Phyfe-Perkins, 1980) may have been suffering short-comings similar to the quantitative data of the present study: failure to measure the quality or complexity of behavior or measurement of too narrow a band of time. Given the range of scores across time periods of this study, it appears important to base conclusions about density or other aspects of group behaviors on data from extended time periods and a number of groups.

The failure to attain intended density levels resulted from an unexpected and unprecedented drop in attendance in the experimental rooms. Although the researchers were unable to pinpoint any specific reasons for the drop, it is noteworthy that no corresponding drop occurred in the control room. It appears possible that the children, where possible, found ways to avoid being present in the high density situation. Further studies of density might investigate increased morbidity and absence as associated factors.

One final reason for a failure to measure effects with the quantitative measure may have been the generally high quality of the day care center program. A high quality of spatial organization was indicated by the even distribution of play across a large number of centers and the almost total occurrence of setting specific behavior, which suggested that children were involved in using the equipment and materials. Phyfe-Perkins' (1980) review of the density literature suggested that the quality of the space, the amount of equipment and materials along with teacher practice interacted to create differing density effects. The retention of the same equipment and materials, organization of space combined with the reported changes in teacher behavior, especially increased intervention, may have minimized the density effects in the present study.

The consistency of scores for the control room across the two years and the tendency for scores to vary more between rooms than between density conditions suggest the possibility of a room or group effect on behavior. In an attempt to retain the natural setting, teachers in this study were encouraged to carry on their usual practices. Future studies might need to exert more rigid controls to ensure consistency of practice among teachers or to incorporate measures of teacher practice.

The difference found for morning and afternoon in the social play categories indicated agreement between the quantitative and qualitative data. The decrease in cooperative play and the increase in parallel play corresponded with the teachers' perceptions of decreasing cooperation among children as the day wore on. This finding bears further investigation to determine the effects on young children of long periods in group care.

The finding that one child in each group exhibited behaviors differing considerably from the majority suggests the need to consider carefully the individual needs of children in group programs and the interaction between these needs and program factors. Some children may find reduced density intolerable or need special help in coping. The playroom model proved an effective device for creating interest and obtaining responses.

The differences in program and teacher behaviors described by the teachers as occurring during the compacted conditions, or recommended by them as necessary if the reduction in space were permanent, parallel findings in other studies of more controlling and directive teacher behaviors and more structured activities under higher density conditions (Phyfe-Perkins, 1980). These differences suggest negative outcomes for children in more crowded conditions.

Clearly, space is an important factor in a day care program, influencing both child and staff behaviors. In studying this factor, there is a need to include methodologies sensitive to the quality of behavior including interviewing and observation to check on quantitative data and to reveal aspects of behavior for which we need improved quantitative measures. The quantitative measures used in this study provided useful data but are in need of refinement and expansion to capture significant changes in behaviors. Furthermore, although higher spatial density appears to create undesirable effects, which should be of concern to those who regulate and operate programs for young children, this factor cannot be considered alone. As this study has demonstrated, other factors, such as room or group, individuality and time of day may have important influences on behavior and need to be considered for their interaction with spatial factors. The variations in child behaviors across rooms and despite differences in density should lead teachers to reflect carefully on the factors contributing to the variations, especially their own behaviors. It appears likely that, even under undesirably high densities, a high quality of teaching practice may alleviate the situation for children. If day care programs for children can be improved through increased knowledge of and attention to the arrangement and management of space, teachers and researchers must continue their efforts to increase their understanding in this area.

References

Campbell, S. D., and N. A. Dill. *Glengarry Research Project Report: The Effects of a Change in Spatial Density on Children's Behavior in a Day Care Setting*. Edmonton, Canada: Department of Elementary Education, University of Alberta, 1980. (ERIC Document Reproduction Service No. PS 012265).

Canadian Council on Social Development. *Day Care: Growing, Learning, Caring*. Ottawa: CCSD, 1974.

Center for Social Work Research. *Space Requirements for Day Care Centers: A Survey of the Literature*. Austin, TX: School of Social Work, University of Texas at Austin, 1977.

Child Welfare League of America. *The Changing Dimensions of Day Care: Highlights from Child Welfare*. New York: Author, 1973.

Clark, A. H.; S. M. Wyon and M. P. M. Richards. "Free Play in Nursery School Children." *Journal of Child Psychology and Psychiatry* 10 (1969): 205–16.

Coates, S.; M. Lord and E. Jakabovics. "Field Dependence-Independence, Social-Nonsocial Play and Sex Differences in Preschool Children." *Perceptual and Motor Skills* 40 (1974): 195–202.

Dill, N. M. "The Effects of Variations in Spatial Density on the Behavior of Children in a Group Day Care Setting." Unpublished master's thesis, University of Alberta, Canada, 1980.

Doke, L. A., and T. R. Risley. "The Organization of Day Care Environments Required vs. Optional Activities." *Journal of Applied Behavioral Analysis* 5 (1974): 405–20.

Fishburne, D. E. "The Effects of Spatial Density on the Social and Cognitive Play Behaviors of Children in a Day Care Center." Unpublished master's thesis, University of Alberta, Canada, 1981.

Hoffman, M. "Nursery School Rooms and Their Effect on Children's Involvement." *Graduate Research in Education* 8 (1976): 54–87.

Kinsman, C. A., and L. E. Berk. "Joining the Block and Housekeeping Areas: Changes in Play and Social Behavior." *Young Children* 34 (1979): 66–75.

Loo, C. M. "The Effects of Spatial Density on the Social Behavior of Children." *Journal of Applied Social Psychology* 2 (1972): 372–81.

———. "The Effects of Spatial Density on Behavior Styles of Children." Paper presented at the Annual Meeting of the American Psychological Association, Washington, DC, 1976. (ERIC Document Reproduction Service No. 133 047).

———. "A Factor Analytic Approach to the Study of Spatial Density Effects on Preschoolers." *Journal of Population* 2 (1979): 47–68.

Massing, C. A. "Children's Use and Perceptions of Space in a Day Care Playroom." Unpublished master's thesis, University of Alberta, Canada, 1979.

Mathien, J. "Legislation and Funding." In K. G. Ross, ed., *Good Day Care: Fighting for It, Getting It, and Keeping It*. Toronto, Ontario: Women Educational Press, 1978.

McGrew, P. L. "Social and Spatial Density Effects on Space Behaviors in Preschool Children." *Journal of Child Psychology and Psychiatry* 11 (1970): 197–205.

Parten, M. B. "Social Participation Among Pre-School Children." *Journal of Abnormal and Social Psychology* 27 (1932): 243–69.

Phyfe-Perkins, E. "Children's Behavior in Preschool Settings—A Review of Research Concerning the Influence of the Physical Environment." In I. L. G. Katz, ed., *Current Topics in Early Childhood Education*. Norwood, NJ: Ablex, 1980.

Prescott, E.; E. Jones and S. Kritchevsky. *Day Care as a Child-Rearing Environment*. Washington, DC: National Association for the Education of Young Children, 1972.

Rohe, W. M., and E. L. Nuffer. "The Effects of Density and Partitioning of Children's Behavior." Paper Presented at the Annual Meeting of the American Psychological Association, 1977. (ERIC Document Reproduction Service No. ED144 721).

Rubin, K. H.; T. R. Maioni and M. Hornung. "Free Play Behavior in Middle and Lower Class Preschoolers: Parten and Piaget Revisited." *Child Development* 47 (1976): 414–19.

Shapiro, S. "Some Classroom ABC's: Research Takes a Closer Look." *Elementary School Journal* 75 (1975): 436–551.

Shure, M. B. "Psychological Ecology of a Nursery School." *Child Development* 34 (1963): 979–92.

Smith, P. K., and K. J. Connolly. "Social and Aggressive Behavior in Preschool Children as a Function of Crowding." *Social Science Information* 16 (1970): 601–20.

Modification of Play Behaviors of Preschool Children Through Manipulation of Environmental Variables

Sharon T. Teets
Department of Home Economics
Carson-Newman College
Jefferson City, Tennessee

For many years researchers and practitioners in child development and early childhood education (Bruner, Jolly and Sylva, 1976; Frost, 1979; and Piaget, 1961) have recognized that the physical environment affects behavior. Through concrete experiences and social interactions of play children form basic concepts that facilitate the acquisition of abstract concepts and role-taking skills. Some researchers indicate that a knowledge of the particular environment is a more reliable predictor of a people's behaviors than knowledge of demographic variables or individual behavior tendencies (Barker and Wright, 1955; Rosenthal, 1974).

Examinations of the relationship between nursery school environments and children's behaviors (Shure, 1963; Rosenthal, 1974) have shown that the various interest areas in nursery schools appear to have a powerful influence on the types of behavior displayed in each area. In a survey of day care environments in which the focus was to determine indicators of quality programs, the quality of physical space found in centers was positively correlated with teacher warmth and children's interest and involvement in activities (Prescott, Jones and Kritchevsky, 1972a). Nash (1981), in a three-year period of observation of children in planned and unplanned environments, concluded that children's creative, cognitive and language development was enhanced in planned environments.

In most recent research focused on the effect of selected environmental variables upon the behavior of preschool children, desirable behaviors were more likely to be found in environments of higher than of lower quality (Smith and Connolly, 1981). In none of these studies has there been an attempt to modify behaviors observed in a classroom of poor spatial quality by improving the existing quality of space. In times of reduced funding, particularly for day care where children spend a considerable portion of their time, it would seem that if changes in environment can produce changes in behavior, attempts to improve space quality would be a valuable tool in program planning for young children. The purpose of the present study was to determine whether the use of a space evaluation instrument and the subsequent amelioration of problems in the environment *could* produce desirable changes in children's behavior.

METHOD

Defining Quality

A difficult aspect of such a study is the determination of quality indicators. In the present study, quality was defined in terms of a rating assigned by the use of the Environmental Inventory (Prescott, Jones, and Kritchevsky, 1972b), a rating based on points derived from an assessment of five features of the environment: organization, complexity, number of places available to each child, variety and special problems. For each aspect of the environment, a numerical score was assigned. Scores were summed up, and an overall rating of 1 to 7 was assigned for the environment. A score of 1 represented the highest possible quality, a 7 indicated the poorest.

265

Procedure

Three classrooms were selected for inclusion in the study, based upon receiving either a score of 5, 6 or 7 on the Environmental Inventory. All classrooms were housed in the same day care center under the same direction with a similar philosophy implemented in all groups. There was one group of 11 two-year-olds, one of 14 three-year-olds and one of 14 four-year-olds. There were Anglo, black, and Mexican-American children in the two-year-old group and Anglo and black children in the two groups of older children. Each classroom was staffed with a head teacher, an assistant teacher and a student teacher.

The study was conducted in three phases, each lasting approximately two weeks. During the first phase, observations of the children were made in the low-quality condition, with a rating of 5 on the inventory held consistently in each room throughout the phase. During the second phase, the classrooms were arranged to achieve a high-quality rating of 1; and during the third phase, the classrooms again were arranged to obtain a low-quality rating of 5.

In each phase, each child was observed on a randomly selected basis until 20 behavior samples were collected. The observers followed the procedure of a 15-second look, a 10-second record and a five-second orientation to the next child. Each child's behavior was coded in the following categories: child-child interactions, teacher-child contacts, use of materials in appropriate areas and level of involvement with materials. Subcategories used to define the child's behavior within each category are listed in Table 1 (Shapiro, 1971).

No observations were made unless a minimum 80 percent of the children were present. All observations were recorded during the self-chosen activity period that occurred at the same time each day. Inter-rater reliability for observations of the children averaged 87 percent across all categories.

RESULTS

A three-way analysis of variance for age group × phase of the study × behaviors was performed for child-child interactions, teacher-child contacts, use of materials in appropriate areas and level of involvement with materials. Post hoc comparisons with the use of a one-way analysis of variance were conducted when cell means appeared to indicate differences in behaviors due to the phase of the study.

Child-Child Interactions

There was a significant interaction effect between phase and behaviors, $F (10, 360) = 11.50, p < .001$. Post hoc comparisons showed that there were more behaviors coded as verbal interactions in Phase 2 than in Phases 1 or 3, $F (2, 72) = 28.17, p < .001$. Post hoc comparisons revealed fewer instances of behavior coded as Associative Onlooking, $F (2, 72) = 11.51, p < .001$, and Non-Interactive, $F (2, 72) = 11.65, p < .001$ in Phase 2 than in Phases 1 and 3. (See Figure 1.)

Teacher-Child Contacts

There was a significant phase × behavior interaction effect for the teacher-child con-

Table 1
Observation Categories and Codes

Child-Child Interaction
Verbal Interaction (VI)
Physical Interaction (PI)
Associative Onlooking (AO)
Associative Parallel (AP)
Associative with Nonverbal
    Communication (AC)
Non-interactive (NI)

Teacher-Child Contacts
Verbal Individual (VI)
Verbal Group (VG)
Nonverbal Individual (NVI)
Nonverbal Group (NVG)

Appropriate Use of Materials
Use of Area (IN)
Use out of Area (OUT)

Involvement with Materials
Constructive (C)
Neutral (N)
Onlooking (O)
Deviant Conduct (DC)
Random (R)

266

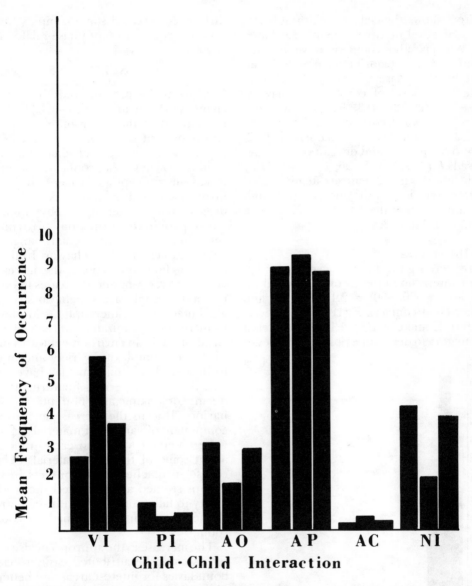

Figure 1. Cell means for sub-categories of Child-Child Interactions for three phases of the study.

tact categories, $F (6, 216) = 31.38, p < .001$. Post hoc comparisons for Verbal Interactions with a Small Group yielded a significant $F (2, 72) = 13.43, p < .001$. An examination of cell means for other categories of teacher-child contacts showed some complex interactions, but these did not appear to be affected by the phase of the study.

Use of Materials in Appropriate Areas
There was a significant interaction effect for

phase × behavior, $F (2, 72) = 6.87, p < .002$. Examination of cell means revealed an increase in the number of times children were observed to use materials in an appropriate area and a decrease in the number of times in which they were observed to use materials in inappropriate places in Phase 2.

Level of Involvement with Materials
There was a significant phase × behaviors interaction, $F (8, 288) = 7.97, p < .001$.

Figure 2 shows the cell means for subcategories of Level of Involvement with Materials. When post hoc comparisons were made, all but one subcategory appeared to be altered by the phase of the study. During Phase 2, the level of constructive play increased, $F (2, 72) = 32.34, p < .001$; onlooking behavior decreased, $F (2, 72) = 4.29, p < .02$; random behavior decreased, $F (2, 72) = 3.38, p < .04$ and deviant conduct decreased, $F (2, 72) = 11.96, p < .001$. Only the differences in the neutral category failed to reach statistical significance, even though an examination of the cell means revealed a decrease in Phase 2.

Age Differences

There were significant age × phase × behavior interaction effects for child-child interactions, $F (20, 360) = 2.14, p < .01$, and teacher-child contacts, $F (12, 216) = 4.72, p < .001$. Examinations of cell means for each subcategory to determine possible sources of

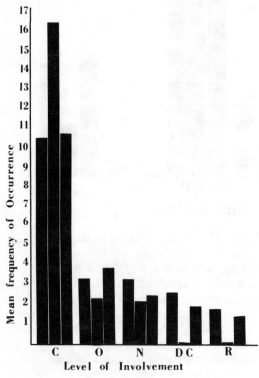

Figure 2. Cell means for sub-categories of Level of Involvement with materials for three phases of the study.

difference revealed some complex interactions but few consistent phase-related interactions.

CONCLUSIONS

Data from the present study indicate that changes in behavior can indeed be facilitated by changes in the classroom environment. In the present study, positive changes were reported in the areas of child-child interactions, teacher-child contacts, use of materials in appropriate areas and level of involvement with materials. Anecdotal records maintained during the observation periods provided additional information regarding how environmental changes contributed to changes in behavior. In the area of child-child interactions, the increase in verbal interactions and decreases in onlooking and non-interactive behaviors could be attributed to few interruptions in play due to increased organization in the classroom. In addition, in an environment with a higher rating for complexity, variety and amount to do per child, children may have had to wait for shorter periods for turns, thus reducing onlooking and non-interactive behaviors. Due to the increase in novelty (a component of variety) of materials, children were observed to talk to each other more about some of the new materials. The increase in teacher-child contacts in small groups seemed also to reflect the teacher's ability to talk more easily with small groups as they played in well-defined areas of the room.

The increase in the appropriate use of materials could be attributed easily to clearer boundaries for interest areas and better displays of available materials. The two areas in which activity increased most during the second phase were art and manipulative; these two areas had received the most attention in redesigning for the second phase. The areas were much improved in terms of display of materials and definition of appropriate areas for usage.

The most meaningful findings of the study were the changes in the level of involvement in activities during the second phase. The increase in constructive play could be attributed to the increase in complexity and improvement in organization. The increase in the amount to do per child afforded more opportunities for constructive play rather than neutral (doing nothing) or onlooking behavior, which decreased in Phase 2. The provision of well-defined boundaries and the alleviation of special problems reduced deviant conduct by reducing the incidence of inappropriate running and play in areas not allowed by the teacher.

In general, these findings are consistent with informal observations of teachers, authors of textbooks for beginning early childhood educators (Danoff, Breitbart and Barr, 1977), and action-oriented researchers. Twardosz, Cataldo and Risley (1974) changed architectural features in children's rooms and observed behavioral changes, primarily noting differences in efforts required to supervise children's behavior. Weinstein (1977) identified problem areas in open classrooms in primary schools and made changes to alleviate problems, although the problems were specific to each classroom and the behaviors of the children did not relate to play.

IMPLICATIONS AND APPLICATIONS

From the data and anecdotal records, a number of recommendations regarding the improvement of spatial quality in a classroom can be made. The following guidelines might be used by teachers or administrators in the use of space as a tool to improve the program for children.

Organization. In this study, it was found that changes in overall organization was a major contributor to the improvement of the overall environmental rating and the subsequent changes in children's behavior. Neill (1982) concluded that open classrooms with few boundaries contributed to aggression and heightened activity levels, and Nash (1981) emphasized the need to reduce distraction to facilitate greater involvement of children in activities. Following are suggestions to improve classroom organization:

1. Paths through the environment should be clear and unobstructed to facilitate an even flow of traffic.

2. The activity to take place in an interest area should be considered before determining where to locate that center in the room.

Art and housekeeping, for example, need to be near a water source. Interest areas where quiet thought takes place, such as the library and science areas, need to be insulated from interest areas with more active, boisterous play.

3. There should be clear definitions of interest areas with easily recognized boundaries, which appear to encourage children to use materials in appropriate areas, thus minimizing the amount of lost or misused equipment and materials. Boundaries also appear to reduce the number of interruptions in ongoing activities, thus fostering a greater degree of involvement.

4. Materials should be displayed in ways to facilitate children's selection and use. Manipulative materials, for example, need to be visible in containers so that children can see into them and recognize where materials are to be returned. Art materials, dramatic play materials and manipulative materials and blocks should be displayed in a systematic way so that children can see how materials are categorized.

5. About one half to two-thirds of the floor space should be used for equipment. The remainder should serve as free space so that the room does not feel crowded.

Complexity. The complexity of the environment translates into interest level for children. The following guidelines are given for enhancing the interest level of the classroom:

1. The selection of the combination of materials and equipment used on any given day needs to be evaluated in terms of complexity. In this study, complexity was defined by three levels of units (Prescott, Jones and Kritchevsky, 1972b). A simple unit is defined as a play unit that has one obvious use and does not have any sub-parts or juxtaposition of materials, such as a tricycle. Complex units are play units with sub-parts or the juxtaposition of two different play materials. Complex units range from closed (puzzles and form boards) to open (collage or water play). Super units are complex units with one or more additional play materials juxtaposed (play dough table with tools or sand box with sand toys and water).

2. In general, there should be a balance

of simple, complex and super units. Super units appear to have the greatest holding power and present the most opportunities for involvement and creative thinking.

3. The presence of the teacher should not be overlooked in evaluating the complexity of an interest center. Rosenthal (1974) noted that teacher presence in a center was the single most important variable in holding children's interest in a center. Teachers may add complexity to a center by their interactions with the children, and they should be aware of where they tend to locate themselves in a room. If they select one area more often than others, children may use that area more frequently.

Variety. The variety score is computed by identifying the number of different choices for children and the degree of novelty of those choices.

1. Each day children should be able to select from a variety of activities at any one time during a self-chosen activity time of sufficient length to allow in-depth involvement in an activity.

2. Activities should be varied from day to day with novel activities provided frequently (after children have adjusted to the routine of school). Interest centers receiving little attention should be examined carefully to determine whether there are ways to increase the novelty and/or variety there.

3. The overall space within the classroom may periodically need to be arranged in different ways to correct special problems or to emphasize certain interest areas.

Amount to do per child. One of the values of the self-chosen activity time is that children can select activities that most nearly meet their needs.

1. The classroom should be evaluated to determine the number of choices children have, with consideration of the number of interest centers in the room, as well as the number that each interest center can serve at any one time.

2. On the Environmental Inventory (1972b), a *minimum* of one and a half places for each child is necessary to receive a high-quality environmental rating. Even this spatial minimum may not be sufficient if some choices have limited appeal.

Special problems. In most classrooms there are design problems that teachers can do little about. Usually, however, many of the problems lie in the way in which equipment and materials are arranged and displayed. Common problems occurring in many classrooms are:

1. Two groups or interest areas may be located in one physical space. For example, in one classroom music and science activities were taking place on one large carpeted area, clearly not compatible activities.

2. Equipment may be in poor repair, such as missing puzzle pieces. Shabby equipment may lead to reduced involvement in play.

3. The environment may be low in aesthetic appeal, or one interest area in a classroom may be less appealing than another. Adding rugs, carpeted stools and soft cushions in one library area increased its usage.

4. Equipment not to be used by children during the self-chosen activity time may be too readily accessible. For example, in one center, tricycles for outdoor use were stored near the exterior door, but children frequently rode them inside into other children's block structures.

Teachers and administrators will need to evaluate their own environment carefully for features creating behavior problems within their classrooms. Only with systematic evaluation of the classroom environment (Prescott, Jones and Kritchevsky, 1972b and Harms and Clifford, 1980), coupled with regular observations of the children can changes be made to produce desirable results.

References

Barker, R. G., and H. F. Wright. *Midwest and Its Children.* New York: Harper & Row, 1955.

Bruner, J. S.; A. Jolly and K. Sylva, eds. *Play: Its Role in Development and Evolution.* New York: Penguin, 1976.

Danoff, J.; V. Breitbart and E. Barr. *Open for Children: For Those Interested in Early Childhood Education.* New York: McGraw-Hill, 1977.

Fein, G. G. "Pretend Play in Childhood: An Integrative Review." *Child Development* 52 (1981): 1095–118.

Frost, J. L., and B. L. Klein. *Children's Play and Playgrounds.* Boston: Allyn & Bacon, 1979.

Harms, T., and R. M. Clifford. *Early Childhood Environment Rating Scale.* New York: Teachers College Press, 1980.

Nash, B. C. "The Effects of Classroom Spatial Organisation on Four- and Five-year-old Children's Learning." *British Journal of Educational Psychology* 51 (1981): 144–55.

Neill, S. R. "Preschool Design and Child Behaviour."

Journal of Child Psychology and Psychiatry and Allied Disciplines 23 (1982): 309–18.

Piaget, J. *Play, Dreams, and Imitation in Childhood.* New York: Norton, 1962.

Prescott, E.; E. Jones and S. Kritchevsky. *Day Care as a Childrearing Environment* Vol. 2. Washington, DC: National Association for the Education of Young Children, 1972a.

———. *Environmental Inventory.* Pasadena, CA: Pacific Oaks College, 1972b.

Rosenthal, B. "An Ecological Study of Free Play in a Nursery School." Unpublished doctoral dissertation, Wayne State University, 1973.

Shapiro, S. "Preschool Ecology: Selected Environmental Variables and Classroom Behavior." Unpublished doctoral dissertation, Columbia University, New York, 1971.

Shure, M. E. "Psychological Ecology of a Nursery School." *Child Development* 34 (1963): 979–94.

Smith, P. K., and K. M. Connolly. *The Ecology of Preschool Behavior.* New York: Cambridge University Press, 1981.

Twardosz, S.; M. F. Cataldo and T. R. Risley. "An Open Environment Design for Infant and Toddler Day Care." *Journal of Applied Behavior Analysis* 7 (1974): 529–45.

Weinstein, C. S. "Modifying Student Behavior in an Open Classroom Through Changes in the Physical Design." *Journal of the American Educational Research Association* 14 (1977): 249–62.

Preschool Children's Preferences for Gender-Stereotyped Play Materials

CHARLES H. WOLFGANG
College of Education
Florida State University, Tallahassee

Play and toy preferences of children have long been of interest to researchers (Bridges, 1929; Vance, 1934; Rosenberg and Sutton-Smith, 1959; DeLucia, 1963; Sutton-Smith and Rosenberg, 1963; Teglasi, 1981; Eisenberg, 1982), particularly as these preferences are reflective of sex role identification (Sutton-Smith and Rosenberg, 1963; Masters, 1976; Kacerguis, 1979; Eisenberg, 1982). Recent research has demonstrated that stereotypic toy preference based on sex can be modified (DiLeo, 1979). It has also been found that gender-specific playthings are given by children's caregivers (Mussen and Rutherford, 1963; Udry, 1966). Beuf (1974) maintains that, as gender awareness develops in children, toys provide cues as to the social limitations associated with gender. Therefore, playing exclusively with "boys' " toys or with "girls' " toys may constrain children from varied and valuable experiences.

Chafetz's (1974) content analysis of toys in three illustrated Christmas catalogs indicated that toys promoted for girls were primarily of a domestic nature, while boys were portrayed using mechanical and technological playthings. When boys and girls were pictured together, the male was typically operating a mechanical toy while the female was either observing or serving the male.

Recent toy preference research has attempted to determine whether preferences are changing because of the dramatic increase in the number of working mothers (Statistical Abstracts, 1976) and the changing roles of women; this research (Rheingold, 1975; Schau, 1968; Teglasi, 1981) shows little or no change in toy preferences based on the sex of the child.

The purpose of this study was to determine whether or not preschool age children of working mothers and who have been in day care centers for most of their lives differ from children of previous studies in their preferences for gender-specific toys (as defined by Vance, 1934 and DeLucia, 1963).

METHOD

Procedures
The day care center consisted of a large, well-designed room with an abundance of all the traditional play materials mentioned; also available was a two-acre outdoor space containing equipment, toys, materials and a "farm" with many domestic animals. The center philosophically opposed and actively attempted to eliminate sex stereotyping of play materials. Through stories, puppetry, music and skits, attempts were made to encourage the acceptance of a wide choice of female and male occupational roles. For example, a dramatization of *Snow White and the Seven Dwarfs* portrayed the Wicked Stepmother as being jealous because Snow White had earned a college degree and was following a professional career; and the male Dwarfs shared with Snow White the household duties. Also, the center had a large number of male teachers (22 percent).

Subjects
The subjects were 35 preschoolers [ages 3½(6 percent), 4(51 percent), 4½(34 percent), 5(9 percent)] attending a play-oriented day care center in a small southern professional city. The Socioeconomic-status levels (Hollingshead, 1958) of the subjects, from highest to lowest were Level 1(20 percent), Level 2(29 percent), Level 3(36 percent), Level 4(11 percent), Level 5(3 percent). The racial mix was white, 26(74 percent), black, 6(17 percent), and Asian, 3(9 percent); there were 18(51 percent) boys and 17(49 percent) girls.

273

The distribution of ages at entry to this day care center was birth to age 1(42 percent), age 1(21 percent), age 2(21 percent), and age 3(16 percent).

Testing

The subjects were individually administered the Preschool Play-Materials Preference Inventory-PMPI (Wolfgang, 1983) in a small quiet room in the day care center building. The PMPI is a dichotomous, forced choice picture inventory requiring children to make 20 choices from among pictures of toys, which provides a final score in five play categories, i.e., Symbolic Play, Constructional-Fluids, Constructional-Structured, Physical Play, and Constructional-Letters-Numbers. Since previous research had shown that the sex of the experimenter has an effect on children's preferences (Dileo, 1979; Teglasi, 1981), testing was randomly divided between an adult male and a female experimenter.

A non-directive script was read by the experimenter for each of the 20 items, with left and right presentation alternated. Reliability was established through test-retest for a random selection of 15 subjects, with the following r's produced for each play category: Symbolic(Sy) .69, Fluids(Fl) .81, Structured(St) .76, Sensori-Motor(Sm) .63, Letters-Numbers(LN) .67.

RESULTS

For examination of the differences on items within the PMPI, see Table 1. On the left half of the table are the 20 items with the A B breakdown and the corresponding play materials labels. Across from the labels are the category symbols (Sy, Fl, St, Sm, LN); the small bracketed numbers are the pictures' page numbers in the Childcraft catalogue. In the next column is a percentage breakdown for choice of the A or B item. Looking at the gross percentage for all subjects, we find that the top five play materials are 10A Rocking Boats(Sm) 91 percent, 13B Houskeeping Corner (Sy) 82 percent, 18A Climbing Frame(Sm) 77 percent, 19B Large Blocks and Boards(St) 77 percent, and 16B Clay Modeling(Fl) 74 percent. In these five items the category of Sensori-Motor is represented twice; this preference will be seen

later in the ANOVA comparison of categories. The categories Symbolic, Fluids and Structured are each represented once, while Letters-Numbers is not represented. Again, in the ANOVA data, LN is the least preferred category.

In the right column are the means and standard deviations broken down by sex. The lower means indicating preference by girls as compared to boys is seen in item 4A Toy House-Furniture(Sy) .059 mean (SD.243) and in 10B Letter Stencils(LN) .059 mean (SD.243). In item 13B Housekeeping Corner(Sy) one finds that the girls' mean was 1.00(SD.000); all 17 girls chose Housekeeping Corner when it competed with 13A Number Cards(LN).

Table 1 indicates that five items were significant or marginally significant, as indicated by two asterisks (**). Using a Mann-Whitney U test for comparison by sex on these items, we find a significant number of girls (.001, U of 42.5) preferring Item 4A Toy House-Furn(Sy) vs. B. Carpentry(St) for the boys. The next significant item (.01, U of 93.5) indicated that girls preferred 13B Housekeeping Corner vs boys' preference for Number Cards. It was found that boys significantly (.05, U of 93.5) preferred Item 14A Color Pegboard(St) vs the girls' preferring 14B Large Doll Play(Sy). Finally, item 9A Puzzles(St) was marginally significant (.10, U of 100.5), preferred by boys vs the girls' preference for Item 9A Letter Shapes(LN); and item 6B Number Shapes(N) was marginally significant (.08, U of 102.0), preferred by boys vs the girls' preference for Item 6A Clay Modeling(Fl).

In a comparison of simple categories by percentages and ranks (Table 2), the category of Sensori-motor play materials ranked number one with 36 percent of the children indicating it was their first choice. Symbolic Materials ranked second with 30 percent indicating first choice. Symbolic Materials ranked second with 30 percent indicating first choice; Fluids ranked third with 15 percent; Structured Constructional Materials ranked fourth with 12 percent and Letters and Numbers, fifth with 6 percent.

Using the ANOVA data, a comparison can be made of play categories indicating the two

Table 1
Pre-School Play-Materials
Preference Inventory (PMPI)

Play Materials	Categories	S's %	Girls Mean (SD)	Boys Mean (SD)
			Comparison on Sex	
1. A. Toy Farm-animals	Sy(43)***	41		
B. Water Play	Fl(68)	59	.588(.507)	.588(.507)*
2. A. Lego	St(106)	35		
B. Climbstairs-Balc	Ph(23)	65	.647(.493)	.647(.493)
3. A. Puppets	Sy(63)	73		
B. Number Steps	LN(131)	27	.235(.437)	.313(.479)
4. A. Toy house-Furn	Sy(59)	59		
B. Carpentry	St(77)	41	.059(.243)	.765(.437)**
5. A. Play house-props	Sy(64)	32		
B. Climb-sliding	Ph(17)	68	.647(.493)	.706(.470)
6. A. Clay Modeling	Fl(74)	56		
B. Number shapes	LN(131)	44	.294(.470)	.588(.507)**
7. A. Finger Paints	Fl(75)	65		
B. Blocks	St(103)	35	.294(.470)	.412(.507)
8. A. Sand Table	Fl(65)	50		
B. Climb-Frame	Ph(19)	50	.412(.507)	.588(.507)
9. A. Puzzle	St(84)	70		
B. Letter Shapes	LN(149)	30	.177(.393)	.438(.512)
10. A. Rocking Boats	Ph(22)	91		
B. Letter Stencil	LN(148)	09	.059(.243)	.125(.342)
11. A. Easel Painting	Fl(69)	56		
B. Dress-up	Sy(54)	44	.353(.493)	.529(.515)
12. A. Tricycle	Ph(29)	68		
B. Matching Color	St(110)	32	.294(.470)	.353(.493)
13. A. Number Cards	LN(154)	18		
B. Housekeep Corn	Sy(53)	82	1.00(.000)	.647(.493)**
14. A. Color Pegboard	St(115)	53		
B. Large Doll Play	Sy(54)	47	.647(.493)	.294(.470)**
15. A. Swings	Ph(18)	50		
B. Toy Furn-people	Sy(59)	50	.412(.507)	.588(.507)
16. A. Number shapes	LN(13)	27		
B. Clay Modeling	Fl(74)	74	.765(.437)	.706(.470)
17. A. Lrg Card-Blocks	St(35)	44		
B. Drawing	Fl(73)	56	.647(.493)	.471(.515)
18. A. Climb-Frame	Ph(20)	77		
B. Easel Painting	Fl(69)	24	.353(.493)	.118(.332)
19. A. Let Crds-Colors	LN(127)	24		
B. L Boards-Block	St(35)	77	.706(.470)	.823(.393)
20. A. No-Let Board	LN(121)	39		
B. Crawl-hoops	Ph(26)	61	.529(.515)	.688(.479)

*** Pictures found on this page in 1981–82 *ChildCraft* catalog
  * A was scored 0, B was 1
  ** Significant–see table 2
N = 37

highly preferred categories of Symbolic (Females 35 percent, Males 25 percent) and Sensori-motor (35 percent, 38 percent) to be nonsignificant for gender preferences, while three categories were found to be significant (Fluids, Structured and Letters-Numbers). The girls over boys first choice was significant (F 121.929, df = 1/31, p < .001) for Fluid

Table 2
Percentage of First Choice on Play Categories—All S's

			0	10	20	30
All S's	Sy	2	XXXXXXXXXXXXXXXXXXXXXXXXXXXXXX(30%)			
	Fl	3	XXXXXXXXXXXXXX(15%)			
	St	4	XXXXXXXXXXX(12%)			
	SM	1	XXXXXXXXXXXXXXXXXXXXXXXXXXXXXXXXXXXX(36%)			
	LN	5	XXXXX(6%)			

Constructional Play Materials (Table 3), and in a percentage comparison Fluids was the first choice of 24 percent of girls but only 6 percent of boys. Thus, three times as many girls as boys chose Fluids. The results for Structured Constructional Materials placed the boys' preference marginally significant over the girls' preference (F 3.203, df = 1/31, p < .10). The percentage comparison indicated a breakdown of 6 percent for girls and 18 percent for boys, which parallels the Fluid percentages; but this time boys preferred Structured Materials three times as much as girls. Finally, in category comparison related to sex and Letters-Numbers, boys over girls significantly (F 4.795, df = 1/31, p < .05) preferred Letters and Numbers. The percentage breakdown was 12 percent for

boys while Letter-Number was not the first choice of any girls.

DISCUSSION

We may infer from the results that boys preferred the categories of Structured Materials and Letters and Numbers and the PMPI items Carpentry, Number Shapes, Number Cards and Color Pegs. An earlier study done with the same subjects indicated that high play performance (not preference) in Carpentry and Physical Skills was significant at the .001 level and explained a dramatic 52 percent of the variance when predicting quantitative scores on a mental abilities test. Past research has demonstrated that boys do better in

Table 3
ANOVA Summary Table
PMPI Categories Comparing Sex Differences

Play Category	Source of Variat	Sum of Sqs	df	Mean Sq	F	p	Preference
Symbolic	Between	4.150	1	4.150	2.048		
	Within	62.820	31	2.026			
	Total	66.970	32			NS	
Fluids	Between	15.750	1	15.750	12.929		Girls
	Within	37.765	31	1.218			over
	Total	53.515	32			.001	Boys
Structured	Between	3.650	1	3.650	3.203		Boys
	Within	35.320	31	1.140			over
	Total	38.970	32			.10	Girls
Sensori-Motor	Between	1.398	1	1.398			
	Within	44.118	31	1.423			
	Total	45.515	32			NS	
Signs (Let-No)	Between	6.633	1	6.633	4.795		Boys
	Within	42.882	31	1.383			over
	Total	49.515	32			.05	Girls

				0	10	20	30
Sex	Sy	F	1	XXXXXXXXXXXXXXXXXXXXXXXXX(35%)			
		M	2	XXXXXXXXXXXXXXXXX(25%)			
	Fl	F	3	XXXXXXXXXXXXXXXX(24%)			
		M	5	XXXX(6%)			
	St	F	4	XXXX(6%)			
		M	3	XXXXXXXXXXXX(18%)			
	Sm	F	1	XXXXXXXXXXXXXXXXXXXXXXXXX(35%)			
		M	1	XXXXXXXXXXXXXXXXXXXXXXXXXXXX(38%)			
	LN	F	4	X(0%)			
		M	3	XXXXXXXXX(12%)			

quantitative and mathematical areas; the results here suggest that boys also prefer the structured materials, possibly reflecting a sex difference at this early age of four.

By contrast, girls preferred the category of Fluid Constructional Materials, and the PMPI items Toy Farm, Doll Play, Housekeeping Corner, Letter Shapes and Clay. Past research has suggested that girls perform better socially, especially in their use of language. It is partly through symbolic play that children learn expressive skills and especially language (Christie, 1983; Smilansky, 1968). Even Fluids such as clay would suggest a more expressive medium than the structured materials preferred by boys. Again, based on these limited data, preference seems to relate positively with performance.

In answering the question posed by this study as to whether preschool children with working mothers and who have been in day care centers for most of their lives differ from children of previous studies in preferences for toys that have been labeled "gender specific," we find for constructional materials a high male preference nearly identical to that found by studies made as early as 1934 (Vance). For girls also, we find no change in preferences and, in fact, our results are nearly identical to those of a 1934 study showing girls' preferences for domestic toys, especially dolls and transformable materials. Item 13B, Housekeeping Corner, was preferred by all 17 girls; girls also scored

significantly higher than boys on 14B, Large Doll Play.

To explore reasons for this lack of change in stereotypic toy preferences in the children of working mothers (children who attend a day care center that actively attempts to modify such stereotyped preferences), we conducted at-home interviews with all parents to try to determine whether or not they were modeling traditional roles at home. To what degree were family responsibilities shared? Our interviews indicated the following:

	Neither	Shared	Mother	Father
Child Care	10	37	50	3
Home Care	0	20	77	3
Home Maintenance	3	13	10	70
Auto Care	30	3	0	67

Although all mothers were working and the greater percentage of parents professed non-sexist values, the above percentages reflect the traditional stereotyping of male-female domestic roles. It appears that mothers have taken up new professional roles but have maintained the traditional role in the home.

In hypothesizing reasons for the lack of stereotypic toy preference changes with these children, a "nature-or-nurture" answer can be given: among preschool age children there is a universal, genetically-determined stage

277

progression stronger than environmental factors (Erikson, 1951). Or, one might maintain that traditional parent domestic roles, television advertisement of toys and many similar stereotypes still prevailing in our society have such strong models effect (Bandura, 1963) that deliberate retraining by a day care center is not productive. It seems that, when it comes to stereotypic toy choices by boys and girls, nothing has changed under the sun!

References

Allen, V. L., and P. S. Allen. "On the Attractiveness of Forbidden Objects." *Developmental Psychology* 10 (1974): 6–9.

Bandura, A. *Social Learning Theory*. Englewood Cliffs, NJ: Prentice Hall, 1977.

Beuf, A. "Doctor, Lawyer, Household Drudge." *Journal of Communication* 24 (1974): 142–45.

Blakemore, J. E.; A. A. LaRue and A. B. Olejnik. "Sex-appropriate Toy Preference and the Ability to Conceptualize Toys as Sex-role Related." *Developmental Psychology* 15 (1979): 339–40.

Bridges, K. M. B. "Occupational Interests and Attention of Four-year-old Children." *Journal of Genetic Psychology* 39 (1929): 551–70.

Chafetz, M. J. *Masculine/Feminine or Human*. Itasca, IL: Peacock, 1974.

Christie, J. F., and E. P. Johnsen. "The Role of Play in Social-Intellectual Development." *Review of Educational Researcher* 53 (1983): 231–37.

DeLucia, L. A. "The Toy Preference Test: A Measure of Sex-role Identification." *Child Development* 34 (1963): 107–17.

DiLeo, J. C.; B. E. Moely and J. L. Sulzer. "Frequency and Modifiability of Children's Preferences for Sex-typed Toys, Games, and Occupations." *Child Study Journal* 9 (1979): 141–59.

Eisenberg, N.; E. Murray and T. Hite. "Children's Reasoning Regarding Sex-typed Toy Choices." *Child Development* 53 (1982): 81–86.

Eisenberg-Berg N.; R. Boothby and T. Matson. "Correlates of Preschool Girls' Feminine and Masculine Toy Preferences." *Developmental Psychology* 15 (1979): 354–55.

Erikson, E. *Childhood and Society*. New York: Norton, 1950.

Hollingshead, A. B., and F. C. Redlick. *Social Class and Mental Illnesses*. New York: Wiley, 1958.

Kacerguis, M. A., and G. R. Adams. "Implications of Sex-typed Child Rearing Practices, Toys, and Mass Media Materials in Restructuring Occupational Choices of Women." *The Family Coordinator* 28 (1979): 369–75.

Lehman, H. C., and P. A. Witty. *The Psychology of Play Activities*. New York: Barnes, 1927.

Liebert, R. M.; R. B. McCall and M. A. Hanratty. "Effects of Sex-typed Information on Children's Toy Preferences." *Journal of Genetic Psychology* 119 (1971): 133–36.

Masters, J. C., and A. Wilkinson. "Consensual and Discriminative Stereotypes of Sex-type Judgements by Parents and Children." *Child Development* 47 (1976): 208–17.

Mussen, P., and E. Rutherford. "Parent-child Relations and Parental Personality in Relationship to Young Children's Sex Role Preferences." *Child Development* 34 (1963): 586–607.

Nadelman, L. "Sex Identity in London Children: Memory, Knowledge, and Preference Tests." *Human Development* 13 (1970): 28–42.

———. "Sex Identity in American Children: Memory, Knowledge, and Preference Tests." *Developmental Psychology* 10 (1974): 28–42.

Phi Delta Kappa. "Practical Applications of Research." *Newletter of Phi Delta Kappa's Center on Evaluation, Development, and Research*. Bloomington, IN: Phi Delta Kappa, 1982.

Piaget, J. *Play, Dreams, and Imitation in Childhood*. New York: Norton, 1962.

Rheingold, H. L., and K. V. Cook. "The Contents of Boys' and Girls' Rooms as an Index of Parents' Behavior." *Child Development* 46 (1975): 459–63.

Rosenberg, B. B., and B. Sutton-Smith. "The Measurement of Masculinity and Femininity in Children." *Child Development* 30 (1959): 373–80.

Schau, C. G.; L. Kahn; J. H. Diepold and F. Cherry. "The Relationships of Parental Expectations and Preschool Children's Verbal Sex Typing to Their Sex-type Toy Play Behavior." *Child Development* 51 (1980): 266–70.

Sutton-Smith, B., and B. G. Rosenberg. "Manifest Anxiety and Game Preferences in Children." *Child Development* 31 (1960): 307–11.

Teglasi, H. "Children's Choices of and Value Judgements About Sex-typed Toys and Occupations." *Journal of Vocational Behavior* 18 (1981): 184–95.

Terman, L. *Genetic Studies of Genius*. Palo Alto, CA: Stanford University Press, 1926.

Turner, E. A., and J. C. Wright. "Effects of Severity of Threat and Perceived Availability on the Attractiveness of Objects." *Journal of Personality and Social Psychology* 2, 1 (1965): 128–32.

Tyler, L. "The Relationship of Interests to Abilities and Reputation Among First-grade Children." *Educational and Psychological Measurements* 11 (1951): 23–28.

Udry, J. *The Social Context of Marriage*. Philedelphia: Lippincott, 1966.

U.S. Department of Commerce, Bureau of the Census. *Statistical Abstracts of the United States* (97th Annual Edition). Washington, DC: Government Printing Office, 1976.

Vance, T. F., and L. T. McCall. "Children's Preferences Among Play Materials as Determined by the Method of Paired Comparisons of Pictures." *Child Development* 5 (1934): 267–77.

Vieira, K. G., and W. H. Miller. "Avoidance of Sex-atypical Toys by Five- and Ten-year-old Children." *Psychological Reports* 43 (1978): 543–46.

Wang, J. D. "The Relationship Between Children's Play Interests and Their Mental Ability." *Journal of Genetic Psychology* 93 (1958): 119–31.

Wolfgang, C. H. *Helping Aggressive and Passive Preschoolers Through Play*. Columbus, OH: Merrill, 1977.

———. "Play as the Predictor of Cognitive Development." *Early Child Development and Care*, in press.

———. "Preschool Play-materials Preference Inventory." *Early Child Development and Care* 45 (1983): 45–49.

Wolfgang, C. H.; B. Mackender and M. E. Wolfgang. *Growing and Learning Through Play*. Minneapolis: Judy/Instructo, 1981.

Video Game Play and Social Behavior: Preliminary Findings

STEVEN B. SILVERN, PETER A. WILLIAMSON
and TERRY A. COUNTERMINE
Auburn University, Alabama

The emergence and prevalence of video games over the past several years have engendered much debate concerning the consequences of children's interaction with such games. Specifically, the debate has focused on whether playing video games is good or bad for children. Until recently, however, there have been virtually no systematic empirical studies that might provide some objective evidence as to the good or bad influence of these games.

During the past two years research at Auburn University has been conducted to address the issue of the effects of video game play on children's social behavior. Because no pertinent literature existed in the area of investigation, the decision was made to begin by following the paradigm used for research on television and aggression. Additional reasons for choosing this paradigm were: 1) Video games entertain in a manner similar to television; an actor (character or object) is involved in a visual fantasy with a beginning, middle and end. 2) The fantasy tends to incorporate violent incidents. 3) Video games also share television features identified by Greer, Potts, Wright and Huston (1982) including: action, pace and visual change.

Three areas investigated in the research on television include catharsis, modeling and arousal theories. Catharsis theory, of course, predicts that higher involvement in an aggressive medium will be followed by periods of less aggressive behavior. If the catharsis theory applies, viewing a violent incident would decrease the likelihood of violence after viewing the incident.

An initial study by Silvern, Williamson and Countermine (1983) examined the theory of catharsis by investigating the effects of a violent cartoon ("Roadrunner") and a violent video game ("Space Invaders") on children's social behavior. Previous research on the effects of television has established that passively viewing violent programs does not provide catharsis (Stein and Friedrich, 1975).

One of the hypotheses tested in this study was whether active involvement with a video game would provide catharsis. Results indicated a significant increase in aggression after watching television and after video game play as compared to baseline. There were no differences between video game play and the television condition. These findings indicate that aggression after playing a video game is similar to aggression after watching a violent cartoon.

It would seem then that the active involvement in video games is not cathartic but arousing in the same manner as in television. It should be pointed out, however, that in the video game condition, with two children seated at the game, only one child used the controls while the other was directed to assist by giving warnings and/or directions. It might then be argued that active involvement of the children was at different levels. The present study attempted to extend the investigation of the catharsis hypothesis by assuring equal, active involvement of the children in both a competitive and cooperative video game condition. Based on our earlier work, one null hypothesis of the present study was that active involvement in video game play would not lead to reduced aggression.

In addition to extending the study of catharsis, the present study tested the theories of modeling and arousal. Modeling theory suggests that after watching a television show, children would imitate what they just saw. With arousal, the assumption is that television raises children's excitement level and that their subsequent behavior can be attributed to this raised level of excitement. The difference between the two theories is directed at the issue of television content. The modeling theory suggests that aggressive behavior follows television programming that demonstrates violence. The arousal theory suggests that aggression will occur when children have not been directed/guided to other kinds of behavior. That is, in the absence of other input, arousal will lead to aggression. This can be true even for programs such as Sesame Street, which are nonviolent (Greer et al., 1982).

The arousal theory includes the idea that children may view violent content but subsequently may be directed toward nonviolent behavior. Home computer technology and video games allow us to test this hypothesis.

It has been suggested that video games might be beneficial if designed so that children would have to cooperate with each other in order to achieve the goals of the game (Favaro, 1982). If children can be aroused and at the same time placed in a position of cooperating, then perhaps their behavior after the initial stimulus might also be cooperative. In the present study, children were exposed to two different violent video games specifically chosen to assure arousal. One game required the children to *compete* with each other; the other required the children to *cooperate* with each other. Modeling theory would suggest that children would imitate the violent conditions in both games in subsequent behaviors. Arousal theory would posit that children in the cooperative condition would pay more attention to the cooperative aspect of the game than the content and be less likely to imitate violence in their behavior following the cooperative game.

The null hypothesis would then be that video condition (baseline vs. competitive vs. cooperative) would yield no differences in children's subsequent play behavior.

The data reported in this manuscript are part of an ongoing study and are preliminary in nature.

METHOD

Subjects

The subjects were 28 children between the ages of 6 and 9 years. They were obtained through advertisements to teach LOGO to the children. Parents willing to volunteer their children for the LOGO class were also asked to volunteer their children for the video game study. Only one parent objected to the study and did not volunteer the child. The children in the study were selected from a total of 34 children taking the programming class. All children in the study were white and lived in a rural environment. Their parents were white-collar workers connected to the university where the study was conducted or to a support service for the university. Of the 28 children, only 4 were girls.

Procedure

Children were paired into same sex, similar age dyads. Each dyad was taken from the classroom on successive days. On the first day they were taken to a play environment and shown a set of toys, which were the same as those used in the Greer et al., study (and are specified under "Materials"). The subjects were told that they could play with the toys in any way they liked. The experimenter told the children that he had to leave but would be back in a few minutes. The children were then allowed to play for ten minutes. At the end of ten minutes the children were returned to the classroom.

On the second day the dyads were taken to a room adjacent to the playroom and shown how to play the competitive video game. After five minutes of play the children were taken into the playroom and allowed to play for ten minutes.

The third day proceeded in the same manner except that the children played a cooperative video game for five minutes immediately prior to the play session. All play sessions were videotaped.

Materials

Toys in the play environment, designed for various types of play, included: play money, blocks, stick horses, dolls, bus, plane, plastic zoo animals, Nurf ball and a bobo doll. All materials were neatly grouped in the center of the play area so that children could readily see and choose.

The competitive video game was a boxing game. Each child controlled a boxer. The objective of the game was to manipulate one boxer to knock down the opposing player's boxer. The player scoring the most knockdowns won the match; the computer kept score and indicated the winner. The game was so arranged that it was obvious to the players which player was manipulating which boxer.

The cooperative video game was a game called "Star Wars," the object of which was to manipulate an alien ship so that it was in the center of a crosshair sight on the screen. When the ship was in the sight, it might be fired upon and blown up. One player must control the vertical movement of the crosshair, the other player the horizontal movement. Either player might fire at the ship at any time but unless the ship was in the sight, firing would merely waste energy and end the round. Players wishing to succeed in the game had to coordinate their movements and control their desire to fire at the "enemy."

Both games had similar features in that they were controlled by game paddles, and the object was to hit a target (boxer or ship).

Instrumentation

The video tapes of the play sessions were coded by two raters using the coding system described in Greer et al. Thirty percent of the play sessions were coded by both raters to establish interrater reliability, which was judged by the number of agreements divided by the total number of observations (agreements and nonagreements). Reliability for each category was above 80 percent. The rating schedule was used to observe for aggression against persons or things, including verbal aggression, fantasy play—both solitary and collaborative—and nonplay prosocial behavior. In addition, two categories were added, both nonfantasy play categories that included incidents of aggression. They consisted of games that were aggressive in nature, e.g., dodgeball. These categories were used when children were clearly playing but not fantasizing.

RESULTS

Because of the small sample, the ongoing nature of the research and the nature of the sample, the data were analyzed with the use of a Friedman two-way analysis of variance by ranks. The only category in which there was a significant difference in the sums of the ranks was in aggression, $x_r^2 = 8.64$, $p < .02$. Post hoc comparisons using a family $\underline{\alpha} = .02$ (Penfield, 1978) demonstrated that aggression at baseline was higher than after the competitive game. No differences were found between baseline and the cooperative condition or between competitive and cooperative conditions. There were no significant differences for fantasy play, collaborative or solitary aggressive play, or prosocial behavior.

DISCUSSION

Since this is a preliminary analysis of ongoing research, the results should be treated with caution. Tentative though the results may be, they represent the first empirical work that suggests that the playing of video games affects children's subsequent play behavior in a manner quite different from watching television. Specifically, active involvement in playing a competitive video game leads to less aggressive behavior then, after a baseline, and provides the first evidence for video games' being cathartic for the participants. Obviously, this line of investigation needs to be carefully and rigorously extended, since these empirical results fly in the face of many subjective opinions.

Results would indicate that our second null hypothesis should be rejected. That is, type of video game condition yielded differences in subsequent play behavior (although only between baseline and competitive play). A possible reason for the difference in levels of aggression between the competitive condition and baseline, but not between baseline and cooperative or between cooperative and competitive conditions, might have had more to do with children's understanding of how to play the game than with whether the game was competitive or cooperative.

Informal observations while the children played the games indicated that children very quickly understood the boxing game after brief adult instruction. Children became involved in the game and rarely asked for rules to be clarified. Such was not the case for "Star Wars." Initial instructions were necessarily more complex because they included not only the rules of the game, but also the component of how to cooperate. Also, the paddle's control over the space ship was not as clearly observable as in the boxing condition. The difficulty of the instructions and the problem with the paddles seemed to give rise to frustration, which the children handled in two ways. Some dyads spent almost the entire time trying to determine who was in charge of what, while other dyads dealt with their frustration by ignoring the point of the game (i.e., how to score) and quickly became content to move their figures randomly and to fire at will. In any case, it is possible that the difficulty experienced in playing the game correctly simply overwhelmed the intent of cooperation. Future research needs to control more rigidly the "instructional" component of the games. In a sense, the present study was strictly a pilot study.

Unlike passive viewing of television, active participation in competitive video games may provide some catharsis. The differences in findings between our first study (c.f., Silvern, Williamson and Countermine, 1983) and the present study suggest that further research needs to be carried out, which directly compares television, cooperative games, competitive games and a no-treatment control.

References

Favaro, P. J. "Games for Cooperation and Growth—An Alternative for Designers." *Softside* 6,2 (1982): 18–21.

Greer, D.; R. Potts; J. C. Wright and A. C. Huston. "The Effects of Television Commercial Form and Commercial Placement on Children's Social Behavior Attention." *Child Development* 53 (1982): 611–19.

Penfield, D. "The One-way ANOVA Model." Paper presented at the American Educational Research Association annual meeting, Toronto, Canada, March 1977.

Silvern, S. B.; P. A. Williamson and T. A. Countermine. "Aggression in Young Children and Video Game Play." Paper presented at the biennial meeting of the Society for Research in Child Development, Detroit, MI, April 22, 1983.

Stein, A. H., and L. K. Freidrich. "The Impact of Television on Children and Youth." In E. M. Hetherington, J. W. Hagen, R. Kron and A. H. Stein, eds., *Review of Child Development Research*, Vol. 5. Chicago: University of Chicago Press, 1975.

PART VI: THE ROLE OF ADULTS IN PROMOTING PLAY

Introduction

Recent interdisciplinary interest in children's play has increased knowledge in this area, but to promote optimum play practitioners need assistance in planning and operating the physical environment of space, equipment and materials. David E. Fernie addresses this need by reviewing selected research, evaluating its practical relevance and recommending new directions for research. Developmental research on social play suggests that contradictory findings make planning for social play problematic, while the counter example of object use in pretend play suggests the potential usefulness of developmental research for practitioners. Environmental research demonstrates the influence of environment on play behavior, but these findings do not transfer readily to the classroom. Finally, Design Principles Research (Moore, 1980) and Segments Research (Gump, 1975b) are presented as two new directions with potential to inform practitioners who wish to set up better indoor play environments. The papers that follow are additional examples of research directed to practitioners.

Carol Woodard focuses on practical guidelines for facilitating children's learning through the use of sociodramatic play in the early childhood classroom. A variety of unisex theme corners were implemented at a college/magnet public school for six semesters. The themes included among others, the drug store, veterinarian's office, appliance repair shop, airport, shoe repair shop and ice cream store.

When appropriate, the participants utilized "outside intervention," making suggestions, commenting, questioning or fostering contact between players in order to extend the sociodramatic play. "Inside intervention," in which a participant entered the play

by assuming a role and modeling relevant play behavior, was also used. Various concrete guidelines for facilitating sociodramatic play were identified: providing an experiential foundation, establishing a theme environment, utilizing props, fostering learning, teacher intervention and child/parent involvement.

Adult involvement in children's play is further explored by Connie Steele and Elizabeth Hrncir. In their study an adult introduced two sets of objects judged as having either high or low prototypicality (reality representation) to each of twenty children (10 males; 10 females). Each child's incidences of pretend play were recorded from equivalent time periods of videotapes. Comparisons of the children's responses to high and low prototypical objects were made under two conditions: (1) responses without adult suggestions for play and (2) responses with adult suggestions for play. Children responded to both high and low prototypical objects at a significantly higher level with adult suggestions for play than without such suggestions. The ten older children exhibited significantly more pretend play incidences than the younger children. Neither the objects' prototypicality nor children's gender accounted for differences in these two-year-olds' pretend play.

Adult intervention in children's play can be either supportive or destructive. Currently there are few teacher education programs that prepare teachers and other child caretakers for positive play involvement with children. The growing body of research showing positive effects of such training provides guidelines.

Robert G. Collier studied the long and short-term practical effects of training preschool teachers in techniques for facilitating

283

preschool children's play during "free play" periods in a "natural" and "uncontrolled" preschool environment. The eight-month study used an experimental/control, pretest, posttest, delayed posttest design. The subjects included eight preschool teachers and 35 children between the ages of three and five. The variables measured were the behavior of the teachers and the children's verbal expression, divergent thinking abilities and play. The experimental teachers were trained in techniques for observing, providing and involving themselves in fostering children's play. The results indicate that: 1) the behavior of the experimental teachers was affected by the training and 2) significant differences were found between groups for verbal expression and divergent thinking abilities on both the posttest and delayed posttest. Children's play was found to be the least affected of the variables studied.

Cynthia Wade studied the effects of a special teacher training program on play behaviors of children and the verbal and nonverbal behaviors of their teachers in an outdoor play environment. A play category system and the "System for Coding Interaction with Multiple Phases" (SCIMP) were used to collect data on 69 nursery school children and their teachers. Play behaviors of the children were significantly different for several play categories before and after the special teacher training program. The verbal playground behaviors of teachers were significantly different for several of the SCIMP categories before and after the training program. Other findings were consistent with the major findings that the special teacher training program had significant effects on both children's and teachers' behaviors in the outdoor play setting.

In a quasi-experimental observational study V. T. Gershner and L. Moore evaluated the effectiveness of an intervention program in-volving teacher reinforcement of cooperative play with opposite-sex playmates, a program involving 48 preschool girls enrolled in eight multiage classrooms in three child care centers. Significant increases in opposite-sex cooperative play and increased preferences for opposite-sex playmates as best friends were measured in the experimental group following the intervention. The study also pointed up the influence of adults in promoting play patterns.

Adult influence on children is, of course, not restricted to a particular age group or developmental level. Francine Nichols reviews research on play and the preterm infant. Her review focuses on developmental differences between the fullterm infant and the "healthy" preterm infant. Although play interactions with both parents are important, she emphasizes mother-infant interaction and provides a framework for assessing the reciprocity of play between mother and infant. Finally, she recommends strategies for increasing play between mother and infant and identifies areas of needed research.

An appropriate conclusion to this section is provided by R. Tim Nocosia, Michael Willoghby, Barbara Hatcher and Jody Nicosia. The purpose of their article is threefold: to provide a brief review of selected research on the values of play for children and the value of parental involvement in children's play; to share an inexpensive and practical way to strengthen family ties in play settings and provide an understanding of the activities that parents and teachers can use to promote adult-child play at home and school. One strategy that supports children's natural propensity for play and also nurtures family ties in play settings is the *Family Fun Night*. This is a play outing for the entire family that allows the child to be the center of attention. Arrangements and activities for this event are discussed.

The Promotion of Play in the Indoor Play Environment

DAVID E. FERNIE
College of Education
Ohio State University, Columbus

The past decade has seen a renewed interest in the educational value, developmental significance and recreational benefit of children's play. Recent efforts range from the research of psychologists who examine short- and long-term outcomes supported by play to the creations of architects who have turned to the playground as an arena for informed design practice. In some ways, we have made great progress toward understanding and promoting children's play.

But another play environment requires our immediate attention. In the United States alone, millions of young children spend a major portion of their childhood days in early childhood classrooms, indoor play environments having only limited financial and physical resources. Teachers allocate these often scant resources guided by intuition, practical considerations and conventional wisdom (Kinsman & Berk, 1979; Moore & Cooper, 1982). They may also consider the guidance provided by child-related theory and research if it is available and speaks to their concerns.

The question addressed in this article was originally a limited and practical one: "How can early childhood teachers plan the classroom physical environment of space, equipment and materials to promote play effectively?" Pursuit of this question, after a review of selected child development and environmental literature, led to an ironic conclusion—that while the amount and range of research on children's play were too great for a single review, the findings pointing clearly toward setting the indoor play environment were too few to guide the practitioner. The emended purpose here is not to review the extant literature on children's play but to evaluate its practical relevance through selected examples and suggest new research directions with potential to inform practitioners as they plan the classroom environment for play.

THE CHILD DEVELOPMENT TRADITION AND PLAY

The disciplines of child development and early education have a common interest in children's play. Since the early days of the nursery and kindergarten, many educators have stressed the development of the "whole child" (Hendrick, 1980; Butler, Gotts & Quisenberry, 1978; Tyler, 1976) and the value of play as a process supportive of development. In turn, developmental psychologists continue to delineate the contributions of play to many aspects of development (Rubin, 1980; Bruner, Jolly & Silva, 1976; Herron & Sutton-Smith, 1971). The potential for dialogue and collaboration among disciplines is great. At present, however, little guidance toward setting a playful environment can be culled from the developmental literature. This state of the research is illustrated below with examples from the psychological literature on social play and pretend play.

The early childhood classroom is, above all, a social environment. Many parents enroll their children in these settings to provide them with opportunities to play with peers. Over fifty years ago, Mildred Parten's (1932) classic work described typical levels of social play in young children, four of which still are widely recognized: in *solitary play*, a child plays alone and directs his separate activity without reference to that of others; in *parallel play*, a child chooses toys like those of children nearby, but plays beside rather than with others; in *associative play*, children engage in overt group play with exchange of materials and conversation; in *cooperative play*, children engage in highly organized group play involving roles, negotiations and a division of labor to achieve a competitive, dramatic or material goal.

Parten (1932) observed children ages two to four and-a-half years and found a significant correlation between age rank and level of participation (as have some more recent investigations, such as Barnes, 1971):

Social participation is dependent, to a large extent, upon the age of the children. As a rule, the youngest children either play alone or in parallel groups, while the oldest individuals play in more highly organized groups. (p. 268)

A teacher who wishes to realize these levels in social play for a similar age group in an indoor environment might find supportive a set of materials ranging from puzzles and Play-doh for solitary play to blocks and dress-up clothes for group play. Physical settings within a classroom might include carrels or counters for individual play, open areas and learning centers for group play. In studies where other recent extensions of Parten's work are also considered, the implications for practice become muddied. These studies either dispute the orderly progression through levels found by Parten or promote one level of social play as superior to others.

The findings of several studies question Parten's orderly progression toward cooperative play (Smith, 1978; Rubin, 1977; Bakeman & Brownlee, 1980). In a longitudinal examination, Smith (1978) found a substantial number of three-year-olds who did not engage in parallel play but progressed directly from solitary to associative and cooperative play. In this study, other three- and four-year-olds alternated their associative and cooperative play with extended periods of solitary play. In contrast, Rubin (1977) found much parallel play to persist in his four- and five-year-old sample. Bakeman and Brownlee (1980) found parallel play to be common as a brief interlude prior to group play, as a catalyst in momentary play encounters. From this different temporal perspective, they suggest that "the

movement from alone to parallel group play may not be a matter of years or months, but of minutes" (p. 877).

Further confusion derives from studies that place relative value on different levels of social play. For example, from the point of view of social maturity, one might assign high value to the sophisticated interactions typical of cooperative play. Studies, such as that of Serbin, Tonick and Sternglanz (1977), where teacher praise was found to encourage much cross-sex cooperative play, imply such a bias. In contrast, other studies stress and document the value of the nonsocial solitary play. For example, Moore, Evertson and Brophy (1974) found solitary play to be "independent task-oriented behavior which is functional in school situations and indicative of social maturity rather than immaturity" (p. 834). MacKinnon (1962) suggests that such solitary behavior may also contribute ultimately to an individual's creativity. Here, a retrospective analysis of the autobiographical narratives of over 600 people judged by peers as highly creative and successful in their fields revealed that these individuals typically spent and enjoyed much time alone (or with adults rather than with peers) during childhood.

This body of research on social play, while important for scientific validation and addressed to important concerns within the child development discipline, leads to confusion for the early childhood educator who seeks to plan an optimal play environment. With respect to the progression in levels of social play, one cannot know what typifies social play in group settings because results of these studies differed from one experimental setting to the next. Can one expect children to skip parallel play (Smith, 1978), persist in it (Rubin, 1977), engage in it as a momentary transition to group play (Bakeman & Brownlee, 1980) or as a developmental transition to more social forms of play (Parten, 1932)? Should one encourage socially sophisticated cooperative play or investigative solitary play? How can limited resources of space, equipment and materials be stretched to encourage both social and solitary play? Social play literature provides no clear guidance to teachers on these questions.

Children's pretend play represents a second example of generally unrealized educational and developmental symbiosis. The provision of dress-up clothes and role-play areas, books and records with fantasy themes attest to teachers' general support of this play. In the developmental research literature only occasionally can clear direction be found concerning the physical environment's support of pretend play.

With respect to how the realism of materials affects pretend play in children aged two to five, useful empirical guidance is available (Fein, 1975; Elder & Pederson, 1978; Golomb, 1977). The general finding is summarized in Fein (1981a): "For young children, the best environment for pretense may be one containing an ample supply of realistic objects. For older children, such an environment may limit rather than enhance play" (p. 269). The teacher ready to buy visually abstract unit blocks for toddlers or realistic housekeeping furniture for kindergarten children, in order to stimulate their pretend play, would be cautioned by this general finding.

An integrative review (Fein, 1981b) of the pretend play domain reveals a lack of child development studies that address the question of how features of architecture and settings affect children's pretend play. Of the more than 250 reviewed articles and studies, Fein cites only 14 that investigate or even speculate on this issue, concluding that: "Setting factors such as crowding, material resources, noise level, adult activity, group size, or group composition have not been studied with respect to environmental factors influencing pretend behavior . . ." (p. 1109), and notes the promise of environmental disciplines to provide insights into pretend play.

One can surmise several reasons for the paucity of such studies in the pretend play and social play literatures. *First*, priorities within child psychology have traditionally focused upon individual variables (e.g., age, sex and personality dimensions) and not upon environmental variables. *Second*, the experimental research paradigm favored in this discipline seeks to control variables not of interest and therefore conceives of them as either controlled or confounding, rather than

as contributory. Thus, the previously mentioned research on variations in "object realism" is a notable exception to the rule that environment rarely has served as an independent variable in developmental play research. Third, it is difficult to describe, quantify and manipulate the physical environment accurately, a problem which further encourages researchers to report only simple descriptions of experimental settings. However, several related environmental disciplines have assumed the task of relating features of environment to behavior, in apparent agreement with what Jerome Bruner calls an ironic truism, that "the best way to predict the behavior of a human being is to know where he is: in a post office he behaves post office, at church he behaves church" (Schoggen, 1978, p. 37).

THE ENVIRONMENTAL TRADITION AND PLAY

Research on the relationship between environment and behavior comes from a variety of disciplines. Ecological psychologists (Barker, 1968; Barker & Wright, 1951; Gump, 1975a) examine people's behavior in a wide variety of environments, from whole communities to individual classrooms. Human ecologists (Brofenbrenner, 1977a, 1977b; Day, 1983) similarly conceive of environments as interrelated and increasingly inclusive nested levels, from microsystems such as schools to the macrosystem (or culture). Ethologists, careful observers who are interested traditionally in the adaptive significance of animal environment and behavior, have begun careful analysis of human ethology (Smith, 1974b).

Though they differ somewhat in theory and method, these disciplines have turned toward an examination of the early childhood classroom environment with the potential to inform teachers as they plan for play. Although the range of literature is wide in these disciplines, for present purposes the concentration is upon environmental studies, which suggest that variables of materials and setting exert a strong "pull" on the nature of children's social play.

Quilitch and Risley (1973) provided children at different times with specially selected "social toys" (such as Pick Up Stix) and "isolate toys" (such as jigsaw puzzles). Differences in children's behavior under the two conditions were dramatic, with social behavior 78 percent of the time while using social toys and only 16 percent while using the isolate toys. Smith (1974a) found similar divergences toward solitary play when a class of children was given only small toys and toward group play when given only large equipment. Vandenberg (1981) combined setting and materials manipulation and offered his three- to five-year-olds both a big muscle room (with jungle gym, two slides, etc.) and a small muscle room (with table activities, paper and pencil, etc.). He found that younger children chose the fine muscle room and engaged there in solitary and parallel play. Older children chose the large muscle room and engaged in associative play. Surprisingly, he found no instances of cooperative play, even in the large muscle room. One might speculate that the high levels of noise and movement in such a setting might preclude the communications and negotiations integral to children's cooperative play.

The influence of materials and setting on the levels of social play, as documented in these environmental studies, raises questions of environmental contributions to any or all of the social play studies cited earlier—to Parten's progression through levels, to the persistent parallel play found by Rubin (1977) and to the optional or transitional nature of parallel play found by Smith (1978) and Bakeman and Brownlee (1980). But beyond a demonstration of the powerful influence of materials and setting on an aspect of play behavior, little practical guidance is provided even by this further set of studies, which specifically investigates the influence of environment on play. It is highly unlikely that a preschool teacher would provide only toys to a class of children (Smith, 1974a), provide only toys of a certain social valence (Quilitch & Risley, 1973) or have the affluence to provide separate rooms for different types of play (Vandenburg, 1981). While there are exceptions (see Shure 1963, for example), environmental studies typically conceive of and manipulate environment too broadly to provide guidance to teachers wishing to set up better indoor play environments.

NEW DIRECTIONS FOR RESEARCH

What are useful new research directions to help the practitioner promote play in the early education environment? Two quite different but complementary approaches are suggested: *Design Principles Research* and *Segments Research*, each representing a possible way toward greater practical knowledge, though neither presents a clear and direct pathway.

Design Principles Research, suggested by Moore (1980), is a call to actualize child-related theory in children's environments. The steps outlined are to examine a theory (or a body of research findings); derive principles to implement the theory accurately in the environment and develop a whole class of design solutions consistent with the theory and principles. For example, his examination of developmental theory and research on exceptional children yielded the design principle of *paced alternatives*—"all play environments should have a variety of graded and pace alternatives for children of varying ability" (p. 12). Applied to the playground, his design solution provided several levels of difficulty for any activity (e.g. ramps and stairs). In the more limited indoor space, perhaps modular or transformable equipment would be an appropriate class of design solutions derived from paced alternatives.

While Moore argues for research-based design principles, at this time the translation of play into practice might be more easily derived from grand theories, such as Jean Piaget's theory of cognitive development, appropriate since it also describes successive stages of early childhood play: sensorimotor play, symbolic play and games with rules (Piaget, 1951). Several existing curricular applications of the theory speak more to the roles of materials and social interactions in support of the child's constructive process (Kamii & DeVries, 1978; Forman & Kusch-

288

ner, 1977; Forman & Hill, 1980) and less to large-scale setting factors. Consequently, to determine the nature of a Piagetian physical environment would be a valuable contribution to several bodies of thought. But what is a Piagetian environment? One built on general principles of the theory? One changing in design from one stage of play to another? One that provides the challenge of change to promote new thinking or the continuity of stability to promote rethinking?

With the Design Principles Research direction, the derived principles and solutions related to a theory will be open to debate. Whether the way suggested by a particular interpretation becomes a pathway to greater knowledge may largely turn on the merits of that debate.

The second new direction, Segments Research, complements the first with an admonition to build knowledge inductively about how to plan better play environments. It is a program of research with an individual classroom learning center or in Gump's words, "the segment," as the focus and unit of analysis (Gump, 1975b).

Since children behave differently, teachers usually have different educational goals in discrete arrangements of space, furniture, materials and activities (Day, 1983). Is children's play usually the same in a block center as it is in a science center? Is it the same in open spaces as in small enclosures? Answers can best be arrived at through an examination of children's behavior in different segments of the classroom. Researchers must examine the constraints and possibilities for children's play within each learning center.

For example, a researcher faced with a small block area in a classroom for three-year-olds, with boundaries defined by a thick pile carpet and two block shelves across from one another, finds that parallel play predominates in this segment with little extended solitary play and little cooperative play. The hypothetical researcher might wish to change the environment in order to extend the range of social play. In a first manipulation, the center could be enlarged to accommodate groups. Children's behavior would be examined for some time after this expansion to determine effects, if any, attributable to the environmental change.

In a second manipulation, some abstract unit blocks might be replaced with realistic replicas of people and objects, guided by the aforementioned child development research, which suggests that realistic objects may enhance younger children's pretend play (Fein, 1981a). A second observation period would examine behavior to determine effects related to this second manipulation. Statistical methods that can determine the relative contributions of each manipulation to children's behavior are available (Glass, 1980). Moreover, use of a broad observational system, such as that described by Bronfenbrenner (1977a) or Day (1983) might reveal the full range of behavioral effects due to these manipulations.

The Segments Research direction is a promising avenue to better play environments, with the potential to build knowledge inductively with each manipulation with guidance by research, theory or observation. In a Segments Research Program, expansions to all segments of a classroom and examinations of the behavioral effect of a single segment manipulation on other segments would be logical next steps.

While almost opposite in scope, these two new directions share several similarities. Each involves the collaboration of developmental and environmental disciplines, an important step toward better play environments for children. Each has a kind of ecological validity and could develop bodies of research that lead directly to practice. With relevant studies as models, teachers could implement theory in a general fashion, as Design Principles Research suggests, and could change single elements within a play environment, as Segments Research suggests. Finally, both of these new research directions could have immeasurable symbolic value. Kinsman and Berk (1981) describe an actual classroom's block and housekeeping segments "as the teacher had arranged them and as they had existed for the seventeen years she had been teaching in the classroom" (p. 68). It is important to validate the roles of teachers, researchers and children in setting an optimal environment for play through parallel research and practice.

References

Bakeman, R., and J. Brownlee. "The Strategic Use of Parallel Play: A Sequential Analysis." *Child Development* 51 (1980): 873–78.

Barker, R. *Ecological Psychology.* Palo Alto, CA: Stanford University Press, 1968.

Barker, R., and H. Wright. *One Boy's Day.* New York: Harper and Row, 1951.

Barnes, K. "Preschool Play Norms: A Replication." *Developmental Psychology* 5 (1971): 99–103.

Brofenbrenner, U. "Lewinian Space and Psychological Substance." *Journal of Social Issues* 33 (1977a): 199–212.

——. "Toward an Experimental Ecology of Human Development." *American Psychologist* 32 (1977b): 513–31.

Bruner, J.; A. Jolly and K. Sylva. *Play—Its Role in Development and Evolution.* New York: Basic Books, 1976.

Butler, A.; E. Gotts and N. Quisenberry. *Play as Development.* Columbus, OH: Charles E. Merrill, 1978.

Day, D. *Early Childhood Education: A Human Ecological Approach.* Glenview, IL: Scott, Foresman, 1983.

Elder, J., and D. Pederson. "Preschool Children's Use of Objects in Symbolic Play." *Child Development* 49 (1978): 500–04.

Fein, G. "A Transformational Analysis of Pretending." *Developmental Psychology* 11 (1975): 291–96.

——. "The Physical Environment: Stimulation or Evocation." In R. Lerner and N. Busch-Rossnagel, eds., *Individuals as Producers of Their Own Development: A Life-span Perspective.* New York: Academic Press, 1981a.

——. "Pretend Play in Childhood: An Integrative Review." *Child Development* 52 (1981): 1095–118.

Forman, G., and F. Hill. *Constructive Play: Applying Piaget in the Preschool.* Monterey, CA: Brooks/Cole, 1980.

Forman, G., and D. Kuschner. *The Child's Construction of Knowledge.* Monterey, CA: Brooks/Cole, 1977.

Glass, G. "Quasi-experiments—A Case of Interrupted Time Series." In R. Jaeger, ed., *Alternate Methodologies in Educational Research.* Washington, DC: American Educational Research Association, 1980.

Golomb, C. "Symbolic Play: The Role of Substitutions in Pretense and Puzzle Games." *British Journal of Educational Psychology* 47 (1977): 175–86.

Gump, P. "Ecological Psychology and Children." In E. M. Hetherington, ed., *Review of Child Development Literature* Vol. 5. Chicago: University of Chicago Press, 1975a.

——. "Operating Environments in Schools of Open and Traditional Design." In T. G. David and B. D. Wright, eds., *Learning Environments.* Chicago: University of Chicago Press, 1975b.

Hendrick, J. *The Whole Child: New Trends in Early Education.* St. Louis, MO: C. V. Mosby, 1980.

Herron, R., and B. Sutton-Smith. *Child's Play.* New York: Wiley, 1971.

Kamii, C., and R. DeVries. *Physical Knowledge in Preschool Education.* Englewood Cliffs, N.J.: Prentice-Hall, 1978.

Kinsman, C., and L. Berk. "Joining the Block and Housekeeping Areas: Changes in Play and Social Behavior." *Young Children* 35, 7 (1979): 66–75.

MacKinnon, D. "The Nature and Nurture of Creative Talent." *American Psychologist* 17, 7 (1962): 484–95.

Moore, G. "The Application of Research to the Design of Therapeutic Environments for Exceptional Children." In W. M. Cruikshank, ed., *Crossroads to Learning.* Syracuse, NY: Syracuse University Press, 1980.

Moore, N.; C. Everton and J. Brophy. "Solitary Play: Some Functional Reconsiderations." *Developmental Psychology* 10 (1974): 830–34.

Moore, S., and C. Cooper. "Personal and Scientific Sources of Knowledge About Children" In S. Moore and C. Cooper, eds., *The Young Child: Reviews of Research* Vol. 3. Washington, DC: National Association for the Education of Young Children, 1982.

Parten, M. "Social Participation Among Preschool Children." *The Journal of Abnormal and Social Psychology* 27 (1932): 243–69.

Piaget, J. *Play, Dreams, and Imitation.* New York: Norton, 1951.

Quilitch, H., and T. Risley. "The Effects of Play Materials on Social Play." *Journal of Applied Behavioral Analysis* 6 (1973): 573–78.

Rubin, K. "Play Behaviors of Young Children. *Young Children* 32 (1977): 16–24.

——. *Children's Play: New Directions for Child Development* Number 9. San Francisco: Jossey-Bass, 1980.

Schoggen, P. "Ecological Psychology and Mental Retardation." In G. P. Sackett, ed., *Observing Behaviors: Theory and Applications in Mental Retardation.* Baltimore, MD: University Park Press, 1977.

Serbin, L.; I. Tonick and S. Sternglanz. "Shaping Cooperative Cross-sex Play." *Child Development* 48 (1977): 924–29.

Shure, M. "Psychological Ecology of a Nursery School." *Child Development* 34, (1963): 979–92.

Smith, P. "Aspects of the Playgroup Environment." In D. Cantor and T. Lee, eds., *Psychology and the Built Environment.* London: Architectural Press, 1974a.

——. "Ethological Methods." In B. M. Foss, ed., *New Perspectives in Child Development.* Harmondsworth, England: Penguin Books, 1974b.

——. "A Longitudinal Study of Social Participation in Preschool Children: Solitary and Parallel Play Reexamined." *Developmental Psychology* 14 (1978): 517–23.

Tyler, B. In C. Seefeldt, ed., *Curriculum for the Preschool—Primary Child: A Review of the Research.* Columbus, OH: Charles E. Merrill, 1976.

Vandenberg, B. "Environmental and Cognitive Factors in Social Play." *Experimental Child Psychology* 31 (1981): 169–75.

Guidelines for Facilitating Sociodramatic Play

CAROL YOUNG WOODARD
Department of Curriculum and Supervision/Early Childhood
State University College at Buffalo, New York

Few early childhood educators would challenge the importance of dramatic play, in which the young child assumes a role and pretends to be someone else in a real-life or fantasy setting. The beneficial aspects of this type of play are widely recognized and respected by most professionals.

Advocates of dramatic play maintain that by pretending to be the baby, the father or the physician, young children learn how the world about them functions and in the process learn new concepts, make decisions and engage in problem-solving. Dramatic play in which children interact and assume roles associated with a theme is known as sociodramatic play. This type of play is viewed as a means of reducing egocentricity as young children interact, exchange ideas and process different points of view. Sociodramatic play is seen as fostering concentration through role-planning and implementation, together with imagination, creativity and cooperation.

Current research findings further support the value of dramatic play. Positive correlations have been reported between dramatic play and friendliness and popularity with peers (Marshall and Doshi, 1965; Rubin and Maioni, 1975), cooperation with peers and adults (Singer and Singer, 1978; Singer 1979), and language used during play (Marshall, 1961; Singer and Singer, 1978; Singer, 1979). When children have received training in sociodramatic and fantasy play, changes in their social and cognitive ability have been cited (Golomb and Cornelius, 1977; Rosen, 1974; Saltz, Dixon and Johnson, 1977), as well as in their language skills (Lovinger, 1974). Play training is also associated with reduction in egocentricity (Van den Daele, 1970) and increase in cooperative social problem-solving (Shores, Huster and Strain, 1976; Spivack and Shure, 1974).

Why, then, if dramatic play is beneficial to the young child, do we see so little of it in the early childhood classroom? In relation to other forms of play, the frequency of pretend play ranges from 19 to 17 percent for preschool groups (Rubin, Maioni and Hornung, 1976; Rubin, Watson and Jambor, 1978; Singer, 1973) to approximately 33 percent for kindergarten groups (Rubin et al., 1978). These are fairly modest classroom percentages, since spontaneous pretend play increases in frequency during the preschool years before declining in middle childhood (Eifermann, 1971). What is needed in the early childhood classroom to facilitate dramatic play and, especially, sociodramatic play?

A review of the research conducted by Sara Smilansky (1968) provides some insight. Convinced that behavior patterns needed for sociodramatic play were similar to those required for school success, Smilansky investigated ways of fostering sociodramatic play. Her findings indicate that a combination of experiences (field trips, discussions, explanations, readings) and play training (the teacher makes suggestions to expand the play or even joins it, modeling play techniques) is particularly effective in facilitating sociodramatic play in the classroom.

Although these results endorse play training, it is significant to note that the teachers in the research initially resisted the idea of intervening in the children's play even though some conceded they did so with their own children at home. The teachers expressed concern that the intervention might nega-

Reprinted from *Childhood Education* (Jan./Feb. 1984): 172–77.

tively affect the children's mental health. Only after they became actively involved in the play training and viewed the children's happiness in their play, did the teachers enthusiastically support the concept of intervention. Possibly, this concept of intervention conflicted with their professional training and violated the traditional view of the early childhood teacher as facilitator rather than participator in the play setting. Is it possible that teachers in general feel uncomfortable about intervening in children's play and, therefore, do not intervene—even when children need to be taught play skills which they lack? If teachers intervened when necessary, would children use sociodramatic play more extensively?

Furthermore, Smilansky suggests the possibility that the classrooms and play themes used in the research might have been more geared to encouraging female sociodramatic play. Certainly, the typical housekeeping corner, the main theme corner provided in most classrooms, is often better equipped to foster imitation of the mother role. Could the lack of appropriate props and theme corners of interest to boys limit their involvement in sociodramatic play?

The possibility of facilitating sociodramatic play by providing a variety of theme corners, together with preparatory experiences and play training, was probed by a group of early childhood students at the State University College at Buffalo. Along with their coursework, these students participated regularly with children in the College Learning Laboratory. This laboratory school is unique in that it is a magnet school of the Buffalo public system; the children are selected by lottery and represent a cross section of a highly diverse urban population.

Working in teams in one nursery and two kindergarten classrooms, the students were assigned the task of implementing the following theme corners over a period of several semesters: drugstore, unisex hair shop, veterinarian's office, bakery, dentist's office, ice cream shop, clinic, shoe repair shop, gas station garage, appliance repair shop, restaurant, bank, airport and shoe store. It was anticipated that these themes would provide roles of interest to both boys and girls and that the children would be somewhat familiar with the themes.

One theme corner at a time was introduced in a room, with each classroom maintaining its permanent housekeeping corner. Each theme corner remained several weeks and considerable time usually elapsed before a new theme corner was introduced. The college students provided the children with preparatory experiences related to each theme, together with play training. The general consensus was that the children, including the boys, not only engaged in more sociodramatic play but became increasingly proficient in its use. The experience also provided direction concerning implementation of sociodramatic play in the naturalistic setting of the classroom. The resultant guidelines are offered to those interested in this type of experimentation:

Provide experiences related to the theme. Although the children were fairly familiar with the selected themes, it soon became apparent that ambiguity existed about some of the roles involved. Even a common theme (e.g., restaurant) became confusing when the children had to cope with the less familiar roles of dishwasher and chef.

In performing a role, children draw from their background knowledge, enacting the role as they understand or remember it. To maintain the role among their peers, they must enact it as convincingly as possible; when their understanding of a role is limited, the interpretation suffers. Providing preparatory experiences helps children extend their understanding of their own roles and of the theme as a whole. The latter is especially important as children tend to slip in and out of different roles connected with the basic theme.

Well-planned field trips provide excellent background knowledge and preparation for sociodramatic play. Children can visit the local drugstore, observe the varieties of merchandise and how they are classified, and talk with the stockperson, the cashier and the pharmacist about the tasks involved in their work. When field trips are not possible, classroom visitations can be an effective substitute. One enterprising team of students responsible for the veterinarian's office theme invited a female veterinarian to class. She obligingly brought along her pet cat, Ralph, and used him to conduct a physical examination. This fired all kinds of questions and, when the theme corner was established in the classroom, the children were ready to be involved.

Children can also learn about themes through carefully selected filmstrips, simple puppet shows, homemade flannelboard presentations, pictures, discussions, poems and books. Finding commercial books too complex for 3-year-olds, another student team produced its own book, *A Visit to the Bakery*, using large-size black-and-white mounted photographs. It was an instant success.

Plan and create a captivating environment for the theme. The physical arrangement of the classroom is an important dimension of sociodramatic play. A theme setting somewhat apart from the other activities in the room appears separate and draws the children to it. One student team created an entranceway from refrigerator cartons which could be folded and stored. Another hung window and door frame outlines from the ceiling to create a separate environment for the play. Research indicates that children like opaque enterable play boxes (Gramza, 1970) and that realistic ones might facilitate the play if the theme is less common and not likely to occur spontaneously in the classroom (Fields, 1979).

The setting should have sufficient space to accommodate the children, and the various areas within the setting need to be clearly defined. In the veterinarian's office, a small table for the receptionist and chairs for patients indicated the waiting room. Beyond this section, several large tables and supply shelves comprised the examining area, while the kennel stocked with cardboard cages and stuffed animals was located at the side. This type of physical arrangement clearly indicates to the children what happens where, and enables them to understand and perform their roles within the setting.

Provide props to establish and expand the play. For many children, especially those with less experience in pretending, props are the tools that enable them to actually assume desired roles. Perhaps for some children,

props contribute a degree of needed reality to the abstractness of the play. It is not unusual to hear a child vehemently argue that you cannot be the doctor without the stethoscope or you cannot scoop ice cream without wearing the appropriate apron. Although children's ability to pretend with less realistic objects increases between 3 and 5 years of age (Elder and Pederson, 1978), Enslein's findings (1979) indicate that even middle-class preschoolers will engage in limited pretense when the setting lacks realistic props. Boys even more than girls are dependent in their pretend play on the presence of objects in the environment (McLloyd, 1980; Matthews, 1977).

Props need to be simple, fairly realistic and as durable as possible. Many of the props the student teams provided were homemade from free or inexpensive materials. Cupcakes for the bakery were cut from scraps of thick foam rubber, while cookies were made from thick cardboard and covered with clear plastic. White, pink and brown yarn pompom balls represented vanilla, strawberry and chocolate scoops of ice cream, to the delight of the children. Props also need to be constructed so they can be stored when not in use. The cars for the gas station garage were cut from large pieces of cardboard which were stored behind toy cupboards. Smaller props for each theme could be stored in clearly labeled cardboard boxes and kept in a central spot, allowing them to be rotated among several early childhood classrooms.

Rather than placing all the props in the theme setting initially, the student teams added a few new props from time to time to maintain children's interest in the play. They also found that the children needed time to explore the props before using them in actual pretend play (Enslein, 1979; Nunnally and Lemond, 1973). Obviously, dramatic play cannot be rushed.

Intervene in the play when necessary. If experiences form the foundation on which sociodramatic play is built, selective intervention is the superstructure that sustains it. On the "opening day" of a theme corner, the children gathered together and reviewed the overall theme and the various roles involved. Ground rules were established, such as the number of children allowed in the setting or the props that had to remain in a specific section. This type of orientation actually involved the children in establishing limits for the play.

As the play commenced, the student team assumed the role of astute observers trying to determine from the children's behavior if and when intervention was necessary. They attempted to leave the children alone to allow the sociodramatic play to move independently, but they were alert to clues that indicated it was beginning to falter. Knowing when and when not to intervene is crucial. Generally, it is helpful to ask, "Do the children have sound ideas of their own?" or "Do they need help?" Help is indicated when the play repeats itself again and again or the children jump from one activity to another in a fragmented manner. Even when intervention was used by the student team, it was not intended to control or direct the *content* of the play but only to assist the children to expand the play more fully.

The student teams used two levels of intervention. Outside intervention involved making suggestions, commenting, questioning or fostering contact between the players in order to support and extend the sociodramatic play. When more assistance was needed, student team members actively entered the play (inside intervention), assuming a role and modeling appropriate play behaviors. In such interactions, the team member always addressed the *role* person the child was portraying rather than the individual child. While research indicates that most mothers rarely join their children in pretend play in the home (Dunn and Wooding, 1977), the children accepted this adult involvement quite naturally. It served as a catalyst to their play because they became more aware of the possibilities inherent in the theme through the adult modeling.

Gradually, as the children became more experienced, the student teams were less actively involved and merely observed the play. Such observations provided the student teams with valuable insights into children's interests and concerns, how they felt about themselves, how they related to others, how they controlled their behavior and adapted to the

limits of a particular role, and how they processed and interpreted past experiences. Team members learned to observe unobtrusively so as not to dampen or curtail interest and not to laugh regardless of the antics. While the focus was on the sociodramatic play rather than neatness, the play tended to disintegrate when the props and setting were disorganized and messy. Periodically, it was necessary to casually help the children straighten the setting so that it was appealing and orderly enough to make sense to them in the process of their role enactments. Occasionally, intervention techniques were not successful and behavior got out of bounds. At this point, the student teams were not reluctant to limit the play or even stop it.

Involve the children and their parents. Once children become more experienced in sociodramatic play, they can take part in planning new themes. "How can we do that?" is a group question that can bridge a network of creative ideas. Parents, too, can be a valuable resource; many welcome the opportunity to make simple props with their children at home and then visit the classroom. A parent meeting might be devoted to a discussion of sociodramatic play, interpreting its value and the learnings involved. Few activities so clearly indicate to parents that, in the cognitive realm, learnings are not compartmentalized into subject areas. Science, language arts, social science and arithmetic are interwoven throughout children's sociodramatic play. In the ice cream shop, for example, the children picture-read the menu, correspond one coin with one scoop of ice cream, and while making real ice cream observe the physical change from liquid to solid. Integrated learning is a natural part of sociodramatic play, and parents who recognize this will be more alert to learning opportunities in the home setting.

Sara Smilansky noted that the parents of the children in her research study did not think of themselves as their child's teacher. Furthermore, they were not involved in their child's use of toys and they neglected to foster make-believe play. It seems probable that many parents, coping with a myriad of complex problems and pressures, share some of these characteristics. By emphasizing the value of sociodramatic play and the skills that foster it, educators can help parents be more aware of their roles as home-based teachers and encourage them to be more involved in this capacity. Certainly, in a society where young children are exposed to endless television and pretending is overpowered by "back to the basics," educators need innovative ways to facilitate sociodramatic play in both home and classroom settings.

References

Christie, J. "Play for Cognitive Growth." *Elementary School Journal* 81 (1980): 115–18.
———. "Sociodramatic Play Training." *Young Children* 37, 4 (May 1982): 25–31.
Dunn, J., and C. Wooding. "Play in the Home and Its Implications for Learning." *Biology of Play*. London: Heineman, 1977.
Eifermann, R. R. "Social Play in Childhood." In R. Herron and B. Sutton-Smith, eds., *Child's Play*. New York: Wiley, 1971.
Elder, J. L., and D. R. Pederson. "Preschool Children's Use of Objects in Symbolic Play." *Child Development* 49 (1978): 500–04.
Enslein, J. *An Analysis of Toy Preferences, Social Participation and Play Activity in Preschool Aged Children.* Unpublished master's thesis. The Merrill-Palmer Institute, 1979.
Fein, G. "Pretend Play: New Perspectives." *Young Children* 34, 5 (July 1979): 61–66.
———. "Pretend Play in Childhood: An Integrative Review." *Child Development* 52 (1981): 1195–1218.
———. "The Physical Environment: Stimulation or Evocation." In R. Lerner and N. Busch Rossnagel, eds., *Individuals as Producers of Their Development.* New York: Academic, 1981.
Fields, W. *Imaginative Play of Four-Year-Old Children as a Function of Toy Realism.* Unpublished master's thesis. The Merrill-Palmer Institute, 1979.
Golomb, C., and C. B. Cornelius. "Symbolic Play and Its Cognitive Significance." *Developmental Psychology* 13 (1977): 246–52.
Gramza, A. F. "Preferences of Preschool Children for Enterable Play Boxes." *Perceptual and Motor Skills* 31 (1970): 177–78.
Lovinger, S. L. "Sociodramatic Play and Language Development in Preschool Disadvantaged Children." *Psychology in Schools* 11 (1974): 313–20.

Marshall, H. R. "Relations Between Home Experiences and Children's Use of Language in Play Interaction with Peers." *Psychological Monographs* 75 (1961). Whole No. 509.
Marshall, H. R., and R. Doshi. "Aspects of Experience Revealed Through Doll Play of Preschool Children." *Journal of Psychology* 61 (1965): 47–57.
Matthews, W. S. "Modes of Transformation in the Initiation of Fantasy Play." *Developmental Psychology* 13 (1977): 212–16.
McLloyd, V. "Verbally Expressed Modes of Transformation in the Fantasy Play of Black Preschool Children." *Child Development* 51 (1980): 1133–39.
Nunnally, J. C., and L. C. Lemond. "Exploratory Behavior and Human Development." In H. Reese, ed., *Advances in Child Development and Behavior*, Vol. 8. New York: Academic Press, 1973.
Rosen, C. E. "The Effects of Sociodramatic Play on Problem-Solving Behavior Among Culturally Disadvantaged Preschool Children." *Child Development* 45 (1974): 920–27.
Rubin, K. H., and T. L. Maioni. "Play Preference and Its Relation to Egocentricism, Popularity, and Classification Skills in Preschool." *Merrill-Palmer Quarterly* 21 (1975): 171–79.
Rubin, K. H.; T. L. Maioni and M. Hornung. "Free Play Behaviors and Lower-Class Preschoolers: Parten and Piaget Revisited." *Child Development* 47 (1976): 414–19.
Rubin, K. H.; K. S. Watson and T. W. Jambor. "Free Play Behaviors in Preschool and Kindergarten Children." *Child Development* 49 (1978): 534–36.
Saltz, E.; D. Dixon and J. Johnson. "Training Disadvantaged Preschoolers on Various Fantasy Activities: Effects on Cognitive Functioning and Impulse Control." *Child Development* 48 (1977): 367–80.
Shores, R. E., P. Huster and P. S. Strain. "Effects of Teacher Presence and Structured Play on Child-Child Interaction Among Handicapped Preschool Children." *Psychology in the Schools* 13 (1976): 171–75.
Singer, D. C., and J. L. Singer. "Some Correlates of Imaginative Play in Preschoolers." Paper presented at Meeting of American Psychological Association, Toronto, 1978.
Singer, J. L. "Affect and Imagination in Play and Fantasy." In C. Izard, ed., *Emotions in Personality and Psychopathology.* New York: Plenum, 1979.
Singer, J. L., ed. *The Child's World of Make-Believe: Experimental Studies of Imaginative Play.* New York: Academic Press, 1973.
Smilansky, S. *The Effects of Sociodramatic Play on Disadvantaged Preschool Children.* New York: Wiley, 1968.
Spivack, G., and M. B. Shure. *Social Adjustment of Young Children.* San Francisco: Jossey-Bass, 1974.
Van den Daele. "Preschool Intervention with Social Learning." *Journal of Negro Education* 39 (1970): 296–304.

Adult Suggestion: An Enabler for Pretend Play in Two-year-olds

Connie Steele
College of Home Economics
Texas Tech University, Lubbock

and

Elizabeth Hrncir
Child Development Project
Hamilton, Bermuda

Previous research (Dansky, 1980; Feitelson & Rose, 1973; Smilansky, 1968) indicates that many young children do not spontaneously engage in make-believe play even when given opportunities to do so. Yet the presence of representational images as characterized during make-believe or pretend play affords the child the means for developing from sensorimotor performance to symbolic thought (Piaget, 1962).

Finding the means for promoting the child's representational imagery or symbolic thought is dependent upon being able to connote the child's progress in moving from sensorimotor to preoperational use of symbols. Record of acquisition of language as an indice for noting children's levels of representational images has been unsuccessful (Fenson, Kagan, Kearsley, & Zelazo, 1976). Objects have been used as a means for eliciting varied levels of pretend play by very young children (Lowe, 1975). Garvey (1977) noted that symbolic representation by young children in "pretending" was aided by the physical properties of objects—for example, a cup usually used by the child for drinking orange juice can be transformed to pretending that the cup has juice even when it does not. Representational detail or a toy's prototypicality may affect the child's incidence of pretend play. Fein and Robertson (Note 1) found that the pretend play of 22 males and females between 20 and 26 months of age was positively related to adult ratings of the degree to which a less prototypical object

(toy) resembled its high prototypical counterpart. The question of adult modeling of make-believe situations in order to elicit children's symbolic functioning has produced mixed results. Fein (1975) found that adult modeling did not assist the children's substitution performance, and she reasoned that pretend transformations arose from sources other than children's imitation of adults. Conversely, Watson and Fisher (1977) concluded that the technique of modeling pretending with certain objects elicited significantly more symbolic responses from the very young child than when the technique was not used.

The present study hypothesized that:

(a) Objects for play with high prototypicality would generate a higher incidence of two-year-old children's pretend play than toys with low prototypicality.

(b) Adult play suggestions would elicit more frequent pretend play by two-year olds than when no adult play suggestions were introduced.

Influences of age and gender within all conditions were also questioned.

METHOD

Subjects. Twenty children (10 males, 10 females) were observed responding to objects rated as having high and low prototypical properties. All children were Anglo and of middle-socioeconomic status (SES). Children ranged in age from 20 to 33 months (mean age = 26.75 months). An older group was composed of 10 children (5 males, 5 females) between 20 to 26 months; a younger group included 10 children (5 males, 5 females) from 27 to 33 months.

Procedures. Prior to observation of the children in play with an adult's introducing two sets of high and low prototypical objects (toys), a checklist of play behaviors (categories) was developed from the literature (Lowe, 1975; Fenson et al., 1976; Nicolich, 1977; and Watson & Fisher, 1977). Four females and 7 males between 20 and 30 months of age, Anglo and middle-SES, were videotaped in play with a set of high prototypical (HP) objects and a set of low prototypical (LP) objects. Three raters' codings of their behaviors with the toys were compared to determine reliability of the categorical checklist for connoting children's pretending behaviors. When high correlation was found between Rater 1's and Rater 3's ranked frequency codings of children's responses to high and low prototypical objects ($r = .814$, $p < .05$; $r = .680$, $p < .05$) but only moderate to low correlation between Rater 1 and Rater 2 ($r = .500$, $p > .05$; $r = .250$, $p > .05$) and between Rater 2 and Rater 3 ($r = .530$, $p > .05$; $r = .610$, $p > .05$), procedures for using the checklist were revised to include definitions devised by Raters 1 and 3 to insure observation reliability.

To check whether or not the objects to be used in play could be associated with each other, 12 adults were asked to pair objects considered to be "high prototypical" with their low prototypical counterparts. The small red car (HP)/small red box (LP) and the small wooden doll bed (HP)/small beige box (LP) were matched by 92.3 percent of the adults. All (100 percent) of the adults matched the white blanket (HP) with the white kleenex (LP); small baby doll (HP) with the foam rubber cut in shape of gingerbread doll (LP); yellow tea cup (HP) with yellow aerosol lid (LP); and small blue brush (HP) with the small blue piece of cardboard (LP).

To determine whether or not adults' ratings of objects would differ as a function of prototypicality, 12 adults were asked to score each object from 1 to 10 in prototypicality. Comparison of the 12 adults' ratings of pro-

totypicality showed significant difference between the high/low groupings ($t = 3.49$, $p < .01$). The Kendall Coefficient of Concordance (W) indicated that the 12 adults were in close agreement (W = .747, p < .01) regarding ranking of the pairs according to their degree of prototypicality.

Each child was videotaped individually in the following sequence:

(a) Play with the high prototypical objects without adult play suggestions until the child was beginning to terminate play with these HP objects—usually by the child's attempt to leave or to push the objects away.

(b) Play with HP objects with adult play suggestions but without demonstration or modeling of the suggested play theme. Play suggestions used by Fein and Robertson (Note 1) were introduced: "Baby is sleepy," "Put baby to bed," "Nighty-night, baby," were stated with the examiner's (E's) hand by the doll bed. With the cup, E placed her hand alongside and said, "Baby is thirsty," "Give the baby something to drink." Placing her hand by the blanket, E said, "Baby is cold," "Make baby warm." By the brush, E suggested, "Baby's hair needs combing," "Comb baby's hair." With her hand near the car, E urged, "Baby wants to go for a ride," "Bye-bye, baby." After each play suggestion, the child was given time for play responses until play diminished. E then asked the child to hand her the HP objects, and they were placed out of view.

(c) Play with low prototypical objects without adult play suggestions until the child terminated play with them.

(d) Play with LP objects with adult play suggestions in the same sequence as with the HP objects. Again the child was not coaxed into following the adult's requests nor was any demonstrating or modeling performed.

The categorical checklist (Figure 1) was used by three raters to record frequencies of pretend play from the videotapes of the children's play behaviors. Each child's response (or lack of response) was recorded only once for each of the above-described conditions:

(a) Play response with HP objects without adult play suggestions

(b) Play response with HP objects with adult play suggestions

(c) Play response with LP objects without adult play suggestions

(d) Play response with LP objects with adult play suggestions.

Checklist categories were coded by the three raters as follows:

Category I: A. Looks at objects; B. Touches objects; C. Looks at adult. Children did something more with the objects after first experimenting with handling and touching them. The raters marked each of these levels if (a) the child looked at the object, (b) touched the object and/or (c) looked at the adult. Each was marked only once within each tape segment even if the Category I behavior occurred repetitively.

Category II: A. Combines objects—haphazard or intentional; B. Shows objects to adult. Children demonstrated the combining of objects repetitively. The child attempted to fit the

Figure 1

Child's name _____
Birthdate _____
Rater's name _____

Categorical Checklist
Circle one:
    (a) With Play Suggestions
    (b) Without Play Suggestions

Frequency to HP Objects	Behavioral Responses	Frequency to LP Objects
_____	I. A. Looks at objects.	_____
_____	B. Touches objects.	_____
_____	C. Looks at adult.	_____
_____	II. A. Combination of objects (may be haphazard— stacking, or inten- tional—fitting box to- gether).	_____
_____	B. Shows object to adult.	_____
_____	III. A. Applies "action" to self or adult (one way).	_____
_____	B. Describes "own" actions.	_____
_____	IV. A. Applies "action" to self or adult and to objects (one way).	_____
_____	B. Describes actions of self and/or others.	_____
_____	V. A. Action patterns of ap- plication of "action" to self, adult, and objects are sequential.	_____
_____	B. Describes actions—de- scriptions use concepts (warm, cold, soft, hard, etc.)	_____

car onto the bed, the doll into the cup, the brush into the car, etc. A mark in these categories meant that the child did not yet use the object to mean something; for example, a child's combination of brushing the doll's hair implied something higher than this category; within this category, the child might show the brush to the adult without giving it away.

Category III: A. Applies action to self or adult (one-way); B. Describes own actions. The child applied the action to self without yet sequentially applying the same action to the doll. For example, a child did not yet brush own hair, brush baby's hair, put baby to bed, etc. in a sequence of activity. Instead, the child picked up the brush, brushed own hair and put the brush on the floor again. Language of child described only own behaviors—not taking into account the adult's language or interaction.

Category IV: A. Applies action to self and/or adult and to objects one-way; B. Describes actions of self and/or other. Children took into consideration what the adult was doing and included the adult's behavior in their activities with the objects. Children's language began to describe not only their own actions but also the adult's.

Category V: A. Action patterns of actions to self, adult and objects are sequential; B. Describes actions—descriptions use concepts. Children began to demonstrate sequential action patterns. Children gave baby something to drink, put baby to bed, covered baby and took baby for a ride. Each specific activity often led into the next with a child's description of what he/she was doing. Children did not only respond to the adult's suggestions but also did something more with the objects. For ex-

ample, one child said, "Baby's dirty. Give baby a bath," and then put the doll into the cup for washing. Behaviors were much less haphazard or unrelated.

RESULTS

Correlations among the three raters' observations of children's play responses were significant at the $p<.01$ level, as shown in Table 1. Therefore, data from Rater 1 were used in the analyses.

Observations of children's play responses coded within the categories of the checklist were summed to obtain a frequency score that was used as the dependent variable in the several statistical analyses.

In one-tailed t tests, response frequencies for pretend-play categories were significantly higher when adult play suggestions were employed with both HP and LP objects than when adult play suggestions were not used ($t=3.65$; $p<.01$). However, objects with high prototypicality did not elicit more frequent pretend play than toys with low prototypicality ($t=1.00$; $p>.05$). Significantly higher scores were demonstrated by older children (mean = 24.9) than by younger children (mean = 20.4) ($t=2.99$; $p<.01$). No difference between males' and females' scores was found.

Analysis of variance (2 age × 2 sex × 2 objects × 2 play suggestions) was employed to determine if interaction effects occurred. Only the main effects of play suggestions and age were found.

To determine if responses of older/younger groups of children differed within each checklist category, the Fisher exact proba-

Table 1
Relationship Between Three Raters' Codings of Children's Response Frequencies

	HP objects without play suggestions	HP objects with play suggestions	LP objects without play suggestions	LP objects with play suggestions
Rater 1—Rater 2	$r = .940$*	$r = .910$*	$r = .810$*	$r = .970$*
Rater 1—Rater 3	$r = .850$*	$r = .810$*	$r = .920$*	$r = .920$*
Rater 2—Rater 3	$r = .900$*	$r = .730$*	$r = .920$*	$r = .940$*

* $p<.01$

bility one-tailed test was employed. Significant differences were found between younger and older children's responses for Category IV and Category V, but not for Categories I, II and III. (See Table 3.)

DISCUSSION

The hypothesis that objects with high prototypicality would generate a higher incidence of two-year-old children's pretend play

Table 2
Analysis of Variance of Children's Behavioral Responses

Source	df	MS	F
Age	1	25.32	8.85*
Sex	1	.62	< 1.00
Age × Sex	1	1.00	< 1.00
Subjects/Age × Sex	16	2.86	
Objects	1	.02	< 1.00
Play suggestions	1	15.18	13.32*
Age × Objects	1	.10	< 1.00
Age × Play suggestions	1	1.00	< 1.00
Sex × Object	1	.60	< 1.00
Sex × Play suggestions	1	.30	< 1.00
Object × Play suggestions	1	.10	< 1.00
Age × Sex × Object	1	.33	< 1.00
Age × Sex × Play suggestion	1	1.03	< 1.00
Age × Object × Play suggestion	1	.33	< 1.00
Sex × Object × Play suggestion	1	.63	< 1.00
Age × Sex × Object × Play suggestion	1	3.59	< 1.00
Objects × Ss/age × Sex	16	1.61	
Play suggestion × Ss/age × Sex	16	1.14	
Objects × Play suggestion × Ss/age × Sex	16	1.44	
TOTAL	79		

* $p < .01$

Table 3
Young and Old Children's Response Frequency Grouped by Category

Category	Young Children	Old Children
I		
Demonstrated	10	10
Not demonstrated	0	0
II		
Demonstrated	9	10
Not demonstrated	1	1
III		
Demonstrated	5	6
Not demonstrated	5	4
IV*		
Demonstrated	5	9
Not demonstrated	5	1
V*		
Demonstrated	0	4
Not demonstrated	10	6

* $p < .05$

than toys with low prototypicality was not supported. Neither the children in the older group nor those in the younger group demonstrated increased make-believe activities with the toys with more realistic representation. This finding appears to contradict the Fein and Robertson (Note 1) conclusion that children pretended more with HP toys than with less prototypical toys. Although adults indicated a significant difference between HP and LP objects in this study, it is possible that the objects used were too similar from the children's perspective for such differentiation to be made by them. These young children may perceive the high and low prototypical objects in a qualitatively different way from the adult. Such perceptual differences between the very young child and adult deserve further research before a conclusion can satisfactorily be drawn regarding the acceleration or deceleration of a child's pretending based upon an object's prototypicality.

Of more interest in the comparison of children's responses to the HP and LP items was the child's ability to transform his/her pretend play from the HP toy to the LP counterpart. Repeatedly, children at 24 to 26 months asked the examiner for the HP "baby" that had been taken from view; they were determined to find the previous "baby" with which they had played and often would do very little with the more recently introduced LP "baby." Actually one child successfully managed to retrieve the HP doll. When this child combined it with the LP "baby," a magical transformation seemed to ensue, for the child proceeded to dismiss the HP doll and use the LP doll for pretend play. The initial play with the HP object seemed necessary for the transformation to pretending with the LP object, as suggested by Fein's (1975) conclusions regarding transformations. Furthermore, the adult's play suggestions provided anchoring support themes to facilitate the child's movement into transformations. In future research, then, the play sequences should include progression from HP objects to a combination of HP and LP objects and finally to offer only LP objects—in order to observe the child's pretend play that might result from such transformational progression.

Children demonstrated greater responsiveness to HP as well as LP objects when adult play suggestions were used then they did when no adult play suggestions were made. Play suggestions neither interfered with nor inhibited the child's play but, rather, provided a catalyst to facilitate the child's pretend behaviors.

The findings of this study suggest that both high and low exemplars are important inclusions in the young child's environment. The findings also point to the influence of the adult on the child's pretending. Adult caregivers can be sure that they have a significant influence on children's make-believe play. Although the adult modeling suggested by study of infants' play was successful with children younger than eighteen months (Watson & Fisher, 1977), adult play suggestions without modeling may become more conducive to enhancement of children's pretend play when the child is around two years of age.

Caregivers of two-year-old children who have not yet acquired language may be well advised to evaluate children's symbolic and representational thought through the use of checklist categories such as those utilized in the present study. Indices such as this categorical checklist would encourage caregivers' planning of "realistic supports" for children's symbolic play. Caregivers who give adult suggestions to two-year-olds can judge to what extent their input enhances the very young child's development of symbolic or representational thought.

Reference Note

Fein, G. G., and A. Robertson. "Cognitive and Social Dimensions of Pretending in Two-year-olds." New Haven, CT: Yale University, 1974. (ERIC Document Reproduction Service No. ED 119 806.)

References

Dansky, J. L. "Make-believe: A Mediator of the Relationship Between Play and Associative Fluency." *Child Development* 51 (1980): 576–79.

Fein, G. G. "A Transformational Analysis of Pretending." *Developmental Psychology* 11 (1975): 291–96.

Feitelson, D., and G. S. Ross. "The Neglected Factor: Play." *Human Development* 16 (1973): 202–23.

Fenson, L.; J. Kagan; R. B. Kearsley and P. R. Zelazo. "The Developmental Progression of Manipulative Play in the First Two Years." *Child Development* 47 (1976): 232–36.

Garvey, C. "Play." In J. Bruner, M. Cole and B. Lloyd, eds., *The Developing Child*. Cambridge, MA: Harvard University Press, 1977.

Lowe, M. "Trends in the Development of Representational Play in Infants from One to Three Years—An Observational Study." *Journal of Child Psychology and Psychiatry* 16 (1975): 33–47.

Nicolich, L. C. "Beyond Sensorimotor Intelligence: Assessment of Symbolic Maturity Through Analysis of Pretend Play." *Merrill Palmer Quarterly of Behavior and Development* 23 (1977): 89–99.

Piaget, J. *Play, Dreams, and Imitation in Childhood*. New York: Norton, 1962.

Smilansky, S. *The Effects of Sociodramatic Play on Disadvantaged Preschool Children*. New York: Wiley, 1968.

Watson, M. W., and K. W. Fisher. "A Developmental Sequence of Agent Use in Late Infancy." *Child Development* 48 (1977): 828–36.

The Results of Training Preschool Teachers to Foster Children's Play

ROBERT G. COLLIER
Elementary Education and Reading Department
Western Illinois University, Macomb

Most preschools and day care centers, recognizing playtime as a healthful activity, include at least some time during their program for children to interact among themselves and their environment with a minimum of teacher direction. The role of the teacher during such periods has been subject to question and varies from being strictly an observer to a facilitator. The skills and abilities necessary for either role require more than patience and a love for children.

The following study involved developing both roles in preschool teachers, measuring the long- and short-term effects of play training techniques applied to preschool teachers in a "natural" setting. The two specific areas of concern were cognitive development and children's play. Research in these areas suggests that: 1) the role of the adult may be crucial (Krasnor and Pepler, 1980; Sylva, Roy and Painter, 1980) and 2) procedures designed to facilitate children's play may lead to the development of problem-solving (Sylva, Bruner and Genova, 1976; Dansky and Silverman, 1973) and divergent thinking skills (Lieberman, 1965, 1977; Durrett and Huffman, 1968; Feitelson and Ross, 1973; Hutt and Bhavnani, 1976; Dansky, 1979) in addition to language usage and verbal intelligence (Smilansky, 1968; Lovinger, 1974; Saltz, Dixon and Johnson, 1977). Two common weaknesses of many of these prior studies were 1) the failure to demonstrate long-term effects and 2) the lack of practical application of such techniques by "real" teachers in a "natural" setting.

The four variables measured were: children's verbal expression, divergent thinking, play and teacher behavior. A modified Flander's Interaction Analysis (Flanders, 1970) was used to measure teacher's behavior during "free play" time. Verbal expression of children was measured by the verbal expression section of the Illinois Test of Psycholinguistic Abilities. The children's divergent thinking skills were determined by Torrance's Creativity in Action and Movement Test (Torrance, 1975). Children's play was viewed in terms of Smilansky's four play levels (Smilansky, 1968), Parten's social play scale (Parten, 1932) and Smilansky's sociodramatic play ratings (Smilansky, 1968).

The study was conducted using two rural, midwest preschool sites licensed for 40 children. The children in both sites were white and from low-middle class families. The experimental status and control status were randomly assigned to the two sites.

The subjects were 35 children and eight preschool teachers. The children included 16 boys and 17 girls, ranging in age from three years to five years, five months. The experimental group included 18 children, ten boys and eight girls whose ages were between three and five. The control group was composed of 15 children between the ages of three years and five years, five months with nine girls and six boys. There were three teachers in the experimental group and five in the control group. All teachers were either experienced with young children and/or college educated.

PROCEDURES

The study used a pretest, posttest, delayed posttest design, with the posttest data gathered six months after the onset of the study and the delayed posttest data collected one month after the end of the posttest. All testing was done by a trained graduate assistant, who was unaware of the purpose of the study.

The control group participated only in the pretest, posttest and delayed posttest testing. The experimental group received the same testing, but the teachers in this group received 11 two-hour sessions in techniques for facilitating children's play. These sessions followed the Schools Council Project for Structuring Play in the Infant/First School and included a text, *Structuring Play in the Early Years at School* (Manning and Sharp, 1978), a set of six videotapes, videotape notes (Manning and Sharp, 1977) and a course leader's book (Manning and Sharp, 1978).

The goals of the training program were to train the teachers in: 1) observing the learning and development occurring in children's play and 2) techniques for facilitating such play through appropriate adult provision and involvement. Provision included providing the time, place, materials and rules required for facilitating play, while involvement pertained to the appropriate use of adult participation, initiation and intervention. The evaluation of such play was determined by its ability to: 1) enable learning and development to occur, 2) sustain itself over a period of time, 3) be carried to a conclusion, 4) be absorbing, enjoyed and shared by a group of children.

The objectives of the experimental treatment were to engage teachers in: 1) group discussion of the play occurring in their classrooms, 2) organizational problems in providing for play and 3) comparing individual attempts at structuring play. The experimental group received instruction and practice in recording and observing play and analyzing the learning and development from such observations.

Other topics included in the experimental objectives were: reviews of the time allotted for play, play materials in individual classrooms, rules affecting children's play and play clean-up, as well as how such rules worked to structure children's play. For all topics, the teachers were guided toward relating each to their own situations, making selected changes in each case and recording the resultant effects of such changes.

The play observations and recordings helped the teachers to define and recognize the forms of adult involvement, as they practiced recognizing and developing objectives for their involvement and identifying the resulting effects. The videotapes stimulated discussion and assisted the analysis of provision and teacher involvement.

Each training session was composed of three segments. The first section included discussions of required readings and of the teachers' play observations, the second consisted of viewing a videotape followed by discussion, questions and comments focusing on a specific aspect of the tape; the last included assignments for the following session.

RESULTS

Preliminary results of this study were analyzed in terms of the effects on teachers and children. (Continued analysis is in progress.) Teacher behavior data obtained during three 20-minute "free play" observations were grouped into the areas of Teacher Talk, Child Talk and No Teacher Interaction. Teacher Talk encompassed seven categories: 1) accepting feelings, 2) praise, 3) use of the child's ideas, 4) questions, 5) lecture, 6) giving directions and 7) criticizing. Child Talk included both the child's responding to the teacher and the child's initiating a response with the teacher. The No Teacher Interaction area was modified to include silence while observing and not observing the children, as well as talking to another teacher while either observing or not observing. These modifications were deemed necessary because of the special nature of the "free play" period as compared to "regular" classroom interaction.

Teachers

The teacher behavior data for both groups, Figure 1, indicated consistent change for each category, except the control group's Child Talk. The experimental group's behavior changes were in the opposite direction from the control group's changes and continued even after the experimental treatment ended (delayed posttest).

Analysis of the individual categories for each area, by group, indicated that for

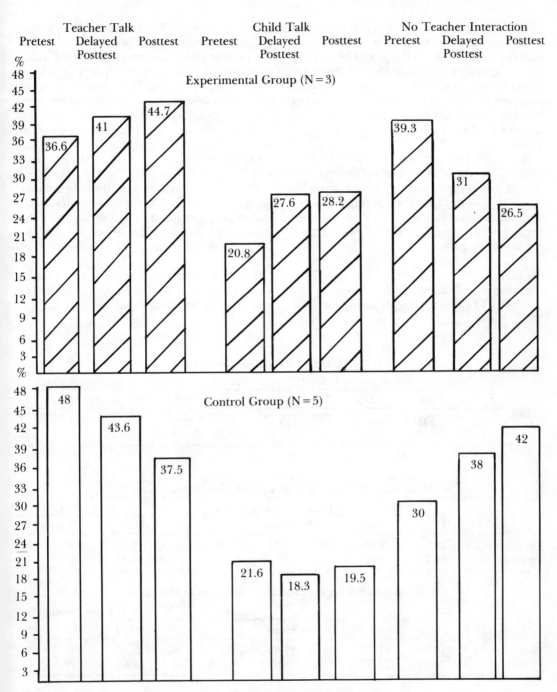

Figure 1. Results Modified Flanders Interaction Analysis

Teacher Talk only category three (use of children's ideas) seemed to account for the experimental group's changes. The experimental group's Child Talk changes were reflected only in category eight (child responding). None of the four categories of No Teacher Interaction consistently decreased or increased for the experimental group.

No single category for Teacher Talk or Child Talk was indicated as responsible for the control group's results. In the area of No Teacher Interaction, the categories of silence while observing and talking to another teacher while observing both demonstrated consistent increases.

Children

The means and standard deviations for the children's ITPA verbal expression scores are found in Table 1. An analysis of covariance, applied to the delayed posttest scores with the pretest as the covariate, indicated a significant difference between groups, $F(1,31) = 5.565$, $p = .025$. The same procedure applied to the delayed posttest data, with the posttest as the covariate and the posttest data with the pretest as the covariate, yielded no significant differences, $F(1,31) = 2.352$, $p = .136$ and $F(1,31) = 3.149$, $p = .085$.

The children's divergent thinking abilities were measured in three areas: fluency, originality and imagination. Table 2 shows the means and standard deviations for the experimental and control groups in each of these three areas.

Application of the above-described statistical procedures to the fluency, originality and imagination data indicated a significant

Table 1
ITPA Verbal Expression Scores

Group	Pretest			Posttest			Delayed Posttest		
	Mean	SD	N	Mean	SD	N	Mean	SD	N
Experimental	15.00	6.79	19	15.37	7.89	19	20.77	9.45	17
Control	14.56	6.25	15	11.88	6.26	16	14.33	4.53	15

Table 2
Mean Fluency Scores Creativity in Action & Movement

Group	Pretest			Posttest			Delayed Posttest		
	Mean	SD	N	Mean	SD	N	Mean	SD	N
Experimental	13.79	8.86	19	13.11	5.32	18	15.94	6.79	17
Control	20.25	16.68	16	16.50	12.35	16	14.33	11.24	15

Mean Originality Scores Creativity in Action & Movement

Group	Pretest			Posttest			Delayed Posttest		
	Mean	SD	N	Mean	SD	N	Mean	SD	N
Experimental	13.61	11.28	18	12.39	7.01	18	13.65	7.01	17
Control	24.07	23.74	15	18.69	14.52	16	14.60	12.88	15

Analysis of Covariance of Post-Imagination Test with Pre-Imagination Test as Covariate

Group	Pretest			Posttest			Delayed Posttest		
	Mean	SD	N	Mean	SD	N	Mean	SD	N
Experimental	15.37	2.77	19	16.11	2.61	18	18.62	1.62	17
Control	16.13	4.72	16	16.69	5.33	16	17.00	5.22	15

difference between groups for the imagination delayed posttest scores, using the posttest as the covariate. All other data yielded no significant differences.

Three aspects of children's play were measured to note any differences in the play levels between each group. The data represent the percentage that each play level appeared in the children's play for the three 10-minute observations taken for each testing period. The percentages were obtained by analyzing the three written observations made of each child's play and noting the level of play evident. For a child to receive credit for demonstrating a specific play level, that level of play had to be noted at least once in two of the three play observations made for each child during the testing period. The number of children receiving credit for any one play level was then divided by the number of children for that group to arrive at a percentage score.

The results of applying Smilansky's four types of play to the children's play observations are found in Table 3. The data indicated no trends supporting differences in the play levels for both groups or developmental changes for either group.

The percentage of Parten's social play levels for the experimental and control groups are found in Table 4. The experimental group indicated a trend toward increased higher levels of social play (associative) with decreased lower levels of social play (parallel, solitary and onlooking). The control group data suggested no such trends.

The data from Smilansky's sociodramatic play rating are listed in Table 5. The exper-

Table 3
Percentage of Types of Play as Measured by Smilansky's Play Scale

	Pretest		Posttest		Delayed Posttest	
	%	N	%	N	%	N
Experimental						
Functional	26.3	19	42.1	19	38.9	18
Constructive	36.8	19	36.8	19	44.4	18
Dramatic	84.2	19	84.2	19	61.1	18
Games	0	19	0	19	0	18
Control						
Functional	56.3	16	6.3	16	13.3	15
Constructive	37.5	16	18.8	16	40.0	15
Dramatic	68.8	16	93.8	16	66.7	15
Games	0	16	0	16	0	15

Table 4
Percentage of Social Play Levels in Terms of Parten's Social Play Scale

	Pretest		Posttest		Delayed Posttest	
	%	N	%	N	%	N
Experimental						
Onlooking	0	19	0	19	0	19
Solitary	47.4	19	36.8	19	44.4	18
Parallel	42.1	19	15.8	19	11.1	18
Associative	52.6	19	84.2	19	77.8	18
Cooperative	0	19	0	19	0	19
Control						
Onlooking	6.3	16	0	16	6.7	15
Solitary	31.3	16	37.5	16	46.7	15
Parallel	25.0	16	0	16	6.7	15
Associative	75.0	16	93.8	16	73.3	15
Cooperative	0	16	0	16	0	15

Table 5
Percentage of Dramatic Play Levels According to Smilansky's Sociodramatic Play Scale

	Pretest		Posttest		Delayed Posttest	
	%	N	%	N	%	N
Experimental						
No Dramatic Play	26.0	19	32.0	19	28.0	18
Dramatic Play	0	19	0	19	11.0	18
Poor Sociodramatic Play	5.0	19	5.0	19	6.0	18
Good Sociodramatic Play	63.0	19	63.0	19	56.0	18
Control						
No Dramatic Play	6.0	16	25.0	16	33.0	15
Dramatic Play	0	16	0	16	7.0	15
Poor Sociodramatic Play	18.0	16	6.0	16	0	15
Good Sociodramatic Play	75.0	16	69.0	16	60.0	15

imental group remained relatively consistent throughout the study. The control group showed a steady increase in the lower levels of sociodramatic play (no dramatic play and dramatic play) and decrease in the higher levels of sociodramatic play (poor and good sociodramatic play).

DISCUSSION

The results of this study suggest that play training applied to preschool teachers may produce both short- and long-term effects for the four variables measured, in a "natural" setting. All variables, however, were not affected to the same degree.

The Flanders behavior data indicated that play training seemed to stimulate increased interaction or dialogue between teachers and children, an effect that escalated rather than "washed out" at the conclusion of the experimental treatment. While the teacher behavior data were strictly descriptive, experimental effects were enhanced due to the control group's behavior change in an opposing direction. The change of behavior for the control teachers suggests the presence of an uncontrolled variable. To the knowledge of this researcher, no major structural or curricular changes occurred at the control site nor were there any significant personal problems among the staff that would account for such steady change. Therefore, the author suggests that the changes may reflect a cycle of interactional behavior among teachers and children. Such

cyclic behavior might be influenced by the children's familiarity with the environment and their playmates, a decline in the children's dependence upon the teacher and/or teacher fatigue.

The preschool children's verbal expression mean scores displayed significant long-term effects. An increase in the experimental group's delayed posttest mean score was the major contributing factor. Such data seem to suggest that the training procedures might have "carry-over" effects, a fact supported by the accompanying teacher behavior change and/or that the effectiveness of these play training procedures upon verbal expression might require more time than was allowed for by the posttest.

The effect of time upon the differences between groups was also evident for the divergent thinking variable. Imagination mean scores indicated short-term significant differences for the delayed posttest data, using the posttest as a covariate. A noting of the changes in group means for fluency and originality suggests the possibility that significant differences might require more time to develop in these areas than was allowed.

The children's play data seemed the least affected by the play training. One possible reason was the lack of control applied during "free play," particularly in regard to the materials available for the children. This was deemed necessary in order to make the study's results as practical as possible and interfere as little as possible with each center's normal routines.

310

The data for Smilansky's types of play indicated inconsistency and no clear developmental trends for either group, which suggest that either the play training had varying effects on the children's play or the changes in available play materials affected this measurement of play. The latter explanation seemed most likely because the environmental changes at the control site took place just prior to the delayed posttesting, and a clear developmental trend was noted between the pretest and posttest for this group. The experimental site's changes were noted prior to the posttest and continued to change throughout the delayed posttesting (no developmental trends were noted for this group). Social play factors seemed less affected, as a steady trend was evident for both groups toward lower and higher social play levels. The control group's sociodramatic play ratings demonstrated consistent regression while the experimental group's ratings remained constant.

CONCLUSION

This study suggests that preschool teachers, without extensive pretraining, can effect cognitive gains in their students by attempting to foster children's play. With the exception of testing, the researcher had no direct interaction with the children of this study. Therefore, the effects registered by the subjects are directly attributable to their teachers and the environment.

Second, for teachers the play training effects noted were not only sustained after the experimental treatment ceased but in most cases continued to escalate, suggesting possible long-term effects. The effects for children were most evident on the delayed posttest, suggesting that time might be a necessary factor in effectiveness.

A third conclusion concerns the interaction between teachers and children during "free play." A possible cycle of behavior is suggested, leading toward decreased interaction throughout the year. The need for further study of the teacher/child "free play" interaction is clearly suggested.

Finally, the positive results of this research must be viewed in light of the small number of subjects and lack of tight controls. While these limitations make generalizations hazardous, the data do indicate a need for future study. The degree of possible social, cognitive and verbal gains in comparison to the small amount of inservice training required for teachers and leaders to obtain such results is impressive.

References

Dansky, J. L. "Temporary and Enduring Influences on Play and Children's Creative Thinking." *The Association for the Anthropological Study of Play Newsletter* 5 (1979): 7–8.

Dansky, J. L., and I. W. Silverman. "Effects of Play on Associative Fluency in Preschool-aged Children." *Developmental Psychology* 9 (1973): 38–43.

Durrett, E., and W. Huffman. "Playfulness and Divergent Thinking Among Mexican-American Children." *Journal of Home Economics* 60 (1968): 355–58.

Feitelson, D., and G. S. Ross. "The Neglected Factor—Play." *Human Development* 16 (1973): 202–23.

Flanders, N. *Analyzing Teaching Behavior*. London: Addison-Wesley, 1970.

Hutt, C., and R. Bhavnani. "Predictions From Play." In J. Bruner, A. Jolly and K. Sylva, eds., *Play—Its Role in Development and Evolution*. New York: Basic Books, 1976, pp. 216–19.

Krasnor, L. R., and D. J. Pepler. "The Study of Children's Play: Some Suggested Future Directions." In K. H. Rubin, ed., *New Directions for Child Development: Children's Play*. San Francisco: Jossey-Bass, 1980.

Lieberman, J. N. "Playfulness and Divergent Thinking: An Investigation of their Relationship at the Kindergarten Level." *Journal of Genetic Psychology* 107 (1965): 219–24.

———. *Playfulness: Its Relationship to Imagination and Creativity*. New York: Academic Press, 1977.

Lovinger, S. "Sociodramatic Play and Language Development." *Psychology in the Schools* 11 (1974): 313–20.

Manning, K., and A. Sharp. *Structuring Play in the Early Years at School*. London: Schools Council Publications, 1978.

———. *Structuring Play Workshops: Course Leader's Book*. London: Schools Council Publications, 1978.

———. *Videotape Notes*. London: Schools Council Publications, 1977.

Parten, M. B. "Social Participation Among Preschool Children." *Journal of Abnormal Social Psychology* 27 (1932): 243–69.

Saltz, E.; D. Dixon and J. Johnson. "Training Disadvantaged Preschoolers on Various Fantasy Activities: Effects on Cognitive Functioning and Impulse Control." *Child Development* 48 (1977): 367–80.

Smilansky, S. *The Effects of Sociodramatic Play on Disadvantaged Preschool Children*. New York: Wiley, 1968.

Sylva, K.; J. S. Bruner, P. Genova. "The Role of Play in the Problem-solving of Children 3–5 Years Old." In J. Bruner, A. Jolly and K. Sylva, eds., *Play—Its Role in Development and Evolution*. New York: Basic Books, 1976.

Sylva, K.; C. Roy and M. Painter. *Childwatching at Playgroup and Nursery School*. Ypsilanti, MI: High Scope Press, 1980.

Torrance, E. P. *Torrance Tests of Creative Thinking in Action and Movement*, Research Edition. Athens, GA: University of Georgia, 1975.

Effects of Teacher Training on Teachers and Children in Playground Settings

CYNTHIA WADE
Elementary School Principal
Kemp, Texas

Play is a vital learning process for the child because it provides the subject matter for activity, thinking and learning. As early as 1887, Froebel gave play central role in the educative process of the young child, asserting that spontaneous play was the most important avenue for children's learning. Frost & Kissinger (1976) conclude that play is the main avenue for children's development during the early years of life and, among recent researchers, Caplan (1973) extols the power of play as the most natural way for the child to use capabilities, grow and learn important skills.

Numerous educators have asserted the importance of play in the social development of the young child (Parten, 1932; Van-Alystyne, 1932; Shure, 1963; Iwanaga, 1972; Barnes, 1971; Rubin, Maioni & Hornung, 1976). Children learn about themselves and others through play and, in turn, develop social skills through their interaction with other children and adults. Studies by Almy (1967), Smilansky (1968), Piaget (1951), Rosen (1974), Garvey (1977) and Lieberman (1965) demonstrate the value of play in stimulating the intellectual development of the young child. Physical growth is directly enhanced by play (Arnaud, 1974; Frank, 1964; Frost & Kissinger, 1976). Play also provides the young child with numerous opportunities to learn about his own as well as the other person's emotional responses and to explore and deal with these in appropriate ways (Axline, 1947; Isaacs, 1956; Lovinger, 1974).

Despite ever-growing awareness of the importance of children's play, little recognition of the significance of the adult in enriching the play experience has emerged. Though numerous studies have been conducted on the importance of play in the development of the young child, investigations that examine the effects of adult intervention on the child's play choices in the *indoor* environment are sparse. The results from studies by Busse, Ree & Gutride (1970), Lovinger (1974), Singer & Singer (1974), Smilansky (1968), Tizard *et al.* (1976), Feitelson & Ross (1973) and Rosen (1974) describe the positive effects of adult intervention on the play behaviors of the young child, but no attention has been given to studying the effects of adult intervention on children's play choices on the *outdoor* play environment.

QUESTIONS OF INVESTIGATION

A recent investigation at a school in Austin, Texas, was directed to the following questions: 1. What are the differences in children's play behaviors before and after a training program for their teachers? 2. What are the differences in teacher playground behaviors before and after the teacher training program?

SUBJECTS

The subjects (N = 69) for the investigation were three- and four-year-old children enrolled in Briar Patch School in Austin, Texas. The 31 three-year-old children consisted of 19 boys and 12 girls ranging in age from three years, two months to three years, eleven months. Of the 38 four-year-old children, 22 were boys, 16 were girls ranging in age from four years, three months to four years, seven months. The children were predominately Caucasian and came from middle- and upper middle-class families.

Five teachers participated in the study— three teachers of three-year-old children and two teachers of four-year-olds.

SETTING

The preschool program at Briar Patch School provided large blocks of time for self-selected free play activities in the indoor and outdoor environments. The three-year-old children were on the playground from 9:00–9:45 A.M. daily, the four-year-olds from 9:45–10:30.

During outdoor free play, the children were permitted to choose from a wide variety of movable and fixed equipment. Stationary equipment included a sandbox, a concrete bike path, a water play area, one swing set with two swings, a second swing set with six swings, a tire climber, a treehouse platform with steps and an immovable Volkswagen steering wheel at the top of the platform, a slide, a geometric dome, four metal rocking horses, two rabbit hutches (with live mother rabbits and babies), a swimming pool, a cedar picnic table and two benches in the picnic area, a large four-sectioned wooden climbing structure, a rope climber suspended from four large trees and a tether ball pole. Movable equipment consisted of three large wooden crates, four metal barrels and three see-saws. Outdoor storage facilities provided children with ready access to scooters, tricycles, wagons, numerous sand toys, water play materials, balls, ropes and shovels.

DATA COLLECTION

The social play categories of Strickland (1979), cognitive play categories described by Smilansky (1968), the combined social-cognitive play categories of Strickland (1979) and modifications of the Instructional Phase and Affective Phase of Townsend's (1974) "System for Coding Interaction with Multiple Phases" (SCIMP) were used to observe the outdoor free play behaviors of the 69 nursery school children and their teachers.

Each three- and four-year-old child was observed for a 25-second interval and coded once daily for 30 school days. Teacher verbal and nonverbal playground behaviors were observed for ten-second intervals and coded for ten minutes daily for 30 school days. At the end of the first 15-day observation period, the investigator conducted a training program for the five teachers participating in the study to provide information on indirect teacher intervention techniques. After the teachers had been trained in a variety of indirect techniques, two coders observed the children for an additional 15-day period. A prepared checklist was used to observe children during outdoor free play. Each child was observed a total of 30 times over a six-week period for a total of 12 and one-half minutes in the outdoor play environment.

Verbal and nonverbal teacher playground behaviors were observed simultaneously for ten-second intervals and coded. Each teacher was observed 600 times over a six-week period in the pre-post observation phases for a total of 100 minutes in the outdoor environment. Throughout the observation period, periodic reliability tests were conducted to ensure the inter-rater reliability of .80 for both teacher observation instruments.

DATA ANALYSIS

The first task of data analysis was to tally the total number of play behaviors each child exhibited for each play category. The total number of verbal and nonverbal teacher playground behaviors exhibited for each category on both teacher observation instruments were tallied. Two-tailed chi-square tests were conducted to determine differences in the frequencies of the social, cognitive and combined social-cognitive play categories for boys and girls in the outdoor play environment. Additional chi-square tests were conducted to determine differences in the frequencies of teacher verbal and nonverbal playground behaviors.

A series of 5 (Teacher) $\times$ 2 (Pupil Sex) $\times$ 2 (Observational Periods in a repeated measures design) analyses of variance was computed for each social (solitary, parallel and group), cognitive (functional, dramatic, constructive and games with rules) and combined social-cognitive (solitary-functional, solitary-dramatic, solitary-constructive, solitary-games with rules, parallel-functional, parallel-dramatic, parallel-constructive, parallel-games with rules, group-functional, group-dramatic, group-constructive and group-games with rules) category of play. In addition, a series of 2 (Pupil Sex) × 2 (Observational Periods in a repeated measures design) analyses of variance was computed for each of the 14 verbal and 9 nonverbal categories of teacher playground behaviors.

RESULTS

Findings indicated that the play behaviors of nursery school children were significantly different for several of the play categories when compared prior to and following the special teacher training program. Significantly greater frequencies of the following types of children's play were found: parallel, group, constructive, dramatic, parallel-constructive, parallel-dramatic, group-functional, group-constructive and group-dramatic play for the total group of children, and for the girls and boys separately, and parallel-games with rules play for the boys. Solitary, functional, solitary-functional and solitary-dramatic play decreased for the total group of children, and for girls and boys separately, after the teacher training program. Group-games with rules play decreased for the total group of children and the boys after the program.

The verbal playground behaviors of teachers were significantly different for several of the SCIMP categories when compared before and after the teacher training program. A number of major findings were reported. Teachers engaged in more behaviors from the Preparatory, Dealing, Questioning, Extending, Accepting and Praising categories with the total group of children and for girls and boys separately. They also demonstrated a significant decrease in the Silence and Teacher Talk categories with the total group of children and for girls and boys separately. The nonverbal playground behaviors of teachers were significantly different for several of the SCIMP categories when compared before and after the program. Teachers engaged in significantly more behaviors from the Smiling, Positive Contact and Positive Nodding categories with the total group of children and for girls and boys separately after the training program. They also demonstrated a significant decrease in the No Visible Behavior category with the total group and for girls and boys separately. Other findings were consistent with the major findings that the teacher training program had significant effects on both children's and teachers' behaviors in the outdoor play setting.

IMPLICATIONS AND DISCUSSION

The finding that the special teacher training program had significant effects on both children's and teachers' behaviors in the outdoor play setting has important implications for teacher education.

First, an emphasis on the appropriateness of teaching techniques needs to be amplified. A key to successful teaching, indoors as well as on the playground, is knowing when to use what techniques. Before a teacher can become adept at making such decisions, knowledge of child development and behavior and learning theory would be most helpful. Teachers must be certain that the implementation of specific teaching techniques is congruent with theories of play and child development. Evidence from the present investigation indicates positive, short-term effects on children's outdoor play behaviors of a special teacher training program on teachers' verbal and nonverbal teaching techniques. It appears that increased teacher verbal and nonverbal intervention strategies simply accelerated what is now considered the "standard" progression of play behaviors for the young child.

The findings are generally consistent with current research in the field. The investigator expected slight changes in teacher playground behaviors; however, the numerous significant changes that emerged were not anticipated. Nevertheless, the changes in teacher behaviors proved to be desirable from the point of view of the teachers as well as the children in this investigation. The teachers' utilization of verbal and nonverbal teaching techniques proved valuable in stimulating higher levels of social, cognitive and social-cognitive play behaviors. The short-term effects of the training program were dramatic.

Second, teachers need to receive immediate feedback as to the effectiveness of their verbal and nonverbal interactions with children in outdoor as well as indoor play settings to facilitate and maintain improved teaching techniques. When teachers have opportunities to view their own behavior, intervention techniques can be refined. These opportunities can be had through the use of videotaping activities in the teacher education sequence.

Third, training in the systematic use of observational instruments such as SCIMP should be of help to the teacher in analyzing her/his own classroom and playground behaviors. Such systematic training should be an integral part of the school system's in-service program for the school year.

Fourth, in-service teacher education programs should help teachers develop an awareness of, and skill in, the appropriate use of several teacher verbal and nonverbal patterns when working with preschool and older children in classroom settings and the outdoor play environment. The teacher training program utilized in the present investigation would be a helpful tool in accomplishing this goal. A continued emphasis upon specific verbal and nonverbal behaviors throughout the school year would seem to assist teachers in understanding both their own teaching behaviors and the consequences of those behaviors on the children with whom they work daily. The teachers that participated in the present investigation felt very good about the change in playground behaviors. It stands to reason that if teachers become more excited about the teaching techniques they implement with children, more possibilities for learning can be provided for young children on the playground.

Fifth, it is important to know how much teacher training is adequate to bring about desired behavioral changes. Since such significant changes in teacher verbal and nonverbal playground behaviors resulted from a short teacher training program, one might speculate that a longer training period with additional periodic sessions spaced over three to six months would produce even more dramatic, sustained effects on the playground

behaviors of teachers. The discovery and manifestation of teaching skills take time. Quite possibly, a longer period would give teachers greater opportunities to incorporate teaching behaviors into their repetoire of teaching tactics and strategies in all environmental settings.

Sixth, the whole area of being able to utilize interaction analysis in the outdoor play setting opens the door to other questions. Do teachers demonstrate different verbal and nonverbal interactional patterns with preschool children in the indoor play environment? Do teachers have different interactional patterns when working with different groups of children? If, through research, answers to these questions could be ascertained, such data could make an important impact on the nature of early childhood education teacher training programs. If teachers could be shown data concerning the importance of adult-child interactions in all play settings, they could make conscious attempts to alter their verbal and nonverbal interaction patterns in a desirable direction. The SCIMP instrument could be especially useful in gathering such data.

References

Almy, M. "Spontaneous Play: An Avenue for Intellectual Development." *Young Children* 22 (1967): 265–77.

Arnaud, S. "Some Functions of Play in the Educative Process." *Childhood Education* 51, 2 (1974): 72–78.

Axline, V. *Play Therapy*. Boston: Houghton, 1947.

Barnes, K. "Preschool Play Norms: A Replication." *Developmental Psychology* 5 (1971): 99–103.

Busse, T.; M. Ree and M. Gutride. "Environmentally Enriched Classrooms and the Play Behavior of Negro Preschool Children." *Urban Education* 5 (1970): 128–40.

Caplan, F., and T. Caplan. *The Power of Play*. Garden City, NY: Anchor Press/Doubleday, 1973.

Feitelson, D., and G. Ross. "The Neglected Factor—Play." *Human Development* 16 (1973): 202–23.

Frank, L. "Role of Play in Child Development." *Childhood Education* 41, 2 (1964): 70–73.

Froebel, F. *The Education of Man*. New York: A. Lovell, 1885.

Frost, J., and J. Kissinger. *The Young Child and the Educative Process*. New York: Holt, 1976.

Garvey, C. *Play*. Cambridge, MA: Harvard University Press, 1977.

Isaacs, S. *The Nursery Years*. New York: Vanguard Press, 1936.

Iwanaga, M. "Development of Interpersonal Play Structure in Three, Four, and Five-year-old Children." *Journal of Research and Development in Education* 6, 3 (1973): 71–82.

Lieberman, J. "Playfulness and Divergent Thinking: Investigation of Their Relationship at the Kindergarten Level." *Journal of Genetic Psychology* 107 (1965): 219–24.

Lovinger, S. "Sociodramatic Play and Language Development in Preschool Disadvantaged Children." *Psychology in the Schools* 11 (1974): 313–20.

Parten, M. "Social Participation Among Preschool Children." *Journal of Abnormal and Social Psychology* 27 (1932): 243–69.

Piaget, J. *Play, Dreams and Imitation in Childhood.* New York: Norton, 1951.

Rosen, C. "The Effects of Sociodramatic Play on Problem-solving Behavior Among Culturally Disadvantaged School Children." *Child Development* 45 (1974): 920–27.

Rubin, K.; T. Maioni and M. Hornung. "Free Play Behaviors in Middle- and Lower-class Preschoolers: Parten and Piaget Revisited." *Child Development* 47 (1976): 414–19.

Shure, M. "Psychological Ecology of a Nursery School." *Child Development* 34 (1963): 979–92.

Singer, J., and D. Singer. "Fostering Imaginative Play in Preschool Children: Effects of Television-viewing and Direct Adult Modelling." Paper presented at the annual meeting of the APA, New Orleans, 1974. (ERIC Document Reproduction Service No. 089 873.)

Smilansky, S. *The Effect of Sociodramatic Play on Disadvantaged Preschoolers.* New York: Wiley, 1968.

Strickland, E. "Free Play Behaviors and Equipment Choices of Third Grade Children in Contrasting Play Environments." Doctoral Dissertation, The University of Texas at Austin, 1979.

Tizard, B. *et al.* "Play in Preschool Centres—I. Play Measures and Their Relation to Age, Sex and I.Q." *Journal of Child Psychology and Psychiatry* 17 (1976): 251–64.

——— . "Play in Preschool Centres—II. Effects on Play of the Child's Social Class and of the Educational Orientation of the Centre." *Journal of Child Psychology and Psychiatry* 17 (1976): 265–74.

——— . "Staff Behavior in Preschool Centres." *Journal of Child Psychology and Psychiatry* 17 (1976): 275–84.

Townsend, D. "A Comparison of the Classroom Interaction Patterns of Bilingual Early Childhood Teachers." Doctoral Dissertation, The University of Texas at Austin, 1974.

Van Alstyne, D. *Play Behavior and Choice of Play Materials of Preschool Children.* Chicago: University of Chicago Press, 1932.

Girl Play:
Sex Segregation in Friendships and Play Patterns of Preschool Girls

V. T. GERSHNER
Department of Educational Foundations
Texas Women's University, Denton

and

L. MOORE
Bock Child Care Center
Dallas, Texas

Since the 1930's sex-segregated play patterns have been documented consistently in observational studies of young children (Bianchi & Bakeman, 1978; Campbell, 1964; Challman, 1932; Clark, Wyon & Richards, 1969; Koch, 1944; Laosa & Brophy, 1972; Maccoby & Jacklin, 1974, 1978; Parten, 1933). While previously assumed to be a normal aspect of development, an alternative view explains same-sex-only play in terms of cultural models and differential systems of rewards and punishments that teach and maintain traditional sex role behaviors (Fagot & Patterson, 1969; Fling & Manosevitz, 1972; Hartup, 1970; Lansky, 1967; Lever, 1976; Maccoby & Jacklin, 1974; Pobregin, 1980). Friendships with peers play a critical role in the child's developing sense of identity and acquisition of social skills (Asher & Gottman, 1981; Bell, 1981; Hartup, 1970; Lewis & Rosenblum, 1975; Oden & Asher, 1977; Pogrebin, 1980). Extensive research in the last three decades has supported the position that sex segregation in play denies children access to a broad range of activities, skills and relationships (Block, Von der-Lippe & Block, 1973; Clark et al., 1969; Dweck, 1980; Eder & Hallinan, 1978; Fagot & Patterson, 1969; Hartley & Hardesty, 1964; Katz, 1979; Laosa & Brophy, 1972; Lever, 1976; Maccoby & Jacklin, 1974; Rosenberg & Sutton-Smith, 1959, 1960; Saegert & Hart, 1976; Serbin & Connor, 1977). Young girls

in particular seem to be damaged by these early socialization practices that tend to lead to loss of self-esteem, lack of motivation for achievement and limitations in future occupational choices (Hoffman, 1972; Horner, 1969; Kagan, 1964; Maccoby, 1966; Scheresky, 1976).

Positively sanctioned opportunities for girls to be involved in games, activities and social patterns traditionally labeled "feminine" in addition to those typically thought of as "masculine" would be especially valuable as preparation for a wider selection of job possibilities (Greenberg, 1978; Hennig & Jardim, 1977; Pogrebin, 1980; Sprung, 1978; Rivers, Barnett & Baruch, 1979). Increased liberties for cooperative play with opposite-sex as well as same-sex playmates might also lead to more positive social relationships that emphasize equality rather than differences between the sexes (Pogrebin, 1980; Serbin, Tonick & Sternglanz, 1977).

Purpose

Concerns about sex segregation in children's friendships and sex role stereotyping in play activities led to the design of a study to examine existing peer relationships and play patterns among preschool girls. An intervention program involving teacher reinforcement of cooperative play with opposite-sex playmates was implemented to determine whether a fixed schedule of contingent

319

reinforcement could increase opposite-sex cooperative play and modify peer preferences.

METHOD

The sample was comprised of 48 preschool girls enrolled in eight multiage classrooms in three United Way and federally funded developmental child care centers in Dallas, Texas during the summer of 1982. The children represented black, white and Hispanic ethnic groups and were from predominantly low income single-parent families.

Eight intact multiage classrooms were randomly assigned to experimental or control group status. Six classrooms had groups of 18 children with two teachers; two classrooms had nine children with one teacher. All teachers were paraprofessionals. Observations and treatment procedures were implemented during the free play sessions that were a familiar part of the daily classroom schedules.

Measures

Observations. Two-week observation periods were scheduled during free play sessions to collect pre- and posttreatment data. A time-sampling procedure was used three times per week, with the order of observations determined by daily random lists. Trained observers used Parten's levels of social play (Parten, 1932) in combination with sex of playmate designations derived by Serbin, Tonick & Sternglanz (1977). Activity choices were indicated by observation records of each child's play in 14 specified learning centers. These were grouped for analysis as proportions of time engaged in feminine-stereotyped, masculine-stereotyped and nonstereotyped activities.

Tests. The Peer Preference Test (McCandless & Marshall, 1957) was administered individually as a pre- and posttest measure of children's friendship choices. Individual, candid color photographs of each child's classmates were used as the stimuli for ranking preferred friends.

The Sex Role Learning Index (Edelbrock, 1976), providing subtest scores of sex role discrimination, sex role preference, and sex role confirmation, was administered individually as a pretest measure of sex role acquisition.

Treatment

During the three-week treatment phase, teachers in the experimental group classes were instructed to provide positive reinforcement at five-minute intervals to girls engaged in opposite-sex cooperative play, provided that the targeted events were occurring. Specialized training sessions were conducted with treatment group teachers to provide instruction and practice in the effective use of attention and positive praise. Teachers in the control group classes were instructed to follow normal procedures to facilitate constructive play during free play sessions.

Analyses of Data

Data collected from experimental and control groups were used to compare the method of intervention, defined as the application of contingent reinforcement techniques applied to occurrences of opposite-sex cooperative play during free play sessions. The null hypotheses were tested using multivariate analysis procedures to adjust for correlations among dependent variables. Posttest data were analyzed using multivariate analyses of covariance, with pretests serving as covariates, thus adjusting for any initial differences on pretest measures. A discriminant analysis was performed to identify the variables that contributed most to differentiation between the control and experimental groups. Nominal data were analyzed using chi square procedures for independent samples.

FINDINGS

Levels of Play. The experimental and control groups differed significantly in observed rates of opposite sex cooperative play. A multivariate analysis of covariance led to rejection of the null hypothesis concerning differences in overall patterns of play. A discriminant analysis selected solitary and opposite-sex cooperative play as the best discriminating variables. The data supported the research hypothesis that teacher attention and praise could effectively increase opposite-sex cooperative play. A by-product was a dramatic decrease in rates of solitary play. Relative stability of the effects of treatment may be inferred by the evidence of posttest changes in classroom behavior. The increase in opposite sex cooperative play appeared to be self-maintained when the reinforcement by teachers was discontinued.

Best Friends. The second hypothesis compared the experimental and control groups by number of opposite sex playmates selected as best friends. A chi square analysis revealed significant differences following the treatment. The null hypothesis was rejected at the .05 level of significance. The findings supported the research hypothesis that positive reinforcement for opposite-sex cooperative play could effectively modify peer preferences.

Activity Stereotypes. The experimental and control groups did not differ significantly in proportions of feminine-stereotyped, masculine-stereotyped and nonstereotyped activity choices. Findings indicated that girls in both groups preferred predominantly feminine-stereotyped activities, which included art, books, cooking and food preparation, dramatic play and music. Nonstereotyped activities, which included manipulatives, water play, hygiene activities such as hand washing and transitional activities were preferred more than masculine-stereotyped activities such as blocks and transportation toys, math, movement and motor skills and woodworking or construction.

Sex Role Learning. The Sex Role Learning Index was administered as a pretest only measure. A multivariate analysis of variance revealed no significant differences between the experimental and control groups. Girls in both groups demonstrated a high awareness of sex role stereotypes for their own sex and a more moderate awareness of stereotypes pertaining to the opposite sex. Sex role preference and sex role confirmation scores tended to be nonstereotypical. The findings indicated that although girls were aware of feminine stereotypes, their preferences included a variety of feminine-stereotyped and

masculine-stereotyped activities, as well as those they defined as nonstereotyped or appropriate for both girls and boys.

Intercorrelations. Canonical correlations were computed to compare the experimental and control groups in terms of relationships among the sets of dependent variables representing levels of play, stereotypes of activity choices and sex role learning subscores. No correlations were significant at the .05 level.

Age. An unhypothesized finding concerned the lack of significant correlations between age and levels of play or sex role learning. Previous studies have consistently reported age progressions in levels of social participation and in both knowledge of sex roles and preferences for sex-appropriate activities. In contrast, the present study found higher rates of cooperative play in children ranging in age from three to five. Similarly, sex role discrimination and preferences were not age related.

DISCUSSION

The findings of this study provide data to suggest the need for a re-examination of the role of the teacher, the classroom composition and the educational environment in child care settings. Implications for the design of play environments and the enhancement of children's learning through play warrant the consideration of all three factors.

Teacher Influence. The study clearly documented the powerful influence of preschool teachers on the play behavior of young children. Teacher acceptance and approval of opposite sex cooperative play allow children a broader choice of friends and playmates.

Classroom Composition. Multiage groupings, in contrast to straight-age groupings, may have accounted for the lack of differentiation in play behavior by age group. Multiage groupings appeared to provide expanded possibilities for social development and encouragement for increased levels of cooperative play among three-, four- and five-year-olds.

Educational Environment. A review of the educational environment, including the curriculum materials and classroom routines, might lead to the identification of practices that direct children toward stereotyped play activities. Girls may be missing experiences necessary to develop adequately mathematical concepts, visual-spatial skills, analytical and problem-solving skills, competence with tools, gross motor coordination and a general sense of mastery over the environment. Planned intervention programs might be required to promote increased opportunities for specific types of play that promote skills related to future careers in areas such as science, engineering, economics, architecture and business management.

IMPLICATIONS FOR PLAY

The encouragement of opposite sex cooperative play relates to preparing girls and boys for a more egalitarian society. The role of the preschool teacher may be pivotal in promoting the acceptance of both same sex and opposite sex friendships. Multiage groupings might provide more opportunities for positive social relationships across age groups. A nonsexist educational environment allows children the freedom to explore a variety of activities and roles without regard to gender.

References

Asher, S., and J. Gottman. *The Development of Children's Friendships.* New York: Cambridge University, 1981.
Bell, R. *Worlds of Friendship.* Beverly Hills, CA: Sage, 1981.
Bianchi, B., and R. Bakeman. "Sex-typed Affiliation Preferences Observed in Preschoolers: Traditional and Open School Differences." *Child Development* 49 (1978): 910–12.
Block, J.; A. Von der Lippe and J. H. Block. "Sex-role Socialization Patterns: Some Personality Concomitants and Environmental Antecedents." *Journal of Consulting and Clinical Psychology* 41 (1973): 321–41.
Campbell, J. "Peer Relations in Childhood." In M. Hoffman and L. W. Hoffman, eds., *Review of Child Development Research* Vol. 1. New York: Sage, 1964.
Challman, R. "Factors Influencing Friendships Among Preschool Children." *Child Development* 3 (1932): 146–58.
Clark, A.; S. Wyon and M. Richards. "Free Play in Nursery School Children." *Journal of Child Psychology and Psychiatry* 10 (1969): 205–16.
Dweck, C. "Social-cognitive Processes in Children's Friendships." In S. Asher and J. Gottman, eds., *The Development of Children's Friendships.* New York: Cambridge University, 1980.
Edelbrock, C. "Sex Role Discrimination, Preference, and Confirmation in Preschool Aged Children." Doctoral Dissertation, Oregon-State University, 1976.
Eder, D., and M. Hallinan. "Sex Differences in Children's Friendships." *American Sociological Review* 43 (1978): 237–50.
Fagot, B., and G. Patterson. "An *in vivo* Analysis of Reinforcing Contingencies for Sex-role Behaviors in the Preschool Child." *Developmental Psychology* 1 (1969): 563–68.
Fling, S., and M. Manosevitz. "Sex Typing in Nursery School Children's Interests." *Developmental Psychology* 7 (1972): 146–52.
Greenberg, S. *Right From the Start: A Guide to Nonsexist Child Rearing.* Boston: Houghton Mifflin, 1978.
Hartley, R., and F. Hardesty. "Children's Perceptions of Sex Roles in Childhood." *Journal of Genetic Psychology* 195 (1964): 43–51.
Hartup, W. "Peer Interaction and Social Organization." In P. Mussen, ed., *Carmichael's Manual of Child Psychology* Vol. 2. New York: Wiley, 1970.
Hennig, M., and A. Jardim. *The Managerial Woman.* New York: Anchor/Doubleday, 1977.
Hoffman, L. W. "Early Childhood Experiences and Women's Achievement Motives." *Journal of Social Issues* 28 (1972): 129–55.
Horner, M. "Fail: Bright Women." *Psychology Today* 3 (1969): 36–38, 62.
Kagan, J. "Acquisition and Significance of Sex Typing and Sex Role Identity." In M. Hoffman and L. W. Hoffman, eds., *Review of Child Development Research* Vol. 1. New York: Russell Sage, 1964.
Katz, P. A. "The Development of Female Identity." *Sex Roles* 5 (1979): 155–78.
Koch, H. L. "A Study of Some Factors Conditioning the Social Distance Between the Sexes." *Journal of Social Psychology* 20 (1944): 79–104.
Lansky, L. "The Family Structure also Effects the Model: Sex-role Attitudes in Parents of Preschool Children." *Merrill-Palmer Quarterly* 13 (1967): 139–50.
Laosa, L., and J. Brophy. "Effects of Sex and Birth Order on Sex-role Development and Intelligence Among Kindergarten Children." *Developmental Psychology* 6 (1972): 409–15.
Lever, J. "Sex Differences in the Games Children Play." *Social Problems* 23 (1976): 478–87.
Lewis, M., and L. Rosenblum, eds. *Friendship and Peer Relations.* New York: Wiley-Interscience, 1975.
Maccoby, E. E., ed. *The Development of Sex Differences.* Stanford, CA: Stanford University, 1966.
Maccoby, E. E., and C. N. Jacklin. *The Psychology of Sex Differences.* Standford, CA: Stanford University, 1974.
——— . "Social Behavior at 33 Months in Same-sex and Mixed-sex Dyads." *Child Development* 49 (1978): 557–69.
McCandless, B., and H. Marshall. "A Picture Sociometric Technique for Preschool Children and Its Relation to Teacher Judgments of Friendship." *Child Development* 28 (1957): 139–47.
Oden, S., and S. Asher. "Coaching Children in Social Skills for Friendship Making." *Child Development* 48 (1977): 495–506.
Parten, M. "Social Participation Among Preschool Children." *Journal of Abnormal and Social Psychology* 27 (1932): 243–69.
——— . "Social Play Among Preschool Children." *Journal of Abnormal and Social Psychology* 28 (1933): 136–47.
Pogrebin, L. C. *Growing Up Free: Raising Your Child in the 80's.* New York: McGraw-Hill, 1980.
Rivers, C.; R. Barnett and G. Baruch. *Beyond Sugar and Spice: How Women Grow, Learn, and Thrive.* New York: Putnam, 1979.

Rosenberg, B. G., and B. Sutton-Smith. "The Measurement of Masculinity and Feminity in Children." *Child Development* 39 (1959): 373–80.

——— . "A Revised Conception of Masculine-Feminine Differences in Play Activities." *Journal of Genetic Psychology* 96 (1960): 165–70.

Saegert, S., and R. Hart. "The Development of Environmental Competence in Girls and Boys." In P. Burnett, ed., *Women in Society*. Chicago: Maaroufa, 1976.

Scheresky, R. "The Gender Factor in Six- to Ten-year-old Children's Views of Occupational Roles." *Psychological Reports* 38 (1976): 1207–10.

Serbin, L., and J. Connor. "Behaviorally Based Masculine- and Feminine-activity-preference Scales for Preschoolers: Correlates with Other Classroom Behaviors and Cognitive Tests." *Child Development* 48 (1977): 1411–16.

Serbin, L.; I. Tonick and S. Sternglanz. "Shaping Cooperative Cross-sex Play." *Child Development* 48 (1977): 924–29.

Sprung, B. *Perspectives on Non-sexist Early Childhood Education*. New York: Teachers College, 1978.

Play and the Preterm Infant: Implications for Parent Education

FRANCINE H. NICHOLS
Department of Nursing
Wichita State University, Kansas

Social interactions between a mother and infant are considered to be one of the earliest forms of play. Stern (1977) defined this early play interaction as a:

bounded period of time, anywhere from seconds to many minutes when one or both members focus their attention on the social behaviors of the other partner and react to these behaviors with social behaviors of their own (p. 77).

Play is an essential element in a harmonious mother-infant interaction. When it is missing or infrequent, interactions between the mother and infant appear asynchronous or disorganized. Play activity must be appropriate for the developmental age of the infant. If the mother plays games too difficult for her infant, the infant ceases to respond and the interaction stops because of the lack of positive feedback (Tronick, Adamson, Wise, Als & Brazelton, 1975).

The purpose of this article is to point out differences in development between the fullterm infant and the "healthy" preterm infant with discussion of the implications of these differences for parents and professionals involved in parent education. Although play interactions with both parents are important, the focus here is primarily on mother-infant interaction.

Play during infancy is considered important in the development of communication and positive parent-infant interactions (Cohen & Beckwith, 1979; Brazelton, Koslowski & Main, 1974). However, Field (1979a) reported that parents of preterm infants engage in significantly less play activity with their infants than parents of fullterm infants. There are qualitative as well as quantitative differences between play interactions of parents with their preterm infants and play interactions of parents with their fullterm infants. Field (1979b) described mothers of preterm infants as more active, more persistent and less imitative in their play behaviors when compared with mothers of fullterm infants. A study by Goldberg, Brachfeld and Divitto (1980) revealed that parents of preterm infants tended to use more object play than parents of fullterm infants. Bakeman and Brown (1980) emphasized that, in contrast to mothers of fullterm infants, mothers of preterm infants had to assume the major responsibility for initiating and maintaining interactions with their often listless infants.

Small preterm infants are often separated from their mothers for long periods during the early newborn period, a period considered important in the development of social interactions between mother and child. Initially, this separation was thought to be the primary factor in the decreased play behaviors between mothers and preterm infants, but more recent findings suggest that separation may be less important than the difficulty of the infant. Field (1979a) explored the effects of both separation and difficult infants on early game playing between parents and infants. Mothers of postterm infants as well as mothers of preterm infants were less playful than mothers of fullterm infants. More important, no difference was found in mother-infant play behaviors between the preterm and the postterm group. The preterm infants, however, had remained in the hospital for an extended length of time after birth, whereas the postterm infants had left the hospital with their mothers shortly after birth. This finding suggests that the difficult nature of these babies was more a factor in the decreased play behaviors than was the separation of mother and infant.

STAGES OF BEHAVIORAL ORGANIZATION IN THE PRETERM INFANT

Preterm infants lack the control over their autonomic, motoric and state regulation systems that would allow them to interact with their environment (Als, Lester & Brazelton 1979). Gorski, Davison and Brazelton (1979) describe three stages of behavioral development in the preterm infant: physiologic organization or "in-turning" stage; beginning response to the environment or "coming out" stage and the stage of reciprocity where the infant is capable of social interaction with the environment.

In the stage of physiologic organization, all the energies of the preterm infant are directed towards maintaining stability. The autonomic nervous system is exquisitely sensitive to all external stimuli. The smallest stimuli may cause great skin color, respiratory or cardiac changes. The infant's movements are purposeless, jerky, sudden and include many Moro reflexes. These infants are incapable of social interaction with their environment. Usually, mothers first see their preterm infants while they are in this unresponsive and unstable stage. As expected, the mother's reaction is, "Will my baby be all right?" The length of this stage is negatively related to the gestational age of the infant. And if the infant has complications such as respiratory distress syndrome or metabolic disorders, the length of the stage of physiologic organization increases.

In the second stage of behavioral development, the preterm infant gains increased autonomic control and begins to develop predictive patterns of interaction with the environment, but response is variable. The infant can achieve a quite alert state for brief periods. If an interaction is started when the infant is in the alert state, he or she can react in a coordinated manner. But mothers may not see their infants at the most appropriate time for interacting. If they try to interact with their infants when they are not in an alert state, the infants may respond with sudden, jerky movements and rapid changes in skin color, respiratory and cardiac status characteristics of the earlier stage of physi-

ologic organization. Infants differ in their ability to cope with external stimuli. Therefore, the response behaviors of each infant must be evaluated.

The mother's concern about caring for her infant emerges during the "coming-out" stage and remains prominent for months to come. Often anxious and worried, her focus changes to, "How am I going to care for my baby?" She wants to do the right thing in the right way. During this time, because of the infant's immature behavioral development, mother-infant interactions are similar to a one-way conservation. The mother contributes much to the interaction, while the preterm infant contributes little, if anything. These early interactions and the mother's concern about caring for her infant condition the mother for future interactions.

The third stage, reciprocity, is achieved when the infant can breathe, eat and respond to stimuli in a specific and predictable manner. The infant has increased patterns of alertness, and the amount of alertness is a reflection of interest. When preterm infants have gained this consistent ability to interact with their environment, they are dismissed from the high risk nursery. However, most preterm infants still respond differently in the stage of reciprocity from fullterm infants born with the capability of interacting socially with the environment. The unique characteristics of the preterm infant also influence future interactions between the mother and child.

CHARACTERISTICS OF PREMATURE INFANTS

Emory and Walker (1982) reported that the most significant difference between preterm and fullterm infants was in the attention and orienting responses. Preterm infants were lethargic, less responsive to stimuli and could maintain an alert state for only brief periods of time. Field (1979b) described preterm infants during face-to-face interactions with their mothers as less attentive and more fretful and squirming than fullterm infants. Although no difference was found in interactive processes between the preterm infants at 40 weeks conceptional age and fullterm infants, Telzrow, Kang, Mitchell, Ashworth and Barnard (1982) reported that preterm infants had an all-or-none response to stimuli. Preterm infants were flaccid and had poor motor control. Yet once aroused, they had higher activity levels than fullterm infants. Moreover, the preterm infants were easily overstimulated; they became agitated and were unable to quiet themselves.

When compared with caring for a fullterm infant, caring for a preterm infant presents unique problems for a mother. The preterm infant has a weak cry and is unable to provide clear distress signals (DiVitto & Goldberg, 1979). The mother of a fullterm infant must learn how to respond to her child's definite cries of discomfort or hunger. In contrast, the mother of the preterm infant must learn to determine and anticipate her infant's needs. Feeding time is usually an enjoyable time for mother and fullterm infant, a time when play behaviors often first occur between them. But for the mother of a preterm infant, feeding time can be frustrating because the infant is sleepy and often difficult to feed.

During early interactions, the mother of a preterm infant is denied the pleasurable feedback that mothers of fullterm infants experience so easily and often. It is probable that the physical appearance of the small, fragile-looking preterm infant, in contrast to the plump and sturdy fullterm infant, influences the mother-infant interaction.

Field (1979b) reported that mothers of preterm infants used more visual, tactile, auditory and vestibular stimulation during interactions with their infants than mothers of fullterm infants. This increased stimulation resulted in aversive behaviors—gaze aversion, fussing and squirming—by the preterm infant. In her efforts to communicate, the very active mother in trying to interact with her preterm infant may cause the infant to become even more unresponsive. Crawford (1982) reported preterm infants behaved more and more like fullterm infants as they grew. Yet the mothers of preterm infants never did spend as much time interacting as mothers of fullterm infants.

PROMOTING SOCIAL DEVELOPMENT

Research shows that the social development (See Table 1) of preterm infants can be improved using infant stimulation techniques. Later studies support the findings of these earlier studies. While the infant is in the high risk nursery, the mother receives information related to infant stimulation, such as: your baby likes patterns and novelty; your baby prefers high contrast colors like black and white (Infant Stimulation Facts, 1982).

Although infant stimulation therapy is beneficial for the preterm infant and may be sufficient for promoting development until the infant reaches the gestational age of 38 to 40 weeks, Schaefer, Hatcher and Barglow (1980) assert the concept is too narrow because it does not adequately emphasize the importance of social interactions between the mother and infant, which should be a smooth and fluid cycle of mother-infant play behaviors.

THE MOTHER-INFANT PLAY CYCLE

Ideally, the mother-infant play cycle (See Table 2) is a reciprocal interaction with each step progressing to greater enjoyment for both mother and child. But what effect does prematurity have on the cycle of mother-infant play interactions? Ten mothers of preterm infants were asked, "How did you play with your baby during the first months after you brought your baby home from the hospital?" One mother responded, "Play, no one told me I should play with him!" She went on to say, "Every time I looked at him I worried. He probably wanted to go back to the hospital." Another mother said, "She wasn't much fun to play with." This mother described how her preterm infant became irritable and difficult to soothe. She "learned" not to disturb the infant any more than was absolutely necessary. Several mothers commented that they "didn't really play" with their preterm infants when they were small.

The mothers interviewed had several characteristics in common: 1) they all provided excellent care for their preterm infants; 2) they were all knowledgeable about infant stimulation therapy and had used in-

Table 1
Effects of Stimulation on Social Behaviors of the Preterm Infant

Type of Stimulation	Results
Extra Handling	Quieter and less crying (Hasselmeyer, 1964)
	Increase in visual exploratory behavior (White & Castle, 1964)
	Improved visual attention because of decreased attentiveness to familiar stimuli and increased attentiveness to novel stimuli (McNichol, 1974)
	Faster rate of social development (Kramer et al., 1975)
Extra Handling and Stroking	Improved developmental status at six months of age as evidenced by higher scores on the Bayley Scales of Infant Development (Solkoff et al., 1969)
Extra Handling and Colored Mobiles	Improved interactive responses at time of discharge from hospital as evidenced by higher scores on the Brazelton Neonatal Behavior Assessment Scale (Scarr-Salapetek and Williams, 1973)
Recording of Woman's Voice	Increased auditory and tactile responsiveness (Katz, 1971)
Rocking Hammocks	Increased visual orientation (Neal, 1968)

Table 2
Mother-Infant Play Cycle

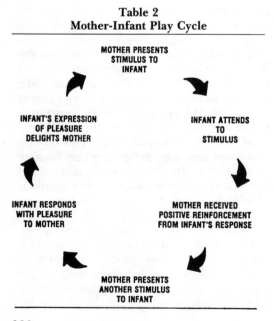

MOTHER PRESENTS STIMULUS TO INFANT

INFANT ATTENDS TO STIMULUS

MOTHER RECEIVED POSITIVE REINFORCEMENT FROM INFANT'S RESPONSE

MOTHER PRESENTS ANOTHER STIMULUS TO INFANT

INFANT RESPONDS WITH PLEASURE TO MOTHER

INFANT'S EXPRESSION OF PLEASURE DELIGHTS MOTHER

fant stimulation techniques with their infants during the early infancy period; 3) playing with their infants during this period of time had not been a pleasurable or rewarding experience and 4) none of the mothers appeared to realize the importance of play in the social development of their infants. In fact, to most of the mothers, playing with their infants during the early months at home seemed to have frivolous overtones when compared with the important and time-consuming activities of physical care of the infants.

Mother-infant play between a mother and her fullterm infant is usually a continuous cycle flowing easily from one step to the next. With the preterm infant the mother-infant play cycle is often interrupted at the second step, as the infant may be unresponsive or difficult to arouse to an active alert state. If the mother achieves a positive interaction and offers an additional stimulus, the cycle may break down when the infant responds with skin color changes, projectile vomiting or other signs of overstimulation. As is typical of the "all or none" response, the preterm infant may become fretful and difficult to quiet.

Although teaching a mother infant stimulation techniques is important to the growth and development of her infant, use of these techniques does not ensure that a mother will "play" with her child. Though mothers are advised to integrate the infant stimulation techniques during play, these techniques often become just another set of tasks to be completed among the many care-giving activities. Bromwich (1976), describing her model of infant intervention, emphasized that the essential first level of maternal behavior was that the mother "enjoys being with her infant" (p. 440). Preterm infant mothers need to know the *importance* of play in the social development of their children if they are to be expected to include play in their activities with the infant during the early months. Because of the early conditioning to an unresponsive and unstable infant, they may need to learn *how to play* with their infants.

FRAMEWORK FOR ASSESSMENT: MOTHER-INFANT PLAY INTERACTION SCALE

The Mother-Infant Play Interaction Scale (MIPIS)[1] is designed to measure the reciprocity of responses between the mother and infant during unstructured play interactions (Walker & Thompson, 1982). The MIPIS (See Table 3) is composed of three subscales: The Maternal Subscale, which measures the mother's attempts to elicit social behaviors from her infant; the Infant Subscale, which measures the infant's responsiveness to the mother's socialization attempts and the Dyadic Subscale, which measures the synchrony or "fit" between the mother and infant during the play interaction. Each item on the MIPIS

---

[1] Copies of the MIPIS and information on reliability training can be obtained by writing Lorraine Walker, R.N., Ed.D., The University of Texas at Austin, School of Nursing, 1700 Red River, Austin, Texas 78701.

has defined and easily rated behaviors. Ratings of 1 are associated with negative behaviors, while ratings of 5 are associated with positive behaviors. For example, behaviors for item two, Maternal Expression of Affect, are:

1—Mother appears tense, worried, and/or annoyed. Frowns at infant or otherwise shows displeasure.
2—Mother appears preoccupied and aloof. May frown at infant.
3—Flat or bland expression.
4—Mother appears attentive and involved with interaction. May smile at infant.
5—Mother appears to express pleasure and tenderness. Mother shifts expression in response to infant's behavior. Smiles at infant (Walker & Thompson, 1982, p. 197).

The MIPIS was developed to evaluate videotapes of five-minute sessions of unstructured play between 69 mothers and their fullterm infants, age four to six weeks. From a research perspective, little is known about the clinical application of the MIPIS. However, it does provide a valuable framework for assessing play interactions between mother and infant. The contributions of both mother and infant to the play interaction and the "fit" between them can be observed and rated in about ten to 15 minutes. Problem areas can be identified, and measures to improve the play interactions between mother and infant can then be implemented. Although the MIPIS may be useful for assessing mother-infant interactions in the high risk nursery, it is more appropriate for assessing mother-infant play when the infant has reached the behavioral developmental stage of reciprocity—at the time of discharge from the high risk nursery and in the early months thereafter.

STRATEGIES FOR INCREASING PLAY BETWEEN MOTHER AND INFANT

Often mothers of preterm infants are overwhelmed by the amount and detail of information they receive about caring for

329

TABLE 3. MOTHER-INFANT PLAY INTERACTION SCALE

	1	2	3	4	5
1. Maternal holding style	1	2	3	4	5
2. Maternal expression of affect	1	2	3	4	5
3. Maternal expression of affect—quality of contingency to infant	1	2	3	4	5
4. Maternal care-giving style	1	2	3	4	5
5. Predominant infant wakeful response level	1	2	3	4	5
6. Predominant infant mood/affect	1	2	3	4	5
7. Maternal visual interaction	1	2	3	4	5
8. Infant visual interaction	1	2	3	4	5
9. Style of play—animate versus inanimate—interaction	1	2	3	4	5
10. Maternal vocalization style—general (tone and content)	1	2	3	4	5
11. Maternal vocalization style—quantity of contingency (to I)	1	2	3	4	5
12. Maternal attempts at smile elicitation	1	2	3	4	5
13. Kinesthetic quality of interaction	1	2	3	4	5
14. Overall dyadic quality of interaction	1	2	3	4	5
15. Synchrony of affect	1	2	3	4	5
16. Termination of interaction	1	2	3	4	5

Total score:_____ Maternal Subscale:_____ Infant Subscale:_____
                    (Items 1–4, 7, 9–13)   (Items 5, 6, 8)
Dyadic Subscale:_____
(Items 14–16)

From Walker and Thompson (1982, p. 193). Reprinted with permission.

their infants. Thus, it is best if information on mother-infant play is presented as broad concepts that a mother can easily integrate into her daily activities. The first essential step in improving mother-infant play is that the mother must understand that the preterm infant's ability to respond to the environment is based on the infant's stage of behavioral development. Next, she needs specific strategies she can use to interact appropriately with her child.

The following approaches are useful in improving mother-infant play: 1) Encourage the mother to take time each day to "enjoy" her infant and emphasize the importance of this "play time" for both mother and infant; 2) Tell the mother to mimic her infant's behavior, which increases the appropriateness of the mother's response to the infant's cues; and 3) Have the mother observe her infant carefully for signs of increasing alertness during interactions that signify the infant's readiness for new activities or signs of fatigue during interactions that indicate the need to decrease stimuli and end the interaction.

NEEDED RESEARCH

Although we find much discussion on theories of play, development of play behaviors in children, relationship between play and the growth and development of a child and play behaviors between parents and their children, play and the social development of the preterm infant are relatively untouched

330

areas of investigation. Among questions to be raised are: How do play behaviors develop in the preterm infant? What are the differences in play behaviors between the fullterm and the preterm infant? Which approaches are most helpful in increasing a mother's understanding of the behavioral development of her preterm infant and assisting her to read her infant's cues? What strategies are most effective in enhancing play behaviors between infant and the mother? What effect does teaching the mother to read and respond to her infant's cues have on the social development of the infant or on the mother's attitudes toward her child and her competency as a mother? Is play behavior between the mother and her preterm infant predictive of maternal-infant attachment?

CONCLUSION

With the advent of aggressive medical approaches, many more preterm infants live today, some beginning life as small as one pound. These infants require much care, often for long periods of time. During this author's discussions with mothers of preterm infants about play interactions, it was apparent that many mothers did not have the enjoyable play interactions that mothers of fullterm infants experience so easily. It is evident that we need to see information on the importance of play incorporated into the education of parents with preterm infants in high risk nurseries and parent education classes. In the literature on infant stimulation, the four R's of infant stimulation are often found: rhythm, reciprocity, repetition and reinforcement. The two P's of mother-infant play are of equal importance! These are promoting mother-infant interactions that are *pleasurable* for both individuals and helping mothers to realize the importance of play in the *promotion* of growth and development of their infants.

References

Als, H.; B. Lester and T. Brazelton. "Dynamics of the Behavioral Organization of the Premature Infant: A Theoretical Perspective." In T. Field, A. Sostek, S. Goldberg and H. Shuman, eds., *Infants Born at Risk: Behavior and Development*. New York: SP Medical and Scientific Books, 1979.

Bakeman, R., and J. Brown. "Analyzing Behavioral Sequences: Differences Between Preterm and Fullterm Infant-Mother Dyads During the First Months of Life." In D. Sawin, R. Hawkins, L. Walker and J. Penticuff, eds., *Exceptional Infant* Vol. 4. New York: Brunner/Mazel, 1980.

Brazelton, T.; B. Koslowski and M. Main. "The Origins of Reciprocity: The Early Mother-Infant Interaction." In M. Lewis and L. Rosenblum, eds., *The Effect of the Infant on Its Caregiver*. New York: Wiley, 1974.

Bromwich, R. "Focus on Maternal Behavior in Infant Intervention." *American Journal of Orthopsychiatry* 46, 3 (1976): 439–45.

Cohen, S., and L. Beckwith. "Preterm Infant Interaction with the Caregiver in the First Year of Life and Competence at Age Two." *Child Development* 50 (1979): 767–76.

Crawford, J. "Mother-Infant Interaction in Premature and Full-term Infants." *Child Development* 53 (1982): 957–62.

Divitto, B., and S. Goldberg. "The Effects of Newborn Medical Status on Early Parent-Infant Interaction." In T. Field, A. Sostek, S. Goldberg and H. Shuman, eds., *Infants Born at Risk: Behavior and Development*. New York: SP Medical and Scientific Books, 1979.

Emory, E., and E. Walker. "Relationship Between Birth Weight and Neonatal Behavior." In L. Lipsitt and T. Field, *Infant Behavior and Development: Perinatal Risk and Newborn Behavior*. Norwood, NJ: Ablex, 1982.

Field, T. "Games Parents Play with Normal and High-risk Infants." *Child Psychiatry and Human Development* 10, 1 (1979a): 41–48.

————. "Interaction Pattern of Preterm and Term Infants." In T. Field, A. Sostek, S. Goldberg and H. Shuman, eds., *Infants Born at Risk: Behavior and Development*. New York: SP Medical and Scientific Books, 1979b.

Goldberg, S.; S. Brachfeld and B. Divitto. "Feeding, Fussing, and Play: Parent-Infant Interaction in the First Year as a Function of Prematurity and Perinatal Medical Problems." In T. Field, S. Goldberg, D. Stern and A. Sostek, eds., *High-Risk Infants and Children: Adult and Peer Interactions*. New York: Academic Press, 1980.

Gorski, P.; M. Davison and T. Brazelton. "Stages of Behavioral Organization in the High-risk Neonate: Theoretical and Clinical Considerations." *Seminars in Perinatology* 3, 1 (1979): 61–71.

Hasselmeyer, E. "Handling and Premature Infant Behavior: An Experimental Study of the Relationship Between Handling and Selected Physiological, Pathological, and Behavioral Indices Related to Body Functioning Among a Group of Prematurely Born Infants who Weighed Between 1,501 and 2,000 Grams at Birth and were Between the Ages of Seven and Twenty-eight Days of Life." *Dissertation Abstracts* 24 (1964): 7.

Infant Stimulation Facts (poster). Los Angeles, CA: Infant Stimulation Education Association, 1982.

Katz, V. "Auditory Stimulation and Development Behavior of the Premature Infant." *Nursing Research* 20 (1971): 196–201.

Kramer, M.; I. Chammorrol; D. Green and F. Knudtson. "Extra Tactile Stimulation of the Premature Infant." *Nursing Research* 24 (1975): 324–54.

McNichols, T. "Some Effects of Different Programs of Enrichment on the Development of Premature Infants in the Hospital Nursery." *Dissertation Abstracts* 34, 9B (1974): 4707–09.

Neal, M. "Vestibular Stimulation and Development Behavior of the Small Premature Infant." *Nursing Research* 3 (1968): 2–5.

Scarr-Salapatek, S., and M. Williams. "The Effects of

Early Stimulation on Low-weight Infants." *Child Development* 44 (1973): 94–101.

Schaefer, M.; R. Hatcher and P. Barglow. "Prematurity and Infant Stimulation: A Review of Research." *Child Psychiatry and Human Development* 10, 4 (1980): 199–212.

Solkoff, N.; S. Yaffe; D. Weintraub and B. Blase. "Effects of Handling on Subsequent Development of Premature Infants." *Developmental Psychology* 1 (1969): 765–68.

Stern, D. *The First Relationship: Mother and Infant.* Cambridge, MA: Harvard University Press, 1977.

Telzrow, R.; R. Kang; S. Mitchell; C. Ashworth and K. Barnard. "An Assessment of the Behavior of the Preterm Infant at 40 Weeks Conceptional Age." In L. Lipsitt and T. Field, eds., *Infant Behavior and Development: Perinatal Risk and Newborn Behavior.* Norwood, NJ: Ablex, 1982.

Tronick, E.; L. Adamson; S. Wise; H. Als and T. Brazelton. "Mother-Infant Face to Face Interaction." In S. Gosh, ed., *Biology and Language.* New York: Academic Press, 1975.

Walker, L., and E. Thompson. "Mother-Infant Interaction Play Scale." In S. Humenick, *Analysis of Current Assessment Strategies in the Health Care of Young Children and Childbearing Families.* Norwalk, CT: Appleton-Century-Crofts, 1982.

White, B., and P. Castle. "Visual Exploratory Behavior Following Postnatal Handling of Human Infants." *Perceptual Motor Skills* 18 (1964): 497–502.

Strengthening Family Ties in Play Settings

R. Tim Nicosia, Michael Willoughby, and Barbara Hatcher
Southwest Texas State University, San Marcos

and

Jody Nicosia
Crockett Elementary School
San Marcos, Texas

The purpose of this article is to emphasize the value of parental involvement in children's play through sharing inexpensive and practical ways to strengthen family ties in play settings and provide an understanding of activities that parents and teachers can use to establish play environments at home and school.

THEORIES AND RESEARCH ON THE VALUES OF PLAY

Based on the work of Piaget, which stresses the importance of play as the vehicle through which children develop new and better cognitive skills, Yawkey (1978) suggests that play is interrelated with thinking skills and intellectual development and is a dynamic process in its own right. It is linked to intellectual development through the elements of transformation (the intellectual ability to change oneself into some object, person or situation) and language (the intellectual capacity to communicate in ways that permit understanding). Play exercises the intellect because a child thinks and acts as if he or she were another person, thing or situation.

Isenberg and Jacobs (1982) state: "Through many repeated play experiences, children can clarify and master many fundamental physical, social, and intellectual skills and concepts" (p. 11). Frost and Kissinger (1976) note, "In play the child tests his limits to find out what he can and cannot do. He exercises persistence and problem solving and makes discoveries for himself as he plays" (p. 350).

Lieberman (1977) studied the play of kindergarten children as it relates to divergent thinking. Results of the investigation indicated a significant relationship between children's playfulness scores and aspects of divergent reasoning. Sylva, Bruner and Genova (1976), studying the effects of play on young children's problem-solving behavior, noted that children allowed to use free play with specific materials exhibited more problem-solving ability, goal-directed behavior and greater persistence than treatment groups. In addition, Garvey (1977) substantiated the importance of peer play for children's acquisition of communicative and social interactive skills.

Jerome L. Singer, Practical Applications of Research (PAR, 1982), summarizes his research and that of others by noting 12 benefits of children's play:

○ *Sheer fun*—fun is essential to growth and is a strong motivation for every kind of learning.
○ *Imagery practice*—an external and internal communication-related skill.
○ *Rehearsing new vocabulary*—connecting words and images, understanding context.
○ *Persistence*—developing a sequenced attention span to follow story lines.
○ *Self-entertainment and waiting ability.*
○ *Role-taking and empathy practice*—learning to put one's self in the other person's place.
○ *Decentering and advancing cognitive orientation*—learning how to get around in the external world.
○ *Preparation for reading.*
○ *Alternative responses to aggression.*
○ *Working through conflict.*
○ *Leadership and cooperation.*
○ *Resistance to television addiction* (p. 3).

333

PARENTS AND PLAY

Can parents influence the quality of children's play? Phinney, Dittmann and Huebner (1979) suggest two important findings. Through play children learn about themselves, other people and the physical world; parents can enrich their children's play by playing with them and providing new experiences, play materials and playmates. "By watching and joining in their children's play, parents enjoy and understand their children better" (p. 4).

Segal and Adcock (1982) suggest that by participating in their children's imaginative play, parents may be able to understand better their children's feelings, resolve parent-child conflicts, communicate parental values and build parent-child relationships based on mutual respect.

Isenberg and Jacobs (1982), suggest that parents and teachers can improve their children's play by:

○ Watching children play. In this way they can learn about the likes and dislikes, favorite themes and interests.
○ Being a model for playfulness. Since children learn from imitating adults, parents can help children play by asking questions or making comments.
○ Playing with children. In so doing, adults are able to help select appropriate props or play materials for children.
○ Expanding the scope of children's play. Parents can help children elaborate on their play by suggesting new ideas or by adding new props to play areas.
○ Supporting children's play by praising the way children use materials and commenting on the roles children have assumed.
○ Planning for children's play. Give children a place of their own in which to play; provide a place for organizing materials and a balance of open-ended and close-ended toys.
○ Encouraging children to pretend. This will strengthen their inclination to use play for fun and learning.
○ Encouraging children to talk about their play, demonstrating parental interest in their activity (Isenberg and Jacobs, 1982, pp. 17–20).

These research findings about parents and their children's play should encourage early childhood educators to plan opportunities for child/parent play. One strategy that supports children's natural propensity for play and also strengthens family ties in play settings is the *Family Fun Night*.

FAMILY FUN NIGHT: AN ACTION STRATEGY THAT PROMOTES PLAY

A Family Fun Night is a play outing for the entire family that allows the child to be the center of attention. There is one cardinal rule for the event. A parent or an interested adult must be the child's partner for the evening. This requirement has a beneficial outcome; parents should have a much better understanding of the activities their children enjoy, and they will probably begin to develop an awareness of how to establish environments at home to promote the physical, social and emotional development of their children.

Flexible scheduling of the event is important for a successful Family Fun Night. Children and parents may come and go as work schedules permit. Activities may begin in the early evening with a meal for all participants. Play activities are organized in old-fashioned county fair booths or learning stations; families are encouraged to participate at their leisure. Freedom of movement and self-pacing is essential. Activities may be repeated again and again. Cooperation is encouraged, and play activities are structured for success. Physical contact such as touching and holding hands between parent and child is encouraged as a positive action to further the bonding experience. A certificate of completion is awarded to each child/parent team at the conclusion of the evening.

It is desirable for parents and children to be able to participate in Family Fun Night events with little or no cost, which may be accomplished by:

○ Asking local merchants to donate needed items: hog dogs, buns, chips, condiments, beans
○ Contacting soft drink companies to donate dented can drinks they cannot sell or companies like McDonald's who provide complimentary items for organizations
○ Contacting military installations for materials or personnel

o Requesting local service clubs and organizations for help with the finances for the evening meal or booth activity expenses.

An alternative for meal preparation is to request that parents bring a picnic lunch for their family or a covered dish to share with other fun night participants.

Site selection and facilities are important considerations when planning for a Family Fun Night. Local parks, recreation centers, large private yards, school grounds or day care outdoor facilities—large open areas with convenient restroom and picnic facilities—are all possibilities. All facilities should be selected and examined well beforehand for safety considerations. Alternative arrangements should be made for inclement weather.

Volunteers needed to assist in the preparation and organization of fun night booths could be interested parents not directly involved with a child for the evening, teachers or service group personnel, future teacher groups, Lion's Club members, boy and girl scout troops, senior citizens, professional educator organizations and philanthropic groups.

If the Family Fun Night is to be sponsored by and for public school or day care students, it can be effectively advertised through notes about the event sent home with the children from school. If the Fun Night is planned for the community at large, advertisement of the event could be made in newspapers and by radio and television public service announcements. Posters put up in public buildings, the library, post office and community businesses are helpful, with a clear, concise description of the purpose of the evening's events. Names and phone numbers of organizers to call for further information will aid parents in their understanding of the value of the event.

SUGGESTED ACTIVITIES
FOR FAMILY FUN NIGHT

Keep Family Fun Night simple. Activities should require child/adult cooperation and physical contact, minimal equipment and expense; above all, events should be fun. The following activities are suggestions.

1. *Face Painting.*   Theatrical make-up, mirrors, tissues and imagination are all that is needed. Children may have their faces made up by adults; children can also remake their parents' faces.

2. *Humpty Dumpty's Hoppity Happening.*   The old favorite of balancing an egg in a spoon. Provide an egg and a spoon for each child/parent team. Mark a start and a finish line with masking tape. Have the child begin by balancing the egg on the spoon and walking to the designated line. The parent should be ready to make the return trip to the start line but should walk backwards.

3. *Charlie Chan's Chopstick Chase.*   Each participant is given a small tin can, eight marbles or poker chips, a pair of chopsticks, ice tongs or a barbecue turner. The object is to pick up all the marbles or chips from the ground or picnic table as quickly as possible and place them in the container. This will require fine motor coordination; parents may use chopsticks and children may prefer tongs.

4. *Mad Hatter's Derby.*   Provide one large and one small Mexican sombrero and six tennis balls. Mark a starting line and a finish line with tape.

    Place the larger hat on the parent and place three tennis balls inside the hat brim. Repeat this procedure with the small sombrero on the child's head and add the remaining three balls.

    The object is to reach the finish line with all balls remaining inside the hat brims. Parent and child should walk hand in hand. If balls fall, they should be placed back in the hat and the walk continued.

5. *Penny Portrait Gallery.*   For this dress-up activity a variety of hats, gloves, scarfs, ties, jewelry, clothes and shoes should be available.

    The child and parent may select from a rack or clothesline items to be used to dress the child. Mirrors should be provided for children to view their appearance. Use a polaroid camera to capture their "new look" for the portrait gallery.

6. *Jump Rope Duo.*   Let a child and his parent jump rope together. Have partners face one another, and let the parent toss

the rope. Younger children may want to hold onto the parent's waist to practice jumping before adding the rope.

7. *Flip a Chip.* Child and parent cooperate in a game of toss. The objects may be varied. Each team should be given eight poker chips and one plastic container. Children should toss each chip, one at a time to the parent who catches the chips in the container. Roles may be reversed and the game replayed.

8. *Wizard's Walk.* Collect objects that a child and a parent can use to wear on the Wizard's walk. Boots, scuffs, swim flippers, stilt cans may be used. Let each child/parent team select the items they will wear. Have a designated path for participants and let them walk hand in hand to the finish line.

9. *Additional ideas.* Sponge and water bucket races, creative art with marshmallows, and toe-sack relays are also activities for fun night participants.

Parents and teachers who want to improve children's play will find Family Fun Night only one experience that can be used to promote and nurture children's play. A well-organized evening should sharpen a parent's awareness of the joy and value of child/parent play and encourage families to design similar supportive experiences at home.

References

Frost, Joe L., and Joan B. Kissinger. *The Young Child and the Educative Process.* New York: Holt, 1976.

Garvey, Catherine. *Play.* Cambridge, MA: Harvard University Press, 1977.

Isenberg, J., and J. Jacobs. *Playthings as Learning Tools: A Parent's Guide.* New York: Wiley, 1982.

Lieberman, J. N. *Playfulness: It's Relationship to Imagination and Creativity.* New York: Academic Press, 1977.

Phi Delta Kappa Center on Evaluation, Development and Research. "Practical Applications of Research: Play." *Newsletter* 5,2 (Dec. 1982).

Phinney, Joanna; Laura Dittman and Robert Huebner. *True Blue. Play and Fantasy: The Child's Building Blocks.* Baltimore, MD: University Park Press, 1979.

Piaget, J. *Play, Dreams, and Imitation in Childhood.* New York: Norton, 1962.

Segal, Marilyn, and Don Adcock. *The Value of Pretending.* Bethesda, MD: ERIC Document Reproduction Service, 1982. ED No. 215 780.

Sylva, K.; J. Bruner and P. Genova. "The Role of Play in the Problem-Solving of Children 3–5 Years Old." In J. S. Bruner, A. Jolly and K. Sylva, eds., *Play: Its Role in Development and Evolution.* New York: Basic Books, 1976.

Yawkey, T. D. "More on Play as Intelligence in Children." *Journal of Creative Behavior* 13 (1980): 4.

PART VII: PLAY AS AN ASSESSMENT TOOL

Introduction

In this final section play behaviors are highlighted as tools for assessing learning and development. Elizabeth J. Hrncir integrates ideas in the literature on infant play, motivation and assessment to demonstrate the need to consider the interplay of motivation and cognition in children's play activity and to illustrate how play can be used as a powerful assessment tool. The ontogenetic sequence of play in infancy is described to show the potential of play as a developmental assessment measure. Problems associated with current assessment measures are discussed. Finally, Hrncir proposes a means for using infant play as a measurement tool, not limited by typical conceptual and methodological boundaries.

Consistent with research recommendations that play behaviors be organized as an assessment tool, Betty S. Wagner describes extensive procedures resulting in a play scale designed to assess symbolic maturity from one to three years of age. Data were collected from a sample of 127 subjects stratified by age, ethnicity, sex and risk score. Three observer/data collectors made 40 paired observations for the interobserver agreement study. The correlation coefficient between observers' scores was .99 (p<.0001). A Guttman scaling program established reproducibility, scalability and reliability. The coefficient of reproducibility was .98, scalability coefficient was .93 and reliability coefficient was .99. The unidimensionality of the scale was determined by correlating each item with the sum of the other items. Coefficients ranged from .391 to .829 (p<.0002). Concurrent validity was established by correlating the scale with standardized tests. Predictive validity was determined with a follow-up study.

In an example of utilizing assessment instruments to determine differences in children's development and functioning, Thomas D. Yawkey and Margaret L. Yawkey assessed young children for imaginativeness through oral reporting using the Imaginative Predisposition Interview Scale (I.P.I.S.).

The study examined imaginativeness of 50 preschool children, ages four and five, and child and family variables such as family structure, number of siblings in the family and gender. After administering the 28-item I.P.I.S. the children's oral reports per item were scored on quality and quantity of imaginativeness using a Likert scale ranging from one point (low) to six points (high). Using the total I.P.I.S. score, it was found that imaginativeness and family structure are significantly correlated. The result showed that preschoolers in single parent families displayed higher imaginativeness than those in dual parent families and that there were a number of significant associations between imaginativeness on individual I.P.I.S. items and family structure. For example, children in single parent families tend to have more imaginative companions and use more imaginary talk with their fantasy friends. In addition, factor analysis was used to determine the number of factors comprising the I.P.I.S. The results of the analyses show that items clustered into 10 major factors. The top four were identified as: (1) imaginativeness with objects, (2) imaginative movement and action, (3) personal manifestations and characteristics of fantasy and (4) verbal imaginativeness.

These and related studies show that we are on the threshold of exciting new knowledge about children's play. As the new researchers highlighted in this volume enter the field, alongside their colleagues with similiar interests, our understanding of the value of play in human development will continue to grow.

337

Infant Play:
A Window to Motivational Competence

ELIZABETH J. HRNCIR
Child Development Project
Hamilton, Bermuda

Through observing children's play adults can gain insights, as if through a window, into the meaning behind children's behaviors. Observations of play must focus on the entire spectrum of children's developmental competence to include at the very least children's cognitive activity, social-emotional interactions and physical motor skills.

As researchers and educators, we often limit our focus to only one domain of the child's developmental competence, a limitation particularly true of the last decade of research on children's play. Many researchers have emphasized cognitive variables inherent in play activity to the exclusion of motivational variables that also govern the child's play.

In the following theoretical review, ideas in the literature on infant play, motivation and assessment are integrated to demonstrate the need to consider the interplay of motivation and cognition in children's play activity and to illustrate how play may be used as a powerful assessment tool. First, the ontogenetic sequence of play in infancy is described to show the potential of play as a developmental assessment measure. Second, problems associated with current assessment measures are discussed. Third, a means is proposed for using infant play as a measurement tool, not limited by typical conceptual and methodological boundaries.

THE ONTOGENETIC SEQUENCE OF INFANT PLAY

The sequence of early play has been described by researchers according to the objects and conditions the infant comes to understand with time and development. Early in life the infant's play with objects is exploratory in nature, whereas later in life the toddler displays advanced pretense acts. Some students of play, therefore, have been most concerned with describing the early stages of the infant's exploration, manipulation and object groups (Zelazo & Kearsley, 1980; Fenson et al., 1976; Belsky & Most, 1981; and Largo & Howard, 1979), whereas others have been concerned primarily with the child's emerging pretend acts directed at both self and others as well as the child's substitution of objects and use of sequenced acts in pretend (Watson & Fischer, 1977, 1980; Fein, 1975). Still other researchers in their descriptions of transitional behaviors that link these early groups of undifferentiated exploratory behaviors with later pretense acts have described the entire sequence of ontogenetic change in infant play (Belsky & Most, 1981; Fenson et al., 1976, 1980).

Undifferentiated exploration. At first infant's knowledge of objects appears limited because their actions are applied indiscriminately. For the infant "the object is what she/he does" (McCall, Eichorn & Hogarty, 1974, p. 64). The infant's exploration might involve mouthing objects or using the mouth sensorially to investigate the world, or the exploratory nature of the infant's behaviors may include both visual and tactile manipulation. The infant may even inappropriately place objects together (i.e. juxtapose). None of these early behaviors, however, include the infant's appropriate grouping of objects or placing things together that seem related. The infant, as yet, has not learned to differentiate and organize the world according to a set plan. Because early play behaviors are characterized as undifferentiated action, they have often been neglected by students of play as part of the ontogenetic sequence (Weisler & McCall, 1976). Recently, however, several researchers have defined these initial behaviors as leading to later and more advanced behaviors in the ontogenetic sequence of infant play (Belsky & Most, 1981; Zelazo & Kearsley, 1980; Fenson et al., 1976; Largo & Howard, 1979).

Differentiated or transitional actions. With the decrease of simple, manipulative behavior, the infant becomes skilled in increasingly functional use of objects. The infant begins to apply action discriminately to objects, now operating as if responding to the question, "What is this and what can it do?" (Weisler & McCall, 1976, p. 493). From this understanding of functionality the infant progresses toward conceptually associating objects. Then the child's actions suggest that she/he is responding to the question "What can I do with the object?" (Weisler & McCall, 1976, p. 494). This ability to conceptually or functionally relate objects appears necessary for later pretense acts that rely on the infant's knowledge of properties of objects and of how the world works. Thus, the toddler's actions begin to approximate pretense. For example, the infant brings the phone receiver only to the shoulder, and not to the ear and mouth for talking, reflecting his beginning understanding of how to use the phone for talking in pretend-self acts. The four previously mentioned studies (Belsky & Most, 1981; Fenson et al., 1976; Zelazo & Kearsley, 1980; and Largo & Howard, 1979) plus Nicholich's (1977) data on pre-symbolic or pre-pretend acts describe this transitional period in the ontogenetic sequence leading from early exploratory behaviors to later pretend acts.

Pretense play. Approximations of pretense document the infant's increasing knowledge of the world apart from his/her actions as well as the developing ability to coordinate relationships among objects. This first external relating of objects enables the toddler to form an internalized system for coding or representing the world of objects, events and situations. Such advance allows for internal coordination so that play behavior is less reliant or tied to the present object or event (Fein, 1979). For example, at first the infant requires a real tea cup to take a drink, then later with greater internal coordination and less reliance on the object properties the toddler can use a seashell, a seemingly meaningless object, for taking a drink.

Thus, only when children have mastered their use of real objects do they move toward use of substitute objects in play, and then the difficulty of these substitutions varies according to the form and function of the objects employed. With such an advanced use of the internalized system of coding and using the world of objects, the toddler becomes skilled at also using these objects (both realistic and less realistic) in action sequences. The child seems to draw an internal scheme for interrelating both realistic and less realistic objects. For example the toddler may use a realistic teapot and teacup to pour himself and mother a drink or may use a block as a substitute teapot for also pouring a drink into a substitute seashell. These play acts that now become sequential have been studied by several researchers (Belsky & Most, 1981; Nicholich, 1977; Fenson & Ramsey, 1980; and Largo & Howard, 1979).

The infant's play does indeed develop, increasing in sophistication and reflecting ontogenetic change in infancy. In fact, the ontogenetic sequence of infant play just described was integrated and tested for scalability and reproducability by Belsky & Most (1981) using the Guttman scalar analysis. The findings of their analysis showed the scalability coefficient to be .77 and reproducability coefficient to be .95.

Play can be used for assessment of infant competence since it reflects the developmental sequence of the infant's understanding of the world. Beyond the infant's cognitive understandings, however, play also reflects the infant's motivational competence.

Yarrow et al., (1979, 1983) examined how measures of infant exploratory play related to persistence at structured tasks and the infant's cognitive functioning. They found that infants who showed greater ability to sustain and focus their attention during free play successfully completed more persistence tasks and persisted longer with the problem-solving tasks. From these results Yarrow et al. (1979) concluded that infants who spontaneously practice emerging skills seem to perfect them earlier than other infants and that cognitively advanced infants are more able to exploit fully the learning potential of their environment.

TESTING FOR CHILDREN

The work of Yarrow and his colleagues (1979, 1983) underscores the interrelatedness of motivation and intellectual competence. The interrelatedness of these constructs, however, is often ignored in educating and testing children. As educators and test examiners, we tend to focus on the child's cognitive functioning and may neglect the importance of cooperation, attention, persistence, ability to sit still and social responsiveness within the assessment situation (Scarr, 1981). Yet, these very characteristics often govern whether or not the child will excel in school.

The standardized infant assessment measure (Bayley, 1933) is an example of our limited focus on cognition and lack of attention to the influence of motivational variables (Hrncir & Belsky, Note 1). During the standardized testing situation children are not allowed to initiate responses, children do not decide whether or not they will attend, persist and essentially lose themselves in the tasks. Instead, the tasks are defined for the children, their attention is repeatedly focused, and they are praised and encouraged regarding their performance. In so doing, the test examiner eliminates variance in children's own motivation to deploy their capabilities. Therefore, as test examiners we are not tapping what the children may be capable of doing on their own. We are, indeed, disregarding the rich potential of the child's spontaneous acts.

THE WINDOW

Children's own motivation to deploy their capabilities can be measured in spontaneous play. Play is a window on children's motivational competence because in spontaneous play children are free to show or not show their most sophisticated behaviors. Through play, adults may observe whether or not children have maximized their potentials. Play observations that consider the interplay of cognition and motivation can help explain why, in both testing situations and school

environments, some children perform consistently below their potentials, whereas other children maximize their potentials.

The theoretical ideas reviewed in this paper were recently tested in a cross-cultural study of infants' motivation in spontaneous play (Hrncir et al., Note 2). In this study a measure was developed that sampled both quantitative aspects of play, or level of play acts, and qualitative aspects of play, or each act of play exhibited. Termed spontaneous mastery, this measure reflected the tendency of infants' play acts to be distributed higher or lower along a level of sophistication of the Belsky & Most (1981) play scale. Thirty-eight infants were videotaped at 12 and 18 months of age in spontaneous play with two sets of toys. Infants' spontaneous mastery scores were compared with another measure of motivation, executive capacity, (Belsky et al., Note 3) and with Bayley MDI scores.

Results showed the spontaneous mastery measure to predict reliably infants' performance on the Bayley MDI at the same age and six months later. The findings of this preliminary research on the interrelatedness of infant's mastery of play acts and developmental competence suggest that over time the interrelatedness of these constructs may indeed influence the learning histories of children. Children who master tasks on their own may also be more inclined to evoke stimulation from parents, teachers and peers and, therefore, be exposed to the better environments.

We have probably only scratched the surface of possibilities available to us for using play for assessments in infancy. We must extend the boundaries we have placed on play by integrating what we know about play with what we know about other developmental phenomena.

Reference Notes

1. Hrncir, E., and J. Belsky. "Assessing Performance, Competence and Motivation in Infant Play: Relations Between 12 and 18 Months." Unpublished manuscript, Pennsylvania State University, University Park, PA, November 1981.
2. Hrncir, E.; G. Speller and M. West. "What Are We Testing?" Submitted to *Developmental Psychology*.
3. Belsky, J.; W. Garduque and E. Hrncir. "Assessing Performance, Competence, and Executive Capacity in Infant Play: Relations to Home Environment and Security of Attachment." *Developmental Psychology*, in press.

References

Bayley, N. "Mental Growth During the First Three Years. A Developmental Study of Sixty-one Children by Repeated Tests." *Genetic Psychology Monographs* 14 (1933): 1–92.

Belsky, J., and R. Most. "From Exploration to Play: A Cross-sectional Study of Infant Free Play Behaviour." *Developmental Psychology* 17 (1981): 630–39.

Erikson, E. H. *Childhood and Society.* New York: Norton, 1952.

Fein, G. G. "A Transformational Analysis of Pretending." *Developmental Psychology* 11, 3 (1975): 291–96.

Fein, G. G., and N. Apfel. "The Development of Play: Style, Structure and Situations." *Genetic Psychology Monographs* 99 (1979): 231–50.

Fenson, L., and D. S. Ramsey. "Decentration and Integration of the Child's Play in the Second Year." *Child Development* 51 (1980): 171–78.

Fenson, L.; J. Kagan; R. B. Kearsley and P. R. Zelazo. "The Developmental Progression of Manipulative Play in the First Two Years." *Child Development* 47 (1976): 232–36.

Freud, S. *An Outline of Psychoanalysis.* New York: Norton, 1949.

Harter, S. "Developmental Differences in the Manifestation of Mastery Motivation on Problem-solving Tasks." *Child Development* 46 (1975): 370–78.

——— . "Effectance Motivation Reconsidered: Toward a Developmental Model." *Human Development* 21 (1978): 34–64.

Harter, S., and E. Zigler. "The Assessment of Effectance Motivation in Normal and Retarded Children." *Developmental Psychology* 2 (1974): 169–80.

Largo, R. H., and J. A. Howard. "Developmental Progression in Play Behavior of Children Between Nine and Thirty Months. 1: Spontaneous Play and Imitation." *Developmental Medical Child Neurology* 21 (1979): 299–310.

McCall, R. B.; D. H. Eichorn and P. S. Hogarty. "Transitions in Early Mental Development." *Monographs of the Society for Research in Child Development* 171 (1977).

Nicholich, L. M. "Beyond Sensorimotor Intellience: Assessment of Symbolic Maturity Through Analysis of Pretend Play." *Merrill-Palmer Quarterly* 23, 2 (1977): 89–99.

Piaget, J. *The Origins of Intelligence in Children.* New York: International University Press, 1952.

Scarr, S. "Testing *for* Children: Assessment and the Many Determinants of Intellectual Competence." *American Psychologist* 36, 10 (1981): 1159–66.

Watson, M. W., and K. W. Fischer. "A Developmental Sequence of Agent Use in Late Infancy." *Child Development* 48 (1977): 828–36.

——— . "Development of Social Roles in Elicited and Spontaneous Behavior During the Preschool Years." *Developmental Psychology* 16 (1980): 483–94.

Weisler, A., and R. B. McCall. "Exploration and Play: Resume and Redirection." *American Psychologist* 31, 7 (1976): 492–508.

White, R. W. "Motivation Reconsidered: The Concept of Competence." *Psychological Review* 66 (1959): 297–333.

Yarrow, L. J., and F. A. Pedersen. "The Interplay Between Cognition and Motivation in Infancy." In M. Lewis, ed., *Origins of Intelligence: Infancy and Early Childhood.* New York: Plenum Press, 1976.

Yarrow, L. J.; D. K. Jennings; R. J. Harmon; G. A. Morgan and J. L. Gaiter. "Exploratory Play as an Index of Mastery Motivation: Relationships to Persistence, Cognitive Functioning, and Environmental Measures." *Developmental Psychology* 15, 4 (1979): 386–94.

Yarrow, L. J.; S. McQuiston; R. H. Macturk; M. E. McCarthy; R. P. Klein and P. M. Vietze. "Assessment of Mastery Motivation During the First Year of Life: Contemporaneous and Cross-age Relationships." *Developmental Psychology* 19, 2 (1983): 159–71.

Zelazo, P. R., and R. B. Kearsley. "The Emergence of Functional Play in Infants: Evidence for a Major Cognitive Transition." *Journal of Applied Developmental Psychology,* 1980.

Assessing Symbolic Maturity Through Pretend Play

BETTY S. WAGNER
College of Home Economics
Texas Tech University, Lubbock

Play behavior of children by the second year of life indicates the beginning function of the symbol system. Study of play behavior gives insight into children's thought processes, frequently yielding information not obtainable with more conventional means of assessment. The object of this study was to design a scale for teachers of young children to assess symbolic maturity of pretend play of children from one to three years of age. Questions pertinent to the problem were:

1. Can significant pretend play behaviors be selected from the literature to identify the stages of symbolic development of children from one to three years of age?

2. Can the significant play behaviors exhibited by children be arranged to form a cumulative scale?

3. Will the play scale show a positive relationship to an existing psychometric test?

4. Will the play scale be reliable?

REVIEW OF LITERATURE

The age period of 12 to 36 months is the time of transition from sensorimotor to representational intelligence (McCune-Nicolich, 1981). Children attempt to represent events by symbolic play, drawing and language (Inhelder, 1978).

The symbolic function begins around 1½–2 years of age with the appearance of differentiated signifiers (signs and symbols) and consists in representing various figurative and cognitive schemes by means of these signifiers. . . . Interiorized imitation and images are, on the contrary, at the same time figurative and symbolic. Mental imagery in particular is the product of interiorized imitation and not the simple residue of perception as it was previously believed (Piaget, 1971, pp. 338–39).

Operational definitions of play differ. Fein (1981), for example, describes pretend play as behavior in an "as if" mode. The terms, make-believe, fantasy or dramatic play, and symbolic play are also used to describe the pretend play behaviors. McCune-Nicolich (1981) defines symbolic play as a combination of a real action and an intended fantasy resulting in pretend play with one of the following characteristics: (1) inanimate objects are treated as animate, (2) daily activities are repeated without the necessary objects, (3) the child imitates actions of someone else, (4) activities are only partially completed, (5) one object is substituted for another or (6) behavior of the child signals the nonliteral quality of the play.

From a cognitive-developmental point of view pretend play reflects the symbolic maturity of the child (Vygotsky, 1978). The emergence of pretend play thus follows a developmental sequence established in cross-cultural studies, appearing around 12 or 13 months of age and increasing in complexity, frequency and prevalence until about 6 years of age (Fein, 1981).

SEQUENCE OF PRETEND PLAY BEHAVIORS

Close to the first birthday the child begins to use and combine objects according to their adult-defined purposes; this behavior increases in frequency and duration with age (Zelazo & Kearsley, 1977). These researchers found in their study that this functional type of play was predominant for the oldest subjects, 15½-month-olds. In Lowe's study (1975), which had a sample age range of 12 months to 36 months, this functional relationship of objects to each other appeared to reach a peak at 18 months for most situations and remained high throughout the other age levels. The pretending described in these studies corresponds to Piaget's description of deferred imitation (Piaget, 1962).

Parallel to this combining of objects in functional play is the situation in which objects are related to self (Lowe, 1975). Sequences of this type of play involve the child's pretending to drink from a cup, comb his or her hair, or cover himself/herself with a blanket. Lowe (1975) places the peak period for play that focuses on the child's own body at 9 to 18 months. This class of behaviors also represents deferred imitation, which Piaget (1962) states is transitional to symbolic functioning.

At 21 months the child begins to abandon self-related activities for doll-related behavior (Lowe, 1975). In this early period activities are not necessarily integrated. By 24 months, however, the sequences are integrated and involve more objects in the play episodes. Doll-related play replaces self-related activity as the dominant form of behavior. Largo and Howard (1979) found in their sample that this change occurred at a younger age.

The child places an object for the doll to "use" or places the doll in a position to "eat" at 30 months (Lowe, 1975). Largo and Howard (1979) describe situations in which children make the doll execute the actions at approximately 30 months. This phase of doll-related play behavior is described as representational by Largo and Howard. Fein (1975) states that these early types of play involve a global matching of an object to a mental pattern.

The next phase of play involves transformation in which one object is used as if it were another object (Fein, 1975). Fein described the use of pantomime gestures in which a child shaped his hand to form a cup. This development represents the period of symbolic play (Largo & Howard, 1979).

The last stage of play defined by Largo and Howard was the sequential play, which involves a series of related episodes. For example, the child might pretend to cook food, feed a doll the food, then wash the doll's face. This activity is many times accompanied by verbalization of the child. Both the Largo and Howard study and the Lowe study found much of this behavior emerging by 30 months. In summary, the child within the first three years of life incorporates adult actions into his/her behavioral repertoire and utilizes symbols of the adult world as play signals.

PROCEDURES

From January, 1980, through September, 1981, data were collected with 127 children in the development of an instrument, the Mental Development Scales: Birth to Three Years (MDS), which consists of six scales (Wagner, 1983). One of the scales, the Play Scale, is discussed here. Behavioral items for this scale were selected from a review of the literature and arranged in an estimated order of occurrence.

Sample

The sample consisted of 127 subjects stratified according to demographic characteristics to approximate the population of the United States (United States Bureau of the Census, 1982). The distribution of the sample is illustrated in Table 1.

Table 1
Characteristics of Sample

Characteristic	Number	Percentage
Ethnic Group		
Anglo	97	76.4
Black	13	10.2
Hispanic	17	13.4
Total	127	100.0
Risk Factors		
None	45	35.4
1	26	20.5
2–4	38	30
5 +	18	14.1
Total	127	100.0
Sex		
Male	59	46.5
Female	68	53.5
Total	127	100.0
Age		
0– 7 Months	24	18.9
8–15 Months	26	20.5
16–23 Months	28	22.0
24–30 Months	24	18.9
31–39 Months	25	19.7
Total	127	100.0

From this sample 15 subjects were chosen for the concurrent validity study. Data from the remaining 112 subjects were collected for further analysis of the scales.

Collection of Data

Data collection sites were six child care centers, the Texas Tech University Development Disability Center and homes in Lubbock, Texas. Each of the 15 subjects in the concurrent validity study was assessed with the MDS and either the Bayley Scales of Infant Development (Bayley, 1969) for children from 2 to 30 months of age or the Stanford-Binet Intelligence Scales (Terman and Merrill, 1973) for children from 30 to 36 months. The remaining 112 subjects were assessed with the six scales of the MDS. Interobserver agreement data were collected on 40 paired observations.

Analysis of Data

In the concurrent validity study scores from the psychometric tests, the Bayley and the Stanford-Binet, were converted to a common denominator of mental age in months and corrected with each of the scale scores of the MDS.

Interobserver agreement was determined by calculating the percentage of identical scores between pairs of observers. In addition, the pairs of scores were correlated using the Pearson method to reveal relationships.

Each scale of the MDS was subjected to a scalogram analysis using the Guttman scaling program of the Statistical Analysis System (SAS). This procedure estimated the reproducibility and scalability of the scales. The reliability was determined by an option of the scaling program. In addition, the relationship of each item to its scale was calculated to determine the unidimensionality of the scales. Finally, the mean age, age range and standard deviations for each possible scale score were calculated.

Findings

In the concurrent validity study, Pearson product-moment correlations between the mental ages of the standardized psychometric tests and the Play Scale of the MDS yielded

a coefficient of .745 (p<.001). The inter-observer agreement study of 40 paired scores revealed a 93 percent agreement between observers. Correlations between observers' scores yielded a coefficient of .99 (p<.0001).

The Guttman scaling program calculated the reproducibility of the Play Scale as .979, the scalability as .927, and the reliability as .993. In addition, this program rearranged the items of the scales according to the frequency of responses and calculated the relation of each item to its scale. These results for the Play Scale are shown in Table 2.

The mean age, age range and standard deviations for each possible score of the Play Scale are illustrated in Table 3. However, this normative data should be used with caution due to the small cell sizes of most of the scores. In addition, the higher end of the scale shows the need for older subjects in the sample. Data are still being collected for this aspect of scale development.

Follow-up Study

Beginning in September, 1981, and concluding in August, 1982, an attempt was made to locate and re-assess each subject. In this follow-up study 34 subjects were assessed with the Stanford-Binet Intelligence Scales approximately 22 months after their first assessment with the MDS. An additional 32 subjects were re-assessed with the MDS approximately 18 months after their first assessments with the MDS. Pearson product-moment correlations measured the relationships. Correlations between the first Play Scale score and the later Stanford-Binet mental age scores revealed a coefficient of .535 (p<.001). Correlations between the first Play Scale score and the later Play Scale score yielded a coefficient of .356 (p<.046).

CONCLUSIONS

Developmental theory and empirical research offered a body of literature regarding early pretend play from which significant behaviors were identified. These significant behaviors were arranged in a cumulative scale that surpassed acceptable standards for reproducibility, scalability, reliability and inter-observer agreement. Concurrent and

345

predictive validity were demonstrated through correlations with the Bayley and Stanford-Binet psychometric tests. In summary, the results of this study provide evidence for the reliable and valid use of the Play Scale with children from one to three years of age.

IMPLICATIONS

The young child reveals his symbolic maturity through play. Professionals who wish to understand the unique qualities of each child need assessment tools to aid in interpreting the spontaneous behavior of the child. An understanding of the developmental progression of pretend play is the first step toward structuring the best possible environment for play.

References

Bayley, N. *Manual for the Bayley Scales of Infant Development.* New York: Psychological Corp., 1969.
Fein, G. G. "A Transformational Analysis of Pretending." *Developmental Psychology* 11 (1975): 291–96.
———. "Pretend Play in Childhood: an Integrative Review." *Child Development* 52 (1981): 1095–118.
Inhelder, B. "Criteria of the Stages of Mental Devel-

Table 2
Guttman Scale Analysis
Resequenced Play Scale
By Number and Percentage Correct-Biserial Correlation: Scale-Item
N = 112

Percentage	Number	Item	r	Probability
59	66	1. Uses a common object on self	.737	.0002
58	65	2. Combines 2 objects correctly	.749	.0002
45	50	3. Gives care to doll or another person Alternate: Borrows 2 objects from doll	.829	.0002
38	43	4. Uses 2 objects on doll or another person	.826	.0002
19	21	5. Identifies imaginery food	.662	.0002
19	21	6. Places object for doll to "use"	.662	.0002
13	14	7. Acts out event with real or imaginary person	.583	.0002
4	5	8. Connects 3 episodes of play in series	.391	.0002

Table 3
Play Scale Scores
Mean, Range, Standard Deviation

Scale Scores	N	Mean Age (Months)	Standard Deviation	Minimum Age	Maximum Age	Standard Error
1	3	15.08	2.27	13.00	17.50	1.31
2	15	17.57	4.12	11.25	26.00	1.06
3	6	19.21	4.01	16.00	27.00	1.64
4	18	24.42	4.96	16.50	34.00	1.17
5	8	31.47	5.92	20.75	39.50	2.09
6	7	31.82	3.57	24.75	35.00	1.35
7	7	33.00	3.14	26.00	35.00	1.19
8	5	30.60	3.93	25.50	34.00	1.76

opment." In J. T. Gibson and P. Blumberg, eds., *Growing Up: Readings on the Study of Children.* Menlo Park, CA: Addison-Wesley, 1978.

Largo, R. H., and J. A. Howard. "Developmental Progression in Play Behavior of Children Between Nine and Thirty Months. I: Spontaneous Play and Imitation." *Developmental Medicine and Child Neurology* 21 (1979): 299–310.

Lowe, M. "Trends in the Development of Representational Play in Infants from One to Three Years—An Observational Study." *Journal of Child Psychology and Psychiatry* 16 (1975): 33–47.

McCune-Nicolich, L. "Toward Symbolic Functioning: Structure of Early Pretend Games and Potential Parallels with Language." *Child Development* 52 (1981): 785–97.

Piaget, J. *Play, Dreams, and Imitation in Childhood.* C. Gattegno and F. M. Hodgson, trans. New York: Norton, 1962.

——— . "Response to Brian Sutton-Smith." In R. E. Herron and B. Sutton-Smith, eds., *Child's Play.* New York: Wiley, 1971.

Terman, L. M., and M. A. Merrill. *Stanford-Binet Intelligence Scale-Manual for the Third Revision-Form L-M.* Boston: Houghton, 1973.

United States Bureau of the Census. *1980 Census of Population; vol. 1; Characteristics of the Population.* Washington, DC: U.S. Government Printing Office, 1982.

Vygotsky, L. "Play and Its Role in the Mental Development of the Child." In J. K. Gardner, ed., *Readings in Developmental Psychology.* Boston: Little, Brown, 1978.

Wagner, B. S. "Reliability, Scalability, and Validity of an Instrument to Assess Developmental Levels of Children from Birth to Three Years of Age." *Psychological Reports* 52 (1983): 217–18.

Zelazo, P. R., and R. B. Kearsley. *Functional Play: Evidence for a Cognitive Metamorphosis in the Year Old Infant.* New Orleans, LA, 1977. (ERIC Document Reproduction Service No. ED 139 545.)

Assessing Young Children for Imaginativeness Through Oral Reporting: Preliminary Results

THOMAS D. YAWKEY and MARGARET L. YAWKEY
College of Education
The Pennsylvania State University, University Park

INTRODUCTION

Recently there has been increasing interest in assessing young children's imaginativeness to determine differences that may occur within their normal development and functioning. Imaginativeness or imaginative predisposition is defined as the extent to which children transcend the constraints of reality in their play—for example, "by using one object to represent another one, by adding vocalizations suggesting he or she was symbolizing a role or object, or by introducing a story line" (Tower, Singer, Singer & Biggs, 1979, p. 271).

Even with this rising interest in imaginativeness of young children, there is relatively little known about relationships between imaginativeness and selected child and family variables. Accordingly, this research investigation was set forth to develop and test an assessment instrument for measuring imaginativeness, using oral reports of young children and discussion of how imaginativeness may relate to: (a) number of siblings in the family, (b) birth order of the child, (c) family structure (i.e., single versus dual parent families), (d) chronological age of the child, (e) sex and (f) general intellectual ability.

As part of an on-going investigation of assessing imaginative predispositions using oral report and observational measures with preschoolers, this present study reports preliminary results of relationships between oral reports of imaginativeness and selected child and family variables.

Theoretical Perspectives

Piaget's (1962) views of imaginative play are widely accepted as the most definitive and comprehensive explanation of imaginative play, growth and functioning in young children, infancy through early childhood. Viewing from several perspectives, Piaget (1962) saw imaginative play as a cognitive entity and a necessary condition for the development of more advanced forms of logical thought. In this light, he notes that imaginative play is an exercise: ". . . of action schemes and therefore part of the cognitive component from conception. At the same time play manifests the pecularity of a primacy of assimilation over accommodation which permits it to transform reality in its own manner without submitting that transformation to the criterion of objective fact" (p. 338).

As a structuralist, Piaget ties together cognitive operations fundamental to imaginative play, the child's motivations for playing and the stage of his intellectual development (i.e., sensorimotor, preoperational, concrete operations and formal operations). Imaginative play, then, shows how a child thinks or is capable of thinking assimilatively from 12–18 months upward.

From a cognitive perspective, the most definitive element of imaginativeness is its "as if" attribute (Piaget & Inhelder, 1971). Described as "representational set" (Sutton-Smith, 1968), the "as if" element announces the beginning and ending of imaginative activities in which young children represent actual or imagined experiences, events and situations as inferred from their verbalizations and/or motoric actions and uses of objects. In turn, these experiences, events or situations are reproduced in differing varieties and under varying conditions in which the initial ones occurred.

The "as if" attribute of imaginative play

349

inferred from the preoperational child's expressions and/or actions shows that symbolic functioning and decontextualization are occurring. The use of symbols requires, at minimum, underlying cognitive or mental constructions that enable children to encode meanings and communicate them in meaningful ways. In using "as if" actions and/or expressions, the preschooler is mentally capable of separating meanings and real events or situations from the symbols that represent them through the perspective of egocentric assimilation (Piaget, 1962; Werner & Kaplan, 1963).

If the child uses a wash cloth (without soap and water) and shows by circular hand-movements or other gestures and/or verbal statements that he or she is washing the face, it appears that the child knows what the wash cloth is used for and how it is used. In this instance, the child decontextualizes the meaning of the wash cloth and uses it outside its regular context. Symbolic functioning and decontextualization are primary attributes of the "as if" capacity.

In addition to symbolic functioning and decontextualization, Piaget at another level explains imaginative play through cognitive development and advancing forms of logical thought, picturing the onset and growth of imaginative play in terms of developmental levels that coincide with stages of cognitive competence and development. According to Fein and Apfel (1975, p. 4), this ". . . progressive decontextualization and elaboration . . . comes from the phasing in of several discrete strands of symbolic matter which reflect the development of symbolic functioning."

In addition to Piaget, other major developmental theorists such as Vygotsky (1967) and Werner (1948) ascribe cognitive significance to and developmental sequence in imaginative play and trace its growth from concrete to more abstract stages—i.e., from treating objects and persons realistically to using them "as if" they were imaginative others.

Imaginativeness and Child and Family Variables

Attempts to explore imaginativeness and its relationships to social behaviors have shown that more imaginative children are able to: transcend the constraints of reality and remember details of stories with accuracy (Marshall & Hahn, 1967; Singer, 1973; Smilansky, 1968); exhibit high levels of social skills (Singer & Singer, 1976b); show greater concentration (Pulaski, 1973; Singer & Singer, 1976b), demonstrate positive affect (i.e., extent to which the child enjoys play activities) (Tower, Singer, Singer & Biggs, 1979); display more imaginary play companions (Calderia, Singer & Singer, 1978) and resist temptation to tolerate delays (D. Singer & J. Singer, 1980; J. Singer & D. Singer, 1981).

Although previous research has explored socially adaptive features (D. Singer & J. Singer, 1980; J. Singer & D. Singer, 1976, 1981; Singer & Singer, 1976a, 1976b; Pulaski, 1973) and enhancement potential of imaginative play (D. Singer & J. Singer, 1976; Tower, Singer, Singer & Biggs, 1979; Smilansky, 1968), additional studies are needed to examine relationships between imaginativeness and child and family variables. Previous investigations have used observational techniques and/or oral reporting to measure imaginativeness. The present study employed the oral report form used largely by Singer and his associates to measure imaginative predispositions in young children. The use of oral reports with young children is based on assumptions that imaginativeness (Singer, 1973): (a) is central to and linked with the development of cognitive and social capacities of young children; (b) has a verbal symbolic mode basic to covert mediational responses and therefore is a part of the child's behavioral repertoire and (c) may be assessed through a verbal dimension especially with children in later preschool years who exhibit increasing development toward anticipatory imagery (cf. Piaget & Inhelder, 1971) and more verbal modes of thinking (cf. Bruner, 1966).

Given the importance of imaginativeness and its relation to general cognitive capacities and social growth abilities in young children, it is likely that child and family variables relate to and parallel such behavior in young children and in varying degrees and ways. For example, family influences are not only transmitted to children at very early ages,

350

but they are also shown in their imaginativeness (Singer, 1973; Tower, 1980). Children who display more spontaneous imaginative play have a history of secure mother-child attachment (Matas, Arend & Sroufe, 1978). Also, children evidencing more imaginative play show a greater likelihood of having a parent who tells them stories and plays pretend games with them (Breckenridge & Vincent, 1965; Shmukler, 1977; Singer, 1961; Svendsen, 1934). In addition, findings from studies conducted by Svendsen (1934) and Breckenridge and Vincent (1965) suggest that the number of siblings in the family (i.e., family density) may relate to the quality and quantity of imaginative play companions children have. Previous research results of Manosevitz, Prentice and Wilson (1973) and Masih (1978) show a significant correlation between having imaginary companions and birth order, with first borns and middle children tending to have more imaginary playmates. The results of Schaeffer (1969) and Singer (1966, 1973) provide evidence for family structure (i.e., dual versus single parent families) that influences whether or not youngsters have imaginary companions.

METHODS

Participants

Of the 50 preschool children in the study, 23 were girls and 27, boys. There were 24 four-year-olds and 26 five-year-olds. The mean age was four years and nine months; the mean mental age in months was 73.4. Using Warner, Meeker and Eels (1960) indices, the children were determined to be primarily from middle socio-economic class backgrounds. All their families' heads-of-households were employed in white collar occupations and represented occupations such as university and public school teaching, sales, service, medical and secretarial.

Of the 50, none were only-children, 25 had two siblings, 18 had three, six had four and one had five. For the variable of birth order, 35 children were first born, 10 were second born and five were third born. For family structure, eight were from single parent, and 42 were from dual parent families.

The mean Peabody Picture Vocabulary Test-I.Q. score was 111.60, and the mean imaginativeness score from the Imaginative Predisposition Interview Scale was 36.40 points.

The children attended seven preschool centers and were randomly selected for inclusion in the study. In general, the preschool centers' curricula, class scheduling and teaching procedures were similar across schools and characterized an academically oriented setting and university-based city.

Variables

The main independent variables in the study are: *number of siblings* in a family unit (Breckenridge & Vincent, 1965; Svendsen, 1934); *birth order of the child* (Manosevitz, Prentice & Wilson, 1973; Masih, 1978); *family structure* (i.e., dual versus single parent families) (Schaeffer, 1969; Singer, 1973, 1966); *chronological age of the child* (Piaget, 1962; Singer, 1966); *sex* (Svendsen, 1934); and, *general intellectual ability* using the Peabody Picture Vocabulary Test (P.P.V.T.) (Dunn, 1960). Except for the P.P.V.T. score, all information was obtained from the records and/or teachers in the preschool centers.

The dependent variable was performance on the Imaginative Predisposition Interview Schedule (I.P.I.S.), which assessed the child's predisposition toward imaginativeness (Singer, 1973). Each item evaluates the child's imaginative play predisposition toward differing yet particular ludic play aspects. These aspects include imaginative play dispositions toward varying objects, actions, situations and activities (Singer, 1973; Smilansky, 1968). Four examples (see note 1) of items from the I.P.I.S. follow:

1. Do you play games with your friends? What games do you play with your friends?

2. Do you have a make-believe friend? What does your make-believe friend do?

3. Do you play with toys: What toys do you play with?

4. Do you watch television? What do you see or watch on television?

The child is read each of the items with order randomized and counterbalanced to

351

reduce effects of the test administration. The child's responses to each item are tape recorded. The question is repeated if the youngster does not appear to understand. If the child does not respond or answers using one word or a small number of words (e.g., "blocks" to example question item one), two prompts are given at the end of a 30-second interval after the initial stimulus item is read. If the child does not respond one minute after the second prompt, the examiner moves to another question. The purpose of repeating questions and using prompts is to: (a) understand whether the child's emphasis is on "reality" or "make-believe" elements; (b) ask for detail and elaboration of one or both elements and, (c) obtain a minimum of 100 running words of oral discourse response per question. This insures a uniform procedure for data gathering as well as a consistent number of words per item that could be used for scoring.

The child's responses are scored independently by two raters on a (one to six) Likert scale. Each of the points on the Likert scale represents increasing emphasis and greater quality of make-believe elements. For example, one point is awarded to the content of a child's response for:

Any response or set of responses that are not logical, appropriate or fantasy oriented. Any responses indicating that the child does not comprehend or understand. Examples include: 'no,' 'cause,' 'yes,' 'mommy told me' and others where the child does not answer orally and/or physically (Yawkey, 1983).

Six points are awarded to content of a child's response for:

Any response or set of responses arising from any content based on fantasy and containing make-believe situations, actions, activities, situations, objects and people from a purely make-believe base; any showing make-believe taking precedence over the original make-believe stimulus. Organization, cohesion and integration of make-believe elements are also observed in the oral narrative. Examples include: make-believe object (e.g., Barbie doll) talks, becomes a fairy princess, flies through the air and catches monsters, etc.; make-believe companion (e.g., Noisy) climbs up atop the house (or castle), flies around in the sky and disappears (Yawkey, 1983).

Procedures

The I.P.I.S. and P.P.V.T. were given in a room near the youngster's classroom. Both were administered to the youngster on the same day and by a trained examiner who established rapport before the testing began. Administering the I.P.I.S. and P.P.V.T. required 40 minutes and 20 minutes, respectively. For the I.P.I.S., the examiners had to equal or surpass a .70 criterion for reliability on scoring oral discourse, using the six point Likert score, and obtain a minimum of 100 words of oral discourse per item to show minimum proficiency in testing procedures (Medley & Mitzel, 1963).

RESULTS

Results are organized into three sections: (a) inter-rater agreement and reliability coefficients, (b) Pearson correlations and (c) factor analysis.

Inter-rater Agreement and Reliability Coefficients

Both inter-rater agreement and reliability coefficients were calculated for the I.P.I.S. For inter-rater agreement, the examiners independently rated all the taped responses of the 50 children across all 28 items. The raters judged the magnitude or degree of imaginativeness of the responses per question by reading the oral discourse and assigning one to six points to the imaginative quality.

Inter-rater agreement coefficients are calculated per item and for total score by determining the number of agreements and dividing by the number of agreements plus number of disagreements and multipyling by 100 (Medley & Mitzel, 1963). Across the items, the mean inter-rater agreement for scoring on the six-point Likert category system ranged from 71.4 to 96.4. Across all items the overall mean inter-rater agreement was .76.

For purposes of test reliability, Cronbach's Alpha coefficient of .81 was obtained for the I.P.I.S. According to Brown (1968), a reliability of .80 or higher is quite satisfactory for tests of cognitive abilities, and considerably more latitude is granted for assessments of attitude and values. The mean and range statistics were 36.44 and 52, respectively, with a standard deviation of 11.45, standard error of measurement of 5 and standard error of test mean of 1.64.

Pearson Correlations

All correlations reported are statistically significant as $p<.05$ level. First, results indicate a significant Pearson correlation between total scores on the I.P.I.S. with family structure (i.e., single versus dual parent families) $(r = -.32)$ but not between total I.P.I.S. score and number of siblings in the family, birth order, P.P.V.T.-I.Q. score, chronological age or sex. Using total I.P.I.S. score, the major result shows that children in single parent families tend to display higher imaginative scores than those children in dual parent families. In addition, there were a number of significant associations between performance on individual items and family structure. The number of parents in the family is significantly correlated with: (1) imaginative games children play themselves when alone $(r = -.28)$, (2) imaginative and fantasy make-believe friends $(r = -.34)$, (3) fantasy games children play out-of-doors $(r = -.32)$ and (4) fantasy talk with imaginary friends $(r = -.35)$. Evidently, children in single parent families tend to have more imaginative companions, use more imaginary talk with their fantasy friends, play more imaginative games themselves when alone and engage in more imaginative games out-of-doors than those youngsters in dual parent families.

Finally, there are other significant associations between the child's performance on individual items of the I.P.I.S. and several of the independent variables: chronological age, number of siblings and general intellectual ability.

First, the age of the child (in months) is significantly associated with beliefs that his fantasy dreams will come true $(r = -.32)$ and the pretend quality of his fantasy games out-of-doors $(r = -.28)$. Younger children tend to have greater beliefs that their fantasy dreams will come true and report games out-of-doors that have greater quality and quantity of fantasy and imaginative elements than older children. Second, the greater number

of siblings in the family is significantly correlated with toys classified as highly imaginative $(r = .30)$ and jokes and humorous stories having higher fantasy content $(r = .28)$. Third, the child's general intellectual ability is significantly related with the fantasy dreams $(r = -.31)$, indicating that youngsters with higher general intelligence tend to have dreams with higher imaginative content than those with lower general mental ability.

Factor Analysis

Factor analysis is used to determine the number of factors comprising the I.P.I.S. and the stimulus test items that cluster within each factor. For factor loadings, .4 (and above) is used as criterion (Hale, 1983). The results showed that the 28 item I.P.I.S. scale contains 10 factors whose descriptions follow: *first*, stimulus items 2, 6, 7, 8, 10, 13 and 19 having an eigenvalue of 4.85 clustered as factor one, which is labeled imaginativeness with objects (e.g., make-believe with self, stuffed animals, imaginative play companion); *second*, having an eigenvalue of 2.72, items 9, 15, 20 and 22 clustered as factor two, which is identified as imaginative movement and action (e.g., physical movement and mental actions in inside and outside environments); *third*, stimulus items 11, 20, 21 and 25 having an eigenvalue of 2.01 clustered as factor three, which categorizes personal manifestations and characteristics of fantasy (e.g., dreaming, being alone, fantasy between self and friends); *fourth*, stimulus items 19 and 28 clustered as factor four with an eigenvalue of 1.59, labeled verbal imagination (e.g., talking to yourself and teasing others); *fifth*, stimulus items 26 and 27 comprise factor five having an eigenvalue of 1.42, which is entitled school imaginativeness (e.g., imaginative products completed in school settings); *sixth*, stimulus items 14 and 18 with an eigenvalue of 1.25 clustered as factor six, which is identified as storytelling and reading (e.g., telling and reading pretend stories); *seventh*, stimulus items 4 and 12 clustered as factor seven with an eigenvalue of 1.21, which describes a general factor called fantasy toys (e.g., animals); *eighth*, stimulus items 5, 23, and 24 having an eigenvalue of 1.04

clustered together as factor eight, which is labeled imaginative play forms (e.g., drawing, joking, pretending to be someone or something); *ninth*, stimulus items 1 and 7 clustered as factor nine with an eigenvalue of .81, which is entitled family imaginativeness (e.g., parent telling make-believe stories and dreams); *tenth*, stimulus items 17 and 21 with an eigenvalue of .72 clustered as factor 10, which is identified as fantasy person (e.g., pretending to be someone other than yourself).

DISCUSSION AND CONCLUSIONS

The preliminary results reported here focus on relationships between imaginativeness as assessed by oral reports of preschoolers and selected child and family variables. Imaginativeness and family structure (i.e., single versus dual parent families) are significantly correlated. The findings that preschoolers in single parent families display higher imaginativeness than those in dual parent families are consistent with the literature on children's imaginative predispositions in single parent households (Singer, 1973, 1966).

Singer's (1973) hypotheses are that single parent families foster imitation, identification and closeness and provide opportunities for privacy and practice, aspects which are parallel to and consistent with growth of imaginativeness. Children in single parent families may have greater amounts of time by themselves and fill up this "empty space" with imaginative thought and pretend activities, an adaptive use of imaginative competencies. Manosevitz, Prentice & Wilson (1973) and Breckenridge & Vincent (1965) note that imaginativeness may provide a means of escape from loneliness by reproducing reality through imaginative play.

Likewise, the greater quality and quantity of imaginativeness shown by children from single parent families on various items from the I.P.I.S. may also be explained by Singer's hypotheses. In single parent families, children report: (1) playing more imaginative games when alone, (2) engaging in more imaginative outdoor games, (3) showing higher levels of imaginative talk with their fantasy friends and (4) having more imagi-

nary play companions than youngsters in dual parent families.

The conceptual relationships between imaginative predispositions and independent variables such as family density (Svendsen, 1934) and birth order (Masih, 1978) require further research examination. In the present study, the lack of supporting evidence between number of children in the family and quantity and quality of imaginativeness may be due to inadequate measurement of items on the I.P.I.S. And, the present study contained no "only" children. Finally, the results indicate that younger rather than older children tend to have greater beliefs that their fantasy dreams will come true and play more fantasy outdoor games, findings consistent with Piaget's (1962) and Singer's (1973) interpretation of imaginativeness as a cognitive and developmental precept.

The ten factors that emerged from the items of the I.P.I.S. fall into fairly identifiable and recognizable patterns. In effect, these results indicate that for the sample of 50 children, it is likely that the oral reports of imaginativeness fall along one or more of these ten dimensions. These factors closely correspond to those of Singer and Singer (1981) using youngsters' oral and observed behavioral actions during free play settings.

In additional research there needs to be an examination of relationships between cultural and environmental press variables such as independence, social class, socioeconomic status and imaginativeness. Other related areas of investigation would include relationships between parent beliefs about imaginativeness and their children's imaginative predispositions.

Note

1. The entire 28 item instrument, Imaginative Predisposition Interview Schedule can be obtained by writing: Dr. Thomas D. Yawkey, Early Childhood Faculty, The Pennsylvania State University, Division of Curriculum and Instruction, 159 Chambers Building, University Park, Pennsylvania 16802.

References

Breckenridge, M. E., and E. L. Vincent. *Physical and Psychological Growth Through Adolescence* (4th ed.) Philadelphia: Saunders, 1960.

Brown, B. B. *The Experimental Minds in Education.* New York: Harper and Row, 1968.

Bruner, J. S. "On Cognitive Growth: I and II." In J. S.

Bruner, R. R. Oliver and P. M. Greenfield, eds., *Studies in Cognitive Growth*. New York: Wiley, 1966.

Calderia, J.; J. L. Singer and D. G. Singer. "Imaginary Playmates: Some Relationships to Preschoolers' Spontaneous Play, Language and Television-viewing." Research Paper Presented at the Eastern Psychological Association, Washington, DC, March 1978.

Dunn, L. *Peabody Picture Vocabulary Test: Form B*. Circle Pines, MN: American Guidance Services, 1960.

Fein, G., and N. Apfel. "Some Preliminary Observations on Knowing and Pretending." Research Paper Presented at the Symbolization and the Young Child Conference, Wheelock College, Boston, MA, November 1975.

Lieberman, J. N. "Playfulness and Divergent Thinking: An Investigation of Their Relationships at the Kindergarten Level." *Journal of Genetic Psychology* 107 (1965): 219–24.

Manosevitz, M.; N. M. Prentice and F. Wilson. "Individual and Family Correlates of Imaginary Companions in Preschool Children." *Developmental Psychology* 8, 1 (1973): 72–79.

Marshall, H., and S. Hahn. "Experimental Modification of Dramatic Play." *Journal of Personality and Social Psychology* 5 (1967): 119–127.

Masih, V. K. "Imaginary Play Companions of Children." In R. Weizman, R. Brown, P. J. Levinson and P. A. Taylor, eds., *Piagetian Theory and Its Implications for the Helping Professions*. Los Angeles: The University of Southern California Press, 1978, pp. 136–44.

Matas, L.; R. A. Arend and L. A. Sroufe. "Continuity of Adaptation in the Second Year: The Relationships Between Quality of Attachment and Later Competence." *Child Development* 49 (1978): 547–56.

Medley, D. M., and H. E. Mitzel. "Measuring Classroom Behavior by Systematic Observation." In N. L. Gage, ed., *Handbook of Research on Teaching*. Chicago: Rand McNally, 1963.

Piaget, J. *Play, Dreams and Imitation in Childhood*. New York: Norton, 1963.

Piaget, J., and B. Inhelder. *Mental Imagery in the Child*. New York: Basic Books, 1971.

Pulaski, M. "Toys and Imaginative Play." In J. Singer, ed., *Child's World of Make-believe*. New York: Academic Press, 1973.

Schaefer, C. E. "Imaginary Companions and Creative Adolescents." *Developmental Psychology* 1 (1969): 747–49.

Shumkler, D. "The Origins and Concomitants of Imaginative Play in Young Childhood." Unpublished doctoral dissertation, University of Witwatersrand, Johannesburg, South Africa, 1978.

Singer, J. L. *Daydreaming: An Introduction to the Experimental Study of Inner Experience*. New York: Random House, 1966.

———. "Imagination and Waiting Behavior in Young Children." *Journal of Personality* 29 (1961): 396–413.

———, ed. *The Child's World of Make-believe: Experimental Studies of Imaginative Play*. New York: Academic Press, 1973.

Singer, D. G., and J. L. Singer. "American Television-viewing Habits and the Spontaneous Play of Preschool Children." *American Journal of Orthopsychiatry* 46 (1976a): 496–502.

———. "Television Viewing and Aggressive Behavior in Preschool Children: A Field Study." In F. Wright, C. Bahn, and R. Rieber, eds., *Annals of the New York Academy of Sciences: Forensic Psychology and Psychiatry* vol. 347. New York: New York Academy of Sciences, 1980.

———. "Fostering Imaginative Play in Preschool Children: Television and Live Model Effects." *Journal of Communications* 26 (1976b): 74–80.

———. *Television, Imagination and Aggression: A Study of Preschoolers*. Hillsdale, NJ: Erlbaum, 1981.

Smilansky, S. *The Effects of Sociodramatic Play on Disadvantaged Preschool Children*. New York: Wiley, 1968.

Sutton-Smith, B. "Novel Responses to Toys." *Merrill-Palmer Quarterly* 14, 8 (1968): 159–60.

Svendsen, M. "Children's Imaginary Companions." *Archives of Neurology and Psychiatry* 2 (1934): 985–99.

Tower, R. B. "The Influence of Parent's Values on Preschool Children's Behavior." Unpublished doctoral dissertation, Yale University, 1980.

Tower, R. B.; D. G. Singer; J. L. Singer and A. Biggs. "Differential Effects of Television Programming on Preschoolers' Cognition, Imagination, and Social Play." *American Journal of Orthopsychiatry* 49, 2 (1979): 265–81.

Vygotsky, L. "Play and Its Role in the Mental Development of the Child." *Soviet Psychology* 5 (1967): 6–18.

Warner, W.; M. Meeker and K. Eels. *Social Class in America*. New York: Harper and Row, 1960.

Werner, H. *Comparative Psychology of Mental Development*. New York: Science Editions, 1958.

Werner, H., and B. Kaplan. *Symbol Formation*. New York: Wiley, 1963.

Yawkey, T. D. "Imaginative Predisposition Interview Schedules: Test and Manual." Unpublished documents: The Pennsylvania State University, University Park, Pennsylvania, 1983.